Political Subjectivity

The Philosophical Foundation
of Democratic Individualism

By
Reginald Grünenberg

Table of Contents

Preface to the 1st English Edition, 2018 5

Notes to the English Translation 8

Preface to the 2nd, Updated and Extended German Digital Edition, 2013 9

Preface to the 1st German Edition, 2006 11

Political Subjectivity
The Philosophical Foundation of Democratic Individualism 13

Introduction 13

A. The Emergence of the Political Triad 38

*A.1 The Development of Individualism in the Force Field
        of the Bourgeois Revolutions* 38

A.1.1 Stages in the History of Subjectivity and Individuality 38
A.1.2 The First Analysis of the Individual (Philosophy) 49
A.1.3 The Education of the Individual (Pedagogy) 53
A.1.4 The Individual in the Markets (Economy) 60
A.1.5 The Individual of Social and Sovereign Contracts (Law) 68
A.1.6 The Individual at War 75

A. 2 The Evolution of Aesthetics to the Science of Taste 84

A.2.1 Classicism, Sensibility and English Aesthetics 88
A.2.2 Science of Sensual Knowledge
         and Critique of the Aesthetic Subject 103
A.2.3 The Connection of Aesthetics and Politics in the *Sensus
         Communis* 110

*A. 3 The Public as Aesthetic and Political Communication
         in the 18th Century* 115

A.3.1   Fragments of a Theory of the Public in the 18th Century 120
A.3.2   New Forms of the Public and their Social Practice 129
A.3.2.1 Audience and Authors in the Medium of Language 131
A.3.2.2 Press, Literature and Reading Societies 136

| B. | Political Subjectivity as Fundament to the Political | 142 |

Graphical Overview of the Political Subject –And an Important Note 142
Introduction to the Philosophical Analysis of Political Subjectivity 144

B.1	The Capacity of Reflection and the Political Judgment: Kant's Critique of the Power of Judgment	146
B.1.1	Preparation I: The Reception of the *Critique of the Power of Judgment*	147
B.1.2	Preparation II: Outline of the *Critique of the Power of Judgment* and Definition of the Reflecting Judgment	160
B.1.3	From Kant's Method to the Counter-Method: The 'Back-Mixing' of Pure Forms of Judgment	175
B.1.4	Transcendental Nature and Political Judgment: The Principle of Judgment in Political Use	190
B.1.5	Figures of the Individual: Individuality in the Text of the *CPJ*	218
B.1.6	Politics in the *Critique*: Political Examples and Topics in the *CPR*	224
B.1.7	The Political Judgment	235
B.1.7.1	Deduction of the Unity of the Political Judgment	237
B.1.7.2	Functions of the Reflection Types: Ends, Beauty and the Sublime in the Political Judgment	242
B.1.7.2.1	The Concept of Ends: *Order* and *Individuality*	242
B.1.7.2.2	Beauty: Morality and Justice	249
B.1.7.2.3	The Mathematical-Sublime: *Time* and *Body*	262
B.1.7.2.4	The Dynamically Sublime: *Power*	273
B.1.7.3	The Public and the *Sensus Communis Politicus*: Structures of the Political Judgment	288
B.1.8	*Practice, Reflection* and *Faith*: The Distinction Between Morality, Politics and Religion as Reflected in the Analysis of Judgment	306
B.1.9	Excursus I: *Hypostases of Identity* – The Second Tradition of Philosophy of Consciousness	337
B.2	Political Quality: Subject-Philosophical Reconstruction of Political Phenomena	359
B.2.1	Charisma	361
B.2.1.1	Max Weber's Objective Charisma	361
B.2.1.2	The Qualitative Turnaround: The Subjective-Political Charisma	366
B.2.2	Excursus II: Ethnological and Cultural-Anthropological	

	Dimensions of Political Subjectivity	373
B.3	*Connecting Points for the Philosophy of Political Subjectivity*	397
B.3.1	Systems and Discourse Theory	397
B.3.2	Political Psychology and Cognition	401
B.3.3	Political Communication and Media Theory	403
B.3.4	Women's Studies and Gender Anthropology	405
B.3.5	Political Education	406

Recap 409

Political Subjectivity – A Cultural Achievement Under Siege 409

Glossary 413

Bibliography 417

1. Monographs 417
2. Anthologies 436
3. Articles 439

Index of Persons 453

Picture Credits and Graphics 462

Picture Credits 462
Graphics 462

Bonus 463

What Is a Democrat? An Attempt to Define the Democratic Personality 464
When Educated Guesses Fail 464
Individual –Political Subject –Democrat 465
Epistemological Anti-Individualism 466
The Ability to Think Political Order 468
Political Science and Ethnology 469
A First Attempt of a Definition 472

About the Author 473

Imprint 474

Preface to the 1st English Edition, 2018

Let me be candid. This is not the story of a smooth highroad to success but of a new strand of philosophy coming down a bumpy road in a soapbox, often shaken by the rejection of others and by my own ignorance. In retrospect, it's a miracle that I was able to raise the initial funds for this huge project, my dissertation in political science (see *Preface* to the 1st German edition). Consequently, after its completion in 1996 nobody was interested in the results. As there is no effective competition about ideas and theories in German social sciences and humanities (but all the more about social and intellectual conformity), the present work, a bulk of groundbreaking new concepts and methodical innovations, never got a chance. Every move I made was stalled. I couldn't get an assistant post – also because my own doctoral supervisor preferred to promote anyone around but me –, I was refused every post-doctoral scholarship I applied for and even all academic publishers I approached turned down the offer of making this ambitious work of mine public. Eventually, in 2006, I became a publisher myself and this book was the first I published. It surprisingly got an excellent review by the highbrow *Neue Zürcher Zeitung* (see Preface to the 2nd German Edition 2013). Yet, this was an exception. I always believed in my first scientific monograph as a truly original achievement in philosophy, but I had to face the possibility that it would not be understood and even less accepted during my lifetime (see *Introduction*).

Now, more than twenty years later and a life completely outside of academia – except for three years as the co-founder of a university, the European College of Liberal Arts, today Bard College Berlin – I came to understand that my description of the 'fourth kernel of subjectivity', the political one, was only an epiphenomenon to a much bigger discovery that I was originally not aware of. In October 2017, I published the treatise *Laws of Singularity* about how any future artificial superintelligence will necessarily be controlled by laws of rationality that can be deduced from Immanuel Kant's critical philosophy. You can also read them as a blueprint for achieving such a technical feat. I spelled them out and it was easy – because I still have access to this practical understanding of Kantian philosophy that I had gained in my earlier studies on political subjectivity. But even then, having described again the four kernels of subjectivity and the *Laws* being avidly read all around the globe, I still had no clue that there was a big kahuna of a theory, my own, hiding in the open, right in front of my eyes. The subdivision of subjectivity was once more only instrumental to the task of describing something else, this time the rules that will govern future technological singularities. Being fascinated by this prospect, I completely overlooked the importance of the tool that I had used and that had even been sharpened in the process.

It was not until a friend of mine, an architect, read the *Laws* in early 2018 and mentioned that it reminded him of something Edmund Husserl had written about the possibility that the subject, as the bearer of reason and consciousness, might not be in one piece, not one homogenous entity, but a composition of several entities of subjectivity. My friend couldn't remember where he had read this, but I quickly found out that this is just a few paragraphs in Husserl's last and unfinished book from 1936, *The Crisis of European Sciences and Transcendental Phenomenology*. And indeed, in § 57 he wrote:

> "The difference between empirical and transcendental subjectivity remained unavoidable; yet just as unavoidable, but also incomprehensible, was their identity. I myself, as transcendental ego, 'constitute' the world, and at the same time, as soul, I am a human ego in the world. The understanding which prescribes its law to the world is my transcendental understanding, and it forms me, too, according to these laws; yet it is my—the philosopher's—psychic faculty. Can the ego which posits itself, of which Fichte speaks, be anything other than Fichte's own? If this is supposed to be not an actual absurdity but a paradox that can be resolved, what other method could help us achieve clarity than the interrogation of our inner experience and an analysis carried out within its framework? If one is to speak of a transcendental 'consciousness in general,' if I, this singular, individual ego, cannot be the bearer of the nature-constituting understanding, must I not ask how I can have, beyond my individual self-consciousness, a general, a transcendental-intersubjective consciousness?"

I admit that it is not immediately obvious how this could lead to a polycentric approach to subjectivity because Husserl seems just bothered by some irritating questions. And we know for a fact from his estate that Husserl had long since walked into another direction, namely a mysterious form of *transcendental intersubjectivity* that was supposed to ultimately buttress his phenomenology – and that nobody seems to have understood to date. But for me, a light went on and rose over the almost three decades of contemplating the inner constitution of the human subject, of how instinct, sensuality, experience, consciousness and reason are intertwined within the confinement of our body and brain. Suddenly, I understood that I had inadvertently worked on (or with; as an instrument) a subject that is not monocentric anymore, but decidedly polycentric. And that until Husserl's essay nobody had tried to do so, even less since then. At that very moment, I decided to finally focus on exactly that and only that. I started writing *You are Many. The Polycentric Subject*. In parallel, I prepared the translation and publication of the present work *Political Subjectivity* in English language. It is nothing less than the origin of it all, starting with the one kernel of subjectivity that nobody has ever thought of before – apart from Hannah Arendt and a few more people who had at least an inkling that there could be something like an 'organ of political thinking' hidden in our mind. The great advantage now is that we have already one kernel of subjectivity that is described completely and in much detail. You will see that this is almost a euphemism, given the complexity and depth of analysis that lies ahead of you. And I firmly believe that there is nothing to add.

Now, having learned the noble craft of excavating kernels of subjectivity within the field of politics, I feel prepared to do the same with the three other kernels, which Kant has already described, at least partly and implicitly. To an extent I had already begun this endeavor with writing *Laws of Singularity*. But we must dig much deeper from here, because Kant's philosophy, especially the transcendental part of it, i. e. the first two *Critiques*, was preoccupied with the solution of a completely different problem – the possibility and limits of objective knowledge – and its method was only tailored for just that task. The three kernels of subjectivity – theoretical, practical (moral) and aesthetic –, meanwhile, have stayed widely undisclosed, just like the political one that I could only give birth to by applying a resolute 'counter-method' to Kant's approach (see Chapter B.1.3). Strangely enough, it will be the achievements of the discovery of political subjectivity that serve as a guide and a rope when digging into the fundaments of three more forms of subjectivity.

This said, please feel encouraged to read *You are Many. The Polycentric Subject* first if you want to study the general method of 'subjectivity debunking'. Otherwise, the present study will make you acquainted with this method in depth and in detail. In this case, I hope you will enjoy the journey as much as I did when I originally wrote this.

Notes to the English Translation

This German-English translation was made with the great support of DeepL.com, a neuronal network based online translation engine that is to date by far the best in the world (a startup from Cologne, Germany). Although it was supposed to deliver just a rough translation, we were amazed at the breathtaking quality of it. And honestly, this English edition of my equally ambitious and voluminous doctoral thesis would not have seen the light of day without this excellent automated preparatory work.

Many of the quotes and references herein would be useless without translation. Therefore, I translated non-English titles of papers and books between bracket '[]' into English. Yet, whenever available, I referred to the English translation of the respective paper or book. In this latter case, the page numbers for the originally German or French edition are only an approximate indication for the English one.

For quotes form Kant's *Critique of Pure Reason* and the *Critique of the Power of Judgment* I chose the excellent translations by Paul Guyer. One cannot thank Guyer enough for it. The improvements compared to earlier translations are absolutely critical and I frankly didn't believe that this level of accuracy in the translation of Kantian philosophy could ever be attained.

Moreover, the *Critique of the Power of Judgment* is abbreviated with "CPJ"; the *Critique of Pure Reason* with "CPuRe"; and the *Critique of Practical Reason*, with "CPraRe". The page numbers of the *CPJ* and the *CPuRe* are taken from their second editions from and 1787 and 1793 respectively as rendered in Weischedel's complete edition, *Werke I-X*, Frankfurt 1988. The corresponding page numbers of the English editions of both works in Guyer's translation are indicated in square brackets.

I also adopted Guyer's particular and new translation of some key terms of Kantian philosophy in my own text: understanding (*Verstand*); intuition (Anschauung); reflecting (*reflektierend*); determining (*bestimmend*), power of judgment (*Urteiskraft*); end (*Zweck*); to judge [something] (*beurteilen*); the judging [of something] (*Beurteilung*); purposiveness (*Zweckmäßigkeit*); satisfaction (*Wohlgefallen*); dissatisfaction (*Missfallen*); pleasure (*Lust*); displeasure (*Unlust*); enjoyment (*Genuss*); gratification (*Vergnügen*); assent (*Beistimmung*); accord (*Einstimmung*); agreement (*Zusammenstimmung*); unanimity/unison (*Einhelligkeit*); to expect (*erwarten*); to expect sth. of so. (*zumuten*), cognition (*Erkenntnis*); representation (*Vorstellung*); presentation (*Darstellung*); the particular (*das Einzelne*), the universal (*das Allgemeine*); there is only one deviation: I don't translate *ansinnen* as 'to require' or 'to ascribe', but as 'to suggest'. See *CPJ*, transl. by Paul Guyer, 2000, *Editor's Introduction*, XLVI-XLIX.

Preface to the 2nd, Updated and Extended German Digital Edition, 2013

A lot has happened since the first edition in 2006, and even more so since I submitted my dissertation entitled *Political Subjectivity* in Munich in 1996. Everything around us has changed and the course of events has been full of crises, disasters and wars. But one thing has hardly changed at all, namely the text of this book. I was amazed at how little I had to edit, correct or supplement the original text in 2006. That was no different this time. The deviations from the manuscript of my doctoral thesis seventeen years ago comprise just three added paragraphs, a somewhat brisker and cheekier introduction, indexes of persons and subjects and of course the two forewords. That's it. I have nothing to complain about either the content or my written expression at that time. As I said, I'm surprised myself, but if you can't improve something good any more, then you should just leave it at that.

As a bonus material I have added the essay *What is a Democrat?*, a publication from 2012, in which I try to show what difficulties we will soon face if we do not finally clarify the most basic concept of our political existence.

Then there is the important reference to the graphic overview of the political subject with all its conceptual organs at the beginning of the study. This graphic was hidden in the printed edition of the book on the last page, where hardly anyone discovered it. It is an enormously helpful topographical map for orientation in the vast foundation of political philosophy that we will be exploring.

Finally, I would like to quote in full a review of the first edition of this book, which appeared in the *Neue Zürcher Zeitung*. Not only because I like the title of this article so much, but because the reviewer has well recognized the militant, aggressive and provocative nature of this new political philosophy.

"**The Theory of Relativity of Politics**

The 20th century has been characterized by an accumulation of political tragedies that are among the darkest moments mankind has to deal with. Totalitarianism and the collective collapse of moral judgment are part of the signature of this epoch. How it could have happened that in a relatively short period of time – think of the twelve years of National Socialism in Germany – the moral orientation system of an entire generation could be suspended is still in need of explanation today. Reginald Grünenberg, a political scientist working as an entrepreneur, goes back to the first questions: What actually is the political? Even after the totalitarianism of the 20th century, massacres and atrocities continue. Humanity could learn nothing from the past because it still misunderstood the essence of politics. That he, Grünenberg, has found a new 'theory of reflection', even a 'theory of relativity' of politics, is impressively stated on the first page of the introduction. Under the guidance of Immanuel Kant and Hannah Arendt, the author returns to the concept of polis. The human capacity to generate different forms of living-together has become 'mysterious to us since antiquity, when it lost its self-evidence'. Grünenberg locates the malaise in a concept of subjectivity that has been castrated of every inner connotation – of empathy, charisma and judgment. **A masterstroke, uncompromisingly thought and nowhere conciliatory, especially not towards the heroes of German post-war thinking like Dieter Henrich, Jürgen Habermas and Niklas Luhmann.**"

Neue Zürcher Zeitung, March 17, 2007

Preface to the 1st German Edition, 2006

This philosophical work could be realized thanks to a three-year graduate scholarship of the Friedrich-Ebert-Stiftung [a German political foundation of the Social-Democratic Party]. An important part of the support was immaterial, because without the trust expressed in this support, I probably would not have had the courage to tackle such an extensive and complex project. I dropped a first version in which I wanted to examine the form of political judgment under the fascinating title *Critique of Form* in an abstract way that would still have impressed the young Hegel. Instead, I took a more historically and sociologically grounded approach. I regretted that very much at first. But then the collection and rearrangement of the rich material from the 18th century and the foundation of my philosophical theses on it gave me so much joy that the time of writing my dissertation between summer 1995 and spring 1996 became one of the most beautiful times of my life.

This work is marked by the impression of personal encounters with the now deceased sociologist Niklas Luhmann. The open-mindedness and creativity of this man had convinced me that I had to deal thoroughly with the theoretical design of his systems theory. With its help I developed the ambition to create a new basis for political philosophy, which finally makes it independent of moral philosophy, state theories and practical teachings for witty heads of state.

I dedicate this book to a great cosmopolitan, the Colombian philosopher, politician, bull breeder, diplomat, patron and founder of the University of Los Andes in Bogotá, Mario Laserna (1923-2013). This scholar, the first doctoral student of Dieter Henrich, a long-standing pen pal of Albert Einstein and John von Neumann, who knew how to combine spirit and action throughout his life, occasionally introduced me to reading Immanuel Kant's works during his teaching at the Geschwister-Scholl-Institute for Political Science in Munich in 1988. In doing so, he opened up natural philosophy and epistemology to me. Instead of encouraging me to research *between the lines*, he has shown me the richness that lies *unseen in the open of the lines* of the Kantian texts. The corresponding hermeneutic rule required an untiring study of the sources. I hope that the inevitably resulting thoroughness has had a beneficial influence on the book I would like to dedicate to him.

Fig. 1: Mario Laserna (r.) in Princeton in 1952, where he received Albert Einstein's support for the founding chapter of the University of Los Andes in Bogotá.

Political Subjectivity

The Philosophical Foundation of Democratic Individualism

Introduction

A series of recent political events has brought the importance of political subjectivity back into the limelight. From German unification together with the preceding civil protests in the GDR to the collapse of the Soviet Union, the peaceful abolition of the apartheid minority rule in South Africa and finally the Arab Spring 2011 – or from the 1989 violence and bloodshed in China on Tiananmen Square via ethnically fanatical nationalism in former Yugoslavia to Islamic terrorism in Algeria: For better or for worse, there are many reasons and current occasions to once again think about what historically powerful forces are secretly at work when people as political subjects try to determine and change the public order of rights, customs and the distribution of goods. Political philosophy should feel called upon to finally get to the bottom of the pressing question: What is political?

But the time for simple answers is over. We have been fobbed off for too long with trivial and less plausible definitions of the political. This book sets a new level, both in terms of the question and the answer. The goal is a new theory of reflection for political science. The approach being developed here is so radically new, so thorough and so incredibly complex that the simple ideas and old knowledge of politics will probably be the greatest obstacle to understanding the new that will be discovered here. For the first time it becomes clear that not only physics, biology and mathematics can be highly demanding, complicated and difficult to represent. The foundations of political philosophy exposed here are at least as great a challenge for the mind and imagination. The results claim to be as universally valid as the great scientific models. That is why I would like to call the following treatise – with a wink – the *first theory of relativity of politics*.

Who is this book written for? This is indeed a problem, because the large group of readers who have the education and the necessary conceptual tools to follow the idea to be developed here, grew up in the humanistic-Aristotelian tradition – and thus they are actually lost for this enterprise. These Traditionalists can hardly accept the consequences of the following considerations, for here a philosophical axe is put to the root of their political worldview, which was always only a moral one. We'll see what a huge difference this makes.

Then there are the Progressives, who have extensive social science and perhaps even philosophical knowledge, but who, unlike the traditionalists, are already completely cut off from the fascinating intellectual world and the subtle questions of Western metaphysics. They believe in the linguistic turn and consider all problems of philosophy as problems of everyday language. Or they still believe that reason itself is the greatest crime of Western philosophy, like the last postmodernists in the wake of Nietzsche, Heidegger and Foucault. With this simple intellectual equipment, they will hardly be able to follow our ascent to the intellectual plateaus of Leibniz, Baumgarten, Shaftesbury, Smith and Kant, let alone enjoy it.

Finally, there are the Liberals, especially those of Anglo-American breed. Admittedly, they have a really good point. Because they will ask why they actually need all this philosophical hair-splitting. It was quite simple to become a political subject; their forefathers and -mothers showed it in the bourgeois revolutions. That's all right. But I maintain that the Liberals have still not understood what really happened back then and how modern liberal-political thinking actually came about. Liberals take the external historical events of that epoch, in which they were still successful revolutionaries, as proof of the universal validity of liberalism and remain to this day superficial in the philosophical justification of it in an almost frivolous way. They prefer to do this with moral-philosophical arguments, which are often naive, alien to life or simply counterfactual. Only when they embark on our expedition to find the true origin of their political worldview and explore how great the theoretical achievement was that implicitly lay in the revolutionary practice of their founders, will the Liberals make in the following chapters the greatest find in their history.

This is the paradoxical challenge of this book: it is written for well-trained philosophers, social scientists and intellectuals in terms of style, argumentation and information density; but most of them will fail. Therefore, it is secretly aimed at the thirst for knowledge of young students, researchers and thinkers of all kinds.

Frankly, I can well imagine that the political philosophy to be developed here is not understood at first. I have observed this in the works of some of the authors that will be mentioned here. How much nonsense I had to read about the works of Immanuel Kant or Niklas Luhmann! The academic commentary literature manages on a regular basis to completely overgrow the original work and make it practically disappear. I hope that my philosophical work will be spared this fate. Therefore, the answer to the question for whom this book is written is quite simple in the end: for the future.

I.

The human capacity to generate different forms of coexistence has been a mystery to us since antiquity, when it lost its naturalness. Consequently, the political has attracted the attention of important thinkers. With the philosophical, theological and scientific terms at their disposal, they tried to make certain orders the epitome of the political. The political was without exception their own political opinion, only as theory or schema. It can perhaps be explained by the theorists' own need for refinement of opinion that the subject of the political could never be more than a *zoon politicon*, a state-related animal. Thus, it could be concluded from the respective state order to the kind of being that had to bear and to suffer it. The inner complexity of this being was completely blanked out.

The reduction of complexity was a specialty of [the German] sociologist Niklas Luhmann, whose historical and theoretical achievements are acknowledged here in several places. Systems theory, according to Luhmann, has always tried to define specific systems and their supporting functions within a society, independent of the will and actions of human individuals. In some areas, such as the 'economy of society' or, in particular, the 'science of society', he has achieved important and conclusive results with this anti-anthropological theory design. But it is precisely the 'politics of society'[1] that he feeds us with a formula that is intended to construct the function of the political as "holding the capacity for collectively binding decisions."[2]

---

[1] Luhmann, Niklas, *Die Politik der Gesellschaft* [The Politics of Society], Frankfurt 2000.
[2] Ibid, S. 84.

Fig. 2: Niklas Luhmann (1927-1998)

From a strictly sociological point of view, this view may be consistent and sufficient. However, the phenomenon of the political is thus only partially understood, because the individual performance of people who actually think and act 'politically' in a sense to be defined in more detail is covered up and annulled by a postulated system performance. Luhmann's systems theory treats people and citizens as 'system animals' (*zoon systematicon*) whose psychological and philosophical inner horizons play no constitutive role in the operation of the political system. Yet the development of – as already mentioned – a 'political' way of thinking and acting between people is extremely rich in prerequisites.

Even to the fact that it is anything but self-evident that these state and system animals recognize each other as humans if they are such. Humans differ from the other mammal species in that they do not recognize each other. The French philosopher Alain Finkielkraut has taken this problem as an occasion for an analysis of the present: "To a cat, a cat is always another cat. A man, on the other hand, must fulfill a set of Draconian conditions or be crossed off the list, without any recourse, of those counted as members of human society."[3] From this point of view it is evident that the state animal can only be human within its own polis (group, clan, tribe, state) and from this position it is justified to regard the rest of natural beings, even if they are similar to oneself, as non-humans. In this context, anthropologist Claude Lévi-Strauss noted that the concept of humanity, which includes all forms of human life without distinction of race or civilization, "came up rather late and was very little widespread. Even where it seems to have experienced some formation until maturation, it is by no means certain – recent history proves it – that it is protected against ambiguities and regressions."[4]

Aristotle, who founded this ancient and still recognized definition of the political subject as zoon politicon, cannot be denied empirical confirmation. For the Greek Polis, the being that was to be regarded *intra muros* as human was considered outside the city state, *ex urbe*, as an animal to be hunted or as a barbarian. Now, in accordance with our thousand-year tradition of Judeo-Christian universalism, we are much more demanding today and wish for a political concept that is more global and can cross the borders of closed communities. We also call for a political concept that is not based on the state and the existing orders, but on us as individuals.

However, the evidence of one's own political will and feelings has stunned the sense of possibility that would have asked: How can I be up to the task of a judgment or feeling of this kind? We are too close to ourselves to realize how preconditionally dependent and complex this capacity of ours is that has become habitual to us. There are not only a number of historical clues that indicate the fertility of this question, but also a philosophical trace to which Hannah Arendt referred. These two things will be a compass and map for our expedition into the foundations of political philosophy. We want to know what the real deal is with the political subject.

---

[3] Finkielkraut, Alain, *In the Name of Humanity*, p. 5, Columbia University Press; revised edition, 2000

[4] Lévi-Strauss, Claude *Strukturale Anthropologie* [Structural Anthropology], vol. II, Frankfurt 1975, S. 369.

In the following study an ideal-typical original situation is constructed on the basis of historical, social science and philosophical materials, which should mark the beginning of 'the political' in modern Europe. This origin of the political lies in the temporal coincidence of three phenomena, the interactions of which have so far hardly been researched. The three elements of this constellation, here for the sake of brevity called 'political triad', are: 1) the philosophical and practical consequences of the notion of subjectivity and individuality in the force field of bourgeois revolutions; 2) aesthetics, as a theory of taste, opinion and common sense; 3) the new social communication practice that we know today as the 'public sphere'. The thesis is that these simultaneous events have built a historical formation that can only be explained under the assumption of a special, cultureally and historically new and genuinely political power of judgment. Furthermore, it should be shown that the key to understanding these new assets lies in Immanuel Kant's *Critique of the Power of Judgment*. Once we have found the key and the lock, the way is clear to what was previously hidden behind this door: the philosophy of political subjectivity.

This study is an attempt at 'lateral entry' into anthropology as a political anthropology, which Otfried Höffe has encouraged.[5] The philosophical model of the political is intended to bring socialization back into view from the point of view of the individual. In the background is the previously negated, but in reality only unsolved question of whether and how the concrete, individual person can appear in theory or, better still, become its measure. In the social sciences, the metatheoretical principle has long dominated that human action should not be understood as a collective event of communication and function by individuals, but only by systems. The basic concept of action is hardly counted back to individual beings or consciousness. In this context, Luhmann's systems theory represents only the purest and most spectacular form of social-scientific reductionism, which boasts of having left "old European humanism" as a theoretical basis behind. It will be shown here that these foundations are far from being exhausted and contain much untapped potential.

Resistance against anti-individualism in the social sciences has also stirred up elsewhere. This became particularly apparent in 1996, when Daniel Goldhagen's book *Hitler's Willing Executioners* was published.

---

[5] Höffe, Otfried, *Wiederbelebung im Seiteneinstieg* [Reopening of the Lateral Entry], in: Höffe (editor), *Der Mensch - ein politisches Tier? Essays zur politischen Anthropologie* [Man – A Political Animal? Essays in Political Anthropology], Stuttgart 1992, p. 5-13, here p. 9-10.

Therein, the author refused to continue writing 'structural' or 'social history' and instead addressed the motives of individual perpetrators. Goldhagen's approach stands in the horizon of a method of narrative historiography that has gained much importance and mastery in the Anglo-American world as 'dense description' (Clifford Gertz). The events and actions are thus repaid a moment of genuine historical contingency that threatens to be completely straightened out in the highly deterministic or crypto-teleological structural or evolutionary models of the social sciences.[6] Political science is also affected by this impoverishment of action theory, since its modelling has become methodologically dependent on sociology and economics. Herfried Münkler noted the following observation:

> "If it is true... that neither the legitimation of political order with economic or sociological models, nor the incorporation of political dimensions of expectation and imperatives for action into the principles of universalist ethics are able to comprehend the current crisis of Western democracies as a crisis, this is more than a mere hint that political science must return to the genuine independence of its area of concern."[7]

Münkler follows this with a plea to take the actual expectations and dispositions of the citizens seriously and only on this basis to follow up the discussion of the normative admissibility of these expectations. Otherwise, political science runs the risk of exhausting itself in testing an inflation of

---

[6] See, for example, Simon Shama's study *Citizen. A Chronical of the French Revolution*, N.Y. 1989, which consciously crosses the boundaries between literature and history. Klaus von Beyme describes in detail the withdrawal of such explicit action theories inspired methods in political science from functionalist approaches in *Theorie der Politik im 20. Jahrhundert. Von der Moderne zur Postmoderne* [Theory of Politics in the 20th Century. From Modernity to Postmodernity], Frankfurt 1991. An excellent and more recent study, which deals exemplarily with the strategies of contingency suppression in the works of the prominent historians Fernand Braudel and Hans-Ulrich Wehler, is Arndt Hoffman's *Zufall und Kontingenz in der Geschichtstheorie. Mit zwei Studien zur Theorie und Praxis der Sozialgeschichte* [Coincidence and Contingency in the Theory of History. With two Studies in Theory and Practice of Social History], Frankfurt 2005.

[7] Münkler, Herfried, *Die Moral der Politik. Politik, Politikwissenschaft und die soziomoralische Dimension politischer Ordnung* [The Moral of Politics. Politics, Political Science and the Socio-Moral Dimension of Political Order], in: Leggewie, Claus, *Wozu Politikwissenschaft? Über das neue in der Politik* [Why Political Science? About the New in Politics], Darmstadt 1994, pp. 228-242, here p. 238.

counterfactual models and ideals.

The descriptive dimension of political science research and theory building is indeed clearly underdeveloped. However, not on the quantitative side, because the empirical data basis is virtually supersaturated. Rather, it is the instruments for interpreting and meaningfully combining the data collected that are outdated. The traditional means of recording the characteristics, properties and peculiar interactions of modern political subjects have been exhausted.[8]

Social and political theories are confronted with the problem of how something particular can be expressed in the language of science, because it only gives the word to particularity when it appears as part of an already known general. If now the particular itself, here in the form of the individuality and political ability of people, is to be scientifically examined in political science, a methodical turn must be made here, namely to discuss the particular *as particular* in an analysis of the *subjective ability of particularization*. This does not affect the scientific task of constructing general laws.

II.

It is already apparent that such an approach will not get along without the concept of consciousness and even the now scientifically hardly accepted concept of reason. This recourse to philosophical instruments considered obsolete is not made in the gesture of theoretical embarrassment but is affirmative throughout. The various types of thought and the forms of reason, as worked out by Immanuel Kant in his critical system, are tested in the course of the investigation and in accordance with the respective question on the material that seems to be familiar to us as 'political reality'. A variation on the main question could therefore be: When, where and in what way can historical world events be interpreted as the articulation of individual political reason and how must it itself be structured?

The dominance of post-metaphysical theories, which consider all subject-philosophical efforts as failed, is taken into account here.[9] However,

---

[8] Münkler, ibid., illustrates this with the example of the speechlessness of political science in view of the 'disenchantment with politics' that has been publicly discussed since 1990 at the latest. There is no well-founded and in-depth contribution from political scientists to this topic.

[9] Cf. Habermas, Jürgen, *Postmetaphysical Thinking*, MIT Press 1994. The term encompasses not only discourse theory but also entire analytical philosophy,

since no one yet has the authority to make a universally valid and final ban on metaphysics binding, it remains free to explain important human connections, at least experimentally, with the difficult and presupposed concept of reason.

As is well known, reason is not an empirically perceptible or experimentally verifiable substance. It is not an object among others in the physical world. Nevertheless, Kant believed, the assumption of a transcendental ability was useful and even necessary. Only such a *focus imaginarius*, which lies outside the sensually perceptible world, makes the order of the world recognizable – and at the same time the various abilities of the subjects themselves to recognize and create such orders. In transcendental philosophy the imaginary lines of known world knowledge were extended beyond the physical world to explore the ability that contains the conditions for this world knowledge. Kant wanted to identify the cognitive capacity itself, within its limits. The procedure is very similar here, because it is not a question of affixing the substantiated political like a clearly legible label to certain objects or events. Rather, the lines are to be drawn beyond the empirical world to the ability that allows us to recognize and understand the things of the world as political. This ability does not passively absorb the political quality of things and events, but rather produces them. Kant described this insight as a 'Copernican turn'. The reason for the object's cognition must be sought in the subject's cognitive ability. Here we will try to make this path once again fruitful for political philosophy. Kant's great work on aesthetics and teleology, the *Critique of the Power of Judgment*, will be the construction site on which a conceptual bedrock and substructure is to be laid open that will be the foundation for our new philosophy of the political.

The arguments that have so far been put forward against further use of the philosophy of consciousness or philosophy of the subject are dealt with in Chapter 1.9 under the title *Hypostases of Identity*. It is not insignificant for the proof intended here to find out how and why this path has been blocked so far and why that which I would like to call the *Second Tradition of Philosophy of Consciousness* has remained undiscovered and never had a chance. Paradoxically, the most important role in this adventurous piece of philosophical grave robbery and banditry is played by Dieter Henrich, the best-known and most profound author of contemporary philosophy of subjectivity. Here his writings are confronted for the first time with a

---

structuralism, systems theory, philosophical hermeneutics and poststructuralism; see Scheme IV on the genealogy of subjectivity theories in Chapter B.1.9.

fundamental critique which feeds on exactly the sources Henrich claims to defend.

But it will also become clear that a concept of political subjectivity does not call into question any of the achievements of discourse theory and systems theory. Rather, the possibility of supplementing these two dominant approaches of social theory is considered. The aim is to remedy a frequently observed deficit in these two large theoretical buildings by complementing them on a new basis. The 'I' must be given a new and fair philosophical chance over the 'we'.

III.

The historical focus of our investigation will be on Germany, because the process has left the clearest and deepest traces in the literature there and is therefore suitable for systematic thematization. Under no circumstances is 18th century Germany the origin of political modernity – as is well known, rather the opposite is the case. Yet, the elements of the political have been intellectualized much more in Germany than elsewhere. Instead of realizing individuality, aesthetic competence and publicity through revolutionary deeds [Taten] as in Great Britain, the United States and France, the Germans have written many profound treatises [Traktate].[10] This is finally an advantage, because this then abstract and theoretical approach now provides an insight into the abilities that thinking people are required to have in order to produce these political phenomena in practice – and to bear them. Therefore, the political triad presented here is an aesthetically appealing figure and by no means a metaphysical sign that is inscribed in German history. It is only a coincidence of events whose aesthetic form begs for being systematically explored. It almost imposes itself on the interpretive mind and promises that the clarity of its outline is also inhabited by a meaning that has been waiting a long time for the appropriate hermeneutics.

Quentin Skinner began his famous study *The Foundations of Modern Political Thought* in the Renaissance. It is also undeniable that the new forms of state wisdom (Machiavelli), political science (Hobbes) and the control of religious conflicts (tolerance, sovereignty) have been on the

---

[10] In German "Statt Taten nur Traktate", 'instead of deeds, only treatises', is a nice pun that highlights our tradition of intellectualizing everything, and the present work will prove how much I am indebted to it.

advance since the 16th century. But the question of political subjectivity is once again something completely different from the question of the genesis of these concepts of order, which were developed as pleasing imitation and inspiration for secular and spiritual princes in order to make their state machinery more controllable. In it the old, restrictive sense of politics still works as rule by virtue, law and, if necessary, cunning. The political triad described here unfolds in the 18th century because it was only between the bourgeois revolutions that the framework of political modernity was formed, in which the preceding achievements of the Renaissance and the religious wars could also be effectively harnessed and realized by bourgeois political subjects. Our investigation is therefore a philosophical analysis of the kind of 'mind' that must have historically evolved and accompanied the transition from serfdom to citizenship.

After the social abolition of the working class of some industrial nations in an enlarged middle class, women in particular now keep alive the memory of how steeply the path to the historical realization of their political subjectivity was – a path that has still not been followed in many places in the world today. In the 18th century, this departure was announced only very cautiously, which does not mean Olympe de Gouges' catalogue of women's rights, but only the expanding of the concrete right of women to have a say in the choice of their spouse. For this reason, the historical part does not specifically deal with the gender difference with regard to political subjectivity, although this would of course be an important question. The delays in this area are due to the strictly patriarchal ways of life and the political subjects who still overidentified their just discovered bourgeois identity as a form of universal humanity with the nature of the male gender. This complex belongs to the topics of historical and philosophical women's studies, which should not be anticipated here.

IV.

For the course of the examination, a distinction is proposed first, which should allow a certain orientation in the abundance of the material. In the current terminology of German political science, when distinguishing between 'political theory' and 'political philosophy', the latter is generally equated with normative political theory, i.e. how politics *ought to be*.[11]

---

[11] Cf. Beyme, Klaus von, *Die politischen Theorien der Gegenwart* [Contemporary Political Theories], 6. revised and supplemented edition, Munich 1986. Beyme uses the term philosophy only in the context of 'practical philosophy'. He calls

Here, however, political philosophy will be separated from political theory in a different way, namely as basic research. In the definition applied here, political philosophy investigates exclusively the foundations of political subjectivity. Political theory, on the other hand, works on this form of subjectivity only in the aggregated state of concrete social interaction and order. The ideal-typical difference is postulated so that in the course of the investigation it can be shown all the more clearly to what extent and in what way each theory is committed to philosophy. A further distinction between political philosophy and theory is intended. The aim is to protect the project from the frequent equation of political and practical philosophy in Germany, as already mentioned. Practical philosophy deals on the same level with the subjective dimension (philosophy as implicit anthropology) and the collective dimension of politics (theory as the social value theory of good living) and leads to short circuits because of this lack of differentiation. Clear signs of such defects are the sudden transitions from moral to legal philosophical problems in treatises that see themselves anchored in practical philosophy.[12] The similarity of moral and legal ways of thinking – provided they are to be regarded as determined by philosophy – has always led in Western history of theory to skip an important stage in the transition from morality to law. This follows Hannah Arendt's intuition. She once wrote to Karl Jaspers:

"Now I suspect that philosophy is not entirely innocent of this mess [the supersession of the human individual as human] in the sense that Western philosophy has never had and could not have a pure concept of the political, because it spoke out of necessity of Man in the singular and treated the fact of his inbuilt plurality as just a lesser ancillary."[13]

---

the foundations of political theory 'metatheories' or 'theories of science'. In his more recent study *Theorie der Politik im 2o. Jahrhundert* [The Theory of Politics in the 20th Century], loc. cit., political philosophy is identified only with a "minority position" of authors within political science who deal with the normative reasons for politics and order.

[12] For example: Brunkhorst, Hauke, *Demokratie und Differenz. Vom klassischen zum modernen Begriff des Politischen* [Democracy and Difference. From the Classical to the Modern Concept of the Political], Frankfurt 1994; even more clearly: Habermas, Jürgen, *Between Facts and Norms: Contributions to a Discourse Theory of Law and Democracy*, MIT Press,1998 (see here chapter B.2.2 and B.3.1).

[13] Letter to Karl Jaspers of March 4, 1951, in: *Hannah Arendt and Karl Jaspers. Briefwechsel*, ed. by Lotte Köhler and Hans Saner, Munich-Zurich 1985, p. 353. This perception may also be the reason for Arendt's lifelong refusal to be considered a 'political philosopher'. She saw herself as a political theorist

As a rule, political philosophy is primarily understood as the normative question of "How should we live together?" But exactly this question must be avoided here, because it presupposes too much and always aims at the order of already organized political subjects. As soon as the political judgments plunge into this horizon of the 'we', the 'I' disappears. These moments, however, in which the 'I' is still quite vital and struggles with itself in order to force itself through to a judgment, are to be observed and analyzed here. In the normatively structured discourse, the subject already speaks under the demand of a "we must" and "we ought to". Political subjectivity, on the other hand, is the flashing of the cheeky "I want to – and the others must" in judgments. Since it is only about the political subject as an individual, I would like to have the concept of political philosophy understood completely norm-free within this investigation. The concept of political subjectivity is an attempt to discuss political competence in the individual in a descriptive way. So, the following is not a statement for or against democracy, liberalism, communitarianism, authoritarian rule, progressive or conservative politics or other forms of political life and government. These would always be theoretical models in which individuals are presented aggregated under certain order patterns. These aggregates are abstracted here, firstly in order to correspond as best as possible to the regulatory scientific ideal in the postulate of freedom of value; secondly in order to explore the general political competence (as subject, citizen, voter, family member, employee, mandate holder or political leader). To this end, one must return to the individual and then first clarify how the transition from a 'general subject of political forms of thought' to the individual is shaped, i.e. what makes the subject to the individual in order to ask further questions from there. For this reason, the discussion of individualism has the largest chapter in the historical part of the study. And for the same reason the distinction between political theory (order) and political philosophy (subject) is recommended, because only the latter will be of interest here.

The distance to be made from practical philosophy should not mean that morality has nothing to do with politics, as some decisionists and systems theorists would confirm without hesitation. The relationship between morality and politicality, i.e. moral and political judgment, must be examined very carefully in its content of differences, so that the significance of morality for politics can be reformulated and possibly better spelt out. The

---

according to the title of her university chair in the United States.

decisive prerequisite for this is the abstinence from any normative specifications in the analysis. Otherwise an edifying catalogue of political wishes would come out of this too quickly. The occasional glance at the "crooked wood of humanity" (Kant) and at the "slaughtering block of history" (Hegel) is enough to sober up the intoxication with moral fantasies in the political. No 'new policy' is presented or sought here, no normative postulate is raised. Rather, a cultural achievement of modernity should be made visible as a cognitive achievement of individuals.

V.

Ernst Cassirer regarded aesthetics as the main philosophical problem of the 18th century. Every important thinker of the Enlightenment was concerned with aesthetics, in an extensive sense as the theory of taste or, to a limited extent, as the teaching of artistic beauty. Kant's *Critique of the Power of Judgment* – again an observation by Cassirer – has given it its "definitive form".[14] With this kind of philosophical theory of taste we will analyze the mediation of individuality and publicity, of philosophy and theory, of one's own world and sociality. In theoretical and empirical terms, the relationship between politics and aesthetics still belongs to the terra incognita of the social sciences.[15] It is precisely this transition, which was previously described in a restrictive sense as an aesthetic relationship limited to natural beauty, the sublime and culture of taste, that is to be developed here as an "extended way of thinking" in its genuinely political dimension. Hannah Arendt had a decisive thought since her Kant studies in the early 1950s. In Kant's *Critique of the Power of Judgment*, she said, there is an organ of reason that can think together singularity (of the ego) and plurality (of mankind), namely the reflective judgment. Exactly this intuition is the starting point of our investigation, and we will follow this thought of Hannah Arendt here to its last implications to demonstrate that she has shown the way to one of the greatest treasures of political philosophy.

---

[14] Cf. Cassirer, Ernst, *Die Philosophie der Aufklärung* [The Philosophy of Enlightenment], Tübingen 1932, 3rd ed. 1977.

[15] A good example is Andreas Dörner' excellent study *Politischer Mythos und symbolische Politik. Sinnstiftung durch symbolische Formen am Beispiel des Hermannsmythos* [Political Myth and Symbolic Politics. Creating Meaning Through Symbolic Forms], Opladen 1995, p. 13.

Fig. 3: Hannah Arendt (1906-1975)

On the basis of the historical and philosophical material in the first part of the book, we will see how this reflective power of judgment and its subjective conditions actually produce a new, namely a *political quality* that is embodied in the *reflective judgment upon public order*. This product, with its individual components and as a whole, is subjected to a philosophical examination of its legitimacy. The concept of 'the public' or 'publicity' is not presupposed here, but only introduced problematically. The continuity of reality of the public sphere that can be represented in philosophical analysis is in fact much broader than that of previous theories of the public sphere. 'Publicity' will prove to be a medium created by actions of thought, namely by judgments. Similarly, the terms 'order', 'individuality', 'power', 'law', etc. must first be subjectively justified before they can take their place within the political judgment. The path to these core theses is very difficult, but they would remain incomprehensible in themselves. The problem of political subjectivity is extraordinarily complex and requires appropriate and therefore philosophically demanding treatment. The scope of the study is therefore essentially due to the historical-literary embedding of the inherently formal core idea.

In particular, the entire historical part A is the result of the effort to give the philosophical depths of the problem a visible shape in the form of its historical emergence. In the course of later analyses, a cultural-historical theory of the emergence of political subjectivity is formulated accordingly. It postulates a necessary connection between individuality, publicity, taste-grounded truth and political judgment. If the origin and evolution of the subjective form of the political is already methodically taken as the basis here, then at some point a theoretical explanation of this political emergence and evolution must also reassure the description made here (cf. Chapter B.2.2).

VI.

Ernst Vollrath, disciple of Hannah Arendt and co-administrator of her intellectual heritage was the first to define the project of an independent political philosophy based on Kant's concept of reflective judgment. Interestingly, in the title of his *Grundlegung einer philosophischen Theorie des Politischen* [Foundation of a Philosophical Theory of the Political], he brings 'philosophy' and 'theory' together. But in the treatise, he does not succeed in setting and articulating the difference between the terms in such a way that their connection seems meaningful or even fruitful in this conjunct expression. Nor does it become clear what the concept of the political, which is emerging on this basis, could actually achieve. Vollrath's demarcation of the new term from the long series of political terms from the French, Anglo-Saxon and German traditions is – however interesting these considerations may be in detail – too strongly concentrated on the rejection of classical German state theories, which hegemonically dominate or at least have dominated the concept of the political. On the other hand, nowhere in the *Foundation* does it become apparent which positive and concrete applications the prospect of the discovered power of judgment holds out. The philosophical impulse is completely absorbed by the venerable liberal ambition to position rights and theories of defense against assaults of sphere of the state (which in his opinion, however, is also attributable to Habermas' concept of 'life-world'), fiercely imagined as freedom-threatening, on the individual. The important concept of order, for example, which is elementarized here to a basic concept, plays no role in Vollrath's attempt to a philosophical theory of the political. He thinks that the reflective power of judgment is the ability to think politically. That's right. But what does it reflect upon besides its own, individual state of mind? Upon orders which it must recognize or invent for this purpose, and about the position of the individual in or relative to these imagined orders.

Fig. 4: Luc Ferry

Another author, the French philosopher, essayist and politician Luc Ferry, has attempted to write the European history of subjectivity along its ruptures in his book *Homo aestheticus*[16]. For him too, who thus continues his program of a "non-metaphysical humanism", Kant's *Critique of the Power of Judgment* is the apex and keystone of a philosophical struggle for a concept of subjectivity that has lasted for over a hundred years, in which human finiteness (sensuality, physicality, temporality, historicity and mortality) and infinity (the ideas of soul, world, freedom and reason itself) can equally find their systematic place. Ferry develops the theme starting from the systematic aesthetics in the 18th century and spans it via Kant, Hegel and Nietzsche to the decline of the avant-garde in art and politics of the 20th century. As fundamental as this book was for the present study and as interesting as the theses and interpretations themselves are, it cannot be

---

[16] Ferry, Luc, *Homo aestheticus. L'invention du goût à l'âge démocratique*, Paris 1990. [*The Human Being as an Aesthete. The Invention of Taste in the Age of Democracy*, University of Chicago Press, 1994].

denied that some critics rightly noted that the subtitle, *The Invention of Taste in the Age of Democracy*, is misleading because no socio-historical or theoretical material is linked to the question of taste theory in the 18th century.

The American Peter J. Steinberger undertook another expedition into the previously little-explored foundations of the political judgment[17]. However, he adhered entirely to the classics of political philosophy since Plato and saved himself the trouble of developing his theses in a field saturated with the social sciences and possibly testing them there right away. He assumed that so many factors were known in his question that his answer did not bring any obvious gain of knowledge. Completely focused on the logical form of the judgment, he had no idea of treating the terms 'political subject', 'order' or at least 'politics' as unknowns, so that his equation would have had something to achieve. Although Steinberger has collected interesting material on the question, he has not found any instruments to make this material speak.[18] It therefore seems all the more important to make the elementary concepts of political philosophy a problem.

Political subjectivity is therefore already a well-known topic of political philosophy, even if it has not yet been explicitly dealt with under this title. This is a good opportunity to make a general statement about which authors I feel particularly obliged to and whom I have to thank. This study explicitly follows the tradition of the works of Hannah Arendt, Ernst Vollrath, Luc Ferry and Alain Renaut. It owes these authors essential insights, impulses and inspirations and sees itself as a continuation and deepening of their approaches. To this end, however, such an investigation must broaden and consolidate its foundation both in a systematic-philosophical approach and empirically. Despite all the criticism I will occasionally make of these authors' preparatory work, it should always be remembered that they have the merit of having discovered the first philosophical ground plan of political subjectivity.

---

[17] Steinberger, Peter J., *The Concept of Political Judgment*, Chicago and London 1993.

[18] The main shortcoming lies in the underestimation of Kant's philosophy, especially of the *Critique of the Power of Judgement*. Steinberger rightly describes it as the climax of the analysis of judgements but regards it as a failure – for reasons with which Schopenhauer already demonstrated that he had not understood the third *Critique* at all.

VII.

For any mind trained in social-scientific functionalism or communication theory, as already mentioned, the older form of consciousness theory is here connected with social history in an unusual way and taking into account texts that have not been appreciated enough so far. We want to avoid the pitfalls of speech-performative unfolding of intersubjectivity (Habermas) as well as the newer sociological functionalism. The latter has catapulted the reference to the transcendental subject of idealism out of social theory, because a sufficiently demanding theory of action of the subject of reason could not yet be produced. This is a fundamental theoretical decision on which Niklas Luhmann's systems theory in particular is based. His approach refrains from metaphysical speculation about the subject of reason because it raises too many problems in the research process and in theory building. Luhmann has suspected that the problems of subject theory relate to "a vague and unspecific concept of reflection."[19] Systems theory has consequently taken leave of the "old European subject" in order to gain a clear path for new expeditions in social theory. This is legitimate and has proved to be a very fruitful approach. In contrast, political science must continue to explore the secret of subjectivity and the associated problems of individuality and personality. And its desolate state on the verge of insignificance has to do with the fact that political science did not do just that. The essential lack of thoroughness in political science lies in the fact that so far it has not

---

[19] Habermas, Jürgen and Luhmann, Niklas, *Theorie der Gesellschaft oder Sozialtechnologie* [Theory of Society or Social Technology], Frankfurt 1971, p. 27. Cf. also Luhmann, Niklas, *Weltkunst*, in: Luhmann (Ed.) *Unbeobachtbare Welten. Über Kunst und Architektur* [Unobservable Worlds. On Art and Architecture], Bielefeld 1990, pp. 11-12: "One can view the concept of reflection of German idealism and Romanticism as a first experiment with observations based on differences and historically recognize in it the semantics of a transitional period. Nevertheless, and precisely for this reason, the otherness of the series of terms distinction-description-form-observation-description must be emphasized. We do not tie in with a concept of reflection that starts from consciousness and therefore does not get rid of the problem of intentionality, self-objectification, the always secondary division of self as subject and self as object and the syntheses that now follow on from it. Theoretically at least the philosophy of consciousness has not succeeded to understand difference as first and last, although such intentions become apparent." At this point Luhmann refers to Dieter Henrich's seminal study, *Fichtes ursprüngliche Einsicht* [Fichte's Original Insight], Frankfurt 1967.

developed a teaching of elementary concepts such as 'meaning' and 'action', as Weber and Luhmann did for interpretive and functionalist sociology respectively. To a certain extent, the concept of political subjectivity now to be presented is the first chance for political science to come to its own concept of reflection and to an elementary theory. In sociology, for example, the validity of legitimate order is already regulated by the definition of the concept of order. In political philosophy, however, the definition itself should be the problem first. In this way, in Part B of the investigation, some terms are positioned to which it appears that all political judgments can be traced. No one should be surprised, then, if some concepts that are usually considered elementary, such as 'rule' and 'state', are not considered at all, for these are always already aggregated concepts that presuppose much that is only clarified in a philosophical investigation of political subjectivity. Likewise, Kant's philosophy of state and law, which is completely dependent on his practical philosophy and is ultimately based on the *concept of duty*, is ignored here. Otherwise one would repeatedly arrive at the normative-political purpose of the subjects, whereas the present study deals with the *cognitive-political capacity of the individuals*.

Political subjectivity has been and still is acquired in a learning process that characterizes some cultures. It is not an innate ability, but an extremely demanding invention of the human species that is dependent on many preconditions as we will see. It is not realized everywhere and at any time, but must be wanted, promoted and communicated. Denying or withdrawing political subjectivity is much easier than successfully teaching it. It always needs role models, but also an at least intuitive insight into the function of what actually constitutes it: political judgment. Political subjectivity is not only a saving blessing, a guarantor of happiness or an exclusive reason for enlightened enthusiasm, but also an imposition, a burden. It is the price to be paid for the *exit from subservience to the responsible citizenship*. Political subjectivity sometimes creates the bitter taste of knowledge about the incurable imperfection of the world. It is a reminder of the poorly scarred wound of the theodicy problem – with the intensification that secularized people can no longer even come up with the relieving idea of blaming a higher being for the disorder in the world. Political subjectivity is an imposition of totality, for every individual is required to produce an overall concept of social and spiritual order in which he or she also reflects upon himself or herself. These designs have to prove themselves in an environment whose complexity is growing and cognitively increasingly difficult to master.

VIII.

The philosophical scheme of political subjectivity is outwardly similar to a kind of political individual psychology. The essential difference lies in the fact that no instinctive patterns or other psychosomatic causal chains are to be tied, but a judgment is analyzed, which is to be attributed to an overall system of a cognizing capacity, which we call colloquially 'reason'. Like Kant's *Critique of the Power of Judgment*, the model of political subjectivity derived from it is also based on an analysis of the functions of concepts and not of sublimated impulses, needs and the conflicts that follow from them. For psychology starts from somatic states and events despite all refinement. Accordingly, neurophysiology is becoming more and more demanding to be the only one who has the real solution to psychic and psychological problems. Kant commented on this distinction between philosophy and psychology (the one known to him at the time) and left it the honor of thoroughly handling the tedious business of collecting interesting individual cases, as for example Edmund Burke in his book *A Philosophical Enquiry into the Origin of Our Ideas of the Sublime and Beautiful* (1756). So, what is explored in the subject's thinking as an individual is by no means necessarily part of psychology (CPJ, *First Introduction*, pp. 38-39). An important follow-up topic is the question of political cognition or cognitive political competence (Chapter B.3.2).

The modern invention of individuality, for example, can only be described in a very reduced form as a social-psychological phenomenon. In modern societies, however, the exploration of individuality is a way of focusing on one's own fundamental prerequisites. "The modern concept of the individual thus belongs in a society that might feel called upon to gain clarity about itself," concludes Niklas Luhmann his survey of the inadequate theoretical appreciation of the problem:

> "After years of de-thematization... seems to start a re-thematization of the individual [references to the German sociologist Ulrich Beck]; but the classics of this discipline [sociology] can hardly help: They had made do with the split paradigm of personal/social identity or with superficial borrowings from transcendental philosophy, with the word 'subject', never drilling deep into the direction of individuality."[20]

---

[20] Luhmann, Niklas, *Individuum, Individualität, Individualismus* [Individual, Individuality, Individualism], in: Luhmann, *Sozialstruktur und Semantik. Studien zur Wissenssoziologie der modernen Gesellschaft* [Social Structure and Semantics], vol. 3, Frankfurt 1993, pp. 149-258, here pp. 258, 219.

Examining this phenomenon as a special system achievement and as an increase in social complexity, or as a language achievement and individualization by means of intersubjectively nested claims to validity in acts of speech, can yield useful and yet very different results.[21] Finally, there is still the way open to analyze individuality and political subjectivity as a special ability of judgment and realization of a well-defined human capacity for thought. The *word* 'subject' was admittedly often used naively. Therefore, one of the tasks of the investigation is to redefine the *concept* of this transcendental-philosophically hypostasized subject – yet not against Kant, but against the pretensions of his commentators (Chapter B.1.9).[22] The thesis of the effect and influence of reason on history by means of the reflective judgment will thus serve in a completely un-Hegelian fashion as an instrument for insight into the philosophical fundament of the political.

---

[21] Jürgen Habermas' main work to date, *The Theory of Communicative Action*, 2 vol., Frankfurt 1981, in particular, bears witness to a great proximity to psychology, for it is based, among other things, on the works of Freud, Piaget and Mead. Mead's thesis of the inexplicability of the ontogenesis of the psychic subject outside a social context plays a central role.

[22] The difference between 'word' and 'concept' is extremely important, especially when dealing with Kant's transcendental philosophy. Yet, nobody has ever written on topic 'Word and Concept' in this philosophical sense. For the time being let's stay with the definitions here in the Glossary of Kantian Terms: "**Concepts** are either constructed, then they are mathematical, or they are confirmed by a critique of the subject and based on knowledge (conceptus ratiocinatus), then they are philosophical. [...] **Words** are *names for concepts* or names for sensual or supernatural objects." So, a concept is not identical with the word by which it is called, but a wrapped-up instruction manual for the unfolding of its own well-defined inner structure.

Political philosophy should be the practice of the optician who tries to grind the conceptual lenses for theoretical glasses, with whose help the intellectual eye can look into this fundament and recognize what the political is.[23] It will become clear that the individual is always a polycentric structure of qualitatively different subjects. **The speech on the 'monologism of the subject', which sees itself as 'critical', can then be returned to its authors as an impermissible simplification** (cf. chart III).

The investigation should therefore also be understood as a piece of 're-enchantment of the world' – not with the help of myth, but by clearly recognizing and admiring the exoticism of the present in its fabulous complexity with this new philosophical view. All the conditions that have to play together to make our way of life possible, and all the achievements that we have to make day after day thinking, reflecting and speaking to maintain or even develop this form, make it almost a miracle that all this is actually happening. It is also about measuring the dimensions of the grown political cosmos anew and making them tangible. And not only in conceptual speculation, which will play a major role here, but also in the presentation of the manifold connections that could simply not be perceived by traditional political science, because the ground plan of this science is so unspecific that a certain conservatism of caution still prevails hegemonically today.

This ethos that motivates our investigation could encourage a sarcastic assessment, because the political present is being considered here as an exotic object at a time when it is clear that the utopian abbreviations into the future are blocked and it could look as if we are just *faute de mieux* leaning back to practice naive-positive thinking to see what we have already achieved. Locked up in the present, we could pretend that the sarcasm is comfortable and perhaps even quite interesting. But the truth is much easier. Because only the exploration of the soil on which one stands and the time in which one lives gives food for new ideas and forces. And those who take a closer look will realize that the modest appreciation of the present is surprisingly subversive in more ways than just one.

---

[23] This beautiful thought can be found in Nicholas Cusanus' treatise *On the Beryl* from 1458 as an attempt to solve the problematic visio dei. The beryl is a cut, transparent stone from which Cusanus grinds philosophical glasses for monks at Tegernsee; it makes the *coincidentia oppositorum*, the origin and the unity of all differences visible to them, namely God.

IX.

As a rule, the traces that led astray during the research process are covered up in the presentation of theoretical studies. Thus, a completely logical and causal structure is presented, which gives the impression that it could not be imagined otherwise. At least two surprising and important twists and turns that took place during the elaboration of the concept of political subjectivity should be mentioned here. On the one hand, the term 'political subjectivity' only prevailed over the title *Individuality and Publicity* after some time and intensive work. It was along this line that the theme was to be developed as I believed that the two terms contained in it were mutually intertwined. I still maintain that, but for a long time I had not found a point in which I could focus these considerations, no *concept* that could carry this new philosophy. On the other hand, I was relatively late in coming to the conclusion that the political judgment does not consist of one single coherent piece and that it does not even have its own original principle from which it can be derived. I assumed the opposite and had resolved to uncover a separate section in the foundation of Kant's reflective judgment, which could be assigned exclusively to the construction of political judgments. That was a mistake.

X.

The investigation consists of two parts. The first part A describes the emergence of the political triad in the 18th century, which spans between the cornerstones of individuality, aesthetics and the public sphere. First, (A.1) it's all about the emergence and evolution of individuality as a historical and philosophical dimension in the context of the bourgeois revolutions. This is also the focus of the first part. The (A.2) aesthetics of the Enlightenment with its various schools already offers a systematic deepening of the theorems of individuality in several points. Finally, the (A.3) new social practices are presented by the public and the related demands are deciphered from the intellectual-historical side during this period. This interweaving of intellectual and social history should protect the entire investigation from excessive philosophical speculation, give it a historical basis and keep the anthropological dimension open.[24]

---

[24] Cf. the excellent essay by Thomas Nipperdey, *Die anthropologische Dimension der Geschichtswissenschaft* [The Anthropological Dimension of Historical Science] in: Nipperdey, *Gesellschaft, Kultur, Theorie. Gesammelte Essays über moderne Geschichte* [Society, Culture, Theory. Collected Essays on Modern History], Göttingen

In the second part B, the expedition delves into the interior of one of the most difficult works of philosophy, Immanuel Kant's *Critique of Power of Judgment*. In doing so, we always hold the rope in our hands, which we have woven in the empirical world before, in order to find our way back into it at any time and to look at our philosophical findings in the light of historical or currently experienceable reality. After the work is presented (B.1.1-2), an important part of the Kantian method, namely the isolation of pure judgments, is suspended and practically reversed into a counter-method (B.1.3). Then it is shown how the transcendental principle of judgment ensures that the political judgment gains access to sensual nature, which is what makes the distinction between individual and order possible (B.1.4). In the following two chapters, the Kantian text is questioned about the use of the scheme of individuality and a collection of all political motives and examples is compiled (B.1.5-6) in order to penetrate, equipped with these philosophical and philological results, into the center of the question associated with the problem of political subjectivity, namely political judgment (B.1.7). This includes the deduction of the formal unity of political judgment, the analysis of the various functions of reflective judgment in the judgment and an explanation of some of its structural features. The functions of the types of reflection beauty, sublimity and purpose consist in the subjective construction of certain elementary concepts of the political. The investigation is then sufficiently advanced to assess the difficult relationship between morality, politics and religion from a new standpoint as a judgmental structure of practice, reflection and faith (B.1.8). The following digression attempts to place the concept of political subjectivity in relation to the previous philosophies of identity and consciousness (B.1.9). In order to bring the philosophical expedition back into social-scientific reality, the new concept is tested, using Max Weber's concept of charisma as an example (B.2.1-2), and confronted with ethnological findings and cultural-theoretical considerations in a further digression (B.2.3). Finally, thematic links to various scientific disciplines and theories are discussed (B.3).

If you want to deal with the philosophical question *in abstracto* without detours, you can ignore the historical part and skip it. This has above all propaedeutic and plausibility rendering function. Everything that is examined there in social and theoretical history appears again as a philosophical topic in the second part. The advantage of the historical section,

---

1976, pp. 33-58.

however, is the practice of a difficult train of thought by repeating several times the empirical material of interrelated subject areas. The deduction of the political judgment and the functions of the types of reflection it contains have the greatest chance of being understood when all preparations have been thoroughly worked through. The efforts of reading this study will hopefully be rewarded with a sharpened sense and a deeper insight into the preconditional dependency, the vulnerability and the endangerment of all culture that can still be called political today.

A. The Emergence of the Political Triad

A.1 The Development of Individualism in the Force Field of the Bourgeois Revolutions

In the period from the constitution of the Habeas Corpus Act by the English Parliament in 1679, the Glorious Revolution in 1688 and the proclamation of the Declaration of Rights in 1689, through the American Declaration of Independence from 1776 to the French Revolution in 1789, Europe underwent a profound change in the way human existence was experienced and in the conception of what a person is, what rights she is entitled to and what her freedom should be.

A.1.1 Stages in the History of Subjectivity and Individuality

It would be a gross simplification to dogmatically fix the entry of the subject as an individual into history in the 18th century. Renaissance humanism and the various forms of Protestantism had anticipated much. One can obviously even say that some ideas and conceptual concepts of the Renaissance only became effective with certain authors of the Enlightenment and thus were able to develop their full systematic content, especially with Giambattista Vico and Wilhelm Leibniz. Since Leibniz now plays a very important role in this context of philosophical conception of individuality, it seems appropriate to recall the precursors of the Renaissance in more detail. In any case, it is a custom in the humanities that is difficult to justify, namely to let modernity and everything that constitutes this epoch spiritually and intellectually, start like an original myth and completely unhistorically with René Descartes *Discours de la méthode* and his cogito speculations. The mental space of modern times begins at the end of the 15th century at the latest. There Hans Blumenberg's famous polemic *The Legitimacy of the Modern Age* locates the transition and the authoritative series *New Cambridge Modern History* lets modernity begin in the Upper

Italian city republics of that time. The individuality of the medieval person could still largely be represented as the different articulation of piety[25] and was therefore more to be understood as a particularity. It is precisely from this religious corset that the self-image of man of the Renaissance is detached.

The following preparation of the history of individuality takes the European framework as a reference, since Renaissance humanism was an international intellectual movement.[26] The focus of the investigation will therefore only gradually be on Germany. Incidentally, the theoretical texts on individualism are as far as possible short-circuited with the social-historical facts, so that the causality of this rather abstract concept becomes comprehensible in history. In this way, the historical concreteness of individualism should become more vivid.[27]

The basic figure of subjectivity was already developed in the Renais-

---

[25] Cf. Gurjewitsch, Aaron J., *Das Individuum im europäischen Mittelalter*, Munich 1994. The classic on the history of mentality of this epoch is Johan Huizinga's beautiful book *The Autumn of the Middle Ages. Studies on Ways of Life and Minds of the 14th and 15th Centuries in France and the Netherlands*, Stuttgart 1975. The series by Philippe Ariès and George Duby (ed.), *Histoire de la vie privée*, four volumes, Paris 1985, covers a large part of the entire history of individuality in the Occident.

[26] Schmitt, Charles B., Skinner, Quentin (ed.), *The Cambridge History of Renaissance Philosophy*, Cambridge 1988, p. 2.

[27] In this respect, the following description differs considerably from the known studies on the subject. First, there is the profound but purely linguistic-philosophical study *Individuals. An Essay in Descriptive Metaphysics*, London 1964, by Peter F. Strawson. Steven Luke's authoritative study in the Anglo-American field, *Individualism*, Oxford 1973, breaks down the history of concepts according to countries, but only in Germany does he see the first traces of individualism in Romanticism and relies exclusively on speculative texts, which are to some extent unconnectedly placed side by side in the gallery of his reflections. The anthology by Pierre Birnbaum and Jean Leca (ed.), *Sur l'individualisme. Theories et méthodes*, Paris 1986 [*Individualism Theories and Methods*, Oxford 1990], offers more social science material, but almost exclusively the theoretical writings of Marx, Durkheim, Weber and Dumont are taken into account, thus again breaking the unity of theory and history. Finally, the extensive anthology by Martin Frank and Anselm Haverkamp (ed.), *Individualität* [Individuality], Volume XIII in the series *Poetik und Hermeneutik*, Munich 1988, deals with the subject primarily philosophically and literary. Only Robert Jauß's study on the discovery of individuality in portrait painting is historically oriented.

sance, both in habit and in philosophical speculation. Since the 11th century loneliness, thoughtfulness, dream states and the expressive use of the first person singular as rhetorical means in the narrative have been practiced in literature. Behind this literary 'I', however, there was still an extraordinary conventionality of stylization in detail.[28] In other words, the 'individuals' of this epoch still had a great deal in common, yes, in fact they could not yet be distinguished from one another by their individuality, but only by their social affiliation. Individuality was not yet a specific difference that could have contributed to the recognition of selfness and alterity. Most 'individuals' were – at least in the representation – perfect pictures of the gentleman or knight. Even François Villon, the first poet who as a bandit no longer wrote in the feudal language of the courts (born in 1431, banished in 1463 and disappeared in the French forest), was marked by the conventions of his precarious existence.[29] This background had an even stronger influence on the chronicles and the writings on moral education and, of course, on love poetry.

Erasmus of Rotterdam then committed a symptomatic stylistic break with his small and extraordinarily successful book *De civilitate morum puerilium* (Basel 1530) in relation to the older style books.[30] He no longer handed down anonymously ancient and scholastic maxims, but told his personal experiences and observations in order to convince the readers with the individually experienced situations described that an improvement of these customs is preferable in many respects (e.g. in questions of spitting, blowing one's nose and above all table manners). There has been a change in tone. There was a sensitivity to the specificity of each individual's (including the author's) experience that could not simply be prohibited or offered with the rule. Norbert Elias has studied these connections thoroughly and subtly in his classic *The Civilizing Process. Sociogenetic and Psychogenetic Investigations*. The successive construction of the pubic thresholds brought about a transition from social coercion to self-coer-

---

[28] Cf. Duby, George, *L'émergence de l'individu. Situation de la solitude XIe-XIIIe siècle*, in: Ariès, Philippe and Duby, George (ed.), *Histoire de la vie privée*, vol. 2, *De l'Europe féodale à la Renaissance*, Paris 1985, pp. 503-525.

[29] Régnier-Bohler, Danielle, *Exploration d'une littérature. L'individu*, in: Ariès and Duby (ed.) *Histoire de la vie privée*, loc. cit., pp. 372-392, here p. 374.

[30] Revel, Jaques, *Les usages de la civilité*, in: Ariès, Philippe and Duby, Georges (ed.) *Histoire de la vie privée*, Volume 3, *De la Renaissance aux Lumières*, Paris 1986, pp. 169-209.

cion.³¹ Exactly this 'self' only emerged in the densifying web of coercion as the 'self'-attribution and making binding of coercion from an inner side of the human subject.³² In this sense, Elias later writes:

> "But what is here called 'interdependence', and thus the whole relationship between individual and society, can never be understood if, as is so often the case today, one imagines 'society' essentially as a society of adults, of 'finished' individuals who were never children and never die. A real clarity about the relationship between the individual and society can only be gained when the steady growth of individuals in the midst of a society is included in the theory of society." ³³

This change in childhood, which must accompany individualization as a social institution, has been examined in particular in recent French historical research on the "longue durée" [long duration].³⁴ The main features are the gradual detachment of the child from its sole significance for the fertility cycle and for the succession of generations, which should transcend the hardness of individual life on earth, and accordingly the preservation of the child's life, constantly threatened by illness, with new medical means *for its own sake*. According to Elias, the process of individualization would be misinterpreted if individualization was regarded too strongly from the point of view of intellectual history as an act of *self-creation* – although the metaphysics, psychology and metaphoric of the

---

31 Elias, Norbert, *Der Prozess der Zivilisation* [The Process of Civilization], 2 vol., 14th ed., Frankfurt 1987, vol. 2, p. 312-341.

32 The material that ethnologist Hans-Peter Duerr has put forward to refute Elias' thesis is impressive; his objection that there was no process of civilization at all, however, amounted to ascribing the empirically very well provable transformation of modern societies since the Middle Ages solely to a completely independent systemic achievement. That would mean an evolving society, but the individuals have nothing to do with it. They can neither be identified as products of this change nor in any way as actors in this process. Since Duerr denies social evolution, he can permit neither historical emergence nor the dissolution or new and traditional anthropological qualities; cf. Hans-Peter Duerr, *Nacktheit und Scham. Der Mythos vom Zivilisationsprozess* [Nudity and Shame. The Myth of the Civilization Process], Frankfurt 1988; Duerr, *Obszönität und Gewalt* [Obscenity and Violence], Frankfurt 1993.

33 Elias, Norbert, *Die Gesellschaft der Individuen* [The Society of Individuals], Frankfurt 1987, p. 46.

34 Cf. Gélis, Jaques, *L'individualisation de l'enfant*, in: Ariès u. Duby (ed.), *Histoire de la vie privée*, vol. 3, loc. cit., pp. 311-329; cf. also the older study by Ariès, Philippe, *L'enfant et la vie familiale sous l'Ancien Régime*, Paris 1960.

humanists in the 16th century suggest exactly this.³⁵ Even then, these first attempts to stylize subjectivity brought with them difficulties in the mediation of the individual and society.

> "The intellectual history of the early modern era, through which the idea of an open-ended, infinite world can be constantly pursued and in which the philosopher is able to discover the development of a modern concept of subjectivity – it gives no clear answer to the question of man within the confinement of society and state, neither to the question of man as a morally acting subject. What is thought in the Renaissance about man and his place in society does not fit together – one can hardly be reconciled with the other."³⁶

The author of the thesis that the Renaissance was the beginning of Western individualism³⁷, the "discovery of man", Jakob Burckhardt³⁸, thereby meant, just like Norbert Elias later, the new sensitivity that was cultivated for the first time. The authors of the 16th century began to document contingent observations in a personally binding style and to consider these impressions worthy of the effort of such a literary representation, until then reserved for the forms of the noble, the general and the sublime.³⁹

> "Above all, Renaissance thought and literature are extremely individualistic in that they seek to express individual, subjective opinions, feelings and experiences to an extent unknown to the Middle Ages and

---

35 The prime example of this is the great speech by Giovanni Pico della Mirandola from 1486, *De hominis dignitate* [Oration on the Dignity of Man].

36 Otto, Stephan, *Renaissance und frühe Neuzeit* [Renaissance and Early Modern Times], Stuttgart 1984, p. 339.

37 The term 'individualism' was first used pejoratively in 1826 by an anonymous author of the Saint Simonist journal *Producteur* and began its career after 1830 with the socialist authors. Joseph de Maistre also used the term derogatorily as early as 1820 in his *Extrait d'une conversation*, which, however, was only published in 1884-87 as part of his *Oeuvres complètes* [Complete Works] in volume 14, here p. 286. For him, individualism was the modern ignorance of how political unity precedes and determines individuality.

38 Burckhardt, Jakob, *The Civilization of the Renaissance in Italy*, Basel 1860

39 An important form of communication for this was the correspondence by letters; cf. Mesnard, Pierre, *Le commerce épistolaire comme expression sociale de l'individualisme humaniste* [The Exchange of Letters as a Social Expression of Humanist Individualism], in: *Individu et société dans la Renaissance, Colloque internationale 1965*, Brussels 1967, pp. 13-31.

most ancient and modern epochs."[40]

The highlight of this form of literature in the Renaissance, as a consistently elaborated art of self-observation and self-representation, is probably Michel de Montaigne's *Essays*, which are still influential today.

> "The writers communicate themselves to the public by some special and distinguishing stamp; so I, as the first of all, all by myself, as Michel de Montaigne, not as a grammarian, poet or lawyer. When the world complains that I talk too much about myself, I complain that the world does not even think about itself. "[41]

As simple as this statement may seem to the unbiased modern reader, it is rich in preconditions and consequences.[42] The social prerequisites have already been mentioned.

The speculative prerequisites for the method and execution of this self-stylization are closely related – and one could even say causally – to the various realizations of the self-experience as an individual in this epoch, as Montaigne exemplified. The extraordinarily influential work of Francesco Petrarca (1304-74), one of the founders of the humanist movement, clearly shows how an artist, a poet who feels himself in full possession of a creative, unmistakable genius, philosophically fights at the same time against this medieval tradition throughout his life, which denies the soul exactly this kind of individualized self-experience, namely Averroism.[43]

---

[40] Kristeller, Paul O., *Humanism and Renaissance*, vol.1, p. 80, Munich, 1974-76.

[41] Montaigne, Michel de, *Essais*, III, Paris 1972, p. 24.

[42] It is important to note that there were indeed 'exceptions', but they cannot in any way be identified as 'precursors'. In his famous study *Mimesis. Dargestellte Wirklichkeit in der abendländischen Literatur* [Mimesis. The Representation of Reality in Western Literature], Basel 1946, 9th ed. 1994, Erich Auerbach identified the novel fragment of Petronius, in which a banquet is described, as the first piece of Western literature in which the persons use an 'individual language' that is hardly to be found in ancient literature and even in comedies (ibid. p. 34). This means that gossip is told there in a passionate manner, in which each speaking person narrates his or her own character and, above all, his or her weaknesses through the special use of the language. "Petron's method is therefore highly artistic, and, if he had no predecessors, ingenious..." (Auerbach, Mimesis, loc. cit., p. 31).

[43] See Cassirer, Ernst, *Individuum und Kosmos in der Philosophie der Renaissance* [Individual and Cosmos in Renaissance Philosophy], Leipzig and Berlin 1927: "The artist and virtuoso of individuality, who first rediscovered it in its inexhaustible wealth and in its inexhaustible value, defends himself against a

Aristotle's teaching of the soul, conveyed by the Arabic author Ibn Rushd (Averroes), said that the true subject of thought was not the self, but a common, impersonal, substantial being common to all thinking beings, whose 'connection' with the individual 'I' remains an external and accidental one.[44] This mystical and suddenly cosmological formula for the soul, as it clearly contradicted the foundations of the Christian faith, was already fought by Thomas Aquin, especially in his book *De unitate intellecttus contra Averroistas*. The teaching of such an absolute intellect should meet the requirements of mysticism and logic at the same time, i.e. secure a timeless, supra-individual point of view for the possible knowledge at all.

The overcoming of scholastic soul metaphysics became the central task of the philosophically guided psychology of the Renaissance, which, more than all other sciences, was directed towards the exploration of subjecttivity, which could only be achieved in the eighteenth century.[45] The human body as a correlate to the soul, which means nothing less than sensuality as a condition of knowledge for finite beings, was given a new status of philosophical-scientific dignity. At the same time, Francesco Piccolomini (1523-1607) first connected the intellect, which was otherwise essentially presented as a unit, with the rules of logic and postulated that thinking takes place in judgments. In a way, it can be said that Piccolomini anticipated – or at least was the first to announce – Kant's transcendental method.[46]

One of the consequences of the experienced individuality was that history became a highly problematic concept. For how could an individual's subjective viewpoint enter into an interpretation of history that until then had been understood as objectively transcendent or objectively documenting?[47] What does the individual and present experience in the

---

philosophy for which all individuality is something purely accidental." (ibid. p. 136)

[44] ibid. p. 134.

[45] However, Cassirer rightly admits that it was not speculative psychology that first achieved the goal of thinking together freedom, autonomy and the necessity of nature, but the exact, mathematically guided sciences and art; see Cassirer, *Individuum und Kosmos*, loc. cit., p. 149.

[46] See Kessler, Eckhard, *Psychology. The Intellective Soul*, in: Schmitt, Charles B. u. Skinner, Quentin (ed.), *The Cambridge History of Renaissance Philosophy*, Cambridge 1988, pp. 485-534, here p. 530.

[47] Here too, Petronius's above-mentioned fragment of a novel is an exception – and it is only an additional indication for the present study that the use of an

horizon of tradition, which contains everything that is general and legal in itself and claims to be an exhaustive interpretation of the present, but also already of every future? In the mirror of this tradition, the future must always be the same, for Christians and other eschatological religions at least until the Apocalypse. Never before and until today has the question of what history actually is been asked so radically.[48] The far-reaching consequences of the theological dispute over the essence of the soul make visible how much more complex social reality has become with the emergence of the figure of the individual. Accordingly, models to explain how the temporal structures of society convey individual, collective, past, present and future experiences with each other became more demanding.[49]

René Descartes took the decisive step from psychology to the philosophy of subjectivity in 1637 in his *Discours de la méthode*. In this small, simple and graciously personal book about the true and only method for obtaining certain knowledge in all areas of cognition, most authors see the beginning of the age of subjectivity. In contrast to Renaissance psychology, the simple fact of a thinking sensation was no longer sufficient to make

---

individual language goes hand in hand with a change in historical-subjective experience: "In this sense, there is hardly a piece in ancient literature that shows as strongly as this inner historical movement." (Auberbach, *Mimesis*, loc. cit., p. 33)

[48] Cf. Kelly, Donald R., *The Theory of History*, in: Schmitt u. Skinner, *The Cambridge History of Renaissance Philosophy*, loc. cit. Apart from a hitherto unimportant discussion of methods (between A. C. Danto, Jörn Rüsen, Hans-Michael Baumgartner, etc.), there is only one radical attempt in the true sense of the word to ask the question in a new way that is still instructive in its failure, namely Stephan Otto's two-part *Rekonstruktion der Geschichte. Zur Kritik der historischen Vernunft* [Reconstruction of History. The Critiquq of Historical Reason], vol. I: Munich 1982; vol. II: Munich 1992.

[49] Cf. Luhmann, Niklas, *Weltzeit und Systemgeschichte. Über Beziehungen zwischen Zeithorizonten und sozialen Strukturen gesellschaftlicher Systeme* [World-Time and Systems History. On the Relationships between Time Horizons and Social Structures of social Systems], in: Oelmüller, Willi (ed.), *Warum noch Geschichte?* [Why still History?], Munich 1977, pp. 203-252; also Luhmann, *Temporalisierung von Komplexität: Zur Semantik neuzeitlicher Zeitbegriffe* [Temporalization of Complexity: The Semantics of Modern Concepts of Time] in: Luhmann, *Gesellschaftsstruktur und Semantik. Studien zur Wissenssoziologie der modernen Gesellschaft* [Studies on the Sociology of Knowledge in Modern Society], Volume 1, Frankfurt 1993, p. 235-300; note that these are systems-theoretical reconstructions of time horizons that take *no account of individual inner horizons* but are nevertheless very instructive with regard to the unusual complexity of the problem.

subjectivity plausible as a kind of life breathed into the body by God. Materialism and the contemporary fascination for machines[50] seemed to make the soul hypothesis increasingly superfluous and to condense into a radical skepticism. In this respect, Descartes' distinction between two substances, the res extensa and the res cogitans, is a salvation of subjectivity that would otherwise have got stuck in its beginnings. He was helped in this by the fact that he was able to combine his "foundation of metaphysics" (4th part of the *Discours*, where the famous "Je pense, donc je suis" occurs) with the overwhelming and already epoch-making results of his mathematical developments (introduction of general algebra and the combination of arithmetic, algebra and geometry in the analytical geometry developed by him).

But as early as 1663, in his *Disputatio metaphysica de principio individui*, the seventeen-year-old Baccalaureus Gottfried Wilhelm Leibniz founded a much more radical and system-forming approach, which was to develop as a fundamental critique of Cartesian dualism of spatiotemporal and rational substances. For from an ethical and legal point of view the question became acute as to how the soul can have an influence on the body when the two substances are completely separated from one another.[51]

---

[50] "Car on peut bien concevoir, qu'une machine soit tellement faite qu'elle profère des paroles, et même qu'elle en profère quelques-unes à propos des actions corporelles qui causeront quelques changements en ses organes: comme si on la touche en quelque endroit, qu'elle demande ce qu'on lui veut dire ..." [For it is conceivable that a machine is so made that it utters words, and even utters some of them about the bodily actions that will cause some changes in its organs: as if it were touched in some place, that it asks what one wants it to say...], Descartes, René, *Discours de la méthode*, Paris 1948, pp. 109-110. The novel *Lemprière's Dictionary* by Lawrence Norfolk, published in London in 1991 and much discussed in the Federal Republic of Germany, makes the haunting of the machine people the all-encompassing bracket of its bloody history, which begins with the siege of La Rochelle in 1628 – the year in which Descartes took down the writing of the *Discours*.

[51] Descartes attempted to solve the problem which friends of the mathematician Gassendi had pointed out in his letters to Regius, Elisabeth et al. with the help of a *genetic psychology of substantial forms*. This means that the human soul as the only permitted substantial form can only gradually – i.e. with increasing age – differ from the matter of the body and finally free itself from it. In doing so, he did not emphasize the problematic unity of res extensa and res cogitans, but their difference, which must first be generated, as he said. However, this teaching, a kind of psychology of Aristotelian physics, no longer had any influence due to a lack of coherent publication. See Rodis-Lewis, Geneviève, *Descartes*,

Leibniz spent a whole life fulfilling his tasks as historian and as at least as important mathematician as Descartes, until in 1713, as an old man, he wrote a script which only appeared in 1720, four years after his death, under the added title of the German translation as his *Monadology*.

A.1.2 The First Analysis of the Individual (Philosophy)

With this treatise Leibniz gave a long matured answer to the question of his academic first paper about the nature of the particular, about a possible ontological principle of individuation, with a complete world system – a cosmology that is based on the principle of the individual and at the same time still grasps the general, eternal and divine.[52] Thus, the rather intuitive reorientation of Renaissance humanism directed towards individuality had received a first, theoretically worked through version that was connectable to the rationalism of the Enlightenment.[53] The pitfalls that Leibniz saw in traditional ontology was the unavoidability of the Parmenidean substance philosophy – that was just overplayed by Descartes with dualism but foreseen by his forerunners in the Renaissance – if it is not proven what makes the *change of conditions and states* in nature and in man possible.[54] It had to be shown that the substances are differentiated in themselves and that these differences also *generate time*. Otherwise, the Eleatic thinking of the All-unity would have been ineluctable and unsurpassable.

For Leibniz, the monads are therefore substances without parts, 'simpli-

---

[52] The following presentation is based on Alain Renaut's outstanding study *L'ère de l'individu. Contribution à l'histoire de la subjectivité* [The Age of the Indvidual. A Contribution to the History of Subjectivity], Paris 1989, pp. 115-150.

[53] The profound constructions and analyses of Leibniz are the background against which the highly regarded theses of the French sociologist and structuralist anthropologist René Dumont should be judged. Dumont has been fascinated by the Indian caste system since his book *Homo hierarchicus* (1967). The schematization of the entire modern history with the help of the difference holism/individualism is analytically only of limited use. In Dumont's version, it primarily serves his moralizing and politically charged disqualification attempts of modern individualism in favor of hierarchically holistic organized societies; see Dumont, Louis, *Essais sur l'individualisme. Une perspective anthropologique sur l'idéologie moderne*, Paris 1983.

[54] Leibniz thus provides a new answer to the question that was first raised with Heraclit's ontology, the fluxus model of being. Karl R. Popper wrote in the Heraclitus chapter of his famous study on the open society: "The philosophies of Parmenides, Democritus, Plato, and Aristotle can all be appropriately described as attempts to solve the problems of that changing world which Heraclitus had discovered", in: Popper, *The Open Society and its Enemies* [1945] London 1984, Volume I, p. 12

cities', "the true atoms of nature and in one word the elements of things."[55] Their very existence is timeless; they are the work of the divine creation and destruction of the world. Thus, time only increases with the creation of the monads and articulates itself through them. What is surprising about the monads is that they cannot communicate with each other, that they have '"no windows".[56] Everything that happens within them. In this way the bodily world no longer has its own special reality and is dissolved in the flow of monads that traverses it.[57] A person is a soul in the form of an indivisible monad, but her body consists of an unimaginable number of monads that differ from the soul in their degree of sensation (perception as an internal differentiation of distinguishable states) and perception in the state of consciousness (apperception as the ability of the monad to think an ego).[58]

This was a paradoxical movement in the description of living beings and things. The institution of the subject as res cogitans, since Descartes considered as a brazen, uniform and yet unmistakable institution, was relativized to a respective degree of realism[59] – at the same time, however, the 'individual' as such was metaphysically created as a special feature of states within an apperceiving monad whose cohesion could be independent of all other monads. This spiritual monad as an individual is characterized by its self-sufficiency, independence from other monads, its lack of communication and the always imperfect apperception, that is, by a never far-reaching reflection on itself, of which only the divine monad would be

---

[55] Leibniz, Gottfried Wilhelm, *Monadology*, Theorem 6, Stuttgart 1990, p. 13.
[56] Ibid., Theorem 7, p. 14.
[57] Ibid. Theorem 71, p. 30.
[58] In this way Leibniz could also take up the machine problem again and solve it in his own way: "Therefore, every organic object (body) of a living being is a kind of divine machine or natural automaton, which surpasses all artificial automatons infinitely. A machine made by human art is not a machine in every part of it. For example, the tooth of a brass wheel has parts or fragments which are no longer artificial to us and which have nothing in themselves that reveals something machine-like in relation to the use for which the wheel was intended. But the machines of nature, i.e. the living bodies, are still machines in their smallest parts, to infinity", Ibid., Theorem 64, p. 29. The animals are also animated again for Leibniz, for the possession of the soul is no longer a question of principle, but only one of degree or intensity.
[59] With this reading Renaut presents the misinterpretation of Heidegger, who claims to have discovered the work of an anthropomorphic principle in *Monadology*; see Renaut, *L'ère de l'individu*, loc. cit., p. 134.

capable. For below the threshold of consciousness an infinite number of things happen in the area of unconscious perception in one and the same monad.[60] There are awake, dreaming and sleeping monads; but none is like the other. And there is the *monas monadum*, the divine and only disembodied monad whose inner side is the whole world with the multiplicity of its monads.[61] It is the ocean, we are each a drop in it.

Fig.5: Gottfried Wilhelm von Leibniz (1646-1713)

However, the deconstruction of the subject while simultaneously inventing the individual was paid for by the abandonment of the idea of autonomy.

---

[60] Renaut localizes here the philosophical origin of the theory of the subconscious; see ibid. p. 136.

[61] In this way, too, the Irenic Leibniz wanted to come to the aid of the denominationally polarized Christian theology, for his system made possible an incurporeal and yet rationally conceivable concept of God in which all parties were to find a common theme. How great the faith barrier of a material-physical conception of God always was, Augustine already gave a moving testimony of this in his *Confessions*.

For although the individualized monad is independent, it has by no means created itself or given itself any law. The notorious panlogism of Leibniz' world model, which only becomes understandable in connection with his *Theodicy*, postulates that each monad contains in itself the totality of the world and its specificity is secured by its own perspective on this world context.[62] But the pre-established harmony is only possible by God having established the world in the act of creation for all time and according to a complete plan. Which means nothing else but that every monad exists in this way that has been destined for it since the beginning of the world. Freedom for these monads is not autonomy, but the special vigilance with which reason strives to see through the divine plan of creation, whereby it has already taken another step towards perfection – which in turn exactly fulfils the plan of creating the best of all possible worlds, in which evil may only exist so that perfection and freedom become possible at the same time.

However, this kind of so-called 'compossibility' of freedom and necessity has deprived free action of any insight into its rational reasons. This amounts to the fact that God has created a world in which a few selected viewers are provided with the minimal conceptual equipment in the form of the discernment of good/evil in order to be able to admire the splendor and the perfect proportions of world creation. In one of the most important and fascinating passages of the *Critique of Practical Reason*, where Kant places moral subjectivity on a ground that is ontologically characterized by the *freedom of time*, he immediately attested to the 'automaton spirituale', as he calls Leibniz' individualized subject, the "freedom of a roasting jack that, once it has been winded up, performs its movement by itself."[63]

One now rightly suspects that Kant, who in his pre-Critical time himself adhered to Leibniz-Wolff's philosophy, had to face up to the dual tasks of making subjectivity and individuality conceivable in his philosophical system and compatible with the demands of reason.

---

[62] Leibniz, *Monadology*, loc. cit., Theorem 56-58, p. 26: Every awake monad is therefore a kind of peephole through which the world can observe itself.

[63] Kant, Immanuel, *Works* VII, p. 222 [A 174].

A.1.3 The Education of the Individual (Pedagogy)

It has already been mentioned that Norbert Elias insisted on not measuring the development of European individuality exclusively in adults.[64] Individuals also have an ontogenesis, or in vernacular: a childhood and youth. The development of pedagogy as a demanding educational science began with the rejection of the older models of growth to adulthood which generally saw in children the enfolded, just not yet germinated and fully developed form of already-adults, which differentiated education according to the state of the child as only a second nature and engraved with great rigor the world knowledge considered essential in the minds of these small adults.[65]

It was therefore a great step forward when John Locke (1632-1704), in his book *Thoughts on Education* (1693), which influenced the entire pedagogy of the 18th century, first pointed out that hardly two children were similar and therefore needed different educational methods, but that children should above all enjoy learning.[66] Locke was the first to recognize the value of play for childhood, the subject's self-activity in the acquisition of skill and knowledge, and at the same time he severely restricted the competence of the educator, for he should be a role model ('gentleman', open-minded and sophisticated nobleman) and at the same time create the conditions for the child's innate dispositions to develop.[67] The ranking of pedagogical values shows a clear rejection of the humanistic educational ideal and a down-to-earth attitude of the educational teachings of the

---

[64] Elias, *The Society of Individuals*, loc. cit., p. 46.

[65] As we have just heard about Aurelius Augustine, we should still mention the historically interesting observation in his *Confessions* in this context: "Nevertheless, I got beaten when I was sluggish in learning. The adults approved of this, as many before us had already lived this way and had sketched out the arduous paths on which we, Adam's children, now had to walk in ever-increasing plague and tribulation", in: Augustine, *Bekenntnisse* [Confessions, ca. 390 A.D.] Munich 1992, p. 41. In *De civitate Dei*, XXI 14, he even remarked: "Who would not rather die than be a child again!"

[66] Locke, John, *Some Thoughts Concerning Education*, edited by H. Wohlers, Stuttgart 1970.

[67] However, this assumption of a *hereditary disposition* contradicts Locke's tabularasa theory of the human mind and is only one of many characteristics of the unsystematic character of his writings; cf. Reble, Albert, *Geschichte der Pädagogik* [History of Pedagogy], Stuttgart 1980, p. 139.

Enlightenment: 1.) virtue and truthfulness; 2.) wisdom; 3.) education of the heart and courtesy; 4.) knowledge of things.[68] This reflects a new naturalness as a maxim of pedagogy. Learning should be unspoiled, uncomplicated, physically empowering and conducive to dexterity. Locke's writing, however, was still an exclusive educational theory for the higher classes of England and he expressly refused to present a general educational theory.

Jean-Jacques Rousseau (1712-78) went much further not only on this regard, although he was a great admirer of Locke. In his voluminous educational novel *Emile ou de l'éducation* (1762), Rousseau appears as a "preacher of the gospel of freedom, nature and the heart, human rights and human dignity."[69] This key work for the development of education up to the Reform Movement in 1900 has become a kind of creed of the Enlightenment. In the first sentence of the book he uses biblical linguistic power to write the apodictic admonition to all educators: "Everything that comes from the hands of the Creator is good; everything is degenerate under the hands of man."[70] For the first time there was a model of education differentiated according to age groups, which at the same time rejected all corporative and professional considerations. Looking back on the up to then valid educational teachings he wrote:

> "Childhood is something completely unknown to us [...] The most sensible people stick to what man must know without considering what children are capable of learning. They always look for the adult in the child without considering what a child is before."[71]

The most important maxim of the education of the young Emile is the naturalness, not only on the way of education in the form of its various practices, as it was taught in the 17th century up to Locke, but also in the goal of education. Rousseau's radical cultural criticism, which has made him famous since his *First Discourse*, is expressed in it:

> "Natural man is everything to himself. It is the unbroken unity, the absolute whole, which has a relationship only to itself or its equals. The bourgeois man is only a fractional number that depends on its

---

[68] Ibid. p. 140.

[69] Ibid. p. 145.

[70] Rousseau, Jean-Jacques, *Emile oder Über die Erziehung* [Emile, or: On Education], Stuttgart 1993, p. 107. The first book in particular is a critique of contemporary education closely related to Locke.

[71] Ibid. p. 102, preface.

denominator and whose value consists in its relationship to the whole, i.e. to the whole of society [...] Whoever wants to preserve the originality of natural feelings in the bourgeois order does not know what he wants [...] He will be a man of today – a Frenchman, an Englishman, a bourgeois – and that is nothing."[72]

Education is all about allowing the human being in the child to develop according to his or her nature. For Rousseau, however, nature is not an individual facility, but a kind of horizontal, age-specific perfection. The pedagogical complexity gain lies above all in the temporal differentiation and stratification of the human ideal, which has been uniform since antiquity, in order to make it accessible for education without empirically dissolving the platonically understood ideal itself. In the fourth book, for example, this enabled him to portray puberty in an extraordinarily convincing way as a great, crisis-like incision in the lives of young men, which he aptly calls a "second birth."[73] Only now is Emile, who at the age of fifteen has practiced his senses and already learned to think, made familiar with feelings and fantasy. It was also at this point that the training of expertise, primarily in history, religion, literature and etiquette as a general teaching of good taste, began.

Rousseau's new ideal of education is a grandiose, albeit fictitious introspection of a naturally growing boy, but the fixation of his development as a counter-term to the existing society makes Emile so much obliged to fulfil an ideal of his author that an individuality following actual autonomy cannot come about. But at a time when education still assumed that the social position of a child, which it is to grow into, is part of its 'nature', it was of course an enormously subversive undertaking to postulate its nature precisely as independent of all social regulations – even at the price of under-schematizing the individual as a general subject of human freedom and dignity.[74] In his autobiographies, Rousseau continued

---

[72] Ibid. pp. 112-113.

[73] Ibid., *Fourth Book*, pp. 438-718; "We are, so to speak, born twice: once to exist, the other time to live; as species and sex beings." ibid. p. 438. The systematic neglect and "natural" inferiority of Sophie's education in the *Fifth Book* is well known. Since nature has created women in such a way that, among other things, they do not need a 'second birth' – their puberty being perceived as far less dramatic – they do not need any education aimed at this.

[74] For Sophie, this sub-individualization goes much further than for Emile, for she is completely bound to her task of fulfilling her function as a female part of the species. As a complement to Emile's shortcomings, her renunciation of indivi-

the same program and saw the individual moments in his own behavior exclusively in the actions that were undoubtedly motivated by a strong moral feeling. In his *Confessions* he justifies none of his deviations, not even the smallest lie or even the slightest unspoken desire, if it is not inspired by a moral thought. That individuality could occasionally mean a critical position against the whole of society and the standards of morality itself, this thought cannot be found anywhere in Rousseau's work – which was an important reason for Voltaire's ridicule of the naively upright Rousseau.

In no other country has Rousseau's teaching had as much influence as in Germany. An entire educational movement was formed from 1770 that enthusiastically translated the teachings from *Emile* into a practice appropriate to German conditions. The teachers and writers, including Basedow, Salzmann, Campe, Trapp and Rochow, who called themselves 'Philantropists', designed a "reasonable-natural" education that recognized Rousseau's teaching, but set different accents:

> "They also pay a great deal of attention to sex education, albeit with a one-sided, rationalist approach based on early instruction. They want to deal with everything early at all and despite their battle cry they usually have little patience to wait for the natural development. In contrast to Rousseau, they want to awaken a sense of acquisitiveness and directly increase the professional skills of their pupils. Their aim is to turn them into efficient, practical, hard-working, enlightened citizens as quickly as possible."[75]

Their homely down-to-earth methods meant that they tested a practice of reform education and carried out experiments such as the *Philantropin* boarding school founded in 1771. But they did not produce any further theoretical development, so that their pedagogy could not consolidate and establish itself as science. They remained an avant-garde that has not yet been followed. For example, if they abolished the penalties and set up a system of rewards, 'virtuousness nails' and 'tickets', then these attempts would be limited to the narrow circle of the philanthropists. Nevertheless, their influence has been sustained in the secularization of schools and in

---

duality and her natural virtue should bring so much nature back into society that it can be regarded as a moral institution; cf. the thorough discussion in Christa Kersting, *Die Genese der Pädagogik im 18. Jahrhundert. Campes 'Allgemeine Revision' im Kontext der neuzeitlichen Wissenschaft* [The Genesis of Pedagogy in the 18th Century. Campe's 'General Revision' in the Context of Modern Science], Weinheim 1992, pp. 340-386.

[75] Reble, *Geschichte der Erziehung* [History of Education], loc. cit., p. 154.

the consolidation of the idea of popular education. With regard to Rosseau's model of education, one could say that they tried to temporize and concretize Rousseau's abstract ideal of human education – with very different, but usually little success.[76] It was only the New Humanism that subsequently succeeded in establishing a theoretically demanding pedagogy as science based on Kant's moral philosophy.[77]

In an astute and very thorough treatise, Niklas Luhmann reconstructed the non-explicit theoretical achievements of the philanthropists in order to find out whether New Humanism, which gravitated primarily around the formula of Kant's categorical imperative, was actually a further development in terms of theoretical content.[78] He noted that the philanthropists had developed a 'bliss theorem' which was not hedonistic in a vulgar way, but which formed a mediation of the individual and society on the basis of self-reference: the self-enjoyment of one's own individual perfection and usefulness could only happen in and via society.[79]

As a reaction to this, a development occurred in pedagogy which will be extraordinarily revealing for the second part of the investigation when Kant's *Critique of the Power of Judgment* is analyzed in the light of the theorem of individuality created in it. The replacement of the philanthropists, criticized as eudemonistic and superficial, set off, as already mentioned, with the pedagogic positioning of the categorical imperative, the formal core of all morality. From 1790 on, Kant's critical philosophy

---

[76] Reble notes, for example, that the Philanthropist has failed because of the "human shortcomings" of their leaders. The Philanthropin had to be closed again in 1793; ibid. p. 156.

[77] Cf. the classic, in which the term 'humanism' also appears for the first time: Niehammer, Immanuel, *Der Streit des Philantropismus und Humanismus in der Theorie des Erziehungsunterrichts unserer Zeit* [The Dispute of Philanthropism and Humanism in the Theory of Teaching in our Time], Jena 1808, new ed., Weinheim 1968.

[78] Luhmann, Niklas, *Theoriesubstitution in der Erziehungswissenschaft. Von der Philantropie zum Neuhumanismus* [Theory Substitution in Educational Science. From Philanthropy to New Humanism], in: Luhmann, *Gesellschaftsstruktur und Semantik. Studien zur Wissenssoziologie der modernen Gesellschaft* [Social Structure and Semantics. Studies on the Sociology of Knowledge in Modern Society], vol. 2, Frankfurt 1993, pp. 105-194; Christa Kersting formulated critical and equally well-founded objections to this in *Die Genese der Pädagogik*, loc. cit., pp. 28-30.

[79] Ibid. p. 133-134, so of course the picture of the Philantropists is quite different from that of Reble, op. cit.

was taught throughout Germany and all newer educators referred to him. This gave rise to many misguided attempts, such as "deducing" the "unity of the concept of education", i.e. legitimizing a concept of education with transcendental philosophy, in which educator and pupil should appear at the same time, as if pulled together in one subject. But more important was the work with the moral formula: "The categorical imperative is used as a kind of socializing a priori, and education is expected to put it into function."[80] However, this was a serious misunderstanding of Kant's moral philosophy, which repeatedly warned that the *Critique of Pure Reason*, the *Critique of Practical Reason* and the *Metaphysics of Morals* were exclusively about rational beings *in abstracto*, who thus have no human traits, but are purely conceptual constructs to philosophically safeguard against skepticism, that there can be something like the cognition of nature, freedom and morality *at all*. It took revenge, for example, for teachers to be asked in an anonymous document to familiarize themselves with the results of Kant's philosophy "without going into the depths and heights of the *Critique of Pure Reason*, for which... few educators can gain time."[81]

Kant only had to give a lecture on pedagogy once in rotation at the Königsberg University, the manuscript of which was also published – in 1803! The theoretical references of the teachers to Kant's work could not be linked to any genuinely pedagogical writings of Kant. Even today, in his essay rich in bibliographical notes, Niklas Luhmann mentions only a single passage from the *Critique of Practical Reason* – and thus cements the error of the New Humanists even more thoroughly.[82]

The mistake was to derive an educational science directly from moral philosophy, which thus could only function analogously to natural mechanics or could not be further developed at all, because it had to fail so much in practice. Kant, on the other hand, stated unmistakably in his lecture on

---

[80] Kersting, *Die Genese der Pädagogik*, loc. cit., p. 135.

[81] *Über moralische Erziehung* [On Moral Education], Archiv der Erziehungskunde für Deutschland 4/1794, p. 1-38, here p. 9; cited from Luhmann, *Theorieubstitution*, loc. cit.

[82] Luhmann, *Theoriesubstitution* [Theory Substitution], loc. cit., p. 125, fn. Luhmann is also mistaken in his claim that the "fact" of moral consciousness as evidence cuts off all further questions for Kant. Although his assessment corresponds to a notorious interpretation that can be found in most Kant commentaries, the systematics of Kant's critical work is dramatically underestimated here. A new approach for the treatment of these interpretation problems is considered here in the excursus *Hypostases of Identity* under B.1.9.

pedagogy:

> "Because the development of nature is not self-evident in humans, <u>all education is an art</u> [and not a science; RG]. The origin as well as the progress of this art is either mechanical, without plan, ordered according to given circumstances, or *judicious*. [...] All educational art, which arises merely mechanically, has to carry many mistakes and shortcomings in itself, because it has no plan as its basis. *Educational art or pedagogy must therefore become judicious* if it is to develop human nature in such a way that it reaches its destiny." [highlights by RG][83]

Kant also de-potentiates the great moral and idealistic tension of educational theory since Rousseau by making it clear that the perfection of human nature can never be achieved in the individual, but only in the species.[84]

It seems as if an apologetic excursion to Kant has crept in here, which has moved a little away from the question. However, the misunderstanding of Kant's philosophy among the teachers is so fruitful for an important discussion in the second part of the study that its presentation and critical illumination could not be omitted here. Later on, it will reappear in the difference between determining and reflecting judgment, as a moral misunderstanding of political subjectivity. Kant's idea that pedagogy is an art that is also supposed to be judicious will reappear in a transformed form in connection with various aspects of aesthetics.

There is no doubt that the 18th century has made great strides towards a pedagogy that is oriented towards the individuality of the person growing up. And yet the theorem of this individuality was only deepened in a kind of historical concreteness in the 19th century – and has been stuck there ever since. For here too it becomes apparent that there is still no philosophical theory of individuality that can take into account the modern world in all its weight and all its impositions.

---

[83] Kant, Immanuel, *Über Pädagogik* [On Pedagogy], Werke XII, ed. by W. Weischedel, Frankfort 1988, p. 703 [A 16].

[84] Ibid. p. 702[A 13].

A.1.4 The Individual in the Markets (Economy)

In the 18th century, Europe's economy was still largely agrarian, with strong regional fluctuations. Food supply and thus agriculture were at the center of economic attention. Depending on the intensity of international trade, manufactory (mercantilism) or trade (liberalism) followed.

The theoretical development of a systematic concept of economic actors has not taken place in Germany. Little significant work was done in this field in the German Reich in the 18th century. There was no one that could have been compared with the Frenchman Francois Quesnay or the Englishman Adam Smith. The German physiocrats were only students of French models and did not significantly expand their theoretical apparatus.[85] The efforts to develop a closed economic doctrine or theory mostly related only to the area that seemed directly vital: agriculture. The countries engaged in colonialism, on the other hand, had some reason to think more intensively, especially about international trade and the condition of the markets. Trade with mutual national advantage was recognized as the most important source of wealth. The end of European mercantilism announced itself from there. The state thus receded into the background as the main player in the economy and increasingly confined itself to customs clearance and the control of cross-border trade in goods. At least that is what the observers, who were both administratively and philosophically trained, saw in their theoretical work. In fact, the economic and social historical retrospective shows no de facto retreat of the state. On the contrary, state activity increased systematically and paradoxically in the age of liberalism. The observation angle of contemporary liberal analysts only shifted from the state, which was gradually faded out, to the individuals and their form of rationality of action. This rationality was still entirely ethical, and the first liberal economists were above all moral

---

[85] After all, the physiocratic theorems were experimentally adopted by some rulers in the German Reich (the so-called "enlightened absolutists" Frederick II of Prussia, Margrave Karl Friedrich of Baden-Durlach, Emperor Joseph II and Grand Duke Leopold I. of Tuscany) – without any success; cf. Holldack, Heinz, *Der Physiokratismus und die absolute Monarchie* [Physiocratism and Absolute Monarchy], in: Aretin, K. O. Freiherr von, *Der aufgeklärte Absolutismus* [Enlightened Absolutism], Cologne 1974, pp. 137-162; cf. also Hensmann, Volker, *Staat und Absolutismus im Denken der Physiokraten* [State and Absolutism in the Thinking of Physiocrats], Frankfurt 1975.

philosophers.[86] The individualistic approach to economics did not develop equally in all European states. Germany's delay in economic theory, which began at that time, continued into the 20th century. John Maynard Keynes wrote very carefully in the preface to the German edition of his epoch-making *General Theory*:

> "Thus Germany, quite contrary to her habit in most of the sciences, has been content for a whole century to do without any formal theory of economics which was predominant and generally accepted."[87]

Shortly thereafter he spoke of "Germany's economic agnosticism", which had already had a longer tradition at that time. In the 18th century, when the European economy was theoretically and technically prepared for industrialization, only two important 'scientists of state' are to be mentioned in the German Reich who became relevant in economic theory, namely Johann Heinrich Gottlob von Justi with his main work *Die Grundsätze zu der Macht und Glückseligkeit der Staaten oder ausführliche Vorstellung der gesamten Polizeywissenschaft* [The Principles of Power and Happiness of States or Detailed Presentation of the Entire Policy Science] (2 volumes, 1760) and Joseph von Sonnenfels, who wrote *Grundsätze der Polizey, Handlung und Finanzwissenschaft* [Principles of Policy, Trade and Financial Science](1765). Like all other German economists, the cameralistic economic understanding of these authors was still consistently state-oriented and reduced the economy to a welfare state instrument. They were familiar with the international debate on laissez-faire policy, but since the separation of state and economy had not yet been implemented, free trade and deregulation ideas had no chance. On an argumentative level, the German theoreticians objected – not without some justification, by the way – to the unintended consequences of a free trade policy, namely unemployment. What really prevented political science from releasing the economy, however, was the inability to theoretically grasp individual economic actors in an economic context, let alone to recognize an overall economic gain that could be generated by free market activity. The only trust-building economic actor in the German Reich was still the state – whereby the 'state' here is to be understood, mind you, the respective

---

[86] See Schumpeter, Joseph A., *History of Economic Analysis*, [Oxford 1954] London 1982, p. 127.

[87] Keynes, John Maynard, *General Theory of Employment, Interest and Money*, Collected Writings Vol. VII, [1936] Cambridge 1973, p. XXVI.

sovereign in person and the administration, which was connected to the princely courts of the territorial corporations. Another theoretical obstacle was the empirically counterfactual doctrine of the 'whole house'.[88] For despite the socially and thus historically already effective differentiation of the functions of house and enterprise, German political scientists saw no reason to separate the old unity of housekeeping, economy and rule.[89] Thus the description of economic conditions preserved conventional patriarchal moral concepts and was already empirically resistant in the beginning.

Many European authors have gone in the opposite direction to market liberalism. First, the moral and religious foundations of economic activity were examined and then, from there, with a whole new anthropology, the Aristotelian-scholastic doctrine was lifted from its hinges. The discussion about the motives for economic behavior began with the famous *Fable of the Bees* by the Dutch physician Bernard Mandeville (1670-1733), who lived in England.[90] In this philosophical-theological allegory, which had appeared in 1723, Christians still knowingly and with a bad conscience deceived their own faith and thus the prevailing moral norms of their society.[91] From time immemorial, capital accumulation and the production of wealth enjoyed a morally more than doubtful reputation in the Christian West.[92]

---

[88] See Wehler, Hans-Ulrich, *Deutsche Gesellschaftsgeschichte*, vol. 1, *Vom Feudalismus des Alten Reiches bis zur Defensiven Modernisierung der Reformära: 1700-1815*, Munich 1987, pp. 81-83.

[89] "Since a separation between house and business only advanced in mining, but otherwise every economy took place within the framework of the whole house, there was no difference between economy and government. Economy as the doctrine of the house and as the doctrine of economics was at the same time the doctrine of government. Politeia and oeconomia were basically indistinguishable," in: Brückner, Jutta, *Staatswissenschaften, Kameralismus und Naturrecht. Ein Beitrag zur Geschichte der Politischen Wissenschaft im Deutschland des späten 17. und frühen 18. Jahrhunderts* [Political Sciences, Cameralism and Natural Law. A Contribution to the History of Political Science in Late 17th and Early 18th Century Germany], Munich 1977, p. 54.

[90] Cf. the critical edition by Kaye, F. B. (ed.), *The Fable of the Bees: or, Private Vices, Public Benefits*, Oxford 1924.

[91] Mandeville's apology of sinfulness and acquisitiveness, without which there would be no art, science and no society at all, has earned him the nickname "Man-Devil"; see Nieli, Russel, *Commercial Society and Christian Virtue: The Mandeville-Law Dispute*, in: *The Review of Politics*, p. 581-609, here p. 596.

[92] "You shall not gather your treasures on earth [....] But gather your treasures in

Conversely, the tradition of the rules of strictly Christian lifestyle depended on an agriculturally determined society.[93] However, precisely this basis dissolved in England as a result of increasing domestic and overseas trade.[94] Against this background Mandeville developed a model of a sense of acquisition that prima facie did not need Calvinism and inner-worldly asceticism, which Weber based his sociology on[95], but only *joie de vivre*. His formula of *private vices*, which are to bring in *public benefits*, is the reversal of the thesis of 'priest's deceit': the faithful lie to their priests and pretend to consider their revelations and rules of life for the straight path to the hereafter, that is, to consider them true and binding[96] in order to be able to devote themselves all the more undisturbed to the enjoyment of earthly fruits.

The Professor of Logic, later of Moral Philosophy at Glasgow University, Adam Smith, resumed this theme in his *Theory of Moral Sentiments*,

---

heaven [...] For where your treasure is, there is also your heart [...] No one can serve two masters: either he will hate the one and love the other, or he will follow the one and despise the other. You cannot serve God and mammon," in: *New Testament*, Matthew 6, 19-24; cf. also Luke 16, 13); cf. also the Book of Ecclesiastes in the *Old Testament*.

[93] Cf. Robertson, H. M., *Aspects of the Rise of Economic Individualism*, Cambridge 1933, pp. 176-178.

[94] It may be interesting to note that domestic trade has been stimulated by increasing urban mobility, new channels for water transport, an increasing number of daily and weekly newspapers with commercial advertisements, an improved postal system and an expanding credit system. In short: England became relatively early on a territorially integrated national market with increasing world market connections; see Brentano, Lujo, *Eine Geschichte der wirtschaftlichen Entwicklung Englands* [History of Economic Development of the United Kingdom], vol. 2, *Die Zeit des Merkantilismus* [The Era of Mercantilism], New York 1968.

[95] Here it would have to be examined whether Dutch and English Protestantism had any influence on Weber after all. He has definitely not taken Mandeville, this important author of rising capitalism, into account.

[96] Of course, Weber's religious study on "the feeling of an unheard-of inner loneliness of the individual" in exemplarily chosen Calvinism is the first to be suitable for a theory of individualization; see Weber, Max, *Die protestantische Ethik und der Geist des Kapitalismus*,[The Protestant Ethic and the Spirit of Capitalism] in: Weber, *Gesammelte Aufsätze zur Religionssoziologie* [Collected Essays on the Sociology of Religion], 6th edition, vol. I, Tübingen, 1972. Here, however, we try to gain *explicit* moments of individualism unfolding as a modern self-description through thinking and acting in the 18th century.

published in 1759, which made him a well-known and respected author throughout Europe.[97] In order to take the egoism, which Mandeville scandalously considered identical with the public good, the sharp edge, he deepened the analysis of the moral subject. He discovered the ability of people to think themselves into other people ("sympathy") and to make the insights gained from this change of perspective the basis of their own moral judgments. This was an important result regarding the constitution of individuals.

A few years later followed the most famous and successful book ever written in economics. Adam Smith's main work *Wealth of Nations*[98] was published in 1776 and was impressive for its simple language.[99] The German translation was already available in the same year that also dated the beginning of classical economics.

Like Mandeville, Smith recognized that the individuality of economic subjects of action is articulated through amorality, which in turn has its cause in an 'evil' nature that seduces people. While Mandeville celebrated this fact as superior cunning, Smith led this anthropological grievance back into an unobjectionable moral-philosophical framework of social theory.[100] In this context, the fact must be seen that Smith himself regarded his *Theory of Moral Sentiment* as his most important work, which for him ranked far above his economic work and whose revision he dealt exclusively with in his last years of life. His moral philosophical writing, with which he had made a name for himself as a young man, was thus at the same time his late work.[101] There was a long discussion among scholars as to whether the basis of the *Theory of Moral Sentiment*, namely sympathy, contradicted the core of economic theory, which could be found in egoism. Apart from the fact that the latter assumption is based on incomplete reading of *Wealth of Nations*, which with more conscientiousness would have brought its author

---

[97] Smith, Adam, *Theorie der ethischen Gefühle* [Theory of Moral Sentiment], 2 volumes, Hamburg 1977.

[98] Smith, Adam, *An Inquiry into the Nature and Causes of the Wealth of Nations*, Harmondsworth/Middlesex, 1970.

[99] Schumpeter wrote somewhat sarcastically: "He never moved above the heads of even the dullest readers," in: *History of Economic Analysis* [Oxford 1954], London 1982, p. 185.

[100] Ibid., p. 184.

[101] See the introduction to Adam Smith's *Theory of Moral Sentiment*, loc. cit., by Walther Eckstein (ed.), p. XXI.

into the ancestral gallery of ethical socialism[102], the concept of sympathy has been misunderstood. Because it is not an objectively valid, socially conditioned or natural commandment of charity. Rather, this kind of compassion is to be understood as a feeling ability that allows people to put themselves in the inner horizon of other people, "if we change places with the sufferer in our imagination"; and "...even the worst ruffian, the most hardened despiser is not completely barren of this feeling."[103] Smith develops here a mimetic theory of subjectivity that is not based on natural morality or malignity as an anthropological constant, but only on the ability to experience the joy and suffering of the *alter* in one one's *ego*. He thus moves between traditional Christian morality and Mandeville's conspiracy theory, which claims that even the greatest virtues are motivated by vain self-love inspired by the envy of others. It is precisely this avoidance of an 'evil' anthropology that should provide the sympathy[104], which is not itself already good or bad, but must be assumed for all morals. The imitation performance of the individual ultimately also leads him to abide by treaties.[105] Thus it is the exact reversal of Mandeville's thesis, but also of Christian doctrine of values, for it is not good or bad morals that promote the economy, but with the help of economic activity the moral thinking and action of entire peoples is strengthened:

> "... and lastly, commerce and manufactures gradually introduced order and good government, and with them, the liberty and security of individuals, among the inhabitants of the country, who had before lived almost in a continual state of war with their neighbors, and of servile dependency upon their superiors."[106]

Adam Smith has thus developed a coherent theory of individuality which, beyond egoism and altruism, is based on a capacity within the subject that must be accepted in order to make the cultural, especially economic

---

[102] Small, Albion W., Adam Smith and Modern Sociology. A Study in the Methodology of the Social Sciences, Chicago 1907, p. 65.

[103] Smith, *Theory of Moral Sentiment*, loc. cit., p. 2.

[104] Ibid., pp. 513-523.

[105] The systems-theoretical perspective on the same facts would, for example, reconstruct trust as a 'semantically' tested and proven procedure for reducing complexity and thereby completely abstract from any individual achievement, i.e. the contribution of consciousness in this event; see Luhmann, Niklas, *Vertrauen. Ein Mechanismus der Reduktion sozialer Komplexität* [Confidence. A Mechanism for Reducing Social Complexity], 2nd ed., Stuttgart 1973.

[106] Smith, *Wealth of Nations*, loc. cit., p. 508.

achievements of that time comprehensible at all. Smith thus anticipated some important insights that Kant later systematically deepened and incorporated into a critique of the subject of knowledge.[107] This did not prevent the sociologist René Dumont from distilling a true horror story of European individualism from this development of economic theory.[108] To draw a causal chain from the works of Locke, Mandeville and especially Smith to National Socialism and Stalinism, the two highlights of the wretched individualism in Dumont's interpretation, proves that even French elite schools do not offer secure protection against the spread of scholarly nonsense.

How extraordinarily rudimentary the subsequent economic theories were compared to Smith's foundation (Say, Riccardo, Malthus, later Mill and Walras) can perhaps be seen from the fact that it would be another century before capital finally replaced the ground as a production factor. Or that only utilitarian marginal utility theory could even attempt to model, aggregate and scale the differently strong needs of different subjects on a mathematical basis. Until then, the strongly morally or mechanistically generalizing assumptions reigned over the empirical behavior of economic actors, which no longer reached the philosophical depth of Adam Smith's reflections.

---

[107] This aspect has been known since August Oncken's study *Adam Smith und Immanuel Kant. Der Einklang und das Wechselverhältnis ihrer Lehren über Sitte, Staat und Wirtschaft* [Adam Smith and Immanuel Kant. The Unison und the Interrelation between their Teachings on Morals, State and Economy], Leipzig 1877; however, Smith's theory of ethical feeling is always – not only with Oncken – too quickly short-circuited with Kant's rigid, transcendentally-based moral philosophy. I consider a line of tradition and argumentation from Smith's concept of 'sympathy' to the 'reflective judgement' in Kant's *Critique of the Power of Judgement*, on which aesthetics and teleology are based, to be much more obvious and convincing.

[108] Dumont, Louis, *Homo aequalis. Genèse et épanouissement de l'idéologie économique*, Paris 1985.

Fig. 6: Adam Smith (1723-1790)

It is probably no exaggeration to say that economic theory has not to date gone beyond the very narrow framework of utilitarian anthropology, which believes its actors to have only a form of shrunk rationality and individuality.[109]

---

[109] The classic example often cited is Gary Becker, the 1982 Nobel Prize winner in economics, who has made topics such as alcoholism, suicide, work, time, family, etc. quantifiable and thus calculable under utilitarian premises. Since the 1970s, on the other hand, the work of Amartya Sen, the 1998 Nobel Prize winner in economics, has shown a completely new quality. Since the successful revival of the psychological economy by Behavioral Science with its more demanding models of the economic subject, classical financial market theory with its theory of perfect markets with rational actors has also been under increased pressure to justify itself; cf. for example Richard Thaler's work on the irrationality of the stock exchange and its actors, such as De Bondt, Werner, *Does the Stock Market Overreact?* in: Journal of Finance, vol. 40, issue 3, *Papers and Proceedings of the Forty-Third Annual Meeting American Finance Association*, Dallas/Texas, December 28-30, 1984 (July 1985), pp. 793-805; the psychological basis for this can be found in Tversky, Amos and Kahnemann Daniel, *Judgement under Uncertainty: Heuristics and Biases*, in: Science, New Series, vol. 185, issue 4157 (September 27, 1974), pp. 1124-1131.

A.1.5 The Individual of Social and Sovereign Contracts (Law)

Modern political philosophy has a central metaphor that inspired all important theorists, namely the contract. It owed its career to the decline of political Aristotelianism and thus to the tradition of natural law. It became an obligatory form of a theoretical, secondary sociality for the purpose of legitimizing domination. However, no real power and social contracts for the foundation of states were concluded for a long time yet, but only substitutes were sought for the disintegrating sacral and natural law legitimation basis of power. In order to conclude a contract, parties or individuals had to be created, i.e. theoretically schematized.[110]

Basically, there were two directions of contract theory. In general, a single memorandum and articles of association were postulated. Only the German authors differed for the fact that they accepted two exactly separate contracts. This peculiarity results from the attempt to preserve natural law with the concept of contract itself. Therefore, in the contractual doctrines of Althusius[111] (1557-1638) and Pufendorf[112] (1632-1694), which were still fundamental in the German Reich throughout the 18th century, there are no private individuals. In the Monarchomach tradition Althusius constructed only official representatives of the estates, the magistrates, who had to speak not for themselves but exclusively for their respective caste. These should, united in general estates, have exclusive rights of resistance against the monarch in the event of his flagrant misuse of power and illegal exertion of violence. This was the legal lesson learned from the French religious wars after the Bartholomew's Night in 1572. Pufendorf was already more clearly interested in consolidating a welfare-state absolutism and had to construct an unbroken chain from a good-natured, godly state of nature of the people up to a contract of sovereignty which was based on the assumption of general voluntariness of all subjects in

---

[110] To my knowledge, there is no monograph on the various forms and articulations of individualism in modern contract theory, not even in democracy theory. Giovanni Sartori casually mentions individualism as a useless term in his (rather obsolete) *Theorie der Demokratie* [Theory of Democracy], [1987] Darmstadt 1992, p. 371.

[111] Althusius, John, *Potlitica methodice digesta atque exemplis sacris et profanis illustrata*,[1603] 3rd ed. Herborn 1614, reprint Aalen 1961.

[112] Pufendorf, Samuel, De jure naturae et gentium libri VIII, London 1672

favor of the will of the sovereign. There was no room for real individuals. Wolfgang Kersting writes:

> "...the natural state is no longer characterized by an atomistic individualism of extreme disconnectedness, but takes on the character of a sociable, almost gregarious state; yet, the newly discovered individual returns its protagonist position immediately to the old European housing community that is politically and legally represented by the oikos-despot."[113]

As in German economic theory, the methodological concept of the house also dominates in 18th century German contract theory. Since Althusius, German bicontractualism has therefore been so little characterized by schemes of individuality that it could never become a stimulus of German liberalism.[114] The other European contractualists rarely had a direct interest in a real individuality and constructed contracts above all in order to *recapture excess individuality* and bring it under control for the purpose of legitimizing power[115]; yet, their individuals, schematized atomistically, kinetically and eudaemonistically, *nolens volens* drove the evolution to democratic modernity and liberalism. Since the German school of contract theory was just as late as the German economy, the focus here must also be extended to European contract theories, for their important impulses for individualism also had their effect in Germany.[116]

In early English liberalism and its continental successors, individuality, which is articulated in the contractual capacity of subjects, is determined up to our century by the ownership of its own person that a subject is entitled to. This is C. B. Macpherson's prominent thesis of possessive indi-

---

[113] Kersting, Wolfgang, *Die politische Philosophie des Gesellschaftsvertrags* [The Political Philosophy of the Social Contract], Darmstadt 1994, p. 228.

[114] The actual social and theoretical foundations of German liberalism are taken into account in chapter A.3 in connection with public education.

[115] Dumont overdraws this observation excessively on the basis of his schema of individualism/holism. The founders of the ideology of individualism from Althusius to Rousseau [sic] would have retained a holistic passion that now subversively continued and led individualism directly into the "people's soul" of the Nazis and into the Moscow processes, i.e. individualism founded totalitarianism; see Dumont, Louis, Essais sur l'individualisme. Une perspective anthropologique sur l'idéologie moderne, Paris 1983, p. 99.

[116] One can see from this that the 'political triad' of individuality, aesthetics and publicity in German history is far from perfect and can at best have ideal-typical value.

vidualism, which has mainly been reflected in contractualism.[117] The property of the individual could also have been dealt with in the preceding economic section, but Macpherson's entire approach would have crossed the development of the idea of individuality in the early theory of the market economy.[118] In the development of his comprehensive concept of possessive individualism, not a single aspect or author of the actually practiced and applied economic theory of the 18th century is mentioned. That would have been the ground on which the term should have proven itself. In political contract theory, however, this thesis seems to be actually confirmed if one takes it as formally as Macpherson himself determined it in the introduction to his book. The individual is thus "essentially the owner of its own person or its own abilities for which it owes nothing to society."[119] In a chain of postulates that Macpherson sees as a common characteristic in the theories of Hobbes, the Levellers, Harrington and Locke, he combines this formal purpose with the ability of the individual to renounce parts of this ownership of itself voluntarily and for self-interest.[120] In this way, the individual was given room for maneuver of political and economic importance, which, however, was to be immediately revoked in political terms and even completely absorbed at Rousseau, in favor of stabilizing the community.

What is astonishing is that, with the end of the tradition of natural law, a *dissociative ground of society* was adopted for the first time and the individual was suddenly found in it. The contracts as generative institutions should bring its seclusion, autonomy and monadicity back into a rational context of society. Thus, in a sense, the contract was not a solution,

---

[117] Macpherson, Crawford B., *The Political Theory of Possessional Individualism. Hobbes to Locke*, [Oxford 1962] Frankfurt 1990.

[118] It is difficult to understand today that this book had a reputation in Germany for being inspired by Marxism. Marxism plays no role therein, and the profound criticism of liberalism in recognition of all its achievements should nowadays be called communitarian. Sartori assumes in his *Theory of Democracy*, loc. cit., that the Marxist author Macpherson overstretched the concept of property as a concept of capital and misunderstood liberalism in economic terms. On the other hand, in his otherwise excellent study *Die politische Philosophie des Gesellschaftsvertrags*, loc. cit., p. 140, Wolfgang Kersting claimed that the origin of Macpherson's thesis lies in Rousseau's "fraud contract in favor of the rich".

[119] Macpherson, *The Political Theory of Possessional Individualism*, loc. cit., p. 15.

[120] The entire chain of postulates in ibid. pp. 295-296. Sartori underestimated and misinterpreted these considerations, i.e. read too much about the economic dimension.

but only the *beginning of all the problems of modern political philosophy*, albeit on a new basis.

Enlightenment contractualism had clear difficulties in incorporating these differently colored theorems of individuality in order to portray people entering into contracts with self-binding and self-commitment as being characterized by an autonomous, free decision. Apart from the fictitious transitions in the difference between the state of nature and civility, the philosophical sovereign contracts of the state were completely without history. Factual cultural history cannot be reconstructed and depicted on its matrix – except through the rigid schematism of good or bad public order, the presence or absence of civil war or interstate wars. In this way, early contractualism, even beyond the borders of the German Reich, has only produced *implicit* theories of individuality, a kind of highly generalized trunk individuality that was developed in atomistic, kinetic or biodynamic terms. Significantly, the treaties have obviously been conceived for nothing other than to neutralize the characteristics of individuality such as ambition, the desire for independence, the desire to work, etc. Individuality was therefore not a value to be defended, but a deficiency of man in the natural state, which, after the failure of Aristotelian moral doctrine, was itself used as the basis for a new description of justice or injustice of the community – that was always historically existing beforehand, of course. Contractualist state philosophy has never taken individuality seriously. It was always the obstacle to overcome and was accordingly materialistic, i.e. kinetically or eudemonistically schematized.

Hume had criticized this deficit sarcastically. In his paper *Of the Original Contract* (1745), he recalled that all existing states of his time, looking back on their founding history, consisted of nothing but conquest or usurpation or both, but no evidence of a voluntarily concluded contract. He did not want to accept the fiction of tacit consent unless at least a moment of voluntariness could be proven.[121] What for Hume was a lack of thoughtful individuality, guaranteed as real, was an intolerable surplus for a later critic of contractualism, namely Hegel. According to his reading, the entire concept of contract was inseparably linked to the sphere of private law, which could never produce a philosophical state foundation for the moral community.[122] No philosopher has formulated this approach more radically than Rousseau in the *Contrat social*. There the individuals volun-

---

[121] Cf. Kersting, *Gesellschaftsvertrag*, loc. cit., p. 250 ff.
[122] See Hegel, G. W., *Philosophy of Law, Complete Works*, vol. 7, § 75/Addendum 133.

tarily renounce all their rights in order to get out of the terrible natural state and to enjoy mutually respected security. Compared to the *Leviathan*, the *Contrat social* is above all truly original in the fact that the sovereign is not a third party for whose benefit the individual renunciation was made, but the individuals themselves as aggregate are again the sovereign. The moral sphere in all its dignity is to rise out of the fiction of the individualistic calculation of interests. In response to this, Hegel referred contractualism to the exclusive mediation of ownership rights, to the "relationship of will to will"[123], which in no way included ownership of one's own person.

Only in the more recent contractualism of the 20th century, by Nozick, Buchanan and Rawls, were more thorough, empirical theorems of individuality developed, which could give analytical depth to the idea of contract, which was constitutive of modernity. In this respect, Macpherson's reference to the structural problems of 'contractualism' based on individualism was justified. Actually, the phase of empirical-individualist contractualism had already ended with Kant.[124] His criticism of the earlier contract theories was radical in that it provided an alternative draft that built the social contract on a completely new basis. Kant placed the contract exclusively under the legal formula of practical reason, but this time not applied to internal but to external freedom, in order to bring about its concordance with the external freedoms of all others. Accordingly, leaving the natural state, which Kant also uses as a methodological term, becomes a special duty, namely the "only affirmative external natural duty: exeundum e statu naturali" (Reflection 7075). The state of nature is characterized by an uncoordinated private law that also includes an alleged right of the strongest. This situation creates the legal uncertainty of property, and private law urges its "positiveization", as Kersting writes, in a public law that constitutes the state and lends transcending objectivity to pre-state private law. This will not be discussed in detail here. What is interesting for our argument is only that with this conceptual strategy Kant completely relieves the normative individualism of the former contractualists and turns the *contractus originarius* into an idea of reason that gives the state a purely rational status. Thus, any voluntarism of any kind of individual in an originally conceived contract is not only superfluous, it even makes the thought *paralogistic* in transcendental philosophical sense, for the methodically necessary and regulative *idea* of the original contract is confused

---

[123] Ibid. section 71.

[124] Cf. Kersting, *Gesellschaftsvertrag*, loc. cit. pp. 207-212.

with the *concept* of a primal contract.[125] The difference between Kant's idea and concept of the contract lies, according to Kant's methodical use of the word, in temporality. The *idea* of the contract is purely methodical postulate of reason, which is not subject to any sequence of times and does not depend on the conscience of men. The *concept* of contract, on the other hand, is already temporalized or historicized by means of its necessary sanctioning by individuals as spatio-temporal beings with attributed needs and inclinations. There are other conceivable forms of temporalization, e.g. determining the duration of the contract – which could mean a contractually guaranteed right to or obligation of resistance. As is well known, there was nothing like this in Kant's philosophy of law. His methodical anti-voluntarism and the rational definition of the original contract, and thus of the state, take the contract as an institution entirely out of the misunderstood dimension of individuality. This is not responsible at all for such difficult tasks as the philosophical foundation of public law and the state; quite apart from the fact that the contractualists primarily wanted to make the individualistic impulses more controllable by means of the contract – albeit sometimes with emancipatory intentions.

Overall, the contract models of the pre-Kantian contractualists were rather unrealistic if one looks at the texts. And yet it must not be forgotten that their ideas truly nourished and even unleashed world-shattering forces. Just as Lockes *Two Treatises of Government* weaponized the American colonists in their fight for independence, so the French revolutionaries with Rousseau's *Contrat social* in their hands drove the Ancien régime into exile. These practical implementations of the theoretical models also brought – and perhaps especially in their failure – significant refinements in the development and understanding of modern individualism. As a result, it became increasingly clear that the methodical individualities of the body and in particular the always presupposed 'tacit consensus' of the thus schematized contractors could not be maintained.[126] It has now become increasingly clear that the idea of a contract would require the introduction of real contractual procedures in the form of constitutions and government elections under the condition of universal suffrage, negotiating representative bodies such as parliaments, an opposition to be toler-

---

[125] Kant, Immanuel, *Critique of Pure Reason*, B 427-428, *Beschluss der Auflösung des psychologischen Paralogismus* [Conclusion of the Solution of the Psychological Paralogism].

[126] Cf. the interesting metacontractualistic considerations in Kerstings *Gesellschaftsvertrag*, loc. cit., pp. 19-58, in particular pp. 32-38.

ated constitutionally and finally freedom of opinion and freedom of the press as a deliberative preparation for such agreements to be repeatedly renewed.[127] In other words, in the 19th century, individuals who are still hesitant to enter into genuine political contractual relationships with one another and with historically shaped institutions.

---

[127] Ingeborg Maus has made the exciting attempt to 'de-transcendentalize' Kant's concept of reason in the contract. Thus, it has theoretically proceduralized the Kantian concept of law and contract in such a way that the practice of democratic popular sovereignty suggested here is also to be reconstructed since the late 19th century; cf. Maus, *Zur Aufklärung der Demokratietheorie. Rechts- und Demokratietheoretische Überlegungen im Anschluß an Kant* [Enlightening the Theory of Democracy. Reflections on Legal and Democratic Theory Following Kant], Frankfurt 1992, p. 43ff.

A.1.6 The Individual at War

According to Cicero's dictum *Silent enim leges inter arma* (In times of war, the law falls silent), the state of war is the logical counterpart to a state of law brought about and regulated by contracts. Historically, however, the new moment of individuality has also prevailed on this side of active, destructive violence. This time less on the level of philosophical and theoretical texts than in the psychosocial practice of war itself, which in this case theory could only follow like a rearguard.

Since the end of WW II, war has been regarded almost exclusively as a sign of civilizational decay. It destroys goods and people, mostly for the benefit of prospective territorial gains. Especially in the social sciences, which see themselves as critical, the ancient dictum that war was the father of all things was rejected as provocative and cynical. A whole branch of research has emerged in favor of the establishment and maintenance of peace. Peace and Conflict Studies [Friedens- und Konfliktforschung] were sanctioned by the highest German office when President Gustav Heinemann expressly demanded the establishment of such a science. This was preceded by a long history of the peace movement, whose roots can be traced back to the organized protest of American scientists against the incipient equipping of the U.S. armed forces with nuclear weapons. Gustav Heinemann said in 1969 in a speech: "The war obviously has less – albeit also – its roots in the attitudes of individuals than in the orders and disorder of communities." The importance of the individual for warfare or even as a cause of war, which Heinemann wanted to leave aside, is a historically relatively late discovery, which is of interest here. For it was only with the revolutionary wars, in which France initially only defended itself against the First Coalition of feudal Europe, that the role of individual conviction was discovered as a dynamizing moment of war. Shortly before, Captain Rouget de Lisle had composed the battle song of the revolution, the Marseillaise. Then the commander-in-chief of the coalition troops, Duke of Braunschweig, published a manifesto just before the imminent attack on France, aiming at the liberation of the French king. This encouraged French patriotism, which emerged as a popular movement at that moment. The famous cannonade of Valmy on 20 September 1792, about which Goethe and Hegel later unanimously reported as the turn of an era, was characterized by the fact that the *French soldiers did not flee in panic* from this massive gunfire of the coalition powers that was unique in military history. The attackers reckoned with the massive escape as a psychological effect of such a massive bombardment for good reason.

Desertion was the main problem of classical warfare. However, the French soldiers did not retreat and won this first war with the Battle of Jemappes and the conquest of Belgium. Under Napoleon's rule and military leadership, the French army finally became unbeatable and won one battle after another – until the campaigns against Spain and Russia (1808 and 1812). During this time the army order was completely rebuilt. The recruitment of all men capable of fighting to fulfil the general conscription replaced the purchase of mercenary troops or the unjust, because arbitrary compulsory recruitment. Instead of an attack in a closed front and higher officers in the back rows for control, which was to make it impossible for the individual soldiers to escape from the fighting, tirailleur tactics were introduced with operations in loose firing lines.

The first question now would be why the earlier practice of disobedience and desertion should not be seen as a sign of individualism. For it is somewhat paradoxical that individuality should express itself in mass, informally synchronized acts of war and voluntary discipline. Today, social research has precise methods of observation and reading at its disposal to reconstruct such historical events that would come to an opposite conclusion. With an approach based on Michel Foucault's microsociology of power, looking at the same object would result in the image of a change and an intensification in the molding and mangling of human bodies through the psychic internalization of coercion. This way of observation conceives the human subjects as surfaces formed by the techniques of power and thus gets meaning inscribed on it. This abstraction of any ego-like inner horizon of the subject, which does not owe its existence to the notches on the surface, i.e. the abstraction of such empirically non-appearing phenomena as reason, autonomy and free will, is methodologically related to functionalist systems theory. All in all, this is a demanding and – if it is only carried out subtly enough – often very instructive approach that has opened up great development opportunities for social theory, as has turned out over the last twenty years [1975-1995]. With it, the social sciences have become worldlier in many respects and the normative, rational idealizations are more than ever under pressure to explain how they want to make their often-counterfactual observations and postulates binding. The old question of social existence and purpose is becoming highly problematic in the field of scientific research for the representatives of purpose.

This challenge is to be met here. It is precisely this emergence of subjective inner horizons, their configurations and laws that interests us. However, the reconstruction of the individual dimension of thinking and acting should not be attempted from a psychological standpoint[128], but from the analysis of the powers and forms of judgment. And here too, in the second part of the study, the normative force of thought is distinguished from a particular power of judgment that has not yet been thoroughly analyzed in political philosophy.

The historical event of individualization in the war was clearly established in the 18th century, and the theoretical considerations were only enhanced by the simple observations of the events of the revolutionary wars. Ludwig Tieck wrote in 1792, moved and witnessing empathetically the struggle of the French soldiers against the "slaves":

> "Oh, if only I were a Frenchman now! Then I didn't want to sit down [...]. But unfortunately, I was born in a monarchy that fought against freedom, among people who are still barbarians enough to despise the French. I've changed a lot, I'm not happy when I can't have a newspaper. Oh, to be in France, it must be a great feeling to fight under Dumouriez and to chase slaves into flight, and also to fall – what is a life without freedom? If France is unhappy, I despise the whole world and despair of its power, if the dream is too beautiful for our century, then we are degenerate alien beings, with no vein related to those who once fell at the Thermopylae, then Europe is destined to be a dungeon." (Letter to Wackenroder[129], end of 1792)

Christoph Martin Wieland's reflections are already more suitable for a theoretical framing of the revolutionary events. The well-known and influential publicist wrote about the European public and the participation of individuals in the revolution before the outbreak of war:

> "No wonder then that from the first moment of such a great revolution,

---

[128] Cf. the interesting studies from the field of empirical psychology by Rainer Dietrich, *Carl von Clausewitz als Psychologe - Die "moralischen Größen" im Lichte der Persönlichkeitspsychologie* [Carl von Clausewitz as Psychologist - The "Moral Factors" in the Light of Personality Psychology], in: Vowinckel, Gerhard (ed.), *Clausewitz-Kolloquium – Theorie des Krieges als Sozialwissenschaft* [Clausewitz Colloquium – The Theory of War as Social Science] Berlin 1993, pp. 111-136 The article is characterized by the fact that in it the individual-psychological aspect is not limited to the qualities of military command personnel.

[129] Quoted from: Losurdo, Domenico, *Hegel und das deutsche Erbe. Philosophie und nationale Frage zwischen Revolution und Reaktion* [Hegel and the German Heritage. Philosophy and National Question Between Revolution and Reaction], Cologne 1989, p. 16.

unheard of and never thought possible, not only was the general attention of Europe drawn to this amazing spectacle, but that among so many millions of foreign viewers, who had no immediate interest in it, there were nevertheless only a few who in the first days would not have felt impelled by an almost involuntary instinct to take part in the uprising of these noble men who had put their character, their courage and their excellent powers of mind at the head of a great, noble, enlightened, spiritual and courageous nation challenged by the most grumpy despotism, to shout cheers and to await their success with unusual restlessness or more or less passionate movement."[130]

It clearly shows that the foreign-European enthusiasm would be sensitive to the development of the revolutionary wars, the rule of the Welfare Committee, the Terror and Napoleon. The audience noticed that these events were hardly compatible with the principles of freedom invoked by the National Assembly in 1789.

The most important supporters of the revolution among the German thinkers, who did not leave their point of view in the process or later on, were Immanuel Kant and G. W. F. Hegel. Joachim Ritter wrote:

> "The event around which Hegel collects all the determinations of philosophy in relation to time, in defense and access, sketching out the problem, is the French Revolution, and there is no philosophy that is the philosophy of the revolution as much and down to its innermost impulses as Hegel's."[131]

Even though Hegel always regarded the revolution as a necessary manifestation of the realization of the idea of freedom, he soon deviated from his earlier enthusiasm and saw that freedom has two sides, namely an objective, world spirit-related, and a subjective side of absolute freedom. He dedicated the chapter *On Absolute Freedom and Horror* to this relationship.[132] This was his lesson from the execution of Louis XVI, the Terror and the revolutionary wars. However, his philosophical system was not designed anyway to track down the traces of individuality in world

---

[130] Wieland, Christoph Martin, *Unparteiische Betrachtungen über die Staatsrevolution in Frankreich* [Impartial reflections on the French Revolution], 1790.

[131] Ritter, Joachim, *Metaphysik und Politik. Studien zu Aristoteles und Hegel* [Metaphysics and Politics. Studies on Aristotle and Hegel], Frankfurt 1969, p. 192.

[132] Hegel, G. W. F., *Phänomenologie des Geistes* [The Phenomenology of Spirit], Frankfurt 1973, p. 431-441.

history, but precisely the opposite was the case.[133]

In his essay *The Dispute of the Faculties*, Kant, as the most loyal supporter of the French Revolution in Germany, wrote *Of an Event of Our Time which Proves a Moral Tendency of the Human Race* (chapter headline):

> "This event does not consist in important deeds or atrocities committed by men, whereby what was great is made small among men, or what was small is made great... No: none of it. It is only the spectators' way of thinking that reveals itself *publicly* in this game of great transformations... The revolution of a witty people that we have seen going on in our day may succeed or fail; it may be so filled with misery and atrocities that a well-thinking person, if he could hope to carry it out happily for the second time, but would never decide to make the experiment at such expense – this revolution, I say, finds in the minds of all spectators (who are not themselves involved in this game) a *participation* that is close to enthusiasm, and whose utterance, even if it was associated with danger, can have its cause in a moral disposition in the human race... By rewarding money the opponents of the revolutionists could not develop the zeal and show the size of the soul that the mere concept of rights produced in them[the revolutionary], and even the concept of honor of the old warfaring nobility (an analog of enthusiasm) disappeared before the weapons of those who had envisaged the right of the people to which they belonged and thought themselves to be protectors of it; with what exaltation the outside watching public then sympathized, without the slightest intention of participation."[134]

An apparent contradiction has been observed between Kant's enthusiasm for the revolution and his unconditional rejection of any right of resistance. But these considerations are consistent, because it is understandable that according to Kant there can be no public and binding law that can give resistance to the authority that creates the law, the sovereign, and its institutions. There is a clear distinction here between criticism and resistance. In relation to the revolution, this means that the failing revolutionaries could not invoke any right to resist and would certainly be held legally accountable for their crimes under applicable law.

---

[133] Cf. representative of many other Legros, Robert, *La critique hégelienne de l'individualisme*, in: *International Journal of Philosophy* 2/1993, pp. 254-265.

[134] Kant, Immanuel, *Der Streit der Fakulttäten* [The Dispute of the Faculties, 1798], in: *Werke* XI, pp. 261-392, here pp. 357-358.

"... and there is little doubt that if the indignation that has brought Switzerland, the United Netherlands or Great Britain their present constitutions so happily praised were unsuccessful, the readers of their history would see nothing but the deserved punishment of great state criminals in the execution of their presently praised authors."[135]

The important nuance in this remark is that the French Revolution is not mentioned here, because it is not a simple rebellion, an indignation, but it is a "sign of history", because it has betrayed itself as a moral asset of the spectators. Kant thus sees here a historical-philosophical, qualitative difference between the French Revolution and the preceding bourgeois revolutions.[136] It is not difficult to recognize, however, that the activity of the viewer in assessing the observed events cannot itself be described as a moral action, but undoubtedly as an aesthetic one. Since this distinction is of considerable importance, it must be pointed out again and again in the first part of the investigation where the distinction between the aesthetics and the morals is articulated. At this point it cannot yet be explained from where the distinction itself derives its form and its right. For the time being, it is only possible to keep alert here with regard to the inappropriate identification of both terms.

Interesting at this point are the "zeal" and the "size of the soul" that the "concept of rights" has produced in the revolutionaries. Only the supposition of such an event in the warring subjects constitutes the special character of this spectacle, which enabled the audience to sympathize with enthusiasm. The theoretical version of this new feature was to be the achievement of Carl von Clausewitz in the early 19th century. In his 1832 posthumous work *Vom Krieg*, Clausewitz summarized the bitter lessons Napoleon's war genius had taught an old European tradition of cabinet wars. Against the still prevailing concept of geometric demonstrability and

---

[135] Kant, Immanuel, *Über den Gemeinspruch: Das mag in der Theorie richtig sein, taugt aber nicht für die Praxis* [On the Common Saying: This May be Correct in Fheory, but it is not Suitable for Practice; 1793], in: *Werke* XI, pp. 125-172.

[136] It is important that Hannah Arendt valued the bourgeois revolutions in exactly the opposite way, i.e. gave the Anglo-American preference over the French Revolution. Nevertheless, she and Ernst Vollrath wanted to read Kant's third *Critique* in such a way that it is above all a philosophical confirmation of the foundations of American constitutionalism. No wonder that this didn't work out as wished.

algebraic predictability of individual war events in his lifetime[137], he used an individualistic theory of action, for the experiment had proven it: The rigid lines of the army of the Ancien régime, held together by the outermost drill and deadly threat, had no chance in the collision with Napoleon's movable firing lines, which were followed by the closed troop body. The authors agree to this day that it was not only a meeting of two military formations, but of two ages. Clausewitz was the first to take this circumstance into account theoretically by combining in his own kind of formula the talent of the commander with that of his officers, the "folk spirit" in an idealistic sense and the warlike virtue of the army.

> "This latter is a point of individual peculiarity, and so it is in vain that one makes a bolder calculation for a fearful man than his own is; for him his own is much truer... I may not have it printed, but... a general can never be too bold in his plans, provided that he is sane, and only pursues such purposes as he is convinced he can achieve with himself."[138]

It depends on the individual and on the abilities that it can assign to itself. This should apply to the army command as well as to the simple recruit, who was inspired by the "folk spirit" and treated somewhat more

---

[137] Ernst Vollrath also dealt thoroughly with Clausewitz and his concept of the "tact of judgement". However, he only took out a theoretical key element from Clausewitz's theory of action and left it abstract, standing just for itself as alleged proof for Vollrath's interpretation of Kant's *Critique of the Power of Judgement* that was inspired by Hannah Arendt and ought to be conducive to a new doctrine of wisdom. However, this conceals the motive of individualization that characterizes the epoch; cf. Vollrath, Ernst, , 'Neue Wege der Klugheit.' Zum methodischen Prinzip der Theorie des Handelns bei Clausewitz ['New Ways of Wisdom'. On the Methodological Principle of the Theory of Action at Clausewitz], in: Zeitschrift für Politik, 1984/1, p. 53 ff. ; Vollrath, *Überlegungen zur neueren Diskussion über das Verhältnis von Praxis und Poiesis* [Reflections on the Recent Discussion on the Relationship Between Praxis and Poiesis], in: Allgemeine Zeitschrift für Philosophie, 1989, vol. 14; Vollrath., *Grundlegung einer philosophischen Theorie des Politischen,* [Foundation of a Philosophical Theory of the Political], Würzburg 1987, p. 287; Vollrath, *Carl von Clausewitz: Eine mit dem Handeln befreundete Theorie* [Carl von Clausewitz: A Theory Befriended with Action], in: Vowinckel, Clausewitz-Kolloquium, loc. cit., pp. 63-78.

[138] Clausewitz, Carl von, *Die Strategie aus dem Jahr 1804 mit Zusätzen von 1808 und 1809* [The Strategy of 1804 with Additions of 1808 and 1809] in Clausewitz, *Verstreute kleine Schriften,* , ed. by Werner Hahlweg, Osnabrück 1979, p. 19.

summarily. Clausewitz saw the cardinal error of military science in treating people like predictable machines. The "moral forces" in the art of war should therefore no longer be subordinated to mechanical forces. Clausewitz thus provided a theoretical deepening of the simple idea of the people's war, as it had been known in military literature since Jacques Comte de Guibert's *Essai sur la Tactique* (Paris 1774).

Fig. 7: Carl von Clausewitz (1780-1831)

It is therefore no exaggeration to say that this is an analysis of the individual of its own kind. It differs only in that it was not derived from the concepts of classical metaphysics but distilled from the empirical experience of a historically powerful principle, namely the *individuality of soldiers fighting in wars*. Later it will become clear that this kind of emergence of individuality was not the first and only one in world history without calling the present one into question.[139]

One aspect of Clausewitz's work already points to the second part of this study. It has not yet been proven whether Clausewitz, mediated by Johann Gottfried Kiesewetter, his teacher and successful popularizer of

---

[139] 115 Cf. Meier, Christian, *Die Rolle des Krieges im klassischen Athen* [The Role of War in Classical Athens], in: Historische Zeitschrift 251/1990, pp. 555-605. War as a potential moment of emergence of individuality and political subjectivity is examined in cultural-anthropological Excursus II, chapter B.2.2.

Kant's philosophy, knew and read Kant's *Critique of Power of Judgment*.[140] After all, he has left behind an art-theoretical fragment that points to a certain (albeit amateur) knowledge of Kant's aesthetics. This seems to be a source of inspiration for the relationship between the whole and its parts in Clausewitz' development of the art of war:

> "The beauty of contemplation is infinite and cannot be submitted to any rule, and it is so much what is actually effective in architecture that, when it is abundant, it can make inconspicuous all contradictions and infringements that the mind can commit in its arrangements and, despite it, produce a pleasant effect of the whole."[141]

In conclusion to this chapter on the development of individuality in the 18th century, it can be said that most of the phenomena of this scheme were still very firmly bound to the context of social unity. It is remarkable how sensitive the intellectual life of this period was to the phenomena of social loss of unity and the symptoms of differentiation. Accordingly, individuality was mostly defensively schematized, in the form of concessions to the demands for autonomy, self-responsibility and political participation. The authors, who were concerned about the common good, hoped to restore the loss of substantial unity with the help of various forms of *secondary sociality*. Throughout the entire epoch there is therefore no song of praise of the self-sufficient and selfish individual, as cultural critics and postmodern authors have often assumed. Enlightenment thinkers were highly scrupulous, if not conservative, in the theoretical schematization of the individual. Only against the great historical background of the dissolution of the ethical-religious unity of medieval societies can the theorems of individuality be interpreted as decay products of radically new quality. On closer inspection, however, one discovers the strong aspect of substituting old unitary formulas with new schematizations of a concept that grants diversity through individuality, taking into account social differentiation, but within the social unity still to be preserved – with the emphasis always being on unity.

---

[140] Cf. Schössler, Dietmar, *Carl von Clausewitz*, Reinbek b. H. 1991, P. 30-33.

[141] Rothfels, Hans, *Ein kunsttheoretisches Fragment des Generals Carl von Clausewitz* [An Art-Theoretical Fragment of General Carl von Clausewitz], in: Deutsche Rundschau, Berlin, December 1917.

A. 2 The Evolution of Aesthetics to the Science of Taste

In the course of the present research what *political subjectivity* could mean, how it arises and in what forms it manifests itself, the aesthetics of the 18th century is the second element of the political triad, in whose figure – according to the leading hypothesis – the basic form of a genuinely political capacity expressed itself historically. The structure of the basic question of modern aesthetics reflects the main problem of modern politics: the mediation of the individual and the general. In the search for the criteria of 'good taste' in the 18th century, the loss of the evidences given by God or by Being itself, in which it had always been determined what was to be considered a good life or a moment of unity in the community, was already announced. The following discussions are direct and particularly important preparations for the second part of the investigation, which will be devoted primarily to the reconstruction of Kant's *Critique of Power of Judgment* in order to lay bare the foundations for a political philosophy of the subject. In preparation for the difficult philosophical arguments that await us there, an attempt will continue to be made to depict the corresponding historical background with appropriate depth of focus.

The aesthetics of the Enlightenment has so far not been the subject of political science research and teaching. There are only a few isolated attempts to analyze its social significance in a historical-sociological context.[142] Otherwise, the 'science of beauty', as it is also described, is entirely reserved for philosophy[143] and literary studies[144]. Therefore, some exam-

---

[142] Terry Eagleton's Marxist-inspired study *The Ideology of the Aesthetic* [1990] should be mentioned here, but above all Luc Ferry's excellent book *Homo aestheticus. L'invention du goût à l'âge démocratique* [Homo Aestheticus. The Invention of Taste in the Age of Democracy] Paris 1990.

[143] Jean-Marie Schaeffer's *L'art de l'âge modern. L'esthétique et la philosophie de l'art du XVIIIe siècle à nos jours* [Art in Modern Times. Aesthetics and Philosophy of Arts from the 18th Century until Today], Paris 1992, contains an analysis of the way in which aesthetics, which had just become independent in the 18th century, is treated from romantic philosophy to Heidegger's fundamental ontology. According to Schaeffer, the sacralization of art through the philosophies of being in the form of theories that have always remained foreign to artistic practice and reality conceals a parasitic relationship between philosophy and art that is still traditional today. Kant was the last philosopher who left art's autonomy undis-

ples are given here, which hopefully not only illustrate the theoretical dispute about the right art theory, but also create familiarity with the atmosphere of an age that wanted to emancipate itself with great seriousness from the tradition of the beautiful, true and good, which until then had been exclusively religious, without slipping into a radical relativism of taste. Perhaps it will also be possible to remind the newer political philosophy of a forgotten line of ancestors whose works could now attract speculative curiosity after the weakening of the great ideological systems.

The "topicality of the aesthetic"[145] and the extensive literature on this topic from the 1990s are only indirectly related to this study. But even this

---

puted. Schaeffer rightly insists that Kant has rejected any claim to a philosophical theory of art in his *Critique of the Power of Judgement* (ibid., pp. 27-84). Gadamer had already formulated it this way, but with the aim of freeing aesthetics from Kant's radical subjectivation and resurrecting it as special hermeneutics of truth in art and science. Thus, Gadamer has also handed down the parasitic relationship between philosophy and art that Schaeffer observed; see Gadamer, Hans-Georg, *Wahrheit und Methode. Grundzüge einer philosophischen Hermeneutik* [Truth and Method. Basics to Philosophical Hermeneutics], Gesammelte Werke Vol. I, Tübingen 1986, p. 47. A more recent critique of the philosophical colonization of modern art can be found in Arthur C. Danto, *Kunst nach dem Ende der Kunst* [After the End of Art. Contemporary Art and the Pale of History], Munich 1996.

[144] The subtle, difficult and certainly most important book on the development of aesthetics is Carsten Zelle's groundwork *Die doppelte Ästhetik der Moderne. Revisionen des Schönen von Boileau bis Nietzsche* [The Double Aesthetics of Modernity. Revisions of the Concept of Beauty from Boileau to Nietzsche], Stuttgart 1995. Its findings are suitable for entailing a revision of practically all textbooks on this subject. Zelle has postulated and systematically investigated the reciprocal relationship between the beautiful and the sublime as the dynamic principle of the history of aesthetics. The author convincingly shows that the dimension of the sublime from the beginning of modern discussion, i.e. at the latest since Boileau's *Art poétique*, the understanding of beauty must be included in the concept of aesthetics in a time-dependent manner and in a revisionary relationship. Here we must now ask for indulgence for the fact that the present study, despite better knowledge, as it were, dispenses with this very well-proven thesis and undercut the level of its argumentation in order to refer to the older periodization of aesthetic history, which postulated a chronological sequence in the historical appearance of the beautiful and the sublime. At least it should be mentioned that Zelle refers with approval and appreciation to the *Homo aestheticus*, loc. cit., by Luc Ferry, whose argumentation the structure of this chapter is oriented towards; see Zelle, loc. cit., p. 45.

[145] Title of the great congress on aesthetics from September 2-5, 1994 in Hanover.

only indirect reference is of certain interest, since some newer schools of aesthetics, such as that of Lyotard's attempted salvage of the sublime[146] or that of Karl-Heinz Bohrer's "Aesthetics of Horror", were concerned – the past tense here suggests that the sources of these intellectual currents may now be regarded as dried up – to develop political consequences and entirely new social theories from art theory. There it was assumed that there was something fundamentally political about aesthetics. When we receive this report, it should remain here, because only this much of this topic can be used for our purposes. Rather than deduce moral and above all political demands directly from the respective aesthetics, the aim here is to *examine how the political enters into aesthetics*, i.e. what must be created within it, so that it can become a medium of political meaningfulness. This task cannot yet be solved completely and not in its entire breadth in the historical part. First of all, the necessary material should be collected in order to create a sufficiently complete picture of aesthetics as science, including its originality. The previous discussion of individuality theorems in their historical and theoretical facets was a good preparation for this. The deepening of the philosophical analysis towards the basic political content of aesthetics takes place in Part B. First of all, the most important trends in European aesthetics are presented here, whose problems lead to Kant's criticism of the subject of taste.[147] The focus is not so much on the

---

[146] Already in *Der Widerstreit* [The Differend], Munich 1987, Lyotard examines the sublime at Kant. In the *Leçons sur l'Analytique du sublime. Kant, Critique de la faculté de juger, §§ 23-29* [Lessons on the Analytic of the Sublime] Paris 1991, Lyotard deepens his knowledge of the third critique and tries to consolidate the concept. The climax of this aesthetic school was probably already passed when Christine Pries published an anthology under the involuntarily self-diagnostic title *Das Erhabene. Zwischen Grenzerfahrung und Größenwahn* [The Sublime. Between Borderline Experience and Megalomania], Weinheim 1989.

[147] To get to know the history of aesthetics in the 17th and 18th centuries, the following three older but still excellent books are recommended: Stein, Heinrich von, *Die Entstehung der neueren Ästhetik* [The Upcoming of the Newer Aesthetics]. Stuttgart 1886; Baeumler, Alfred, *Das Irrationrationitätsproblem in der Ästhetik und Logik des 18. Jahrhunderts bis zur Kritik der Urteilskraft* [The Problem of Irrationality in the Aesthetics and Logics of the 18th Century up to the *Critique of the Power of Judgement*] 1923, newly ed. Darmstadt 1975; Cassirer, Ernst, *Die Philosophie der Aufklärung* [The Philosophy of Enlightenment] Tübingen 1932, 3rd ed. Cassirer, however, relied very much on Bauemler, so that in his elegant and instructive chapter on aesthetics he underwent some historical misdating. Among the more recent studies, it is worth mentioning: Wolfgang Welsch's dissertation *Aisthesis. Grundzüge und Perspektiven der Aristotelischen Sinnenlehre*,

various theories of art, but rather on the new articulation of a subjective capacity for judgment that is beginning to take its place in history.

Stuttgart 1987, in which the author formed a kind of Aristotelian reinsurance of his later arguments on postmodernism, and of course Carsten Zelle's already mentioned habilitation thesis, *Die Doppelte Ästhetik*, op.cit.; however, these two latter books are no longer introductions. By the way, Baeumler's study was planned as the prelude to an extensive work entitled *Logic of Individuality*, but this was thwarted by the interaction of too strict self-criticism of the author and subsequently the destruction of the manuscripts in Berlin in 1945. This is Baeumler's own statement in the 1967 epilogue, but this plan to develop his original approach into a theory of individuality, even if it was abandoned, naturally makes Baeumler's study particularly interesting for the present study. A recent overview of 18th century aesthetics is given in the first volume of Paul Guyer's monumental study *A History of Modern Aesthetics*, 3 vol., 2014.

A.2.1 Classicism, Sensibility and English Aesthetics

In the 17th century, some French poets and scholars made determined attempts to bring all previously known art under a canonical system of rules. Since French culture was an undisputed hegemony in Europe in the age of Louis XIV, the influence of French aesthetic literature was enormous, all the more so since it directly related to artistic products. However, these attempts from the age of absolutism, which appear extraordinarily conservative from the retrospective as a whole, have in common that they already bear the unmistakable signum of modernity. For in aesthetics the authority of religion has been systematically limited. The guarantee for the value of beauty in art and nature was no longer in the way it reflected the glory of God and his creation, but in its agreement with reason, which had been established as a subjective principle of truth – and thus also of beauty – at the latest since Descartes.

The so-called classicist aesthetics is a theory for the arts which can be summarized in a few rules. The classical ideal of beauty in its symbolic, formal and phonetic realizations is at the same time the direct representtation of a truth value. Since ancient times, under the domination of theology, art was charged with the heavy burden of producing the sensual manifestations of perfection. The concept of God has already been replaced by the concept of reason. But beauty could still not be found in something isolated, individual or coincidental. The sphere of beauty was the general, the universal, and thus perfection.

This definition initially follows the self-description of Europe's first art teachings at the beginning of secularization. On closer inspection, it cannot be maintained for the description of contemporary art practice at the time. A more differentiated picture becomes necessary when one considers that many of the great works of art of the 17th century, which are still appreciated and admired today, no longer accepted these editions. As much as Rembrandt was allowed to present the particular of his own life in over a hundred self-portraits, so little did the Commedia dell arte care about these noble demands for perfection. The struggle of classicist, mathematical-rationalist aesthetics of reason with an aesthetic of feeling that was articulated both practically and theoretically was already in full swing. At the same time, when Nicolas Boileau (1636-1711), the author of the extraordinarily influential *Art poétique* (1674), continued his career as "législateur du Parnasse"[148], i.e. the undisputed legislator of the Muses and the classicist aesthetics of rules, Blaise Pascal (1623-1662), a great mathematician and undoubtedly familiar with the *esprit géometrique*, had already written so unforgettably in his *Pensées*: "Le coeur a ses raisons que la raison ne connaît point."[149] Another aesthetician and contemporary of Boileau, the Jesuit Dominique Bouhours, staged a dialogue between Eudoxe, the lover of ancient authors and sensual art, and Philante, the admirer of the lush baroque of the Spanish and Italians, in his book *Des manières de bien penser dans les ouvrages de l'esprit* (1687) a few years after the publication of the legislative *Art poétique*. Thus, the aesthetic contrast was presented for the first time in the ideal-typical, dialogic personification of two beauty concepts, whereby Eudoxe should soon have the greatest difficulties in convincing his interlocutor of the exemplariness and authority of antiquity for contemporary art.

More than two centuries later, Edmond Rostand had his beautiful play *Cyrano de Bergerac* (1897), which had already become world-famous shortly after its premiere, begin in the first act with a historically documented quarrel of the sword hero, which once again reflected the whole tension between classicism and sensibility. The story takes place in Paris in 1640; at the Hôtel de Bourgogne the play *La Clorise* by Boro is to be performed with the obese and popular actor Montfleury. He is just raising to recite Boro's introductory verses.

"Happy is he who, far from the court, in solitude.

Dedicating himself to exile by his own decision,

Loved by Zephyr's breath, free from the ambition to..."

The cheeky Cyrano interrupts him, threatens him with power and finally challenges the whole hall to a duel, because the crowd first stands behind their favorite actor. Until someone asks him:

"Did Montfleury give you reason to hate him?"

---

[148] A title which, by the way, was awarded to him only in 1829 by Saint-Beuve in: *Revue de Paris*, 1/1829, p. 29.

[149] Pascal, Blaise, *Pensées*, Fragment 423 (after the numbering in the edition of Port Royal 1670), Paris 1962, p. 180.

Cyrano on it:

> "Yes, hopeful young man.
>
> Pro primo, I hate him as a miserable actor;
>
> For wheezing he drags like a cart dog
>
> The light verses with wings in them.
>
> Secundo – that's none of your business."

An old man is outraged that he is deprived of the enjoyment of art, whereupon Cyrano assures him that he has only saved him from a bad piece. The 'precious people' are outraged in the lodges, for 'their' Boro could not possibly have written a bad play.

Cyrano's anger is directed against the pedantic madness of poetry, against the hollow pathos of reasonableness and its lack of spontaneity of feeling. Rostand had thoroughly studied the art theoretical background of Cyrano's lifetime and had the *Querelle des Anciens et des Modernes*, the dispute of art theorists at the Paris Academy of the Arts, fictitiously and dramatically settled before its time in the medium of theatrical poetry.

The *Querelle des Anciens et des Modernes* was without doubt the real climax of the French dispute over better aesthetics for the 18th century.[150] Boileau left the Académie française on 27 January 1687 in protest at the reading of Charles Perault's address of homage *Le Siècle de Louis Le Grand*, because it had turned into a "hospital des fous" (a madhouse), where it was seriously claimed that Plato was boring, Aristotle was incomplete and Homer's epics were full of digressions and brutalities. The 17th century was therefore not identical in its entirety with a classicism to be overcome first[151], but it was itself characterized by an ongoing struggle for the best

---

[150] Cf. Jauß, Hans Robert, *Ursprung und Bedeutung der Progressidee in der "Querelle des Anciens et des Modernes"* [Origin and Meaning of the Idea of Progress in the 'Quarrel of the Ancients and the Moderns], in: Kuhn, H. u. Wiedemann, F. (ed.), *Die Philosophie und die Frage nach dem Fortschritt* [Philosophy and the Question of Progress], Munich 1964, pp. 51-80; Jauß, *Literaturgeschichte als Provokation* [Literary History as Provocation], Frankfurt 1970, chapters 1-3; Jauß, [Aesthetic Norms and Historical Reflection in the 'Querelle des Anciens et des Modernes'], in: Perrault, Charles, *Parallèle des Anciens et des Modernes en ce qui regarde les Arts et les Sciences*, Munich 1964, pp. 8-64, introduction.

[151] These side currents of French classicism, such as the influence of Balthasar Gracian's *Oraculo manual, y arte de prudencia* [The Art of Worldly Wisdom] in

representation of art, and at the same time by which human organ is more important for the evaluation of art: brain or heart?

Boileau had not written his *Art poétique* as a dry treatise, but in its artistic form, namely in verses, to convey the theoretical content that seemed important to him.[152] To him clarity, measure and logical coherence were essential criteria of the admissibility of what could be regarded as beautiful. Essentially, however, he was concerned with the analogy of beauty and reason, whereby by 'reason' he understood mathematical rationality throughout.[153] Art was in no way autonomous in this respect but was under the demand of the sensualization of perfect forms. In his *Epistles*, Boileau also wrote the rules of his aesthetics in clear, didactic verses.

"Rien n'est beau que le vrai, le vrai seul est aimable,

Il doit regner partout, et même dans la fable;

De toute fiction l'adroite fausseté

Ne tend qu'à faire aux yeux briller la vérité."[154]

[Nothing is beautiful but the truth, the truth only is lovable,

It must reign everywhere, even in the fable;

Of all fiction the clever falsity

Tends only to outshine the truth to the eyes]

Much earlier there were works that wanted to give rules to art, so that it could be formed according to the divine truth. In contrast, for Boileau the rules are no longer maxims of artistic prudence, but laws based on reason

---

France under the title *L'homme de cour* [The Courtier], was first described by Stein in *Die Entstehung der neueren Ästhetik*, loc. cit.

[152] Boileau had two predecessors, Le Bossu and d'Aubignac, particularly with regard to the theory of the parallel between art and science; cf. von Stein, *Die Entstehung der neueren Ästhetik*, loc. cit., pp. 25 ff. and 64 ff. His most important pupil in the 18th century was Charles Batteux with his treatise *Einschränkung der schönen Künste auf einen einzigen Grundsatz* [Restriction of the Fine Arts to a Single Principle], 1746, ed. by J. A. Schlegel, Hildesheim 1976.

[153] There have been a whole series of attempts to identify this representation of Boileau's concept of 'raison' as prejudice, which, however, have not yet gained acceptance; cf. the statements of the editor August Buck in the introduction to Boileau's *Art poétique*, Munich 1970, p. 36. These theses could now receive late recognition based on Zelle's profound study *Die Doppelte Ästhetik*, loc. cit.

[154] Boileau-Despréaux, Nicolas, *Epître IX*, in: *Oeuvres* II, ed. by S. Menant, Paris 1969.

itself. This shows the influence of rationalism on classicism: Boileau has dogmatized Descartes artistically.[155] Boileau now wanted to place the subject of Descartes' thinking alongside the subject of emotions. The latter, however, had to remain an abstract subject and carried no trace of concrete individuality, because it was prescribed by reasonably dedicated law what it had to feel, whereby it always remained an absolutely general and formal subject. There was nothing coincidental, surprising, relational or even unspeakable in classicist aesthetics.[156] Here begins the great aesthetic dispute that Alfred Bauemler analyzed as *the problem of irrationality in the 18th century*. As long as art was reduced to science and the beautiful had to serve the always known truth, what was later to be called taste was completely unnecessary and irritating. Early rationalism could not place the irrational of feeling, heart and temperament in its cosmology. Accordingly, Boileau wrote about the Italian Baroque as if everybody there had gone mad.

> "La plupart emportés d'une fouge insensée
>
> Toujours loin du droit sens vont chercher leur pensée.
>
> Ils croiraient s'abaisser dans leurs vers monstrueux
>
> S'ils pensaient ce qu'un autre a pu penser comme eux.
>
> Évitons ces excès: laissons à l'Italie
>
> De tous ces faux brillants l'éclatante folie."[157]
>
> [Most of them carried away by a senseless fury
>
> Always far from the right sense they seek their thoughts.
>
> They would think they were stooping into their monstrous verses
>
> If they thought that anyone else might have thought it like them.
>
> Let us avoid these excesses: let us leave to Italy
>
> Of all these fake gems the dazzling madness]

As a result, art could not yet have a real history. It was not conceivable as a

---

[155] Baeumler, Alfred, *Das Irrationalitätsproblem in der Ästhetik und Logik des 18. Jahrhunderts bis zur Kritik der Urteilskraft* [The Irrrationality Problem in the Aesthetics and Logic of the 18th Century until the Critique of Power of Judgment], 1923, newly ed. Darmstadt 1975, p. 25.

[156] Ibid., p. 30.

[157] Boileau-Despréaux, Nicolas, *L'Art poétique*, Chant I, loc. cit., p. 40.

development or even as progress, but as the unpredictable emergence of perfect and thus always identical art forms in the ages, which were distinguished by this very perfection of their culture before the others.

Voltaire respected this canon throughout when he wrote his great historical essay *Le siècle de Louis XIV* on the 17th century, which was in his opinion the fourth in human history that had brought the sciences and the arts to this very perfection. With the following restriction:

> "Tous les arts, à la vérité, n'ont point été poussés plus loin que sous les Medicis, sous les Auguste et les Alexandre; mais la raison humaine en général s'est perfectionné [All arts, in fact, did not evolve any further than they had under the Medicis, the Augustes and the Alexanders; it wasn't but the general human reason that had reached perfection]."[158]

The perfection of art in classical understanding is finite and achievable. Therefore, on its own, it has no history with potential for further improvement. All four ages admired by Voltaire had already reached perfection, only in different ways.

It is of course paradoxical that Voltaire of all people paid homage to the epoch of Louis XIV and classicism, in a form that must have deprived his own person of the legitimacy of political-expressive action and writing. His polemics and especially his *Candide* could not have been subsumed under the rules of classicism. This fact illustrates that the history of the aesthetics of that time no longer had anything mechanical-natural about it and was no longer unconditionally at the service of theology or magical consciousness. Aesthetic principles could already be used reflexively by people themselves with intentions that we suspect should be called 'political'.[159] This is already one of the entanglements that arise when arguments or worldviews that lack the foundations for the articulation of individuality, taste and publicity, which are thus 'apolitical' in themselves, begin to work in contexts that are obviously political. But the investigation has not yet reached that stage. The philosophical dimensions of such

---

[158] Voltaire, *Le siècle de Louis XIV*, Paris 1929, vol. I, p.3; the two-volume work was first published completely in Berlin in 1751; Voltaire had begun the work in 1732, but the first editions of 1739 in Amsterdam and Paris were censored and confiscated.

[159] An indication of this is that Voltaire at the same time called the most anti-classical script of French aesthetics, Dubos *Réflexions critiques sur la poésie et la peinture*, "the most useful book ever written about this subject in one of the European nations"; quoted after Ferry, *Homo aestheticus*, loc. cit. p. 63.

concrete problems of political-individual existence are only discussed in Part B of the present study.

There is the amusing speculation that more than anything else, *boredom at the tedious quotes, comparisons and invocations* of the artists to the ancient authorities brought classicism out of fashion and heralded the age of taste. Karl Borinski wrote: "The sigh of Madame de Longueville at the lecture of Chapelain's sensational epic *La pucelle* (Oui; cela est parfaitement beau, mais il me fait bâiller [Yes, this is perfectly beautiful; but it makes me yawn]) was the poet's death sentence."[160] The practice of an ever more individualizing culture of taste as subjective expectation would then have overcome the dictatorship of theory in France.

The French aesthetic of sensibility, as prepared by Bouhours and Malebranche and later represented by Dubos, went from speculation about the discovery of beautiful forms to their invention. In it, first of all, the restrictive aspect of classicism as an aesthetic of reception is exceeded. Just as in Blaise Pascal's "je ne sais quoi" the theory of emotion announced itself as a logic of the heart, in the concept of 'esprit' the first prefiguration of the later aesthetic of genius appeared, which focused on the creative moment, the creation of art. The aesthetics of sensibility is the first to draw attention to the inner processes in the subject, to the receptive and productive abilities of the 'sentiment'. At first, the word is still used very cautiously as a borderline concept of rationality, as "jugement confus".[161] After all, "sentiment" is already associated with an unarticulated power of judgment and is usually translated as "opinion".[162] Note here that at this point begins the protracted liberation of the subjective knowledge of opinion from the stigma of ontological inferiority.[163] Since Greek antiquity, the identity of

---

[160] Borinski, Karl, *Baltasar Gracian und die Hofliteratur in Deutschland* [Baltasar Gracian and Court Literature in Germany], 1894, p. 25, cited after Bauemler, *Irrrationality Problem*, loc. cit.

[161] Bauemler, *Irrationality Problem*, loc. cit., p. 34.

[162] Ibid., p. 36.

[163] One of the best connoisseurs of ontology, Nicolai Hartmann, succinctly summarized this tendency: "The old doctrine of being was based on the thesis that the 'general', condensed in the *essentia* into a substance of form and tangible, is the determining and formative interior of things. Besides the world of things, in which Man is also enclosed, the world of beings enters, which forms a timeless and immaterial realm of perfection and higher being. The extreme representatives of this school of thought even attributed the actual and only true reality to the general entities and thus devalued the temporal-material world. The

individual and collective ignorance has been designated with the term 'doxa'. However, since the concept of 'opinion' is a basis for democratic forms of rule and the quintessence of modern public opinion, it will have to play a prominent role in the further investigation of political subjectivity.

The culmination of French sensibility is Jean-Baptiste Dubos' *Reflexion critiques sur la poésie et la peinture* [Critical Reflection on Poetry and Painting] from 1719: the theory of emotion becomes a radical critique of classicism and rationalism, for the feeling already contains all the judgment and is thus a sense of judgment, an *iudicium sensuum*, as Baumgarten later called it. Dubos' theory can be described as 'sentimentalism'[164] as a counter term to rationalism. The fixation of the rules of aesthetics gives way to the immediacy of feeling. Therefore, the public is the highest instance of taste at the moment of art enjoyment – it can no longer be deceived by false sensations while diligently learning to appreciate the true value of the object of art only after a certain time, as Boileau still assumed. There are also no deductions of taste criteria in Dubos according to certain rational rules, but only the observation of the particular (impression) under the aegis of the unmistakable feeling:

> "After the geometric principles about the spice have been established and the properties of each ingredient added to the overall composition have been determined, the portion preserved in its mixture has to be discussed in order to decide whether the ragout is good? You do nothing like that [...] you try the ragout, and even without knowing these rules, you can see if it's good. The same applies to the works of the spirit and the paintings."[165]

However, this also marked the beginning of a theoretical impasse, for the criticism of taste no longer found any hold here and under these conditions was exposed to the relativism of the absolutely monadic-subjective feeling. French aesthetics couldn't answer the question of criteria for taste and explain the dichotomy of heart and mind, because so dogmatic classicism was, so formless became sentimentalism, which offered no further

---

descendants in the 19th century, who acknowledged the general only in the form of the concept, called this direction 'conceptual realism'." (Hartmann, *Neue Wege der Ontologie* [New Paths of Ontology], [1943] 4th ed., Stuttgart 1964, p. 8)

[164] Bauemler, *Irrrationality Problem*, loc. cit., p. 53.

[165] Dubos, Jean-Baptiste, *Reflexion critiques sur la poésie et la peinture*, ed. 1770, p. 341; quoted from Ferry, *Homo aestheticus*, loc. cit., pp. 66.

connection.[166]

It is interesting that the skeptical aesthetics in England and Scotland had come into the same situation as French sentimentalism, but enriched by the amusing volte with which the Scotsman David Hume (1711-1776) wanted to demonstrate that skepticism in matters of taste was actually the only true classicism.[167] In his treatise *Of the Standards of Taste*, which appeared in 1757 with other texts in the *Four Dissertations*, Hume points out that the conscious sensual experience of a state can be the only authentic witness to the judgment of taste. "All sentiment is right, because sentiment has a reference to nothing beyond itself, and is always real, wherever a man is conscious of it."[168] Hume, armed with epistemological skepticism, goes the path of aesthetics to its end, from where he extends the aesthetic solution to all areas of knowledge and rejects any assumption of reason as metaphysical.[169] In contrast to French classicism, empirical aesthetics no longer refers to the qualities of the artistic work, but to the empirical constitution of the artistically enjoying subject.[170] The criteria for taste are consequently the physical health of the sensory organs, their good training, freedom from prejudice and, of course, the necessary education in the form of a 'good judgment'. The natural basis of taste for Hume is therefore implicitly the biological condition of the human body and its position in society. Under these conditions it becomes inevitable to assume an objective reason of beauty that is only obscured by a sick nature or bad social position. Taste is therefore nothing other than what the persons themselves are, on whom one agrees as embodiments of good taste. It is

---

[166] Bauemler concludes: "It was and is France's fate not to find the mediation between sentiment and raison. In Germany, on the other hand, throughout the 18th century, nothing else was sought than this 'mediation'." (Bauemler, *Irrationalitätsproblem*, loc. cit., p. 64). In aesthetic theory, the Germans finally took over the squadron and, on this basis, experienced an epoch of literary-philosophical high culture in idealism and romanticism. This is an interpretation of the historical connections, which also Luc Ferry does not doubt anywhere in his book.

[167] Cf. for the following presentation the brilliant analysis of Ferry, *Homo aestheticus*, loc. cit. pp. 78-90.

[168] Hume, David, *Of the Standards of Taste and other Essays*, ed. by John W. Lenz, Indianapolis 1975, p. 6.

[169] Cassirer, Ern Cassirer, *Die Philosophie der Aufklärung*, loc. cit., p. 408. This aspect points to a relationship between analytical philosophy and the aesthetics of the 18th century that has never been addressed before.

[170] Ibid., p. 422.

not possible to assume any power of rational judgment in a subject that might have an influence on the standards of taste, because that would be metaphysics. Hume thus developed an expertocratic and corporative theory of taste that offered him complete security when he attributed much greater genius to his cousin and friend, the unknown Scottish playwright John Home, than to the hated Englishman William Shakespeare. Although it is in no way obvious why one should still argue about tastes at all, because their diversity is *objectively wrong* anyway in view of an assumed uniform reason of beauty and taste – or because the relativism of taste anyway has *objective reasons* in the social and physiological diversity of the persons (this is not decided with him), Hume reserves a strict classicism. The works of the ancients are simply authorities in matters of good taste because they have proven themselves as such for such a long time. In Hume's view, the arts as permanent forms of expression can claim much more universality than the mathematical sciences that come and go in revolutionary thrusts with Aristotle or Galileo, while Plato, Vergil and Cicero remain: "The abstract philosophy of Cicero has lost its credit: the vehemence of his oratory is still object of our admiration."[171]

This paradox of monadic-individualistic sentimentality and classicist orthodoxy is what director and aesthete Peter Greenway brought together in his 1982 movie *The Draughtsman's Contract* in the person of the draughtsman Mr. Neville. He has this arrogant man beaten to death because he was stupid enough to document the evidence of a murder on twelve accurate and school-like drawings of the estate of the country nobleman Mr. Herbert, but without being able to interpret the signs – whereupon the murderers nevertheless considered him a threatening witness of their deed and consequentially killed him, too. The superficial skeptic had to give up his life, because he had not understood that the objects of observation point to other objects and their connections, and that he therefore should not have assumed that the sharpness of his judgment was at the point of his drawing pencil.

---

[171] Hume, *Standards of Taste*, loc. cit., p. 34.

Fig. 8: Anthony Ashley-Cooper,
Third Earl of Shaftesbury (1671-1712)

The enthusiasm philosophy of the English aristocrat Shaftesbury laid the basis for a completely different tradition. He is the actual founder of English aesthetics and all later thinkers referred to him – even Hume. Enthusiasm is for Shaftesbury the key word to a doctrine of wisdom that explains above all where the artist gets his inspiration from. Thus, the question of artistic genius was asked for the first time, and Shaftesbury's answer is an elegant theory of the creative moment in beauty, called intuitionism.[172] The philosophical motto of this view is the formula "All beauty is truth". However, in a different meaning to Boileau's "Rien n'est vrai que le beau", for behind Shaftesbury's assumption is a whole cosmology.

"To him, truth is rather the inner context of meaning of the universe: a

---

[172] See Cassirer's explanation in *Philosophy of the Enlightenment*, loc. cit., pp. 417-429 It is obvious that Shaftesbury's theory of creative thought impressed Cassirer very much, all the more as Cassirer's own philosophy, especially his *Philosophie der symbolischen Formen* [Philosophy of Symbolic Forms], stands in a certain progeny to Shaftesbury's teaching.

context that cannot be recognized in the mere concept, nor inductively grasped by the accumulation of individual experiences, but can only be experienced immediately and intuitively understood."[173]

Intuition is the ability to get to the particular via the world as a whole, in other words to have the cosmos as a whole present for a moment, so as to finally come to the problems of life and art. Not everyone succeeds in becoming aware of the cosmos with the same intensity, and the artistic genius reveals himself through the representation of his particularly clear view of the whole from the point of view of the ephemeral and the individual. This unequally distributed ability of intuition is the enthusiasm that Shaftesbury knew very well that it is related to the mystical *visio dei* and therefore can be dangerous:

> "Nor can Divine Inspiration, by its outward Marks, be easily distinguish'd from it [Enthusiasm]. For Inspiration is <u>a real</u> feeling of the Divine Presence, and Enthusiasm <u>a false one</u>. But the Passion they raise is much alike. For when the Mind is taken up in Vision, and fixes its view either on any Real Object, or mere Specter of Divinity; when it sees anything prodigious, and more than human; its Horror, Delight, Confusion, Fear, Admiration or whatever Passions belongs to it, or is uppermost on this occasion, will have something vast, immense, and (as Painters say) <u>beyond Life</u>. And this is what gave the name of <u>Fanaticism,</u> as it was us'd by the Ancients in its original Sense, for an Apparition transporting the Mind."[174]

This was a major step towards the subjectivation of aesthetics, because the subject, who does not necessarily have to be an artist, can report something of importance about the outer world, similar to a Leibniz monad, through the exploration of its inner states. This is the idea of an intuitive mind, or, as Kant will later call it in his criticism of this idea, an *intellectus archetypus*.[175] Since this intuitive mind, which is potentially as capable of looking at the world as the divine, grasps everything before discursive coagulation to conceptuality, Shaftesbury's philosophy is certainly to side

---

[173] Ibid., p. 420.

[174] Wolf, Richard B. (ed.), An Old Spelling. Critical Edition of Shaftesbury's 'Letter Concerning Enthusiasm' and 'Sensus communis: An Essay on the Freedom of Wit an Humor', N.Y. 1988, p. 88; the underlines are taken from the critical edition.

[175] Kant, Immanuel, *Critique of the Power of Judgement,* B 349-350 (from here on quoted as 'CPJ').

with French sensibility, for enthusiasm is above all a feeling.[176] However, since this feeling is supposed to be a force of soul underlying all beings equally, which only articulates itself more strongly here and there than elsewhere, the subjects are only media of a cosmic event working through them. As much as the accentuation of emotion looks like a mental event after a consideration of the individual being, this theory is still quite panlogistic and reduces each individual to a moment of the universal.[177]

By the way, Hume referred to this lifelike and theoretically unburdened basic trust in the accustomed cohesion and the experiential order of the world in order to disqualify the danger of radical, all-decomposing skepticism itself as another, purely speculative web of metaphysically exaggerated fantasies.[178]

A final motif of Anglo-Saxon aesthetics is the extraordinarily important discovery of an entire new scheme of aesthetic perception, namely the *feeling of the sublime*. Edmund Burke published in 1756 *A Philosophical Inquiry into the Origin of our Ideas of the Sublime and Beautiful* and could have relied on a long tradition on the subject of the sublime since Longinus.[179] In his psychological investigation, which follows Hume's empiricism, he works out a new trait of the sublime, namely its quality to react not to well-formedness, but always to disproportion, not as simply pleasurable and pleasant, but as in a delightfully terrible way: "a sort of delight full of horror, a sort of tranquility tinged with terror."[180] This feeling arises, for example, when the subject faces the forces of nature without really being able to be destroyed by it, like the fascinated spectator of a storm or an

---

[176] Cassirer writes that it is "rather a specific basic direction, a pure energy and a primordial function of the spirit" (*Philosophy of Enlightenment*, loc. cit., p. 432). He notes, among other things, that the difference to Dubos lies primarily in Shaftesbury's in-depth analysis of the artistic-productive subject, whereas Dubos examines the sensitivity of the art-loving viewer or listener.

[177] Kant's criticism of the idea of this archetypal mind therefore comes down to the same objection as against Leibniz: "In this world, if Shaftesbury were right, freedom would be impossible; Kant, CPF, B 349-350.

[178] Hume writes: "The feelings of our heart, the excitement of our passion, the intensity of our emotions drive away all their conclusions and turn a profound philosopher into an ordinary person." (Hume, David, *A study of the human mind*, ed. by Herbert Herring, Stuttgart 1986, p. 19)

[179] Previously Boileau had also read Longinus' late-antique treatise on the sublime and translated it in 1674.

[180] Cassirer, *Philosophy of the Enlightenment*, loc. cit., p. 442.

"outraged ocean" (Kant). Cassirer immediately points to the social dimension of this feeling that Burke has highlighted:

> "In the experience of the sublime, these barriers [of the bourgeois-sociable order] also fall; the ego is purely self-sufficient and must assert itself in this of its independence and originality against the universe, both physical and social."[181]

The dissolution of the subject's boundaries in the psychic experience of the sublime is a kind of pleasure that could no longer be measured against the old eudemonistic standards of striving for happiness, comfort and satisfaction. Kant will later call it a "negative lust" and give the sublime an important position in the evolutionary theoretical part of his anthropology. Burke's investigation was highly appreciated by Kant:

> "As psychological remarks, these dissections of the phenomena of our minds are extremely beautiful and provide rich material to the most popular researches of empirical anthropology."[182]

Nevertheless, Kant showed convincingly that the question of beauty and taste could not be answered in this way. Burke's empirical interpretation of the sublime as a pure instinct of self-preservation leads into the same dilemma as Hume's teaching of the standard of taste, because taste becomes a purely private feeling about which there is nothing to argue, because it could not be expected at all that any beings have the same inner states. Kant calls this an "egoistic" aesthetic, whereas he demands a "pluralistic" judgment of taste, in which the ability of the individual to take into account the respective tastes of other individuals is expressed.[183] In the second part of the present investigation, the feeling of the sublime will play a very important role in the philosophical analysis of political subjectivity.

In the transition to German aesthetics, a surprising movement is now emerging, for the *increase in the abstraction of theory* is accompanied by an *increase in the closeness to reality in art itself*. The differentiation and specialization of art has emancipated it from the theoretical guidelines, which meant more freedom and experimentation in artistic practice and aesthetic theory at the same time. The advantage of German aestheticians was that

---

[181] Ibid.

[182] Kant, CPJ, B 129.

[183] Ibid., B 130.

they had less to do with art than their French colleagues in particular. French and Anglo-Saxon theories of art and taste have at least gained important insights into the connection between aesthetic and political subjectivity by recognizing the *social, intersubjective dimension of taste*.

A.2.2 Science of Sensual Knowledge and Critique of the Aesthetic Subject

The theoretical turn to a critique of taste in the subject is a further systematic deepening of the questions presented in the first element of the political triad. There it was still a very distant and relatively external schematization of a concept of the individual. The newer aesthetics must now determine more precisely how the inner life of the individual must be designed in order to be able to grasp and formulate its problems in the face of art, science and faith in a coherent manner. At the same time, philosophical speculation is now actually moving in the direction of the individual human being and takes the theoretical problems of individual contingency and concreteness seriously. That aesthetics has thus already implicitly worked on the core problem of political philosophy is, as already mentioned in the introduction, the continuous thesis of this study, which is to be proven by the material presented here.

The efforts to concretize individual subjective states in the horizon of a possible 'truth' and the binding generality of taste were, however, much less entertaining in Germany than in France, where the teaching of aesthetics was at the same time the realization of the established art rules in mostly poetic form. Baeumler pointed out that the French had a classical literature behind them, but the Germans still had to create a society that could have been connected by taste.

> "Today we have a hard time imagining the desolation of the taste that surrounds them [the Germans]. Dubos' ground floor heard the verses Racines; Gottsched's audience bellowed over the pickle herring. The French could do without the raison without danger; the aesthetics of the Germans first had to distrust the feeling."[184]

This mistrust was expressed primarily in the rigid, systematic-scholastic form of the aesthetic treatises written in Latin in Germany, which stood in strong contrast to the elegant verses of a Boileau or Burke's fine, empirical-psychological observations. Baeumler summarized the great change from the aesthetics of reason to the theory of sensuality in a magisterial way:

> "The aesthetics of more recent times can be clearly distinguished from all earlier attempts of a similar kind in that it is defined as a *doctrine of*

---

[184] Baeumler, *The Irrationality Problem*, loc. cit., pp. 60-61.

taste. The Greeks and the Middle Ages knew approaches to art science and technology of the arts, attempts at a psychology and metaphysics of beauty, but no aesthetics in the modern sense. All these approaches lack a certain prerequisite: a specifically *aesthetic subject*. There is a science of aesthetics only from the moment when the experience and the concept of taste enter the consciousness of European mankind. The experience of taste constitutes the aesthetic subject."[185]

To what extent this aesthetic subject is already political in detail, this question still has to be put back. What is decisive here is the formation of a new subjectivity that is sensitive enough to truth values below the thresholds of temporal eternity and systematic perfection – and at the same time symptomatic of a new interest in the world. In this context, European secularization has brought with it a world-historically unique revaluation of the here and now waiting for subjects with a capacity for thought, with which this new accessibility of the sensual world can be made fruitful.

When Alexander Baumgarten published his extraordinarily sophisticated treatise *Aesthetica* in 1750, written in illegible Latin, hardly anyone knew what to do with it.[186] Already half a century later Jean Paul noted: "Our time was teeming with nothing more than aestheticists."[187] The concept of aesthetics was introduced by Alexander Baumgarten and one should actually say: invented. It was unknown in Wolff's school philosophy and in contemporary literature.[188] The somewhat elliptical definition of this new science in §1 of Baumgarten's work reads as follows: "Aesthetica est scientia cognitionis sensitiva". In *Metaphysica*[189], an earlier work

---

[185] Ibid., p. 2.

[186] Thematically Leibniz, König and Gottsched preceded him; Lambert, Winckelmann, Mendelsohn – and Kant followed him. In Bauemler, *Irrrationalityproblem*, loc. cit., pp. 38-43, the discussion of German aesthetics quite rightly begins with Leibniz. However, since the aesthetic moments of Leibniz' philosophy are almost identical with his already discussed 'analysis of the individual', Baumgarten is treated here as the first aesthete. Ferry, *Homo aestheticus*, loc. cit., pp. 77-82, is again particularly enlightening on the aesthetics of Leibniz.

[187] Paul, Jean, *Vorschule der Ästhetik* [Preschool of Aesthetics], 1804, hist.-crit. issue 1/11, Leipzig 1935, p. 13.

[188] Baumgarten, Alexander Gottlieb, *Texte zur Grundlegung der Ästhetik* [Texts Concerning the Foundation of Aesthetics] ed. by Hans Rudolf Schweizer, Hamburg 1983, p. XX.

[189] Baumgarten, Alexander Gottlieb, *Metaphysica*, Halle 1739, photo-mechanical repr., Hildesheim 1969.

by Baumgarten, it says: "Scientia sensitive cognoscendi et proponendi est aesthetica" (§533). Here we explicitly differentiate between the aspect of sensual cognition and expressive, performing art, which as philosophical problems should now both belong to aesthetics as science. In the abridged definition found in *Aesthetica*, confidence is expressed even more strongly that art and sensual knowledge, i.e. productive and receptive capacity, belong together.[190]

Baumgarten is not really known as the founder of aesthetics, but rather as the master of conceptual accuracy, whose definitions and deductions in logic and metaphysics were logically so clear and undeniable that his method became the role model of the entire German school philosophy in the 18th century. Of all people it was this philosopher, who, as a perfect logician, should have been expected to be more pedantic, who wrote an epochal work about exactly those things that could not be accessible with logic – namely everything sensual and particular. The assumption would have been obvious that he simply wanted to categorize the problem of the sensual as another completed topic of metaphysics. However, this would not do justice to Baumgarten's profound insight. In the aesthetic tension between the individual and the general, he ventured to the root of the problem and did not simply negate the claim to universality of theory and science, as Hume criticized, but in Kant's sense, by trying to limit its claims. The "lower powers of the soul" or "lower powers of cognition", as they were called in classical metaphysics, which struggle with the "indeterminate", "dark" and "confused" of always erroneous sensuality, must, in his opinion, have their own aesthetic legitimacy, which is to be settled outside logic, the "older sister" of the now discovered aesthetics[191]. For the "intense clarity" of the exact sciences, he sought an "extensive clarity" for a science of the sensual, which, unlike the great metaphysical systems of the 17th century, does not allow its finiteness to dissolve completely into infinity, but gives this finiteness its own right on a new ground of knowledge.

The decisive factor was his assumption of an "analogon rationis"[192], one or more assets in the subject, which would be the corresponding counterpart for the sensual world as reason is for the intelligent world. He had already tried to describe this *organ of thinking*, as it could be called, in its

---

[190] See Baumgarten, *Grundlegung der Ästhetik*, loc. cit., p. IX.

[191] Baumgarten, *Aesthetica*, §13.

[192] On this term in great detail Bauemler, *Irrrationalityproblem*, loc. cit., pp. 188-197.

individual parts. The "lower assets" include:

> "... 1) the lower ability to recognize the identical in things; 2) the lower ability to recognize the different in things; 3) the sensual memory; 4) the ability to poetry; 5) the ability to judge; 6) the expectation of similar facts; 7) the ability of sensual denomination."[193]

These different and distinguishable lower cognitive capacities are *necessarily to be assumed* in the equipment of a subject capable of sensual cognition, for only with this equipment can a finite being succeed in grasping the relationships between the things of the sensual world.[194] The radicality of this procedure does not immediately make sense. Perhaps the listing of the titles thus acquired is helpful: renunciation of the absolute (as Leibniz still aspired to); emancipation of sensuality (in the sense that every person feels and thinks in and with herself – in good and in bad); the recognition of conceptually uncatchable spontaneity (e.g. as a source of all artistic inspiration); and finally the synthesis of reason and sensuality in a single being.[195] These individual parts were essentially known to school philosophy. Baumgarten's achievement was to summarize them in such an *analogous rationis* and thus prepare what Kant would later call the *reflective power of judgment*. Kant discovered its basis in the course of the critique of the subject of knowledge in the *transcendental principle of judgment*, which states that the sensual world, i.e. the empirical diversity of nature, specifies itself in favor of the intellectual capacity of reflective judgment, as if nature were based on a uniform mind, which, however, is not assumed as the legal basis for nature, but only as the basis for reflection for the thinking subject. The figure of analogon rationis is thus adopted by Kant and mirrored once again. Not only that – as with Baumgarten – a rational ability must be accepted in the subject, which can make the sensual world tangible, but *the sensual world as a whole is based on a fictitious mind*. Otherwise it would be completely unconnected in all its phenomena and there would be no reason to assume that the animal kingdom could be divided into species, for example, that a landscape could evoke something like the idea of beauty in thought or that people should organize their life on the surface of the earth in the form of communities. These relationships are examined in more detail in the second part.

---

[193] Baumgarten, *Metaphysica*, loc. cit., § 640.

[194] Ferry, *Homo aestheticus*, loc. cit. p. 103.

[195] This is the summary of Baumgarten's achievements as seen in Cassirer's *Philosophy of Enlightenment*, loc. cit., pp. 474-477.

So German aesthetics has been a serious and immanent critique of rationalism from the very beginning and demands that the sensual world be conceivable with its own claim to rationality[196]: "Quid enim est abstracttio, si iactura non est?"[197] Abstraction as renunciation is the price of the theoretically relevant sensuality deficit of rationalist enlightenment. *Aesthetics is also a logic*, but with its own responsibilities in the area of lower cognitive ability ("logica facultatis cognoscitivae inferioris")[198] and thus detached from the classical organon. In the title of his study on aesthetics, *La manière de bien penser*, the Jesuit Bouhours showed an affirmative relationship to the logic of Port Royal[199], which was intended to help him design an aesthetics of rules in the form of "salon logic"[200]. Bauemler aptly writes about Leibniz that he had an unhappy love for logic because he failed in his task of writing the "logic of the irrational" in the form of an *ars combinatoria*.[201] But that the criticism of the German aestheticians[202] of the rule of logic was not only formulated in favor of the fine arts proves, among other things, Baumgarten's philosophical weekly, which he published in letter form in 1741 under the pseudonym "Aletheophilus" [Friend of Truth][203] – almost a decade before his *Aesthetica*. In his Second Philo-

---

[196] In his voluminous study *Die Aufklärung im Rahmen des modernenzeitlichen Rationalismus* [The Enlightenment within the Framework of Modern Rationalism], Stuttgart 1981, Panajotis Kondylis classified this critique as "antintellectualistic" or "sensualistic" (ibid., pp. 559-563) and dealt with the entire European aesthetic in a few remarks. In a book written on the guideline of the thesis that the Enlightenment has worked on the mediation of spirit and sensuality (ibid., p. 19), this is somewhat surprising, for what discipline has done this more intensively and experimentally than aesthetics?

[197] Baumgarten, *Aesthetica*, loc. cit., § 585.

[198] Baumgarten, *Metaphysica*, loc. cit., § 533.

[199] Of which one could of course already say that it is a further development of Aristotelian logic and in the broadest sense a preparation of aesthetics, because after all, this important work from 1662 is not called *La logique ou l'art de penser* [Logics of the Art of Thinking] for nothing.

[200] So the expression of Baeumler, *Irrationalityproblem*, loc. cit., p. 29.

[201] Ibid., p. 42.

[202] According to Baumgarten, these include, among others, his pupil G. F. Meier (*Beginning of Fine Sciences*, 1748 – i.e. before Baumgarten's *Aesthetica*, but by attending the lectures with knowledge of the subject), J.-H. Lambert (*Phenomenology*, 1764) and of course Kant.

[203] This magazine had to be abandoned after its 26th edition. What is remarkable

sophical Letter[204], the author coined the terms "aesthetic empiricism" and "aesthetic art of experience". In this context, he explicitly points to the dexterity in the use of the "artificial... weapons of the senses", such as binoculars, microscopes, barometers, etc., to advance the experimental sciences. Unfortunately, the letter breaks off at this point. Elsewhere he writes: "Confusion is the mother of error. My answer: a.) But it is an indispensable prerequisite for the discovery of truth."[205] This is a statement that would *not be possible in the organon of classical formal logic*.[206] It can therefore be said without exaggerated speculation that Baumgarten was on his way to a general heuristics of sensual knowledge that guided art and science, as Kant finally developed it in the *Critique of the Power of Judgment*.[207] In the speculative core of Baumgarten's aesthetics, it was already suspected that a philosophical theory of society[208] was enclosed and whose impulse Kant passed on to the *CPJ* – which still remains to be shown.

It was only with the German philosophy as a criticism of taste that a history of art became conceivable, with which, of course, the historicization of its objects began and various moments of selectivity in the perception and appreciation of tradition became possible.[209] At the same time, the disintegration of a previously philosophically secured unity of the world

---

here is that these are Baumgarten's only texts written in German. This already sheds light on the publication activity in the 18th century, which will be thoroughly examined in the following section on the development of the public sphere.

[204] Baumgarten, *Texte zur Grundlegung der Ästhetik*, loc. cit., pp. 67-72.

[205] Baumgarten, *Aesthetica*, loc. cit., §7.

[206] The first author to put error in the position of an indispensable moment in all knowledge gain and progress was Francis Bacon. Accordingly, he called the key work of his *Instauratio magna* the "Novum organum", a new form of logic.

[207] However, not so specifically applied to empirical-scientific experiments; this priority remains undisputed to Baumgarten. For Kant, the experiment was exclusively part of theoretical reason, because the question of nature is spelt out mathematically in the experiment. However, the arrangement, such as the selection of the necessary equipment and measuring techniques, is without doubt part of the aesthetic, i.e. heuristic part of the experiment.

[208] Cf. Schweizer, Hans Rudolf, *Ästhetik als Philosophie der sinnlichen Erkenntnis. Eine Interpretation der ‚Aesthetica' A. G. Baumgartens mit teilweiser Wiedergabe des lateinischen Textes und deutscher Übersetzung*, Stuttgart 1973, pp. 98-101.

[209] Jauß, Hans Robert, *Studien zum Epochenwandel der ästhetischen Moderne* [Studies in the Field of Epochal Changes in Aesthetic Modernity], Frankfurt 1989, p. 7.

became apparent, which to this day is gladly taken into account as the sum of the consequential costs of its increasing subjectification and individualization. The insight, often repeated since Gadamer's seminal work *Truth and Method*, that Kant had pursued the subjectification of aesthetics dates the event therefore too late, for this process was initiated by Baumgarten at the latest.[210] Paradoxically, the essential expansion that aesthetics undergoes in Germany and there especially in Kant's third *Critique* is its subordination to a more general, namely reflective judgment that is responsible not only for the beautiful and sublime, but also for the concept of purpose in teleology.[211] In the *Critique of the Power of Judgment*, the problem of concreteness and particularity has not only become the keystone of the Kantian system, but in it the analysis of the individual, begun with Leibniz, is contained in the philosophical form of the "subject of feeling," as Baeumler aptly described it. It is conceivable that at this point the foundations of political subjectivity could also be found and exposed.

---

[210] Gadamer, Hans-Georg, *Wahrheit und Methode. Grundzüge einer philosophischen Hermeneutik* [Truth and Method. Fundamentals to a Philsosophical Hermeneutics], Gesammelte Werke [Collected Works] Vol. I, 5th ed. Tübingen 1986, pp. 48-87. Gadamer is only partly responsible for this misjudgment, for in this conversion of the aesthetics from objective truth to subjective judgement he expressly describes Baumgarten as Kant's predecessor; see ibid., p. 36-37.

[211] To what extent this *subordination* can be understood as an *extension* can only be shown in the second part of the present study.

A.2.3 The Connection of Aesthetics and Politics in the *Sensus Communis*

It is not immediately and directly clear what the elucidation of taste might have to do with the development of a specific political culture. All thinkers who have studied aesthetics have conceded or even insisted that having a taste is only possible and meaningful in a society. In order to somehow bring the different tastes – if such tastes were permitted – into harmony with each other, a force uniting the people involved had to be assumed. This unifying factor has been *phronesis, sensus communis* or just *public spirit* since ancient times. It made sense to return to this basis of older political theory, all the more so since its admissibility was guaranteed by the authority of the ancients. For most authors of Enlightenment, however, the 'healthy folk spirit' which was intended to be addressed, was not a skill in which each person shared in his or her own way, but the theorists made great efforts to determine the content of this common sense very precisely and to distinguish it from the simple 'opinion' or even the 'prejudice of the crowd'.[212] For them, the judgment of the individual was always normatively combined with the judgment of the general public, for the individual ultimately experiences what he or she has to think as a norm through the common sense.

All in all, the European sensus-communis speculation was uncritical in the political sense, except for the important function of protecting one's own status or profession (above all that of the philosopher) from the unreasonable demands of religion. This becomes clear against the background of one great exception, namely the pamphlet *Common Sense* written by Thomas Paine. In 1776, when the United States of America declared its independence, Paine took the colonists' side in this document, delegitimized the succession of the English monarchy and its constitution on the basis of their social common sense and saw only a necessary evil in the future American governments, which must always be limited by common sense.[213]

---

[212] Peter Steinberger's study *The Concept of Political Judgment*, Chicago 1993, which is discussed in Chapter B.1.1, belongs to this tradition.

[213] Paine, Thomas, *Common Sense,* Stuttgart 1982. 150,000 copies had already been sold in the first three months after the publication of the book; by 1800 it was approximately half a million copies with all translations; cf. ibid, *Epilogue* by Lothar Meinzer, pp. 102-3.

But even in these radical demands based on the doctrine of the public mind, the common denominator is not first sought, but always assumed to have been fully developed. For Paine, too, it is self-evident that society, as an incarnation of the common sense, will always behave in a united critical manner towards the government facing it. This means that even here, theoretically, no internal differentiation was attributed to the community.[214] In Kant's version of the sensus communis, the essential difference that has already emerged in the criticism of taste is the first *chance of intellectual dissent* – the public spirit as a spiritual forum in which no *scientific dispute*[215] is possible, but all participants are allowed *to argue* and share their *opinions*. It has to be put in paradoxical terms: Kant builds the common sense on the rationally possible *dissent*, not on the consensus that has always been assumed.[216]

Gadamer therefore observed quite correctly that Kant's sensus communis was taken out of its ancient and also enlightening provisions, which had already coagulated into tradition. Kant formalized the common sense and no longer allowed it to be congruent in content with its definition of the "moment of moral bourgeois existence" which was valid until then.[217] It

---

[214] What with Paine is exclusively a lack of theoretically conclusive representation, for in political practice he was an unusually radical and yet always liberal democrat.

[215] In Kantian lingo, the word 'dispute' is reserved exclusively to the Latin meaning of 'disputatio' which was since the Middle Ages a strictly regulated exchange of arguments between scholars or scientists with the prospect of finding out objective truth. In aesthetics, this is not only undesirable, it is even impossible by its very ontological principle as Alexander Baumgarten has proved.

[216] Luc Ferry pointed this out to explain the inadequacy and superfluousness of Lyotard's scheme of conflict in an interpretation of Kant's common sense; cf. Ferry, *Homo aestheticus*, loc. cit., pp. 135-141. At this as at many other places in the writings of Ferry it becomes clear that he is concerned with a theory of intersubjectivity in the sense of Jürgen Habermas, however not based on "postmetaphysical" speech pragmatism, but in the sense of a "problematic metaphysics" of the subject's intersubjective judgement. Manfred Frank's philosophical motives are similar to Ferry's; cf. Frank, Martin, *Wider den apriorischen Intersubjektivismus. Gegenvorschläge aus Sartrescher Inspiration* [Against the Apriori Intersubjectivism. Counterproposals from a Sartrean Perspective], in: Brumlik, Michael u. Brunkhorst, Hauke (ed.), *Gemeinschaft und Gerechtigkeit* [Community and Justice], Frankfurt 1993, pp. 273-289.

[217] José Ortega y Gasset wrote in the little booklet *Über das römische Imperium*

should be noted that Gadamer wanted to reinstate the older sense of the sensus communis in its rights in order to strengthen the 'prejudice heuristics' he had developed against the heuristics of reflective judgment. Thus, he represents the position of many thinkers before Kant, who by no means regarded the public spirit as an accompanying element of an individualism to be promoted, but – quite analogous to the already discussed contractualisms – wanted to be guaranteed in the sensus communis a kind of *secondary unity of society*.

As Gadamer aptly points out to Vico in particular, these sensus-communis teachings usually refer to the pragmatic tradition of Roman classics such as Cicero, who wanted to raise and protect the intact unity of the republic to the norm with the term – which for Gadamer, however, is already too critical and he interprets as a falling away from the original doctrine of common sense. Aristotle, on the other hand, had still recognized the public spirit as a truthful knowledge of the moral unity of the community. It is unmistakable in which direction Gadamer's steps lead. His model as political philosophy amounts to a pre-Socratic, philosophy-of-being-variant of the doctrine of phronesis.[218] What is decisive here is only that Gadamer's own interpretation of the sensus communis, which wants to go back to tradition, makes it clear that the *communitas* as a timeless truth value has always preceded the *sensus* in the political subject[219] – from which it could be concluded that the subject actually does

---

[About the Roman Empire], Stuttgart 1942, about his passion for a certain political office, which Gadamer might also have been interested in: "The view that this [unity] is the foundation of society has been a commonplace since Aristotle. One of his disciples, Dikaiarch, had written a whole treatise on harmony. Less known is that in some Greek states, for example in Heraklea, during the 4th century there was an authority that... 'guardian of unanimity.' I have often thought about this very meaningful title, and although I dislike any public office, I would have liked to have worked in this position." (ibid., p. 12-13)

[218] Gadamer, *Truth and Method*, loc. cit., pp. 28 and 29, where he announces with a great gesture: "But we will see that in all these twists and turns the way of being of moral knowledge recognized by Aristotle is effective. Remembrance of this will become important for the appropriate self-image of the humanities."

[219] Cf. the precise study by Teresa Orozco, *Platonische Gewalt. Gadamers politische Hermeneutik der NS-Zeit* [Platonic Violence. Gadamer's Political Hermeneutics of the Nazi Era], Hamburg 1995, on the fundamentally non-political understanding of (early) Gadamer.

not or should not need a political sense.[220] This was the case until Kant's criticism of the traditional doctrines of the common sense.[221]

Kant reversed this connection by rebuilding the always too promising and fictitious sense of community on the *subject's rational capacity for common sense*. From the expression 'public spirit', which was morally used until the end of the 18th century and which for the most part had to serve order-preserving, integrative but very rarely critical needs, he made an operative concept which could be used for the first time to analyze social and political reality because he no longer left it to the vocabulary of its idealized self-description. Gadamer is thus very mistaken when he sees Kant's concept as completely defused and subjectified to its disadvantage simply because it was separated from its Aristotelian definition, always morally determined in content and thus much too material.[222] For Kant, the formalization of the concept of the common sense is inseparably connected with a *program of bourgeois individuality and the philosophical development of a methodical concept of the public sphere* that is not exhausted in

---

[220] Here, perhaps, the theory of Shaftesbury's sense of community could still be mentioned, in which, despite its temporal and anthropological fixation (love as an original relationship, enthusiasm as a quasi-mystic basic force), he insists that dissent animates the entertainment and the use of reason is welcome as he wrote in in his 1709 essay *Sensus communis. An Essay on the Freedom of Wit and Humour*: "The freedom of joking mockery, the privilege of doubting everything in decent language, and the permission to disrupt and refute any argument without offending the argumentator, these are the only prerequisites that can make such profound conversations reasonably pleasant." (Shaftesbury, *Standard Edition. Complete Works, Selected Letters and Lesser Writings*, Volume I.3, Stuttgart 1992, p. 31).

[221] The same applies to Gadamer's inherently interesting 'prejudice heuristics', which also reveal the limits of hermeneutics. For if Gadamer wants to show that we always need prejudices, the real philosophical question can only be asked with Kant: How can we even have prejudices, being prejudiced? Anyone who answers that we "develop them out of a need" or "anamnesis" misses the method of judgment analysis and undercuts the philosophical level of reflection demanded by this question.

[222] The same applies to Gadamer's inherently interesting 'prejudice heuristics', which also reveal the limits of hermeneutics. For if Gadamer wants to show that we always need prejudices, the real philosophical question can only be asked with Kant: How can we even have prejudices, being prejudiced? Anyone who answers that we "develop them out of a need" or "anamnesis" misses the method of judgment analysis and undercuts the philosophical level of reflection demanded by this question.

the enlightened empathy for freedom of opinion in scholarly circles. [223] In miniature, the entire political triad whose formation is being investigated here in detail is traced: The aesthetic capacity in the common sense forms the transition from the communicable individual to a public sphere that can only be called political if it articulates itself in its common sense as individuality. The logical figure in it is not a tautological circular conclusion, but an expression of social-theoretical self-reference, which the newer systems theory rightly demands as basic conditions for universalizing theories. The following part discusses the third pillar of the political triad, the social practice of public communication. It should be noted that this presentation will primarily deal with the historical theories and practices of the public, whose socio-historical material will only form the basis for the later philosophical discussion of the concept of the public sphere and the political subjectivity articulated in this event.

---

[223] The further development of the concept of public spirit in German idealism naturally did not in any way follow Kant's new, radically subject-related theory of common sense, but only his criticism of the Scottish and German-popular philosophical predecessors. This led a decline of interest in the philosophical value of the common spirit that was unintended by Kant, and Hegel even expressed his contempt for this invention; see Hegel, G. W. F., *Phänomenologie des Geistes* [Phenomenology of Spirit], Frankfurt 1972, Preface, p. 63.

A. 3 The Public as Aesthetic and Political Communication in the 18th Century

The citizens of western democracies at the beginning of the 21st century have taken some possibilities of individual living so for granted that hardly anyone can imagine how rich in highly demanding preconditions they are. This includes the freedom to form an opinion and to make it 'public'. The bourgeois public in Germany is an achievement of the 18th century.[224] The historical retrospective should help here to make the improbability and audacity of this cultural achievement visible. This prepares the empirical topic 'public sphere' in all its diversity for the political-philosophical analysis, so that its problems can be better understood. From a historical point of view, it is already astonishing that people, especially rulers of competing faiths, do not (let) kill each other, but organize their social reality according to such highly fragile concepts as tolerance. Neither can it explain why churches and princes did not forcefully deny the citizens, who were still subjects, the extremely threatening freedom of opinion-forming and expression, i.e. the establishment of public communication outside institutional control.

At the 1992 conference of historians about *The Public in the 18th Century*, the researchers agreed only on the point that nothing is self-evident about the emergence of the public and everything still has to be argued about.[225] Thus one is probably still far from a scientifically satisfactory definition or from an exhaustive concept of the early bourgeois public. There is still a desideratum that was registered in a similar fashion at the 1962 conference on *Public Opinion*.[226] The reason for researching the public as an institution

---

[224] In the following, the terms 'public' and 'public opinion' are used synonymously, since in the second half of the 18th century they were not yet systematically distinguished from one another and in addition interfered with the older term 'publicity'. Today's differentiation of definitions, applied to the epoch, would be an anachronism.

[225] *Öffentlichkeit im 18. Jahrhundert* [The Public in the 18th Century], conference of the Society for the Study of the 18th Century, from 18 to 20 November 1992 in Meersburg on Lake Constance, conference report by Carsten Zelle in: *Das achtzehnte Jahrhundert* [The Eighteenth Century] DAJ, 1/1993, pp. 12-13.

[226] Löffler, Martin (ed.), *Die öffentliche Meinung. Publizistik als Medium und Faktor der öffentlichen Meinung* [The Public Opinion. Journalism as a Medium and Factor of Public Opinion], published on behalf of the Deutsche Studiengesellschaft für

of vital importance for liberal democracies was the "television judgment" of the German Federal Constitutional Court, which gave the state an active protection mandate for the formation of public opinion. Thus, for the first time, a fundamental right was not interpreted as a civil right of defense against the state, but as a state order itself.[227] However, the court left the definition of the concept of public opinion in terms of content to science. In the summary of the results of the 1962 conference, the editor tried to define the term provisionally:

> "Public opinion in the broader sense is the view of people, events or conditions that prevails in the population of a certain area (community, country, state, continent, world) during a certain period of time. Public opinion in the narrower (political) sense is understood to mean the views on persons, events or conditions of general (public) interest prevailing in the population of a certain area (municipality, country, state, continent, world) during a certain period of time."[228]

In this synthesis, the same positivism that is still being lamented thirty years later on the same issue is decisive. The peculiarity of the bourgeois public seems to be its inexplicability with empirical-sociological categories. This is precisely the aim of the present study. After all, in order to make progress in this area, do we not first need to reflect on the foundations of political subjectivity?

Jürgen Habermas critically analyzed the normative content of this historical phenomenon of bourgeois societies in his habilitation thesis *The Structural Transformation of the Public Sphere* from 1962, i.e. at the same time as the first conference on the topic took place.[229] His study was a great step forward, for earlier sociology had not dared to formulate something scientifically sound on the normative charge of the public sphere.

The *Kritik der öffentlichen Meinung* [Critique of Public Opinion] by

---

Publizistik, Munich 1962.

[227] Cf. *Entscheidungen des Bundesverfassungsgerichts. Amtliche Sammlung* [Decisions of the Federal Constitutional Court. Official Collection], vol. 12, p. 205 ff.

[228] Löffler, *Public Opinion*, loc. cit., p. 79.

[229] Habermas, Jürgen, *Strukturwandel der Öffentlichkeit. Untersuchungen zu einer Kategorie der bürgerlichen Gesellschaft* [The Structural Transformation of the Public Sphere: An Inquiry into a Category of Bourgeois Society], Neuwied 1962, 13th edition, Frankfurt 1991, with a preface to the new edition.

Ferdinand Toennies expressly excluded the entire history of the development of this social phenomenon and was limited to establishing the structural similarity of religion and public opinion, which – according to Toennies – connects internally and then intolerantly excludes.[230] Above all, according to him, the gain in power of public opinion also meant the disappearance of religion as the guarantor of publicly recognized morality. Toennis described the public sphere as a medium of almost thwarting and destructive effect on any form of normativity. Thus, he implicitly understood morality as a traditional heritage, an endangered and non-renewable asset.

At the 1992 conference, historians disqualified Habermas' thesis of a literary public preceding the political public as a "normative postulate" without corresponding historical reality. The insight that the moral-philosophical character of the public sphere in the 18th century can be made socially and theoretically fruitful threatened to be gambled away. In addition, the facts of press history are put to a great strain if the "literary" public is understood to consist exclusively of entertaining and instructive fiction, as was the case there. Habermas himself did not claim this anywhere, but rather with the title "literarily" probably meant what Lucian Hölscher also reports about:

> "For the concentration on questions of taste, fashion and general customs also in Germany attracted a relatively broad middle-class, above all female audiences, and made it possible for them to be informed."[231]

In this context, 'literary public' refers to a public that discusses general aesthetic questions. *Political* publicity only arises when a bourgeois claim to participation in power is articulated. Aesthetic and political public spheres are similar or even identical in their personal composition, but in terms of their function, the public discussing questions of taste clearly differs from the circles arguing about the public order of law and government.

In the preface to the new edition of *Strukturwandel*, Jürgen Habermas admitted to the public that historians were right in accusing the study of

---

[230] Toennis, Ferdinand, *Kritik der öffentlichen Meinung* [Critique of Public Opinion], Berlin 1922, pp. 569-72.

[231] Hölscher, Lucian, *Öffentlichkeit*, in: *Geschichtliche Grundbegriffe. Historisches Lexikon zur politisch-sozialen Sprache in Deutschland*, [Public, in: Basic Historical Terms], ed. by Brunner, Otto, Conze, Werner u. Koselleck, Reinhart, Stuttgart 1978, p. 433.

empirical shortcomings, but saw his theses largely confirmed in Hans-Ulrich Wehler's *Gesellschaftsgeschichte* [German Social History].[232] In particular, he admitted that the over-stylization of the bourgeois public sphere as a unified public is historically inadmissible and that there were rather a whole series of competing and mutually exclusive publics.[233] Furthermore, Habermas now quite frankly admits that his analysis of a degeneration of the bourgeois public from a "culture-raising to a culture-consuming audience"[234] jumped too short and that the study's "Hegelian-Marxist" attempt to instrumentalize the idea of the welfare state as a lever for radical-democratic reformism was a kind of happy failure. Otherwise, if the bourgeois public had favored to develop according to the young Habermas' wishes, then it would have degenerated into a legislature that always knew a priori what had to be done, namely the restriction and finally the abolition of property.[235] Overall, Habermas today concedes that his view of the bourgeois public at that time were in many respects too pessimistic.[236] These admissions are very helpful for further investigation, because some aspects of the phenomenon are now undisputed.

In the following, the discussion of the theoretical charge of the concept of the public sphere in the 18th century is given priority over the presentation of the various forms of its practice[237] only because it must nevertheless be assumed that the idea of a right to freedom to form public, expressive opinions – and only later indirect participation in government – was brought forward from outside, namely through the Anglo-American and French writings and revolutions, and thus not only historically but also systematically preceded a public sphere as practice in Germany.[238] The entire pre- and early history of Western European, especially American republicanism since the Founding Fathers is assumed here. Of course, it should not look as if the German Reich and its states invented the political

---

[232] Habermas, *Strukturwandel*, loc. cit., p. 13; Wehler, *Gesellschaftsgeschichte*, loc. cit., p. 303-331.

[233] Habermas, *Strukturwandel*, loc. cit., p. 15.

[234] Ibid., p. 30.

[235] Ibid., p. 26.

[236] Ibid., p. 30.

[237] Cf. Eder, Klaus, *Geschichte als Lernprozeß? Zur Pathogenese politischer Moderne in Deutschland*, Frankfurt 1985.

[238] See Hölscher, *Öffentlichkeit*, loc. cit., p. 431: "The German conceptual development followed a change in the form of sociability that originated in Italy, France and England in the 17th century."

and its public in the 18th century. The presentation of this section is limited to German history, because the connecting lines should not be drawn too far with the later philosophical deepening of the topic. In addition, the public is finally the element of the political triad Individuality-Aesthetics-Public, for whose valid description enough social and literary events are documented in Germany.

The intention to collect here the historical material for an anthropological reading of the emergence of the political does not necessarily contradict other theoretical reconstruction methods of the same subject area. The thesis to be underpinned here, that Reason should have helped to shape this history in a certain way, is compatible with a sociological analysis of the development of the public in the 18th century. The differentiation of modern society was, this is undisputed, one of the conditional possibilities for the representation or thematization of individuality (through the achievements of the distinction of person, role and individual) and for the practice of the public (through the civilization of behavioral expectations[239]). Niklas Luhmann puts aside the discussion of the subjectivity involved in these processes with the succinct remark that no one can say "who" is this empirical subject and that there is therefore a compulsion to postulate "man" in the singular.[240] However, it is possible, without having to doubt the functionalist mode of observation of history, to identify *a capacity of thought that participates in shaping the same story*. Part B below discusses how these capacities actually *make history*.

---

[239] Cf. Luhmann, Niklas, *Grundrechte als Institution* [Fundamental Rights as an Institution], Berlin 1965, Chapter 5: Freedom of communication, pp. 84-107.

[240] Luhmann, Niklas, *Gesellschaftliche Komplexität und öffentliche Meinung*, in: Luhmann, *Soziologische Aufklärung 5 – Konstruktivistische Perspektiven*, Opladen 1990, pp. 170-182, here p. 174. There was in interesting discussion on the under-definition of the subject in Luhmann's criticism of the achievements of German idealism in subjectivity theory; see Wagner, Gerhard u. Zipprian, Heinz, *Identität oder Differenz. Bemerkungen zu einer Aporie Niklas Luhmanns Theorie selbstreferentieller Systeme* [Identity and Difference. Notes on an Aporia in Niklas Luhmann's Theory of Self-Referential Systems], in: *Zeitschrift für Soziologie* 6/1992, pp. 394-405.

A.3.1 Fragments of a Theory of the Public in the 18th Century

There has always been a certain kind of public opinion in traditional history, since in all forms of the community the rulers had to inform themselves at least informally (e.g. by informers and agents) about the state of affairs in order to adapt wisely or opportunistically to them, or to force their conformity with the will of the ruler through repression. *How* smart the repression and manipulation of popular opinion could be designed is demonstrated in Chapter VII of the book *Il Principe* (1513) by Niccolo Machiavelli. There it is reported how Cesare Borgia sent the obedient and cruel Ramiro de Lorqua to 'pacify' the province of Romagna. Once the province was brutally tidied up, one morning Borgia had the noble henchman horribly executed in the Roman capital Cesena and from then on could be sure of the love of his subjects – and thus of the affection of public opinion – in this area.

This kind of informal public has hardly been seriously addressed in legal and theological terms for many centuries. In a sense, it was the ideological basis of Roman politics and also the subsequent feudal-Christian duty of the rulers to care for their subjects, because the prince must have his fortress in the heart of the people and must pay attention to the opinion of his subjects, as a famous dictum exhorted.[241] But the very oracle of *salus populi suprema lex* and the moralizing mirror-for-princes literature [Fürstenspiegel], in which Machiavelli's treatise was the scandallous exception, indicate how little thought was actually given to the public. According to the modern concept of publicity, a popular opinion could and had to exist for reasons of legitimacy for just rule, but it was not allowed to express itself except through ceremonial homage, especially not in acts of resistance against the authorities. This was a dilemma that became clear for the first time in all its scope when the religious struggle in France after the Night of Bartholomew brought an otherwise loyal Protestant aristocracy into life-threatening opposition to the Catholic king. The Monarchomach resistance theories of the French Calvinists – shortly afterwards followed by Catholics with pamphlets of identical content, only this time directed against a Protestant sovereign – were the first and irreparable break with the unquestionability and sacredness of the

---

[241] Also by Niccolò Machiavelli, in the *Discorsi sopra la prima deca di Tito Livo II*, cap. 24, after *Operas*, 7th ed. Milan 1976, p. 288.

sovereignty of the anointed king.[242] This crisis of legitimacy of rule reached its climax in the French Revolution.

"In this way, June 17, 1789, the idea that an individual man, by virtue of divine will, ecclesial anointing and inherited membership of a dynasty or even some of the social classes protected and privileged by him, could sufficiently represent a nation and could satisfactorily decide about their fate, was finally banished from the world of political imagination with lasting effect. To the present day, it has determined the model, techniques and principles according to which a representation of the will of the people or the nation must be composed as democratic."[243]

This is already a peculiarity of this historical phenomenon, for publicity is first and foremost a purely European event in that only a division of faith and the church and the resulting loss of unity of the sacred legitimacy of rule made a secularized form of publicity relevant and prepared the separation of society and state.[244] In the second part of the present study, after the systematic philosophical discussion, comparative cultural and

---

[242] Cf. Bermbach, Udo, Widerstandsrecht, Souveränität, Kirche und Staat: Frankreich und Spanien im 16. Jahrhundert [Right of Resistance, Sovereignty, Church and State: France and Spain in the 16th century], in: Piper's Handbuch der politischen Ideen [Piper's Handbook of Political Ideas], edited by Iring Fetscher and Herfried Münkler, Munich 1985, Volume III, pp. 101-160; cf. also Stankiewicz, W. J., Politics and Religion in Seventeenth-Century France. A Study of Political Ideas from the Monarchomachs to Bayle, as Reflected in the Toleration Controversy, Berkley/Los Angeles 1960.

[243] Schmitt, Eberhard, *Repräsentation und Revolution. Eine Untersuchung zur Genesis der kontinentalen Theorie und Praxis parlamentarischer Repräsentation aus der Herrschaftspraxis des Ancien Régime in Frankreich (1760-1789)* [Representation and Revolution. An investigation into the genesis of the continental theory and practice of parliamentary representation from the ruling practice of the Ancien Régime in France (1760-1789)], Munich 1969, p. 281. The author notes, however, as it were disappointedly that this post-revolutionary practice of representation made the "representation of the sovereign nation-state" strong in order to seemingly abolish the "representation of interests". The result is an "uncontrollable crypto existence" of the interest groups that colonize the state.

[244] Cf. on this Schulze, Winfried, *Deutsche Geschichte im 16 Jahrhundert 1500-1618*, Tübingen 1987, p. 232ff.; cf. also in Rainer Wohlfeil's *Einführung in die Geschichte der deutschen Reformation* [Introduction tot he History of German Reformation] 1982, the chapter "Reformatorische Öffentlichkeit" [Reformatory Publicity], pp. 123-133.

historical material from non-Christian countries is presented to illustrate this peculiarity of early European formation of publicity (cf. in particular chapter B.2.2).

In the 17th century, the absolutist state had left the private interior to its subjects.23[245] But that was soon no longer enough: "The Enlightenment began its triumphal procession to the same extent as it expanded the private interior to the public."[246] For this reason, the 18th century has this incomparable key position in the development of Western subjectivity. What is true and beautiful and just, people increasingly developed out of their individual perception and experience. One began, so to speak, to explore from its 'inside' how reality, the outside, exists. An unimaginable, even highly absurd train of thought shortly before. The public sphere was thus also the process of understanding about this subjectivation and individualization in a special culture.[247] Of course, this idea of the public sphere created a competition for truth for tradition and religion, which until then were the main suppliers of truth and thus responsible for the legitimacy of government. The idea of the public, however, already had its own, very old tradition, which was brought into position itself under this title in the course of the registration of claims.

The concept of the public was derived from the legal concept of *ius publicum*, public law as a counterpart to private law. However, public law

---

[245] In a sense, this is a late historical confirmation of Carl Schmitt's account in his book *Der Leviathan in der Staatslehre des Thomas Hobbes. Sinn und Fehlschlag eines Symbols* [The Leviathan in the Theory of State by Thomas Hobbes. Meaning and Failure of a Symbol], Cologne 1938, where he saw the seeds of liberal publicity and liberalism in the "private reservation of faith" in Thomas Hobbes' main work. Thus, in Schmitt's opinion, our era of parliamentarianism began.

[246] Koselleck, Reinhart, *Kritik und Krise* [Critque and Crisis], Frankfurt 1973, p. 41. There is a great difference between the earlier view of public opinion as a right to a private view and the competence of citizens to form an opinion with public value. See Löffler, *Die öffentliche Meinung*, loc. cit., p. 7.

[247] Habermas writes critically, starting from the point of view of his own theory of communicative action: "Public spheres can be understood as higher-level inter-subjectivities. Collective self-descriptions can articulate themselves in them. And in the highly aggregated public also an awareness of society as a whole. This no longer needs to meet the precision requirements that subject philosophy must place on self-confidence. It is neither philosophy nor social theory that concentrates society's knowledge of itself." (Habermas, Jürgen, *Der philosophische Diskurs der Moderne* [The Philosophical Discourse of Modernity], Frankfurt 1985, p. 435)

only referred to state and intergovernmental functions and institutions. Private law was also not yet functionally separated from constitutional law, but only hierarchically placed under it, which is why one could say that private law was a constitutional right for all areas of life until the 19th century.[248] This terminological irritation continued until Immanuel Kant, on the basis of philosophical considerations in his *Metaphysics of Morals* (1797), proposed a new system.[249] Kant's famous essay *Answering the Question: What is Enlightenment?*[250] had already sent a political program on this new system back in 1784 and thus documented in many respects only what other Enlightenment scholars had already written before him; therefore it was not particularly provocative. But the 'language policy' he pursued in it turned everything one knew upside down, for he mixed up the previously known meaning of 'public' and 'private'.

> "Private and public functions, which had previously fallen apart in the different areas of life of the house and the bourgeois office, now correlated in a new way. According to Kant, the citizen took part in the public communication process of bourgeois society precisely in his function as a private citizen and thus contributed to the formation of public will, which formed the highest legislative power in the state."[251]

This marked the end of a longer process of delegitimizing the state-centered understanding of the public sphere. At the same time, the career of the concept of publicity as an ideal for finding and procuring truth had

---

[248] Cf. Bullinger, Martin, *Öffentliches Recht und Privatrecht. Studien über Sinn und Funktion der Unterscheidung* [Public and Private Law. Studies on the Meaning and Function of Distinction], Stuttgart 1968; see Hölscher, *Öffentlichkeit*, loc. cit., p. 428; Habermas, *Strukturwandel*, loc. cit. p. 58: "There are low and high 'authorities', low and high 'righteousness', but no status fixable under private law from which private individuals can emerge into a public, so to speak".

[249] "The supreme division of natural law cannot (as sometimes happens) be that into natural and social law but must be that into natural and civil law: the first of which is called private law, the second public law. For it is not the social but the bourgeois state that is opposed to the natural state; because there may well be society in it, but only no bourgeois law (which safeguards mine and yours by public laws), hence the law in which the former is called private law". (Kant, Immanuel, *Werke VIII* [Works VIII], ed. by Wilhelm Weischedel, 1st ed. Frankfurt 1974, p. 350).

[250] Kant, Immanuel, *Werke IX* [Works IX], loc. cit., pp. 53-61.

[251] Hölscher, Lucian, *Öffentlichkeit und Geheimnis* [Public and Secret], Stuttgart 1979, p. 103.

already flourished so successfully that state and religious claims to truth increasingly came under pressure to justify themselves. From the perspective of the state sphere, the *arcana imperii*, the doctrine of the moral and religious-free secret policy of the cabinets or the absolutist prince, which systematically excluded the bourgeois public, was above all a precautionary measure of state wisdom to maintain internal peace in the face of competing religions. Sociologically, however, a powerless bourgeoisie succeeded in determining the normative ideals of rule, government and order and in tying acrimonious sovereigns and officials to these ideals by measuring their achievements against the latter. In the 18th century, the administrators and beneficiaries of the arcana imperii less and less convinced their subjects of the necessity of authoritarian, absolute and morally unjustifiable rule. The religious struggle had long since been transferred from the battlefield to the universities and could no longer be presented as the first threat to the state.[252] Morality returned to politics.

> "In Enlightenment terminology, the two meanings of the attribute 'public', namely 'truly' and 'generally accessible', had merged into a conceptual unity. The new ambiguity was expressed in the collective singulars 'public will', 'public criticism', 'public judgment', etc., which had been in circulation since the 1790s and gave the authority of a normative judgment to the collective expression of will of the bourgeois society not participating in rule."[253]

This was an extraordinarily complicated, hardly manageable process, which has not actually been completed to this day.[254] Who is 'public opinion' and by what authority is its judicial office legitimized? The Christian-Jewish, monotheistic and above all platonically determined

---

[252] Kunisch, Johannes, *Absolutismus und Öffentlichkeit* [Absolutism and Publicity] in: *Der Staat*, 2/1995, p. 183-195; for the same result, namely the contradiction between normative claim and functionally sacrosanct everyday political life in Germany, Peter Nitschke, cf. Nitschke, *Zwischen Innovation und Tradition: der politische Aristotelismus in der deutschen politischen Philosophie der Prämoderne* [Between Innovation and Tradition: Political Aristotelism in German Political Philosophy of Premodernism], in: *Zeitschrift für Politik* 1/1995, p. 27-40.

[253] Hölscher, *Öffentlichkeit und Geheimnis* [Publicity and Secrecy], loc. cit., p. 105.

[254] The best-known attempt, besides Habermas' approach to understand the public thoroughly in theory in connection with justice and law, is *A Theory of Justice* [Cambridge/Mass.1971], Frankfurt 1975, by John Rawls. The public is examined there as a formal prerequisite and special achievement of liberal contract theories. See in particular ibid, pp. 34, 74, 153, 203-208.

ontology had no possibility of its own to attribute any truth value to a variety of individually formed opinions. Until the 18th century, the concept of opinion had a status that cannot be otherwise described as *ontological inferiority*. We have already seen (in chapter A.2) how much the legitimation of 'opinion-knowledge' in judgments of taste also became an important reason for theoretical reflection on systematic aesthetics. Wieland was one of the few authors who saw an important question in the relationship between opinion-knowledge and the public and also sought answers to it. In his *Gespräche unter vier Augen* [Dialogue Conversations in Private] (1798) there is a section entitled *Über die öffentliche Meinung* [On Public Opinion], where Wieland refers to the French Revolution in answer to the question:

> "Ten, twenty, thirty million people *in one state* cannot be treated like moral zeros. After all, the greater part of these millions may in a sense be regarded as minor; but they have common sense as their guardian, and one can count on the fact that in matters that directly affect the welfare or woe of the infinitely larger majority, the statement of this guardian is also public opinion."[255]

In the vehemence of this claim, the power of tradition is obvious, against which Wieland must argue. It is also obvious that he does not want to succeed in a systematic answer and liberation from the classical equivalence of truth=unity=government. Based on this observation, one can also conclude on the importance of the French Revolution for the German Enlighteners and advocates of a basic form of liberal publicity: They were given an event by history, with which they were freed from a systematic overcoming of classical ontology by their own means and could show the fact of a humanity developing to maturity. That history itself is the coming spirit of freedom and the justification of God, and not, as the churches claimed, a profane, earthly-lustrous event to be punished by God, that was Hegel's brilliant thesis in retrospect of the events:

> "So this was a glorious sunrise. All thinking beings have celebrated this epoch. A sublime emotion prevailed at that time, an enthusiasm of the Spirit shone through the world as if the real reconciliation of the divine with the world had only just come about [...] Consciousness has come to this point, and these are the main moments of the form in which the

---

[255] Citations after Möller, Horst, *Vernunft und Kritik. Deutsche Aufklärung im 17. und 18. Jahrhundert* [Reason and Critique. German Enlightenment in the 17th and 18th centuries], Frankfurt 1986, p. 286.

principle of freedom has been realized, for world history is nothing but the development of the concept of freedom [....] That world history is this development and the real becoming of the Spirit, under the changing spectacles of its stories – this is the true theodicy, the justification of God in history."[256]

The enslavement of the revolution in favor of the public idea naturally also programmed its overstretching in the late Enlightenment and finally the disappointment of an early bourgeois utopia. Pathos could not make up for the lack of systematics and the public sphere was understood undifferentiated both as a medium and as a criterion of reason.[257] Hegel's view of public opinion had cooled off considerably over the years. The enthusiasm for the public as a higher form of rationality also peaked with the turn of the century with other authors.[258] There is no doubt, however far 'publicity' was politically functionalized among the German Enlightenment, the French Revolution had acted as a catalyst.[259] Georg Foster wrote to his wife from Paris in 1793:

> "We already have seven thousand writers, and regardless of that, just as there is no German common spirit, there is no German public opinion. Even these words are so new to us, so foreign that everyone demands explanations and definitions; while no Englishman misunderstands the other when it comes to public spirit, no Frenchman to the other when it comes to public opinion."[260]

An important part of the popularization of the speech of the public and

---

[256] Hegel, G. W. F., *Philosophie der Geschichte* [Philosophy of History], 1830-31, Frankfurt 1970, p. 529 and 540. Jürgen Habermas' thesis is also interesting in this respect that Hegel had only fixed the revolution "in the beating heart of the world spirit" in order to be safe from it. For Hegel, according to Habermas, saw philosophy as a whole threatened by the revolution, namely in such a way that the only remaining possibility was the incorporation of the revolution into philosophy. Only in this way had it become criticizable at all in the sense of Hegel; cf. Habermas, Jürgen, *Hegels Kritik der Französischen Revolution* [Hegel's Critique of the French Revolution], in: Habermas, *Theorie und Praxis. Aufsätze zur Sozialphilosophie* [Theory and Practice. Essays on Social Philosophy], Frankfurt 1988, pp. 128-171.

[257] Hölscher, *Publicity and Secrecy*, loc. cit., p. 97.

[258] Hölscher, *Öffentlichkeit*, loc. cit., pp. 460-461.

[259] Möller, *Reason and Critique*, loc. cit., p. 288.

[260] Foster, Georg, *Über die öffentliche Meinung* [On Public Opinion], Akademie Edition, vol. 8, Berlin 1974, p. 365.

public opinion was the reading of Jean Jacques Rousseau's *Contrat social* (1762), in which the theory of *volonté générale* and *volonté de tous* was developed.[261] Although Rousseau did not, on closer inspection, write a manifesto for any socially practicable form of political participation, the citizens read it that way, and they found in his social contract above all what they already knew. Only the scholars took this supposed fundamental right to public communication very seriously and showed little enthusiasm for the idea that ordinary people should now express themselves on all things of political life.

Of the greatest importance at first was not directly the politics, but the public feeling. Therefore, the reception of Rousseau's other writings, in particular the *Confessions*, the *Emile* and the *New Heloise*, in France may have had at least as much influence on the development of public opinion as his *Contract sociale*. The historian Simon Schama writes in his fascinating study on the French Revolution on this connection of publicity, emotion and politics:

"While there is growing evidence that this work [*Contrat Sociale*] was in fact read and understood before the Revolution, it is undoubtedly true that it never reached the huge and daring readership of his educational 'biography' *Emile* and the *Nouvelle Heloise*. But to assume that those works had little influence on political allegiance is to adopt a much to narrow definition of the word political. [...] But for Rousseau's acolytes in the 1780s, visions opened up of possible societies that might be capable of integrating the imperious 'I' within the comradely 'We'."[262]

Finally, Schama examines the "new sensibility" inspired by Rousseau's writings, which made such phenomena possible as public crying, nationwide campaigns for respect for the elderly and breastfeeding of children. Especially the aristocratic childhood was marked by the nurse and was now called "unnatural" and responsible for the human stoniness of the adult feudal lords.

Together with the physiocratic theses of the non-productivity of the nobility, relatively subversive ideas entered the discussion, which at first was strongly interested in moral and ethical issues. Questions of public order and legitimacy of government have only gradually become nego-

---

[261] See Hölscher, *Öffentlichkeit*, loc. cit., p. 452-3; cf. also the discussion on Rousseau's social contract in section A.1.5.

[262] Schama, Simon, Citizen. A Chronicle of the French Revolution, N.Y. 1989, p. 161.

tiable in an audience that had no part in the government itself. Therefore, in Germany, only questions of taste arise in the press at first, because these could be publicly negotiated in the classical sense as private truths. They represented a first cautious intervention in the sovereigns' monopoly on truth. 1768 Friedrich Justus Riedel writes:

> "Read Gellert's fables to the Baron; he will say: they are beautiful. His servant stands in an angle and thinks: my master is right; a judgment which he often says and rarely thinks."[263]

From these first, very limited spaces of individual private existence, namely the inner freedom of faith and freedom in questions of taste, i.e. from the resulting negotiability of the questions of beauty and good, an entire culture developed at breathtaking speed under the idea of the existence of an autonomous subjectivity.[264] This concept of subjectivity was found competent enough to be able to produce the criteria for beauty and good, but soon also for justice, good rule and sovereignty without recourse to religious authorities. Individuality – first as aesthetic, then as political subjectivity – and the public sphere are thus two mutually reinforcing vectors in the field of European secularization and an epoch which we justifiably call modernity.[265]

---

[263] Riedel, Friedrich Justus, *Über das Publikum. Briefe an einige Mitglieder desselben* [About the Audience. Letters to Some Members of the Same], Jena 1768, p. 212; quoted from Hölscher, *Öffentlichkeit*, loc. cit., p. 431.

[264] Ferry, Luc, Homo aestheticus. L'invention du gout à l'âge démocratique, Paris 1990, pp. 27-28.

[265] Cf. Hans Blumenberg's controversial work *Die Legitimität der Neuzeit* [The Legitimacy of the Modern Age], Frankfurt 1966.

A.3.2 New Forms of the Public and their Social Practice

Rarely have intellectual events and trends had such a formative influence on social history as in the European Enlightenment in the 18th century. The still very theoretical notion of the bourgeois public sphere sought several forms of realization, namely in social areas and practices in which rule could not initially be called into question. Wilhelm Bauer distinguished 'oral', 'written' and 'actual' means of expression from the public.[266] If one refines this filter somewhat, the following vertical criteria result for the topic:

1. Public address
2. Writing as doctrine, criticism and edification
3. Knowledge as writing and speech (stories, fairy tales, religious myths)
4. Legal proceedings
5. Political decision-making

Horizontally, the organization and technology of the respective form of articulation are of interest: written and oral language competence in high-level and artificial languages as well as in dialects; publishing and sales organization; their financing possibilities; training and recruitment of professional or semi-professional authors; limited or general compulsory schooling; establishment of joint reading in reading clubs; institutionalization of formal or informal advisory groups in the environment of princes, etc.

What has not yet emerged in 18th century Germany, however, and is therefore not discussed here any further, were forms of parliamentary public opinion that would have to be categorized under point no. 5 of the table. Until well into the 19th century there were no constitutions or parliaments in most German territorial states. Even in the country of origin of parliamentarianism, England, Parliament was by no means a representative body, at least until 1832, because the meetings of Parliament were secret, and it had in fact a status of complete autonomy vis-à-vis the crown, government and above all society, which was actually supposed to be

---

[266] Bauer, Wilhelm, *Die öffentliche Meinung* [The Public Opinion] Tübingen 1914.

represented. By resolution of the House of Commons of 13 April 1783, public opinion was not allowed to have any influence on the course of parliamentary business. So, the Glorious Revolution of 1688 had in a sense only provided the housing for a kind of parliamentary sovereignty. It took more than a century before a liberal parliamentary practice prevailed in Britain that actually granted the people of the country a certain share in the government of the state.[267] *En passant* it is striking here how little influence the common-sense philosophy had or even wanted to have on the actual British government policy. In Germany, where the enthusiasts of parliamentarianism were sparsely sown, people already knew all too well about the "corrupt" English parliament, which represented only professional and clique interests.[268] Only in the Wars of Liberation against Napoleon were parliamentary ideas able to capture larger circles of society. But when the Wars were over, it turned out that the constitutional and parliamentary aspirations were first and foremost unitarian. Particularly in the southern German central states, which suffered greatly from territorial particularism, it was hoped to be able to create unity with constitutions and parliaments. From 1817 onwards, the Grand Duchy of Weimar, then Baden, Bavaria, Hesse and finally Württemberg each had a representative body, which, like all other parliaments on German soil until the Weimar Republic, had a hard time making their voices heard and their rights respected.[269]

To prevent the emergence of the 'small publics' of the 18th century from drowning in the flood of socio-historical information, it is helpful to recall the anthropological approach of Thomas Nipperdey's historiography.[270] With his method one can make a historically informed speculation as to

---

[267] Kluxen, Kurt, *Geschichtliche Grundlagen des Parlamentarismus* [Historical Foundations of Parliamentarianism], in: Kluxen (ed.), *Parlamentarismus* [Parliamentarism], Cologne 1967, pp. 91-92.

[268] Fraenkel, Ernst, *Parlament und öffentliche Meinung* [Parliament and Public Opinion], in: Fraenkel, *Deutschland und die westlichen Demokratien* [Germany and the Western Democracies], ed. by Alexander v. Brünneck, Frankfurt 1991, pp. 204-231, here pp. 206 and 207.

[269] Bergstraesser, Ludwig, *Die Entwicklung des Parlamentarismus in Deutschland* [The Evolution of Parliamentarism in Germany] in: Kluxen, Kurt (ed.), *Parlamentarismus*, loc. cit., pp. 138-160, here p. 139.

[270] Nipperdey, Thomas, *Die anthropologische Dimension der Geschichtswissenschaft* [The Anthropological Dimension of History], in: Nipperdey, *Gesellschaft, Kultur, Theorie. Gesammelte Aufsätze* [Society, Culture, Theory. Collected Articles], Göttingen 1976, pp. 33-58.

whether such an institution as the public meets a subjective need that manifests itself in a certain historical time under describable circumstances. The anthropological reading gives more space to the subjective experience of communication, understanding and opinion-forming than a social history strongly oriented towards structures and functions (as can be found in H.-U. Wehler's *Deutsche Gesellschaftsgeschichte* [German Social History]. Accordingly, in Germany in the 18th century a human disposition, a need for sociability, conversation and education created social forms so that these practices could be institutionalized. The following overview is oriented on this guideline.

A.3.2.1 Audience and Authors in the Medium of Language

The prerequisite for something like publicity was people's ability to communicate through spoken and written language. The 1789 born German language critic Carl Gustav Jochmann wrote:

> "The first and most important of all public spheres, and which underlies all others, is understandable language."[271]

In his writings Jochmann complained that from the very beginning there had been no language in German culture that would have been capable and appropriate for the public.[272] The German language, he said, suffered in particular from its encrustation in the scripture, which came almost exclusively from official offices.[273] In addition, too many people simply did not know how to read.

> "All public life is finally a single great book, and a book in which very

---

[271] Jochmann, Carl Gustav, *Über die Sprache* [On the Language], Riga 1828, reprint 1968, p. 80.

[272] See also Jochmann, Carl Gustav, *Über die Öffentlichkeit* [On the Public], in: *Prometheus. Für Licht und Recht. Zeitschrift in zwanglosen Heften* [Prometheus. For Light and Law. Journal in Casual Issues], ed. by Heinrich Zschokke and his friends, third part, 1833, pp. 149-178; reprint in: Haufe, Eberhard, *Carl Gustav Jochmann. Die unzeitige Wahrheit. Aphorismen. Glossen* [Carl Gustav Jochmann. The Untimely Truth. Aphorisms. Glosses], Leipzig 1979, pp. 205-243.

[273] In the legal sphere, Anselm Feuerbach, in his *Betrachtungen über die Öffentlichkeit und Mündlichkeit der Gerechtigkeitspflege* [Reflections on the Public and Orality of the Maintenance of Justice], Siegen 1821, passim, demanded the orality of criminal proceedings. So even court proceedings were written matters and there was no oral plea like the American jury courts already knew it.

few who are concerned are allowed to read and know how to read."[274]

This observation has only now been confirmed by historical research, for the talk of the "reading revolution"[275] has now given way to a sober assessment of a regular increase in the reading public and the quantity of print media. The low literacy rate of 25% to 40% of the population around 1800 gives an impression how all ideas of a bourgeois public could only be a matter for a minority in the run-up.[276]

An important symptom, however, was the enormous decline in the number of works published in Latin from 1780 onwards. 17.3% of Latin publications fell to just under 4% by 1800. 1740 it was still 27.7%.[277] This suggests a certain tendency towards popularization of the German language, which was a prerequisite for expanding public communication beyond the scholarly public. Together with the poets and artists, the professors soon belonged to a rather beyond-the-stands and corporative-free society of privileged educated citizens who formed a kind of public sphere of their own at the courts and in the universities.[278]

Overall, the university has promoted social mobility.[279] Wehler even speaks of a "socially progressive top position" of German universities in international comparison, as confirmed by more recent studies.[280] Around this milieu, the social boundaries and authorship as well as the public could simultaneously increase:

---

[274] Jochmann, Carl Gustav, *About the language*, loc. cit., p. 187.

[275] At the origin of the talk about the "reading revolution" is Rolf Engelsing with his essay *Die Perioden der Lesegeschichte in der Neuzeit. Das statistische Ausmaß und die soziokulturelle Bedeutung der Lektüre* [The Periods of Reading History in Modern Times. The Statistical Extent and Socio-Cultural Significance of Reading], in: *Archiv für Geschichte des Buchwesens* 10/1970, p. 877 ff. However, the word itself comes from Friedrich Schlegel from the *Athäneum Fragments*, 1798.

[276] Möller, *Reason and Critique*, loc. cit., p. 263.

[277] Wittmann, Reinhard, *Die frühen Buchhändlerzeitschriften als Spiegel des literarischen Lebens* [The Early Bookseller Magazines as a Mirror of Literary Life] in: AGB XIII, 1973, pp. 613-932; quoted from Möller, *Vernunft und Kritik*, op. cit., p. 273.

[278] Möller, *Reason and Critique*, loc. cit., p. 234.

[279] Ibid., p. 242.

[280] Wehler, *Deutsche Gesellschaftsgeschichte*, loc. cit., p. 298; unfortunately without further references.

"Since the words 'writer' and 'scholar' were used quite synonymously – a linguistic usage that was also followed by Hamberg's encyclopedic *Lexikon der jetzt lebenden teutschen Schriftsteller* [Lexicon of German Writers Living Today] at the turn of the century – a large number of authors can first be attributed to university life. [...] The freelance writer who lives by his pen, whether a general writer or predominantly a journalist, did not appear as a social figure until the second half of the 18th century."[281]

This corresponds to Kant's representation of the public use of reason, which should only be allowed to the citizen as a scholar.[282] This scholarly term no longer denoted the academic status, but only a special function, one of the possible roles of the bourgeois individual under a republican constitution, which is granted to every citizen (who pays taxes and possesses property – this is the well-known early liberal reservation of ownership, which Kant also recognized).

Jochmann's criticism would have been countered by the fact that the dominant, administratively shaped writing of the German language certainly facilitated communication, since with its help the strong coloring of the regional oral dialects or layer-specific differences in the way of speaking could be bridged. What is interesting in any case is that in almost all sources on the public and language the basic metaphor is that of free, oral speech, although one must assume that there was no truly free, coherent speech, as the French National Assembly knew it, at that time in Germany.[283] Jochmann also writes: "A public voice of this kind, a public conscience... "[284] and "Publicity is the voice of political bodies, and a mute society in its kind is something completely as poor as in its own a mute

---

[281] Ibid., p. 313.

[282] This aspect is discussed in detail in part B of the present study.

[283] Reinhardt Brandt noticed that the following quote from the pen of J. H. Campe in a letter of 10 September, 1791 to the Duke of Braunschweig, could as well have come from Kant: "... because truth is determined in no other way than that a person judges it, that this judgement is shared with other people, for which the printing press provides him with a convenient opportunity, and this enlightens the audience." (Brandt, Reinhardt, *Die politische Institution bei Kant*, in: Göhler, Gerhard et al. (ed.), *Politische Institutionen im gesellschaftlichen Umbruch. Ideengeschichtliche Beiträge zur Theorie politischer Institutionen* [Contributions to the Theory of Political Institutions by the History of Ideas], Opladen 1990, pp. 335-357; here pp. 356, footnote 25)

[284] Jochmann, *About the public*, loc. cit., p. 224.

man."[285] Immanuel Kant, on the other hand, was one of the few authors who did not confuse the categories of writing and orality. He expressly described the possibility of public expression as "freedom of the pen". In his famous essay *Answer to the Question: What is Enlightenment?* he defined this:

> "But I understand by the public practice of his own reason the one whom someone makes of it *as a scholar* before the whole *audience of the reader world*."[286]

Elsewhere, he even explicitly opposes the free speech, in which he places much less trust than in written communication. He would always prefer a beautiful poem to the "reading of the best speech of a Roman folk or current parliamentary or pulpit speaker...". He goes so far as to claim that rhetoric is a "deceitful art" that "understands how to persuade people as machines to judge important things" by using the weaknesses of people. It is therefore "...not worth any respect."[287] Andreas Georg Friedrich Rebmann accordingly reported the following about the conversations of his contemporaries:

> "In the inns visited by citizens, the only and dearest form of entertainment is the disgusting political rambling. Usually a speaker of these parliamenters appears, reads one or more newspapers, and illustrates each line with high notes. This is fire into the powder. At the moment, rage takes hold of the whole honorable society to ramble; it is calculated how much the National Assembly costs every day, how much the King of France has to consume every minute etc. The veins of the fighters swell with passion, and a thick cloud of smoke rises from their pipes. Aristocrats and democrats, royalists and nonhists stand man for man, and often even the heads of the counterparty had to feel the political balance of Europe very violently."[288]

---

[285] Ibid., p. 242.

[286] Kant, Immanuel, *Werke* [Works] XI, loc. cit., A 485[55], emphasis by Kant.

[287] Kant Immanuel, Critique of the Power of Judgment, B 218, note.

[288] Rebmann, Andreas Georg Friedrich, *Briefe über Erlangen* [Letters about Erlangen], vol. 1, Frankfurt and Leipzig 1792, p. 139f; quoted from Welke, Martin, *Gemeinsames Lesen und frühe Formen von Gruppenbildung im 17. und 18. Jahrhundert. Zeitungslesen in Deutschland* [Reading and Early Forms of Group Formation in the 17th and 18th Centuries. Newspaper Reading in Germany], in: Dann, O. (Ed.) *Vereinswesen und bürgerliche Gesellschaft in Deutschland* [Associations and Bourgeois Society in Germany], Munich 1984, pp. 29-53.

This is both an indication of the arrogance of the writing Enlighteners against the citizens who make a political statement without learned instruction and of the unusual nature of a coherent, free speech in the reading societies. As in the above quotation from the *Critique of the Power of Judgment*, it becomes clear that even the freest speech could not have been imagined otherwise than as a 'reading out aloud' of a manuscript or as a paratactic commentary on a document. Wolf Davidson reports in his *Letters about Berlin* in 1798 the following from the life of a reading society he knows. The members gather every Wednesday and the meetings are...

> "...divided into a lawful and a lawless session. In the lawful ones, treatises from the fields of philosophy, aesthetics, history, etc. are read aloud, in the lawless ones, plays, poems, music, etc. are read aloud. It is not allowed to play or smoke tobacco. The meeting lasts until 8 o'clock, then a moderate supper is eaten, and a cheerful song is sung afterwards."[289]

From the exclusive Berlin Monday Club he wrote that one spend one's time there very pleasantly and entertainingly, "only here and there it smells of pedantry. Urbanity, lightness, conversation, in a word what the Englishman calls good humour, is not a matter for the German scholar."[290] Such observations indicate that the relationship of the Germans to the spoken word was problematic[291] and the metaphor of enlightenment, the introduction to "maturity" [Mündigkeit] and the freedom of "speech" must be understood symbolically and perhaps rather as an expression of a desire than a social reality.[292]

---

[289] Quoted after Möller, *Reason and Critique*, loc. cit., p. 265.

[290] Ibid., p. 266.

[291] Jochmann, *On language*, loc. cit., ibid., p. 224: "We are a maltreated people because we are a mute one, and we have no voice in the rate of peoples because no language."

[292] Cf. the book by Erhard Eppler, *Kavaleriepferde beim Hornsignal. Die Krise der Politik im Spiegel der Sprache* [Cavalry Horses at the Bugle Call. The Crisis of Politics in the Mirror of Language], Frankfurt 1992, in which the politician [the author was a mastermind of the German social democrats SPD] notes the continuation of this relationship of the Germans to the language up to our days.

A.3.2.2 Press, Literature and Reading Societies

In 1773, there were 3000 professional writers, in 1787 already 6000, but most of them could not live from writing alone. They supplied an audience whose size is still controversial in research.[293] One reason for this is the different weighting of the multiplier effect in the consumption and reception of individual journals and books. Wehler puts it at 10[294] and thus comes to an overall very underestimated distribution of the German press.[295]

Among the most important journals were Schlözer's *Staatsanzeiger* (average circulation 4400), Wieland's *Teutscher Merkur*, Nicolai's *Allgemeine Deutsche Bibliothek*, Schubart's *Deutsche Chronik*, Wekhrlin's *Das Graue Ungeheuer* and *Hyperboreische Briefe*. The centers of German publishing were Hamburg and Schleswig-Holstein.

The most important review journal was Nicolai's *Allgemeine Deutsche Bibliothek*, which grew to 264 volumes between 1765 and 1810 and employed 433 staff throughout Germany during its best period. Their decidedly critical judgments were very much feared.[296]

The *Hamburgische (unpartheyische) Korrespondent* [Hamburg (Non-Partisan) Correspondent] already had a circulation of 20,000 in 1780, worked his way up to a record high of 51,000 copies sold by 1801 and was thus Germany's best-selling and most widely read magazine for at least two

---

[293] Cf. the controversial essay by Reinhard Wittmann, *Der lesende Landmann. Zur Rezeption der aufklärerischen Bemühungen durch die bäuerliche Bevölkerung im 18. Jahrhundert* [The Reading Provincial. On the Reception of Educational Efforts by the Peasant Population in the 18th Century], in: Berindei D. et al. (ed.), *Der Bauer Mittel- und Osteuropas im sozioökonomischen Wandel des 18. und 19. Jahrhunderts* [The Farmer of Central and Eastern Europe in the Cocio-Economic Change of the 18th and 19th Centuries], Köln 1973, pp. 142-189. Wittmann shows that the circulation figures of the newspapers are not valid arguments. His analysis of the history of reception has shown that books as well as newspapers were often not read and that the circulation figures sometimes resulted from the purchase of aristocrats, who then gave the works away to farmers who did not want to know anything about the reading.

[294] Wehler, *Deutsche Gesellschaftsgeschichte*, loc. cit., pp. 305 and 307.

[295] "Under the spell of the much-admired early development of the newspaper industry in England, including in the Netherlands and France, the importance that German newspapers already possessed in the 18th century has long been underestimated. This must be corrected." (ibid., p. 306)

[296] Möller, *Reason and Critique*, loc. cit., p. 278.

decades. The American and French revolutions have pushed up circulation, stimulated the founding of new newspapers and further popularized reading. There was already an audience of millions following events in the West.[297]

The average circulation of German journals was 1000, of which 600-700 could normally be sold. The profit zone began with around 500 copies sold.[298] Many magazines were thematically specialized from an early age, for example in questions of agriculture, customs or fashion. However, the readership did not appear to be congruent with the intended recipients of the widely used print media. Georg Friedrich Rebmann writes in *Kosmopolitische Wanderungen durch einen Teil Deutschlands* [Cosmopolitan Hikes Through a Part of Germany] (1793):

> "...the audience, whose voice does not judge our writers critically, but economically, consists of hairdressers, chambermaids, waitresses, merchants' servants and the like, dozens of whom can be found in our reading libraries."[299]

Journalism, from written correspondence to the political daily newspaper, and the emergence of publicity are inseparably linked. Schlözer's public demands to the state, which not only accused abuses but also wanted to acknowledge the public sphere of state affairs and freedom of the press as the only remedy for these shortcomings, are likely to have been particularly effective. In 1790, he even demanded the disclosure of the state budget and hoped that it would have the same effect as the account published in France by Finance Minister Necker. The burden on the state budget proved therein by the costs of the royal household

---

[297] Wehler, *Deutsche Gesellschaftsgeschichte*, loc. cit., p. 308.

[298] Ibid., p. 310.

[299] Rebmann, A. G. F. *Kosmopolitische Wanderungen durch einen Teil Deutschlands*, ed. by H. Voegt, Frankfurt 1968, p. 54. There is only one work in which the subscription lists for newspapers are counted with the means available at that time, namely the dissertation by Irene Jentsch, *Zur Geschichte des Zeitungslesens in Deutschland am Ende des 18. Jahrhunderts. Mit besonderer Berücksichtigung der gesellschaftlichen Formen des Zeitungslesens* [The History of Newspaper Reading in Germany at the End of the 18th Century. With Special Attention to the Social Forms of Newspaper Reading], Leipzig 1937. She notes that the pastors were the most numerous professional group among the subscribers (cited after Dann, Otto, *Lesegesellschaften und bürgerliche Emanzipation. Ein europäischer Vergleich* [Reading Societies and Bourgeois Emancipation. A European Comparison), Munich 1981, pp. 38 and 46, note 2).

shocked the French public and prepared the revolutionary indignation.[300]

"Publicity is a wonderful way to cure the sacred justice in those areas where it lies sick. On them, the holy justice, the freedom of the press has just as beneficial influences as on civil and ecclesiastical freedom. Ask England and Sweden."[301]

It has become particularly clear in the press that the freedom of expression conceded by princes developed a momentum of its own that was difficult to control and critical of power and government. Valjavec, for example, notes the increasing importance of political caricature since the Thirty Years' War. Its initial aim was to revile the greats of the other side, the opponents of the respective rulers. Slowly this loyalty gave way and a critical press could develop.[302] But until it became politically significant, the public had to be educated and the publishing houses had to be expanded to a certain size. Valjavec stated: "It was Schlözer who raised German journalism to a political power."[303] Book production also expanded extraordinarily. If there were about 2000 new publications in 1775, there were already 4180 in 1805. Nicolai's *Allgemeine Deutsche Bibliothek* [General German Library] reviewed about 80,000 books between 1765 and 1811.[304] Although censorship increased from 1789 onwards in most territories of Germany, this did not seem to have hindered the spread of print media.

This enormous expansion of production and market required better legal and economic protection for publishers and authors alike. For this reason, Kant dealt, among other things, with the special problem of the definition of the book within the framework of "legal doctrine" in the *Metaphysics of Morals*. He distinguished the author who speaks to an audience in his own name from the publisher who "speaks publicly" in the name of the author. Therefore also the reprint is forbidden, which, apart from the object-law-inadmissible copy of the object as an artifact, above all offends against the right of personality: The publisher who circulates an unauthorized reprint makes a speech to the public on behalf of an author,

---

[300] Valjavec, Fritz, *Die Entstehung der politischen Strömungen in Deutschland 1770-1815* [The Origin of Political Trends in Germany 1770-1815], Munich 1951, p. 404.

[301] Schlözer, *Neuer Briefwechsel 1777*, 2. Teil [New Correspondence 1777, Part 2], p. 62; see Valjavec, *Politische Strömungen*, loc. cit., p. 103.

[302] Valjavec, *Politische Strömungen*, loc. cit., p. 93.

[303] Ibid., p. 100.

[304] Möller, *Reason and Critique*, loc. cit., p.273.

so to speak, without having a power of attorney from this author.[305] Here, too, Kant clearly has the correspondence of speech and writing as ideally equivalent components of public communication. This ambivalent representation of communication, its degrees of freedom and the nature of its reification points in a continuous line to the more recent media-theoretical problems of virtualization of reality and the hypostasis of information.[306]

The places of convivial, joint reading were the reading societies, which on the one hand must be described as a new media technology, but which are also clearly the expression of an individual educational need and a new sociological constellation of knowledge. Reading circles and associations became a form of mobilization in the transition from corporative to civil society.[307] The number of newly founded reading societies[308] grew from five (1760) to 50 (1780). By 1790 there were 170 and by 1800 200 new reading societies. Women in clubs, associations and salons are not reported until around 1800.[309]

Möller disqualifies the significance of reading societies for the Enlightenment as a "medium of social communication" by asking why so many noblemen, canons, senior civil servants and officers have themselves "socio-culturally and socio-politically turned into vehicles of 'bourgeois emancipation'[?]"[310] There is no doubt that reading societies have for a short time linked the function of sociability with the function of conveying information. With the conventions of the Protestants and other associateions, they had also gained in importance in the formation of inter-class forums.

---

[305] Kant, *Werke VIII* [Works VIII], op.cit., pp. 404-405.

[306] See here chapters B.1.7.2.2 and B.3.3.

[307] Cf. Nipperdey, Thomas, Verein als soziale Struktur im späten 18. und frühen 19. Jahrhundert [Association as Social Structure in the Late 18th and early 19th Century], in: Nipperdey, Gesellschaft, Kultur, Theorie. Gesammelte Aufsätze zur neueren Geschichte [Society, Culture, Theory. Collected Essays on Modern History], Göttingen 1976, pp. 174-205.

[308] Stützel-Prüsener, Marlies, Die deutschen Lesegesellschaften im Zeitalter der Aufklärung [The German Reading Societies in the Age of Enlightenment], in: Dann, Otto (ed.), Lesegesellschaften und bürgerliche Emanzipation. Ein europäischer Vergleich [Reading Societies and Civic Emancipation. A European comparison], Munich 1981, pp. 71-86.

[309] Möller, *Reason and Critique*, loc. cit., p. 264.

[310] Ibid., p. 268.

"In many cases, the Pietist Conventions have not recognized any class or corporative differences, thus contributing to the upheaval of the traditional social order."[311]

In this sense, the new social practices have also promoted the creation of comparability and associability of persons of different social origins – an "isonomy"[312] on a small scale – which seems to be the basic prerequisite for a functioning public sphere as a medium. An isonomy in this context would be, if the term may be borrowed from the ancient historian Meier, the temporally and obviously also spatially limited possibility of abolishing social layer-specific asymmetries of the relations of control for the purpose of free expression of opinion.[313]

The Pietists' personal reservation of faith was therefore an important moment in public education. They were not politically active, but they set themselves in a conscious relationship to the political events and reserved themselves the right to measure and criticize the authorities by the yardstick of an internalized religion while maintaining all loyalty. This individualistic move was already enough to pave the way for ideological emancipation and liberalism. The Pietist criticism of the authorities, however, was rarely really liberalist, but fed on a moral rigorism that arose from a political culture that was no less conservative than southern German Catholicism.[314] This also applied to Orthodox Lutherans, except that the political ethics of these Protestants, however conservative in detail, brought forth something itself in which it had no direct, programmatic interest, namely liberalism and the publicity.[315] These subjective moments caused what Wehler called the "consolidation of public communication."[316] In this new, multi-layered but still relatively structurally weak German

---

[311] Valjavec, *Politische Strömungen*, loc. cit., p. 64.

[312] See Meier, Christian, *Die politische Kunst der griechischen Tragödie* [The Political Art of Greed Tragedy,] Munich 1988: "The political order that Kleisthenes established was a preform of democracy, which today is usually called 'isonomy' with a concept of time: an order in which at least the middle classes of the citizens exercised regular, effective political influence. Although the management of the business remained in the hands of the nobles, most of them – as in Athens – were concentrated in a council of nobility."(ibid., p. 16)

[313] Cf. Welke, Gemeinsame Lesen, loc. cit., pp. 29-53.

[314] They could not have appeared immediately. See Valjavec, *Polische Strömungen*, loc. cit., p. 85.

[315] Ibid., pp. 65-68.

[316] Wehler, Deutsche Gesellschaftsgeschichte, loc. cit., pp. 303-316.

audience, the revolutionary events of the West have for a time given rise to the first idea of cultural identity:

> "The German patriots, at home in the small territories of the particularistically organized empire, knew for the most part before 1789 only a vague imperial patriotism which, oriented on the structures of the disintegrating empire, had long since become obsolete [...] For the German intelligence the French Revolution was the role model of a concretely filled patriotism."[317]

Looking at the history and development of the public since the 18th century, one gets the impression that society, in a particular aspect, wanted to advance its modernization very early and very thoroughly from its own dynamic, but that the organization of political rule in Germany could not keep up with this social progressivism. Even today, organizing the public is anything but self-evident and is becoming ever more demanding, as the current debate on media theory and law shows. Several more times in the past two centuries, the concept of a liberal public sphere was to partially or completely disappear.

But the idea of the public sphere and free formation of opinion has always produced its own practice. Hopefully it has become clear that every time this happens a human disposition seems to come true. The anthropological dimension of the public sphere sometimes lies in the fact that modern man *can think* and also *thinks* as an individual. However, he can only do so in a society that must guarantee this autonomy for its part, but which also involves its citizens in a never-ending discussion about it. This *double ability* of self-image and deliberative orderly thinking points to a human capacity that may constitute the basis of the political and whose trace we now follow in another direction, namely the one into philosophy.

---

[317] Prignitz, Christoph, *Vaterlandsliebe und Freiheit. Deutscher Patriotismus von 1750-1850* [Love of Fatherland and Freedom. German Patriotism from 1750-1850], Wiesbaden 1981, pp. 48, 49.

B. Political Subjectivity as Fundament to the Political

Graphical Overview of the Political Subject – And an Important Note

On the following page, there is an illustration, a chart of the *four kernels of subjectivity* as developed in my treatise *Laws of Singularity* (Grünenberg 2017) and presented in more detail in my upcoming book *You Are Many. The Polycentric Subject* (Grünenberg 2019). It shows by which concepts these cores of subjectivity are connected and how some of these concepts – all of them will be deduced in the following chapters – build up and structure political subjectivity.

There could be eventually more than those four kernels of subjectivity – which remains to be shown and proven by other philosophers – but they would necessarily look somehow like no. 4. This part of the chart is more detailed only due to the context of its 'excavation' from the *Critique of the Power of Judgment*; the other kernels 1-3, when unfolded, do not appear much different in principle. Use this chart 0 as a topographical map of the political subject, bookmark it and return to this point for orientation when the analysis gets complicated. For it will, I promise.

Please be aware that you leave now the safety area of traditional academic philosophy. The ideas and concepts that will be developed in the following chapters are radically new and make up a hole continent of an uncharted philosophy of subjectivity. It took me more than twenty years to understand this. After waking up from my own 'dogmatic slumber' in 2018, I finally noticed that the real discovery of the present study was not so much – as interesting as it may be – political subjectivity as such, but the new framework of a polycentric subject which I had developed as just a tool to the task. The benefit is that we now have one fully developed model of subjectivity which will be helpful to excavating the other three (or more) 'kernels'. The irony is that the political subject, after having been undiscovered until these pages were originally written two decades ago, is now at the same time the best and most thoroughly described one.

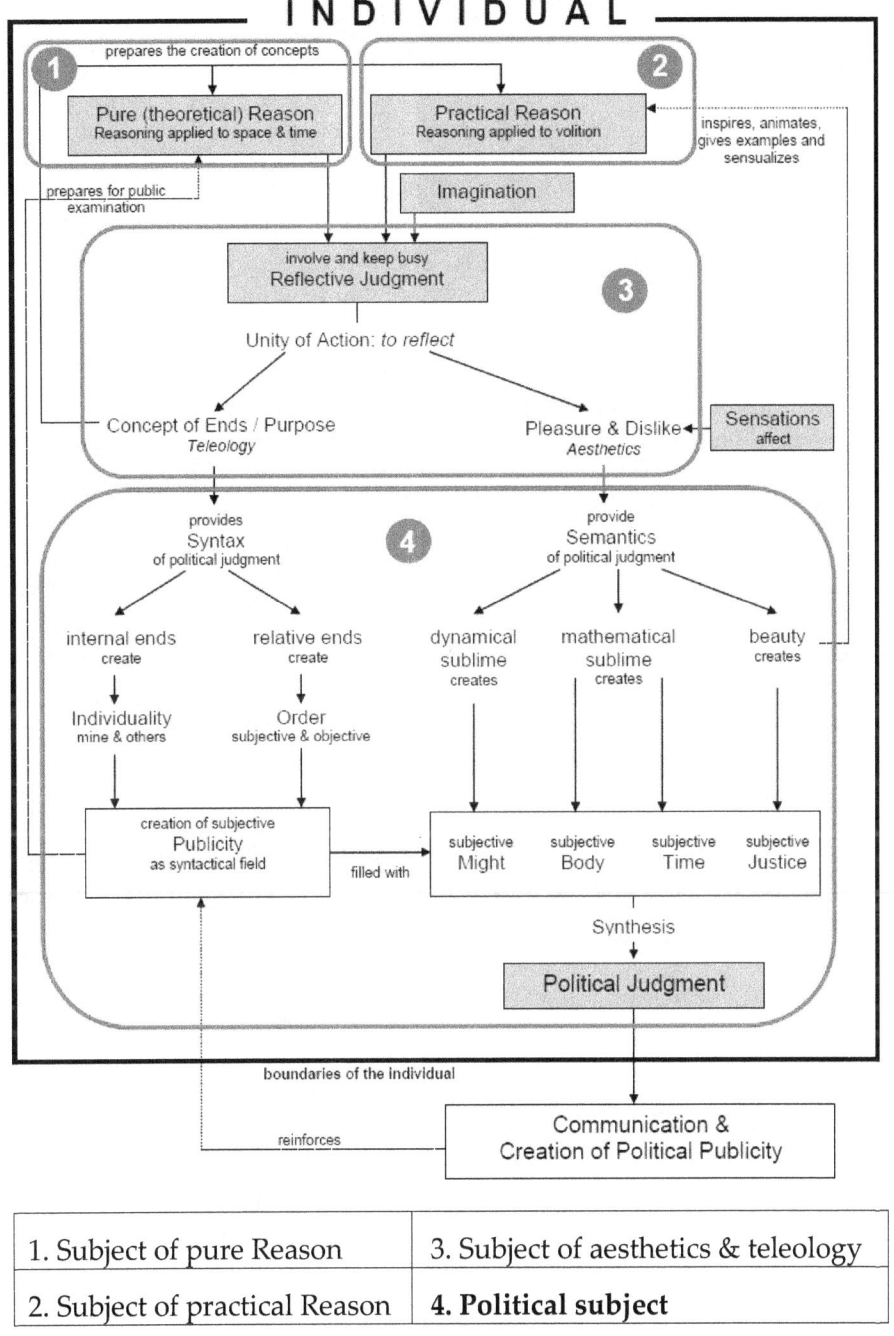

Chart 0: Overview of political subjectivity within the individual

Introduction to the Philosophical Analysis of Political Subjectivity

The panorama of the 18th century, which has been developed so far from various historical and philosophical observations on European culture of the epoch, is in no way complete, but it is a sufficient basis for further pursuing the plan of the present study. The working hypothesis was that in the *formation of three phenomena* occurring simultaneously and increasingly intertwining in this epoch, a connection becomes visible that provides information about a *human intellectual capacity that is beginning to take its place in history*. The advantage of placing a clear emphasis on German intellectual and social history lay in the detail with which the scholars in Germany – as if to compensate for social and political stagnation in an increasingly progressive and revolutionary environment – have made systematic philosophical and theoretical considerations that have been skipped in other countries in order to be put into practice immediately. This intellectualization of delayed social and political development has given us valuable indications of what questions and response strategies should have been developed if the practical political achievements in England, North America or France that came about rather by themselves through advantageous constellations, would have required planful and skillful inventions instead.

We could show that individuality, aesthetics and the public are in an interrelation whose triangular structure appears like a trace in the historical material, but which is by no means self-explanatory. After all, the first part of the study gave a clear and quite solid reason for believing that the intertwining of these three inventions into a historical formation is closely related to the development of a specific political capacity in European culture.

In the discussion to date, the observation of the increased sensitivity to the concerns and abilities of the individual human being in all areas has demanded our attention in particular. Research in this direction is now to be continued in the form of a philosophically in-depth analysis of the subject, which takes the historical material as an occasion and can at the same time test its explanatory power. The concept of the political should not be assumed in a defined way, but should itself be the problem, so that it becomes apparent what is in it and how much is demanded of the subjects, so that something like a specific political ability can be ascribed to them as individualized human beings. According to the assumptions of Hannah

Arendt and some other authors, the instruments for such a philosophical in-depth analysis of human individuals are sought in Kant's *Critique of the Power of Judgment*, selected, recombined and applied to determine the precise shape and content of political subjectivity in them.

Following the presentation of Kant's third *Critique* and its significance, a targeted 'conversion' of its method is carried out. On this basis, a form of judgment is reconstructed and examined in detail which can be found in judgments as a politically qualifiable achievement of the subject and which structures the subjective dimension of the area of phenomena designated as political. These chapters on political judgment (B.1.7.1-3) are the philosophical centre of the investigation. This is followed by considerations on the distinction between moral, political and religious judgments (B.1.8), assumptions on why the problems of the traditional philosophy of subjectivity (or consciousness) did not allow for these distinctions (Excursus B.1.9), and finally some offers of application and mediation on research questions of neighboring disciplines (B.2-3).

An important characteristic of the chosen method will be the *subjective use of terms* that are thought to be entirely objective in their everyday use, i.e. their meaning is usually not attributed to judgment but to an appearance outside the subject. This, however, results in an important semantic shift in terms such as 'individual', 'order', 'power', 'body' and 'time', which is initially irritating for understanding.

B.1 The Capacity of Reflection and the Political Judgment: Kant's *Critique of the Power of Judgment*

> "I am of the opinion that a return of all human activities to working or producing and the reduction of all political conditions to the relationship of power is not only historically unjustifiable but is fatally crippled and perverted the space of the public and the possibilities of man as a being gifted in politics."
>
> Hannah Arendt, *Doubtful Traditional Holdings in Contemporary Political Thought*, 1957

Hannah Arendt persistently refused to be called a 'political philosopher'. The political hostility of philosophy seemed to her to be an intolerable intellectual mortgage. She therefore always insisted on being a 'political theorist'. But she trusted one particular philosopher to have something essential to say about the origin and form of the political even today: Immanuel Kant. Unlike most interpreters and commentators, she did not get caught up in Kant's philosophy of morals and law but was the first to draw attention to his third critical work, the *Critique of the Power of Judgment*. A few authors have followed Arendt, but so far no one has really penetrated the philosophical cosmos of Kant's work to verify their intoition. This will now happen. However, the path chosen for this is quite unusual. The content of the book should not simply be searched for circumstantial evidence and its philosophical content passively recorded. Some systematic considerations will make it clear in advance that Kant's own method of presenting aesthetic and teleological judgments cannot lead to a political judgment. For this reason, the layout of the entire work is anticipated (instead of being worked through in the order of the chapters), so that a plan for the aforementioned "conversion" can be drawn up. The manifold consequences of this unconventional method hold out the prospect of a subjective change in political philosophy, which Hannah Arendt would have certainly welcomed.

B.1.1 Preparation I: The Reception of the *Critique of the Power of Judgment*

The *Critique of the Power of Judgment*[318] was published in 1790, and with this tome Kant saw the "business of Critique" as finished.[319] This third part of a system of critique of the subject of knowledge was to be the keystone, whereby the philosophy of nature (*Critique of Pure Reason*) and the philosophy of freedom (*Critique of Practical Reason*) are connected and mediated. However, what Heidegger wrote about the work is unchallenged: The impact of the *Critique of the Power of Judgment* was (and still is) exclusively based on misunderstandings.[320] For a century, the authors concentrated on the *CPJ* as a philosophy of art and art beauty. Although Hegel considered the program itself a failure, he described Kant's third

---

[318] The *First Introduction* to the *Critique of the Power of Judgment*, as published in Weischedel's edition based on the Rostock manuscript with Kant's handwriting, is taken into account here, since there is no reason to assume that this introduction is incorrect in detail. All the less so since it was found in the estate with correction notes by Kant's hand. Moreover, the *Critique of the Power of Judgment* is abbreviated with "*CPJ*"; the *Critique of Pure Reason* with "*CPuRe*"; and the *Critique of Practical Reason*, with "*CPraRe*". All quotes from the *CPJ* and the *CPuRe* are taken from the outstanding translations by Paul Guyer, 2000 and 1998 respectively. The page numbers of the *CPJ* and the *CPuRe* are taken from their second editions from and 1787 and 1793 respectively as rendered in Weischedel's complete edition, *Werke I-X*, Frankfurt 1988. The corresponding page numbers of the English editions of both works are indicated in square brackets. I also adopted Guyer's particular and new translation of some key terms of Kantian philosophy in my own text: reflecting (*reflektierend*); determining (*bestimmend*), power of judgment (*Urteiskraft*); ends (*Zwecke*); to judge [something] (*beurteilen*); the judging [of something] (*Beurteilung*); purposiveness (*Zweckmäßigkeit*); satisfaction (*Wohlgefallen*); dissatisfaction (*Missfallen*); pleasure (*Lust*); displeasure (*Unlust*); enjoyment (*Genuss*); gratification (*Vergnügen*); assent (*Beistimmung*); accord (*Einstimmung*); agreement (*Zusammenstimmung*); unanimity/unison (*Einhelligkeit*); to expect (*erwarten*); to expect sth. of so. (*zumuten*), cognition (*Erkenntnis*); representation (*Vorstellung*); presentation (*Darstellung*); the particular (*das Einzelne*), the universal (*das Allgemeine*); there is only one deviation: I don't translate *ansinnen* as 'to require' or 'to ascribe', but as 'to suggest'. See *CPJ*, transl. by Paul Guyer, 2000, Editor's Introduction, XLVI-XLIX.

[319] "Thus with this I bring my entire critical enterprise to an end," *CPJ*, B X [58].

[320] Heidegger, Martin, *Nietzsche*, 2 vol., Pfullingen 1961, vol. 1, p. 126.

Critique as "a starting point for the true understanding of art beauty."[321] Kant's reservations and warnings regarding the *CPJ* as a theory of art were ignored. For a long time, commentators and even the students missed the much more comprehensive and significant connection of the work with the unity of the critical system and the scope of Kant's proven transcendental principle of this particular kind of judgment in the fields of aesthetics and teleology. With his own study *Kant and the Problem of Metaphysics*, Heidegger himself made a significant contribution to prolonging the underestimation of the *CPJ*, since his objections to the Kantian line of thought must be described as no less educational for an entire school of German academic philosophy that continues to dominate. His attempt to interpret the *Critique of Pure Reason* with the means of the fundamental ontology he developed towards its specifically and exclusively *human* foundation was explicitly directed against Kant's concern, formulated even more emphatically in the second edition of the *CPuRe* (B), that he wanted transcendental philosophy to treat only *intelligent beings* as objects. Kant insisted that the first two *Critiques* should under no circumstances be regarded as studies in anthropology.[322] Apart from the untenability of this interpretation of Kant by Heidegger, who was certified by Ernst Cassirer that in important parts it is no longer a commentary, but the penetration of a usurper into the Kantian Work in order to subjugate it and make it subservient[323], Heidegger, with his concentration on the schematism chapter of the *CPuRe*, has completely distracted from the fact that man as an empirical being certainly has his place in the system of critical philosophy, namely in the *Critique of the Power of Judgment*. The key to Kant's own fundamental ontology lies solely in the third *Critique*, which

---

[321] Hegel, G. W. F., *Vorlesung über Ästhetik* [Lecture on Aesthetics], *Werke XIII* [Works XIII], Frankfurt 1986, p. 89.

[322] This critical mistake in philosophy is called *pathetic fallacy*, i.e. when explicitly non-human concepts, matters and contexts are illegitimately humanized. I consider this to be the biggest mistake in modern philosophy – with catastrophic consequences, in particular for the philosophy of subjectivity. I dealt with this massive multiple collision in philosophy in detail in *Laws of Singularity* and will elaborate on it even more in *You are Many – The Polycentric Subject* (Grünenberg, 2017 and 2019 respectively)

[323] Cassirer, Ernst, "Kant und das Problem der Metaphysik". Bemerkungen zu Martin Heideggers Kant-Interpretation ["Kant and the Problem of Metaphysics". Remarks on Martin Heidegger's Interpreation of Kant], in: Kantstudien, vol. XXXVI, 1-2/1931, p. 17.

Heidegger has systematically suppressed.[324] Luc Ferry suspects that Heidegger had to proceed in such a way as to be able to present any previous philosophical reference to man as necessarily based on anthropological ideas (instead of on insights into the essence of being).[325] In this way he could further imagine the *metaphysics of self-empowered subjectivity* as a dark fate of forgetting the being. Kant's philosophy in this context was another and very important arrow that Heidegger tried to draw on his fundamental ontological arc of radical critique of modernity.

Jean-Francois Lyotard, on the other hand, sought direct connection to an important chapter of the *CPJ*.[326] However, his instrumentalization of the analysis of the sublime falls back into the early phase of the reception of the *CPJ*. Once again, the third *Critique* here is reduced to a theory of art. However, this aesthetic of postmodernism has a massive claim to social theory and is only mentioned here for this reason. Lyotard's art theory on the basis of the sublime should provide a model for the perception and conception of modern reality in general, modern political reality in particular.[327] The conflict, which he postulates as the basis of all communication, has supposedly been uncovered by Kant in his third *Critique* as the *conflict between sensuality and reason*. This is also the signum of the postmodern era, namely the blocking of the unrepresentable in new art against pure sensuality, visualism, and the power of definition. Kant still has to be freed from his own "metaphysical prejudice" regarding the sublime for this purpose, Lyotard believes. This school of aesthetics demonstrated an increased political ambition and a lively joy of association in political theory.[328] By the way, Lyotard later – possibly after reading the

---

[324] There is no indication that Heidegger had ever read the *CPJ* before he took on the challenging task of interpreting Kant's critical philosophy at large. In other words: apart from his own agenda of disqualifying the greatest philosopher ever and his new way of presenting humanism as a critique of reason and judgment in the subject, Heidegger had no clue what he was doing there.

[325] Ferry, Luc, *Der Mensch als Ästhet. Die Erfindung des Geschmacks im Zeitalter der Demokratie* [The Human Being as an Aesthete. The Invention of Taste in the Age of Democracy], Stuttgart 1992, p. 136.

[326] Cf. Lyotard, Jean-Francois, *Der Widerstreit* [The Differend. Phrases in Dispute] Munich 1987.

[327] Welsch, Wolfgang, *Ästhetisches Denken* [Aesthetic Thinking], Stuttgart 1990, p. 164.

[328] Cf. Pries, Christine (ed.), *Das Erhabene. Zwischen Grenzerfahrung und Größenwahn* [The Sublime. Between Borderline Experience and Megalomania], Weinheim 1989, p. 28: "The sublime has too often been overweight on the metaphysical

relevant text by Kant for the first time[329] – distanced himself from his earlier statements about the sublime.[330] A reading of the *CPJ* remotely related to this project of the newer aesthetics of the sublime can be found in Jacques Derrida, who attempts to understand Kant's third *Critique* itself as a work of art that attempts to communicate something about the problem of the frame in art and indirectly about truth, its presence and its possibility.[331] Derrida does not formulate a political program in his interpretation of the *CPJ*, but following the understanding of all his works and his political activities, it can be said without great distortion that philosophy (as text) and philosophy (also the texts and his own continuation of these texts) as such are already a political issue for him. *How* it qualifies *as* political is an issue that has not yet been specifically addressed in the context of his own philosophy. Derrida's study is only considered here because it is inspired, sheds light on unnoticed passages in the text and, above all, provides revealing information through its missteps on the floor of the Kantian text.[332]

---

side. An overweight that had already implicitly been created by Kant and subsequently affected German Romanticism, Hegel and Schopenhauer up to Fascism and the SDI [Strategic Defense Initiative of the Reagan administration], and for which the enslavement of sensuality, the primacy of the absolute spirit, the rule of the subject over nature, in short: modern megalomania, is characteristic."

[329] Cf. Lyotard, Francois, *Leçons sur l'Analytique du sublime: Kant, Critique de la faculté de juger, §§ 23-29*, Paris 1991. This book, which is in the style and tone of a note box, as its author freely admits (ibid., p. 9), testifies to the first more thorough reading in the period 1988 to 1990 – at least the relevant paragraphs of the *CPJ*, which do not even make up 1/10 of the work. Lyotard's "philosophy book" *The Differend*, loc. cit., and some publications of his followers on the theme of the sublime were published between 1983 and 1989. In his teaching notes Lyotard tries to prove the thesis that the sublime, as Kant understood it, is the signum of our time, in which one can and must imagine things that can no longer be depicted.

[330] "No, you know, they have said, and I too have certainly said, very many stupid things about the subject of the sublime. There is no sublime art, there is no sublime object. That is a principle. The sublime is a feeling. It is a feeling called aesthetic." (*Freischwebende Reste*, interview with Jean-Francois Lyotard in: die tageszeitung, 13.8.1994).

[331] Derrida, Jacques, *Die Wahrheit in der Malerei* [The Truth in Painting], Vienna 1992, especially the first chapter *Parergon*, pp. 31-176.

[332] Much of Derrida's interpretation of what he presents as deeper insights into a deconstructive process, however, does not go beyond the usual commentary

There are further attempts, however, which have instrumentalized Kant's third *Critique* as a negative foil for a political and allegedly emancipatory aesthetic. However, they have no further significance for the present study.[333] More important here are the works of Hannah Arendt, Ernst Vollrath and Luc Ferry. What they have in common is that they want to open up the *CPJ* as the basis for a new philosophy of politics.

Hannah Arendt has not brought her assumption, which she had cherished since the early 1950s, that an independent political philosophy would have to be recovered in the *CPJ*, into the framework of a coherent theory of the political. The publications from her estate and the sighting of the unpublished part prove that she had always thought of such a large design. In addition to the assumption that it was the time pressure under which she was under for years[334], there are two other possible explanations for her stagnation[335] in the interpretation of the *CPJ*. Either the difficulties in deepening the topic had only just begun and Arendt noticed that they were immense. The critical system should have been taken into account from the *CPJ* as a whole, something that few authors have tried to do so

---

literature.

[333] Cf. Bourdieu, Pierre, *Die feinen Unterschiede. Kritik der gesellschaftlichen Urteilskraft* [The Subtle Differences. Critique of Social Power of Judgment], Frankfurt 1982, pp. 39-114; cf. Eagleton, Terry, *Ästhetik. Die Geschichte ihrer Ideologie* [Aesthetic. The History of its Ideology], Stuttgart 1994, pp. 73-106. Bourdieus' exciting and interesting sociological investigation would not have depended on the unsuccessful distancing from Kant's theory of beauty and is in no way enriched by it. Eagleton's Marxist-inspired study is superficial on Kant's third *Critique* and follows in Hegel, Marx and Adorno: The *CPJ* tries to cement the ideal of freedom so thoroughly in the subject and to separate it so much from the necessity of nature that it no longer has to claim any reality. That Eagleton would have read the text of the *CPJ* is an assumption that is not supported by any evidence.

[334] See Ludz, Ursula, *Kommentar der Herausgeberin* [Comment of the Editor] in: Hannah Arendt, *Was ist Politik? Fragmente aus dem Nachlaß*, [What is politics? Fragments from the Estate] in: Hannah Arendt, ed. by Ursula Ludz, Munich 1993, pp. 137-229, here pp. 139-142.

[335] "The most important aspects of Arendt's interpretation of the *CPJ*, as found in the posthumously published lecture of 1970, are already recognizable in the 1950s" (ibid., *Nachwort der Herausgeberin*, p. 221, note 66); cf. also Beiner, Roland, *Hannah Arendt über das Urteilen* [Hannah Arendt on Judgment], in: Arendt, Hannah, *Das Urteilen. Texte zu Kants politischer Philosophie* [The Judging. Texts on Kant's Political Philosophy], ed. by Roland Beiner, Munich 1985, pp. 115-197, here pp. 116-117.

far. Or Arendt saw – this is the second possibility – that a more thorough study would have dissuaded her from her program of a neo-Aristotelic republicanism[336] and possibly even led it consistently ad absurdum; therefore, she wanted to use Kant's third *Critique* only to the extent that it could still serve her purposes.

With regard to the first possibility, one has to realize which problems an affirmative, integral appropriation of the Kantian system of critical philosophy has to solve. This would include simultaneously looking at transcendental natural philosophy, rigorous moral philosophy and a priori theory of taste and linking their respective consequences. This can hardly be avoided, because it seems implausible that one can make selective use of the three critiques instead of commissioning the system as a whole or at least taking appropriate account of its other parts and functions.[337]

It is not necessary for the present study to choose between the various explanations. It is enough that neither Hannah Arendt herself, nor her student Ernst Vollrath, have made this deepening into a philosophy of

---

[336] See Beiner, Roland, *Hannah Arendt über das Urteilen* [Hannah Arendt on Judging], loc. cit., pp. 115-197, here p. 175; cf. also Brunkhorst, Hauke, *Demokratie und Differenz. Vom klassischen zum modernen Begriff des Politischen* [Democracy and Difference. From the Classical to the Modern Concept of the Political, Frankfurt 1994, p. 103-116; cf. Friedmann, Friedrich G., *Hannah Arendt. Eine deutsche Jüdin im Zeitalter des Totalitarismus* [Hannah Arendt. A German Jewess in the Age of Totalitarianism], Munich 1985, pp. 129-141; cf. Sternberger, Dolf, *Drei Wurzeln der Politik* [Three Roots of Politics], Frankfurt 1984, p. 389-396; see in particular Vollrath, Ernst, *Grundlegung einer philosophischen Theorie des Politischen*, [Foundation of a Philosophical Theory of Politics], Würzburg 1987, p. 257, note 10, where the author testifies that Hannah Arendt still believed in 1972 that the power of judgment was a continuation of the "old prudence theory" and only needed to be reconstructed.

[337] This is of course a reservation, which also concerns the selective Kantianisms of John Rawls, Otfried Höffe and the already mentioned instrumentalization of Kant by Lyotard. Comparable with this are the failed attempts to transform Hegel's philosophy of the objective and the absolute mind into the paradigm of intersubjectivity without accepting the consequence of a world spirit. Cf. Theunissen, Michael, *Die verdrängte Intersubjektivität in Hegels Philosophie des Rechts* [The Repressed Intersubjectivity in Hegel's Philosophy of Law] in: Henrich, Dieter u. Horstmann, R.-P. (ed.), *Hegel's Philosophie des Rechts. Die Theorie der Rechtsformen und ihre Logik*, Stuttgart 1982, pp. 317-381; also Hösle, Vittorio, *Hegels System. Der Idealismus und das Problem der Intersubjektivität* [Hegel's System. Idealism and the Problem of Intersubjectivity] 2 vol., Hamburg 1987.

politics. In his *Grundlegung einer philosophischen Theorie des Politischen* [Foundation of a Philosophical Theory of the Political], Vollrath ventured only little beyond what Arendt had already achieved. Instead, he tried not to be suspected of having a 'metaphysical' interest in Kant's system. To this end, he systematically ignored all aspects and texts in the works of Kant that are not directly connected with the definition and presentation of reflecting judgment as a unified power of thinking.[338] He only took the purely technical concept of reflection in order to connect it, separately from its conditions, with objects that he considered required this connection. He treated the area of political phenomena selected for this operation much more carefully than the borrowed philosophical concept. It was also noted that Vollrath's appropriation of the Kantian thought of a reflecting power of judgment had to remain vague and general only because the author wanted to remain completely unburdened by all the interesting philosophical problems that followed.[339] Philosophy appears only as a short presentation of a small part of Kant's critical philosophy. Vollrath did not himself work philosophically with the system of Kant's critical writings, nor did he illuminate the historical framework of the emergence of aesthetics in the 18th century, the result of which is the *Critique of the Power of Judgment*. Kant, as shown here in Chapter A.2, referred to more than a century of philosophical struggle with the question of taste and a system of ends as a form of subjective, yet communicable truth. Vollrath, on the other hand, places the earlier efforts towards a philosophical aesthetic in a series with Christian Wolff's moral-philosophical and consistently rationalist concept of politics. He knows the references to the philosophy of taste in the 18th century, but considers it to be completely caught up in the rationalist theory of beauty.[340] Although he writes in the *Grundlegung* that he would have recognized that it could not be a simple "reconstruction" of judgment[341], as he assumed in his earlier study – encouraged

---

[338] That is why Ulrich Sassenbach's work *Der Begriff der Politik bei Kant*, Würzburg 1987, is so commendable, because from the early writings to the estate, almost all of Kant's texts accessible today were taken into account - except for the three *Critiques*!

[339] See, among others, Wenzel, Uwe-Justus, *Fundamentaltheorie des Politischen oder politische Theorie des Fundamentalen* [Fundamental Theory of the Political or Political Theory of the Fundamental] in: Archiv für Rechts- und Sozialphilosophie, 4/1988, pp. 531-441.

[340] Vollrath, *Grundlegung*, loc. cit., p. 260, footnote 18.

[341] Ibid., p. 257, fn 10.

by Hannah Arendt herself.[342] But the decisive part of his *Grundlegung* does not take this step, which would have led beyond the reconstruction. Vollrath states as his most important realization that Kant would have exceeded the transcendental horizon of his philosophy in his critique of (aesthetic) judgment.[343] However, this is – as will be clearly shown below – such an obvious claim of the *CPJ* that it can hardly be offered as a new insight.[344]

Of much greater interest is the question: How was that possible? How could the system of critical philosophy, often presented as a monolithic block of rationalist theory, provide this connection and mediation to aesthetics and teleology? After all, the border was not simply crossed, but the crossing was part of the program. Arendt and Vollrath, on the other hand, implied that Kant had to be read against his own intentions, at the systematic level of his critical project. However, this is obviously wrong. The expansion of the field of transcendental philosophy in the *CPJ* is neither a discovery by Arendt nor by Vollrath, but to its entire extent part of the program of critical philosophy.[345] However, the assumption seems correct in Vollrath's project of the *Grundlegung* that the *CPJ* must be extended by a dimension – which is already inherent in it – namely that of the political way of thinking. This is made much easier to understand by the problematic assumption of its modal identity with the forms of reflecting judgment that are differentiated and analyzed in the *CPJ*.

On the one hand, the investigation of political subjectivity to be carried out here differs from Vollrath's approach by the consistent historical and systematic location of the theoretical building-blocks in Kant's third *Critique* for a political theory of modernity. But above all, this new concept is oriented towards the closest applications, namely the dimensions of

---

[342] Cf. Vollrath, Ernst, *Die Rekonstruktion der politischen Urteilskraft* [The Reconstruction for the Political Power of Judgment] Stuttgart 1977.

[343] Vollrath, *Grundlegung*, loc. cit., p. 259, 288.

[344] *CPJ*, B V; XX; XXVII [56; 63; 67].

[345] Even if not from the beginning, for it was only in 1787 that Kant saw – through his discovery of the transcendental principle of (reflected) purposiveness of nature for the human power of judgment – the possibility of a critique of the subject of taste. What is decisive is that Kant wanted to provide his life's work in his last years with transitions to empirical sciences and practices. And with the *CPJ*, if you only read it and take its many examples seriously, it is as obvious as possible that this transition to empirical sensuality and its reflection had already been built.

order, morality, faith and history in relation to political judgment. Perhaps the greatest shortcoming of Vollrath's attempt is that nowhere is it clear what a philosophy of the political could mean or explain in practical and civilizational terms. His efforts led him to be suspected that he wanted to creep into a metaphysical, normative and thus universalist foundation of Anglo-Saxon liberalism, which secretly does not move beyond Aristotle and only instrumentalizes Kant's theory of reflection. The applications Vollrath offers as the basis for testing reflecting judgment are threefold.[346] He attempts to position this still very meagre framework of political judgment against the concept of the German constitutional law tradition, against Jürgen Habermas' theory of communication and at the same time against Niklas Luhmann's systems theory. Not only that this insufficiently thought-out confrontation with the meagre theoretical means that Vollrath had at his disposal up to then could confirm the above-mentioned suspicion. Much more important is the fact that Vollrath was not able to treat the significance of the *CPJ* for political philosophy exhaustively in this way and that he greatly underestimated the philosophical scope of reflecting judgment.[347]

Peter Steinberger understands his attempt to distill the concept of political judgment from the classics of political philosophy and modern linguistics as a kind of answer to Vollrath's foundation.[348] His main concern is to overcome the dichotomy of judgment, as he puts it. By this he understands the division of all judgment teachings since Plato into 'cognitive' and 'non-cognitive judgments'. What he has in mind as a suspension is a kind of phronesis with a status as rational cognition instead of just pragmatic prudence, or as he puts it succinctly: "Judgment as intelligent performance." But as little as this solution represents a real extension of the concepts of political philosophy, just as unconvincing are the analyses and interpretations that are sent before it. Steinberger already notes observations on Hobbes that do not exactly give cause to suspect him of being an intimate connoisseur of Hobbes research. What he writes about the *CPJ*,

---

[346] Vollrath's interesting interpretation of Clausewitz was already discussed in Chapter A.1.6.

[347] At the same time, I must add that I have learned a great deal from this book. Without Vollrath's preparatory work I would not have had the idea that there is a philosophically interesting approach here. And on its own, the *Grundlegung* in its individual observations is a very subtle book, which lacks only the systematics and elaboration of the decisive part.

[348] Steinberger, Peter J., *The Concept of Political Judgment*, Chicago and London 1993.

however, makes it clear that there is no familiarity with the original text. He knows Arendt's interpretation of the third *Critique* and bravely tries to comment on the philosophical problems of the *CPJ*, because for him it is allegedly the first, though now surpassed, climax of the judgment teachings. It is obvious that Steinberger has obtained his sparse knowledge from second hand in order to be able to present the *CPJ* as a failed project and to move on. Afterwards, he strains five more authors until he has collected the material for a handy truism. It is sufficient as a last hint that nothing in this book is to be found of what at the end of the present study is to be called political subjectivity.[349]

Of particular interest for the study of political subjectivity is a newer French school of political philosophy, from which some of the most fruitful, profound and elegant contributions to the rationalist tradition of the Enlightenment and European humanism have come. With their works on Heidegger's political philosophy, philosophy of history and the history of subjectivity[350], Luc Ferry and Alain Renaut place themselves in a tradition of subject philosophy that seemed to have come to a temporary end with Cassirer's Kant interpretations. Cassirer's examination of Heidegger in the Davos Disputation and in his review of Heidegger's famous Kant study[351] are, according to these French philosophers, emblematic of the encounter of two incommensurable philosophical traditions: Criticism and modern phenomenology. Instead of, however, as the majority of the New Kantians did, placing transcendental aesthetics and the epistemological achievement of criticism for the modern natural sciences in the foreground, Luc Ferry in particular opened a new debate on the achievement of the *CPJ* for the theories of history, politics, art and subjectivity in various attempts. His experiments aim at a completely new breakdown of German idealism in general and Kant's critical system in particular, which from the third

---

[349] Ibid., in particular pp. 130-148.

[350] Ferry, Luc, *Philosophie politique II. Le système des philosophies de l'histoire*, Paris 1984; Ferry, Luc and Renaut, Alain, *Heidegger et les Modernes*, Paris 1988; Ferry, Luc, *Homo aestheticus. L'Invention du goût à l'âge démocratique*, Paris 1991; Ferry & Renaut, *La pensée 68th Essai sur l'antihumanisme contemporain*, Paris 1988; Renaut, Alain, *L'ère de l'individu. Contribution à l'histoire de la subjectivité*, Paris 1989.

[351] Heidegger, Martin, *Kant und das Problem der Metaphysik* [Kant and the Problem of Metaphysics], Frankfurt 1929, where the Davos Disputation is also documented; ibid., p. 244-268; Cassirer, Ernst, "*Kant und das Problem der Metaphysik*". *Bemerkungen zu Martin Heideggers Kant-Interpretation* ["Kant and the Problem of Metaphysics". Remarks on Martin Heidegger's Kant-Interpretation], in: Kantstudien, vol. XXXVI, 1-2/1931, p. 1-26.

Critique could reveal undreamt-of 'secrets' for understanding our political present.[352] This is no longer an unusual approach – Ingeborg Maus has conducted a study on modern democracy theories under similar guidelines.[353] But this new French school has proved that it takes Kant's works more seriously, now understands them much better than its German colleagues and is also inspired by them to more of its own philosophical ideas.

Ferry's writings are of particular interest here because he consistently prepares a new draft of political philosophy on the basis of Kant's aesthetics. This is not yet available in extenso, but the foundation for it is already much more developed and sustainable than at Vollrath. Like him, Ferry draws a clear distinction between moral and political judgments – a separation that will have to be dealt with thoroughly here, because it is quite considerable what exactly these differences between practical reason and political judgment are.[354] Only in this way can we show and prove that we are dealing with clearly differentiated assets of thought that are used in each case. To a certain extent, Ferry presupposes that this distinction can be presented and justified without further ado. This may surprise some readers, for in Germany the practical philosophical and Aristotelian tradition has such strong roots and such far-reaching claims within political philosophy that Heidegger's permanent refusal to deduce ethics from his phenomenology has always been perceived as an urgent problem and a deficit, rather than simply being resigned to it. For this reason, the distinction between practical and political philosophy will be discussed below (cf. chapter B.1.8). In a more recent treatise, Ferry gave a very vivid side to his program and showed that the invention of modern aesthetics as a theory of taste in the 18th century was closely related to the preparation of European democracies.[355] The idea of exploring a cognitive capacity under the title

---

[352] Ferry, *Philosophe politique II*, loc. cit., p. 10.

[353] Maus, Ingeborg, *Zur Aufklärung der Demokratietheorie. Rechts- und demokratietheoretische Überlegungen im Anschluß an Kant* [On the Enlightenment of Democratic Theory. Reflections on Legal and Democratic Theory Following Kant], Frankfurt 1992.

[354] Ferry, *Philosophie politique II*, loc. cit., chapter *Une interprétation 'esthétique' de la vision morale du monde: vers une synthèse 'critique' des philosophies de l'histoire*, pp. 210-242.

[355] Ferry, *Homo aestheticus*, loc. cit. A further validation of the aesthetically conceived philosophy of politics through its application was presented by Ferry in a large and, in my opinion, brilliant essay on the confrontation of humanism,

'Political Subjectivity' has been sustainably inspired by this treatise, including the chosen historical method as developed in Part A.

It has often been pointed out how much the *CPJ* is at the service of the revolutionary subjectivation of the world. The task now is to find out what this could mean in detail and how much Kant's third critical work really achieves in this respect. The studies on the self-empowerment of the bourgeois individual, on the enthronement of autonomous reason as the ruler of the world and on the responsibility of the subject's metaphysics for the crimes of the 20th century – all these were far too general considerations that were always allowed to feel safe in the protection of distanced macroscopy from critical questions as to how this should be understood in detail.[356] So the subject's individualization in the sense of atomization, alienation, loss of self and forgetfulness of being is only one of its concerns. What is new and much more interesting, however, is the analysis of the reflecting judgment as a power of political judgment in the various special cases. From the outset, the investigation aims to form classes and types of political judgments, differentiated according to criteria by the specific use they make of the subjective powers of mind, imagination and reason. This enterprise is thus obviously opposed to a tendency of the Kant interpretation to regard the questions of the third *Critique* as historically settled, because the natural sciences (above all biology) have overtaken the teleological speculations and modern art the aesthetic analyses of the *CPJ* in the matter.[357] Here the opposite is claimed. It seems that it is only in our time that the conditions in the form of empirical findings from ethnology, historical research, sociology and psychology exist that allow the *CPJ* to be put to the test.

The problem of political subjectivity and political judgment is to be solved in the following in a completeness and clarity helpful for political theory.[358] The insights into the origin, form and structure of the political judgment can then be tested against the diversity of the political cosmos,

---

anti-humanism and democratic-republican inspiration in ecological movement and theory; cf. Ferry, *L'arbre, l'animal et l'homme*, Paris 1992, in particular pp. 260-263.

[356] Michel Foucault and Louis Dumont, who have extensively documented their contentious theses historically and sociologically, are excluded from this.

[357] See Höffe, Otfried, *Immanuel Kant*, Munich 1983, p. 260.

[358] In the aforementioned sense of differentiating between the *philosophy of the subject* and the *theories of public order*; see here Introduction, IV.

because the instruments to be developed promise a clear distinction between the political and the non-political. If this enterprise proves successful in a convincing way, modern political science would have a new and very profound philosophical foundation.

B.1.2 Preparation II: Outline of the *Critique of the Power of Judgment* and Definition of the Reflecting Judgment

It is no easy task to outline the *Critique of the Power of Judgment* here in a few sentences in such a way that a sufficient and continuous understanding of the following investigation can be promised. Basically, it is even irresponsibility that passes on and consolidates the shortcomings of academic education in the subject of philosophy. Because actually the inclined readership, which is not familiar with the Kantian opus, should be politely asked to put these pages aside again and to familiarize themselves thoroughly with the so little frequented text of the third *Critique*. The pedantic version would be an invitation to first read all three *Critiques* and to pay special attention to the *CPJ* as the conclusion of the philosophical system. But especially at German universities it is unfortunately the case that you can't expect to read even one of the three *Critiques* from the first to the last page in major seminars that extend over several semesters. In doubt, the attentive and for good reasons suspicious readers should always turn to the original text, which in its richness of thought and systematic sophistication I could never adequately refer to in a summary. What applies to all previous comments on Kant's work also applies to the one to be submitted here: it is worse than the original text.[359] The only protection that can be provided here and above all in the following chapters is an extensive citation. I would like to point out that the chapters following the sketch are to be understood only to a very limited extent as 'comments'. Rather, it is a new construction or 'conversion' for which *CPJ* supplies the outstanding material. If this new building should prove unstable or even collapse completely, the responsibility will certainly not lie with Kant.

The *CPJ* is not Kant's first preoccupation with the problems of aesthetics. As early as 1764 he published his *Beobachtungen über das Gefühl des*

---

[359] Nevertheless, a literature reference: In the short, handy and comprehensibly written introduction by Dieter Teichert, *Immanuel Kant: "Kritik der Urteilskraft"*, UTB, Paderborn et al. 1992, one finds a quickly manageable basic structure of the *CPJ*. However, Teichert only begins with the 'Analytic of the Beautiful' and does without the two introductions, which make up 115 pages in the Weischedel edition. Yet, these are particularly interesting because they provide an overview of the entire critical system that is to be concluded with the *CPJ*.

Schönen und Erhabenen [Observations on the Feeling of the Beautiful and Sublime][360], raising his voice in the forum where the scholarly dispute about the essence of beauty and about aesthetics as science had lasted for more than half a century. The theoretical-historical background on which Kant developed his philosophical aesthetics up to the criticism of judgment has been described in detail here in chapter A.2. It would be helpful to remember this, because much of what is dealt with here, only in philosophical terminology, is developed there in the historical material. The question has remained the same: How can there be a knowledge of the concrete-individual and how can this be conveyed with the general, with the always law-guided knowledge that knows nothing individual? The great progress in Kant's second philosophical investigation of aesthetics, the *CPJ*, lies in the fact that – quite unlike in his psychological-casuistic observations of the pre-critical period – he has in the meantime identified a special power of judgment that must form the basis of all aesthetics, but ultimately also of teleology (doctrine of ends). As a result, the question of a "science of sensual knowledge," as Baumgarten called aesthetics, has acquired the right to be treated specifically within the system of critical philosophy. Because one should always keep that in mind: Kant's critical philosophy is nothing more than a.) the analysis of judgments and b.) the deduction, i.e. the justification of the concepts and principles, that make a.) possible. The newly discovered power is in any case the reflecting power of judgment, which represents a counterpart and critical complement to the previously exclusively researched *determining power of judgment*. The *CPJ* is exclusively concerned with what is justifiably called the "extended way of thinking" of reflecting judgment in this respect as well. The discussion of their various achievements constitutes the three main pieces of the book: the judgments on the beautiful and the sublime (aesthetics) and the judgments on purposiveness (teleology).

The most important characteristic of the *CPJ* for the overall view of critical philosophy is the system-closing character already mentioned.[361] Transcendental philosophy as a system would actually already be complete with a philosophy of nature (*Critique of Pure Reason*) and a philosophy of freedom (*Critique of Practical Reason*).

---

[360] Kant, Immanuel, *Werke II* [Works II], pp. 823-884.
[361] See also Höffe, *Immanuel Kant*, loc. cit., pp. 259-280.

Fig. 9: Immanuel Kant (1724-1804)

But with these two sides of subjective cognitive capacity, which thereby each become capable of a doctrine, i.e. metaphysics (*Metaphysical Beginnings of Natural Science*; *Metaphysics of Morals*), there is still no explanation why mankind needed its entire long history to come to these insights. Neither was it clear what kept the Germanic tribes away from the preoccupation with theoretical physics and analytical geometry, nor was it obvious why morality and the civil law based on it only wanted to spread so slowly – when pure reason always had this knowledge ready. In other words: transcendental philosophy with its two main pieces was, as it must be demanded of a philosophy aiming at pure forms, completely timeless, or rather without history. Kant has always insisted that transcendental philosophy is not anthropology. This accentuation has determined the most important changes in the B edition of the *Critique of Pure Reason*.[362]

The fundamentally a-historic character of the two main pieces of transcendental philosophy had several consequences. The most important one, systematically, for Kant, as he put it, was the *lack of transition from the concepts of nature to the concept of freedom*[363] (B XX-XXI [p. 83]). Over the abyss between necessity of nature and freedom (as two different forms of causality[364]) there is indeed no bridge[365], but there must be a *common ground*

---

[362] Changes: Preface to the second edition (B), whereby the A-preface was completely dropped and not kept as it is usually the case; new version of the transcendental deduction and the paralogism chapter.

[363] The singularity of the concept of freedom is owed to the fact that the actually exuberant idea of freedom of reason makes possible, i. e. rationally thinkable a whole *second nature*, a world of moral beings under laws in a problematic way (because no knowledge in the theoretical sense can be built upon it) through this one qualified concept (see "The Antinomy of Third Dispute" in *CPuRe* B 472-479 [485-489]). The concept of freedom is thus attributed to world authorship. The plural of the concepts of nature refers to the twelve categories of the table of judgment and the pure forms of sensuality, also referred to as categories, namely space and time. Only these terms in interaction can lead to a *cognized*, i.e. (re-)constructible and *dictated nature* according to causal-mechanical principles. The unity of nature in a single term can only be *reflected teleologically*. It is one of the tasks of the *CPJ* to work out precisely these differences.

[364] The transcendentally deduced, i.e. legitimized concept of freedom, opens up the prospect of a second nature, as Kant himself puts it, which is subject to another causality, namely the *causality of freedom*, in which one cannot only think of a 'cause' that is itself effectuated by an 'effect' – this is the realm of nature in its theoretical sense, dealt with in *CPuRe* – but can also imagine a cause as originally and exclusively causative, without dependence from any prior effect. This is the meaning of the term 'spontaneity' in the Kantian sense: to be the author of one's own nature, which only has to borrow the "form of law" from that nature which the mind recognizes with the help of pure sensuality and the twelve categories.

[365] Derrida misunderstood this when he wrote that Kant, despite his explicit denial of this possibility, had spanned a "bridge" over the "abyss". Derrida tries to argue profoundly that the bridge is a symbol and above all: the symbol is the bridge between the worlds (theoretical and practical world). Although this is a plausible use of Derrida's words for his private needs, it no longer has anything to do with Kant's determination to seek only a common "ground" and not a "bridge" in the abyss. Kant was also completely clear that "ground (support, basis)" (*CPJ*, B 257 [226]) is a *symbolic hypotyposis* that calls up a very specific field of association. Nevertheless, Derrida later surprisingly showed in this book that he otherwise read the concept of 'ground' very carefully; Derrida, *Die*

for both ways of thinking, a "unity of the supersensible", which is inherent in nature as well as freedom. Because only if at least one such common reason can be accepted, there is the possibility of a transition of the way of thinking under two different principles. Only then can one think that the concept of freedom, in that it determines a will, becomes effective in nature and can thus reconcile concepts of nature and freedom. After all, freedom has the task of *making the world of the senses become real according to its ends*, i.e. of furnishing it as it *should* be.

The ground on which this transition becomes possible is an "ability of the soul" that lies between cognitive ability and desire, namely the feeling of lust and displeasure (B 23 [p. 85]). Among the so-called upper cognitive faculties, namely *understanding* as the determination of cognitive faculty in relation to nature and *reason* as the determination of volition in relation to morality, the power of judgment is assigned to this faculty. The power of judgment can therefore be the common ground for this transition from one principle to another, because it cannot be traced back to any other common ground with the two other capacities and "presumably", as it is still called at the beginning of the *CPJ*, contains a principle a priori. For if it wants to become the *law* in any way to the feeling of lust and displeasure, it must necessarily contain such a principle a priori. The first and second versions of the introduction to the *CPJ* each contain a table indicating the systematic connection between the capacities and their principles.[366]

All the faculties of the mind	Faculty of cognition	A priori principles	Application to (Products)
Faculty of cognition	Understanding	Lawfulness	Nature
Feeling of pleasure and displeasure	Power of judgment	Purposiveness	Art
Faculty of desire	Reason	Final end	Freedom

Table 1: Faculties of the Mind

Wahrheit in der Malerei [The Truth in Painting], Vienna 1992, pp. 54-55 and p. 62, where Derrida supposes that we have accepted and forgotten his bending of the Kantian text.

[366] *CPJ*, B LVIII [83]. The titles of the table in the first version of the introduction differ significantly only in one point: "Products" is written in the last column instead of "Application to". This is an interesting reference to the constructivist constitution of the concept of nature in Kant's philosophy.

I would like to take this opportunity to refer to the short glossary here in the appendix to the study. It contains the most important terms of Kant's transcendental philosophy that must be assumed here.[367] For the unusual language that Kant constructed for the sake of the precision of his argumentation and the systematics of his work otherwise leads us astray because of the often seemingly obvious but false associations with (scientific) everyday language.[368] All other terms that are still missing here are explained specifically in the text.

The first distinction is now made by the *CPJ* between the determining and the reflecting power of judgment.[369] The uniform principle, i.e. the ground for the transition, is revealed as the types of transition between the particular and the universal in judgments. Basically, two transitions are conceivable, namely from a given universal to a sought-after particular by way of *subsumption*, or from a given particular to a sought-after universal by way of *reflection*. The former is the kind of *determining power of judgment*, the latter the *reflecting power of judgment*. The closer definition of a power of judgment as 'reflecting' means that it fulfils a function that is actually reserved for the understanding:

"Through this attribute, the power of judgment is ascribed a task which in the true sense belongs only to the understanding, namely to form concepts."[370]

---

[367] Rudolf Eisler's handbook, which provides Kant's own definitions for each term, is very helpful for more precise reinsurance with regard to Kant's terminology; albeit only in German; see Eisler, *Kant-Lexicon: Nachschlagewerke zu Kants sämtlichen Schriften, Briefen, und handschriftlichem Nachlass* [Kant Lexicon: A Reference of Kant's Collected Writings, Letters, and Handwritten Accounts], 1st ed. 1930, Hildesheim 1972

[368] Kant was already an excellent, respected and successful writer in the literary enterprise of the Enlightenment before the publication of his systematic major works. The elegant and ironically entertaining style, which can still be found in his pre-critical work *Dreams of a Ghost Seer*, Works II, pp. 919-989, he abandoned in his critical writings in favor of his own uncompromising theoretical language; cf. the excellent study by Willi Goetschel, *Constituting Critique. Kant's Writing as Critical Praxis*, revised and expanded ed., Durham & London 1992.

[369] On the genesis of the CPJ and the distinction between the two types of judgment, see Dumouchel, Daniel, La découverte de la faculté de juger réfléchissante. Le rôle heuristique de la "Critique du goût" dans la formation de la Critique de la Faculté de Juger, in: Kant-Studien, vol. 85, 1994, pp. 419-442.

[370] Liedtke, Max, *Der Begriff der Reflexion bei Kant* [The Concept of Reflexion in Kant] in: Archiv für Geschichte der Philosophie, 48/1966, pp. 207-216, here p.

In the same way that this ability, in the sense of Kant's philosophy, has so far produced the concepts of beauty, sublime and end, it will now generate a *concept of politics* whose kinship with critical aesthetics and teleology will make the political cosmos appear in a new light. However, this brief anticipation is not intended to distract from the fundamental question of conveying the particular and the universal, the answer of which by Kant is still of some interest here. Its presentation (see above) is extremely formal in itself and requires explanation. The misunderstandings at this point have often resulted from the fact that the type of mediation of the particular and the universal, which was only found in the *CPJ*, was not sufficiently anchored in the first two *Critiques*. When Kant writes that *the particular* is sought and subordinated to *a universal*, it is not a general, formal logical subsumption in the sense of a syllogism with subordinate and superordinate clause (where it does not depend on the content of the propositions), or the well-known Hempel-Oppenheimer scheme with explanans and explanandum, but the process refers to the special insights into this mediation that have become possible with transcendental philosophy.

> "The determining power of judgment under universal transcendental laws, given by the understanding, merely subsumes; the law is sketched out for it a priori, and it is therefore unnecessary for it to think of a law for itself in order to be able to subordinate the particular in nature to the universal."[371]

Since the determining power of judgment also applies to practical philosophy, this means that each individual, special action must be subsumed under the categorical imperative and can be examined by means of the maxim of the will that determines it. **The universal is not every higher stage of generalization in a series of abstractions, such as from man to mammal or from neighbourhood to humanity, but it is the universal that is given and secured in its justification since a certain Immanuel Kant has written the *Critique of Pure Reason* and the *Critique of Practical Reason*.**[372] Through the concept of freedom, the possibility of the

---

216; cf. Liedtke, *Der Begriff der reflektierenden Urteilskraft in Kant's Kritik der reinen Vernunft* [The Concept of Reflecting Power of Judgment in Kant's Critique of Pure Reason], Hamburg 1964.

[371] (*CPJ*, B XXVI [p. 67])

[372] For example, the otherwise thorough Kant interpreter Friedrich Kaulbach was subject to a blatant misinterpretation of the determining power of judgment, here in his *Einführung in die Philosophie des Handelns* [Introduction to the

categorical imperative is conditioned, which means that its *practical* objectivity is guaranteed by transcendental philosophy. The same is true of natural philosophy. The particular therein is not a single find or an accidental observation of nature, which is then sorted under an already known empirical law that provides the explanation for the existence of this thing. The particular in the correct use of critical natural philosophy is the *experiment*[373] in which **nature is *constructed*, according to the general laws dictated by the understanding**. The dictate of the understanding knows only a clearly defined and thus limited vocabulary, namely those terms with which the "functions of thought" are called, also known as "categories" or "ontological predicables". They are completely listed in the *Table of Categories*.[374] The concept of universality thus refers exclusively to the results of the first two *Critiques*. Otherwise it would be hard to understand why Kant calls the required power of judgment for this task a *determining*

Philosophy of Action], Darmstadt 1982, p. 158: "Its achievement consists in the subsumption of a particular appearance under the universal term responsible for it. Thus, a physical appearance, which shows characteristic properties, called symptoms, is 'subsumed' by the doctor under the universal term of a certain disease such as rheumatism etc." This is certainly wrong, because **Kaulbach confuses the function of the determining power of judgment with a logical conclusion**. At the same time, however, it points to a serious misunderstanding of a priori natural philosophy in the CPuRe at large, for it is precisely medical art and all other empirical sciences (such as chemistry at this time, which was not yet able to demonstrate a priori the laws of movement of its elementary particles; see Kant, Immanuel, *Metaphysische Anfanggründe der Naturwissenschaften* [Metaphysical Beginnings of Natural Science], Werke IX, Perface, p. 15) that are discussed in the *CPJ* on the basis of reflecting power of judgment as types of Aristotelian-classifying world research (e.g. *CPJ*, B XL [74]), with whose help the affiliation of an apparition to a class of phenomena suitable as a *provisional* law can be *reflected upon*.

[373] To what extent the entire transcendental philosophy of modern natural science is modeled after the experiment is testified by the manifold references in Preface B of the *CPuRe* alone. Last but not least, the initial quotation in the second edition of the CPuRe is also an indication of this. It comes from the preface of the *Novum organum* (1620) by Sir Francis Bacon, the famous founder of the doctrine of experimental-scientific natural research, who wanted to initiate the *Instauratio magna* of science with this work, its Great Renewal.

[374] *CPuRe* B 106 [212]. Cf. the excellent study by Reinhard Brandt, *Die Urteilstafel. Kritik der reinen Vernunft A 67-76; B 92-201* [The Table of Categories. Critique of Pure Reason A 67-76; B 92-201], Kant-Forschungen, vol. 4, Hamburg 1991, which corrects many mistaken comments to date.,

one.³⁷⁵ In a very strong sense, the universal determines the possibility of the particular, here of the individual experiences. The subsumption is not an occasional subordination of a particular to a universal, depending on where it fits best. The 'universality' of all knowledge, the 'form' with which it can be brought to experience, is completely described in the *CPuRe* and in Kant's view only needs to be interlinked.³⁷⁶ If one does not understand this mechanism of the determining power of judgment, all insights into the so-called "Copernican turn"³⁷⁷ as well as into the peculiar character and the performance of reflecting power of judgment remain blocked.³⁷⁸ This turn

---

[375] A good example can be found in the Introduction of the *CPJ*: "Now under these laws the power of judgment is determining, for it has nothing to do but subsume under given laws. E.g., the understanding says: All alteration has its cause (universal law of nature [of causality, R.G.]); now the transcendental [i. e. determining; R.G.] power of judgment has nothing further to do than to provide the condition of subsumption under the *a priori* concept of the understanding that has been laid down for it: and that is the succession of the determinations of one and the same thing." (*CPJ*, B XXXII [70])

[376] This means that the twelve categories of the understanding (under the titles quantity, quality, relation and modality, which, by the way, also subdivide the analysis of the beautiful and the sublime) must be connected combinatorily and by means of the "schemata" to form a complete system of natural philosophy, which would be a "Metaphysics of Nature (science)", in which the general principles for gaining experience in all exact, mathematically proceeding sciences would be found. In the CPuRe Kant has dispensed with these interlinks: In any case, from the little that I have here adduced it becomes clear that a complete lexicon with all the requisite definitions should not only possible even easy to produce. The headings already exist; it is merely necessary to fill them out, and a systematic topic, such as the present one, will make it easy not to miss the place where every concept properly belongs and at the same time make it easy to notice any that is still empty." (CPuRe, B 109[214]). In 1786, one year before the second edition of the *CPuRe*, Kant finally published *Die metaphysischen Anfangsgründe der Naturwissenschaft* [The Metaphysical Origins of Natural Science] in which he dedicated himself to this "easy" task of completing the subjects he showed. The transition from this metaphysics of nature to physics was to become his late work, but the *Opus posthumum* clearly shows that the physical and mental condition of the old philosopher soon put an end to this struggle.

[377] See *CPuRe*, B XVI [110]

[378] For example, Derrida, like all other commentators known to me, has completely misunderstood this peculiarity of the 'universal' in the correct understanding of transcendental philosophy; cf. Derrid, *Die Wahrheit in der Malerei* [The Truth in Painting], loc. cit., p. 71.

means that the constitution of theoretical (nature) and practical objects (morality) is presented as an achievement of the subject in its judgments. In order to put this connection between determining power of judgment, experiment and natural law in the right light once again, only one meaningful passage in the text is to be considered here:

> "Reason, in order to be taught by nature, must approach nature with its principles in one hand, according to which alone the agreement among appearances can count as laws, and, in the other hand, the experiments thought out in accordance with these principles, yet in order to be instructed by nature not like a pupil, who has recited to him whatever the teacher wants to say, but like an appointed judge who compels witnesses to answer the questions he puts to them."[379]

Let reason go to nature with *two hands*. In one it holds the *experiment* (in the quote the order is reversed) and remembers the achievement of Bacon and Galileo. In the other hand it holds its own principles, which – as the attentive reader may have noticed anyway – can be read in the *Critique of the Pure Reason* of a certain Immanuel Kant, who would also like to be remembered!

This digression may have taken a little effort, but it might be helpful to understand the completely different problem of the third *Critique*. Here, by the way, we should not least remedy the already mentioned lack of academic philosophy, which consists of looking at the large systems of philosophy in a completely unsystematic way, namely only selectively or at best segmentally. The challenge of a system of knowledge is precisely to systematically open it up to understanding.

Kant stated that the general task of criticizing taste is either an art – and then using examples – or a science. In the latter case, this must be due to the nature of cognitive ability. Thus, it becomes a transcendental critique of taste, whose task is to bring the mutual relationship of understanding and imagination under rules (no laws, since the reflecting power of judgment cannot afford it) and to determine the conditions that make them possible.

The *CPJ* is thus exclusively concerned with the reflecting power of judgment, in which the particular is given and the universal is only 'suggested'.

> "The judgment of taste does not itself **postulate** the accord of everyone (only a logically universal judgment can do that, since it can adduce

---

[379] *CPuRe*, B XIII [109].

grounds); it only **ascribes** this agreement to everyone, as a case of the rule with regard to which it expects confirmation not from concepts but only from the consent of others."[380]

Nevertheless, the third *Critique* also stands entirely in the sign of the "Copernican turn", for the aesthetics and the teaching of ends, teleology, are no longer built up from the sensations of empirical nature as in the case of Hume and Burke, but on the basis of a subjective judgment, which is qualified for this. Although the reflecting power of judgment means the reversal of the relationship between the universal and the particular, it also requires its own law for this reversal, or in this particular case: a *maxim*.

Even this 'claim' to universality and general consent, which it asserts in its judgments on taste, obliges the reflecting power of judgment to give itself a law that gives this universalization a legitimate ground – which is the aforementioned common 'ground', and not Derrida's 'bridge', between *CPuRe* and *CPraRe*. Although the claim is not determining in the same way as in the theoretical judgment, the title of the universality of a judgment, even if it is only *suggested*, requires a principle that guarantees the condition of the possibility of this claim.

The condition of the possibility of judgment is always a question of transcendental discussion. Kant has found the transcendental principle of judgment, which legitimizes its claim to universality, in the *purposiveness of nature for our judgment*. The reflecting power of judgment imagines nature as a unit that specifies itself and makes itself tangible in favor of our judgment. Implicitly, it imputes nature to be the design of another, non-human mind, which nevertheless functions in form like the human mind. This mind is the basis of nature as a possibility for reflection. Only in this way could people ever come to the conclusion that there is something like order or disorder outside as within themselves, that something is beautiful or sublime. Beauty and sublimity represent the subjective side of this purposiveness, i.e. nature appears to us as if made by the underlying, reflected mind in such a way that we can contemplate or fear it with pleasure, in other words: that it appeals to us. These two subjective moments are combined in aesthetics.

This purposiveness also has an objective side, in which the underlying mind is assumed to act in such a way that the entire natural order has been

---

[380] *CPJ*, B 26[101]

appropriately harmonized by it and that it has created special beings that take this *end in themselves* as the sequence of cause and effect and become what we call *organisms* or *life*.[381] These natural objects are, subjectively considered, products of a reflection of the (material-objective) inner purposiveness of the phenomena, which can be concepts of spiritual (spirits, souls, consciousness, i.e. mental organisms) as well as spatio-temporal quality (animals, plants, humans as animals, i.e. biological organisms). Overall, these are notions of *organic orders*, which would include ideas that represent groups or societies as cultural or biological macro-organisms – or even *nature as an ecological or eco-social whole* (*CPJ* B 304 [252]). These ideas are characterized by the fact that the ends reflected therein always take the form of a system, because the result of these integral, self-organized and autopoietic associations are in turn ends, namely social, psychological or biological life. From this point of view, the newer, functional-structural systems theory according to Niklas Luhmann certainly finds a philosophical justification in the *Critique of the Power of Judgment*. It describes exactly which form of judgment must be tried so that something like 'functions' can be thought of as a 'system'. These functions are reflections of material-objective inner ends, which for us result in the concept of organic order, with which *we recognize every form of life – long before we understand in detail how this life is constructed*, whether it is biological or of another kind and above all: how it was created.

Another, much more extensive class of ideas are the mechanical or aggregated orders, which Kant, despite their frequency, treats as subordinate. Not every idea of order reflects the internal, organic purposiveness of an appearance, but – as in political reality – the relative purposiveness of objects, actions and events is much more frequently reflected. For this capacity contains the power to *form primary hypotheses* par excellence, so also in political judgment. Only in this way can individuals imagine that an increase in collective wages, for example, will have a beneficial effect on their own consumption, motivation to work and social justice – or will be negatively expedient and thus harmful for productivity, investment, their national position in international competition and, ultimately, even for social security, as unemployment rises. Since the whole of nature does not provide an answer to the question of whether the well-being of employees or perhaps the security and economic growth of companies is the higher end of nature even in the most anxious reflection, *political judgment remains*

---

[381] "I would say provisionally that a thing exists as a natural end **if it is cause and effect of itself** (although in a twofold sense)..." (*CPJ*, B 287 [243])

dependent on this very weak capacity of primary hypothesis formation, i.e. on the reflection of material-objectively relative purposiveness. Kant only briefly presents this form of judgment and completely excludes it from the rest of the investigation. This is another methodological decision that must not be followed here.

> "From this it can readily be seen that external purposiveness (advantageousness of one thing for another) can be regarded as an external natural end only under the condition that the existence of that for which it is advantageous, whether in a proximate or a distant way, is in itself an end of nature. This, however, can never be made out by mere contemplation of nature; thus it follows that relative purposiveness, although it gives hypothetical indications of natural ends, nevertheless justifies no absolute teleological judgments."[382]

Kant wanted to deal primarily with the problem of organic orders. The aggregated orders as notions of end with short range and high uncertainty are at least as important for the function of everyday political judgment. In the view of nature, however, they can be better depicted. Only with their help was it possible to provisionally distinguish and classify genera, species, classes and types of things of external nature – although it is not at all clear that in our modern understanding these classifications were 'rational' or even just appropriate to the object. It was not until 1753 that Linné systematically recorded the plant world through comparative observation, and Mendeleev and Meyer did not even discover the periodic system of chemical elements until 1869. Whereas previously all ideas generally only reflected aggregates of order in nature (relative purposiveness)[383], which seem quite arbitrary to us today despite their logical consistency, Linné created the first order system (inner purposiveness) and Mendeleev constructed – like Galilei and Newton – mechanical orders of nature. The determining power of judgment was already at work here. Decisive is the assumption that the power of judgment gives itself a maxim (no law) to make nature accessible, in other words to have a compass for *getting to know* and *tentatively understanding* the world before it can be constructed causally-mechanically as *knowledge*. Kant calls this *self-prescription of a heuristic rule* made by the power of judgment its "heuristic autonomy", because the rule applies only to the power of judgment itself

---

[382] *CPJ,* B 283 [241]

[383] Of course, this was only true as long as the natural orders were viewed in a positivist manner, i.e. without recourse to a divine Creator whose idea immediately calls for reflection on ultimate and supreme ends.

and not as a law for nature or freedom, for which *objective autonomy* would be necessary. *Heautonomy*, on the other hand, is *subjective autonomy*.[384]

This fascinating figure serves to put a weaker and provisional way of experiencing nature in thought alongside the causal-mechanical way of knowing nature through the understanding, which only succeeds with great difficulty, as the cultural and scientific history of mankind shows. As long as the physiological and chemical, i.e. mechanical principles, such as blood circulation and organs (e.g. liver) could not be determined, an assumed functional natural order was adhered to, with whose help the empirical phenomenon could not be *determined*, but at least *reflected upon*. The alchemistic theory of the equilibrium of the body's juices, for example, would be appropriate to the previous example, which justified such therapies as bloodletting or mercury baths. Constructions of this kind can easily be identified as results of a reflection of relative purposiveness.

This example should be looked at a little more closely, because the problem of political subjectivity already comes into view here, at the level of transcendental justification of the reflecting judgment. The blood circulation was discovered in 1628 by William Harvey and documented in his *Exercitatio anatomica de motu cordis et sanguinis*. The book, or rather the idea of the cycle, had a decisive influence on the first cyclical models of national economys. However, one must not overlook the fact that the medical model has indeed been mechanical since this discovery, whereas the economic cycle models have since borrowed the image of this mechanism only to at least *reflect* and *symbolize* the order of the economy if it cannot already be determined causally and mechanically – to this day. Exactly the same problem has arisen from the outset in the area of political order. People have only a *reflecting approach* to the idea of a political order outside themselves, whether they belong to it or not. They can therefore reflect political orders either as *organs* or *aggregates*, depending on whether a closed overall context is presented or only a limited section of it. Thus, it is already indicated that the *concept of order*, as it is to be opened up via teleology, will take a key position in the further discussion, because the fundamental question has already been asked: How can the subject think of an order and at the same time create or maintain its own individuality in relation to it? In nuce, the fields of 'individuality' and 'publicity' discussed in Part A have merged into one question, in which another unknown, namely the 'how', must be named. We have already met this unknown, but

---

[384] *CPJ*, First Introduction, p. 39 [28].

under the more obscure than explanatory title of 'aesthetics'. In the following it is now shown that the unknown with the full name " reflecting power of judgment" and above all, what astonishing achievements it produces that Kant himself had not noticed.

The *Critique of the Power of Judgment* leads to the question of criticism in general. Under the titles 'Beautiful', 'Sublime' and 'Ends', therefore, the conditions under which Kant's first two critiques were made possible can be found, but at the same time the wealth that makes people's coexistence visible from a genuinely subjective side, which cannot be reduced to interests, human needs or the duty to realize a good life. Political subjectivity has also a moment of 'heautonomy', which is accessible to the critical procedure and at the same time makes this procedure possible. In the *CPJ*, the critique of knowledge in the subject becomes self-referential, i.e. circular, for the first time.

> "The dogmatic treatment of a concept is thus that which is lawful for the determining, the critical that which is lawful merely for the reflecting power of judgment."[385]

Apart from the double problem of factual analysis (beautiful, sublime, ends) and the systemic function in the *CPJ* for the whole of the *Critiques*, a third difficulty is added, namely the methodically necessary segregation and purification of the individual forms of reflecting judgment for the aforementioned factual analysis for Kant's projects. This procedure is now to be examined and read against the grain, for we are now leaving the bottom of simple interpretation in order to start our own enterprise, which will take Kant's third *Critique* beyond its own limits. For this book is a philosophical burning glass that can perhaps, when held on a combustible matter, ignite a new light of philosophical knowledge.

---

[385] *CPJ*, B 329 [266].

B.1.3 From Kant's Method to the Counter-Method: The 'Back-Mixing' of Pure Forms of Judgment

A central task of the investigation is now to come to terms with the various modes of the reflecting judgment. The exact consideration of these individual forms is unavoidable here. All the power of reflecting judgment, including the problematic unity of aesthetic and teleological judgment, must be explored in terms of a genuine political judgment. The entire process of 'dissection' of the judgments of reflection[386] must be taken into account, for it has proved to be a serious shortcoming in the approaches of Arendt, Vollrath and Steinberger that they wanted to transform the reflecting power of judgment as a whole into a political philosophy, without analysis of the individual achievements of its different modes.

Political subjectivity, according to the guiding thesis of the present study, is a rationally understandable way of thinking that is expressed in judgments that must be of a special kind. The political is therefore not an empirically provable characteristic of spatio-temporal objects and events, but a mental achievement and can only be seen in its quality through this. In political judgment, the understanding (in the sense of the categories as concepts and functions of thought related to intuition) is transcended under the direction of ideas. Under the unity of this judgment there is a relationship between *receptivity*, which is a characteristic of formal sensuality and thus of the nature-recognizing mind, and *spontaneity*, which characterizes the consciousness of freedom. This means that nature and freedom[387] (formaliter) meet in aesthetic and teleological, but also in political judgment – in the judgment of the concrete, historical subject, whereby it first brings something like politics into the world. This unusual

---

[386] See *CPJ*, First Introduction, p. 53 [39]

[387] The transcendentally deduced, i.e. legitimized concept of freedom, opens up the prospect of a *second nature*, as Kant himself puts it, which is subject to another form of causality, namely the *causality of freedom*, in which not every 'cause' is effectuated by an 'effect' – this nature in the mechanical sense isn't but the sum of all chains of causes and effects that run from the origin of the world through the past into the future – but a cause can actually be causative in itself; it is possible to think of *new chains of cause and effect* that begin with us. This means the expression 'spontaneity' in the Kantian sense: to be the *author of one's own nature*, which only has to borrow the *form of law* from that mechanical first nature which the understanding recognizes with the help of receptive sensuality.

idea requires practice, because it contradicts our intuitions, which are conditioned by a radical empirical way of speaking and thinking about politics in everyday life, that politics is above all something that happens to us and of which we are the object. With the transformation of the reflecting power of judgment, a completely different, subjective image of politics emerges, which is no longer fixed on the sphere of the state, but on the peculiar, exotic capacity itself to be able to think something like politics at all. This proves that the simplest individuals achieve metaphysical high performances, for everyday language may be what it wants it to be: the judgments on which it is based reveals also in the political an understanding of a hyperphysical world which has long become habitual and which is many times more complex and demanding than the marketable spiritual teachings of esotericism.

So, there is a *metaphysics after the Critique*, with the help of which a critical use of the supersensible is brought within the reach of science.[388] This is the problematic thesis, along which the reading and the material must be brought up. In the meantime it has become clear that this cannot be metaphysics as 'dogmatics', as Kant had the *Critique of Practical Reason* followed in the form of the *Metaphysics of Morals*.[389] Kant also pointed out from the outset that the *CPJ*, which seeks out and exposes the conditions of the possibility of aesthetic and teleological forms of judgment, is not capable of metaphysics, i.e. of dogmatics.[390] If it were permissible to call 'metaphysics' a doctrine of judgment that analyzes and organizes only the various moments and connections of forms of judgment already found, then this investigation could be called *political metaphysics*. However, it is not permitted. Because an essential moment of all metaphysics is completely missing here. The political doctrine of judgment to be developed here

---

[388] See *CPJ*, First Introduction, p. 60 [44].

[389] At the beginning of this study, I was still convinced that there had to be a *political metaphysics* in Kant's sense, i.e. a completely independent, conceptually autonomous ability to form political judgments. This assumption has increasingly proven to be an obstacle, and it was ultimately wrong.

[390] "Thus with this I bring my entire critical enterprise to an end. I shall proceed without hindrance to the doctrinal part, in order, if possible, to win yet from my increasing age some time still favorable to that. It is self-evident that there will be no special part for the power of judgment in that, since in regard to that critique serves instead of theory; rather, in accordance with the division of philosophy into theoretical and practical parts, and the division of pure philosophy into the very same parts, the metaphysics of nature and of morals will constitute that enterprise." (*CPJ*, B X [58])

does not have its own, uniform principle. Political subjectivity – this much can perhaps be anticipated – is, as a concept, a philosophy of reflection. All further discussions must not obscure the fact that the philosophical competence for political judgment in the subject comes from a conditioning of a much more universal faculty. In other words: Aesthetic and teleological power of judgment must first be placed under certain conditions before a form of judgment is formed that can give the predicate of the political a philosophical meaning. In summary, it should be noted that under the guidance of reflecting judgment no path leads to metaphysics in the strict sense, that it is therefore decidedly not a matter of political metaphysics and finally that such a teaching would only be possible in the area of determining judgment, i.e. in practical philosophy.

The first of these conditions is now the inversion of Kant's method. This means here exclusively his restriction to distil in the *CPJ only pure forms of judgment* in order to process them. For if we further analyze all the refined figures of the beautiful, sublime and purposiveness in judgments, we will never see anything 'political' in any way, but at best questions of phenomenology, fundamental ontology or deconstruction. Going the other way seems more promising. The subjective, political judgment in everyday life often contains several (sometimes all) moments of reflecting judgment, which are treated in the *CPJ*, if one examines it only a little more carefully. My judgment of the 1995 wrapping of the Reichstag, an art performance by Christo and Jeanne-Claude, combines the (more or less strong) feeling of *sublime* in the face of this large, representative and historic building with the enjoyment of the *beauty* of the work of art that was made of it, and finally with the *end* or *purpose* that the aesthetic entity could have for Berlin's political culture, for the Federal Republic of Germany and for myself as a part of it.

This composite in the political judgment should not be disassembled in order to make the parts fit into the judgment templates of the *CPJ*. That would neutralize the political quality of any judgment before it would have revealed its secret. We will do exactly the opposite: The *CPJ* is *disassembled and reassembled* so that what a political judgment is becomes visible.

Fig. 10: The *Wrapped Reichstag*, 1995, drawing by Christo

The initial aim is therefore to formulate a negative criterion for the formation of political judgments: The political judgment is not identical with any one of the various forms of reflecting judgment. The work on the text of the *CPJ* requires special hermeneutics that satisfies the requirement of finding a composite judgment in a work that only deals with unmixed, 'pure' judgments or analytically dissects mixed judgments in order to arrive at their pure elements. For the next steps, Kant's own method must first be discussed in more detail.

In the *CPJ*, the formal-subjective and the material-objective purposiveness are distinguished according to the principle of the purposiveness of nature under the concepts of reflection[391] (formal/material and subjective/objective).[392] Under these two headings, aesthetic and teleological judgments can be described, which constitute the division of the *CPJ* into two separate parts. The aesthetic judgment is once again divided into the judg-

---

[391] Cf. for an understanding of the concepts of reflection the chapter *On the Amphiboly of the Concepts of Reflection* in the *CPuRe*, B 316-324[366-370], especially titles 3. and 4. in B 322-324. Concepts of reflection in the transcendental sense are comparative schemes for testing the affiliation of ideas to sensuality or reason.

[392] The two other types of purposiveness are not dealt with further, as they do not present any problems. *Material-subjective* purposiveness is the judgment of the senses by feeling stimulus, *formal-objective* purposiveness lies in every geometric figure.

ment of the *beautiful* and the *sublime*, and the latter into the *mathematically sublime* and the *dynamically sublime*. This subdivision corresponds to the reference of the aesthetic judgment to indefinite concepts of the understanding in the beautiful (e.g. form) or to equally indeterminate ideas of reason in the sublime (God, reason, freedom); the latter is divided, depending on the power it exerts on cognitive ability or on desire, into judgment on the mathematically sublime or the dynamically sublime. This should only be mentioned here in summary, because for the time being it is merely a matter of showing that Kant's sole aim in breaking down the reflecting judgment into its species was to isolate pure judgments.

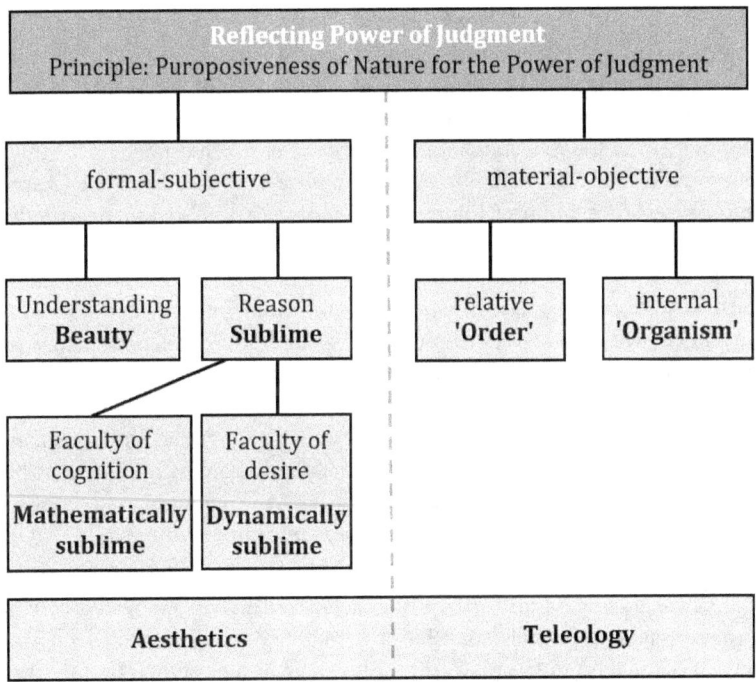

Chart I: Thematic structure of the *Critique of the Power of Judgment*

In order to really get these different types of judgment pure, Kant refers them in the following text of the *CPJ* only to nature. The process is not only similar, but undoubtedly identical to the isolation of 'ideal types', as the method has been called since Max Weber.[393] It is extremely important to

---

[393] As is well known, Weber was not the inventor of the method of the ideal typing, but he made it known through his masterful application. Note, by the way, that the formation of ideal types itself is a process that requires reflecting

note that Kant did not mean, as was often assumed by the commentators, that beautiful and sublime things can only be found in nature.[394] Kant's restriction to nature is a methodical decision that should serve as a solution to a special problem, namely the 'impurity' of most judgments in everyday's speech.[395] Nature is only the *catalyzer* to make the distinctive forms of

---

judgment. Here, too, Kant's philosophy is appropriately circular, because *he uses the faculty he describes*. Kant's own reflecting power of judgment in this case, namely the description of itself, is the discovery of the notions of 'free' or 'raw' natures as the ideal basis for the description of 'pure', unmixed judgments.

[394] Cf., for example, Kulenkampff, Jens, *Kant's Logik des ästhetischen Urteil* [Kant's Logic of the Aesthetic Judgment], Frankfurt 1978; on pp. 138-141 he deals with "pure judgments of taste" and considers as sources of error only "stimulation and emotion", with which Kant wants to escape sensualism. The various forms of judgment of the reflecting judgment are out of the question. He misinterprets or misquotes *CPJ*, B 76 [129] in order *to assume a complete connection between art and nature*. His citation of Kant's statement that art is "*always* restricted to the conditions of agreement with nature" (Kulenkampff quotes) is misleading and meets only the need of the interpreter. Art is by no means *always* limited to these conditions of conformity, but *only* (now another way of citing): "... if, *as is appropriate*, we here consider first only the sublime in objects of nature (that in art is, after all, always restricted to the conditions of agreement with nature)." First, then, it is only about the sublime in art and second, it becomes clear that this "always" refers to the method of the *CPJ*, in which the agreement has already been made to analyze only judgments that are as pure as possible. For this reason, the subject area remains ("free" or "raw") nature, in favor of a better methodological decomposition of the judgments into their types.

[395] In his second Stanford lecture on the 200th anniversary of the *CPJ* under the title *Explanation of Aesthetic Judgment*, Dieter Henrich also repeated only an old, but no longer applicable mistake of commentators: "From now on the only activities engaged in the play were the very activities shown by the *Critique of Pure Reason* to be operative in the constitution of objects from given intuitions in space and time. Consequently, natural objects and products of the skilled crafts had to be moved into the position of the paradigm case of the beautiful, while the work of art became the subject of a complex theory with a richer set of premises." (Henrich, *Aesthetic Judgment and the Moral Image of the World*, Stanford 1992, p. 29-56, here p. 35.). This claim is obviously wrong, and in more than just one respect. Not only are natural objects certainly not the "paradigm case of the beautiful" but just fitting examples; it is also a big mistake to think that the *forms* of intuition as exposed in the transcendental aesthetics are involved in aesthetic judgment. They have, as media of *construction* of objects of *possible experience*, namely natural and mathematical laws, strictly no business here, where only empirical space and time are in the play. Georg Kohlers' related assumption of a conceptual dependence of the *CPJ* on the *CPuRe*, which

judgment visible in the analysis.

There is an unmixed judgment of the sublime just as there is of the beautiful only in relation to nature and, in the case of the sublime, only to "raw" nature. An "...example of an unmixed, pure judgment that completely fits the critique of aesthetic judgment" can only be had if one is careful that...

> "...the sublime must not be shown in products of art (e.g., buildings, columns, etc.), where a human end determines the form as well as the magnitude, nor in natural things **whose concept already brings with it a determinate end** (e.g., animals of a known natural determination), but rather in raw nature (and even in this only insofar as it by itself brings with it neither charm nor emotion from real danger), merely insofar as it contains magnitude."[396]

Many things of nature in our perception are therefore completely unsuitable from the outset to give examples of pure judgment, because they have long since been cultivated, studied and classified. In other words, their objective-relative purposiveness (teleological) has already blended with the purely subjective purposiveness (aesthetic). From this point on Kant therefore treats the feeling of the sublime only in relation to the raw nature[397], and the backmixing of what is separated here is the task of the *reconstruction of the political judgment*. And as a hypothesis it is now also permissible that the political judgment does not occur in the *CPJ*, because in principle it can *only be thought of as a mixed judgment* and thus, for methodological reasons, has escaped the attention of the great systematist, who in the two parts of the *CPJ* and in the two books of the first part only wanted to break down judgments until their pure forms can be represented. It may have escaped Kant's attention that something specific

---

is supposedly unbecoming for aesthetics, is equally wrong; this time it is called "parallelization strategy"; cf. Kohler, Georg, *Geschmackmacksurteil und ästhetische Erfahrung. Contributions to the interpretation of Kant's "Kritik der ästhetischen Urteilskraft"* [Judgment of Taste and Aesthetic Experience. Contributions to the Interpretation of Kant's Critique of Aesthetic Judgment], Kantstudien Ergänzungshefte, Vol. 111, Berlin, N. Y. 1980. **These misconceptions touch so much on the centre of the philosophical efforts of the *CPJ* that a manifest misunderstanding of Kants method in this work and his entire philosophy of nature must be assumed.**

[396] *CPJ*, B 90 [p. 136].

[397] Although he had already introduced this method without comment, as the quotation here in footnote 77 shows (*CPJ*, B 76 [129]).

is lost if one breaks down the entire wealth of reflecting judgment into its individual parts, to which it is difficult to draw conclusions from these parts. If Kant had not been so considerate as to give the reflecting power of judgment as taste a nickname such as "common sense", a name that resounds and attracts a certain amount of attention, perhaps no one would have had the idea of searching for a political philosophy in his third *Critique*. Here it becomes apparent why the previous attempts to embed the *CPJ* conclusively in a political philosophy have gained so little depth and persuasiveness.

The systematic and comprehensible production of pure judgments in the field of aesthetic and teleological thinking raises the first question here as to whether there could ever be such a thing as a *pure political judgment*. For Kant, 'pure' means 1) without any admixture of sensual appeal, 2) legislative and 3) exclusively related to form.

> "Taste is always still barbaric when it needs the addition of **stimulations** and **emotions** for satisfaction, let alone if it makes these into the standard for its approval."[398]

Only such a judgment is a "*Pure Judgment of Taste*" (*CPJ* B 38[108], title of § 13) and differs from a judgment of the senses in that it is a formal-aesthetic judgment and does not refer to the convenience or inconvenience of the object, i.e. is independent of "stimulus and emotion". Kant, for example, considers color to be the reason for the comfort of an object and drawing to be part of its form[399]; only the latter is suitable for beauty (*CPJ* B 42[p. 110]). So, taste does not consist in sensual perception, i.e. sensation, but exclusively in reflection on this sensual perception.

> "**Emotion**, a sensation in which agreeableness is produced only by means of a momentary inhibition followed by a stronger outpouring of the vital force, does not belong to beauty at all."[400]

It is precisely this process of inhibition and subsequent release that belongs to the sublime, where *emotion* has its place. We need to stay here a moment in order to make a critical reflection. On this basis, could the political judgment already be dismissed as a *feeling*? Would the entire presentation

---

[398] *CPJ*, B 38 [108]

[399] A remark in art philosophy: This statement does not contradict the view that a relationship between several colours and/or surfaces belongs to the *form* of the object, but rather *justifies it* in the first place.

[400] *CPJ*, B 43[111]

made here be untenable from the outset on the basis of the assertion that nothing in a political judgment is anything but a sensory stimulus, interest or instrumental reason anyway, if no practical philosophy, i.e. no normative claim is taken as a basis? This is a serious and very justified objection against the background of the European tradition of political philosophy. Normative political theory only recognises a judgment as politically qualified if it is bound to values that aim at socialisation. The objection is not simply rejected here, its treatment is only postponed. The demands of practical philosophy in this field must be taken seriously. First of all, the investigation will lead to an attempt to separate practical and political philosophy in such a way that their distinction is advantageous for both (cf. here chapter B.1.8). It is a fashion of 20th century philosophy to plead for a 'weak' and in this weakness little contoured concept of reason. Here, surprisingly, it amounts to showing 'weak reason' than has already been at work for a long time, precisely in the use of political reason.

Kant's demands for the representation of pure judgments are supplemented by another, namely the important separation of purely aesthetic and purely teleological judgments. This means that there must be no trace of teleology in the aesthetic judgment. Among the mixed judgments are such *sublime* ideas as the famous vaulted, starry sky above us or the ocean as the source of life – but these are secretly "pure *teleological* judgments" (*CPJ* B 119 [p. 129]). And although the judgment of taste does not constitute an interest, there is, for example in the judgment on the beauty of nature, an interest that is "related to the moral interest" (*CPJ* B 169 [p. 180]). This moral interest sees itself in an order of end, the highest end of which is the moral end, with which, however, it would already be a subject of teleology – which is why Kant had to mention it specifically and in advance in the deduction of pure aesthetic judgments (*CPJ* B 171-172[p. 181]). It seems that teleology holds the whole of the *CPJ* and the system of the *Critiques* together – as one would expect from a philosophical teaching of ends.

> "To be sure, in the judging especially of living objects in nature, e.g., a human being or a horse, objective purposiveness is also commonly taken into account for judgingc its beauty; but in that case the judgment is also no longer purely aesthetic, i.e., a mere judgment of taste. Nature is no longer judged as it appears as art, but to the extent that it really is art (albeit superhuman); and the teleological judgment serves as the foundation for the aesthetic and as a condition of which the latter must

take account."[401]

The same objects can be seen from an aesthetic or teleological point of view, e.g. when looking at the beauty of nature. We have favour for nature because it is so rich in beauty that we can admire without interest; but the same nature itself appears to us with favour in teleological judgment, because its beauty stimulates us as a member in the system of its whole to form culture.[402]

The *CPJ* has a clear inner connection through its dichotomy, although it must be recognized that, as Kant emphasizes several times, it is about different reflecting achievements. The depictions of the beautiful and sublime are, as the method requires, always based on pure judgments, but the like occurs, if at all, only in the rarest exceptional cases in everyday perception and in historical experience. Kant is therefore also a little embarrassed about apt examples.[403] For if the presentation of the reflecting power of judgment is indeed at the same time to think – and that always means: to judge – a development theory of concrete-human abilities, as is assumed here, then the problem is that examples are often only connected with a certain context of human culture and history and therefore cannot be universalized as illustrations of the performance of reflection, which changes from epoch to epoch.

What is to be attempted here, namely the *controlled backmixing* of the forms of judgment, shows how extraordinarily artificial and yet – measured against the difficulties of systematic processing – artfully the mutually separated achievements of reason in the text of the *CPJ* are alternately dependent on one another in order to explain the de facto judgments of everyday consciousness. Surprising, however, is how little is to be found in all the reflections on everyday perception and on a possibly separate ability to the political, i.e. on a political judgment with its own reflective-logical structure.

There is no political judgment of this kind, especially a pure judgment of the political. It is not even conceivable in the horizon of critical

---

[401] *CPJ*, B 188-189 [p. 190]

[402] *CPJ*, B 303 [251] with footnote.

[403] As already became clear shortly before in the quotation from *CPJ*, B 89 [136], the examples must be conditioned by all requirements of the method, if they are to be appropriate to the thing.

philosophy. The political judgment that takes place in thought is always a composition of the different kinds of reflecting judgment. The political judgment is a mixed, a blended judgment par excellence. It is only available as such. In political judgments, there is always and without exception a reference to the ideas of nature, freedom and the proper/improper coincidence of the two, i.e. all pure forms of judgment must complement each other in order to form a political judgment.

A particular consequence of this first, preliminary observation is further in its negativity: there is no *Critique of Political Reason* or *Judgment*! Without a special form of political judgment that can be presented as 'pure', there is no reason at all to even think of a critique of this power of judgment. This is probably the most important reason for the fact that Kant did not even mention such an expansion of the critical enterprise. The impossibility of a critique of political reason is, from this point of view, obvious. Kant's other approaches to this question are discussed below.[404] It is precisely the historically documented fixation of political philosophy on the morality of the political that provides an unmanageable amount of illustrations for the fact that an autonomy of the political, as Hannah Arendt demanded it, has never been in prospect.[405] But also the mechanistic downside of this political speculative thinking typical of modernity, which tried the concept of *nature* instead of *freedom* (Machiavelli, Hobbes, Schmitt), has never gone beyond the *functionality of the political*. Up to now it has not been possible to create a kind of *philosophical dignity of the political*, perhaps even through its subjects.

---

[404] Cf., for example, the study by Ulrich Sassenbach, *Der Begriff des Politischen bei Immanuel Kant*, Würzburg 1992, discussed here in Chapter B.1.8.

[405] Ernst Vollrath claims, among other things in his *Grundlegung*, loc. cit., pp. 138-166, that the Anglo-American tradition of political philosophy had guaranteed real autonomy as an "optional field of action", but this pragmatic concession, which is based on some historical experiences, has preserved its own history as a surrogate of a truly philosophical analysis of origin and therefore never discussed the *possibility of this history*. Instead, the history of Anglo-American liberalism was put into one with a philosophically ennobled idea of politics in a questionable way. With his "philosophical theory of the political" Vollrath therefore does not work out the political in liberalism – which would be desirable and a great merit – but only protects in this way the **frivolous superficiality of Anglo-American self-reflection in matters of political theory**. If that were in fact all that philosophy could find there in political terms, then this liberal tradition would rightly be denounced as naive universalism or poorly disguised ethnocentrism.

It is therefore part of the fundamental and thus methodological orientation of the present investigation that it is not at all a question of understanding the pure execution of the judgment and its immaculate structure. In this case, a 'pure political judgment' should have been expected. That doesn't exist. There is no type of political judgment of its own, such as a type of judgment on the dynamically sublime. All one finds are modes of political judgments, which owe themselves to the composition of different types of judgment. If the right framework conditions are formulated, one can use the *CPJ* to filter out **what can be contained in a political judgment and what must be contained in it so that it can be qualified as political**. Kant had to break open and separate the judgment of taste and the teleological judgment for the sake of a systematic presentation that could be sequenced in a coherent progression of chapters. Since the method of a supposedly still to be written critique of political judgment, which cannot exist, should not be understood here, it should remain constantly present that we are not interested at all in pure judgments. Only as a component of the political judgment, which itself is never pure, does it become useful for us.

There is still a lot to be said about the separation of practical (moral) and political judgments. At this point, let us just say in advance that it will not be a question of demanding or constructing the scheme of moral-free politics. Contrary to the pure judgment of aesthetic, the mixed judgment by means of teleology and beauty always refers to morality and it can very well be bound to an interest, in the way that the individual can want the existence of a thing, or not at all come to a political judgment other than on the way of the will around the thing in such a judgment. In pure aesthetic judgment, on the other hand, it does not depend on the existence of the thing to be judged.[406]

---

[406] Again, it seems as if Derrida wanted to hypnotize the Kantian text so that he would no longer oppose his interpretation, as in the following statement: "I-am-pleased-at-my-pleasure [Je-me-plais-à-me-plaire-à] of that which is beautiful. To the extent it doesn't exist." (Derrida, *Die Wahrheit in der Malerei*, loc. cit., p. 66). Did Kant not clearly explain that existence or non-existence is not the measure, *not the criterion*?

> "One must not be in the least biased in favor of the existence of the thing, but must be entirely indifferent in this respect in order to play the judge in matters of taste."[407]

This "being in favor" for the existence of a thing is represented in the concept of interest, which already plays an important role in Kant's moral philosophy. At no other point in this critical work does Kant address the question of the different types of interest as thoroughly as here. The continuation of the passage just quoted makes it clear:

> "But we cannot explain this sentence, which is of excellent significance, any better than if we counter the pure disinterested pleasure in taste with that which is connected with interest: especially if at the same time we can be sure that there are not more kinds of interest than they are just now to be named."[408]

In the note to this passage Kant states that the judgment of taste is not based on any interest – like the judgment of the senses – but also produces none – like the moral judgment.[409] "Only in society it becomes interesting to have taste, of which the reason is subsequently indicated." (ibid.) As we will see in the following, the political judgment is only interesting in society, but it is based on interest, generates interest and is at the same time without interest in an aesthetic or theoretical way. A political judgment can be sensual, moral and aesthetic at the same time. This is a paradox that must be resolved. This will be done shortly. Preliminary evidence of the entanglements Kant himself has seen can be found in the first section of the analysis:

> "Given representations in a judgment can be empirical (hence aesthetic); however, the judgment that is made by means of them is logical if in the judgment they are related to the object. Conversely, however, even if the given representations were to be rational but related in a judgment solely to the subject (its feeling), then they are to that extent always aesthetic."[410]

---

[407] CPJ, B 6-7 [91].
[408] *CPJ*, B 7 [p. 91].
[409] Cf. CPraRe, A 141.
[410] *CPJ*, B 5 [90].

The various forms of the political judgment will show how broad the continuum is of what can justifiably be called political on the basis of the concept of political subjectivity to be developed here. It remains to be noted that there is no urgency and that it is not even possible to follow Kant's claim to distill pure judgments in view of political judgments. This claim was, of course, quite rightly made in a critique of the subject's power of judgment. On the contrary, the problem here will be to combine the pure judgments in such a way that we can make them speak for our purposes.

Finally, the 'reversal' of Kant's method also includes the fact that the deduction of the transcendental principle[411] is not to be examined in detail, but rather is already being worked on with this principle itself as a guideline, as is clearly demonstrated in the following section.[412]

The investigation applied here is not a philological-philosophical analysis of the individual steps of proof of the third *Critique*. This is already evident from the guidelines, because here the political subjectivity, as it is to be recovered in the *CPJ*, is to be examined. The exact analysis of the *CPJ* as a transcendental procedure of evidence and as a systemic conclusion of Kant's critical philosophy, as it already exists several times, must always proceed in considerably smaller steps.

---

[411] Namely the formal purposiveness of nature for our power of judgment – whereby the power of judgment gives laws only to itself, but not to nature or freedom, which Kant calls "heautonomy"; see *CPJ*, First Introduction, p. 39.

[412] Nevertheless, the contra-method developed here for the analysis of pure judgments may be a hermeneutic instrument to make Kant's deduction and all other arguments more understandable. On this basis, Georg Kohler, for example, might have come to a different (and the only correct) conclusion than the complete failure he attested Kant's deduction, because it was biased in a terminology "whose original place is the theory of (scientifically-determining) objective recognition." This has allegedly resulted in "constructions unrelated to the subject matter", "which cannot be identified in the matter itself, the beauty and the way it becomes intersubjectively accessible to us and ultimately the subject of specific assessment."(Kohler, Georg, *Geschmacksurteil und ästhetische Erfahrung. Beiträge zur Auslegung von Kants "Kritik der ästhetischen Urteilskraft"* [Judgment of Taste and Aesthetic Experience. Contributions to the Interpretation of Kant's "Critique of the Power of Judgment], Kantstudien, supplementary issue, vol. 111, Berlin, N. Y. 1980, p. V and VI)

Conversely, the approach implemented here could contribute to making the *CPJ* visible in the variety of problems it synthesises and to making its results plausible. From a certain problem (political subjectivity) the general problem-solving strategy (*CPJ*) can probably best be checked for its coherence and suitability. In a sense, therefore, a thetic and less problematic approach must be taken here with regard to the text of the *CPJ*. No attempt is being made here at any point to make the evidence of the *CPJ* an issue, to criticise it or even to improve it.[413]

---

[413] The relevant literature has nevertheless been worked through and can be found in appropriate places. The comments by Ernst Cassirer, Friedrich Kaulbach, Alexis Philonenko, Volker Gerhardt and Reinhard Brandt were particularly helpful and inspiring for our purposes.

B.1.4 Transcendental Nature and Political Judgment: The Principle of Judgment in Political Use

All political philosophy has had a connection to nature since Aristotle. Political Aristotelianism as a whole was based on its own concept of nature, which had nothing to do with modern natural mechanics, which, at least since Galileo and Bacon, has been characterized by a.) the applicability of mathematics to objects in space and time and b.) the experimental test procedure of hypotheses about the lawful constitution of nature. Aristotle's teleological concept of nature consisted in the ontological assumption of the perfectibility of all beings. The most important thing was to correspond to one's own nature. Man distinguished himself by fulfilling his nature only and exclusively in the political community, *intra muros*, within the walls of the polis. *Ex urbe*, outside of the city, he was animal, object, barbarian and stranger. Man and nature thus belonged essentially together in their mutual dependence and the polis was "the metaphysical biotope of man"[414], thus itself a piece of pure nature. Natural teleology was also the basis of the Stoa, only there it was already universalistic and extended to the whole of humanity.[415] The same congruence of good law and good order with the pattern of nature applies to European natural law. Although modern, individualistic contractualism breaks with the unity of nature and the human community, the theoretical basis still remains a speculative state of nature, from which mankind is led out with sovereign and social contracts.[416] This is only mentioned to make it clear that it is not strange at all if in the method by which the content of political philosophy in the *CPJ* is to be deciphered, the concept of nature has not only an optional but a constitutive function.[417] The transcendental-

---

[414] This apt formulation comes from Wolfgang Kersting in *Die politische Philosophie des Gesellschaftsvertrags*, Darmstadt 1994, p. 8.

[415] "But the true law is the right reason which is in harmony with nature, which flows into all, which is consistent, eternal, which calls to duty by orders, which discourages deception, but which does not in vain command or forbid the righteous but does not move the nefarious by orders and prohibition." (Marcus Tullius Cicero, *De re publica* [On the Commonwealth], III, 22", Stuttgart 1979, p. 281.)

[416] See here chapter A.1.5.

[417] Investigating this complex of natural foundations in political philosophy, Eric Voegelin turned on an Aristotelian basis and with critical intent against the modern concept of nature in *What is Nature?* in: Voegelin, *Anamnesis*, London

theoretical – and that always means: subjective – turn of Kant's terminology as a whole must be taken into account, also in application to the concept of nature.[418] This will have considerable consequences and open up analytical possibilities for a new political philosophy.

The restriction of the applications of reflecting judgment to nature, it was just claimed, had been a methodical compulsion to be able to present pure judgments. It was promised to test a *controlled backmixing* of these judgments. Now the title of the section suddenly announces nature as the basis of the political judgment. How can this obvious contradiction be resolved?

In this context it must be noted that for the methodical purification of judgments, nature does not appear in the text as singulartantum (a single one for totality), but always bears a predicate, namely as 'free' or 'raw' nature. As the many examples in the *CPJ* show, this nature is identical with the landscapes, things and creatures that we have associated with this word since Romanticism. Nature as a concept, however, falls under a completely different kind of presentation. Only a certain context, namely all events in space and time thought under a continuous causality[419], is suitable for a *concept* of nature, which in turn is suitable for a transcendental principle that requires critique of judgment. It must be able to found knowledge and be confirmed by reason, a "conceptus ratiocinatus"[420]. In this sense, *nature as an appearance* itself is only the *representation of a nature in itself*, of which reason has an idea[421]. Only through this extension *from word to concept* and from word to idea is the unity of nature as a concept capable of a *symbolic hypotyposis*, i.e. it is underpinned – albeit always inappropriately – by a sensual form, whereby it is presented.[422] Only in this form is it possible to think nature as a unity. In order to be

---

1978, pp. 71-88.

[418] Volker Gerhardt's most thorough and fruitful reflections on this topic to date can be found in Chapter VI "Nature and Politics" of his treatise *Immanuel Kants Entwurf "Zum Ewigen Frieden". Eine Theorie der Politik* [Immanuel Kant's Draft "On Eternal Peace". A Theory of Politics], Darmstadt 1995, pp. 107-25. The train of thought, the possibility of which he first discussed there, is carried out here in all steps up to its systematic endpoint.

[419] *CPJ*, B 116 [p. 151].

[420] *CPJ*, B 330[p. 267].

[421] *CPJ*, B 116 [p. 151].

[422] This fascinating process of symbolic hypotyposis will be discussed in detail later; cf. chap. B.1.7.2.2 on *Beauty: Morality and Law*.

considered a 'ground of possible knowledge', nature must be thought of as a unit according to the formal condition of time. Empirical and specifically different natures can, however, still be causes in an infinite variety of ways[423]. Although they belong to 'nature in general' when it is thought as a unity of principles in space and time, apart from these purely formal spatiotemporal conditions they are determined by much more specific conditions. A distinction must therefore be made between *empirical natures* and the *concept of nature*, which makes the former conceivable as a unity.[424] This section is only concerned with the latter.

The transcendental principle of judgment is, as already mentioned, the formal purposiveness of nature for judgment. Therefore, the idea of a possible political judgment as a certain way of looking at nature needs to be discussed. If nature in its unity determines the function of all reflecting judgment as a transcendental principle, then political judgment must also fall under this principle. In a way, a conditional relationship that is now known is reversed here. The 'ecological turn' in the consciousness of the public and thus in politics, which is becoming increasingly global, assumes a dependence of nature on the political judgment of mankind. In it, however, the word 'nature' is meant again, albeit in a much broader sense than the romantic one. Nature here is the idea of all organic and inorganic events and cycles on our planet. This idea still does not qualify nature as a concept in the sense of transcendental philosophy. Nature only becomes a concept where – transcendental-philosophically speaking – it constitutes *the condition of the possibility of reflecting judgment* and in our particular case: *the possibility of political judgment*. For our concern, therefore, politics as a form of thinking, i.e. of reflecting judgment, is dependent on a concept of nature, which provides the thinking with any incomplete and provisional totality of nature as a basis for reflection. There is, so to speak, an ecology

---

[423] *CPJ*, B XXXIII [p. 70].

[424] The distinction between a.) empirical natures produced by the imagination, b.) a practical nature according to the law of a causality of freedom, c.) "free" and "raw" nature, and finally d.) the concept of reason of nature as totality, cannot be found even in such important commentaries as that of Wolfgang Bartuschat; cf. *Zum systematischen Ort von Kants Kritik der Urteilskraft* [On the Systematic Site of Kant's Critique of the Power of Judgment], Frankfurt 1972: The optional function of "free" and "raw" nature for the reflecting judgment on beauty and sublimity, which is also constitutive for the method of the *CPJ*, but not for the judgments themselves, is not noticed either.

of the physical world and one of thinking.[425] The first is inconceivable without the second or would never have become explorable and technically reconstructable.

The capacity for reflecting judgment therefore means that *political thinking must also be a way of assessing nature*, for example in the way individuals reflect on the forms of living together and thus on the organization of public order. But even the noticing and the recognition of other individuals as members of this order, especially as equals, is a completely uncertain type of reflection and, as is well known, a recent historical achievement which, moreover, is still far from being a general cultural asset of all peoples today. And it is precisely in the name of equality that the essential equality of human individuals has already been ignored in order to force a homogenization of their external characteristics. A brief historical reminder is intended to illustrate this:

> "Courage, good Sansculottes, double your vigilance; no rest while the hatchet of the law has not struck all the conspirators, the traitors, all those who oppose democracy; it is a just war against the enemies of the human race." (*Journal du vrai Jacobin*, No. 14, June 7, 1794)

The bourgeois and socialist revolutions were similar in that in the feudal epochs of all cultures they recognized only ideologically legitimized forms of exploitation. Accordingly, they saw in it an ideology-critically precisely determinable suppression of actually equals. The doctrine immediately following Marx did not denounce the concealment of true production conditions as 'priestly deceit', i.e. the event of feudal and bourgeois class rule as deliberate deceit by the owners of the means of production to 'objectively' equals. The historical as well as the dialectical variant of materialism are completely opposed to this naive theory of consciousness and conspiracy. However, the powerful vulgate of this political doctrine, which moved the masses, rearranged the globe and now cost many millions of forgotten lives, believed it knew exactly who belonged to the deceivers. Thus, the persecutors found many innocent people among their

---

[425] Cf. the evolutionary works of Gregory Bateson: *Ökologie des Geistes. Anthropologische, psychologische, biologische und epistemologische Perspektiven* [Ecology of the Spirit. Anthropological, Psychological, Biological and Epistemological Perspectives], Frankfurt 1981, and *Geist und Natur. Eine notwendige Einheit* [Mind and Nature. A Necessary Unity], Frankfurt 1987. It would be of great advantage if such clever and imaginative authors as Bateson could gain more from the Kantian text than before.

contemporaries, especially peasants in China and the Soviet Union, who suffered and died because they were alleged to be characteristics of the world-historical conspiracy against the prophecy of the victory of communist equality.

The idea of a conscious, conspiratorial deception of equals by substantial equals, i.e. implying an essential and yet concealed equality, for example between master and servant, would have been completely absurd in ancient and medieval feudal society. Inequality was thought of *substantially* and was above all a problem of reflection, or not experienced at all as a problem, but rather as the solution to a problem, namely how the ruling order must structure the forms of life in order to be able to resist the destructive forces of the human nature of its own people, the foreign peoples, those of external nature and the evil deities.[426] Being able to make equality the basis for reflection in the noticing and recognition of other beings, even against obvious differences (gender, skin colour, group affiliation, faith, etc.), is the opposite of self-evident, or to be more precise: an extremely preconditioned achievement of cultural evolution. The deprivation of human individuality from slaves or untouchables and the reduction of humans to their useful animality and instrumentality thus betrays the uncertainty of human reflectivity. This is an important dimension of all collective persecutions of people and all mass murders.[427]

---

[426] Of the well-studied example of a society that still lives to a significant extent in this state of knowledge, see Dumont, Louis, *Gesellschaft in Indien. Die Soziologie des Kastenwesens* [Society in India. The Sociology of Castes], Vienna 1976. There are repeatedly massive protests from the lowest caste of the 'untouchables', who increasingly put this holistic hierarchy under pressure.

[427] In the following, the connection between cruelty and individuality is examined in order not to expose the investigation to the justified mistrust Arthur C. Danto aptly lent his pen to: "What I found in preparing my remarks was the almost complete absence from the great moral texts of Western thought of even a mention of cruelty. Montaigne and Machiavelli excepted, until Schopenhauer and Nietzsche no one seems to have singled out cruelty as something to think about philosophically [...] But were everything except philosophy erased from the documents of our time, future readers would infer that we lived in a golden age!" (Danto, *Philosophical Individualism in Chinese and Western Thought*, in: Munro, Donald (ed.), *Individualism and Holism. Studies in Confucian and Taoist Values*, Michigan 1985, pp. 385-90, here pp. 386-7) In this flattering view of our age, future archaeologists could also be encouraged by Richard Rorty's writings, who simply and naively bases his entire literary liberalism on the demand of 'non-cruelty' without specifically problematizing it. At the same time, he degrades a writer who has taken cruelty very seriously compared to

The German approach, for example, to categorize Jewish fellow citizens as 'vermin' at the time of National Socialism and to deny humanity to the subjects thus animalized is not only the paranoid outgrowth of a hygienic fixation, a mass-psychologically effective dirt phobia. Rather, this animalization of old age marks a threatening *inability to think*, i.e. to judge, i.e. an *actual animalization of the respective individual ego of persecutors*.[428] However, it is an animalization that lies beyond the natural-animal and rather fulfils the *symbolic content of the animal conceived by man as evil reason*, of which in turn only man is capable. This back-projection of the concept onto man is necessary and must not remain unmentioned here, because in an investigation of political subjectivity a quasi-ontological predicate of animality, which has the function of an objective characteristic of cognitive inferiority, must not suddenly appear. For it is highly problematic and at the same time characteristic of the uncertain performance of cognition regarding subjectivity and individuality that the majority of the world population slaughters animals without much consideration and eats their flesh. Not only the deviations in some cults, which sanctify selected or all animals, or in the appearance of modern, vegetarian lifestyles[429] draw attention to the clearly lacking necessity of such an interpretation of animality as inferiority or exclusive edibility. In this abstract, dry and theoretical question of radical utilitarianism, universities, too, have already been plagued by such a fierce dispute that even the world press has been listening.[430] The subjectivity of animals is a complex of its own, still far too little thought-out, which cannot be discussed here.[431] The topics of

---

what he considers to be Nabokov's timeless genius. *Animal Farm* and *1984* only show, according to Rorty, how much Orwell was historically and politically trapped in his time; see Rorty, Richard, *Kontingenz, Ironie und Solidarität* [Contingency, Irony and Solidarity], Frankfurt 1991, pp. 274-304.

[428] Hannah Arendt's remark that Eichmann distinguished himself by "poor judgment" and nothing else fits this; see Arendt, Hannah, *Eichmann in Jerusalem*, N.Y. 1968, p. 85.

[429] Or the fact that the public in industrial societies is suddenly devoting special attention to the protection of certain mammal species (whales, dolphins, seals).

[430] The discussion about the provocative theses of the Australian philosopher and animal rights activist Peter Singer is meant.

[431] See the first part of Luc Ferry's book, *Le nouvel ordre écologique. L'arbre, l'animal et l'homme* [The New Ecologic Order. The Tree, the Animal and Man], Paris 1992, pp. 41-128, under the title *L'animal ou la confusion des genres* [The Animal or the Confusion of Species]; cf. from a completely different, namely radically modernity-critical and sometimes involuntarily comic view the discussions of

bioethics and genetic manipulation will soon put it on the agenda.[432]

The observations to date can be condensed into an initial assumption as to why the most terrible human destructions in world history, which took place in the 20th century, can no longer be seen if they are ontologized as moral abysses. Classical ontology, all ethics that follow it, and even Kant's subjective moral philosophy – they all do not have the capacity to bring these all-human devouring events back into the realm of rational comprehension. On the contrary: moral considerations often advertised the tabooing of all attempts to catch up events as a moral achievement, be it the taboo of memory or that of speaking.[433] In a way, this was also a wise and tactful way of protecting the collective conscience from tension, but above all of not overtaxing morality itself. Because within morality there is no way to call the unspeakable by name. This inconvenience and embarrassment become noticeable in Germany at every public speech and ceremony that is somehow connected with the memory of National Socialism. These files always remain incomplete. Not least because for many people the event has not yet been released for reflection.

But it can also happen the other way round that the existing basis for reflection of individuality is reduced and literally suffocated by the cultural context or environmental conditions. In 1904, Leo Tolstoy wrote the following in his story *Chadschi-Murat* about the constantly tense and dangerous relationship between the Chechens and the Russians:

"Nobody talked about the hatred of Russians. The feeling that all

---

Jacques Derrida in *Gesetzeskraft. Der "mystische Grund der Autorität"* [The "Mystical Cause of Authority"], Frankfurt 1991, p. 37-39; also in Derrida, *"Il faut bien manger" ou le calcul du sujet* ["You need to eat well" or the Calculation of the Subject], *Interview aved Jean-Luc Nancy*, in: Confrontation, no. 20, Paris 1989.

[432] See *Spiegel* 27/1993, p. 162-3, on a group of scientists who demand the validity of human rights for chimpanzees, gorillas and orang-utans. Background for this are the comparisons between the consciousness and communication achievements of babies, severely handicapped persons and animals; cf. Cavalieri, Paola u. Singer, Peter (ed.), *The Great Ape Project*, London 1993.

[433] Cf. Heinsohn, Gunnar, *Warum Auschwitz? Hitlers Plan und die Ratlosigkeit der Nachwelt* [Why Auschwitz? Hitler's Plan and the Perplexity of Posterity], Reinbek b. Hamburg 1995. Heinsohn presents a list of the forty-two most important Auschwitz interpretations and adds his own as 43rd. This also has a relation to morality, but from a point of view of radical exteriority to it. His thesis is that Hitler wanted to exterminate the Jews in order to eliminate Jewish ethics, especially the ban on killing. Morality itself should be murdered by the extermination of its people.

Chechens – large and small –felt was stronger than hate. This was not hatred, but a non-recognition of these Russian dogs as humans and such disgust and astonishment at the senseless brutality of these beings that the need to destroy them, as well as the need to destroy rats, poisonous spiders and wolves, was as natural a feeling as the instinct of self-preservation."[434]

Recently it was again the Chechens themselves who were raped, and this crime is still going on. In any case, Tolstoy tries to put on record here how the development of a genocidal attitude is subjectively experienced; and not, as in the German case, as an attitude demanded and sanctioned by official authority[435], but as a dynamic part of everyday culture. The more recent versions, for example from the point of view of the Cambodian, Bosnian-Serbian or Rwandan torturers and mass murderers, have not yet been so literarily documented. There is a sad multitude of examples of this kind in world history, which indicates that the intellectual capacity of the respective people, which would have enabled them to recognize one another, has either not yet emerged or has already been broken again. In the language of critical philosophy, it could then only mean dryly that in these cases nature has not yet specified itself enough or no longer specified itself sufficiently on behalf of the judgment.

To recognize a person as an individual, including a personality, simply because she has legs and hands that she can use or because of a head with eyes sitting on her shoulders is a very unlikely and repeatedly risky

---

[434] Tolstoy, Leo, *Chadshi Murat*, 1904. In this scene, the reaction of villagers after a Russian raid is described, which is exemplary both historically and systematically for the emergence of spirals of violence. The whole story is about the Caucasian Chadshi Murat, who perishes in the power struggle of two despots, namely Tsar Nicholas I and the leader of the mountain tribes Shamil.

[435] Of course, it is not a question of presenting the technical character of the German mass murder as a kind of aesthetically based reason for reducing guilt, but of reconstructing the subjective experience of systematic dehumanization. The official emphasis, such as the Nuremberg race laws, became strategically necessary because there was too little ecstatic anti-Semitism in the population, which would have been prepared for violence and which would have helped to stabilize the Nazi rule. In Germany there was far too little enthusiasm for pogroms for the taste of the NSDAP leadership; the so-called "Reichskristallnacht" [Imperial Crystal Night] was the exception and has only therefore its own name (from Berlin's vernacular). The mood of persecution had to be fueled and kept alive by the authorities.

achievement of culture.⁴³⁶ The method of classical logic, the conclusion in which the sentences "Socrates is a man" and "All men are mortal" occur, is deceptive about the true problem of this concept of humanity in the individual. Mutual recognition and acceptance as human beings has never taken the form of a syllogism, but is a great achievement of judgment, which must always work with assumptions and imputations.⁴³⁷ The living being outside myself is therefore first of all a body of external nature, which apparently moves automatically. "Apparently", because there is always uncertainty as to whether a person moves herself or is moved, for example by the invisible and even incorporeal hand of a spirit. Conversely, a human mind is conceivable without great difficulty in objects or even better in animals. And finally, the unity of the body itself is by no means a priori given, for in many cultures the traces of a body, its property or selected, mostly magical objects are not distinguished from the biological body.⁴³⁸ These phenomena should not be underestimated, because they

---

[436] Wilhelm Dilthey's philosophy of history, for example, is completely insensitive to this improbability, for it bases all historical individuality on a moral commonality that can be directly experienced: "Through the entire concept of the spiritual world such basic experience of commonness passes, in which the consciousness of the unified self and that of uniformity with others, the same human nature and individuality are connected with one another" (Dilthey, *Der Aufbau der geschichtlichen Welt in den Geisteswissenschaften* [The Composition of the Historical World in Humanities], *Gesammelte Schriften* VII [Collected Works VII], Leipzig 1927, p. 141).

[437] An interesting question remains as to whether and how the reflecting judgment could be incorporated into formal logic. It should be remembered that Baumgarten (cf. chapter A.2.2) had already designed aesthetics as a complement to complement classical logic.

[438] What the 'I myself' is as a body and how it is taken as the basis of self-consciousness is not a priori defined because, as ethnological documents prove, the boundaries of the body are often not identical with the skin as the sheath or shell of the body. Jean Cazeneuve reports in his excellent treatise *La conaissance d'autrui dans les sociétés archaiques*, in: *Cahiers internationaux de sociologie XXV*, July-December 1958, S. 75-99, about the ethnologist Maurice Leenhardt, who for the first time in the course of his studies on the Canaries in New Caledonia (*Gens de la grande terre*, Paris 1937 and *Do Kamo*, Paris 1947) recognized that the Europeans, contrary to their own naive Christian ideas, did not teach the natives the existence of their souls, *but taught them the existence and unity of their bodies*. This centering of the body is the basis for the further emergence of individuality. Cazeneuve and Leenhardt's theses have been confirmed by recent ethnology (cf. chapter B.2.2). If the evidence of one's own physicality is put into perspective in this way, new possibilities arise to treat philosophical and, for

determine the lives of hundreds of millions of people worldwide every day. The persecution of alleged witchcraft by lynch law cost the lives of over 300 people in Kenya alone in 1992 – they were almost exclusively women.[439] In magical consciousness, the invisible has much more reality and above all more power than the visible. The appreciation of the eye by Aristotle as the most important sensory organ and as the most reliable supplier of world knowledge[440] is in this sense a piece of early enlightenment directed against myth and magic.[441] This body, apart from myself, is primarily based on external observation. Only in a much more demanding and culturally preconditioned version of thought does a reflecting comparison of external and self-observation take place.[442] It requires a long

---

example, neurophysiological questions together. A first overview of these possibilities can be found in Thomas Metzinger's habilitation thesis *Subjekt und Selbstmodell*, Paderborn 1993.

[439] Cf. Kahl, Sinikka, *Mit der Kürbisflasche gegen das Böse* [With the Pumpkin Bottle Against Evil], in: die tageszeitung, 29.9.1995, p. 15-16. In this context it does not matter that the cause of these persecutions and executions may be social envy or private speech, and that witch belief is only of secondary effect. What is important is the collective mechanism that triggers it and allows individuals to experience their own persecution impulse as being based on the objective threat posed by the victim. **It is no exaggeration to say that witchcraft, faith in it and witch-hunting are still much more widespread in the world than belief in the effectiveness of parliamentary democracy.** This political dimension is illustrated particularly clearly in the excellent article by Bartholomew Grill, *Die Macht der Hexen* [The Power of the Witches], in: Die Zeit, 38/2005, where 5000 **murdered 'witches' are reported in Tanzania alone (1994-98).**

[440] Cf. Aristotle, *Metaphysics*, 1st book, 980 a.

[441] Cf. in this context also the inspired essays by Martin Jay, *Im Reich des Blicks: Foucault und die Defamierung des Sehens im Französischen Denken des zwanzigsten Jahrhunderts* [In the Empire of Sight: Foucault and the Diffamation of Vision in French Thinking in the Twentieth Century] in: David Couzens Hoy (ed.) *Foucault: A Critical Reader*, Oxford 1988; see also Jay, *Die Ordnungen des Sehens in der Modernzeit* [The Orders of View in Modern Times] in: *Tumult. Zeitschrift für Verkehrswissenschaft*, 1990 edition: Das Sichtbare [The Visible], pp. 40-55.

[442] See Strawson, Peter Frederick, *Einzelding und logisches Subjekt. Ein Beitrag zur deskriptiven Metaphysik*, Stuttgart 1972 [Individuals, London 1964], pp. 111-149, where Strawson develops an approach to the problem of the alien psychic 'person' by means of the single thing 'body' and the connection of these two categories in the "conceptual framework" of everyday language. Strawson's thorough and clever analysis certainly exploits all the possibilities of linguistic-analytic philosophy and his findings should not be contradicted at all. However, an extension and generalization is necessary for our purposes. For

development of social competence in order not to fear or worship foreign people with whom, as is the rule in sedimentary and traditional societies, there is no lifelong familiarity, as *superhumanly-dangerous*, nor to slate them as *animalisticly-useful*. The reflecting judgment provides opportunities to recognize human-like bodies other than myself as natural bodies with the same end as my own. It enables me to accept a subject and even an individual in alien human bodies[443], which was by no means guaranteed throughout cultural history.[444] Furthermore, the reflecting power of judg-

---

with the anthropologically and especially ethnologically sharpened view, some dimensions of the concept of individuality overlooked by Strawson appear in the concept of the person. **It is empirically well proven that not only disembodied mental beings can quite legitimately benefit from the linguistically assigned status of personal individuality, but also animals.** The first case is already to be found in the popular Christian ideas of God. Strawson avoids this aspect by retreating to the highly speculative theology and the monad philosophy of Leibniz (p. 161), which of course can only attribute the *ens perfectum* individuality or none at all. Finally, those bodies are also considered that are absent and with whose multitude one could never make acquaintance. To present these as personal individuals is the achievement of what Kant called the *common sense* or *cosmopolitan way of thinking*. **This also underlines the fact that individuals are only created through *thought*, not through the language material of the "conceptual framework".** Strawson's analysis, however, was from the outset too restricted by the linguistically realized everyday-consciousness of the 1950s in the United States. And even of this, his analysis captures only a highly generalized fiction determined by the norms and wishes of the academic milieu.

[443] Cf. Ferry, Luc, *Philosophy politique II. Le système des philosophies de l'histoire*, Paris 1984, pp. 226-242, where he tries to show that according to the *CPJ* the human body can be regarded as a "symbol of individuality"; cf. here chapter B.1.7.2.3-4.

[444] Cf. Lévi-Strauss, Claude, *Das wilde Denken* [The Savage Mind], Frankfurt 1989. The ethnologist stated that the proper name is not necessarily an index, as Peirce postulated, or that its logical model was already applied in the demonstrative pronoun, as Russel claimed. Rather, such postulates themselves are determined thoroughly culturally (in the case of Peirce and Russel Anglo-Saxon, Roman and Christian). In the savage mind, proper names for individuals are easily identical with classes, e.g. as technonyms (relation to living relatives) or necronyms (relation to dead relatives), because the proper name only makes sense through its explicit relations within the naming system (ibid., chapter *Das Individuum als Art* [The Individual as a Species], pp. 223-250). However, this is well below the requirements that modern thinking combines with the concept of individuality. Early cultures only combine individuality with *distinguishability in a relationship structure*. They thought or think, so to speak, much more (causally) functional than the modern, who imagine indi-

ment still allows the acceptance of individuals in *bodies that are not physically present at all*. It is therefore not only about the direct sensual perception and the proximity effect of reflecting thinking. **Being able to think one's own individuality in the context of a society of individuals that one does not know personally and probably will never get to know, is the most demanding and laborious way of thinking that has ever been developed.** It was still completely alien to Greek antiquity, for there was no horizon beyond the polis that was presented socially or politically. The Greek preform of individualism had only *intra muros* significance, i. e. within the polis.[445] But then, the universalism of individuality appeared for the first time in the Jewish writings of the Old Testament. Judaism developed an imaginary world in which humanity as a whole was considered, and in which exteriority lost its namelessness and its horror.[446]

The transcendental principle of judgment is the philosophical key to this mental capacity. It establishes the subjective *maxim*[447] for the power of

---

viduality as essentiality and uniqueness out of the human body and its name. This is an interesting ethnological indication of how much genuine individualism and social functionalism have to irritate each other – and not only at the theoretical level, as it often seems.

[445] Cf. Diehle, Albrecht, *Die Griechen und die Fremden* [The Greeks and the Foreingers], Munich 1994. Diehle sees the difference, however, only in Greek education, the lack of which the authors of that time accused the barbarians of. He ignores a considerable number of ancient passages (especially in Aristotle's and Plato's works) that document massive and substantial xenophobia. Wolfgang Detel explained this convincingly in his essay *Griechen und Barbaren. Zu den Anfängen des abendländischen Rassismus* [Greeks and Barbarians. On the beginnings of Western Racism], in: *Zeitschrift für Philosophie*, 6/1995, pp. 1019-1043. Detel points out that since 1965 there have been a whole series of scientific publiccations on this subject, for example in the U.S., France and Great Britain – but not one of them in Germany, where classical philologists and historians continue to protect their idealized antiquity from such intrusiveness.

[446] Cf. the works of René Girard, in particular his interpretation of the Judeo-Christian texts in *Things Hidden Since the Foundation of the World*, 1987. Cf. Grünenberg, Reginald, *Gründungsgewalt und Politik. René Girards Kulturtheorie im Spiegel der Politikwissenschaft* [Founding Violence and Politics. René Girard's Theory of Culture as Reflected in Political Science] in: academia.edu, Berlin 2010.

[447] As already mentioned, it is decisive here that there is no *law* here, for the power of judgment only prescribes this principle to itself; see *CPJ*, B XXXIV, in the midst of the transcendental deduction of the principle of the purposiveness of nature for our cognitive capacity, B XXXI-XXXIV [p. 69-72], which does not

judgment that nature in the above sense as a unit meets this in its phenomena and *specifies* itself so that it can be recognized. The opposite term, with which the judgment comes from the particular to the universal, is *classification*. Kant notes, by the way, that the classification as a technique of nature study must have been much more attractive at an earlier time than for his contemporaries. He probably looks back on the epoch from Aristotle to Bacon and marks the difference between an earlier age, when nature was still studied through the collection and classification of individual cases in typologies and taxonomies, and a more mature epoch, in which nature is constructed and researchers seem to be less and less dependent on judgment.[448] The law of the 'specification of nature' now means that nature specifies its general laws according to the principle of purposiveness for our cognitive ability: it provides the universal to the particular, the unity of the principle to the different.[449] Classification is therefore conditionally made possible by nature's principle of specifying itself for our cognitive ability. This is the necessary naturalness in the reflecting recognition of another as an individual: we must assume an individuality through reflection, thereby assuming that nature has produced certain beings, a species, which possesses the quality of individuality. This is in no way contradicted, for example, by the fact that humans often underlay such individuality to animals.[450] The problems arise more in the use of this assumption when, for example, beloved animals are not interested in their domestication or the recognition as individuals is not reciprocal, which in the harmless case is expressed by the fact that certain domestic animals obviously feel comfortable with every food-giver, without regard for the person and the character, i.e. their unmistakable individuality. Conversely, a less responsive and usually obedient individuality, which is imputed to the animal, can lead to an inadequacy of the reflecting person's imputation of individuality to human beings. This can be reflected in personal contact, but also in political orientation, as radical animal rights activists, who are not thrifty with death threats, repeatedly

---

even bear its own heading. The principle itself is only a *maxim* of judgment, a subjective principle.

[448] *CPJ*, B XL [p. 73].

[449] *CPJ*, B 37 [p. 107]; see also *CPJ*, First Introduction, p. 27.

[450] Whether or not such an imputed individuality to animals of whatever kind really exists or not should not be judged here in advance at all. Sigmund Freud, at least in his last work, pointed out that animal psychology would have an exciting task to solve in investigating exactly this question; cf. Freud, Sigmund, *Abriß der Psychoanalyse*, [1938] Frankfurt 1985, p. 11.

prove.[451] **But this *assumption* or *imputation*, no matter how successful or absurd we judge it in detail, is precisely the achievement of reflection.**[452]

In the case of individuality, it is assumed that the living being encountered belongs to the same specification of nature for the power of judgment as the owner of this power of judgment himself. The subjective condition of this judgment of reflection is clearly doubled in this particular context of individuality: not only that nature specifies itself in favor of the power of judgment and thus gives it a subjective principle of knowledge[453], whereby it can assume that there is something like a species of related human individuals; nature also allows the power of judgment in the case of the imputation of individuality to become circular by suggesting it in the *alter* a comparable carrier of power of judgment, an *ego*, an *alter ego*. It is immediately obvious that it can only be assumed what already exists in the reflecting power of judgment. **Of course, individuality can only be assumed if the imputing subject is a being that already reflects *itself* as an individual.**

The difference between this reconstruction of the recognition of individuality and the almost identical sociological theorem of 'double contingency' lies firstly in the fact that it is not an empirical process, that it does not depend on the presence of the *alter*, and secondly that it is just as little a matter of interaction in the sense of the theories of action as of the emergence of a social communication system in the sense of functional-structural system theory.[454] It is above all the assumption of an individuality in the alter that reflects back on the ego. This advance of reflecting

---

[451] As is well known, Adolf Hitler was also an active animal lover and vegetarian. Consequently, under National Socialism, by far the strictest animal protection law in the world was drawn up and enacted by direct order of the Führer; cf. Ferry, Luc, *Le nouvel ordre écologique. L'arbre, l'animal et l'homme*, Paris 1992, in particular the chapter *L'écologie nazie*, ibid. pp. 181-208.

[452] In this respect, for example, Strawson's concept of the "primitive concept of persons" would have to be expanded. This would clearly cross the boundaries of analytical philosophy, for here a critique of the subject of knowledge and judgment is unavoidable.

[453] This principle is its heuristic guide to all objective knowledge, which is either mathematical-dynamic, mathematical-mechanical, metaphysical (in the sense of Kantian metaphysics *after* their criticism) or transcendental.

[454] See the *General Statement of the Editors* in: Parsons, Talcott and Shils, Edward (ed.), *Towards a General Theory of Action*, Cambridge Mass. 1951, pp. 3-29; cf. Luhmann, Niklas, *Soziale Systeme*, Frankfurt 1984, pp. 148-190.

judgment cannot be described as an encounter between two black boxes.[455] However, if it actually took place a priori between two completely non-transparent beings, then it would certainly be conflictual, unless at least one of the parties provided a conflict resolution mechanism of its own accord. Only the imputation of anything at all (the alter as man, spirit, God, animal, enemy or friend) creates connection possibilities in communication. In the theorem of double contingency, this *very thing* is the insertion from outside of information interfering with the homogeneous vacuum, so that the autopoiesis of system formation can begin. In discourse theory it is the counterfactual imputation of a meaning-identical use of linguistic expressions that automatically leads to communication-oriented action.[456] From the perspective of the theorem of political subjectivity, however, this *very thing* is always the form of an individuality, however rudimentary, which is provided by the reflecting power of judgment and attributed to the appearing being, the alter. The two approaches do not contradict each other *in re*, because there is no contradiction in the empirical findings. They judge the same objects only from different perspectives and are methodically separated from each other by the difference between consciousness as a reflecting ability and social, systems-theoretically understood communication.

The interface of nature and reason, which goes right through this being 'man', the rational animal, is the main theme of Kant's critical philosophy. The mediation of two cosmological principles in one subject presents itself as the coming true of freedom in nature – this is the often overlooked and truly challenging paradox – by man as a sensory being. Rationality as freedom determined by reason, as insight into the necessity of lawful, autonomous and thus moral action, which must negate the naturalness of man in his inclinations, becomes real only through the animal natural body of the same being in nature.

---

[455] So however: Luhmann, *Soziale Systeme*, loc. cit., p. 156. It should not be overlooked that in Luhmann's version of this topos of Parsons, alter and ego are completely de-anthropologized; but the model must also be applicable to the encounter of mutually foreign individuals in its claim to generality, at least among many other cases.

[456] Cf. Habermas, Jürgen, *Faktizität und Geltung* [Truth and Justification], Frankfurt 1992, chapter *Transzendenz von innen: Lebensweltliche und archaische Dissensbewältigung* [Transcendence from Within: Coping with dissent in everyday life and archaic disagreement], pp. 32-44.

"The effect in accordance with the concept of freedom is the final end, which (or its appearance in the sensible world) should exist, for which the condition of its possibility in nature (in the nature of the subject as a sensible being, that is, as a human being) is presupposed."[457]

Kant becomes even clearer in the comment on this passage, where the causality of freedom is at the same time described as the causality of a "subordinate natural cause", namely the subject as man and appearance.

The mind cannot think of the unity of the principles of nature, which also includes this imputed individuality in the animal human bodies. Only the power of judgment is able to make this assumption.[458] From this point of view, the (especially German) philosophical discussion about identity and subjectivity in idealism must be evaluated. Then it becomes clear why this speculation has always had to end aporetically. **Subjectivity as self-consciousness cannot be reconstructed as experienced, human reality on the model of a *singulartantum* without precisely losing the quality of the special feature and a content-related knowledge about oneself that is made possible by reflection in the first place.** This highly speculative concept of pure subjectivity results in a much more limited concept of the *I* and none of *You, We, He* or *She*. The speculative ego is fixed on the opposite of the 'It'. This 'I', which can also be found in the key chapter of the *CPuRe* as the *synthetic unity of transcendental apperception*, is the formal concept of a selfhood that gives unity to thought, in order to even look at a very specific It, namely the It as a pure form, which later once again disintegrates into *phenomenon* (object of nature) and *noumenon* (essence of freedom). But the lower-case 'i' of human individuality [that expression makes more sense in German] is thus still in no way captured.[459] Conversely, pure subjectivity cannot be constructed from individuality. The overlaps in the speculative exploitation of epistemic or individual subjectivity, which, as is also shown in the following, give rise to very

---

[457] CPJ, B LV [81].

[458] *CPJ*, B XXXIX [73].

[459] In this respect, the transition from the transcendental 'I' to the (in his case only empirical-analytical, with reference to general rules of language) individualized 'I', as demanded by Ernst Tugendhat, is interesting and even more strongly founded in transcendental philosophy than he has perceived it. See Tugendhat, Ernst, *Selbstbewußtsein und Selbstbestimmung. Sprachanalytische Interpretationen* [Self-Consciousness and Self-Determination. Interpretations of Language Analysis], Frankfurt 1979.

different cognitive capacities, have led to serious misunderstandings.[460] One of the most important is probably the alleged lack of transition from Kant's morals philosophy perceived as 'rigorous' to 'ethics of the world of life', which the linguistic-pragmatic discourse theory would like to deliver in continuation of Kant's intentions.[461]

The completeness of the *theorem of the individual as a product and carrier of reflection* now demands that it is shown where the individual draws its ability from to begin reflecting at all in order to finally understand itself and others – as individuals – in judging. Ex nihilo such a faculty or capacity does not arise. Here, a generative principle must be found from which the reflectivity can be developed in a coherent manner into an evolutionary theory. In Kant's text, this role undoubtedly falls to the *feeling of the dynamic and sublime*. For in this feeling the courage is awakened to "be able to measure oneself with the apparent omnipotence of nature."[462] Until this rebellion against the forces and beings of nature takes place and the fear of them is not overcome, there are no people in terms of cultural philosophy. One of the most moving parts of the *CPJ*, which is quoted in detail for its own beauty, can now be found:

---

[460] In his book *Subjektivität in Raum und Zeit* [Subjectivity in Space and Time], Frankfurt 1990, Anton Koch took some important steps to clarify these misunderstandings. Cf. in particular the chapter *Subjektivität als Singuraletantum* [Subjectivity as Singular Tantum], ibid. p. 217 ff.

[461] On 'German identity philosophy' as an obstacle to the development of the subject-philosophical potentials in the Kantian Work cf. further down in the excursus under B.1.9, *Hypostases of Identity*.

[462] *CPJ*, B 105 [144].

"Bold, overhanging, as it were threatening cliffs, thunder clouds towering up into the heavens, bringing with them flashes of lightning and crashes of thunder, volcanoes with their all-destroying violence, hurricanes with the devastation they leave behind, the boundless ocean set into a rage, a lofty waterfall on a mighty river, etc., make our capacity to resist into an insignificant trifle in comparison with their power. But the sight of them only becomes all the more attractive the more fearful it is, as long as we find ourselves in safety, and we gladly call these objects sublime because they elevate the strength of our soul above ist usual level, and allow us to discover within ourselves a capacity for resistance of quite another kind, which gives us the courage to measure ourselves against the apparent all-powerfulness of nature."[463]

The prerequisite for the discovery of one's own "strength of our soul" is therefore a relative observer position. It is not difficult to imagine that such occasional situations in the history of civilization have awakened a culture-forming impulse in the subject. All that must be accepted is a mimetic ability (the imaginary imitation of the force of nature to resist it) that can develop into reflection and common sense.[464] If people do not discover this ability, Kant argues similarly, then they remain dominated by the fear of nature, which is incited on man by evil gods, for example.[465] In this state, they can neither judge the sublimity of nature nor find pleasure in its beauty.

---

[463] CPJ, B 104-5 [144].

[464] For Kant, the concept of 'subreption', a kind of confusion of the idea of man in the subject with the violence and power of the object of nature (*CPJ*, B 97 [141]), is an excellent mimetic interpretation. These speculative basic lines of a generative cultural theory from a philosophical point of view of reflection, which cannot be further discussed here, at least do not contradict the work of René Girard and more recent ethnology. Cf. Grünenberg, Reginald, *Gründungsgewalt und Politik. René Girards Kulturtheorie im Spiegel der Politikwissenschaft* [Founding Violence and Politics. René Girard's Theory of Culture as Reflected in Political Science] in: academia.edu, Berlin 2010; also the contributions in the research volume of the Laboratoire d'Ethnologie et de Sociologie Comparative, *Singularités. Les voies d'émergence individuelle*, commemorative publication for Eric de Dampierre, Paris 1989.

[465] There are indeed ethnological peoples living in such imaginary worlds, e.g. the Alakalufs (or Alakulufs), who inhabit the extremely inhuman region of Tierra del Fuego, whose nature is experienced by them as an intolerable imposition.

"Someone who is afraid can no more judge about the sublime in nature than someone who is in the grip of inclination and appetite can judge about the beautiful."[466]

But if they find the opportunity, as uninvolved persons, to fearfully admire the power of nature in its destruction, then their subjective imagination seems to unfold a faculty that puts them into a transcendently fruitful confusion and illusion of being able to resist this nature, because the whole immensity of nature itself disappears in the light of the infinity of a *felt idea of reason*. In the first instance, nature is an existential humiliation of man:

"...likewise the irresistibility of its power certainly makes us, considered as natural beings, recognize our physical powerlessness, but at the same time it reveals a capacity for judging ourselves as independent of it and a superiority over nature on which is grounded a selfpreservation of quite another kind than that which can be threatened and endangered by nature outside us, whereby the humanity in our person remains undemeaned even though the human being must submit to that dominion."[467]

Finally, this passage gives a brief insight into political anthropology and its history. The force of nature has always been experienced – and still is today – in a very rudimentary sense also politically and judged accordingly. Because "goods, health and life" (ibid.) are under the power of nature. These must be produced, distributed, guarded and cared for under a certain order to maintain well-being. Nature, however, often sets everything in motion to destroy the order of mankind, be it through climatic, epidemic or warlike catastrophes.[468] This puts them under an obligation to

---

[466] *CPJ*, B 103 [144].

[467] *CPJ*, B 105 [145].

[468] In this context, it is irrelevant that such a schematized concept of nature practically never currently occurs in the subjective judgment of pre-modern cultural beings in particular. Nature in primitive understanding is always personified, animistic and determined by its own causality, which does not allow contingency. The boundaries between people, their community, their ancestors and nature animated by good, evil or useful spirits are not evident. For the present argument it is only of importance that nature is accepted in those of its phenomena that actually have the power over the inferior people in the important questions of survival. These can also be humans, strangers or barbarians, who are more part of the animal kingdom anyway, unless they are worshipped or feared as gods. Even today, man-made disasters, especially racist conflicts, are subjectively naturalized as quasi-"raw forces of nature",

think about the appropriateness of the established order confirmed by tradition on the occasion of the crisis. These reflections on the establishment of new orders, however ritualized, elitist or chaotic they may be, are reflecting judgments on various ways of appropriately restoring the social order of nature. The essential thing here is that in this case the raw, violent external nature makes people aware that they live in an order that is neither timeless nor was created by nature itself. Raw nature forces people to think about order by smashing the existing ones. But this is only an external reason for reflection on order. Because the question now has to be in a good transcendental manner: How can people think of order? Thus, we leave the violent nature with the associated feeling of the dynamically sublime as a possible source of culture (cf. *Excursus II*, chapter B.2.2) and return to the transcendental concept of the purposiveness of nature.

It should be noted that in reflecting judgment the *individualization of the self as I* and at the same time the *constitution of You, He or She* (and the It as You, He or She) is achieved. At the beginning of this chapter we first approached the question of the reflected natural basis in the recognition and acceptance of individuality. Because it is most directly accessible to individual experience, the most difficult thing to begin with was the reflecting process of *reciprocal individualization*, which is realized above all (not exclusively) in the (successful) liberal forms of modern socialization.[469] Moreover, it has already been mentioned that this reflectingly constituted individuality is related to the order of coexistence of beings individualized in advanced cultures and their organizations.[470]

---

because it is not possible to base the event of the mass mutual self-destruction of the species on an order-generating mind or to identify the causality of an individual's actions within it. And that is probably also appropriate, because otherwise one would do too much honor to the event that indeed insults mankind.

[469] Obviously, such assertions must be made with caution, for they all too easily fail to be naive and levelling idealizations of the European modern era, which could serve exclusively Eurocentric conservatism. In my opinion, a differentiated consideration on the basis of the now collected social-scientific "world knowledge" allows at least a cautious formation of ideal types. One thing is clear in any case: the boom of radical, ideologically instrumentalized criticism of Western modernity from its own ranks, which was completely blind to its achievements, including so-called postmodernism, is over. However, these impulses have been gratefully adopted by radical religious movements, especially Islamic fundamentalism.

[470] Another comment on the present method of presenting political subjectivity: if

From the beginning and without exception, the tradition of political philosophy has been searching for an order that could be recommended to subjects, citizens and rulers as *objective*. Until the 1970s, post-war German political science was also shaped by an idea of political science as 'order science'. It should, equipped with expertise on the ontologically guaranteed validity of certain liberal to conservative values in relation to political order, educate citizens to democrats through the teaching profession at school and in adult political education. The now dominant orientation of political science as empirical social science must not hide the fact that so far there has been no replacement of this basic idea of research into *political order as an objective norm or reality* (cf. Chapter B.3.5). It is surprising that there is not even a well-thought-out, conceptually applicable definition of order in the social sciences. The word is used almost exclusively in a conventional sense, assuming that everyone else already knows. Even Max Weber has compiled a collection of basic sociological concepts in business and society that he has cleared up in an exemplary manner, but the very concept of order remains undefined and its understanding is assumed to be that of an objectively given object.[471] Everyday political understanding also supports the view that order is something objective, for order in subjective perception is usually the actions of others who take little or no account of my opinion, or the compulsion of others to cause me to take action that serves their order.[472] This should apply today more than ever.[473]

---

the theorem of reflecting judgment in its form of political judgment has a cultural-theoretical dimension, then the entire cultural development must always be referenced; for this purpose it must be bundled and snatched up in time or historically, whereby – and this should be emphasized here – the view goes from the position of modern democratic orders to the past epochs. This point of view is *relative*, and yet it makes sense, because otherwise we will have to identify with another cultural-historical position, which we know much less well, above all from the subjective experience of our own horizon. Liberal democracies are therefore *not objectively* the avant-garde of culture, but for us they are certainly *time-wise*, and we are, so to speak, hermeneutically bound to the tip of this time arrow into the future.

[471] This is thoroughly examined further below in B.2.1.2, in connection with the interpretation of charisma from the perspective of political subjectivity.

[472] For this presentation, it does not matter whether a subjective agreement or a dissentive assessment exists.

[473] Andreas Anter has now presented the first thorough analysis of the concept of order. In *Die Macht der Ordnung. Aspekte einer Grundkategorie des Politischen* [The Power of Orden. Aspects of a Fundamental Category of the Political], Tübingen

All classic political ideas refer to the state sphere – most of them with unswerving exclusivity. This also applies, incidentally, to North America's liberal tradition, which in the United States Constitution mainly institutionalized rights of defence against the state.[474] The recognition of the state as a pattern of order does not depend on whether one is affirmative, such as the German tradition of constitutional law, which was not only scientifically effective, or opposed, for example because of an emphatic notion of society.[475]

So it is time for political philosophy to undress the concept of order in its objective appearance to give it a subjective turn. Therefore, it is no longer a matter of real or normative orders, which are always objective, but of the ability of the subject to think order, regardless of the social role and position of the individual. The answer to the question posed above, how concrete people can think of order, can only be answered by an analysis of the ability in the subject, which enables the individual to present orders thinkingly and finally sensuously. It is worth mentioning briefly that this is about political judgment, which is the basis of active citizenship in all liberal-democratic societies, but which is also present in other forms of socialisation.

The ability by which the order of nature can be judged reflectingly is the teleological power of judgment. It is the *faculty of thinking (in) ends*. Teleological judgments combine the *causality of empirical nature*, which we can experience through concepts of reason, with the *ideas of reason*. The purposiveness of nature for the power of judgment, i.e. the transcendental principle of judgment, is not shown here from the subjective side, as in the beautiful and sublime, but in its objective meaning. However, this objectivity is not of the same nature as the objectivity of concepts of order presented above but is an objectivity in nature reflected by the subject.

2004, he notes, however, that order has long been used as a "cognitive-subjective concept". This is the only point in which this excellent and inspired study is to be contradicted here, because Anter refers here unilaterally to a few constructivist authors (e.g. Heinz von Foerster) and to the political scientist Eric Voegelin, who, even taken together, do not represent a dominant current of order theories.

[474] See Thomas Paine's positions in Chapter A.2.3.

[475] As is well known, there is currently a strong and dangerous right-wing populist movement in the United States, fuelled by resentment against the central government of the state in Washington. In this case, 'society' is played off against the 'state'.

Teleological judgment does this by subordinating nature to its own ordering mind in order to make its phenomena visible in their regularity. In contrast to the beautiful and sublime, teleological judgment also strives for concepts. This means that it prepares the causal-mechanical understanding of nature in a reflecting, hypothetical way. **Teleology is a "heuristic principle"[476] for getting the world to know.** Kant further differentiates between the inner and outer purposiveness of nature, because he rightly sees an essential difference between the physical and biological contexts of nature[477] and the living beings occurring therein. For the living beings differ in their reflecting judgment in that they can also produce the causes of their self-effecting effects themselves, i.e. that they can store whole causal chains in themselves for a certain period of time. A living being takes in food to effectuate the growth and maintenance of its vital functions, which in turn contain the cause for food intake. The concept of life was first attributed a biological meaning in the narrower sense relatively late in cultural history, and 'late' refers to the time of Aristotle. Taking ethnological findings into account, it emerges that the concept of life in primitive societies is not limited to biological organisms in our understanding, but that nature as a whole is usually presented in an animistic way, i.e. animated by spirits through and through. Chapter A.1.1 reported that in Europe since the beginning of the 17th century the question of whether man is a machine and how the teleological question could finally be replaced with the help of refined mechanics has become virulent. This was the last station in the history of thought before the *concept of organism* was developed, whose first mature philosophical explanation can be found in Kant's concept of end (teleology). Today, the terms 'feedback', 'self-reference' and 'autopoiesis' are common in evolutionary biology and cybernetics for research into the phenomenon of life, and it has become clear that other subject areas are also characterized by self-retaining and self-generating cause and effect, in particular consciousness and social communication.[478]

---

[476] *CPJ*, B 355 [280].

[477] Regardless of whether it is inhabited by a divine or ghostly will and is thus causally determined or presented as a functional interaction of homeostatic circuits.

[478] None of the comments on the *CPJ* known to me have noted that Kant quite unmistakably considered Darwin's theory of evolution to be possible or necessary, on the basis of teleological judgment. The famous, because at least by the biologists of the 19th century still known quote, which contains the whole pro-

Kant, however, limits teleology to the observation of nature (and theology) and makes it as clear as possible that the teleological judgment is the *symptom of the perplexity of the mind in the face of the plans of nature and life*. But the mind helps itself, or rather the teleological power of judgment helps it[479] by providing it with a preliminary, reflected or also indefinite scheme of order until the causal-mechanically proceeding knowledge of nature with its concepts has constructed a certain and objective order of nature. Kant therefore sticks to his method of keeping the judgments pure and to refer exclusively to empirical nature for this end, of whose 'free' character, as in the judgment of the beautiful, or the 'raw' nature, as in the feeling of the sublime, can no longer be spoken of.

This ability to reflect on the order in nature is the same for several reasons, which enables us to 1. to recognize individuals (including ourselves as such) and 2. to think judging the order of their coexistence (including our own). First of all, even with the methodical reservation that the judgments are only related to nature, no separation of social reality as something non-natural is possible. For just as with the individual, the separation or being together of human beings on the planet in an undefined territory is a matter of natural objectivity. *The society of beings outside of oneself is in reflecting understanding first of all nature* - a manifestation that must be based on the teleological power of judgment so that

---

gram of a theory of descent, is as follows: "This analogy of forms, insofar as in spite of all the differences it seems to have been generated in accordance with a common prototype strengthens the suspicion of a real kinship among them in their generation from a common proto-mother through the gradual approach of one animal genus to the other, from that in which the principle of ends seems best confirmed, namely human beings, down to polyps, and from this even further to mosses and lichens, and finally to the lowest level of nature that we can observe, that of raw matter...". (*CPJ*, B 369 [287]). Only Ernst Cassirer took this passage seriously in his speech *Kant und die modern Biologie* [Kant and Modern Biology], first published in: Cassirer, *Geist und Leben. Schriften zu den Lebensordnungen von Natur und Kunst, Geschichte und Sprache* [Writings on the Life Orders of Nature and Art, History and Language], ed. by Ernst Wolfgang Orth, Leipzig 1993, pp. 61-93. Kant's extension of the chain of ancestry to "raw matter" has now been confirmed by the so-called 'molecular Darwinist' approach of evolution theory and by the work of Christiane Nüsslein-Volhard, Nobel Prize winner 1995 in medicine; cf. on Molecular Darwinism the book by Bernd-Olaf Küppers, *Der Ursprung biologischer Information. Zur Naturphilosophie der Lebensentstehung* [The Origin of Biological Information. On the Natural Philosophy of the Origin of Life], Munich 1986.

[479] *CPJ*, B 351 [277].

the individual can form a picture of the connections between the other beings in space and time.

The second reason for teleological judgment as the moment of *subjective generation of order* is simply that it is the only ability that can make order conceivable below the determining, causal-mechanically constructing knowledge of nature and the objective moral law. Kant's formal definition of the end as a *restriction in a special form*[480] is losslessly convertible into the general determination of *order as a restriction of variation* or "limited independent variability"135[481]. So, what is order other than the idea of a system or even just an aggregate of ends?[482]

Thus, the scientifically long neglected order can finally be appointed an elementary concept of political philosophy. The exact name should be *subjectively indefinite* or **subjectively-reflected order**. The products of subjectively-reflecting order are easily confused with the moral determination of a common order of rational beings. Whether I judge the image of society and thus its order teleologically or morally makes no difference in a single respect: both judgments say in their own way: "It should be so and not different!" However, moral judgment is a determining, non-discussing authority of moral law, which above all has to bind the subject itself; in teleological judgment, however, communication and discussion is not only possible, but even necessary. This does not necessarily have to be abolished in a social communication practice, but it is already a lot if the structure of judgment in the individual formally fulfils this condition. This form of *monological obstinacy*, which is always an inner dialogue in an imaginary forum[483], cannot be reconstructed with the common communication theories (Habermas and Luhmann) because they programmatically renounce the reference 'consciousness' or 'subject'.

---

[480] *CPJ*, B 374 [290].

[481] See Topitsch, Ernst, *Über die Möglichkeit besonderer Verfahren in den Sozialwissenschaften* [On the Possibility of Special Procedures in the Social Sciences, in: Topitsch (ed.), *Logik der Sozialwissenschaften*, [Logic of Social Sciences], Köln 1965, p. 254; this definition naturally also includes an objectivist bias that will be found in almost all previous definitions of order.

[482] Cf. here chapter B.1.2 and *CPJ*, § 67 [249].

[483] And not with one's own conscience, which moral philosophy rightly claims to be part of its competence. Friedrich Kaulbach's *Einführung in die Philosophie des Handelns* [Introduction to the Philosophy of Action], Darmstadt 1982, pp. 147-152, provides an interesting, but still too vague interpretation of the internal dialogue with political reference.

A passage from the *Critique of Teleological Judgment* is to underline once again that Kant has already perceived the political under the aspect of teleology. It is a small footnote in which he has hidden an important allusion to the French Revolution:

> "Thus, in the case of a recently undertaken fundamental transformation of a great people into a state, the word **organization** has frequently been quite appropriately used for the institution of the magistracies, etc., and even of the entire body politic. For in such a whole each member should certainly be not merely a means, but at the same time also an end, and, insofar as it contributes to the possibility of the whole, its position and function should also be determined by the idea of the whole."[484]

In this way, he thinks of France's political constitution of 1789 as an *objective-material-internal purposiveness*, i.e. as a 'natural end' or even simpler: as a form of social life that only bourgeois-republican societies are capable of. A first, still very general presentation of a breakdown of the various reflecting achievements in a political judgment is now possible. It will still seem quite abstract, but in the further course the examples become more and more concrete. In relation to the *subjective conception of society*, the political judgment is structured as follows:

Society as a number of people in outer nature can be thought by thinking subjects in several respects as soon as they have exhausted and transcended their view of it as the construction of the bodily world.

The aesthetic assessment of **beauty** shows a community or its elements without interest (here the distinction of aesthetic and practical interest is important) as an image for humanity in the reflecting subject itself.[485]

The reflection of the **sublime**, as a negative pleasure in the inadequacy of the image for the idea of one's own humanity, makes society appear (mathematically) as a great order of virtue, public freedom or domination, but which never attains the greatness and power that could destroy the empire of a morally thought humanity whose member the individual is (dynamically) at the same time.

Teleological thinking judges society or its elements according to their usefulness for the fulfilment of a supersensible ideal, namely that of hu-

---

[484] *CPJ*, B 295, fn. [247].
[485] This shows a certain similarity to Shaftesbury's idea of enthusiasm; cf. chapter A.2.1.

manity in general (instead of only within me). For in the teleological purposiveness of nature the reflecting power of judgment sets the mind in relation to reason (its ideas).[486]

The **moral way of thinking** in the sense of an assessment according to the determining power of judgment in application to the idea of freedom, which is mentioned here only to form a contrast, shows a community of identical beings of nature gifted with reason, endowed with a will that has a causality on freedom, i.e. that can act causally[487] (Note: We are not talking about human beings alone; this also applies to extraterrestrial intelligent beings or artificial intelligence).

The moral assessment of the community always shows an *empire of strict obedience*, for the moral law, the categorical imperative, prevails there in universal observance, without exception and regardless of ends.[488] Consequently, there lies no political reflection on one's own individuality in the horizon of the social community presented. There is no mediation, no options, only unconditional subordination. This way of thinking does not take into account interests, situations and needs:

> "**For where the moral law speaks there is, objectively, no longer any free choice** with regard to what is to be done; and to show taste in one's conduct (or in judging that of others) is something very different from expressing one's moral mode of thinking; for the latter contains a command and produces a need, while modish taste by contrast only plays with the objects of satisfaction without attaching itself to any of them."[489]

In the following two chapters, the elementary concepts of 'individual' and 'order', which have now been worked out, are once again examined to determine how they appear in the *CPJ*. For the 'reconstruction' of the *CPJ* in favor of the representability of political subjectivity, the text must be subjected to a certain amount of violence, which, however, should not be

---

[486] In real natural purposiveness, only mind and imagination are put into a relationship. See *CPJ*, First Introduction, p. 47.

[487] As a reminder: Natural causality is characterized by the infiniteness of the cause-effect chains in both directions of time, whereas causality of freedom makes it possible for such a chain to begin spontaneously in a cause which itself is no longer preconditioned by an effect, i. e. that is primordially and originally causative.

[488] Cf. *CPJ*, B XVI-XVII [61].

[489] *CPJ*, B 16 [96].

that of a usurper, but that of an architect appointed for the task, who must submit and explain a plan for this purpose. For the time being, this plan looks as follows: up to chapter B.1.7 *The Political Judgment*, everything that follows must be regarded as preparation and provision of material. Only from there on does the orderly transformation of the *Criticism of the Power of Judgment* into a philosophy of the political subject begin.

B.1.5 Figures of the Individual: Individuality in the Text of the *CPJ*

After it has already been pointed out several times in Part A and also here that Kant's third *Critique* is intended to represent a philosophy of the concrete that enables the transition between conceptual-universal forms of theoretical and practical reason on a common 'ground', it is nevertheless an obvious assumption that the concept of the concrete individual finally experiences its own justification in relation to the formal subject of knowledge at this point in the Kantian system. Therefore, it makes sense to perform a short word field analysis. Even at first glance it is noticeable that no separate paragraph is dedicated to the concrete-human under the term 'individual'. At second glance, for example with the help of a Kant index, it turns out that there are also few passages in the text where the word 'individual' appears.

The only place in the *CPJ* is in dialectics, more precisely in the paragraph on the dissolution of the antinomy of taste:

> "Now the judgment of taste does pertain to objects of the senses, but not in order to determine a **concept** of them for the understanding, for it is not a cognitive judgment. It is thus, as an intuitive singular representation related to the feeling of pleasure, only a private judgment, and to this extent its validity would be limited to the *judging individual alone*: The object is an object of satisfaction **for me**, it may be different for others; – everyone has his own taste."[490]

Kant extends the concept of reflecting judgment immediately afterwards, but at least he has applied the concept of the individual here in a way that provides the first indications of its defined function. For the individual is "alone" here and the judgment experiences a limitation if it should actually only apply to the individual. Individuality is therefore a state of confinement within one's own private horizon of judgment. Moreover, the individual already exists before it has developed its ability to communicate and with its judgments (aesthetically and teleologically) could in some way claim universal validity. This very strong restriction of the individual's abilities is surprising and does not yet fit at all to the demanding word use that is aimed at here.

---

[490] *CPJ*, B 235 [215].

The next encounter with the word only takes place in *Teleological Critique of Judgment*, where Kant calls "prestabilism" the theory in which "... a nature that continuously works at their destruction simultaneously makes good the loss of the individuals."[491] It then goes on to the theory of "individual preformation", which is also that of the two possible types of prestabilism, which nature beings are regarded as "reactants" and is therefore called "theory of evolution":

> "The champions of the **theory of evolution**, which excepts every individual from the formative power of nature in order to allow it to come immediately from the hand of the creator, would still not have dared to have this happen in accordance with the hypothesis of occasionalism, which would make impregnation a mere formality"[492]

Undoubtedly, the word individual here only refers to a human being among many others, namely as an empirical natural being. Kant tries to emphasize here that the pre-Darwinist "evolution theorists" of that time allowed too many transcendent, i.e. hyperphysical assumptions, because they believed that a "supreme rational world cause" had already determined everything and would "form the fruit with his own hand" in order to leave to the mother only the "development and nurishment of it." (ibid.) This idea would take away the individual's own formational power and see all individuals since the beginning of the world as given by divine hand. This would bring us back to the middle of the monadic cosmos of Leibniz, who had more certainties about divine perfection and world creation than critical philosophy would have allowed. For some time now, this position has again been held by Christian fundamentalists in the U.S. under the marketing-approved name Intelligent Design. Kant, on the other hand, found *epigenesis* to be much more explanatory because it needs only a minimum of the supernatural to explain the diversity of nature, simply by seeing reproduction as a productive, i.e. *involving* or *enfolding faculty* at work, instead of just an unfolding of the consequences of a first cause. He was thus on the way to a modern theory of evolution that had to operate with the concepts of *variation, selection* and *chance*.[493]

---

[491] *CPJ*, B 376 [291].

[492] *CPJ*, B 376 [291].

[493] This section in the *CPJ* is extremely important, for there is no doubt that Kant saw the entire **system of critiques from an angle of analogy with organic beings**. The concept of *epigenesis* occurs only once more in his major works, namely in transcendental deduction, where Kant names the mind and its categories as the basis for the creation of a "system[s] of the epigenesis of pure

Kant has distinguished the living organisms from the outer natural order with their inner and outer (objective-material) purposiveness. As a rule, these two orders are two completely separate areas – with one exception: the"... organization of both sexes in relation to each other for the reproduction of their species." (*CPJ*, B 381 [293]) Surprisingly, two different living beings can also be considered from the point of view of the purposiveness as one uniform organism:

> "...for here one can always ask, just as in the case of an individual, why must such a pair have existed? The answer is that this is what here first constitutes an **organizing** whole, although not one that is organized in a single body."[494]

Herewith the passages on the 'individual' are already exhausted. It can be seen from the few remarks that Kant regards this word as a clearly defined but essentially general relationship structure of ends, which is characterized by a relative seclusiveness or rather: relative autonomy in relation to its environment.

In no way can a meaning of individuality be demonstrated in the vocabulary of critical philosophy that is still in use today in the context of social science. And in some ways Kant has been much more precise in determining individuality than the authors of the subsequent hypertrophic or hypostatic versions of this term were. Kant's thriftiness with the word individual is related to its history. It is well conceivable that he has seen how much the individual, when taken seriously as a concept, is indebted in an older notion of atomistic substantialism or problematic monadology.[495] The mortgage would then be open in the form of the meaning of the word: the individual is the indivisible. But exactly this assumption is contradicted by the whole doctrine of reflecting judgment. For an indivi-

---

reason" (*CPuRe* B 167 [265]). And what other than an organized individual could be the *Critique of Pure Reason* itself, if he calls it a "**structure of members in which each thing is an organ, that is, in which everything is for the sake of each member, and each individual member is for the sake of all, so that even the least frailty, whether it be a mistake (an error) or a lack, must inevitably betray itself in its use**", (*CPuRe* B XXXVII-III [120])? This should only be hinted at here: there are obviously text systems that are based on the organic causal principle of life (or on its analogue). Catherine Malabou who gave a fresh restart to understand Kant from the perspective of epigenesis in *Before Tomorrow: Epigenesis and Rationality*, Cambridge 2016.

[494] *CPJ*, B 381 [293-4].
[495] See chapter A.1.2.

dual thus presented would actually be nothing more than a substance understood scholastically. However, the reflecting power of judgment is attributed to a being that is defined precisely by a.) the possession of this power of judgment itself and b.) not to be able to determine the world and above all itself in continuous causality. The *CPJ* only concerns beings who are virtually the opposite of 'individuals' in this substantialist sense.

In the *CPuRe* the concept of the individual is reserved in a prominent place for the transcendental ideal of reason:

> "It is, however, also the one single genuine ideal of which human reason is capable, because only in this one single case is an – in itself universal – concept of one thing thoroughly determined through itself, cognized as the representation of an individual."[496]

Here the terminology is particularly clear: the in-dividuum is just one. This individual is a God first "realized" as an idea, then "hypostasized"[497] and finally "personified".[498] In Kant's work, then, it already amounts to what Novalis later put into the formula: **the individual is a dividual**. Individuality in our contemporary sense, which should actually be called dividuality, is only possible through the self-divisibility of a self, the self-relativation and at the same time self-objectivation of the subject in the execution of what Kant called the "subjective universality" in judgments. Without wishing to suggest this term for further use, and exclusively to illustrate the theoretical landscape, the following remark: what the theory of discourse calls 'intersubjectivity' would correspond to 'interdividuality' in the present thought process. But it doesn't make things easier when new terms are added. Kant in any case uses 'individual' in the *CPJ* only as a word and thus describes the terminological counterpart to 'genus', as 'individual' in relation to its 'species'.[499] Thus a further, albeit negative

---

[496] *CPuRe* B 604 [556].

[497] On the concept of 'hypostasis' and the counter term 'hypotyposis', see chap. B.1.7.2.2 below.

[498] *CPuRe* B 612, fn. [559].

[499] Kant uses the example of the race to show just how much is demanded of a simple *word* or *term* until it is suitable for the homophone *concept*; cf. Kant, Immanuel, *Bestimmung des Begriffs einer Menschenrasse* [Determination of the Concept of Human Race] in: ders. *Werke* [Works] XI, pp. 63-82. The distinction between word and concept has been a constitutive moment of the whole rationalism since Scholasticism. I know of no investigation into this distinction in Kant, a distinction that is obviously reflected in his texts and even belongs to the method of his critical philosophy.

result would be presented in this section. But this result is valuable, because now an important terminological difference between Kant's use of 'individuality' as a word or concept and today's emphatic-human understanding of individuality can be described. If we continue to talk about the individual in the following, then the individual is meant as an individual who is capable as a being of reflecting judgment, i.e. a being with 'common sense', but not the social atom, the monad or the moral subject, of which only the latter, through its freedom and autonomy, is the instance that can preserve man's title of special dignity from nature. This sounds a little tense, but it is important to point out that **reflecting judgment is not the keeper of the seal of human dignity**, because it really follows exclusively from the categorical imperative, is therefore legal without deviation and falls under the determining judgment. Otherwise, the distinction between subject and individual that is to be made here would be lost. The task is to read into the Kantian text a concept of individuality that conflicts with his own use of words and concepts and corresponds to what he calls "human".

> "Agreeableness is also valid for nonrational animals; beauty is valid only for human beings, i.e., animal but also rational beings, but not merely as the latter (e.g., spirits), rather as beings who are at the same time animal; the good, however, is valid for every rational being in general."[500]

Finally, a brief consideration shows why the emphatic individual cannot occur at all in the *CPJ*. The representation of concrete individuality has already been thwarted by the arrangement of the judgment analyses. The lack of interest in beauty is actually incompatible with the notion of real individuality and corresponds more to the shape of the moral subject. Kant accordingly also emphasized the kinship of disinterested pleasure and the moral interest "taken" in a thing in the analysis of beauty.

> "All interest presupposes a need or produces one; and as a determining ground of approval it no longer leaves the judgment on the object free."[501]

The assumed needlessness of an individual is a fiction for the generation of ideal-typical forms of pure judgments. To use there the concreteness of the individual in its always complex world experiences would have run counter to the method of the analysis of pure judgments. The individual

---

[500] *CPJ*, B 15 [95].

[501] *CPJ*, B 16 [96].

must also be 'back-mixed', or rather: recomposed and related to aesthetics and the public, so that it becomes visible as a philosophical figure. This is why it is also called figures of the individual instead of *concept* – as in the political triad in Part A. The figures of the individual appear only at the intersections of the various forms of judgment. The *CPJ* does not produce any *concepts*; at best, teleology aims at or strives for such concepts. If the human, emphatically understood individual had now been introduced as a concept, then it would certainly not have been able to prove its origin from the reflecting power of judgment. It would have been just an illegitimate, hypostasized God who usurped the ideal of reason. As we know, this act of violence by individuals against themselves actually occurs in the world by means of a lack of common sense, namely in the form of mental insanity[502].

---

[502] Thus, political insanity could be diagnosed as a symptom of pathologically deformed judgment. This deformation could be examined in detail and perhaps precisely determined with the means of the judgment analysis. Paranoid states of mind are tied to particular forms of judgment in the subject. The fact that political insanity has long been a phenomenon familiar to mankind is recalled by the ancient admonition of slaves to the Roman army leaders and Caesars: "Memento mori!" See Post, Jerrold M. and Robins, Robert S., *Political Paranoia. The Psychopolitics of Hate*, Yale 1995.

B.1.6 Politics in the *Critique*: Political Examples and Topics in the *CPR*

In previous attempts to gain a political philosophy from the *CPJ*, the systematic and judgment analysis of the work has not even been attempted. This may have been connected with the difficulties that had already emerged in advance. However, it is all the more astonishing that the invitations of the text, where it explicitly offers political themes and examples, were in no way and at any point taken seriously or even noticed as an opportunity to illustrate the political-philosophical content of the *CPJ*.[503] Even in Ulrich Sassenbach's instructive study *The Concept of the Political in Kant* the *CPJ* is not even mentioned – although it will still be shown here that this circumvention is a method to secure the exclusivity of the claim to the title 'political philosophy' for the moral dimension of the political.[504]

It is therefore not entirely free of irony if on the first page of the First Introduction of the *CPJ* no less is claimed by Kant than that "state wisdom and state economy" could be counted as practical philosophy due to a "great" and "disadvantageous" misunderstanding (*CPJ*, First Introduction, p.9). In the second introduction, he reaffirms and clarifies this assumption on the second page:

> "All technically practical rules (i.e., those of art and skill in general, as well as those of prudence, as a skill in influencing human beings and their will), so far as their principles rest on concepts, must be counted only as corollaries of theoretical philosophy."[505]

The old teachings of political acumen therefore belong only to natural philosophy if they are based on mechanistic ideas (Machiavelli, Hobbes). More important for the path chosen here to explore political subjectivity is what excludes the restriction "if its principles are based on concepts". After the discussions so far, it has become clear that the reflexive power of judgment is *based on the renunciation of a conceptual basis*. The art and

---

[503] One important passage is no longer cited below, namely that on the French Revolution and the state as an "organization" (*CPJ*, B 295, fn. [247]), because it has already been discussed in Chapter B.1.4.

[504] Sassenbach, Ulrich, *Der Begriff des Politischen bei Kant*, Würzburg 1992; discussed here in Chapter B.1.8.

[505] *CPJ*, B XIII-IV [60].

wisdom of influencing the will of others (or even one's own), as long as it is not based on *concepts*, but is carried out through *reflection*, has a justified claim to its treatment outside theoretical philosophy, i.e. outside the domain of the *CPuRe*. **This is something like a *concession to dig for a new political philosophy*, which Kant has deposited at the entrance to the *CPJ*.** We want to see if there is not another vein of gold to be uncovered in the rock of the text, the existence of which has now been pointed out by a whole series of observations and test drillings.

In distinguishing the "judgment of the senses" as a "private judgment", which has purely receptive character and makes no claim to general attunement, from the "judgment by reflection", Kant uses a word whose fundamental political significance in historical practice was reported here in chapter A.3. Kant calls the judgment by reflection a "common" judgment that is "public"[506]. Thus, the judgment by reflection in all its types and modes is a *public judgment* or a *judgment that claims publicity*. What is interesting here is that **the public sphere is not used as an empirical-material concept of social practice, but it is obvious that it describes a practice of judgment**, i.e. the realization of subjective faculty. After 'order', there comes also for the philosophical constitution of the 'public' a subjective turn into view. Furthermore, the public sphere can be categorized under the teleological concept of order, whereby the order of the public sphere is not unproblematic, because *the idea of the public sphere is in part a negation of the general concept of order*. Publicity cannot therefore be completely reconstructed without the other elementary concept: individuality. This relationship will be thoroughly examined in the next chapter.

Kant's comment on the relationship between the sublime and some objects, which we would easily attribute to politics, is much more explicit than the subtlety of the public sphere scheme in practice of the universally reflecting judgment:

> "It [the scale] may be, by the way empirical, as in the case of the average magnitude of the people known to us, of animals of a certain species, of trees, houses, mountains, etc., or a standard given *a priori*, which because of the deficiencies of the judging subject is restricted to subjective conditions of presentation *in concreto*: as in the practical sphere, the **magnitude of a certain virtue, or of public freedom and justice in a country**."[507]

---

[506] *CPJ*, B 22 [99].

[507] *CPJ*, B 82-83 [133].

Virtue, public freedom and justice as objects of the sublime in the reflecting judgment are – who would deny this – among the numerous possibilities for an individual and everyday assessment of political-empirical reality. The scales of the respective size serve for the aesthetic assessment of the objects. What is sublime is what goes far beyond these standards. This points to two things: there is an *aesthetically acquired normal size* (where the moment of the sublime does not yet really come into play) for all political and moral concepts; and if the *size of the object grows relative to the others, there is a political sublime*, just as there is a moral sublime in its own right. The decisive factor here is the comparative size of the objects in the imagination.

The relationship between sublime and political history is worth considering for itself. For the feeling of sublimity comes to an end in that age, as Kant exemplifies in the *CPJ*, when nature needs human help and protection, if it is thought of in relation to nature. The human capacity to feel the sublime is sometimes responsible for the plundering of nature that began as soon as technical civilization provided the means[508], as, for example, Lévi-Strauss lamented in his famous account of the global development of industrial culture.[509] The sublime would then be this driving force of the resistance to nature and its subsequent submission that has gone beyond the goal; perhaps beauty is now the medicine for the healing of the same wounds. And only the beautiful is man's home. That's how Kant taught it.

The threat of nature as such is less prevalent than ever in the democratic industrial age. Almost every ecological danger today (for the rich peoples of the industrial nations, although this distinction is becoming increasingly blurred) is a product of culture. And even as such it is – so far at least – hardly comparable with the epidemics and catastrophes of the early modern period (plague, hunger). But even today it still remains the case that the more a culture has to tremble before the actual threat of nature, the less chances political subjectivity has to be practiced and developed.[510] For as long as nature is really experienced as terrible, it com-

---

[508] Kant reports on the early destruction of European forests by deforestation, in the north in particular the spruce forests [Guyer mistakenly translates "pine"], "because of their unreasonable extinction we often accuse our ancestors." (*CPJ*, B 281-2 [240])

[509] Lévi-Strauss, Claude, *Triste tropiques* [Sad Tropics], Paris 1955.

[510] Flooding, earth movements, hunger and epidemics are the main natural threats; racial conflicts, wars, overpopulation and mismanagement – e.g. in the form of

mands over everything individual, threatens with its superiority and humiliates humans. If the power of nature cannot be viewed from a safe position, but hits humans directly, then there is nothing sublime about it, but only anguish[511], for sublimity is only in the mind...

> "...insofar as we can become conscious of being superior to nature within us and thus also to nature outside us (insofar as it influences us)."[512]

In this context, one could recall Egon Friedell's cultural-historical thesis that European history gained its greatest impetus for increasing power and knowledge from overcoming the plague of the late Middle Ages. From the point of view of a subjective historical power connected with the aesthetic capacity, this very speculative but not completely absurd thesis, which was above all ironically directed against Nietzsche's superhuman philosophy, is again interesting: Man grows from illness![513]

War is in no way objectively a natural disaster, even if it is subjectively experienced as such. Under certain conditions, Kant believes, it can be waged by the feeling of the sublime with conviction.

> "Even war, if it is conducted with order and reverence for the rights of civilians, has something sublime about it, and at the same time makes the mentality of the people who conduct it in this way all the more sublime, the more dangers it has been exposed to and before which it has been able to assert its courage; whereas a long peace causes the spirit of mere commerce to predominate, along with base selfishness, cowardice and weakness, and usually debases the mentality of the populace."[514]

---

hostile resettlement or destruction of arable land – are cultural products, whereby of course the interdependencies and increases are sufficiently known: Evil rarely comes alone. The development economist Amartya Sen, for example, has shown how famines can and often are 'home-grown'. In this case, the economic rationality of hoarding producers and traders as well as consumers anticipating future demand would have to be presented in a natural way throughout, just as in Hobbes' anthropology of future hunger ("Homo etiam fame futura famelicus"; De homine X,3); see Sen, Amartya, *Poverty and Famines*, Oxford 1981.

[511] See here the *Cultural Anthropological Excursus II* in chapter B.2.2.

[512] *CPJ*, B 109 [147].

[513] Friedell, Egon, *Kulturgeschichte der Neuzeit* [Cultural History of the Modern Era], 3 vols., 1927-32.

[514] *CPJ*, B 107 [146].

Consideration is given here to the war as it was waged until Napoleon and as Clausewitz wanted to restore it.[515] The wars with which mankind was familiarized in the 20th century had little to do with it. Through the "Even..." at the beginning of this quote, the representation is an admission that by *no means wants the war to appear sublime in itself*. Kant was well acquainted with the senseless destruction and increasing brutality even in the "most civilized" war. However, some wars in world history must have been of a special kind.[516] Kant was never a recruit; he only knew the war from literature and the Russian occupation of East Prussia between 1758 and 1762. At the same time, Frederick II was playing with suicidal thoughts for the first time, for his troops were wiped out on all fronts by the supremacy of the European armies. At the beginning of the dispute the king had the laudable intention not to let the civilian population notice anything of the war, but the resulting Seven Years War spared only the very few, and to be occupied by Russia was therefore a favorable arrangement, so to speak a loge seat, in order to be able to observe the further course of the spectacle calmly. The position of the subjects of the European coalition powers, who could admire the courage of the French army since the cannonade of Valmy on 20 September 1772, was similar. Kant, who in all his writings, as much as possible, distances himself from the barbarity of war, has not judged all wars equally bad and harmful. Some wars in world history have had special qualities. Even if there had been something like a free press, especially in war reporting, or a field sociology interested in this topic, which had enlightened about the brutality of conscription, punishments and mass desertions, Kant would have been forced, for methodological reasons, to concede the possible sublimity of war.

As in Michel de Montaigne's *Essais*, for example, the depiction of war has always been about a literary projection that turned war into a laboratory for testing human virtues – as long as one was not affected by violence oneself. The war served the chroniclers, writers and philosophers to sensualize an idea of reason.[517] Kant calls this process a *symbolic hypo-*

---

[515] See section A.1.6.

[516] This thought is taken up her once again in the *Cultural Anthropological Excursus II*, chapter B.2.2, where it is shown that there is a possible connection between the *emergence of political subjectivity* and the events of war.

[517] An exception is the famous, extensive *Adagium 3001 'Dulce bellum inexpertis'* by Erasmus of Rotterdam, which is also the first European peace script; cf. Erasmus of Rotterdam, Desiderius, *Süß scheint der Krieg den Unerfahrenen* [Sweet Seems War to the Inexperienced], edited by Brigitte Hannemann, Munich 1987.

typosis. The idea of virtuous courage was underpinned by war as a sensual image. This was often very little related to historical-empirical reality. The Swiss, for example, were the most feared mercenaries in Europe since the 15th century. They waged the war precisely with the commercial spirit that Kant reports – with the voice of the people – that it was corrupting a people. It should be noted here that Kant tolerated the war under certain conditions and in a certain respect as beneficial to humanity, namely 1) when it lets the audience discover their own moral feeling in the enthusiasm of participating in the events (French Revolutionary Wars; cf. here Chapter A.1.6); if 2) it lets the war participants discover in their courage a new dimension of humanity in their person that can be experienced through the feeling of the sublime (for example the Battle of Salamis 480 BC; cf. here Chapter B.2.2); and finally 3) with regard to its long-term necessarily civilizing effect. In his treatise *Zum ewigen Friede* [On Perpetual Peace. A Philosophical Sketch] for example, war is considered under the teleological assumption that its barbarism will keep a process of cultivation going.[518] A corresponding statement can also be found in the *Methodology of Teleological Judgment*. The "cosmopolitan whole" of a system of states is mostly thwarted by "ambition, lust for power and greed"; then...

"...war ... is inevitable, which, even though it is an unintentional effort of humans (aroused by unbridled passions), is a deeply hidden but perhaps intentional effort of supreme wisdom if not to establish then at least to prepare the way for the lawfulness together with the freedom of the states and by means of that the unity of a morally grounded system[519] of them, and which, in spite of the most horrible tribulations

---

[518] The whole bundle of theses in Kant's treatise on peace is therefore an achievement of reflecting judgment, i.e. the methodical application of the idea of beauty, sublime and end to world politics. This was often overlooked because only the moral-philosophical aspect was considered, which conceals the aesthetic-teleological foundation of writing. Exceptions to the rule: Rudolf Makreel's contribution to the 8th International Kant Congress – *Kant and the Problem of Peace*, March 1-5, 1995, Memphis/Tenesseee, USA, under the title *Reconciling Dogmatic and Reflecting Interpretations of History*, published. 1996 in the Kongress-Akten; in addition, Alexis Philonenko's study *La théorie kantienne de l'histoire*, Paris 1986, pp. 44-5, Volker Gerhard's excellent discussion of this complex of questions in his study *Immanuel Kants Entwurf "Zum Ewigen Frieden"*. *Eine Theorie der Politik* [Immanuel Kant's Draft 'Perpetual Peace'. A Theory of Politics], Darmstadt 1995, pp. 107-25.

[519] The establishment of a "morally based system" does not contradict the view that it is **political subjectivity that prepares moral orders**. On the contrary: it is

[...] is nevertheless one more incentive [...] for developing to their highest degree all the talents that serve for culture."[520]

War can usually only be judged politically from the position of the audience, from the subjective viewpoint of the individuals who do not have to participate, because **in wartime itself there is usually no longer any political subjectivity**. Nowhere is everything individual more systematically suppressed by discipline than in military organization – all the more so, of course, when it comes to the ability of (compulsorily) obligated individuals to reflect on the order of warfare and its admissibility. The political subjectivity of the warrior as a soldier may only be expressed if the purposiveness of war itself, as determined by the ruling power, is recognized without a dissenting accent.[521] Even formulas such as that of the 'citizen in uniform' cannot disguise this [introduced in Germany when the army was rebuilt after WWII].

Kant was already discussing another topic that determined the political autumn of 1995, namely the tendency of governments to use the imagery of religion for their own purposes. The Federal Constitutional Court had asked the State of Bavaria to take the crucifixes in the classrooms of the schools off the walls in order to guarantee the freedom of faith in public institutions. Kant writes in a very Protestant manner that people "for fear of the powerlessness of their ideas" should seek help in "images and childlike apparatuses".

> "That is why even governments have gladly allowed religion to be richly equipped with such supplements and thus sought to relieve the subject of the bother but at the same time also of the capacity to extend the powers of his soul beyond the limits that are arbitrarily set for him and by means of which, as merely passive, he can more easily be dealt with."[522]

This also includes a very strict assessment of such practices as the political-religious morning prayer in North American schools in the face of the U.S.

---

even inevitable. But from the goal you no longer recognize what a society has brought there. It is a question of understanding the ability to implement such orders; cf. chapter B.1.8.

[520] *CPJ*, B 394 [300].

[521] This also applied to the first French revolutionary army, which benefited from the coincidence of command and its own subjective will to order; cf. chapter A.1.6.

[522] *CPJ*, B 126 [156].

banner. The relief of reflection for the subjects, however, has two sides, because without a sensual-symbolic view, without eventfulness and memory, no feeling for political, religious and moral things can develop – in the sense of Rousseau's pedagogy.

Kant then developed an observation of human sociability into a general theory of emotional communication. This ability to communicate emotions must be recognized as an anthropological fact if one has previously attributed a natural social instinct to human beings.

> "The beautiful interests empirically only in society; and if the drive to society is admitted to be natural to human beings, while the suitability and the tendency toward it, i.e., sociability, are admitted to be necessary for human beings as creatures destined for society, and thus as a property belonging to humanity, then it cannot fail that taste should also be regarded as a faculty for judging everything by means of which one can communicate even his feeling to everyone else, and hence as a means for promoting what is demanded by an inclination natural to everyone."[523]

Taste must therefore be part of civilization when man's impulse to society is added. Mind you: Kant does **not** claim an *a priori secured socialization drive*, but only reminds us that, if one assumes such a drive as natural, taste must also be a natural means of realizing this drive.

This communication of feelings is by no means bound to language, but taste lives almost from the fact that it can grow beyond words. Emotions can be communicated and generated in the same way in aesthetic attributes. Kant cites as examples the "Jupiter's Eagle" and the "Peacock of the Queen of Heaven", who, unlike logical attributes, do not present the concepts of grandeur and majesty, but the power of imagination...

> "...which gives the imagination cause to spread itself over a multitude of related representations, which let one think more than one can express in a concept determined by words"[524]

The aesthetic attribute thus invites the imagination to an *excess of associations* which could not be effectively communicated by the pure concept.[525] Kant's examples are domineering attributes and point to the

---

[523] *CPJ*, B 162-3 [229].

[524] *CPJ*, B 195 [251].

[525] This is the critical problem of the development described by Max Weber to rationalize rule in the form of administration. Bureaucratic rule no longer

realm of heraldic symbols and emblems, which undoubtedly serve to sensualize a political judgment, for they are public and are intended to evoke the idea of a discrete, i.e. precisely defined order and make its power binding by means of the exuberant imagination in the subject. Here we are, of course, on the ruling side of political subjectivity, for the aesthetic attributes belong to the expressive action of the ruling subject (in its respective embodiment, for example as prince, council, president, parliament, ministry, court or corporation). The sovereign as political subject tries by means of aesthetic attributes to achieve the purposiveness[526], size and power of the order created and maintained by him the attunement of subjects or citizens. These attributes therefore do not belong to the apparatus of compulsory decrees but form a separate aesthetic-persuasive dimension of the political, whereby on the side of domination a **special ability of judgment is obviously assumed among the dominated subjects**. A more detailed discussion of this topic belongs in the *political iconography*.

Kant believes that Frederick II, the 'Great King', strengthened less his own rule than the "cosmopolitan attitude" of his subjects when he decorated his end of life with the aesthetic attribute of the beautiful summer day accomplished[527]. In this way he would have stimulated a certain idea of reason in a manner "for which no expression can be found" through "a multitude of sensations and side conceptions."[528]

Another type of non-conceptual expression, which is supposed to generate accord in the subjects, lies in the political architecture. Kant

---

produces aesthetic attributes, but can at best still refer to its own, conceptually reconstructable rationality. Keyword: "Legitimation through procedure" (Luhmann).

[526] Kant does not mention the aspect of purposiveness here, but only for the methodological reasons discussed, namely because it belongs to teleology, which is to be dealt with separately within the CPJ. This very distinction must be disregarded in a controlled manner in further research into political subjectivity.

[527] *CPJ*, B 196 [194].

[528] In this lies a major problem of modern politics: What rational idea can still be *sensed* when in everyday political life or in the political system, including the administration associated with it, it is almost exclusively a matter of factual-theoretical decisions that no longer allow political-subjective competence to come into play? At this moment, morality often jumpf in, instrumentally to break up and delegitimize the imperatives of system rationality. But can this process really be qualified as political? This is discussed in chapter B.1.8.

declares the "magnificent buildings to be the home of public assemblies", "arches of honor", "columns" and "cenotaphs", and other aesthetically attributed honors as belonging to architecture, in order to distinguish them from the buildings which are just suitable for use.[529] But it is obvious that the honors in political architecture have an extraordinarily strong functional character with regard to the aesthetic order to be embodied; it is only worth recalling the cenotaph of Napoleon and the Pantheon in Paris or the difficulties in reconstructing the Reichstag in Berlin after the unification of Germany. In this context belong the attempts to work out the peculiar on fascist and National Socialist architecture. The philosophical assumption here is none other than the **imputation of political subjectivity among the dominated**, which, with the help of the symbolic violence of architecture among other things, should be completely silenced as a self-portrayal of rule in order to remain trapped in a kind of *political religiosity* and piety. **The largest political subject is then also the only one**, namely the National Socialist leader, who completely unites the political on himself and has the state of emergency, as Carl Schmitt described the phenomenon of the leader state with admiration.

And yet, like everyone else, this sovereign needed aesthetic means for a certain kind of persuasion, remembering not only architecture but even more the propagandistic speech. Kant wrote about "eloquence" as "persuading art to deceive by beautiful appearances (like ars oratoria)"[530], which is unsuitable for the pulpit and court. This free speech, especially when it is used for political purposes, is always fraud because it only "understands how to persuade people **to judge important things like machines**", which no one would do objectively out of free will.[531] From a historical point of view, he notes that political rhetoric in Athens and Rome reached its peak just then, when "the state had hastened to its doom and true patriotic ways of thinking had ceased."[532]

This is a serious objection to the modern, democratic ideal of free vocal expression, to the idea of the dignity of political speech. However, it fits with Kant's clear awareness of an important difference between the freedom of speech and the freedom of the pen. However, the explanation lies in the mistrust of all scholars associated with this ideal-typical distinction,

---

[529] *CPJ*, B 208 [200].
[530] *CPJ*, B 216 [209].
[531] *CPJ*, B 218, fn [210].
[532] Ibid.

however much they saw themselves as enlighteners, against uncontrolled and unattended bourgeois reasoning in the public sphere. The writing of all criticism was a very restrictive condition, whereby the scholars, including Kant's own person[533], wanted to reserve privileged access to an exclusive form of state publicity.

The expressiveness of these explicitly political passages of the *CPJ* does not exactly invite us to assume a whole political philosophy in this work. But at least it is now proven that Kant himself thought about problems of the evaluation and representation of political objects when he wrote the *CPJ*. That he did not determine the predicate 'political' is, on the one hand, connected with the fact that *he still limited the concept of politics in German tradition completely to the state sphere* with officially appointed and professsional decision-makers; on the other hand, it would also have run against his method of the dismembering analysis of pure judgments to determine the political in the form of political subjectivity as an achievement of one's own judgment. This chapter was now also the last preparation for presenting this political subjectivity in its functions, modes and structures. The text of the *CPJ* has been discussed in this way in order to present the following as a consequence of the Kantian work, namely as a conversion or extension on the same foundation.

---

[533] See chapter A.3.1 on the publicity of criticism.

B.1.7 The Political Judgment

The following three sections examine the political judgment itself. An exemplary historical background with a political triad is now open, and Kant's *Critique of the Power of Judgment* has been disassembled in such a way that all elements are ready for the construction of the form of political judgments. The task is extremely difficult, because this form of judgment is not simply a static model that knows no time. Such a synchronous philosophy of the political subject would be useless and uninformative. It would be like a mirror in which you only recognize what you look into, namely the desperate political subject of democratic modernity. Some stick a beard on this dissatisfied subject, and good old Aristotle looks out of the mirror. On the other hand, a general theory for determining and localizing political competence in the subject, which also wants to prove itself before history and the newer social and cultural sciences, must be able to compete with the diachrony. If Kant's third *Critique* contains a philosophy of the sensual-concrete and at the same time is the basis of the possibility of political subjectivity, then this philosophy of the political subject must *at least aspire to* going through the series of all historical concretions of the political. As much as this sounds like Hegel's phenomenology, it has nothing to do with it, because the spirit will not fix this. The diachronic process does not necessarily mean that a solid theorem of evolution of political culture as an aggregate of political subjectivities is crystallized. The opposite will be the case here, because the surprising thing is the fragility, the risk and improbability of political subjectivity and its culture. In a sense, diachrony means nothing more than simply calculating with time. The minimum requirement is that something relevant is said about emergence and the development of political subjectivity, when it entered historical time and what concretions it went through during this time. Presenting this proves to be very problematic, because it is about still images of a world in flux. All time horizons must be equally present so that the appropriateness of the form of political judgment, as presented here, can be tested on the multitude of their concretions. I hope, however, to be allowed to relieve the following sections of the diachronic representation by referring to the historical part A of the investigation and the scattered ethnological-historical observations in part B, especially in chapter B.2.2. This restriction seems to me all the more inevitable since there is not even a theorem on political evolution to date, with which something like a political quality of time could be discussed.[534] Kant himself, by the way, has neatly separated the temporal references of his depictions in the system of his critical philosophy, for the first two critiques (theoretical and practical philosophy) are purely synchronic, whereas the diachrony for the whole system of the *Critiques* is anchored in the *CPJ* (cf. chapter B.1.2 under the keyword 'historicity'). The claim to diachrony is therefore unmistakably raised here too, but with an exemption from the obligation to depict the time dimension with the concept dimension completely on the same matrix.[535]

---

[534] The first approaches to researching the political dimension of time should have been expected in Frank Pfetsch's comprehensive new work; cf. *Dimensionen des Politischen*, 3 vol., vol. I: *Erkenntnis und Politik. Philosophische Dimensionen des Politischen* [Knowledge and Politics. The Philosophical Dimension of the Political], Darmstadt 1995. In the chapter *Raum und Zeit in Politik und Politiktheorie* [Space and Time in Politics and Political Theory] (ibid., pp. 51-63), the author takes these two hitherto unexplored dimensions of political philosophy into account. However, the study is empirically and analytically oriented throughout, which in theory always means that a series of illustrations and examples are assigned to a phenomenon or a term in any order, without one really knowing what justifies this connection. In addition, Pfetsch's interest in a theory of international politics is the focus of the study, which defines in particular the spatial dimension of the territorial and national space. The spectrum of effectiveness of these two forms of visualization and imagination is thus covered only in a small sector. Helmut König and Matthias Pfüller, on the other hand, came much closer to the question when they sketched the outlines of a "political science of the subject". They rightly pointed out that **political science does not have any kind of usable subject theory and that this is one of the main weaknesses of political science as a serious social science**. However, they wanted to counter this lack with a consistently psychological theory of the political subject, which they unfortunately also wanted to be inseparably linked with their own "emancipatory" and "capitalism-critical" motives; cf. König, Helmut, *Politologie des Subjekts* [Politicial Science of the Subject], in: Albrecht, Ulrich et al. (ed.), *Was heißt und zu welchen Ende betreiben wir Politikwissenschaft?* [What Means and to which Ends Do We Practice Political Sciences?], Opladen 1989, pp. 53-65; cf. also Pfüller, Matthias, *Faktoren einer Konstitution des Subjekts in der vorbürgerlichen und bürgerlich-kapitalistischen Gesellschaft - Beitrag zu einer "Politologie des Subjekts"*, [Factors of a Constitution of the Subject in Pre-Civic and Civil-Capitalist Society – Contribution to a Political Science of the Subject], in: Albrecht, Ulrich, loc. cit., pp. 66-80.

[535] This does not mean that it is impossible in principle. The question simply has to be left open, because everything that has to do with time is extraordinarily complex and the available theoretical techniques are not mature enough.

B.1.7.1 Deduction of the Unity of the Political Judgment

In the preceding chapters, in the reversal of Kant's method (B.1.3), which was based on the analysis of pure judgments, the "back-mixing" of these individual forms of judgment, structured and classified by Kant, was held out as a strategy for a solution. Going straight to mixing back the ideal-typically distilled judgments would mean, however, taking the second step before the first. For it must first be established what constitutes the unity of a political judgment, i.e. how it can be distinguished from aesthetic, teleological or generally 'mixed' reflecting judgments. In addition, the functions of the pure forms of judgment (beautiful, sublime, ends) within this unity should be determined. Without this orientational framework, all possibilities of linking the pure forms of judgment would have to be played out purely combinatorically. And even then, it would not be possible to determine exactly which combinations are qualified for political judgments, because there would be no criterion for discriminating the unsuitable hybrids.

It is therefore the right moment to determine the unity of the political judgment, for from now on it will be indispensable for the further representation of political subjectivity. The definition that can now be justified has no less task than to make *the formal principle of all politically qualified judgments*. **Everything in which political subjectivity has manifested itself in some way must become visible through the glasses of this formula.** Kant himself will not provide a single clue, let alone a metaphysical or even transcendental expression that could create this unity. How would this unity be constituted?

First of all, it must specify the framework or the unity of an action, i.e. what the judgment does. In this respect, the unity of judgment is already clearly determined by the previously analyzed and legitimated critique of judgment on the basis of reflecting judgment. Accordingly, the unity of the action of the judgment is *reflection*, in the sense of the *construction of experimental universality* based on the heautonomy of judgment, the basis and starting point of which is always some particular (as opposed to universal). Thus, there is still no further restriction than that which determines the reflecting power of judgment as the universal basis and possibility of performing the political judgment, which was previously assumed in the investigation anyway – in accordance with the indications of Arendt, Vollrath and Ferry.

The specific *object* must now be found for this named unity of the activity of the judgment, to which the judgment applies. Reflection must be given an object so that it can be determined more precisely. The application to beautiful, sublime and ends is excluded, because the *CPJ* has already anticipated everything in their regards. The empirically-reflected nature (the word) cannot therefore be its direct field of activity any more than the totality of nature (the concept), which ultimately itself represents the transcendental principle of reflection, i.e. the condition of possibility of reflecting power of judgment. In addition, the political judgment can no longer be examined using the guidelines of the categories of understanding (quantity, quality, relation, modality) or the ideas of reason, because this reference to the understanding and reason is also already made in the *CPJ* by the forms of judgment that are themselves to be combined in the political judgment. Concepts of the understanding and ideas can therefore no longer directly be the objects of and the basis for the synthesis of political judgments. This is the most important restriction of the political judgment in transcendental-philosophical terms: **it has no transcendental or metaphysical principle of its own** that would have made this direct reference to understanding or reason possible (cf. chapter B.1.3).

On the other hand, direct access to the *feeling of pleasure and displeasure* as the basis of judgment is equally blocked, because this feeling is completely taken up by the beautiful and the sublime. The political judgment can only refer to pleasure/displeasure *through* aesthetics. Here it becomes clear that the political judgment has a *much weaker cognitive status than the aesthetic or teleological judgment*. The lack of reference to the categories, the ideas and the feeling of pleasure/displeasure now means, apart from the renunciation of a principle of its own, that the object of political judgment cannot lie in itself, but only in one of the pure forms of judgment co-operating competitively in it.

There is now *one single object* which, in the entire analysis of the forms of judgment in the *CPJ*, is not completely possessed and its meaning is not exhausted by one of the faculties of mind, and that is the **concept of order**. The teleological judgment produces the concept of order as a combination of ends, whether organic (internal purposiveness) or only aggregated (external purposiveness). These two modes of judgment allow people to provisionally recognize outer existence as an interplay of animate (spirits, animals, consciousness, plants, society) and inanimate structures (connections between precipitation and harvest, scarcity and poverty, warmth and clothing, etc.). It is not only about the scientifically exact determination of organic or mechanical functions, but about the basic orientation in the judging consciousness. As was shown in chapter B.1.4, the restriction of the analysis of teleological judgments in the *CPJ* is again due to the method of producing pure judgments.

The chapter on the *Methodology* of teleological judgment, on the other hand, is the most comprehensive instruction for the application of judgment in Kant's entire critical work, for here he finds the opportunity to have the dispute between teleology and theology settled under the arbitral supervision of the Faculty of Philosophy.[536] Since Kant trained the concept of teleology *reflectingly* in nature and *decisively* in practical philosophy, theology has no choice but to acknowledge its own justification in the addition of moral and natural teleology.[537] If Kant himself had actually thought that there is a philosophy of political subjectivity in the *CPJ*, then he would have had to design it in this very chapter of the methodology of teleological judgment. On the one hand, he applied teleology indeed precisely differentiated to "teaching on nature" (natural sciences) and "teaching on the soul" (theology), according to the encyclopedic classification of all sciences under theoretical and practical knowledge.[538] But at least one particular reason prevented him from allowing teleology – and thus the **ability of the subjective genesis of order** – to come to *self-application in the individual*. This reason is nowhere else to be found than in the method of skimming off pure judgments. One can see how extremely important and rich in consequences Kant's methodical decision was, because many possible connections have thus remained unexploited – in favor of a systematic continuation of Kant's critical enterprise. The individual would have gone beyond the systematics of his methodology because, as a citizen of two worlds, he or she is the subject of the application of a practical and always theoretical method of knowledge. However, *the self-application of the ability of order genesis is only possible in the individual*, who can **reflect upon itself in relation to an order under two aspects: as unity and yet differentiated**. The individual can, so to speak, from the *perspective of the spectator,* reflect upon the order of nature or of souls (methodology), but it can also imagine itself in an order of other beings who are gifted with the same judgment and who must be thought to be involved in the subjective genesis of order, because *they imagine the same process only from a different perspective – and they are imagined like that by*

---

[536] Cf. the scheme of philosophy as one of the "lower faculties" in Kant's *Der Streit der Fakultäten, Werke XI* [The Conflict of the Faculties, Works XI], pp. 261-393.

[537] *CPJ*, B 414 [311].

[538] *CPJ*, B 364 [285].

the politically judging individual. An imagination of identically imagining beings, so to speak. The ability to subjective genesis of order must therefore **not be expanded** to enable its simultaneous self-application (individual) and external application (order of individuals) **but limited** in accordance with the motto: *omnis determinatio est negatio*.

So, it is not about the order of nature or souls, but about the *subjective order of individuals*, whereby the judging individual is included in this order in a differentiated manner, *not as the eternally formal cognitive subject, but as an individual*. This inclusion is inconceivable with the formal subject Kant develops in the theory of categories of the *Critique of Pure Reason*, or the judgment would automatically be a *determining* one and no longer a *reflecting* one. This more precise definition of the self-applied subjective order is made available by the *concept of publicity*. The historical analysis of the public sphere has shown (cf. chapter A.3.1) how difficult it was and is still today to give the concept of the public sphere an appropriate philosophical description. This is not surprising, for publicity proves to be a phenomenon whose exact and above all generative description **cannot be achieved without a philosophy of political subjectivity**. The concept of publicity now has the extraordinarily welcome merit of giving sufficient limitations to enable **self-reference on two sides**, namely the **concept of reflection** and the **concept of order**. The individual is suspended in the concept of the public (not in the Hegelian sense), where its restrictive effect, namely in the form of the application of reflection and order to individuality, enables *reflections to be reflected* and *orders to be ordered*. Precisely because the individual is not defined as a singular, pure form of the subject (singulartantum), but always reflected as a concrete individual as plurality, the reflections as well as the subjective possibilities of order are pluralized; therefore, one can now speak of reflections and orders in the plural. Or to put it another way: through its self-application to an object – namely what is called 'subject' in the singular – **reflection *generates* the plurality of the concrete in the same object, which is now called the 'individual'**. Hence, the adverbial definition can only be found in the concept of the public, which appropriately limits reflection and order, for *the concept of the individual is only generated by the active connection in public reflection on order*. The expression "reflection upon *individual* order", on the other hand, makes no sense at all. For the imagined transition from the individual to order in judgment is already the reflection itself in its mediation between the *particular* and the *universal*.

The unity of political judgment is thus fully definable, for now all moments can be connected to an organic whole, which in turn would ensure the self-application of reflecting judgment in the conception of political subjectivity. Political subjectivity is therefore **the capacity for reflection upon**[539] **public order**. This is the formula, so simple and modest, with which everything must be reconstructible/constructible, which from the point of view of subject-critical philosophy wants to be qualified 'political'. This small sentence is the *logical organism* that, according to the consideration in the previous paragraph, generates individuality as a product of growth. The definition of the unity of judgment can now rightly be called the *deduction of the political judgment*, because it contains everything that belongs to a deduction in the transcendental-philosophical sense. The formula contains the **framework** to the *subjective conditions of the possibility of political reality* (not yet the conditions themselves; that will follow hereafter). According to the three modal forms 1). necessity, 2.) possibility and 3.) reality, the subjective 'conditions' contain the *necessary* conceptual components (1) for the *possibility*, i.e. all that can be potentially thought *as political* in this philosophically qualified sense and without falling into the non-political, (2) of the *reality* of the political, i.e. the actual political judgment synthesized by the individual (3). It is therefore required to discuss now these *subjective conditions* that allow subjects to conceive of political private cosmologies, i.e. action- and judgment-guiding worldviews in which they themselves occur and which contain the measure of their willingness to participate in shaping political reality.

---

[539] Whether one uses the formula intransitively, i.e. as "reflection *of* public order", or transitively as "reflection *upon* public order", makes no fundamental difference, because the "upon" only belongs to the *symbolic hypotyposis* of this process, which is in itself abstract, thus illustrating and thereby facilitating its conceivability. The individual is imagined as a person "bent over upon" its own thoughts and their objects, which is completely appropriate in the matter, for nothing else means reflecting.

B.1.7.2 Functions of the Reflection Types: Ends, Beauty and the Sublime in the Political Judgment

The unity of political judgment is thus described sufficiently precisely as a unity of an action of thought. Now the components have to be determined which must be marked before a "back-mixing" of the basic forms of the judgment analyzed by Kant, so that this back-mixing can take place in a controlled manner. First of all, the question of what specific tasks are assigned to the beautiful, the sublime and the ends in the unity of judgment. With the determination of the unity, the field of investigation is also clearly defined and the functions of the individual types of reflection in political judgment can now be better understood.[540] The concept of *function* here describes the causality of the types of reflection on the unity of judgment, i.e. the respective specific way in which beauty, sublime and ends "order[ing] different representations under a one common one."[541] Analogous to Kant's method of isolating pure judgments, the powers and performances of the individual types of reflection are examined separately below, although they are not applied to nature but to the unity of political judgment.

B.1.7.2.1 The Concept of Ends: *Order* and *Individuality*

The separation of the *CPJ* into two parts, aesthetics and teleology, is now relevant, for aesthetic judgments obviously have a different reference to consciousness than teleological ones. After the classification into the different types of purposiveness, the teleological judgment is *objectively purposive*. It is, so to speak, an impeded judgment of knowledge that marks the path along which reflection strives for theoretical-mechanical knowledge.

---

[540] The type concept should be adhered to, since the separation of the beautiful, sublime and the concept of end was found in the *CPJ* according to the method of the formation of ideal types.

[541] *CPuRe*, B 93 [205]; full quote: "By a *function* however, I understand the unity of the action of ordering different representations under a common one."

"The judgment on the objective purposiveness of nature is called teleological. It is a judgment based on knowledge, but only on reflecting judgment, not on determining judgment."[542]

Ideal-typically "it has nothing to do with feelings of pleasure in things, but with the understanding in assessing them."[543] The teleological judgment has no reference to the feeling of pleasure and displeasure in the subject, for it is not a special ability,

"...but only the reflecting power of judgment in general, insofar as it proceeds in accordance with concepts, as is always the case in theoretical cognitions, but, with regard to certain objects in nature, in accordance with particular principles, namely those of a power of judgment that is merely reflecting and is not determining objects."[544]

Thus, the downgrading of a faculty due to a lack of a principle of its own also takes place within the *CPJ*. In this respect, the clearly emphasized epistemological inferiority of political judgment in the deduction (B.1.7.1) is not an unusual process within the framework of critical philosophy. Kant has unmistakably given priority to the critique of aesthetic judgment over the teleological judgment.[545] Essential for the argument just introduced is now the different reference to consciousness in the two types of judgment. For this reason, the beautiful and sublime should also be systematically described within the political judgment as the two *aesthetic functions*, for only they have a direct reference to the feeling of pleasure and displeasure.

In the political judgment, beautiful and sublime things are not experienced for the sake of pure contemplation or for the experience of inner resistance, as the *CPJ* text repeatedly suggests for immanent methodological reasons, but they are always related to the concept of end, which not only creates subjective order, but also structures individuality as a form of mutual recognition and acceptance of human beings. Aesthetics expresses the individual way in which order is experienced in a reflecting

---

[542] *CPJ*, First Introduction, p. 34. Steinberger's objection that Kant's reflecting judgment had expressly only a "non-cognitive" status would thus be settled; cf. Steinberger, Peter J., *The Concept of Political Judgment*, Chicago and London 1993, p. 148.

[543] *CPJ*, B XLIX [78].

[544] *CPJ*, B LIII [80].

[545] See also *CPJ*, B L-LI [79].

way with reference to the feeling of pleasure and displeasure, whether it has already happened, is just happening or, through imagination, projected into the future.[546] A subjective dimension of experience must also be assigned to the subjective concept of order, otherwise one remains stuck with the old, objective concept of ontologically specific order, with which the subjective genesis of order could not be thought. Aesthetics makes subjective order thinking reflexive, i.e. only in the aesthetic dimension can the political subject think of itself as an individual of an imaginary order of individuals without annulling the difference between the individuality of the ego and all other alters. For the aesthetic moment gives the subject the *concrete states* with which it can fulfil the concept of the individual.

Since the concept of end is simultaneously responsible for the reflecting construction of order and individuality, it obviously – and in contrast to its transcendental inferiority in the *CPJ* – has a greater conceptual power in political judgment than the aesthetic functions. The subjective order is, as already noted, a reversal of the old European, Aristotelian-ontological ordo concept, which determined political thinking and action until the 19th century.[547] Carl Schmitt, as one of the most important ordo thinkers of the 20th century with his friend-enemy scheme, had already taken into account the necessary new version of the concept of order and, to a certain extent, had already completed the subjective change in the first attempts.[548] For he

---

[546] The consideration of the different time vectors in a diachronic view is obvious. Past, present or future orders can become the measure and basis for the political judgment. Here the possibilities of political subjectivity are naturally due to the social accessibility of different time horizons, which is extraordinarily variable in cultural history. In particular, the conceivability of the future is a signum of modern societies. Cf. the outstanding essay by Niklas Luhmann, *Weltzeit und Systemgeschichte. Über Beziehungen zwischen Zeithorizonten und sozialen Strukturen gesellschaftlicher Systeme* [World-Time and Systems-History. On Relationships between Time Horizons and Social Structures of Social Systems], in: Oelmüller, Willi (Ed.), Warum noch Geschichte, Munich 1977, pp. 203-252.

[547] Cf. Nitschke, Peter, *Zwischen Innovation und Tradition: Der politische Aristotelismus in der deutschen politischen Philosophie der Prämoderne* [Between Innovation and Tradition. Political Aristotelism in German Pre-Modern Philosophy], in: Zeitschrift für Politik 1/1995, pp. 27-40. On the overall problem of the concept of order, see the first comprehensive study by Andreas Anter, *Die Macht der Ordnung. Aspekte einer Grundkategorie des Politischen* [The Power of Order. Aspects of a Basic Category of Politics], Tübingen 2004.

[548] Of course, only within the anti-individuality *theory* of law, state and order, for European and North American liberalism, through its *democratic practice*, had long since promoted and claimed political subjectivity as the wealth of

was no longer concerned with a given basis of political order within the constitution of being. With his accentuation of the idea of political causation, which must be thought of as a creatio ex nihilo, he attributed the genesis of order to selected subjects, namely those who 1) represent political unity and 2) are therefore legitimated to handle the distinction between friend and enemy, 3) command the state of emergency and finally 4) have to think in *concrete orders*. There has already been an exciting but unfinished discussion as to whether Schmitt, with his concept of concrete order thinking[549], might have wanted to replace the friend/enemy scheme.[550] The creation of concrete order in his presentation is the self-assertion of sovereignty, the 'representation' of the 'identity' of 'political unity', which transcends the legal order and can certainly contradict it.[551] The concept or reality of concrete order precedes law, because only on it can the law be established.

The difference between friend and enemy as a generative moment of concrete order is without doubt an element of the natural basis of political subjectivity, for it consists of a sufficiently formal and integrable instructtion manual for the diversity of empirical cases, which is incorporated into the subjective genesis of order with the help of a reflected universal maxim on the lawful behavior of natural living beings. Thus, it should be noted that Schmitt's 'concept of the political' is certainly a subjectively turned concept of order genesis, albeit with far-reaching limitations compared to a universal concept of political subjectivity. First and foremost, the terms friend and enemy conceal much more than they explain, because the philosophical – and i.e. here: the aesthetic-critical question of knowledge – would be of interest, how these two categories barricaded in the cleverly chosen schematism come about individually and on their own. Furthermore, the formula of the *intensity of dissociation and association* and the associated friend / enemy distinction only become politically qualifiable

---

specifically modern politicality.

[549] The term was coined in Carl Schmitt's treatise *Über die drei Arten des Rechtswissenschaftlichen Denkens*, Hamburg 1934, and subsequently made a surprising career in law itself.

[550] Cf. Kaiser, Joseph H., *Konkretes Ordnungsdenken*, in: Quaritsch, Helmut (ed.), *Complexio oppositorum. Über Carl Schmitt*, Berlin 1988, with discussion pp. 319-340.

[551] Cf. Adam, Armin, *Rekonstruktion des Politischen. Carl Schmitt und die Krise der Staatlichkeit 1912-1933* [Reconstruction of the Political. Carl Schmitt and the Crisis of Statehood 1912-1933], Weinheim 1992.

when they are related to the self-assertion of sovereignty. In this way, the criterion for what qualifies as political remains traditionally tied to the state sphere, and Schmitt can only note with the greatest regret that modern liberalism is driving the depoliticization of the state. More important for our ends is that Schmitt's critical difference of the political cannot be attributed to the individuals associated with it and has lost its plausibility, especially in the face of modern democracies, where the use of a political concept or judgment is, even if doesn't always happen, at least expected of all adult citizens. The distinction between friend and enemy, which naturally plays a psychological role and is even relevant to rational judgment, is not in itself able to explain its own origin. It is therefore not wrong, but at the same time too formal and too concrete to inform modern societies about their achievements and conditions. Too formal, because it alone does not produce a political quality, and too concrete, because it is a far too rigid empirical schematism for selected situations (above all states of emergency), which also only possibly gives a baseline in these. With Schmitt's concept of the political, the political shrinks to a supposedly creative causative power in existential situations. Even if the friend/enemy pattern were generally attributed to individuals, this would only result in a primitive concept of the political. Accordingly, the question arises whether the cultural-historical emergence of the political could be described with this difference – which is clearly not the case, since the friends/enemy distinction has no generative moment and therefore no evolution can be reconstructed with its help. It does not provide instructions for tracing the transition from 'barbarism' to the politics of Greek urban culture, for example. Or to put it even more drastically: **with Schmitt's concept of the political one cannot even distinguish between humans and animals**.[552] As already mentioned, it obscures what actually ought to be explained, such as the concepts of intensity, association, and dissociation. The difference between friend and enemy benefits from its timelessness and makes this advantage gained by trickery invisible through its apparent proximity to empiricism. But it is an *ontological criterion* that refers to a nature of the political, which is why Schmitt's concept formation was also applauded by Heidegger and Jünger.[553] Schmitt's proposed solution was a

---

[552] After all, Aristotle's first concern in his political thinking was to distinguish humans from animals and gods by the intensity of their state-relatedness; cf. *Politics*, A 2.

[553] In a letter to Carl Schmitt dated October 14, 1930, Ernst Jünger wrote: "I dedicate the following epigram to your work *Der Begriff des Politischen*: Videtur: suprema laus. Because the degree of direct evidence is so strong that any

reactive yet important contribution to the study of political subjectivity. Christian Meier commented:

> "The emergence – or more precisely: the coming to power – of a multitude of political subjects was exciting for one who took the unity of the state (and its 'monopoly of the political') for granted and necessary."[554]

Meier criticized Schmitt's political concept formation as too simple and extraordinarily unhistorical. At the same time, the ancient historian tried to make Schmitt's insights fruitful elsewhere. In the "*Sketch*" of his own concept of the political, with which he prefaced his book *Die Entstehung des Politischen bei den Griechen* [The Formation of the Political in Ancient Greece], he unfolds the political as a "field of action" in which potentially anything can become political and thus takes over Schmitt's description of the political as a "field of relationship and tension".[555] Meier tries to do justice to Schmitt theoretically, but to overcome his approach by expanding it (for example to domestic politics). He remains committed to the old kinetic and paraphysical vocabulary of "elements", "units", "forces", "fields of tension", "intensities" and "positions". But his studies on the history of mentalities clearly show that he actually explores the subjective dimension of the political, which no longer knows an ontologically or mythically guaranteed order, but could only arise from its collapse and with the development of a subjective competence to order as the ability to think politically.[556] Ernst Vollrath was therefore absolutely right when he orient-

---

opinion becomes superfluous and the communication that one has taken note is sufficient for the author."

[554] Meier, Christian, *Zu Carl Schmitts Begriffsbildung – Das Politische und der Nomos* [On Carl Schmitt's Concept Formation – The Political and the Nomos], in: Quaritsch, *Complexio oppositorum*, loc. cit., pp. 537-556, here p. 541.

[555] Cf. in Christian Meier's book Die Entstehung des Politischen bei den Griechen, Frankfurt 1983, the chapter Vom Politikós zum modernen Begriff des Politischen. Eine Skizze, pp. 27-47.

[556] Apart from Meier's study on the Greek drama in *Die politische Kunst der griechischen Tragödie* [The Political Art of the Greek Tragedy], Munich 1988, his biography on Cicero is particularly meaningful, because it describes a politician of the Roman Republic who thinks the social order in a genuinely apolitical sense (namely from the ontologically apparently assured uniform point of view of the Republican virtue) and also fails; see Meier, Christian, *Cicero. Das erfolgreiche Scheitern des Neulings in der alten Republik* [Cicero. The Successful Failure of the Newcomer in the Old Republic], in: Meier, *Die Ohnmacht des allmächtigen Dictators Caesar. Drei biographische Skizzen* [The Impotence of the Almighty Dictator Caesar. Three Biographical Sketches], Frankfurt 1980, p. 103-

ed his philosophical study *Grundlegung* on the results of Meier, because the historical characteristic of the "*ability-consciousness*" of citizenship in the Greek polis, the optionality of all action and finally the resulting "adverbial modality" of the political lie entirely in a perspective of subjective determination of the political.[557] For Carl Schmitt and Christian Meier, the political is no longer exhausted by an 'art of the possible', the epitome of political wisdom that always has a mainly technical character. They are not concerned with *phronesis*, nor with political wisdom in the sense of the Machiavellian-Hobbesian calculus of power, which is only forward-looking and visionary, because it is quite unambiguous, right down to its self-image, a natural knowledge of people and their society as a mechanism, as has already been shown several times.

The teleologically reflected concept of end, which here in the unity of political judgment provides the concepts of individuality and order for their self- and external applications in the medium of the imaginary public (this is thoroughly examined in Chapter B.1.7.3 *Public and Sensus Communis Politicus*), is practically meaningless in the approaches of Schmitt and Meier. At Schmitt, the sovereign's self-knowledge and understanding, i.e. his individuality, is reduced to the extent to which he is aware of his special competence to create concrete orders in a state of emergency and how far he makes the difference between friend and enemy the basis of all his actions. Only one end (purpose) can be attributed to concrete orders as spontaneous creations, namely the *self-assertion and self-preservation of the*

---

222. An older social science study with consideration of the subjective-political perspective is the well-known book by Berger, Peter and Luckmann, Thomas, *Die gesellschaftliche Konstruktion der Wirklichkeit. Eine Theorie der Wissenssoziologie* [The Social Construction of Reality. A Theory of the Sociology of Knowledge, N.Y. 1966], Frankfurt 1995; cf. there section II, *Gesellschaft als subjektive Wirklichkeit* [Society as Subjective Reality] (p. 139-196) and the chapters *Gedanken über Identitätstheorien* [Thoughts on Identity Theories] (p. 185-190), *Organismus und Identität* [Organism and Identity] (p. 191-196).

[557] "Adverbial Modality" is the term inspired by Michael Oakeshott, with which Vollrath tries to do justice to the fact in the theoretical language that the field of the political is not to be limited by its identifiable objects (the "what"), but by a certain activity, namely modalization as a determination of the 'how'; see Vollrath, *Grundlegung*, loc. cit., p. 50. **The answer to this 'how' is of course: by reflecting!** But Vollrath has not been able to show how reflection must be organized in detail and which distinctions have to be made. This task is solved here.

sovereign state. With the representation of the subjects' *ability-consciousness*, Meier also succeeds only in a quasi-psychological, external and completely unphilosophical description of the ability to subjective genesis of order.

Overall, there is a lack in both approaches of solid, philosophically based terms to describe the political subject, even if the will to do so is clearly discernible. The absence of the concept of end is in a certain way also the side effect of an important basic decision by both authors, namely to develop their concepts of political subjectivity *while completely ignoring the moral dimension*. **This in itself was an important achievement, because for the first time we got a clear view of some of the basic structures of the political subject, which have been stubbornly concealed by moral philosophy since antiquity.** But without the concept of end, the political subject lacks a decisive ability, namely his ability to orientate itself in ideas, interests and moral values. The actual meaning and power of the teleologically reflected concept of end for political subjectivity is best illustrated in contrast to the other elementary concepts presented here. Therefore, we do not want to lose sight of the concept of end in the following chapters.

B.1.7.2.2 Beauty: Morality and Justice

Schmitt's concept of the political and the "ability-consciousness" explored by Meier both have a fundamentally creative profile that represents the second vector, whereby their political concepts are unmistakably related to subjective consciousness. Both focus exclusively on the subjective aspect of order in politics; the entire aesthetic dimension of politics, on the other hand, is reserved for objectified representation, i.e. the representation of politics as a concrete drama, as a symbol or as a decision. The aesthetic component is always related to concretions, i.e. symbolic embodiments, but not to the aesthetic capacity in the subject, whereby such objects are only produced or judged. It did not occur to them that aesthetics played a significant role in the political judgment of the subject. Walter Benjamin already expressed this tendency most clearly when he described fascism as an "aestheticization of politics", which inevitably leads to war as an aesthetic existential.[558] But the question of the representation of the political

---

[558] Cf. Benjamin, Walter, *Das Kunstwerk im Zeitalter seiner technischen Reproduzierbarkeit* [The Work of Art in the Age of Mechanical Reproduction] Frankfurt 1977, *Epilogue*, pp. 42-44, where he exemplifies Marinetti's grotesque manifesto on the Ethiopian colonial war. Political philosophy has repeatedly let itself be

must be turned in the perspective of political subjectivity to the *political representability in the subject*. Bernd Guggenberger was on the right track when, knowing the *CPJ* and its interpretation by Arendt, he drew the following picture of the communication of judgment in the subject in a small text:

> "Even the spiritual ability of the individual to judge independently of metaphysical conditions grows out of a discussion, namely that 'two-in-one' of the silent dialogue, which Socrates understood as the cause of thinking aimed at behavioral orientation. And here the circle closes again to aesthetic judgment: just as in the judging personality I and my conscience conduct a dialogue that creates judgments, so does the artist, who is always both in one: *as the maker of the work of art always also its first viewer*."[559]

Aesthetics has nothing to do with the passive evaluation of sensations, i.e. a receptive-reflecting activity of thinking that depends on sensory data, but the judgment itself is always a creative act when it is sensualized – and that means: at least in the imagination it is turned into language or visualized, i.e. prepared for communication. However, the creative moment does not lie in taking something out of the nothing, but in the special way in which sensual data or products are linked to concepts. Kant defined this ability to think aesthetically-representative as the process of *symbolic hypotyposis*. He starts from a general process of representation, which is decisive for all areas of critical philosophy, in that the way of presentation underpins the terms a priori, no matter what they are, with *intuitions*. According to the distinction between determining and reflecting judgment, however, fundamentally different types of this connection can be named, depending on the nature of the view underlying the term:

> "All **hypotyposis** (presentation, *subjecto sub adspectum*), as making something sensible, is of one of two kinds: either **schematic**, where to a concept grasped by the understanding the corresponding intuition is given a priori; or **symbolic**, where to a concept which only reason can think, and to which no sensible intuition can be adequate, an intuition

---

guided in a completely wrong direction by this famous dictum, because the materialism condensed in it saw the aesthetic dimension only as a medium in the service of the bourgeois class.

[559] Guggenberger, Bernd, *Die politische Aktualität des Ästhetischen* [The Political Topicality of the Aesthetic], Eggingen 1992, p. 32.

is attributed with which the power of judgment proceeds in a way merely analogous to that which it observes in schematization, i.e., it is merely the rule of this procedure, not of the intuition itself, and thus merely the form of the reflection, not the content, which corresponds to the concept."[560]

Hypotyposis is therefore a sensualization that either 1) underpins the term with an intuitive-schematic view (theoretical and practical philosophy through determining power of judgment), or 2) also senses it in an intuitive, yet symbolic-analogical way – which describes the entire field in which the reflecting power of judgment is responsible. Kant explained this extremely formal argumentation using an example which, thankfully, he chose from the political sphere:

> "Thus a monarchical state is represented by a body with a soul if it is ruled in accordance with laws internal to the people, but by a mere machine (like a hand mill) if it is ruled by a single absolute will, but in both cases it is represented only **symbolically**. For between a despotic state and a hand mill there is, of course, no similarity, but there is one between the rule for reflecting on both and their causality."[561]

This passage proves that the general problem of representation is also virulent in the assessment of political reality. This dimension of the political has so far only been examined at the level of propaganda and political architecture, without recourse to Kant's theory of representation – probably because it would have always given the entire critical philosophy access to the problem area and thus brought about insoluble additional problems.[562] The symbolic representation exists – and this is quite essential

---

[560] *CPJ*, B 256 [225].

[561] *CPJ*, B 256 [296]. This passage was not mentioned in Chapter B.1.6, which dealt with the explicitly political statements in the *CPJ* and was instead repealed for the present argument.

[562] An excellent contribution to this in the field of political mythology is the study by Andreas Dörner, *Politischer Mythos und symbolische Politik. Sinnstiftung durch symbolische Formen am Beispiel des Hermannsmythos* [Political Myth und Symbolic Politics. Creation of Meaning Through Symbolic Forms Using the Example of the Hermann's Myth], Opladen 1995, but Kant's theory of representation was also passed on there. In the field of political symbol research, which is intensively pursued in the U.S. and where such political phenomena as the missile defence system SDI or the American presidency are investigated, the scientists work exclusively with current semiotic or functionalist methods; see Burnier, DeLysa, *Constructing Political Reality: Language, Symbols, and Meaning in*

for the political use of this thought – in two closely related types of sensual assessment. The one who guides the creation of the sensual object through its creative activity is the judgment of artistic genius. The concept of genius is now also an ideal type that stands for creative-modelling and constructing thinking of every kind; apart from the top achievements of genius in the emphatic sense, which generate admiration (if understood, i.e. the artist is not 'too far ahead of her time'), the everyday products of art and the arts and crafts, such as the aesthetic design of a political election campaign, must also be categorized here. The political artists of representation[563] therefore form and produce the objects through which they sensualize the political goals, the desired values, in short: **order, by subordinating these sensually experienceable objects to their own political judgments** (or those of their clients). That would be the active side of the representation. But even the viewers of such sensually experienceable objects of political art are creative, albeit in a passive way, because they do not produce the order of sensual objects themselves. But there must be a communication between the political performer and the political subject in question, something in common on which they can agree or disagree. Unity or disagreement takes place through a comparison at the level of concepts of order, but the communication takes place in the aesthetic object created with the claim to embody the unity of concepts of order. The idea of connecting the viewer to a general public in judgment is embodied here in an object that can be experienced by the senses. The viewer feels addressed by this object but can react to it equally with acceptance or rejection, depending on the persuasiveness of the embodied approach. The subjective political judgment related to the creative act lies in the fact that the political subject, independently of the creative intentions, takes the same object again and underpins its own reflected ideas of order to determine whether it is an appropriate symbolic embodiment of this subjective order or not. Consensus or dissent build on this. A politician's face on television that is still 'unconsumed', i.e. that is not already fixed in the viewer's mind about a greater previous knowledge

---

Politics. A Review Essay, in: *Political Research Quaterly* 1/1994, pp. 239-253.

[563] That is, for example, such persons who today advise politicians rhetorically and fashionably on behalf of parties, organize party conferences in terms of interior design and media technology, or also those who provide protest movements with funny and attention-grabbing actions and objects etc. The political performer can be both the politician and his own body the material for his political artwork.

and its history, is regarded by the politically interested viewers as an embodiment of the ability to realize subjective orders that are compared with one's own ideas. If the politician is not expected to implement the announced order, whether for moral or factual reasons, or if his or her own personal ideas of order are not compatible with those of the viewer, aesthetically mediated dissent arises. It is clear that this kind of assessment allows a very broad hermeneutic spectrum of possible judgments about one and the same order, which is sensed in different objects. In a sense, the aesthetics of embodiment is a medium for political judgment that deliberately avoids precision. With their help, especially in modern democracies, the consent of those who actually disagree is sought. On the ballot paper only the cross counts, not the complex attitude in detail.[564] Moreover, the power of judgment interferes precisely in relation to the representation of ideas of order by persons with libidinal ties and needs.[565] These surpluses and ambivalences are all processed in political business – not necessarily in the interest of cultivating political subjectivity, as is well known.

The active and passive representation process was only vaguely distinguished in the aesthetics of the 18th century (cf. chapter A.2.1). Only Kant's theory of symbolic hypotyposis allows a consistent and critical distinction between creative and contemplative judgment. What is surprising about this is the fact that the subject must also carry out a sensual act of judgment. In the commentary literature of Kantian scholarship little interest has been shown in this topic so far, which is all the more surprising **since the hypotyposis theory quite obviously contains the conditions of the possibility of the whole critical system**, i.e. the subjective production conditions for a philosophical work that consists of sensually experienceable and somehow meaningful signs.[566] Therefore,

---

[564] The embodiment is examined even more thoroughly under the mathematically and dynamically sublime in chapters B.1.7.2.3 and 4. The restriction of the decision-making power in elections to certain names or by the binary yes/no schematism is a good example of the functioning of the reduction of complexity that social systems use as a method of communication in order to enable and condition connected actions.

[565] Before the Berlin parliamentary elections in October 1995, the newspaper *die tageszeitung* organized a campaign to explicitly try to separate libido and political judgment among female voters, saying: "Dear non-voters, do you really only go to the polls when you are in love with the politician?"

[566] Dieter Henrich dedicated the first of his Stanford lectures on the 200th anniversary of the *CPJ* to *The Moral Image of the World*. He not only completely

the following longer passage is intended to illustrate once again that we are facing a central problem of all philosophy here and that Kant must have formulated his arguments in the light of his own strict criticism of language, which modern analytical philosophy has not yet attributed to him for lack of knowledge of the text:

"This business has as yet been little discussed, much as it deserves a deeper investigation [...]. Our language is full of such indirect presentations, in accordance with an analogy, where the expression does not contain the actual schema for the concept but only a symbol for reflection. Examples are the words **ground** (support, basis), **depend** (be held from above), from which **flow** (instead of follow), **substance** (as Locke expresses it: the bearer of accidents), and innumerable other non-schematic but symbolic hypotyposes and expressions for concepts not by means of a direct intuition, but only in accordance with an analogy with it, i.e., the transportation of the reflection on one object of intuition to another, quite

---

ignored Kant's theory of representation based on the concept of hypotyposis, which would be able to explain how we come to meaningful images of objects and ideas at all. Even in his second lecture, entitled *Explanation of Aesthetic Judgment*, he makes no mention of symbolic hypotyposis and restricts the concept of representation to its determining function in the schematism chapter of the *CPuRe*. Moreover, he leads the subject so closely to his own moral-ontological interests that he does not say a word about the connection between beauty and morality, which is evident in Kant's text. Instead, he claims that the text of the *CPJ* does not contain a source of the legitimacy of the concept of end – whereby Henrich assumes that this source itself must be hidden in the moral context. This is manifestly wrong and testifies to a reading of the work that is insensitive to its subtleties and instead obscures the text in the shadow of the philosophical problems of the interpreter; cf. Henrich, *Aesthetic Judgment and the Moral Image of the World*, Stanford 1992, pp. 3-28 (for further criticism of Henrich's interpretation of Kant see here chapter B.1.8, and chapter B.1.9 on the attempt of an emergence theory with regard to the various achievements of judgment, which historically temporalizes the relationship between morality, aesthetics and politics). Even Jacques Derrida, who has a reputation as a thorough reader and who finally deals with the problem of representation in the *CPJ*, does not say a word about hypotyposis; cf. Derrida, *Die Wahrheit in der Malerei* [Truth in Painting], loc. cit., in particular p.135-144. The discipline in which such phenomena should be taken into special consideration and taken seriously is semiotics: see Umberto Eco's *Einführung in die Semiotik* [Introduction to Semiotics], Munich 1985, which addresses Kant's philosophy several times, but does not mention at any point the *Critique of the Power of Judgment* or one of its theorems.

different concept, to which perhaps no intuition can ever directly correspond."[567]

The term hypotyposis occurs only in three places in the *CPJ* and in none other in the entire Kantian opus.[568] The explanations in this regard are very poor in view of the weight of the problem. Javier Ibanez-Noé has undertaken a meaningful deepening by trying to emphasize the division of functions between imagination and judgment:

> "Accordingly, the function of the power of judgment does not actually consist in the representation itself, but in the reflection on the representability of a (certain or indeterminate) concept through the particular of the view [...]. But the connection of vision and concept, i.e. of the functions of the imagination and the mind, is the business of judgment. The imagination cannot find the view corresponding to a concept by itself, because it is no ability to think and therefore not conceptual [...]. Imagination as a power of representation (not merely opinion) is, in other words, in the service of judgment."[569]

Thus, it is clear that the power of judgment is not itself the sensual mode of imagination, but only in its reflection there is a guide to sensualization.[570] It

---

[567] *CPJ*, B 257 [226-7].

[568] Cf. Martin, Gottfried (ed.), *Allgemeiner Kantindex zu Kants gesammelten Schriften* [General Kant Index to Kant's Collected Works], Berlin 1967, vol. 1, p. 500.

[569] Ibanez-Noé, Javier, *Urteilskraft und Darstellung* [Power of Judgment and Representation] in: Funke, Gerhard (ed.), Akten des 7. Internationalen Kant Kongresses, Mainz, 28 March–1 April, 2 vol., Bonn and Berlin 1991, pp. 117-127, here p. 123. This is one of the few further contributions I have been able to find in the literature; cf. also Rudolph Gasché's essay *Reflexion zum Begriff der Hypotypose bei Kant*, in: Christiaan L. Hart Nibbig (ed.), *Was heißt darstellen?* Astonishingly, even Ernst Cassirer did not devote a single line to hypotyposis, even though he would have had every reason to do so given his own philosophy of symbolic forms and his comments on the *CPJ*. The French philosopher and Kant commentator Alexis Philonenko has noticed that there is a problematic relationship between Cassirer's reading of Kant and his own philosophy, because he was silent about some important achievements of the Kantian work, but must nevertheless have appreciated them because he used them; see Philonenko, Alexis, *Cassirer. Lecteur et interprète de Kant*, in: Seidengart, Jean (ed.), *Ernst Cassirer. De Marbourg à New York. L'itinéraire philosophique*, Actes du colloque de Nanterre, 12-14 October 1988, pp. 43-54.

[570] From the very beginning, the investigation of political subjectivity has focused on the form of reflecting judgment. At this point, however, we are reminded

cannot therefore be claimed that aesthetics, as a kind of reflecting power of judgment, provides the sensual material for the presentation of political orders to others, namely the teleological power of judgment. However, it contributes to the formation of political judgment by introducing into the order to be drafted *a point of view* that is marked by the respective feeling of pleasure or displeasure in the face of this order and constitutes a reflected individual state.

The decisive functions of aesthetics in the political judgment therefore lie in the **communication of the individual state and the representation of subjective order**, because only in this way can the natural and social order be related to the sentient subject who judges. Here it must not be overlooked that aesthetics can really contribute something to the representation of the subjective order, i.e. to that in which the subject has to think itself along at all times. For the general empirical orders of nature, which are purely teleologically reflected and aim at mechanical-mathematical con-

---

that there is another way to read the *CPJ* towards a supposedly contained political philosophy. This other reading opens up in the concept of imagination, which has hardly been considered as such and in its achievements here – not least because Kant spoke of it as "a blind, though indispensable function of the soul, without which we would have no cognition at all, but of which we are seldom even conscious." (*CPuRe* B 104 [211]) However, there is no doubt that the *CPJ* is the text in the system of the *Critiques*, where subjectivity and personal individuality could be deciphered from the power of the imagination. Martin Heidegger's objections to Kant's reduction of the imagination in the B edition of the *CPuRe* had an educational effect; cf. Heidegger, *Kant und das Problem der Metaphysik*, 4th ed, Frankfurt 1973, p. 129-197. His assertion that Kant had fluctuated between several possible sources of knowledge (understanding, intuition, imagination) and that the imagination was banned from the system of pure reason into psychology and anthropology because of its threatening "personal-ontological[n]" potential, is perhaps of dramaturgical interest for the composition of a Kant commentary, but is nevertheless quite untroubled by a possible reading of the *CPJ*. There would be a whole range of other positions there. Here only one of them: "The imagination (as a productive cognitive faculty) is, namely, very powerful in creating, as it were, another nature, out of the material which the real one gives it. We entertain ourselves with it when experience seems too mundane to us."(*CPJ*, B 194 [250]). Wolfgang Leidhold has already made a very advanced attempt to pursue political philosophy on the basis of an entirely Kantian concept of imagination; cf. Leidhold, *Politische Philosophie*, Würzburg 2003. Leidhold comes to similar results in a different theoretical language as the present study, which is based on the concept of reflecting judgment. With the method he has chosen, he has formed some elementary concepts which are also examined here: 'order', 'time' and 'body'.

cepts (such as the arrangement of the planets and their orbits in the solar system), do not in themselves require aesthetics; they therefore need neither the beautiful nor the sublime, for it is sufficient for teleological judgment to see in nature the sensual effect of a superhuman mind.[571] Since humans are not the originators of the empirical order of nature, they assume a mind, however vaguely imagined, that has created this nature according to its own rules. Teleology, on the other hand, is indispensable for aesthetics in order to give individuality and possible orders a conceptual framework. Individuality and subjective order as thoughts are only conceivable through the concept of teleology. And suddenly, a surprising *analogy* to theoretical knowledge emerges in the combination of this reflective powers of judgment, which Kant had depicted separately. The transcendental philosophical rule "Thoughts without content are empty, intuitions without concepts are blind" or "The understanding is not capable of intuiting anything, and the senses are not capable of thinking anything"[572] reminds us as an aesthetic law of theoretical philosophy of how much intuition and concepts are dependent on one another. Similarly, in political judgment there is an interdependence of aesthetic and teleological reflection, which is completely analogous to that of intuition and concept, or of sensuality and reason:

Teleology is the political ability of concepts; aesthetics is the political mode of intuition.

In order not to make the Kantian terminology more complex and possibly completely opaque through useless duplications, a vocabulary borrowed from linguistics should be used to distinguish between the **teleological syntax** and the **aesthetic semantics of political judgment**, whereby the semantics do not lie in sensual impressions themselves, but in the meanings of the feelings of pleasure or displeasure in the subject in relation to orders. There are therefore *beautiful and sublime notions of end*, i.e. two aesthetically different references of the subjective notion of order to the individual.

---

[571] Even if aesthetics plays a particularly important *heuristic* role in the research process and is combined with natural teleological judgment. Kepler explored the harmonies of the spheres for their beauty and thus came to the regularity of planetary movements, which he developed in his *Astronomia novae*. Even today mathematicians revel in the beauty of forms and spaces, which they view with the means of their symbolic languages, formulas and proofs.

[572] *CPuRe* B 75 [194].

The discussion of these extraordinarily difficult contexts can only be justified by preparing an explanation of the most important problem of political philosophy: the clarification of the relationship between morality and politics. The short section on hypotyposis, which is dizzying in its richness of meaning, immediately precedes the following statement in the text of the *CPJ*: "Now I say that the beautiful is the symbol of the morally good."[573] Kant has obviously only considered the problem of representtation in order to find a methodological basis for this assertion, so that it can be sustained under the conditions of critical philosophy. He then compiles a list of the kinship characteristics of the beautiful and moral and gives some examples:

> "We call buildings or trees majestic and magnificent, or fields smiling and joyful; even colors are called innocent, modest or tender, because they arouse sensations that contain something analogical to the consciousness of a mental state produced by moral judgments."[574]

The lack of interest of pleasure in the contemplation of beauty also stands with the moral interest in such an analogous relationship, and this is now easy to understand in a political context. For the moral aspect of the political judgment is connected with the idea that it is not interests that govern order, but moral principles that claim universality. The decisive point here is that morality can be reflected in the political, without it being a simple moral judgment, which is only conceivable under the guidance of determining judgment. In the political mode of judgment, morality is a public matter, and the political subject (even if only in an internal dialogue) proposes *that a ruling order be or become established according to the moral laws to which the judging subject feels committed.*

In another, perhaps more common theoretical language, the same could be worded as follows:

> "He [Kant] uses this communication-theoretically charged conceptuality [sociability, communicative ability, participation] for an interest-free discourse, preceded by the recognition of the discourse partner. And it is – once again – not about the recognition of his interests, but about the recognition of the fact that he wants to communicate to me something of his own accord, which I will participate in, which does not presuppose my interest – if you like – but *arouses a pure one first.*

---

[573] *CPJ*, B 258 [227].
[574] *CPJ*, B 260 [228].

Recognition is the release of the other to release himself by releasing me."[575]

Here, the aspect of morally-related lack of interest in aesthetic judgment is redirected to communication and, moreover, the aspect of mutual recognition and acceptance is also discussed. But then the decisive reason is given why *morality needs aesthetics in order to become able to publicity*:

"Kant does not even consider moral communication. Morality forces after him. The moral decision can be calculated. That people also talk about what is morally right should not be called communication."[576]

Morality can therefore only be communicated aesthetically.[577] This applies in general and therefore also in the special case of political judgment.

The moral dimension appears in the political judgment when a subjecttive order is conceived for its own sake. The moral imperative demands that order is not intended for another end (e.g. security, prosperity, freedom of faith, etc.) but has the task of implementing moral laws and at the same time being based on causality through freedom. Therefore, moral claims in politics usually negate concrete (especially material) interests or contradict requirements presented as objectively necessary in order to create an order that is perceived as beautiful in its harmonious legality and is also presented as such. The conflict between morality and politics as a

---

[575] Blasche, Siegfried, *Zur kommunikationsphilosophischen Rekonstruktion der Zweckmäßigkeit in Kant's Kritik der Urteilskraft* [About the Communication-Philosophical Reconstruction of Purposiveness in Kant's Critque of the Power of Judgment] in: Forum für Philosophie Bad Homburg (ed.), *Ästhetische Reflexion und kommunikative Vernunft*, Bad Homburg 1993, pp. 11-40, here pp. 16. Blasche's inspired treatise could have achieved even more if the author had recognized Kant's method of referring the forms of reflecting judgment exclusively to natural phenomena in order to keep his judgments pure. Instead, he interprets Kant's method so insistently as a kind of rescue of nature for the sake of 'communicative freedom' that his thesis soon sounds like 'deep ecology' and the idea of reconciliation of the early Frankfurt School. This interpretation is also wrong in the matter, as is shown here in the cultural anthropological digression; cf. chapter B.2.2.

[576] Ibid., p. 19.

[577] I will be very sparing with such terms as 'communication' and 'discourse', for they denote processes that have not yet been sufficiently clarified from a philosophical point of view. Moreover, they are too rich in associations and their unregulated use invites misunderstandings.

reconciliation of interests therefore lies in different ways of looking at and representing the subjective order. The moral annulment of particular interests in politics succeeds in modern societies governed by the rule of law through politics itself, namely in the form of legislation.[578] However, this does not mean that morality itself becomes a form of rule, but that it must **pass through the public sphere and thus the political process of deliberation, decision-making and law-making like any other particular interest**. The moral component in political judgment, when it is presented, usually strengthens the *claim to the universality of reflecting judgment* in a very efficient manner and gives it a strong note of practical necessity.[579]

It makes a considerable difference in everyday life, of course, whether morality in political judgment is represented by a political subject as an individual (citizen, voter affected) or in a political function (mandate or decision-maker, candidate, speaker), because in the second case there is always the well-founded suspicion that the moral dimension is used instrumentally in the representative role, i.e. in favor of a party, an apparatus, a factual and thereby morally neutral decision or simply to promote personal interests. These entanglements and motivic interdependencies of everyday political life should all be taken into account, but should not be dealt with here in detail, since it is ultimately the elementary forms of political subjectivity that are at stake. It is only important to consider the ability to increase complexity in the analysis of the elements, so that the concept of political subjectivity becomes a reliable instrument of navigation in the political cosmos.

In modern societies, law is a political substitution of morality and violence.[580] This is particularly evident in the historical development of the legal systems. While in the Middle Ages the literary genre of so-called

---

[578] This corresponds to the discourse theoretical reconstruction of the normative content of law, which Habermas developed in *Faktizität und Geltung* [Truth and Justification], Frankfurt 1992.

[579] Niklas Luhmann has repeatedly experienced this as a nuisance, which is one of the reasons why he let himself be carried away into disqualifying day-to-day political business as a "hype of opinion". In the person of its inventor, systems theory reacts sensitively when the communication systems it depicts as functionally differentiated interfere with empirical reality, mix their function codes and produce 'disturbances' or 'noise' in communication.

[580] This does not restrict the systemic or discursive theoretical reconstruction of law, but only opens up a separate perspective on the same subject from the perspective of political subjectivity.

Princely Mirrors still served to guarantee the paradoxical self-restraint of monarchical power through the authority of a theologically equipped moral doctrine, in modern times the same was achieved through the institutionalization of rights, which were made binding and protected by a constitution. However, the process of enacting a constitution itself has only gradually become more political, for the constitutions established by monarchs themselves made little or no use of political subjectivity. In a relationship of a sovereign willed by God to a subservience of all dominated subjects, equally according to the will of the Creator, there is still nothing political (cf. chapter A.1.5).

The functions of the reflection types discussed so far can be summarized as follows: The reflected concept of end, which the teleological judgment produces, provides *two syntactic forms* for political judgment, namely the two political elementary concepts *individual* and (subjective) *order*. The two aesthetic functions in political judgment are the beautiful and sublime by their reference to the feeling of pleasure and displeasure in the subject. They mark states or points of view by which the individual *semantically* proves its relationship to the subjective order and these otherwise empty terms only relate to one another. At the same time, the aesthetic functions are concerned with the representation of the individual state by finding symbolic sensualizations for the concepts of mind and reason in the respective imaginary subjective order by analogy. The idea of a moral good, philosophically supported and legitimized by the concept of reason of freedom, is symbolically sensualized by beauty. **In political judgment, it is included in the subjective concept of order in order to make the rule of morality and law that prevails in it tangible as its beauty.** Political subjectivity does not make morality and law authoritarian in ideas of order, binding through formal respect for the law, but rather *persuasive*, to a certain extent about the pleasure in the beauty of such an order. Beauty itself does not create a law, for it is free play and "liberality in the manner of thinking."[581] Now it can be formulated the other way round from the point of view of political subjectivity: The pleasure in morality and law in subjective orders that are communicated for universalization and objectification is *political beauty*.[582]

---

[581] *CPJ*, B 116 [151].

[582] This consideration could best be illustrated and deepened in the field of *political utopia*. Utopia has been closely linked to the idea of beauty and order since Plato. Schiller's *Letters on the Aesthetic Education of Man*, for example, are to be understood as the promotion of beauty as a path to political freedom. Carsten

B.1.7.2.3 The Mathematical-Sublime: *Time* and *Body*

Thus, the function of beauty in political judgment is sufficiently described and also some preparatory work is done for the investigation of the sublime. The feeling of the sublime refers not to the concepts of the understanding, but to the concepts of reason. Moreover, as a judgment on the deformity, it is violence either against desire (will) or against the imagination. Kant has therefore divided it into the *dynamically* and the *mathematically sublime*. In examining the problems of representation, as already mentioned, he focused only on the symbolic sensualization of morality in beauty – obviously out of his primary interest in conveying aesthetics and practical philosophy. Does the sublime also turn something meaningful, symbolized and communicable by analogy? We would have reason to conclude it independently from the discussion and knowledge of the Kantian method so far, but Kant has done us the great favor of telling us himself about it. One remark explicitly points out that the beautiful and *even the sublime* can stimulate morality, while at the same time it is a clear passage to Kant's theory of the segregation of forms of judgment:

> "…;the moral feeling, is nevertheless related to the aesthetic power of judgment and its **formal conditions** to the extent that it can serve to make the lawfulness of action out of duty representable *at the same time as aesthetic, i.e., as sublime, or also as beautiful*, without sacrificing any of its purity; which would not be the case if one would place it in natural combination with the feeling of the agreeable."[583]

It therefore makes sense to seek the same method of sensualization in the sublime that was presented to us in the *symbolic hypotyposis of morality through the beautiful* by Kant. This is also obvious because Kant's 'Analytic of the Sublime' contains a series of examples of an immediate political nature. There, for example, he writes about the *greatness* of virtue, public

---

Zelle has referred to the callistic doctrine of beauty as a guarantor of utopia for the philosophies of history; cf. Zelle, *Die doppelte Ästhetik der Moderne. Revisionen des Schönes von Boileau bis Nietzsche* [The Double Aesthetics of Modernity. Revisions of the Beautiful from Boileau to Nietzsche], Stuttgart 1995, p. 187.

[583] *CPJ*, B 114 [150]. Interestingly, this is an admission regarding the moral relevance of the sublime, which is no longer mentioned in the study of hypotyposis one-hundred pages later (B 255-261 [225-228]). There Kant writes only about beauty as a representation of morality. We'll see why in a minute.

freedom and justice as objects of the sublime in reflecting judgment, which in our view has long since become a political judgment.[584] For without reversal of meaning one could also speak of an *order* of virtues, public *order* of freedom and *order* of justice, whereby the political subject individuates itself by reflecting itself through its conditions set in relation to these layers, types and forms of order. The orders in general can be estimated, desired, criticized or even rejected – but always only according to the subjective order of the individual. We are, however, concerned here only with the isolated function of the sublime in the political judgment. For this purpose, the distinction between mathematical and dynamic sublimity must be considered once again. According to the general provisions, the sublime differs from the beautiful a.) by the assessment of formlessness instead of form, b.) the quality of well-being instead of quantity, and c.) inhibition instead of the promotion of life forces. But what is decisive d.) is the obvious inexpediency (or un-purposiveness) of the sublime, which in the horror and inconceivability of its greatness and power is "as it were doing violence to our imagination."[585]

The mathematically sublime refers to the indefinite concept of size. This is specified, corresponding to the forms of intuition, in two dimensions, the (qualitative) temporal and the (quantitative) spatial size. Kant did not specifically deal with the temporal magnitude in the analysis of the sublime. Perhaps he thought he could do without it, because anyway all empirically thought time must be spatialized in aesthetics, because the "outer sense", the spatial idea, makes time representable as "inner sense" in the first place. The spatialization of time has been a much-discussed topic since Henri Bergson's *Essai sur les données immédiates de la conscience* (1889) [Time and Free Will: An Essay on the Immediate Data of Consciousness], in which he mainly refers to Kant to criticize the spatial imprisonment of time with him. For Bergson, the stream of time is the true stream of life and must not be locked into the grid of the concept. Bergson's misunderstanding regarding Kant's theory of time is that he works through the *CPuRe* with his vitalistic motives and interests in the natural-mechanical determination of time, but neither in the *CPraRe* (where Kant develops a theorem of the practical freedom of time;[586] and certainly not in the *CPJ* for perspectives on the philosophy of time. This misinterpretation had been fixed since Herder's emphatic criticism of Kant, which referred exclusively

---

[584] *CPJ*, B 82-3 [133].

[585] *CPJ*, B 77 [129].

[586] *CPraRe*, *Werke* VII [Works VII], A 147 [123].

to the *CPuRe*.

"Actually, every changing thing has the measure of its time in itself; this exists, even if there were no other; no two things in the world have the same measure of time... So there are (one can say boldly here) countless times in the universe at one time."[587]

Yet, the mathematically sublime provides exactly such a dimension, in which time is not forced into a mechanical concept – provided that the *CPJ* is read according to the counter-method of controlled back-mixing developed here. Thus, time finds its aesthetic-reflected dimension. Both in reception and in creation, the subjective experience of time is oriented towards empirical reality and everyday experience.[588] Thus it is already indicated that there is a *creative, spontaneous relationship to time in aesthetics*, which means no less than that *time is also produced in the concept of mathematical sublime*. The 'Golden Age', for example, is not an experienced lifetime, but a construction of the imagination under the guidance of reflec-

---

[587] Herder, Gottfried Johann, *Metakritik zur Kritik der reinen Vernunft* [Metacritics to the Critique of Pure Reason], Berlin 1955, p. 68. Such arguments are still directed against Kant today, as for example in the study by Günter Dux, *Die Zeit in der Geschichte. Ihre Entwicklungslogik vom Mythos zur Weltzeit. Mit kulturvergleichenden Untersuchungen in Brasilien (J. Mensing), Indien (G. Dux / K. Kälble / J. Meßmer) und Deutschland (B. Kiesel)*, [Time in History. Its Developmental Logic from Myth to World Time. With Comparative Cultural Studies in Brazil (J. Mensing), India (G. Dux / K. Kälble / J. Meßmer) and Germany (B. Kiesel)], Frankfurt 1989, p. 59. This author also did not note that the empirical sense of time of the subject should be dealt with in cognitive-critical aesthetics and teleology, i.e. in the *CPJ*. The biggest problem of interpretation is that time is mostly presented as a *sensualizing medium for objective-mechanical causal chains*. The experiments in this field always aim at the awareness of an *operative use of time*, i.e. the ability to sequence events and to relate them causally; cf. for example Jean Piaget's study *Le développement de la notion de temps chez l'enfant*, Paris 1973, where it is shown that only older children can operationalize the idea of duration in relation to speed.

[588] Martin Seel has an inkling of this individuality of aesthetic time, even if, like Kant, he concentrates exclusively on the temporality of aesthetically judged natural events. Seel obviously considers the aesthetic state of time to be very important, because he has placed the fifty-page chapter IV of his book under the promising title *Die Zeit der Naturwahrnehmun* [Time in Perception of Nature]. But only in the short subchapter *Eine andere Zeit* [A Different Time] are finally a few interesting considerations on the peculiarity of the aesthetic presence of nature; see Seel, *Eine Ästhetik der Natur* [An Aesthetics of Nature], Frankfurt 1991, p. 193-198.

tion, and the size of this age varies depending on the perception of the respective present. The 'Century of Louis XIV' has indeed been experienced, but the greatness of this epoch had a long-lasting effect on the ideas of people who were born after it. The aesthetic size of ages, epochs and the lifetime of rulers, such as dynasties or legislative periods, is not determined by objective duration, even if duration contributes a quantitative aspect. The 'century' of the Sun King, for example, is an aesthetically expedient extension of the idea of a regency that lasted from 1661 to 1715. What is rather astonishing is that the size of a time is characterized by the fact that it is *larger the less the time as such is presented as working in it*. This can only be explained if these *ideas of time are connected with the general concept of order* (which includes the subjective one). Order as a connection of ends is the negation of time, because time cannot be thought of as an own end in order. **Time pushes into consciousness as the destruction of order** – even if it has always made its construction possible in the first place. One of the metaphysical preconceptions is that of the *break-in of time into the world*, which has since been devoured by Chronos.[589] Accordingly, all strong concepts of order in cultural history are specialized in *cancelling time*[590] – except for the idea of progress of modern times. The latter offered a solution with which the acceleration of time could become a moment that is not part of the order itself, but instead temporalizes the order as a whole and makes its continuous change a task. But in the final analysis, even at the end of the idea of progress, some kind of 'end of history' usually awaits

---

[589] This contradicts the interpretation of Günter Dux's mythical origin in *Die Zeit in der Geschichte*, loc. cit. In the chapter *Unterworfen unter die Macht der Zeit* [Subjected to the Power of Time], pp. 205-222, he describes "the threat of time by the state of rest of eternity" as the most important primary trauma (ibid., p. 206). However, eternity as a threat in itself is a thoroughly modern pattern of imagination. I think the author's highly selective interpretation of myths is wrong, because it presupposes an awareness of the operative need and use of time to become aware of temporality. According to this representation, time is nothing new in the process of becoming conscious, but rather an invited guest whose gifts one knows before he has entered. In doing so, Dux is thwarting his own developmental approach.

[590] Michael Theunissen's *Negative Theologie der Zeit* [A Negative Theology of Time], Frankfurt 1991, is also an attempt to determine the moment of eternity as the sole dimension of successful life and at the same time as resistance against the alienating rule of time. With Theunissen there is no trace that subjects could be the authors of time by means of their imagination and judgment. His concept of the subjectivation of time is limited to classical time as a form of perception, as it was first dealt with in the transcendental aesthetics of the *CPuRe*.

us. The idea of progress made it possible for the first time to plan an order for the future and to use time, *because time and progress became identical under the teleological concept of human perfectivity*. But few seem to want to continue on this train forever –once they have noticed that they are *prisoners and not passengers*; rather, the created order of justice, prosperity or technical civilization should one day become a firm and unchangeable continuance, so that their fruits can be enjoyed in peace. Whatever the individual's opinion: the decision will inevitably take the form of a political judgment.[591]

Whether it were the eschatological end-time ideas of the Gnostics and Apocalyptics or those of the Marxist utopists, the conservative traditionalists or the operators of the scientific-technical revolutions: All hope is aimed at the state in which time stands still.[592] This is why ages and epochs

---

[591] With the help of this combination of time and order, dimensions of the aesthetics of political time could have become apparent that had escaped Karl Heinz Bohrer because he concentrated on the model of an "absolute present". This fixation could also be interpreted as an annulment of time, but due to the "suddenness" of the temporal structure of this absolute present, which seems indispensable, it is far too strongly tailored to certain dramatic events, or even more clearly: this form of the present is the essence of the 'true' drama, as Bohrer believes. Equipped with this criterion, the literary scholar wants to show where the 'timelessness' of great literary works comes from. At the same time, he wants to be able to judge *today* which contemporary works are not "great" and *have no future for lack of timelessness*; cf. Bohrer, *Das absolute Präsens. Die Semantik ästhetischer Zeit* [Absolute Presence. The Semantics of Aesthetic Time], Frankfurt 1994.

[592] Here, too, Carl Schmitt has shown a fine intuition by illuminating the connection between order and time, drawing attention to the political tragedy of the fate of time. In *Hamlet oder Hekuba. Der Einbruch der Zeit in das Spiel*, [Hamlet or Hekuba. The Intrusion of Time into the Play], Düsseldorf 1956, unchanged reprint Stuttgart 1985, Schmitt tries to measure Shakespeare's greatness by how he managed not only to preserve an intertemporal substrate in the historically-contingent change of events, but also to raise the play to a real tragedy in the first place with this "emergency" (ibid., p. 42) of the collapse of time – in contrast to the later bourgeois tragedy. This differs from the Attic tragedy, which Schmitt believes drew its strength exclusively from the myth itself; whereas Shakespeare is said to have discovered the new source of all tragedy, which lies precisely in the dawn of time and is for the first time in a position to produce new myths in the play – such as the character Hamlet. Schmitt does not specifically discuss the subjective standstill of time, but this dimension is opened up by his thesis that Hamlet is a character of Shakespeare who admonishes the divine right of kings and the holiness of dynastic legitimacy

of rule are all the greater the less the time in them could cause unrest and trigger the disintegration of the once established orders. This applies even to everyday politics. Many German citizens, for example, who sympathized with social democracy or belonged to it as members, enthusiastically remembered the times under Helmut Schmidt's government in the 1990s and measured the chancellorship of Helmut Kohl or the SPD party leadership against the aesthetic greatness of that past time. Or, to stick to the example, in 1995 the Social Democrats clearly realized that they had no future if they could not project into it an order that could survive a new era and whose magnitude would then have to lie precisely in that it would stop or at least slow down time as an order-destroyer over the duration of its rule. Helmut Kohl's reign of sixteen years would perhaps have been presented as a great age for the same reasons – if the CDU donations affair had not intervened in 1999 – because his government would have appeared from a distance like that of an extraordinarily strong law enforcement officer. This would have been all the more glamorous since it survived the collapse of the Eastern Bloc and the unification of Germany with less excitement and disorder than an earlier 'age', such as the student revolts of 1968.[593]

The discussion of the individually experienceable quality of time in political reflection naturally leads to the heart of theory of history. However, the philosophical theories on history usually take the form of a 'historian's theory', because the professional historians, if they are interested in the theory of their subject at all, are primarily concerned with

---

founded by the Christian idea of representation. In his excellent study *Carl Schmitt zur Einführung* [Carl Schmitt. An Introduction], Hamburg 1992, p. 49, Reinhard Mehring pointed out that this whole complex of myth production in tragedy points to the "silent motto" (Hans Freyer) of Schmitt's entire political work: *Ab integro nascitur ordo* (Order is born again). Whether Schmitt's interpretation as such is correct is not discussed here. After all, it stands in an interesting relationship to René Girard's political interpretation of Hamlet, which he described in his comprehensive study *Shakespeare. Les feux de l'envie* [Theater of Eny. Wiliam Shakespeare], Paris 1990, pp. 436-467.

[593] Of course, this is not necessarily the case. Rather, this is an attempt to sketch out a future political judgment that is limited to the aesthetic dimension. Here the cognitive aspect of political subjectivity emerges, from where speculations could be made about how much knowledge a political subject needs in order to keep such forms of rule and government as parliamentary democracies functioning, as they depend on the political subject's, i. e. the citizen's qualified participation; cf. Chapter B.3.3 and B.3.5.

the respective version of conclusive source hermeneutics.[594] An important exception in this context are the works of Reinhart Koselleck. On a broad basis of sources, he tried to find out the subjective time horizons of the respective contemporaries in order to be able to read an evolutionary rule of the subjective experience of time in the summary of several epochs:

> "The hypothesis is that in determining the difference between past and future, or anthropologically, between experience and expectation, something like historical time can be grasped. Now it is certainly one of man's biologically determined circumstances that the relationship between experience and expectation changes as he grows older, whether one grows and the other disappears, whether one is compensated by the other, or whether extra-biographical horizons of an internal or external nature are opened up that help to relativize the finite time of a personal life. But also in the sequence of historical generations the relationship between past and future has obviously changed."[595]

For political philosophy, the historical time horizons should of course be of the greatest importance. At the same time, however, they cannot be discussed from the perspective of history, because the tenses of history, especially in their individual experience, cannot be anything other than political (or just: apolitical) times from the point of view of political subjectivity. The difference is articulated in the fact that the aesthetic capacity of the mathematically sublime enables the political judgment to

---

[594] Cf., for example, the contributions in Rossi, Pietro (ed.), *Theorie der modernen Geschichtsschreibung* [Theory of Modern Historical Research], Frankfurt 1987.

[595] Koselleck, Reinhart, *Vergangene Zukunft. Zur Semantik geschichtlicher Zeiten* [Past Future. On the Semantics of Historical Fimes], 3rd ed., Frankfurt 1984, p. 12. With systems-theoretical means but oriented to the teaching of mental and biological evolution represented in Helmuth Plessner's philosophical anthropology, Günther Dux tries to solve these tasks and isolate a developmental logic of time in the sources; see ders., *Die Zeit in der Geschichte*, loc. cit. The systems theoretical masterpiece by Niklas Luhmann, *Weltzeit und Systemgeschichte*, loc. cit., should be remembered here once again. In his extensive work, Stephan Otto has attempted to reconstruct history on the basis of Hegel's logic. In *Zur Kritik der historischen Vernunft* [Concerning the Critique of Historical Reason], 2 vol., Munich 1982 and 1992, physicality plays an essential role under the title "concrete subjectivity", but the subject falls pitted by the wayside because the "understanding of transcendently justified reasonableness" (ibid., II, p. 243) is no longer attributed to any form of judgment. The body should be conjured up for the successful mediation of the individual and the universal through an intermodal system of rules, but the magic trick does not work.

give the respective notions of time about the subjective orders imagined therein the quality of relative size (or their absence) – which is thought in a delay or cancellation of time as an agent of change during a certain duration. Formulated in Koselleck's anthropological words: **The political times are mathematically thought to cover the past experiences with expectations directed towards the present or future (traditionalism, conservatism) or expectations with new future experiences (because the past offers no order to be continued: progressivism, utopism)**. Political subjectivity may not always be subject to objective determinations of time, such as sensual nature, but it is also not free of time, such as moral nature of freedom. The reflecting power of judgment as a whole stands under the *prescribed* or the *taken time*, thus also the political subjectivity. The taken time is the time that the subject can spontaneously and freely unfold in order to reflect its own ideas of order. The prescribed time is accepted by the subject only receptively as a basis for reflection on order. Giving and taking refers to the relative positions and states of the rulers and the ruled. Contrary to what appears to be the case, these initial remarks on political time theory do not yet contribute to the problem of the diachronic representation of political subjectivity mentioned above but are only part of the discussion of the aspect of time in political judgment itself.[596]

The mathematically sublime is not exhausted by the generation of aesthetic, relative time size for political judgment, for the important spatial aspect of size also belongs in this capacity. The spatialization of ideas of order can be experienced above all in the works of political architecture. Kant cites the Egyptian pyramids and St. Peter's as examples of inappropriateness of one's own imagination for the ideas of a whole, whose exces-

---

[596] This brief discussion is only a suggestion to examine the problem of time in political philosophy in more detail. Here a thorough philosophical analysis of the interrelationships was dispensed with, because it would certainly have gone beyond the scope. Just one comment: the approach seems to have similarities with Edmund Husserl's phenomenology of time consciousness, but this appearance is deceptive. For Husserl, time is consciously pre-conceptual and not bound to any spontaneity of the judging subject. He would have been surprised if one of his students had claimed that time could also be a spontaneous product of aesthetic judgment; see Husserl, *Zur Phänomenologie des inneren Zeitbewusstseins (1893-1917)*, ed. by R. Boehm, The Hague 1966, Husserliana vol X. More exciting would be a confrontation with Martin Heidegger's speculations on time in the context of 'existence' in *Sein und Zeit*, Halle 1927.

sive demands, however, generate a touching pleasure.[597] Precisely following this point Kant again warns against mixing the forms of judgment and describes these examples, which he himself has just given, as inappropriate to the method of the *CPJ*.[598] But the door is already wide enough open for us to gain an insight into the relationship between the mathematically sublime as a relative, spatially imagined quantity to teleological reflection and finally to politics, especially in the form of *political architecture,* one of the most important forms of the sensualization of the political in general. But one should not be too impressed by individual concretions in a philosophical analysis of judgments; it is precisely here that the generalizations must be tested. Accordingly, political architecture is above all an aesthetic-technical theory of the body about the spatialization of political meaning, either as a surface or as a volume.[599] Thus the pictorial representations of bodies and the architectures extended in urban planning or entire cities are included.[600] Moreover, the bodies brought to the spatial representation do not have to be concrete images, but they can themselves exist in analogies that are expressed by symbols, i.e. the body concept is primarily to be understood aesthetically-symbolically, not physically.[601] The relative size as an active moment in the feeling of the mathematically sublime is the decisive factor here and extends across all bodies. This means that the sublime can be created not only by monuments and buildings, but also by

---

[597] *CPJ*, B 88 [136].

[598] *CPJ*, B 89 [137]; here cited in B.1.3.

[599] At this point, the differences between the semiotic analysis of architecture and the method proposed here, which is based on the study of forms of judgment, can be studied particularly well; cf. Eco, Umberto, *Einführung in die Semiotik* [Introduction to Semiotics], München 1985, pp. 293-356.

[600] Cf. the ambitious and beautiful book by Richard Sennett, *Flesh and Stone*, N.Y. & London 1994. Sennett has thus again pointed out the connection between order and body, without, like Foucault, making it exclusively the subject of power strategies. He follows an important intuition. "The guiding principles of 'the body' often suppress mutual, sensual perception, especially among those whose bodies differ from one another. When a society or political order generally talks about 'the body', it can deny the needs of bodies that do not correspond to the ideal. A form of the model of the body is revealed in the expression 'political body' (the body politic), it expresses the need for social order." (ibid., p. 31)

[601] Maurice Merleau-Ponty comes to a similar conclusion in his study *Phänomenologie der Wahrnehmung* [Phenomenology of Perception], Berlin 1966, pp. 181, where he points out that self-perception as a body does not produce a physical object, but a work of art.

images of people, whether they are two or three-dimensional in space. Whether it was the larger-than-life busts of Augustus with a very flattering depiction of the Emperor, which he had erected throughout the Roman Empire, or the huge screens on which the speakers can be amplified by party conferences: the spatial extension of the person is related to its depiction of what is usually called its *power*. From the perspective of political subjectivity, however, power must be a concept that is more closely defined as the general influence of one's will on the will of other subjects, according to Weber's definition "...every chance to enforce one's own will within a social relationship against opposition, no matter what this chance is based on."[602] This comprehensive determination is therefore not simply to be short-circuited with the mathematical-emphasis of relative greatness, because there is no direct connection at all between the size of an embodiment and the influence of this size on the will of subjects. It is an empirical experience of everyday life that the size of political representtation has an effect on the mind of the beholder, but a body, in any case, has nothing political in itself. It requires a *mediating idea*, and that is of course the *subjective order underpinned by this embodiment*. The relative size as height, massiveness or extension of an embodiment of political meaning can only have an influence on political judgment if the representation contains the idea of an order of analogous size or calls it up in the subject.

An outstanding example of the political aesthetics of embodiment can be found in Ernst H. Kantorowicz's monumental study *The King's Two Bodies*.[603] In it he examines the teaching of the King's dual physical nature in medieval law and theology, which was still valid in England until the Tudor period. Edmund Plowden, the crown lawyer under Queen Elisabeth, wrote in his reports:

> "For the king has in himself two bodies, namely the natural (body natural) and the political (body politic). Its natural body is in itself a mortal body exposed to all challenges arising from nature or accidents, the imbecility of early childhood or old age and similar defects occurring in other people's natural bodies. The political body, on the other hand, is a body that cannot be seen or touched. It consists of

---

[602] Weber, Max, *Wirtschaft und Gesellschaft. Grundriss der verstehenden Soziologie* [Economy and Society], 5. rev. ed., Tübingen 1985, p.29. Weber observes shortly afterwards: "The concept of power is sociologically amorphous."(ibid.)

[603] Kantorowicz, Ernst H., The King's Two Bodies. A Study in Medieval Political Theology, Princeton 1957.

politics and government, it is there for the control of the people and the public good. This body is completely free of childhood and age, as well as of the other defects and weaknesses to which the natural body is subject. For this reason, nothing that the King does in his political corporeality can be invalidated or prevented by a defect in his natural body."[604]

One notices on this occasion the beautiful illustration of the *expectation of timelessness*, which is put in order, so that its temporal size (as a standstill) and its spatial-symbolic size interact advantageously. From the observation of this strange legal figure in the 16th century, Kantorowicz followed the pattern of the royal double body back to the 13th century. The doctrine of ecclesiastical law in force at the time, according to which Christian society is a *corpus mysticum* with Christ as its head, was gradually transferred by the jurists to the state as *corpus rei publica mysticum*.[605] Finally, in the epilogue the author states that this scheme was not exclusively of Christian origin, but was certainly also used by pagan authors – after which the ethnological and anthropological discussion of the royal dual nature should follow.[606] The body symbolism was certainly culturally influential in the Middle Ages, but modern phenomena of the political can undoubtedly also be interpreted with their help.[607] The continuation of the theory of an immaterial, superhuman 'body politic' is naturally found in Thomas Hobbes' work *Leviathan*, whose figure, as the famous frontispiece shows, had grown into a "mortal God". The idea of its size is an own dimension of the order value symbolized by analogy. The analysis must not ignore the fact that this function of reflecting judgment is opposite to individuality in political judgment, for **sheer greatness has nothing else to do but to replace the individual, to allow it to dissolve into a higher**

---

[604] Plowden, Edmund, Commentaries or reports, London 1816, p. 212 a; quoted from Kantorowicz, loc. cit., p. 31.

[605] Kantorowicz, loc. cit., pp. 218-240.

[606] An initial approach to this can be found in René Girard's main work, *Das Heilige und die Gewalt* [Violence and the Sacred], Frankfurt 1992, pp. 450-452, where this aspect is taken into account from the point of view of mimetic conflict theory. Cf. Grünenberg, Reginald, *Gründungsgewalt und Politik. René Girards Kulturtheorie im Spiegel der Politikwissenschaft* [Founding Violence and Politics. René Girard's Theory of Culture as Reflected in Political Science] in: academia.edu, Berlin 2010.

[607] Cf. Lefort, Claude, Logique totalitaire et l'image du corps [Totalitarian Logic and the Image of the Body], in: Lefort, L'invention démocratique. Les limites de la domination totalitaire, Paris 1981.

unity and to relieve it of its work of self-assertion. The longing for political greatness can signal a reflected need for *liberation from the expected reflecting activity*, but also the desire to let the reflected individuality swell as will itself to this greatness, whereby the transition to the much more momentous function of *subjective power* is marked in judgment.

B.1.7.2.4 The Dynamically Sublime: *Power*

The above-mentioned distinction between power and size was a measure to prevent the loss of one's own aesthetic value of spatially imagined size in relation to order. The last dimension of relative size in the course of the discussion of the sublime is no longer spatially imagined as such, but very often makes use of a supporting sensualization *in space*. So, there is no doubt that power has an important but not essential relation to spatially imagined greatness. For example, the concept of divine power in Christianity is not sensualized in space because it transcends the concept of space itself. Things were different with the gods of Olympus. But space is not the decisive factor. What is essential is the *quality of an imagined will*, namely its strength and intensity.

In § 28 of the *CPJ*, Kant describes the dynamically sublime only from the point of view "*Of nature as a power.*"[608] This again corresponds entirely to his method of distilling almost purely aesthetic judgments, which has to be reversed here. First, *power is to be distinguished from violence*, and Kant sees in it only a difference in intensity, for violence is also a kind of power, but one that breaks the resistance of the respective counterpower. So there is power and countervailing power, and furthermore there is power *only as long as there is a countervailing power*. This is an important observation, because it excludes the possibility that updated violence can still be described as power and at the same time determines that power must always be presented in pairs with its resistance. It is also clear that violence cannot replace a lack of power.[609] It is only a gradual difference whether a representation, i.e. a sensualization of ideas of order, invites contemplation and makes the viewer an involved spectator on the sidelines, or whether it exerts a manifest compulsion on the will of the observer, which proceeds from a will that is thought to act in the matter. Thus, the spectrum is de-

---

[608] *CPJ*, B 102-110 [143-148], title of the chapter.

[609] Hannah Arendt recalled this in particular in *Macht und Gewalt* [Power and Violence], Munich 1970.

fined from free political judgment to open manipulation and violence, likewise the degrees of evaporation of permitted and practicable political subjectivity. Power is a product of reflection in the political subject when its judgment, i.e. its subjective concept of order as a relationship of individual self and universal order, sees itself exposed to a will and reflects as influenced by it. When this power increases to violence, the possibility for reflection is inversely lost.

In the Kantian model, which in so many respects already prima facie recalls political conditions, nature is given the following status: "Nature considered in aesthetic judgment as a power that has no dominion over us is dynamically sublime."[610] But the sublime can only be dynamic when nature is viewed with fear, whereby this fear does not mean angst or horror, but rather a quasi-shuddering demonstration of respect: "Thus the virtuous man **fears God without being afraid of him**,..."[611] Kant does not develop the natural aesthetic appearance of power in the concept of will itself, but in a divine being that is thought of as working in nature. It may be that he did not wish to remove the concept of will too far from its moral-philosophical use; but there is no doubt that it is fundamental to the sensual concept of power.[612] The concept of a will in the object of the sublime is analogous to the phenomenon of life in the teleology of organized ends, i.e. dynamically sublime order must have the quality of a will, that is, a force to realize and maintain itself, just as the individual who either participates in or resists this realization of order. This extension of the concept of power of nature to an *imagined will* is a systematic completion of the *CPJ*, because **the imagined, non-human mind on which nature's teleology is based is thus given the complementary will.**

Consequently, the sensualization of power is divided into two cases according to the terms 'individual' and 'order' which coincide in the political judgment. Behind the concept of will are now directly the ideas of the individual and order, but through the concept of will itself they do *not appear in their static-syntactic form*, as teleological judgment makes them available to political judgment as *concepts, but as semantic states*, i.e. they are dynamically presented in the activity of their self-assertion and self-development as acting beings, and their action is the preservation of themselves,

---

[610] *CPJ*, B 102 [184].

[611] *CPJ*, B 103 [144].

[612] In two places Kant mentions the will, but only of this being which must be resisted in order to feel one's own power; see *CPJ*, B 110, 111 [147].

which is thought as power. To make it once again very clear: not only individuality, but order in general is thought in the dynamic judgment analogous to the causality of organic living beings, for only through the concept of end something like a *being* and an *action* becomes conceivable, and only with these ideas can individuality and order be *animated* or *enlivened* in the sense of critical philosophy.[613]

It becomes clear once again here that from the perspective of political subjectivity it is not a matter of the objective effect of power, for example in the manner of a psycho-mechanics or phenomenology.[614] It also has nothing to do with how power can be generated and used, but only the way in which **power can be specifically assessed politically in imagination and in representation**, i.e. how it enters into the political judgment and what function it has there. In sociology, the production and execution of power is viewed objectifyingly on the basis of the reaction of subjects, in that the effected movements of the subjects are condensed into a mechanics whose fundamental effect is called 'power'. However, there is a striking proximity to Niklas Luhmann's systems theory approach on a terminological level, for his sociology of power is based on a *general theory of symbolically generalized communication media*. However, systems theory takes a different approach, because power (or truth, money, love) has nothing to do with judgmental, conscious aesthetics, or more emphatically: with individuals, but it is a medium that can only be experienced in the form of a code that generates communication opportunities for system formation.[615] In the investigation of political subjectivity, however, only the judgmental receptivity of thought for power comes into view, whereby

---

[613] Political orders that do not produce power carry the seed of doom within them – as Hannah Arendt put it in *Vita activa or Vom tätigen Leben* [The Human Condition, 1960], Munich 1981, p.197. According to Arendt, this applies above all to dictatorships, because they are tyrannies.

[614] As it was designed by Gustav Le Bon psychologically, by Sigmund Freud psychoanalytically and finally by Elias Canetti in *Masse und Macht* [Crowds and Power, 1960], Frankfurt 1994, decidedly anti-psychoanalytically and phenomenologically instead.

[615] Cf. Luhmann, Niklas, *Macht* [Power], Stuttgart 1975; Luhmann, *Einführende Bemerkungen zu einer Theorie symbolisch generalisierter Kommunikationsmedien* [Introductory Remarks on a Theory of Symbolically Generalized Communication Media], in: Luhmann, *Soziologische Aufklärung* 2, Opladen 1975, p. 170-192; an excellent representation of this theory can also be found in Luhmann, *Liebe als Passion. Zur Codierung von Intimität* [Love as Passion. About Coding Intimacy], Frankfurt 1982, pp. 21-47.

this is also the individual's achievement when this receptivity is connected with an action in the form of judgment. If this is not the case, then the individual is actually subject to a natural-mechanical, i.e. psycho-mechanical force and cannot judge freely. If, according to Kant's definition, power is indeed increased in intensity into violence, then it is impossible to judge the sublime:

> "Someone who is afraid can no more judge about the sublime in nature than someone who is in the grip of inclination and appetite can judge about the beautiful."[616]

The same applies to political judgment, for where fear in the sense of angst and horror prevails, there is no political judgment and no political subjectivity. It is always important to remember how preconditional and fragile the ability of political thought acquired in the process of cultural development is. Power and violence in particular are the means repeatedly used to generate political immaturity, not only in the form of external coercion on individuals who potentially remain free in their judgment, but also through the **suppression or expulsion of the *ability* to think politically**. This is the philosophically reconstructable process that has a judgment-related effect in such practices of government as 'enforced conformity', 'self-critique' and 're-education'.

The phenomenon of political power has its own history, for its form has changed considerably over time – a clear sign that it has a dimension independent of biological and anthropological constants.[617] For the discussion of political subjectivity, it is only of interest *how power is reflected upon by the individual*, what forms of judgment are put in relation to it and above all what kind of sensualization of this power is. It is to be called *subjective power*, because it refers to an ability of thinking, whereby *the subject also produces this power by judging*. As in the study of the function of the mathematically sublime for the political judgment, here too we follow the guideline of aesthetic embodiment, for it became already clear there that spatial sensualization is important for the representation of power. This

---

[616] *CPJ*, B 103 [144].

[617] Cf. Michael Mann's extraordinarily material-rich study *Die Geschichte der Macht*, 2 vol., Frankfurt 1990 [The Sources of Social Power. A History of Power from the Beginning to AD 1790, 1986]. There, the "IEMP model" (ibid., p. 15, 56) is developed, in which the historically effective sources of power are summarized: Ideological, Economic, Military and Political. On this methodically ordered material basis Mann wanted to publish another volume with the corresponding theory of power, which has not yet appeared.

time, however, the relative spatial size is ignored, for power is embodied not only in favor of the mathematically sublime feeling and its assessment, but to a greater extent in the feeling of the dynamically sublime.

The coat of arms is an embodiment strategy that was particularly important in the Middle Ages and is still practiced today. This kind of symbolization of meaning and values by means of the composition of selected attributes, i.e. a *will to order*, was experienced in its beginnings as a particularly strong form of representation. The coat of arms has inherited and transformed the function of the archaic totem.[618] Obviously neither the quantity of spatial size depicted, nor the imagined quantity of space plays a role here. The concept of size is effective here as a *quality*, namely as the **strength and compelling force of the heraldically-symbolically embodied will**. As a result, the German federal flag is intended to keep alive in memory the mood and determination to impose a certain new order as a historical and at the same time political date. The German federal eagle is a sensualization of the majesty and danger of the bird of prey, borrowed from the animal kingdom, which overlooks its territory from great heights. The open beak signals its readiness to fight, because it already emits a warning cry. The other bestiary in the coats of arms and flags is sufficiently well-known and its meaning is usually evident. All political emblems embody an ordered entity (be it a ministerial administration or a municipality) that signals the preservation (in the case of a superior power to be respected) and possibly the increase in the power of its will (at state level: territorial or economic expansion). The same applies to economic enterprises in the world of markets since the rise of trading houses and banks between the 17th and 19th centuries, although the separation of political and economic reality is now of course only fiction. However, the explicit, symbolic power claims of companies to social order are still very rare, because they harm business. Even if the balance sheet totals of some globally operating corporations and banks overshadow the budget volume or even the gross national product of many countries on the globe, their politically qualifiable power is only embodied in spheres isolated from the

---

[618] See Huizinga, Johan, *Herbst des Mittelalters. Studien über die Lebens- und Geistesformen des 14. und 15. Jahrhunderts in Frankreich und in den Niederlanden* [Autumn of the Middle Ages. Studies of the Ways of Living and Thinking in the 14th and 15th Century in France and the Netherlands], Stuttgart 1975, pp. 335-336; cf. also Walter Seitter's unconventional attempt to rediscover heraldry as an analytical instrument for political science in *Menschenfassungen. Studien zur Erkenntnispolitikwissenschaft* [Human Conceptions. Studies in Political Epistemology], Munich 1985.

public, informally and only in discrete tie-wearing. The self-portrayal of companies in the construction of their buildings, for example, is only rarely of a representativeness that communicates itself as somehow political.[619] For a political subject since the end of 19th-century patriarchal capitalism, which still made exploitation physically visible (for example in Hauptmann's *Die Weber* [The Weavers; 1892]), there is hardly any aesthetic opportunity to perceive the power of commercial enterprises, for **the aesthetic principle of the economy is not the embodiment of a possibly threatening will**. On the contrary. Economic actors usually spend a lot of money to appear in public as politically innocent and merely serving minds who fulfil all wishes and at best support the existing order; i.e. they make their power invisible and unrepresentable. Presenting the order-determining power of individual economic actors or aggregated systems has always been the task of a scientific or artistic critique of society.

In the dynamically sublime, power becomes conceivable because resistance against the subject's own will through an imagined will *is felt*. The assessment of power is therefore clearly related to the feeling of pleasure and displeasure and is therefore part of the semantics of political judgment. The political subject characterizes its own *individual state* in relation to the subjective order through its reflection on an object perceived as dynamic. Empires, nations, or subordinate governmental bodies are judged as powers by attaching to them (imagined as living orders) a will that communicates aesthetically its willingness to resist and, if necessary, subjugate the individual will. Using the example of patriotism, or in increased intensity: nationalism, the previously mentioned dimensions of power sensualization can now also be summarized.

The imagined power of a nation is thus composed 1) of the *essential quality of a strong will*, as it is judged in the dynamically sublime, in which rarely the manifest will to freedom of the citizens (like in the French Revolutionary Wars) and more often the entire military power or the imagined will to survive of a pure, super-personal, racial collective subject would have to be reckoned with; 2) of the time in the form of its duration, which is *thought to be suspended in its order*, and finally 3) from the *spatial-territorial extension of the dominion area* including the quantity and concen-

---

[619] This becomes clear from the exceptions, such as the Springer Press House in Berlin, which was deliberately built in the immediate vicinity of the Wall and within sight of the GDR as a symbol of combative Western democracy, which according to the publisher's owner's idea would one day liberate occupied East Germany from socialism.

tration of controlled individual subjects contained therein. Only the first criterion is essential to the concept of power and is one of the functions of the dynamically sublime in political judgment; the following two are functions of the mathematically sublime and only optional for the idea of power. All three work together in the political judgment in order to make a concrete relationship between one's own nature, one's own person and the order presented *tangible* and *accessible to reflection*.[620] The German discussion about 'constitutional patriotism' since Dolf Sternberger is a good and for us enlightening illustration of this. A post-war generation of political theorists believed that the sensual forms of connecting nation and power could no longer be cultivated in Germany on the basis of historical experience ('Leader', 'Military', 'Livin Space', 'Thousand-Year Reich'). At the same time, however, they did not completely want to give up the imagined power of an embodied will to order and therefore pleaded for the constitutional document (Grundgesetz [Basic Law]), which was to assume this function in the political judgment of the subjects. This programmatic and well-meaning *de-sensualization of the political* has mainly influenced the ideas of the political left, but overall success has been limited, for this lack of sensuality is now perceived by the left itself as a disturbing problem of communication. The aesthetic of constitutional patriotism creates an intellectualization of political judgment that imposes too great limits on the imagination and requires too much prior knowledge to make the idea of a charismatic founding act popular.[621]

A distinction was made at the beginning between the *embodiment of order* on the one hand and the *embodiment of the individual* on the other in

---

[620] Cf. Anderson, Benedict, *Imagined Communities*, 1988. One would have expected a *theory of community consciousness* as an idea, but the descriptive approach remains entirely sociological. Also, in Cornelius Castoriadis' attempt *Gesellschaft als imaginäre Institution. Entwurf einer politischen Philosophie* [Society as an Imaginary Institution. Draft of a Political Philosophy], Frankfurt 1984, the imaginary is not attributed to any individual, but remains an inexplicably normatively charged creative force that constantly produces *ex nihilo* new social 'worlds'.

[621] In the U.S., which served as role models here, pure constitutional patriotism is framed by a more intensive religiosity, a heartily unclouded national pride in the size and military power of the country and not least by its own history, which actually begins with its own founding act and can therefore be thought of identically with national history. American constitutional patriotism therefore allows all other functions to play a role in political judgment that make power imaginable.

the judgment of the dynamically sublime. The observations to date on sensualization referred exclusively to the power of order. The no less important but mostly overlooked counterpart is the *embodiment of power in human bodies*. The biological body of man is hardly suited to evoke the feeling of mathematical sublimity. Except for the exceptional cases of giant growth and the already conveyed pictorial or sculptural representation, it is not the spatial greatness through which power could be sensualized. And yet even a physically relatively small person can unmistakably depict power, as we know from the stories about the majesty and radiated power of Louis XIV, the Sun King with a very modest stature. This observation immediately points to an important distinction to be made. On the one hand, there is the *embodiment of the will of an order in a person*, as Louis XIV clearly expressed it in the dictum "L'État, c'est moi" that is attributed to him. Every head of government and minister, every party leader and mayor stands with his body for an order. In sociology, this would be his *function* or his *role* and *position*, each described relative to others. In the theory of political subjectivity, it is (only with reference to the politically judging subject) first of all the aesthetic embodiment of a will to order. What sociology calls its function must be reflectable in a concrete sense for the political judgment of an individual, and that is the feeling of the dynamically sublime.

The second dimension of political sensualization in human bodies is actually much more important, namely the *embodiment of the subjective will to order in one's own body*. According to the *separation of power and counter-power* introduced above, this is the symbolic sensualization of the counter-power to the power of order itself. However, we must not lose sight of the fact that this opposition of power of order and autonomy occurs in reflection, which only produces these ideas with the help of sensual embodiments. So it is not a matter of the objective physical force of an order on the subjective feeling of self-power, but of a *contraction and comparison of imagined self-power and power of order in reflection*. **For only in this way is a political judgment possible that can be consensual or dissensual, thereby preserving its optional moment that is constitutive.** Physical and psychological constraints can certainly limit this optionality, but to the same extent the judgment loses its political quality and becomes mechanical, because the body of the subject is only the psychosomatic embodiment of a *foreign* will.[622]

---

[622] The modern psychological training methods for torturers, with which they are appropriately prepared for their inhuman business, are informative in this

The essential function of embodying a power in one's own body vessel for political judgment is now not the acute resistance to order, but the *semantic labeling of one's own individuality*. It was explained above that the concept of end provides part of the syntax of the political judgment in the form of the terms 'individual' and 'order'. The aesthetic functions in political judgment are therefore responsible for providing the semantic states for this syntactic form. In the type of reflection of the dynamically sublime, the subject now experiences itself as its own concrete will, which was awakened by the option or necessity of resistance to the natural order or precisely the reflected, subjective social order. In contrast to Aristotle, who interpreted the soul as the form of the body, which itself provided only the material, the objectivist form/material difference is not applied under the guidance of reflecting judgment, but the body, insofar as it is recognized as a *symbol of the individual*, is an achievement of the reflecting subject. This must have already recognized itself as an individual in order to recognize another being, a human being, as an individual. Or to put it another way, namely limited to the symbolic basis of individuality: those who do not know themselves as their own bodies cannot recognize others in their bodies.[623] *In the dynamically sublime, the body is thus recognized and accepted as a symbol of the individual.*

Luc Ferry has already referred to this possibility, albeit in pursuit of another method.[624] Ferry tries to show that, according to the *CPJ*, the human body must be regarded as a symbol of individuality, because only in this way can the sphere of freedom acquire an analog in the physical world that can be communicated and aesthetically experienced. However,

---

respect. Morally, the torturers are annulled as subjects, politically they are no longer individuals. By the way, we'll see: He who is not a subject cannot be an individual.

[623] It is worth recalling the passage already quoted by Jean Cazeneuve in his treatise *La conaissance d'autrui dans les sociétés archaiques* [Knowledge of the Self in Archaic Societies], in: *Cahiers internationaux de sociologie* XXV, July-December 1958, pp. 75-99, where he notes that the Christian Europeans did not, as they intended and believed, teach people from ethnological peoples the existence of their souls, *but the existence of their bodies*. This centering of the body is the basis for the further emergence of individuality.

[624] Cf. Ferry, Luc, *Philosophy politique II. Le système des philosophies de l'histoire*, Paris 1984, pp. 226-242. The title of the chapter reads *De la finalité comme signe de la liberté: le corps humain comme symbole de l'individualité* [About the Finitude as a Sign of Freedom: The Human Body as the Symbol of Individuality] (ibid., p. 226).

the notion of freedom is only possible in accordance with the determining power of judgment if the term does not only mean the negative definition as an absence of coercion, which can very well be judged in a reflecting manner. The concept of freedom is part of practical philosophy, and it should not be plundered there until political philosophy has exhausted all its own resources.[625]

A variant of this is the symbolic hypotyposis in the individual proper name[626], which must certainly also be regarded as an embodiment of individuality (in sound and scripture).[627] But the strongest aesthetic sensualization is the will as unbroken power in the human body. It is not determined whether the border of this reflected body of individuality is the *skin* or, for instance, the *clothing*, which is an entire symbolically used surface full of messages. These demarcations are subject to cultural change, for in ethnological peoples the body is usually not limited to the biological substrate, but the traces of the body or its property are thought together with it.[628] The special cultural form of individuality, as it was developed in Europe and as it is still exported across the globe, consists in centering all actions and acts of thought in the biological body as the vessel of the soul and reason. To a certain extent, this is a cultural-historically very recent *restriction of the diffusion of individuality to natural objects and events or magical beings*. Modern individuality consists in an increase of attention for one's own body as a symbol for the consciousness of oneself, whereby it

---

[625] In chapter B.1.8, *Practice, Reflection and Faith*, this topic is discussed separately

[626] Cf. *CPJ*, B 257 [296] and Lévi-Strauss, Claude, *Das wilde Denken* [The Savage Mind], Frankfurt 1989, p. 223-250.

[627] Such considerations could advance the 'personalistic' approach in political philosophy developed by Max Müller and represented by Alexander Schwan. But here too the greatest obstacle lies in the strong blending of ethics and political philosophy. Cf. Müller, Max, *Erfahrung und Geschichte. Grundzüge einer Philosophie der Freiheit als transzendentale Erfahrung* [Experience and History. Fundamentals of a Philosophy of Freedom as a Transcendental Experience], Freiburg and Munich 1971; Max, *Philosophische Anthropologie*, Freiburg and Munich 1974; also Schwan, Alexander, *Philosophie der Gegenwart vor dem Problem des Pluralismus* [Today's Philosophy Facing the Problem of Pluralism], in: Simon, Josef (ed.), Freiheit. *Freiheit. Theoretische und praktische Aspekte des Problems* [Freedom. Theoretical and Practical Aspects of the Problem], Freiburg and Munich 1977, pp. 171-203.

[628] Especially clear in voodoo magic, where the entire foreign body is to be magically controlled by means of its smallest part or occasionally an object touched by it.

becomes possible for the subject to communicate aesthetically about one's own identity with oneself. Moreover, it follows from the discussion so far that individuality cannot be separated from political subjectivity, because it is in fact identical with it, but in philosophical analysis individuality must even be regarded as the *product* of a political judgment.

Individual self-awareness by means of the body gives the subject the possibility of carrying out a comparative reflection of subjective order and individual state, because otherwise the subject does not even know what it has to attribute to itself and what not. It does not know its states, cannot relate them to an imagined order and therefore cannot reflect on options in judgment.[629] The human body is a contested field of techniques and techni-

---

[629] Here is the place for a brief introduction to ethnologically and culturally uninformed analytical philosophy. Its postulate that the self-reference and self-confidence of consciousness, which is articulated in 'deictic terms' (expressions in statements from the 'I' or "he/she" perspective), cannot be conveyed through physicality, points to what I would like to call the *hypostasis of identity* (cf. the *Excursus I* in chapter B.1.9). The concrete concept of the self is equated with the scheme of the unity of transcendental consciousness and, instead of being reflected by symbolic hypotyposis through physicality, is reified in an inadmissibly cognitive-critical manner, i.e. hypostasized. The concept of the self, concentrated on self-reference in a unity, is a hypostasis, an impermissible reification of the idea of the self as a schema. But already in Kant's chapter on paralogism it is clearly stated about the doctrine of self-conception: "I cannot have a theoretical-schematic knowledge of my ego-constitution, thus no objective certainty in knowing myself, because my inner view is always empirical." (*CPuRe* B 399-432 [pp. 411]) Only in a theorem that is based on symbolic hypotyposis as a basis for representation can a cultural-historical evolution of the concrete forms of self-consciousness be described. Manfred Frank, who here approvingly refers to Elisabeth Anscombe's thought experiment of the "sensorily completely deprived 'I'(-body?)" in a nutrient solution tank, wants to have the body treated subordinatedly and presuppose the 'I' as an act of reference in need of the body: "What is important here is that it is assumed that there is in fact no possibility of identifying the physical as mine, and that is not because'I' still reports with certainty of death, although it cannot know anything about its physicality". (Frank, Manfred, *Selbstbewusstsein und Selbsterkenntnis. Essays zur analytischen Philosophie der Subjektivitä* [Self-Consciousness and Self-Knowledge. Essays on the Analytical Philosophy of Subjectivity], Stuttgart 1991, p. 273). It may be that a subject retains its self in the nutrient solution with the help of its memory for a while, but **perhaps the analytical philosophers should be made aware that this is a kind of torture that leads to madness within the shortest time, i.e. to the self-decay through body loss.** The problem of these analytical considerations is that a physical-

cians of power who want to limit reflection and to have the subject a priori properly arranged. The most intensive research on body politics, as carried out by Foucault in particular, has been taken up, further developed and even used politically by the women's movement:

> "For feminist theory and criticism, the body is not one subject among others, but a subject in which existential, personal everyday experience, strategies of gender policy and questions about the conditions of cultural interpretation and socially organized practices of the generation of bodies and body images overlap."[630]

Gender difference is one of the main distinctions in the structure of political orders, such as client/slave, citizen/foreigner or owner/non-owner. In traditional societies it was the aesthetic mark and evidence of necessary inequality. Through its constantly embodied form it had undergone few changes, for it was transverse to all other evolving distinctions. It is only in modern democracies that it is seen as a problem and even as the subject of political concepts of order. The development of political subjectivity among women in patriarchy has experienced a historical delay in comparison with that of men through programmatically controlled discrimination – and in some places it is still as severely hindered as is possible in internationalizing and globalizing cultural circles. The 1995 World Conference on Women in Beijing, for example, brought these regional differences to light.

It is now happening on the basis of political subjectivity itself that the physical difference of women has become an occasion for reflection on public order. But it is not yet clear whether women's policy should be

---

material body concept is underpinned in them by the human organism, which is to have the function of a pure stimulus membrane for consciousness, although it is still not clear how this mediation between the material and the immaterial could be organized. The body, we can conclude, is a *hypotyped symbol in the self-awareness of thought*; the physical 'body' would only need to be a varying impulse of some kind (as 'information' in the sense of classical information theory according to Shannon), so that the meaning of selfhood can be underpinned by consciousness. In other words: **a consciousness could theoretically use the smallest, but continuous and varying sensual stimulation as an occasion to make itself a body and a self out of it.**

[630] List, Elisabeth, *Wissenskörper: Von der Theorie des Subjekts zur Politik symbolischer Repräsentationen* [Body of Knowledge: From the Theory of the Subject to the Politics of Symbolic Representations], in: List, *Die Präsenz des Anderen. Theorie und Geschlechterpolitik* [The Presence of the Other. Theory and Gender Policy], Frankfurt 1993, pp. 111-122, here p. 121.

shaped by physical difference, because, under the constitutional and human rights principles of equality without regard for gender, it is not even foreseeable whether a policy of female difference is not rather a huge step backwards, because it favors the traditional division of roles. The dissolution of direct legal claims through birth, gender and religious affiliation was an achievement of modern societies. **If the body is brought back into play, acquired rights could be lost and new duties dictated instead.**

Finally, there is the instrumental aspect of the body, its active physical use in politics as an argument. Self-immolation, hunger strike, demonstration, passive resistance at the risk of the removal of the body, chaining to industrial plants endangering safety, disguise and exposure are various stages from safe provocation to self-sacrifice, all of which have only one purpose: to create publicity. In cases of endangering one's own body, the actor's acute or imminent suffering is used as an argument for the falsity of the criticized world order. The reflecting judgment of the actor(s) tries to create a fact by incarnating the argument that is to convince the public. This instrumentalization of the body has strongly ritualistic forms[631], but if such actions can be successful at all, then this is already a sign that **subjects capable of political judgment were assumed in the audience** and were finally also present there. For otherwise there would be no reason at all to assume that the act could be understood by the public as protest and criticism of order, because it would not even be able to perceive the protesting subject as an individual who wants to communicate something specifically political (and also qualifiable as such) in the aesthetic form of the incarnation of suffering. Rather, such a person would appear to be the opposite of an individual, namely *possessed by another being, mentally insane and thus at best regrettable*. Their actions could not be interpreted and presented as a proper voice in the 'council [consilium] of the citizens of the world'. Consequently, the counter-strategy of state authorities or economic agents against such unruly actions consists in *delegitimization through pathologization and psychiatrization* – by no means implying that this reaction would in fact never be justified, because real-pathological insanity is always on the heels of everyday reason. As already mentioned, the body strategists are very close to ritual consciousness, and the question as to whether they are subjects capable of political judgment or whether they are subjects who are at all accountable cannot be answered

---

[631] Even in the weaker forms, such as the not-really-serious hunger strike of a leftist party leadership in Berlin in 1995 because of an unfair tax ruling against the party.

a priori. Protest, insofar as it is politically subjective, is in fact political and is therefore not subject to any guarantee of truth. The protest is party, tries to create new parties in the audience from the potential of political subjectivity and is consistently partisan. These forms of physical use are therefore rightly qualified as political if political subjectivity can be found on both sides, among the actors and the audience. **In a non-political form of publicity, the self-endangerment and self-sacrifice would only be an entertaining spectacle in front of an audience greedily waiting for the bloody outcome.**[632]

An important new development is the dissolution of the body into an image and simulation in the public of the dawning age of information and media technology. This virtualization of the body certainly leads to new forms of self-perception and behavior until perhaps a new ethnology and ethnomethodology must be developed for cyberspace.[633] However, as far as political subjectivity in a world of virtual realities is concerned, its conditions of possibility are still the same. Whether and how they can then still be realized, that is another question. Nothing would stand in the way of an investigation of the evolutionary chances of political judgment in the subject under the conditions of an increasingly artificial nature, i.e. simulated objects, bodies, spaces and times, for the model of political subjectivity is after all basically geared towards diachrony.

---

[632] The comparison of the Roman circus with today's entertainingly choreographed catching events is instructive: the division of the fighting parties according to the distinction between good and evil, as in modern wrestling, is alien to the circus, for hero is only who wins. Besides, only a few were allowed to fight properly at all. Most of the victims slaughtered in the Roman arena for half a millennium to turn the public into a crowd of addicts – Augustine, in his *Confessions*, reported from his own experience of the overwhelming excitement and lust in the face of this violence, which obviously made many of the visitors psychologically dependent on the bloody games – were not trained gladiators, but innocent, prisoners of war or common criminals who were thrown to death by the tattering weapons of the opponents or the predators. For five centuries! Cf. Tarnowski, Wolfgang, *Gladiatoren* [Gladiators], Nuremberg 1987.

[633] Cf. the dark visions of disappearance through generalized acceleration in Paul Virilio's book *Die Eroberung des Körpers. Vom Übermenschen zum überreizten Menschen* [The Conquest of the Body. From Super-Human to Over-stimulated Man], Munich 1994; the reflections of Stefan Jensen are rather ironic, but not a bit more reassuring with regard to the systemic-synthetic future of modern existence; see *Im Kerngehäuse* [Within the Core], in: Rusch, Gerhard et al. (ed.), *DELFIN 1993. Konstruktivismus und Sozialtheorie* [DELFIN 1993. Constructivism and Social Theory], Frankfurt 1994, pp. 47-108.

Surprisingly, the last chapters have now shown that the functions of the types of reflecting judgment are responsible for the production of certain elementary concepts in the political judgment. The completeness of these terms is also astonishing, as they should be sufficient conditions for all kinds of political judgments. It would now be obvious to speak of a *table of categories of the political*, but since these are all translated and even derived terms, this would be an exaggerated reference to the impressive Kantian topos. At least there should be no doubt, however, that these concepts bring an indisputable philosophical dignity into the philosophy of political subjectivity. It is astonishing how little effort political theorists and philosophers have made so far to anchor their concepts in this or a similar way in a cognitive capacity connected with the political competence of politically associated beings. Hannah Arendt probably wanted to have her concepts of 'birth' or 'worldliness' understood in this way, but certainly also her distinction between power and violence. It only lacked the framework to define these terms more precisely. An indication of the problem and the necessity of an own, philosophically justifiable elementary conceptuality of the political and the developmental logic of political imagination can be found in Volker Gerhardt. In his book on Kant's peace treatise, he writes:

> "Empiricism and criticism, however, do not change the fact that we exceed the methodologically permissible context of experience at all times, especially in human communication. We could literally communicate nothing about ourselves and our situation if we could only use the critically secured data of science. 'Nature', 'world', 'cosmos', 'universe', 'space' or 'life', but also 'body' or 'instinct', 'soul' or 'person', 'power' or 'might' are still indispensable terms."[634]

Some of them are indeed indispensable, but the concepts *individual, order, reflection, public, time, body* and *power* only experienced their precise derivation and justification here. In retrospect it will hopefully become clear that the task of determining the origin and possibility of thinking of these and other concepts and their effect in favor of the political judgment was at least correctly identified. The solution offered for this task, on the other hand, still has many tests and trials ahead of it. Some of them will be carried out here in the following.

---

[634] Gerhardt, Volker, *Immanuel Kants Entwurf "Zum Ewigen Frieden". Eine Theorie der Politik*, [Immanuel Kant's Draft 'On Eternal Peace'. A Theory of Politics], Darmstadt 1995, p. 114.

B.1.7.3 The Public and the *Sensus Communis Politicus*: Structures of the Political Judgment

The central and consistently philosophical part of the investigation is completed. From now on it is about paraphrases, illustrations, connections and applications of the analyzed elements of the political judgment. This chapter begins to finally include all the loose ends, especially those from the first half of the investigation, because now the means are available to trace the connections between the apparently disparate circumstances. In Part A one could still think that it could not be conclusively justified why the three fields of individuality, aesthetics and publicity were chosen to form the historical-philosophical background for reading the *CPJ*. This decision, however, was a covert anticipation of a thesis that had not yet been explicitly developed at that time. The real reason for the whole work was a long reflection on the obvious difficulty of philosophy in finding an appropriate explanation or even a satisfactory description for the social phenomenon 'publicity'. It became increasingly clear that philosophy alone cannot be held responsible for this, as Hannah Arendt still believed, but that there is indeed an enormous complexity in this phenomenon, which is not dishonorable to anyone to fail. Aesthetics and individuality were dealt with quite thoroughly in previous chapters, and only a more precise definition of the idea of the public is missing, so that the triangular structure of the three fields does not have to be founded solely in social-historical reality but finds an equivalent in the form of political judgment.

A generative definition of the public sphere was postponed in the previous chapters because this does not correspond to a determinable function of one of the types of reflection but describes the method of the reflecting judgment itself. As a *product* of reflection, it is not identical with its *action* in the unity of judgment, but it owes its form to reflection. The public therefore does not directly contribute to the semantics of political judgment (in the sense of state identification) and does not directly determine the syntax of the judgment, but rather represents the *structural principle*. Therefore, with a certain suddenness, and accompanied only by a brief explanation, it was included in the deduction of the unity of political judgment. The concept of the public sphere, like all other elements of political judgment, must first be 'turned subjective', i.e. the reality that comes to it must be presented in a thinking – and that always means: judging way of creation. Publicity is not only the technical event of empirically observable social communication (as in chapter A.3), but also the *form of a judgment* without which **no one could ever have imagined that freedom of expression, freedom of the press or an opposition to the ruling government to be tolerated are possible and important institutions of the community.** Social functional or structural achievements can thus be counted back to the judgment of individuals as political subjects – a previously unsolvable problem because these achievements were attributed to a much too formal subjectivity that is only responsible for experimental knowledge of nature and objective morality (cf. chapter B.1.9). The judging achievements of individuals, on the other hand, have so far not been taken into account. Even in the ontological political concept of Aristotelian provenance, which Hannah Arendt (in a classicist variant), for example, represented and for which the bourgeois polis-publicity was constitutive, the invested individual judgment does not take into account. This was expressed by another Aristotelian, Dolf Sternberger, in all desirable clarity and with reference to Arendt's work:

> "The inner side of drives, interests and motives is of no concern to the public [and insofar to political philosophy; R.G.], and thus to the political sphere, appearance here is being, and the doctrine of being, the ontology of politics, which is interpreted or excavated here, knows no psychology."[635]

In other words: the concept of political subjectivity developed here undermines the separation of public and private sphere that was dogmatized by classical political ontology. The reflecting judgment as the inner thought experience of the individual is the type of public thinking, i.e. the logical form of this judgment and not its linguistic, pictorial or gestural staging determines the moment of the public. What was called in the deduction of the unity of judgment the action in judgment (B.1.7.1), namely *reflection*, is nothing more than the *procedural moment of consciousness in the generation of publicity*. Thus, this concept of reflection, which is not locked into the circle of self-thinking in the 'I', always brings along a

---

[635] Sternberger, Dolf, *Drei Wurzeln der Politik* [Three Roots of Politics], Frankfurt 1984, pp. 391-392. Sternberger typically sees no place for a consciousness-philosophical view of the political event between the ontological and the psychological interpretation of politics. The political roots in demonology (Machiavelli) and eschatology (Augustinus) he depicted in this beautiful book also do not allow a subject-related and at the same time non-prudential interpretation. But this is exactly what Hannah Arendt sought and suspected – albeit undecidedly – in her reading of Kant, which Sternberger, however, did not take into account.

concept of the public sphere, which ultimately connects the two syntactic components individual and order. But caution is needed here, because as long as this primary concept of the public sphere remains syntactically unconnected, it is so general that it cannot be clearly politically qualified on its own and without any further conditions. On its own, the formal concept of the public sphere is nothing more than a comparison of judgments, namely of one's own aesthetic perceptions or judgments about the purposiveness with those of other individuals. In addition, however, this formal structural concept of the public sphere *also permits theoretically and practically determined judgments in the structure of the comparison.* There is therefore a pre-political or post-political concept of the public sphere, which nevertheless arises from aesthetic reflection as a general principle of comparison.[636] This formally understood public sphere is much broader than the political concept of the public sphere and must first be restricted by the unity of political judgment and the syntactic elements (individual and order) associated with it to be political. All this must be mentioned for the sake of thoroughness, because the structural principle of political judgment is determined by the concept of the public, but this concept has other functions that must be excluded here. In relation to the phenomena documented in evolutionary and cultural history, for example, the archaic ritual publics of sacrifice, the already mentioned Roman circus or the witch trials can be distinguished from a genuinely political public. **The spectacles, which are usually fatal, are indeed forms of reflection in the above sense, because judgments are compared with each other.** In the sacrificial rite, the decision to choose the sacrifice is compared with the

---

[636] Reinhard Brandt has pointed out that the requirement of publicity depends on communicability that is itself closely linked to the theory of beauty; see Brandt, Reinhardt, *Die politische Institution bei Kant* [The Political Institution in Kant], in: Göhler, Gerhard et al. (ed.), *Politische Institutionen im gesellschaftlichen Umbruch. Ideengeschichtliche Beiträge zur Theorie politischer Institutionen* [Political Institutions in Societal Change. Idea-Historical Contributions to the Theory of Political Institutions], Opladen 1990, pp. 335-357, here p. 353. If one follows this path step by step back, namely from the beautiful (and in the consistent expansion of course also from the sublime and from the end), which is based on the reflecting power of judgment of the individual, to the (with Kant exclusively 'learned') public, it first becomes clear that the social reality of publicity is not only rooted in a *commandment of reason*, which was often noticed, but above all in the *ability of the power of judgment* to make judgments communicable and thus available for comparison. For the general character of reflection as 'thinking over' and comparison see *CPuRe* B 318-9 [367] and *CPJ*, First Introduction, pp. 33-34 [23].

decision of the worshipped gods, and it is like the general logic of the reflecting judgment: *"We do not know exactly what the gods demand in their wisdom and wrath to put the world in order, but we try this one!"* The truth of one's own judgment on the basis of a particular (sacrifice) is *suggested* in a quasi-experimental way to the general public (ordering power and legal force of the gods).[637] In the witch trial, the process is so rationalized that it has already accepted the concept of 'judgment of God'. The accused's assertion is then compared with God's decision, who must have seen everything and reveals himself by letting the accused pass an examination (or not).[638] We have no interest in giving these forms of collective instinct relief and satisfaction the prestigious title of a political phenomenon.[639]

In his *Anthropology from a Pragmatic Point of View*, Kant writes that the logical egoist considers it unnecessary to test his judgment on the minds of others:

---

[637] No one has analyzed more radically and thoroughly than René Girard the ritual-logical relationship between the *particular as a victim* and the *universal as law or order* that can only be brought about through it. According to him, the victim is the real basis of mythical transcendence, which manifests itself as a divinely endowed law. Cf. Grünenberg, Reginald, *Gründungsgewalt und Politik. René Girards Kulturtheorie im Spiegel der Politikwissenschaft* [Founding Violence and Politics. René Girard's Theory of Culture as Reflected in Political Science] in: academia.edu, Berlin 2010.

[638] Tests that a normal person could not survive, such as staying under water in a cage for ten minutes without air supply. Cf. here the regulation of the judgments of God in the *Malleus malificarum*, the 'Witch Hammer' of 1489, which the two Dominican monks Institoris and Sprenger wrote according to the witch's bull of Pope Innocent VIII from 1484. This book cost the lives of about one million women until the 18th century. However, it is characterized by the fact that it wants to *rationalize the still inconsistent judgments and trials of God* (the wearing of glowing iron, drinking boiling water, duels, etc.), with the argument that these trials could all be passed with the assistance of demons and would in no way allow conclusions to be drawn about a judgment of God. The confession forced under torture should become the only effective legal institution.

[639] Johan Huizinga, at the beginning of his book on the Middle Ages, pointed to this second, often forgotten face of the public: "... and all things in life were of a magnificent and cruel publicity." (Huizinga, *Herbst des Mittelalters. Studien über die Lebens- und Geistesformen des 14. und 15. Jahrhunderts in Frankreich und in den Niederlanden* [Autumn of the Middle Ages. Studies of the Ways of Living and Thinking in the 14th and 15th Century in France and the Netherlands], Stuttgart 1975, p. 1)

"But it is certain that we cannot do without this means of assuring ourselves of the truth of our judgment, that perhaps it is the most important reason why the learned people cry out for the freedom of the pen: because if this is denied, at the same time a great means is taken away from us to examine the correctness of our judgments and we are exposed to error. *One shall not say that at least mathematics is privileged to agree on the basis of its own power;* for if the perceived consistent conformity of the judgments of the measurer with the judgments of all others who devoted themselves to this subject with talent and diligence had not preceded it, it would not have been removed from the concern of falling somewhere into error."[640]

Kant certainly reports from his own experience, because his first publication, *Thoughts on the True Estimation of Living Forces* (1749), was a mathematical-physical attempt of mediation between Leibniz and Descartes regarding their two formulas for the force of moving bodies. And Kant was wrong about both his predecessors. **As far as political subjectivity is concerned, it should be noted here that even judgments that have been rendered a priori and in accordance with pure theoretical reason require public assessment.**

Pure reason can only be a source of truth production for human beings through the creation of a free public sphere,[641] i.e. through the comparison of judgments, so that this achievement arises from the "accord of free citizens".

"The very existence of reason depends upon this freedom, which has no dictatorial authority, but whose claim is never anything more than the **agreement of free citizens**, each of whom must be able to express his reservations, indeed even his *veto*, without holding back."[642]

---

[640] Kant, Immanuel, *Anthropologie in pragmatischer Hinsicht*, Werle XII, BA 6 [409].

[641] In a much broader sense than in discourse theory, which aims only at the formation of normative commitment in intersubjective communication.

[642] *CPuRe* B 767-768 [643]; one of the interesting passages on this subject in Kant's oeuvre, which I have not yet considered anywhere. Note the increase in the permitted public sphere of 'scholars', as stated in Kant's essay *What is Enlightenment?*, to 'free citizens' – and this in Kant's main scientific work, which seems to have so little reference to political reality! Willi Goetschel has corrected this misconception in his precise study *Constituting Critique. Kant's Writing as Critical Praxis*, Durham and London 1994, in particular pp. 115-143, by thoroughly following the trace of Kant's political ideas into even his most theoretical writings.

Theoretical judgments therefore require the public and are not only attributable to a single subject of knowledge, but also to individuals who can reflect on the place of this epistemic subject and compare the resulting judgments in public in a reflecting manner. How can we imagine the status of these judgments? Are they now judgments of knowledge a priori or, through their reliance on communication, merely aesthetic judgments? Moral, scientific and aesthetic judgments must all be equally conceived in the mode of communicability in order to intersubjectively preserve the kind of objectivity that is due to them, which means, however, that they must already be imagined by the subject in the mode of communicability. *The reflecting, the practically-determined or the theoretically-determined judgment are not mutually exclusive forms of judgment.* Accordingly, the various forms of judgment do not have to follow one after the other in the consciousness of the subject. And it turns out that the reflecting judgment can be presented as being connected with the theoretical or with the practical judgment. So, there are two types of *divided judgment*, namely the *theoretically-reflecting* and the *morally-reflecting* one. Here we are again approaching the medium of the social-empirical and political public. **For the two *divided judgments* only express that theoretical and moral truths need to be communicated, but that communication itself can only be made in the mode of reflecting judgment.** Reflection therefore means that a person has exposed her insights in the form of judgments that claim to be true to comparison with *imaginary objections in thought* herself, or even seeks them out in the *empirical social communication* [i. e. not necessarily *political*, but also *scientific*, *moral* or *religious* communication] of her judgment.[643]

Publicity is therefore an event in which understanding, reason and sensuality are communicated between individuals. It is a communication of theoretical, practical and aesthetic-teleological judgments between persons able of judgment. The *political public sphere* is a more specific process of communication, which takes place precisely when the various forms of judgment are communicated under the *imaginary conditions of individuality and order of individuals in a society*, from microsocial partnership/opposition to world society. The decisive factor here is that the public sphere in

---

[643] The proximity to Popper's methodology of falsificationism is obvious. Anyone who makes a reflecting judgment, even about objects that require the determining power of judgment (nature, morality), knows that he is always dealing with his own hypotheses that are waiting for their acceptance, limitation, correction or refutation.

general and the political public sphere in particular are *always produced in a reflecting manner, i.e. always aesthetically and teleologically, even if the judgments communicated can be practical or theoretical*. By borrowing from Alfred Tarski, the social-empirical public as a medium of *object language* could be distinguished from the epistemic public as a product of the *metalanguage*.[644] The metalanguage that the medium creates or produces is nothing other than the form of judgment of reflecting judgment that prepares an empirical public through structural analogy and under consideration of the aforementioned restrictive conditions. This is also the constitutive difference between judgment and communication, because judgment is a meta-linguistic process, while communication takes place in the object language.[645] This is the only way to explain how economic, technical, religious, social or moral issues can be political issues at the same time, *instead of being completely different forms of rationality*.[646] Political problems thus cover more than just legal and state problems:

The whole spectrum of factual questions turns political by the way they are judged.[647] Only such an expanded concept of the public supports

---

[644] For the distinction between object and meta language see Tarski, Alfred, *Logic, Semantics, Metamathematics*, Oxford 1956.

[645] See Brandt, Reinhard, *Die politische Institution bei Kant*, loc. cit., p. 351 and p. 356, fn. 25. Campe, in a letter to the Duke of Braunschweig dated September 10, 1791, states that one has to distinguish between the activities of judging and communicating these judgments. Brandt observes that this argument could also have come from Kant's pen (see chapter A. 3).

[646] For example, as autopoietic, operatively closed functional systems, whose descriptions can be found in Niklas Luhmann's works; with reference to economics, see in particular Luhmann's *Die Wirtschaft der Gesellschaft* [The Economy of Society], Frankfurt 1988. In this model, the rational gap between the subsystems lies in their respective specific coding: here government/opposition for politics, there payment/non-payment for economy. Intersystemic communication, for example as "interpenetration" (see Luhmann, *Soziale Systeme. Grundriß einer allgemeinen Theorie* [Social Systems. Groundwork for a General Theory], Frankfurt 1984, chapter 6) or as a reconstruction of the other system as a piece of environment according to its own code (cf. ibid., chapter 5) is prepared here for the philosophical perspective of political subjectivity as the possibility of entanglement of judgments, each of which has its own status of rationality. The systems theoretical approach is not criticized in any way; it is just an attempt to add a complementary perspective to the same event.

[647] We should remember once again the expression of the 'adverbial modality' suggested by Michael Oakshott, but finally coined by Ernst Vollrath and, in my opinion, appropriate for the concept of political subjectivity as terminus

a phenomenology of the political that can simultaneously do justice to the facts of prehistoric, ancient, modern and future societies.

Moreover, it becomes understandable that a rational being is not *either* a subject *or* an individual. Epistemic subjectivity (responsible for objective nature and morality) and personal individuality are *essentially* separate (namely through embodiment and particularization); subjectivity in the strong sense of Kantian criticism *can*, however, be contained in individuality – the reversal, on the other hand, is wrong, for despite the particularization, individuality is the more general and broader concept that cannot be completely grasped in subjectivity (see *Excursus I* in chapter B.1.9, *Hypostases of Identity*). The metalanguage can be treated as an object in the object language (which is currently happening here), but the object language cannot be treated as an object in the meta language. Or to put it simply and paradoxically: **subjectivity can only be made public and universalized individually**. A book on subjectivity, such as the *Critique of Pure Reason* or the *Metaphysics of Morals*, can only be written by an author (it could have been several) and perceived by readers as a book-like and aesthetically textualized judgment and criticized with the same right. This is now very close to the sphere of political public opinion, for what characterizes a large part of public communication is precisely its saturation in scientifically reinsured judgments. It is not only about such soft sciences as the economy, with the help of which the economic status quo of an economy (which from a scientific point of view is a functional part of society) or the expected growth is presented. Rather, the arguments on a mathematical-physical basis, with which chemistry, biology or geology, for example, supply the public, have also become de facto reflecting and even directly political judgments. This is because the expert reports written according to formerly unquestionable standards of scientific rationality are being relativized or refuted with increasing regularity by counter-expertises.[648] The political discussion about the French nuclear bomb tests in 1995 and 1996 (apart from the security policy aspects) would not have been possible without the scientific expertise of the critical audience. A more general example in this direction is the ecology movement as a whole, which is consistently determined by a scientific rationality, and

---

technicus; see Vollrath, *Grundlegung*, loc. cit., pp. 49-50.

[648] In my opinion, this is still the most exciting aspect of Ulrich Beck's book *Risikogesellschaft. Auf dem Weg in eine andere Moderne* [Society of Risks. On the Way to Another Modernity], Frankfurt 1986; this other modernity is accordingly *reflexive* (ibid., chapters VII and VIII).

which has gained its strength precisely from *making the natural sciences reflexive and public*, i.e. opened it to the comparison of judgments. At the same time, the new ecological civil culture has managed to make the natural sciences political; for with the environmental problems generated by man, both the individuality in the perception of their conditions and the subjective orders came into motion, because all these things could be thought to be connected with one another. Thus, it is only slowly becoming clear what astonishing complexity of the individual structure of judgment lies behind something like political 'environmental awareness', which is increasingly being expected of individuals as standard competence.

In order not to pursue the aspect of theoretical philosophy, i.e. natural mechanics and exact science too far for the problem of political judgment, it should suffice here to point out that the reflecting power of judgment systematically influences the entire architecture of pure reason. It is not a subsequent filling of the gap between concepts of nature and freedom, which Kant was supposed to help out of an embarrassment.[649] Its heuristic function does not only apply to the natural sciences and the humanities, as the teleology of the *CPJ* in particular makes clear. **Rather, it contains the heuristics of all cultural formation par excellence, including those that were necessary to bring the system of the *Critiques* to the record by Kant's pen.** In this sense, the reflecting power of judgment as an *epistemic public sphere* is the **motor of all culture**, which is thus viewed from a standpoint of individual judgment. There are, of course, other perspectives, all of which are either uncritically transcendent, i.e. religious, or uncritically immanent, i.e. positivist or functionalist.[650] They each have their own individual benefit. But only the constitution of reflecting judgment allows the paradoxical character of this point of view to be referenced between transcendental (objective nature and morality) and reflexive use (by reference to individual states). Ultimately, the CPR is the place where reflecting judgment reveals itself. In other words: *If* reason is a part of world affairs, it is in *this way*, namely by means of an (not yet unconditional) capacity for reflection of individuals, whereby they enable a general form of communication and publicity and can become a cause in nature, and not otherwise.

---

[649] Even if, as already mentioned, he still ruled out its philosophical possibility at the time of the writing of the *CPuRe* – the *CPJ* has finally only become conceivable because it became necessary for the system conclusion.

[650] I exclude here Habermas' discourse theory because it is a reflecting-normative social theory and thus critical.

A decisive factor in understanding these considerations is the insight that the *word* 'public' can be a *concept* that does not describe the empirically observable social facts of communication under particular spatial and temporal conditions, but rather *a method*. This method has the function of connecting consciousness and social reality. The public is the concept that conveys the connection between reason and the world, between the individual and society, between the particularly human and the ideally universal. It is the methodical concept of a philosophy of communication, which forms the common ground between the *infinity* of the individual, inner horizons of the self and the *finiteness* of the social world. This philosophy is an action theory of judgment, whose action consists in judging. It can perhaps rightly be described as a metaphysical theory of communication in that it accepts reason as a problematic but not impossible *focus imaginarius*. In this sense the French interpreter of Kant, Alexis Philonenko, writes:

> "In Kantian philosophy, the cogito is necessarily mediated by the cogitamus... – **the Kantian cogito is a plural cogito**. The fundamental presupposition of the *Critique* is the presupposition of the cogito as cogitamus [...] The balance of critical thought is to yield neither to the Cartesian cogito nor to the Hegelian Spirit, and to maintain oneself in the difficult kingdom of presupposition."[651]

It is neither the theoretical nor the practical moral subject that can carry out this difficult and always risky assumption ("présupposition"), but exclusively the aesthetic subject as an individual:

> "It is only as an aesthetic subject that others appear as entirely human. As a theoretical subject, others are only *understanding*, as a practical subject they are only *reason*. Only the aesthetic subject is really human, an otherwise determined and concrete man. Neither understanding nor practical reason makes it possible to grasp others in their concrete being: understanding denies others in the *concept*, practical reason denies it in the *moral law*."[652]

---

[651] Philonenko, Alexis, *Kant. Critique de la faculté de juger – "Streiten und Disputieren": l'antinomie du goût*, in: Philonenko, *Le transcendental et la pensée moderne. Etudes d'histoire de la philosophie*, Paris 1990, pp. 212-235, here p. 234. This difficult "presupposition" is precisely the achievement described above as 'assumptions' or 'imputations'. It is long overdue that Philonenko's important studies on Kant are translated into German [and even more importantly into English]; cf. also Philonenko, *La théorie kantienne de l'histoire*, Paris 1986.

[652] Philonenko, *Kant*, loc. cit., pp. 234-235.

An important negative feature of the structure of political judgment is that the classical distinction between public and private, which is used so vividly in the social-empirical space, is not at all suitable for the structural qualification of the political, because it itself is only a political content. This would have been easy to understand so far, but the infinite regress of questions was probably blocked with the dogmatization of difference. Of course, one could also say that the difference determines the political precisely because it is political (for example with Carl Schmitt[653]). But hardly anyone claimed this, because it would have made the difference morally questionable again - with which it is already said that the difference secretly always also had to structure a moral order and was politically not autonomous in this respect. Therefore, as mentioned above, the philosophical concept of political subjectivity must subvert the empirically dogmatized difference public/private with subversive intent. The fiction of two areas of being, one of which protects people from the unreasonable demands of civic duties and the mechanisms of bureaucratic rule, continues in Habermas' *distinction between system and lifeworld* in a moderate form. Its advantage is that the ethical claim is clearly formulated in this theory of communicative action, namely as the preservation of the opportunity of non-objectifying individual emancipation through free and yet true acts of speech. But it is only under the aspect of political subjectivity that it becomes clear how it could happen that all areas of life become a political issue in fact and comprehensible to everyone (even if not directly perceived due to an often-reduced understanding of politics in everyday life). **Political subjectivity is an imposition of totality, which must be processed individually** in each case, according to the individual ability to do so. The criteria for determining the relative extent of this totality of the political are as regionally diverse on the globe and have developed as rapidly as the competence of judgment of individuals themselves. The integration of the whole area of nature in questions of economic, ecological and legal order is, as just mentioned, a new dimension in some industrial nations. A further dimension has emerged with the new

---

[653] In his book *Der Leviathan in der Staatslehre des Thomas Hobbes. Sinn und Fehlschlag eines Symbols* [The Leviathan in the Theory of State by Thomas Hobbes. The Meaning and Failure of a Symbol], Tübingen 1938, however, Schmitt regretted that Hobbes was so unwise to grant the subjects a private reservation of faith in religious matters. So they had to carry out the public rituals of the state religion, but they did not have to be at heart. In the book Schmitt pursues his own paranoid idea that Hobbes had invited the invasion of liberalism in Europe through this little door of unstated privacy in the system of the Leviathan.

women's movement and the problematization of the gender question along the difference public/private.[654] However, its activation is *not only a gain* in politically reflecting world knowledge, *but also an imposition* to again deal with larger, new and complicated dimensions of the political. The political subjectivity of individuals must be guided by these themes if they do not want to regress. And that means efforts and hard work in reflection and information gathering and processing from which there is no reliable protection in any living environment.

Instead of postulating unadulterated communication as the regulative ideal of an original intersubjective situation of political judgment (as in Habermas' discourse ethics), this origin is, in the model of political subjectivity, transferred into the subject itself. It would also be worth considering whether it is not only *in foro interno*, i.e. in the medium of judging thinking, that one comes into a certain factual proximity to the ideal situation of discourse theory. The arguments to be exchanged are then only intended for the time being and the truth values of the performative acts of speech in a merely imagined 'council of the citizens of the world' would be unproblematic, for the person opposite, whom I imagine arguing, cannot lie, and it cannot help but serve the interest of my judgment:

"By 'sensus communis,' however, must be understood the idea of a communal sense, i.e., a faculty for judging that in its reflection takes account (a priori) of everyone else's way of representing in thought, in order as it were to hold its judgment up to human reason as a whole and thereby avoid the illusion which, from subjective private conditions that could easily be held to be objective, would have a detrimental influence on the judgment."[655]

---

[654] List, Elizabeth, *Homo politicus – femina privata? Thesen zur Kritik der politischen Anthropologie* [Homo politicus - femina privata? Theses on the Critique of Political Anthropology], in: List, *Die Präsenz des Anderen. Theorie und Geschlechterpolitik* [The Presence of the Other. Theory and Gender Policy], Frankfurt 1993, pp. 155-173; List's study also contains many indications that political subjectivity could be a promising basic model for articulating feminine, aesthetically founded peculiarities in political judgment and action. For through this philosophical model the individually experienced body can certainly become the subject of a rational political discourse, without the result of radical difference being established from the outset as a necessary postulate. Nowhere was it so emphatically pointed out as in women's movement and research that the femine/male/human body is political and the difference public/private is itself a political dogma.

[655] *CPJ*, B 157 [173-4]. Here we should remember the beautiful *theory of sympathy*,

However, the judgments that can be recorded in terms of metaphors of language or discourse (as was shown above all in chapter B.1.7.2 on the basis of the production of subjective concepts) only constitute a rather limited section of the actual spectrum of political forms of judgment anyway. Political subjectivity allows a greater proximity to *political introversion* or, if you like, *obstinacy*, which it not necessarily generated or even communicated through verbal or written discussion. It is in accordance with our intuition if every politically thinking person is left with his or her own attachments, but it is also conceded that a *special feeling* can also be associated with political judgment in the individual. In order not to let taste be indifferent to common sense, Kant proposes the distinction between *sensus communis aestheticus* and *sensus communis logicus*.[656] This is a distinction that can certainly be further processed under the perspective of political judgment. For the political judgment, as has already been thoroughly discussed, is a mixed form and is not as close to the sources of knowledge as pure logical or pure aesthetic statements. Nevertheless, one can speak of one's own *sensus communis politicus*, the origin of which has already been proven here from the various judgments. The term has the advantage that it also designates a feeling that is addressed or aroused by a way of judging without having to be called irrational in the classical sense. The feeling that touches people in self-affection through their thinking when they reflect on their own special states in the horizon of their imagined fellow human beings, when they reflect on their individuality with the imagined order under the conditions of the subjective dimension of body, time, space, power, morality and justice – this feeling, the ferment of bourgeois culture, deserves its own name: *sensus communis politicus*. This political sense, which is connected with the judgment, can even be performed below the level of linguistic communication at any time. The fact that it *does not have to be this way* only means that political subjectivity *can also* express itself linguistically and discourse-pragmatically.

An important clarification needs to be made here: This kind of subjective judgment has nothing to do with success, i.e. with the empirical confirmation or enforcement of a conclusion. No schema for tactically or strategically advantageous decisions in political action can be derived from all

---

which Adam Smith developed in his actual main work, the *Theory of Moral Sentiment*, and which is in complete agreement with Kant's theory of common sense; cf. chapter A.1.4.

[656] "One could designate taste as sensus communis aestheticus, common human understanding as *sensus communis logicus*." *(CPJ*, B 160, fn. [175])

the discussions on political subjectivity so far. What kind of political philosophy would it be if it were oriented towards the ability to make selections and the vitality of its possibilities? Apart from the moral questionability of such an ambition, the focus of philosophical analysis on the success of political judgment also falls short of the available spectrum of describable possibilities. It would mean, for example, that bad politics or unsuccessful action based on political judgment would no longer be part of politics. Considering the success of strategic-political judgment, there would only be good politics or none at all. No detailed explanation is required here to recall that precisely this perspective of political action is shaped by the concept of state-centered realpolitik, which among other things has dominated the German tradition of political thinking at least until National Socialism.[657] In it, politics is only directly or indirectly state-related action, which is of course geared to success and enforcement. The philosophical consideration of political obstinacy, on the other hand, refers to the microscopic observation of the individual political subject, who every day thinks of a multitude of political judgments that move beyond all empirical requirements of probation or discourse, yet still structure the its everyday understanding of politics. The reflecting judgment does not yet secure this individual autonomy in the objective sense, as it does by observing moral law, but at least a subjective autonomy, which Kant demonstrates with the creation of the word 'heautonomy'.[658] Its importance must not be underestimated, for nothing less is connected with it than the individual claim to human dignity:

> "The *common human understanding*, which, as merely healthy (not yet cultivated) understanding, is regarded as the least that can be expected

---

[657] This focus on end and success also dominates the sociological definition and presentation of politics, because without the assumption of such a basic function it would not be able to form a coherent political system. Talcott Parson's four-field functional scheme assigns "achievement of goals" to the subsystem of politics; Niklas Luhmann encodes the system with the basic difference government/opposition and considers the state, the accompanying self-reference of the political system, as its self-description. Symptomatic of the lack of an independent political philosophy in Habermas' *Theorie des Communicativen Handelns* [Theory of Communicative Action], Frankfurt 1981, is the fact that he quotes Parson's scheme with approval right from the beginning (ibid., p. 20), leaves the concept of the politics of sociological reduction and concentrates on moral claims to validity and their conservation in legal forms. Politics plays no further role in his *summa sociologiae*.

[658] *CPJ*, First Introduction, p. 39 [28].

from anyone who lays claim to the name of a human being, thus has the unfortunate honor of being endowed with the name of common sense (*sensus communis*)..."[659]

Shortly thereafter Kant tries to avoid the accusation that his entire philosophical analysis of this faculty and its foundations is not at all useful for empirical reality, because it has only produced a complicated construct. I would also like to take advantage of his response to this objection – which, by the way, was reflecting – for the whole complex-looking structure of political subjectivity:

> "By '*sensus communis*,' however, must be understood the idea of a communal sense, i.e., a faculty for judging that in its reflection takes account (a priori) of everyone else's way of representing in thought, in order as it were to hold its judgment up to human reason as a whole and thereby avoid the illusion which, from subjective private conditions that could easily be held to be objective, would have a detrimental influence on the judgment."[660]

However, the naturalness of this operation is not illustrated and convincing in the philosophical analysis itself, but only in the examples. The peculiar process of sensualization under the strange name of symbolic hypotyposis, which served us greatly in chapter B.1.7.2, describes an everyday phenomenon. In the public media, for example, an individual is often the symbolic hypotyposis of a party, a program, the state, the government or other institutions. Individual hypotypes for objectively supra-individual objects include the *Gauck Authority*, the *Kohl Administration*, *Hitler's Germany*, the *Briand Kellog Pact* or *Reaganomics* – for all these terms there would be neutral, descriptive synonyms such as the *Office of the Federal Commissioner for Documents of the State Security Service of the former GDR* or the *Federal Government* etc. The image of an individual, sensually imaginable person is underpinned by an office, a function or an event whose actual complexity could hardly be brought to an inner view, but even more difficult to communicate. But it is easy to see that these hypotypes are mostly constructed and perhaps even cleverly launched, whether by the media or by interested persons or groups. The image of success or successful embodiment increasingly requires artefacts, simulation and a preparatory, systematic and public-effective construction. The aesthetic power of judgment helps us by facilitating not only the

---

[659] CPJ, B 156 [173].

[660] *CPJ*, B 157 [173-4].

presentation of complex mechanisms and facts, but also their communication. Undoubtedly, the tightening of this media logic, supported by the aesthetic capacity of individuals, is a potential threat to modern democracies.

"At the same time, television is unsuitable for adequately presenting the complex and abstract contents of politics. Because it depends on images and concrete events, it preferably offers its audience *heads* and events that illustrate the actual facts or decision-making process at best. Television encourages the tendency to make political convictions and election-related decisions a question of sympathy or antipathy towards politicians."[661]

This is a border problem of modern politics, because if the judgment of individuals is conditioned with strong visual and emotional stimuli, then it is no longer aesthetic. By increasing the stimulus threshold, which acts as mechanically as possible on the organism (speed, volume, fear, pleasure) in order to bring it manipulatively into states of tension and relaxation, the aesthetic judgment falls short and the object is taken from reflection. The intensification of stimulus patterns, as the above-mentioned *Report on the State of Television* emphasizes, creates an opening gap with the increasing complexity of problems of social order, which require competent assessment by political subjects. Here the sensualization of dispensed information becomes the *anesthesia the of sensus communis politicus*. The successful symbolization of different current or future orders in persons (but also in any other way) is therefore becoming increasingly difficult in industrial societies, 1) because when fundamental ideological differences tend to dissolve, the differentiating aspects are more difficult to distinguish, and 2) because the complexity of the status quo can no longer be adequately embodied – all the less future complexity. In sociological terminology, this means that the reduction of complexity in people (and in the broadest sense: images) no longer works. At the same time, an increasing personalisation of elections has recently also been observed in Germany. This may mean that the elections tend to lose their character as democratic decisions on more or less concrete alternatives to order and are used as individual mechanisms of relief to support persons or groups who are believed to have nothing but general decision-making ability, so that decisions can be

---

[661] *Report on the Situation of Television* (for the President of the Federal Republic of Germany, Richard von Weizsäcker), presented by Ernst Gottfried Mahrenholz et al., ed. by the Office of the Federal President, February 1994, p. 102.

taken at all. As long as something happens. Abstention, on the other hand, signals the frustration of political subjectivity, because the individual does not have the impression that he or she has sufficient influence on the realization of the alternative offers of order. Contrary to the usual descripttions in election reporting and the accompanying press, however, there is no reason to view individual abstention as a higher insight, more realistic political behavior or justified dissatisfaction with real grievances. This is an over-attribution of rationality to individuals that is observable in empirical electoral research, whose political subjectivity actually regresses, either through symptoms of fatigue under the demands of modern participation techniques, or as an already effective anesthetization of political judgment through deculturation and sensory overload. If semantic peak values (size, power, identity, salvation, etc.), i.e. extremes that can usually be drastically depicted, lead to a *shrinking form of reflection*, then only binary decisions that promise uncompromising and possibly expressive violence are in prospect: "We or they!"; "Germany for the Germans!" (and not the foreigners); "We or the state!"; "Islam or death!"; "Revolution or death!" If the descriptive achievements of the concept of political subjectivity are to be exhausted, then these individual deficits, underdevelopments and regressions must also be taken into account.[662] The democratic electoral process can also be used, for example, by active voters to reject the imposition of political subjectivity and delegate it to subjects found suitable for it: "One of them should decide for us!" The updating of political judgment competence in the individual must be seen as an open spectrum of possibilities, the individual values of which do not depend on the state of formal education or intelligence. As Kant has already pointed out, reflection is not stimulated by knowledge, but is a disposition of the mind that distinguishes itself as sensitive. This sensitivity is best promoted and cultivated by *role models*. But if the power of images is the problem and the

---

[662] There is very little useful political science literature on 'un-', 'anti-' or 'a-politics', which corresponds to the astonishing fact that there are no well-founded contributions from this discipline on the subject of 'political disenchantment'; see Münkler, Herfried, *Die Moral der Politik. Politik, Politikwissenschaft und die sozio-moralische Dimension politischer Ordnung.* [The Morals of Politics. Politics, Political Science and the Socio-Moral Dimension of Political Order], in: Leggewie, Claus, *Wozu Politikwissenschaft? Über das Neue in der Politik* [Why Political Science? On the New in Politics], Darmstadt 1994, pp. 228-242, here pp. 238. Hella Mandt has presented a courageous but philosophically and theoretically too short-winded attempt in her essay *Antipolitik* [Anti-Politics], in: Zeitschrift für Politik 4/1987, pp. 383-395.

danger: through which medium could role models reach the political subjects?[663]

There also seems to be an interdependence between morally-determined and politically- reflecting judgment, which consists in the fact that reflection itself can be made a morally binding self-obligation by the subject. This gives rise to the interesting figure that the subject can make it its own moral task to experience and get to know itself as an individual and therefore as a political subject. This brings us to a structural feature of the political judgment that needs to be discussed separately. The relationship between morality, politics and faith is at the centre of political philosophy. In the following, an attempt is made in accordance with the preparatory work now carried out to inquire into this complex from the perspective of the respective required faculty of judgment in the subject.

---

[663] On this seemingly hopeless situation, see Niklas Luhmann's sober analysis, *Die Wirklichkeit der Massenmedien* [The Reality of Mass Media], Opladen 1996.

B.1.8 *Practice, Reflection* and *Faith*: The Distinction Between Morality, Politics and Religion as Reflected in the Analysis of Judgment

The normative content of political action has occupied philosophers since antiquity much more than the actual political nature of action itself. For a long time, the political was not granted autonomy, and it is still mostly treated as a subchapter or an appendix to practical philosophy. In accordance with the requirements of the investigation of political subjectivity, the aim here will be to defend the subjective concept of politics researched so far as **a descriptive concept with a philosophical claim against the normative impositions of practical philosophy**. In this sense, political philosophy has its own title that assures its autonomy in a particular field and which does not owe to practical philosophy.[664] The political philosophy presented and defended here in no way strives for the same status as philosophical moral doctrine, which flows directly from the objective reason and the concept of freedom, from which it also justifiably obtains its majesty.[665] So it is rather a problem of current normative political theories that they claim too much of the honor and cultivate their own soil too little, because they do not even know the limits of their field.[666]

---

[664] On this important aspect of political subjectivity as an autonomous political philosophy, see Ernst Vollrath's *Grundlegung einer philosophischen Theorie des Politischen* [Fundamentals of a Philosophical Theory of Politics], loc. cit., passim, and his subsequent essays on this topic.

[665] In a philosophically more dramatic variation one could speak of the fact that only moral philosophy deserves the highest respect, because it is the only one that understands to look directly into the "abyss of existence", the abyss which for Heidegger lies in freedom, with which he himself – mind you – wanted to outdo moral philosophy fundamental-ontologically; see Heidegger, Martin, *Vom Wesen des Grundes* [1949], 7th ed., 1983, p. 53. A persevering Kantian reading of this beautiful topos of freedom as the abyss of existence can be found in the precise study by Michael Schefczyk, *Moral ohne Nutzen. Eine Apologie des Kantischen Formalismus* [Morals Without Use. An Apology of Kant's Formalism], Saint Augustine 1995, in which the author demonstrates the inadequacy of the objections of analytical philosophy against Kant's foundation and justification of morality.

[666] Conversely, Heidegger repeatedly had to defend himself against the intrusiveness of moral philosophers, who did not want to admit that fundamental onto-

With this distinction between normative-moral and reflecting-political judgments, however, it must still be taken into account that, from a historical perspective, the normativity of action today arises from two different sources. In the secular view, which is decisive in such scientific studies as the present one, it is easy to lose sight of the fact that most of the political forms of life and thought on our planet are under some kind of *religious imperative*.[667] The dominance of secular perception in this context is somewhat astonishing, because for millennia, even in Europe, today's understanding of everything that is called political was completely identical to religion. Therefore, in this chapter, the influence of religious thinking on the political judgment is to be taken into account. For the

---

logy does not have its own moral doctrine (which Dieter Henrich is still looking for there; cf. *Excursus I*). At the same time, Heidegger left political philosophy to the practical philosophers free of charge, so to speak: "I would like to make it questionable whether my concern about the history of being in the present age, which I think is the will to will, must be followed by a practical, i.e. also political philosophy. I cannot see in it a further approach that goes beyond the spiritual state of the question of being [...] Certainly it would be advantageous both for practical and political philosophy as well as for the thinking of the question of being if we leave each in its own field and do not pull the one over into the other." (Letter of August 3, 1974 to Reinhard Maurer, quoted in: Schwan, Alexander, *Politische Philosophie im Denken Heideggers* [Political Philosophy in Heideggers Thinking; 1965], 2nd ed., Opladen 1989, supplement of 1988, p. 209)

[667] In John Rawl's classic *A Theory of Justice* [1971], for example, one looks in vain for the individual religious view as the moment of one's own decision in the calculus of justice. In one of his later essays, collected in *The Idea of Political Liberalism. Essays 1978-1989*, he at least addresses the problem of religious freedom, but believes he can solve it by describing the conflict between Protestants and Catholics in the 16th and 17th centuries as historically settled. Freedom of religion can therefore no longer be an issue for democratic majority decisions as a means of reaching a consensus, because it has been taken off the 'political agenda' together with other fundamental freedoms and is taken for granted. He considers this idea of a political agenda to be so original and important that he believes he must thank his colleague Stephen Holmes for it. A notable exception here is *Theorie des kommunikativen Handelns* [The Theory of Communicative Action], 2 vol., Frankfurt 1981, by Jürgen Habermas, who in his *opus magnum* deals several times thoroughly with the manifestations of sacrality, myth and religious revelation from the point of view of his concept of communication in the lifeworld and its reserves of rationality. Walter Reese-Schäfer writes laconically and yet well-founded about this sensitivity of the communication theorist to questions of faith: "Habermas is a kind of post-religious sociotheologist." (Reese-Schäfer, Walter, *Jürgen Habermas*, Frankfurt 1994, p. 109)

historical roots of politics as well as moral teachings are not based on Greek philosophy or European Enlightenment, but on religion, in which the complete reservoir of all ideas of order was developed. With regard to the still existing liberal or authoritarian rule of religious ideas in many societies around the globe and thus to the political judgment of many subjects, religiosity is already discussed here systematically together with morality and not only in the later ethnological *Excursus II*, where an unreflected secularist view of political philosophy and political science would banish faith (cf. B.2.2). Moreover, religion is not to be discussed here as political theology, which always gets bogged down in the sophistry of the Christian church fathers, reformers, commentators and philosophers, but as a phenomenon of the individual – or if you like: popular *faith*.[668]

First, however, let's deal with practical philosophy, i.e. the moral practice and its relationship to political judgment. In Europe, after the heyday of philosophy in Greek antiquity, it took a long time before a concept of politics as a life practice in the polis, as *bios politikos*, came up again. Likewise, the comparably subtle distinction between *political phronesis* and *moral practice* on the one hand and the form of objective knowledge in *theoria* or *episteme* on the other, i.e. politics, ethics and actual philosophy as knowledge of principles, was long forgotten. The dominance of theoria-knowledge became decisive for the history of Europe and finally the spread of its culture across the globe. The ontological priority of the *fundamental* and *universal* has – as has been mentioned here several times – kept the *particular* and the *individual* in a state of ontological inferiority for a long time, namely until the 18th century, when the the theorems of indivi-

---

[668] Carl Schmitt's *Politische Theologie* [Political Theology], whose subtitle *Vier Kapitel zur Lehre von der Souveränität* [Four Chapters on the Doctrine of Sovereignty], 1922, 3rd ed., Berlin 1979, already reveals that it is not about the individual and somehow politically determined type of faith of subjects, but about the rule and claim to political decree of faith by virtue of a new tradition of democratically immanent (instead of feudally transcendent) legitimacy, which must appear as an 'artificial God' (Hobbes): the dictatorship (ibid., p. 66). Incidentally, it has already been pointed out by Strawson that in *Individuals*, loc. cit., he avoids a phenomenon actually concerning the individual faith by means of a discussion of the corresponding theology and thus analytically far underestimates the problem; cf. here chapter B.1.4, footnote 125. What we are concerned with here is best described for the Christian religious circle in the fascinating study of Gustave Bardy *La Conversion au Christianisme durant les premiers siècles* [The Conversion to Christianism During the First Centuries], Paris 1949, and in the more recent study by Lucian Hölscher *Geschichte der protestantischen Frömmigkeit in Deutschland* [History of Protestant Piety in Germany], Munich 2005.

duality and the systematic aesthetics broke up of this philosophical prison, which one could observe here in chapters A.1 and A.2 at close range. Only with remembrance of this boundless rule of the eternal, ideals, principles and the universal can the scandal that this shameless booklet of Machiavelli's has caused be measured, which has earned him the right to the worst curses from thinkers and rulers for centuries to come. In *Il Principe*, he put the ancient literary tradition of the partly naïve, partly hypocritical *Princely Mirrors* (*principum specula*, an important literary genre in the Middle Ages consisting of books for the moral education of rulers) from the head on its feet. Instead of pious reading, he recommended to the prince from case to case the controlled use of cruelty, praising the benefits that the ruler in this way bestows on his subjects and made him the conscientious fulfiller of the holiest rule: *salus populi suprema lex*.

But even if one takes seriously the historical teaching that the morally dubious, if not even most reprehensible decisions may have great and beneficial political consequences (cf. for example the political actions of Machiavelli's Cesare Borgia, of Mao Zedong or the dropping of the first nuclear bombs by Harry Truman), then one still has not stepped far into the perspective of political subjectivity. These would only be considerations that are still completely caught up in the question of the mechanical wisdom and the skillful control of the state which is incumbent on some selected subjects by succession, democratic vocation or appointment (or violent occupation of this control function). The essence of their task is that they do not act as *persons*, but as *holders of functions*, for example as worldly representatives of God on earth, "first servant of the people" (Frederick II of Prussia), "supreme official" (Joseph II of Austria) or simply as heads of government. Whether in the particular individual cases, i.e. in the persons in their individual actions in the context of their function, a reflecting judgment in the sense of political subjectivity exists, is to be decided only from case to case. Anyone who wants to increase the power and territorial expansion of his country at any price and is perhaps still successful at the same time has no right to political judgment – even if the morality of his actions can already have denied him long ago. This was the case with Frederick II, ironically the author of the *Anti-Machiavel*, after he invaded Silesia in 1740 and thus plunged the whole of Europe into the Seven Years' War.

Kant treated the difficult relationship between morality and politics as a misunderstood antinomy and made a drastic statement:

> "So, objectively (in theory) there is no dispute between morality and politics. True politics cannot therefore take a step without first paying homage to morality, and although politics is a difficult art in itself, unifying it with morality is no art at all; for it cuts the knot that it cannot untie as soon as the two conflict."[669]

Such statements have given ample reason for moral-philosophically determined comments on Kant's understanding of politics. The study *The Concept of the Political in Immanuel Kant* by Ulrich Sassenbach is a serious and successful attempt to present political philosophy in Kant's work in systematic dependence on practical philosophy.[670] In German scholarship on Kant and practical philosophy, Sassenbach can thus be assigned to authors such as Otfried Höffe and Volker Gerhardt, who in a similar way assert the primacy of practical philosophy over political philosophy. Especially in view of Vollrath's *Grundlegung* (op. cit.) that is inadequately anchored in the Kantian text, Sassenbach's study has the great merit of interpreting the concept of the political *as it actually appears in many places in Kant*. Vollrath had dismissed all of the relevant passages in the text with the simple remark that politics was to Kant the "mechanism of legal administration."[671] Altogether, Kant's practical philosophy was nothing more than metaphysics of morals and no own draft for a political philosophy could be found. This statement is shaken by Sassenbach's comprehensive source study and his clever interpretation of the collected passages. Against the simple rejection of practical philosophy, he undertakes a convincingly structured justification of the formula of "moral politics as a practicing jurisprudence."[672] It is intended to ensure that the a

---

[669] Kant, Immanuel, *Zum ewigen Frieden, Ein philosophischer Entwurf* [On Eternal Peace. A Philosophical Draft], Werke XI, B 95, 96 [242, 243].

[670] Sassenbach, Ulrich, *Der Begriff des Politischen bei Kant*, Würzburg 1992, in which the distinction made here at the beginning between *political philosophy* and *politicial theory* must be taken into account. What Sassenbach calls 'philosophy' should therefore be understood here as 'theory'.

[671] Vollrath, *Grundlegung*, loc. cit., p. 92. The formula itself is from Kant's treatise against Benjamin Constant, *Über ein vermeintes Recht, aus Menschenliebe zu lügen* [On a Supposed Right to Lie from Philanthropy; 1797], Werke VIII, p. 642.

[672] Sassenbach, Ulrich, *Concept of the Political*, loc. cit., p. 23. This formula, in turn, is a constriction of "politics as a practicing doctrine of law" and "true" or "moral politics" in Kant's writing *Zum ewigen Frieden* [On Eternal Peace], in: Kant,

priori principles of practical reason are communicated with empirical experience and its conditions. The texts he uses from the Kantian opus actually encourage such an immanent interpretation of the concept of politics.

The claim of Sassenbach's study is, as the title of the underlying dissertation signaled, to interpret the concept of politics from Kant's "critical" works.[673] **However, the fact that none of the three *Critiques* are somehow brought into play, i.e. no textual bases are used from there, points to a certain misunderstanding regarding the approach of Arendt and Vollrath, as well as to a self-misunderstanding of the author.** Arendt and her student were after all concerned with the subjective conditions of the possibility of thinking the political, that is, with a critique in the subject of knowledge; with what could be called 'political reason' or the 'form of political knowledge.' This political criticism of knowledge, rudimentary as it may have been and in need of expansion, should accordingly be closely linked to one of Kant's critical writings, namely the *Critique of the Power of Judgment*. There was the prospect of determining the form of the political judgment. Arendt sought Kant's philosophy of the political in this work because she had noticed that the whole classical ontology, which had structurally bound politics with the claim to unity of truth, had been revolutionized in it. Sassenbach has therefore underexposed some aspects of the problem in order to concentrate on its specific interpretation. **In his study – as a logical consequence of the 'critical' misunderstanding – the indeterminacy of the political subject is striking. States, communities, citizens, politicians, rulers, i.e. social organizations and natural persons, alternately act as 'political subjects.'**[674] This subject has a morally a priori

---

Werke XI, p. 229 and p. 243.

[673] Sassenbach, Ulrich, *Der Begriff des Politischen im kritischen Werk Kants und das Problem des Übergangs zu einer empirisch-praktischen Politik* [The Concept of the Political in Kant's <u>Critical</u> Work and the Problem of the Transition to an Empirical-Practical Politics], doctoral thesis, Münster University 1992.

[674] This is in agreement with the statements of Volker Gerhardt, the supervisor of Sassenbach's dissertation, who, however, constructs the 'politician' as a prototypical political subject in a much more accentuated way; see Gerhardt, Volker, *Politisches Handeln* [Political Acting], in: Gerhardt (ed.), *Der Begriff der Politik. Bedingungen und Gründe für politisches Handeln* [The Concept of Politics. Conditions and Reasons for Political Action], Stuttgart 1990, pp. 291-309, which seems to have been taken over from his teacher Friedrich Kaulbach; cf. Kaulbach, Friedrich, *Einführung in die Philosophie des Handelns* [Introduction to the Philosophie of Acting], Darmstadt 1982, pp. 148-150; Peter J. Steinberger's study *The Concept of Political Judgment*, Chicago 1993, discussed here in chapter B.1.1,

understandable task and duty to devote its actions to the realization of welfare state living conditions.[675] Sassenbach is thus, like Gerhardt, on the way to a kind of modern *Princely Mirror*, in which politicians should be exhorted and educated to moral action in all affairs of state. Here it is admitted that Sassenbach's and Gerhardt's interpretations are indeed encouraged and even confirmed by the Kantian text. But this approach is so unsatisfactory in political science, i.e. also beyond the texts to be interpreted, as well as in the matter itself, because it is too formal and too concrete at the same time. Too formal, because all historical-political events are only classified as poor fulfilment of an ideal of 'true politics'; too concrete, because at the same time this ideal seems to already exist in the welfare state of Germany and only needs to be globalized. With the terminology proposed above one could formulate: in this philosophy already too much theory (in the form of conception of concrete order) is assumed. Gerhardt writes at the end of an essay promising to become the whole philosophy of this author's politics:

> "Despite the modern expression for an old claim, it is to be feared that the final attempt at definition [of the political] has not significantly gone beyond Aristotle."[676]

This self-criticism is undoubtedly entirely justified if such important aspects of political modernity as its competitive and streaking character and the divergence of political action into good intentions and bad consequences (or vice versa: private vices – public benefits) are not sufficiently acknowledged. The model of 'good living' as an archetype of 'true politics', which is at the same time the true moral, holds political science captive in the problematic horizon of pre-modernism. No political philosophy can be derived from the mandatory term, except as a practical instruction to decision-makers. Practical philosophy, especially if it follows Kant, has as its basic concept the *duty* and the morally demanded *you ought to*. **But how could a modern liberal-democratic concept of politics that is based on individualism be derived from the concept of duty?** It is the method of classical *political philosophy* that it addresses decision-makers and becomes *political theory*. This weakness cannot be proven in Kant's critical writings; only a certain type of selective reading can give the im-

---

    also belongs to this series of 'politician theories'.

[675] Sassenbach, *Der Begriff des Politischen*, op. cit., pp. 165-167.

[676] Gerhardt, *Politisches Handeln* [Political Acting], loc. cit., p. 309.

pression that Kant could revive the old unity of morality and wisdom.[677] Sassenbach has elegantly ignored all passages that do not fit into his perspective. Kant has stated several times and as clearly as possible that there is no state to be founded on morality; and he has also insisted that there is not a single common trait between a morally good person and a good citizen.[678]

From here we should examine precisely the problem that constitutes a considerable gap in Sassenbach's investigation, namely the relationship between moral and political judgment from the point of view of Kant's critical work, especially taking into account the *Critique of the Power of Judgment*, about which so much has already been said here and which no longer needs to be presented specifically. For if a critical distinction is to be made between different forms of rationality, then, if the Kantian method is adhered to, the *form of judgment* must inevitably be used, as one must imagine it in the subject, so that something like morality or politics becomes possible. Therefore, no sociology of morals and morally significant practices is pursued here, which always understands the context of the individuals as a systemic communication performance, whereby such everyday practices are produced in a contingency-managing-functional or consensus-oriented-deliberative and pragmatic manner. From a subject-philosophical perspective, these are methods that represent the creation of morality in a proceduralized way, abstracting the subjective achievements of consciousness that actually constitute the source of this habitual morality. A distinction should therefore be made between judgment-related morality and empirical morality, because obviously the conditions of the possibility of moral and even political experience from a subject-philosophical point of view lie in the judging consciousness.

In order to trace the relationship between morality and politics – politics here in the sense of political subjectivity – at the level of judgment, the *CPJ*'s constitutive distinction between determining and reflecting

---

[677] Of which Hannah Arendt was finally also convinced until the end, as Ernst Vollraths knew to report in his *Grundlegung*, loc. cit., p. 257, Note 10.

[678] Cf. the excellent short essay by Jelica Sumic-Riha, *Über die Inexistenz von Kants politischer Philosophie* [On the Inexistence of Kant's Political Philosophy], in: Dolar, Mladen et al., Kant und das Unbewusste [Kant and the Subconscious], Vienna 1994. Although the authors of the volume see themselves as Lacanists and partly fall back on the instruments of this form of psychoanalysis as text analysis, Sumic-Rihas essay is nothing else than a good summary of this Kantian thesis, which lies openly in the text.

power of judgment makes sense. There are two major differences between moral judgment and the forms of reflecting judgment regarding the political judgment:

1.) The moral judgment is, according to its logical method, a determineing judgment. The categorical imperative calls for action according maxims that could be considered general laws of (a second) nature. The universalization in the idea of the subject therefore always concerns *one's own* maxim. An undefined multiplicity of subjects is presented as identical copies of the imagining subject itself until they could constitute a community system.

The reflecting judgment, on the other hand, always assumes an equally indefinite number of different subjects *whose reflection is not identical to one's own*. In other words, the reflecting judgment is an individual judgment. *It individuates the reflecting subject itself as well as the imagined multitude of distinguished subjects*. The reflecting power of judgment does not subdue **identically imagined subjects** to a law in order to think up a whole nature under the causality of freedom but must present the **differently imagined individuals** as a system of nature appropriate for the power of judgment, whose empirical laws are first sought. The power of judgment thus only gives itself a law. This is the meaning of *heautonomy*. [679] After all, the political question is how different individuals, to whom, among other things, the idea of freedom as free will must be attached, can live in an order that makes external coercion conform to internal coercion. And now it is precisely the diversity of individuals and the necessary constraints that prohibits answering this question of the order of constraints *logically* and according to the *determining* power of judgment subsumed under a given concept (which itself is already anticipated from the concept of order, e.g. obedience, equality or descent).

2.) The second difference follows from the first. The moral judgment is always a *private judgment* without any dependence on consent, for the compulsion which the concept of duty exerts within the empire of morals on rational beings is not an external compulsion (like the compulsion of the legal duty), but only a *self-obligation*[680] (through the idea of the moral law, through conscience). The private character does not mean, however, that this judgment is only of private interest, as is the sensual judgment of

---

[679] *CPJ*, First Introduction, p. 39.
[680] Kant, Immanuel, *Metaphysik der Sitten* [Metaphysics of Morals], Werke VIII, [A 4] p. 509.

perception, but that it is made by the ego exclusively *in foro interno* and without any request for the consent of an imagined alter.

The reflecting judgment in political use, on the other hand, is without exception a judgment requiring approval. This consent is not necessarily a factual event, but, where this is not possible, the *fictitious calling of humanity into a council*, in which the reflecting judgment sets the judging individual with a single voice and allows the other individuals to be imagined partly as opponents, partly as proponents of their own reflection. Here you can easily see what has already been worked out in the previous chapter: **The public sphere originates from the individual's thinking through the form of its judgment**. Conversely, this form of public thinking is the only way to constitute what we call emphatically and politically an individual. So, *individuality and the public sphere are interdependent*. The continuum of reality of the concept of the public begins in the subjective form of judgment of the reflecting judgment. This is an assumption that goes far beyond all the classic teachings of separating the public from the private sphere.

The crucial thing about the communication of moral judgment is that it can **only be carried into the sphere of inter-subjectivity or inter-individuality** *on the back of the reflecting judgment*, so to speak. This was meant with the distinction between meta- and object language: the moral as well as the theoretical judgment may be unquestionably valid a priori – to become communicable and executable in the object language, and to be able to get its validity confirmed, it has to take pains to pass through the meta-linguistic medium of the reflecting judgment. *Moral communication between people is necessarily always aesthetic-teleological*, and only for this reason can it *also* be political.[681] However, the assistance provided by the reflecting power of judgment for the moral-determining judgment can be pursued even further, right into the process of moral judgment formation itself.

In the moral judgment, the maxim of the will must be examined for its universalizability, so that the categorical imperative as the supreme moral law is followed. I.e. the supreme and universal moral law *is given*, and the

---

[681] Here we should remember Siegfried Blasche's interesting essay *Zur kommunikationsphilosophischen Rekonstruktion der Zweckmäßigkeit in Kant's Kritik der Urteilskraft* [On the Communication-Philosophical Reconstruction of Purposiveness in Kant's *Critique of the Power of Judgment*] in: Forum für Philosophie Bad Homburg (ed.), *Ästhetische Reflexion und kommunikative Vernunft*, Bad Homburg 1993, pp. 11-40.

subsumption of the maxim as a special disposition of action under this law, which demands the imaginary and unconditional universalizability, so that the judgment may be qualified as moral, examines the agreement between subjective disposition and objective rule. So here the determining power of judgment as the ability to subsume is at work in a prototypical manner, opens a doctrinal part to moral philosophy, namely a metaphysics of morals[682], after a critique of the practical capacity through the causality of freedom, and thus places moral philosophy methodically, i.e. making use of the same kind of power of judgment, on the same level with theoretical philosophy. In a particularly clear definition Kant now writes about the maxim:

> "Maxime is the subjective principle of will; the objective principle (i.e. that which would also subjectively serve all rational beings as the practical principle if reason had full power over desire) is the practical law."[683]

The interesting question, however, is *how a rational being comes to maxims* and whether it itself uses the understanding and reason directly or whether it only mediates these through the power of judgment. Of course, this power of judgment cannot be determining, because the law is not yet given if the maxim first has to be sought. It will therefore come as no surprise that *reflection is needed to design the maxims*:

> "The reflecting power of judgment is already at work here in so far as the maxim of a possible action must first be found in order to be able to universalize it in the legislative process."[684]

So, morality can only be self-communicated and brought into the com-

---

[682] Cf. also *CPJ*, B X [58].

[683] Kant, Immanuel, *Grundlegung zur Metaphysik der Sitten* [Groundwork of the Metaphysics of Morals], Werke VII, BA 52, p. 51, fn. See also Bittner, Rüdiger, *Maximen*, in: *Akten des 4. internationales Kant-Kongresses Mainz 6-10.1974*, part II.2, p. 485-498.

[684] Wenzel, Uwe Justus, *Moral im Abstand. Die "Operation der Reflexion" im moralischen Grenzfall* [Morals at a Distance. The "Operation of the Reflexion" in the Moral Borderline Case], in: Funke, Gerhard (ed.), *Akten des 7. Internationalen Kant Kongresses, Mainz, 28. März-01. April 1990*, 2 vol., Bonn u. Berlin 1991, pp. 439-53, here p. 444. This important aspect of the formation of maxims in individuals, for example, is not taken into account at all by Otfried Höffe, who dealt in detail with the maxims; see Höffe, *Ethik und Politik. Grundmodelle und -probleme der praktischen Philosophie* [Ethics and Politics. Basic Models and Problems of Practical Philosophy], Frankfurt 1979, pp. 86-102.

manding form of moral judgment in individual consciousness if one can reflect and represent, i.e. if one has a logical and aesthetic common sense and an equally aesthetic ability to symbolize one's own process of judgment, be it as language, writing, image, facial expressions or gestures. The maxim is so interesting because it is an important *meeting place of two powers of judgment*, which can be described as follows.

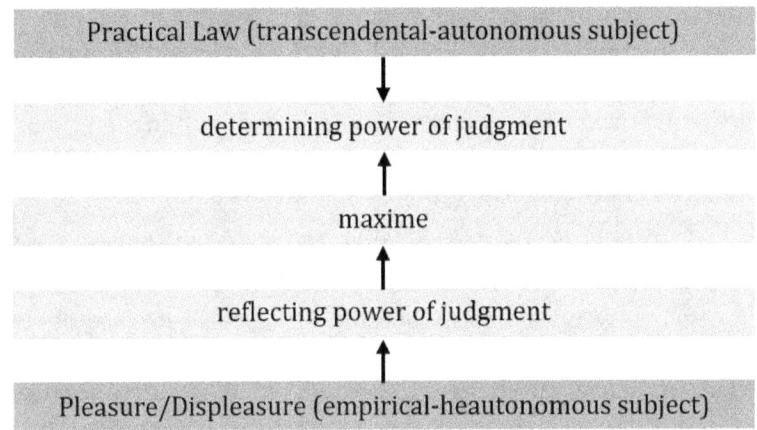

Chart II: The judgment path of determining and reflecting judgment

The rising arrow marks the judgment of a reflecting being who, thinkingly, establishes or seeks a connection and a uniform principle in its own actions. It is therefore not about beings who leave themselves completely to emotions or who bring about habitual-moral action through pure imitation. Mimesis and morality belong together only if the morally relevant imitation is a *succession*. At a place where artistic imitation is discussed analogously to the relationship between imitation of models and the autonomy of virtue, Kant writes:

> "*Succession*, related to a precedent, not imitation, is the correct expression for any influence that the products of an exemplary author can have on others, which means no more than to create from the same sources from which the latter created, and to learn from one's predecessor only the manner of conducting oneself in so doing."[685]

This learning is therefore only possible through reflection and it is clearly recognizable in how many ways the reflecting power of judgment comes to the aid of the formation of moral judgment: the *sublime* awakens in the

---

[685] *CPJ*, B 139 [164].

subject the feeling of being able to resist nature in the first place, in order to connect one's own *ends* with a supreme world end with the help of the teleological judgment, the harmony of which can bring the mind through *beauty* into a state of indifference and admiration receptive to moral self-examination.[686] Without a sense of taste for moral values, morality would be tasteless[687] – although Kant writes very clearly that the interest in feeling good in taste judgment is fundamentally different from that in practical laws. After all, this is the only transition from concepts to feelings.[688] The "subjective community" formed in the reflecting judgment[689] is a universalizing methodical precursor to pure moral consciousness guided by insight into the moral law. But morality would move nothing and nobody, especially not to act, if the subjective part in the preceding subjective universality could not be made as strong as the universal one.[690]

Thus equipped with maxims, the thinking rational being can undergo rigorous examination by practical law, whereby – even in the case of an initially negative result – it has taken the first step of the use of reason, which is at the same time the beginning of its autonomy in moral judgment. But what about the political judgment? What influence does the practical law have on this and how can a political judgment take on a moral dimension? Continuing the above scheme, the relationship could be

---

[686] "Only that which has the end of its existence in itself, the *human being*, who determines his ends himself through reason, or, where he must derive them from external perception can nevertheless compare them to essential and universal ends and in that case also aesthetically judges their agreement with them: this *human being* alone is capable of an ideal of *beauty*, just as the humanity in his person, as intelligence, is alone among all the objects in the world capable of the ideal of *perfection*." (*CPJ*, B 55-56 [117])

[687] What Kant explains, for example, in *Metaphysik der Sitten* [Metaphysics of Morals], Werke VIII, under the section *Ethische Ästhetik* [Ethical Aesthetics], A 177 [626] with the beautiful expression of the *joyful heart*: "Something must be added which grants a pleasant enjoyment of life and yet is merely moral. That is the always joyful heart in the idea of the virtuous Epicurus."

[688] *CPJ*, B 18 [97].

[689] *CPJ*, B 19 [97].

[690] "...the moral feeling [,] is nevertheless related to the aesthetic power of judgment and its *formal conditions* to the extent that it can serve to make the lawfulness of action out of duty representable at the same time as aesthetic, i.e., as sublime, or also as beautiful, without sacrificing any of its purity; which would not be the case if one would place it in natural combination with the feeling of the agreeable." (*CPJ*, B 114 [150])

represented as follows:

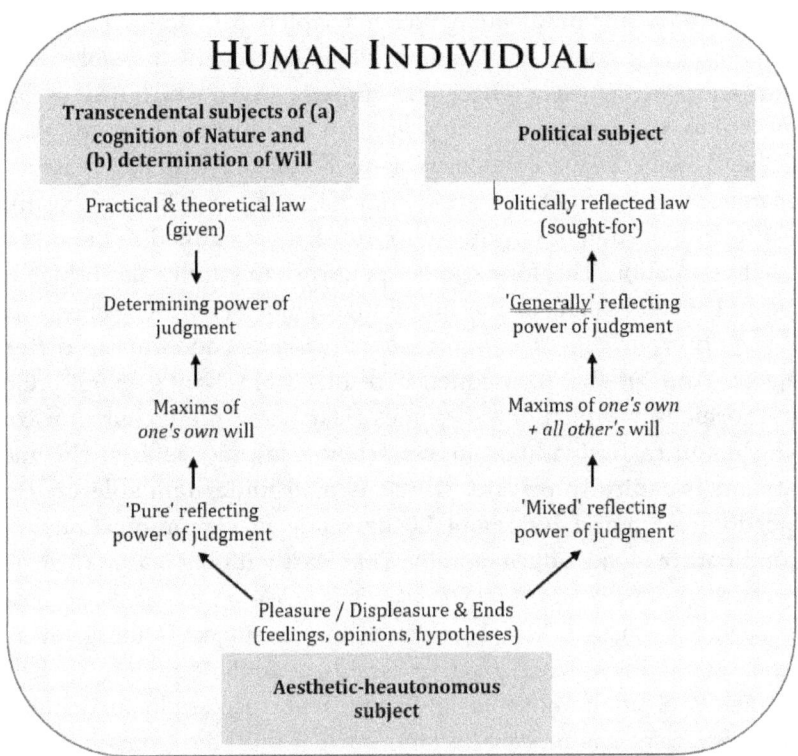

Chart III: The human individual – a polycentric subject[691]

In the relationship between moral and political assessment, the concept of

---

[691] The surprising fact that not only the practical law but also the theoretical law is determined as *given* is only understandable in reference to the presentation of the *determining power of judgment* in chapter B.1.2. This moment of the Kantian critique of the epistemic subject of cognition of nature is misrepresented in all scholarly commentaries to date that I know of – and an important incentive to completely start over with the interpretation of Kant's entire critical philosophy against two centuries of erudite misinterpretation. I have started this endeavor with *Laws of Singularity*, 2017, where I prove a much more conclusive understanding of Kant by applying the critical tools he developed to the prospect of upcoming artificial superintelligences, so-called *technological singularities*. My upcoming book *You are Many. The Polycentric Subject*, 2019, will then set a completely new framework of subjectivity and open a powerful new strand in the philosophies of mind that is mostly based on Kant's work, but this time centered on the *Critique of the Power of Judgment*, and that will be another pragmatic proof of its veracity.

maxims is split up as a summary principle of action *for one's own will* and that *of all others*. This is the consequence of the distinction between pure and mixed-reflecting judgment, which in chapters B.1.3 to B.1.7 became the methodological guideline for reading the *CPJ*. Over this possible stage of *political maxim formation*, a reflected lawfulness arises, which tries to *imitate the method of the determining moral principle*. One must not overlook the fact that this scheme is the condensation of a cultural history whose latest appearance was the right ascending branch leading to political subjectivity, the historical location of which was exemplarily attempted in the first part of the investigation. This formation of political subjectivity also brings with it the full development of the individual, who thereby becomes a *polycentric entity of qualitatively different subjective faculties* and thus: **of different subjects**. And another consequence results from Kant's moral-philosophical formalism, which only becomes clear here, in the course of considering empirical individuals in politically relevant contexts: **the moral judgment is radically private, which is also understandable on closer inspection, for moral judgment is the mode of communication in the 'second nature'**; who judges morally, is at least with his reason (instead of with one leg) in the *world of intelligent beings to whom time, need and above all individuality are foreign*. Moral judgment in one subject is the gateway to another world in which perfection is still possible; but only under the dictatorship of an immovable law that is not accessible to democratic procedures. Kant has repeatedly stressed that only the overcoming of all inclinations coincides with the target concept of morality, *holiness*. It is therefore no wonder that Kant did not want to have his first two *Critiques* understood as *anthropological* teachings, for there are too few examples in world history of people who would have been capable of insight into the *pure foundations of the knowledge of nature* or the *observance of morality for the sake of the law*.[692] The reflecting power of judgment, on the other hand, is purely anthropological, because it makes it possible to describe people and their political potential, as it can now be found in a few historical times and in a growing number of cultural places (see chapter B.2.2, *Excursus II*).

The political concept of law remains completely open through the *double reflection* and can be filled with potentially all contents, so to speak, on the way to the political judgment. The examination procedure of the universally reflecting power of judgment after the formation or deter-

---

[692] This aspect, the 'pathetic fallacy' in virtually all interpretations of Kant, I discuss in more detail in my works quoted in the previous footnote, namely *Laws of Singularity*, 2017, and *You are Many. The Polycentric Subject*, 2019.

mination of the maxims is a universalization just like its morally determining counterpart. However, since the procedure is carried out in the logical form of reflection (instead of determination), it has an *experimental character*. For the political law, if you want to call a perfect political judgment that, since it still bears the mark of its individual origin, is only a *suggested* law. Thus, one's own individual will is thought in a reflected order relationship with all other wills (that are taken into account, i.e. not necessarily the whole council of humanity but 'to whom it may concern') regarding the subjective form of justice, power, time, body and morality. It has already been discussed in chapter B.1.7.2.2 that morality can become the subject of political judgment through reflection. This path is now recorded in detail here. For the practical law of all morality, the categorical imperative, to be effective in political judgment without *hypostasizing* it by means of the determining power of judgment, the individual must make its own moral experience, the experience of its own conscience, the object of such a two-stage reflection. Thus, the commanding moral law that is felt in one's own chest can serve the way of reflected individuality in the horizon of other imagined individuals for the design of a *suggested* public order. This process must take place in the medium of *persuasion*, the imagined *and* the real exchange of opinions within the imaginary *and* the socio-empirical public, in order to legitimately claim political subjectivity. In this sense, politics, as Kant himself admitted, is an extraordinarily difficult art, but also beyond the ruling government, namely in the judging consciousness of all citizens. Kant did the "political moralist "[693] wrong, because he imagined politics exclusively as government business and rule by law, which in the case of "moral politicians" coincides precisely with the laws of morality. In modern constitutional states, on the other hand, all citizens are called upon to a kind of *imaginary co-government*, whereby each and every one of them is called upon to make their own individual experience with the moral law the object of an imagined political order. The "political maxim(s)" of which Kant speaks, on the other hand, are only rules of prudence for institutional politicians and rulers: "1. Fac et excusa...", "2. Si fecisti nega..." and "3. Divide et impera..."[694] And yet this restriction of the concept of politics to certain subjects as carriers of action is optional, i.e. the circle of the subjects concerned can be expanded in accordance with Kant's own argumentation, for the "transcendental principle of public law" as a formal and constitutive principle no longer

---

[693] Kant, Immanuel, *Zum ewigen Frieden* [On Eternal Peace] loc. cit., p. 233.

[694] Ibid., p. 236. ["Do it first, excuse later"; "If you did it, deny it"; "Divide and rule."

recognizes this restriction to government personnel and state administration: "All actions relating to the rights of other people, whose maxim is not compatible with publicity, are wrong."[695] This principle, which is both "ethical" and "juridical", is based on the pure "form of publicity."[696] Now it should not be forgotten that we are in the exclusive realm of reflecting judgment here, because the concept of publicity is only conceivable through reflection, as has been shown above. This transcendental principle does not belong directly to the doctrinal part of practical philosophy, i.e. the metaphysics of morals, but as a principle of "ethics," it has its origin in "virtue teaching" in which the application of the practical law is already transcendently secured and metaphysically already executed to "human beings as rational beings of nature, who are unholy enough to oppose" the absolute end of the moral imperative.[697] Kant has tried in an exemplary way to formulate a transcendently reassured *basic law of all politics*, which can be determined by analogy[698] to the moral determination of judgment – by reflecting on the relationship between subjective and universal legal

---

[695] Ibid., p. 245.

[696] Ibid., p. 244.

[697] Kant, Immanuel, *Metaphysik der Sitten* [Metaphysics of Morals], part two: *Metaphysische Anfangsgründe der Tugendlehre*, [Metaphysical Beginnings of the Doctrin of Virtue], Werke VIII, A 2 [508], in the chapter *Erörterung des Begriffs einer Tugendlehre* [Discussion of the Concept of a Doctrine of Virtue]. Here is one of the transitions from pure critical philosophy to anthropology, which Kant has always marked as clearly as possible, but which Kant's successors and commentators have for many reasons almost all disregarded. In the foundation Kant writes unmistakably:"... but all moral philosophy is entirely based on its pure part, and, applied to man, does not borrow the least from the knowledge of it (anthropology), but gives it, as a rational being, laws a priori, which certainly still require judgment sharpened by experience in order to partly distinguish, in which cases they have their application, partly to provide their entrance into the will of man and emphasis for the exercise, since he, as himself being afflicted with so much inclinations, is *capable of the idea of a practical pure reason*, but not so easily able to make it effective in his way of life *in concreto*." Kant, Immanuel, *Grundlegung zur Metaphysik der Sitten* [Groundwork of the Metaphysics of Morals], Werke VII, BA IX [13-14]; cf. also the following *Excursus I* in chapter B.1.9.

[698] Actually, it is a *reverse analogy,* because an analogy is the identity of two relations in different contexts. In the present case, however, the relations are determined by the respective subsumption or extrapolation rule of the various powers of judgment, which process the other way round between the universal and the particular.

order and by linking these elements with the medium of reflection itself, namely the public sphere, so *that law can only be lawfully established through its compatibility with publicity.*[699] Political judgments and aesthetic ideas can therefore be stimulated by moral and consequently also by theoretical concepts.[700] With regard to chart III, it could be formulated as follows: What the understanding and conscience (the left branch ascending) in transcendental use of reason must constitute entirely on their own in the face of the laws of morality and constructed nature, they can make (the right branch ascending) about the use of reflecting judgment the object of *public comparison* and *public suggestion*, finally the object of an *individual political judgment*. Morality cuts through this political knot, as Kant rightly called these philosophical entanglements, at all times – but firstly only "in theory,"[701] as he admits, and secondly only at the price of the fragile nature of political judgment as a reflection on public order, which under this blow solidifies into a determining and thus dogmatic moral judgment.[702]

---

[699] This forms a reflexive constitution of law, for the public sphere as a transcendental concept (in relation to the legal system) becomes its own *right to have rights*. Incidentally, and famously, it was Hannah Arendt who was the first to use this formula, albeit in a global aspiration to protect stateless people, to make human rights more concrete and binding after their failure in Nazi Germany and WW II, and to ground them in an ineluctable 'meta-law'. It is nothing but the maximal *externalization* and *expansion* (humanity) of the mechanism of political judgment that we have located as *internalized* and *limited* (community) in the subject as individual, i. e. political subjectivity; see Arendt, *The Origins of Totalitarianism*, 1951. Newer approaches to research into this complex can be found in Gerhard Teubner's essay *Reflexives Recht* [Reflective Law], in: Archiv für Rechts- und Sozialphilosophie 68/1982, p. 13ff.

[700] "One can thus, it seems to me, grant to Epicurus that all gratification, even if it is caused by concepts that arouse aesthetic ideas, is animal, i.e., bodily sensation, without thereby doing the least damage to the spiritual feeling of respect for moral ideas, which is not gratification but self-esteem (of the humanity within us) that elevates us above the need for gratification, without indeed any damage even to the less noble feeling of taste." (*CPJ*, B 228 [210-11])

[701] Kant, Immanuel, *Zum Ewigen Frieden* [On Eternal Peace], loc. cit., p. 242.

[702] There was a very similar dispute between morality and politics on the question of the right to lie. In his essay *Über politische Reaktion* [On Political Reaction], in: Constant, Benjamin, *Werke in vier Bänden*, vol. III, ed. by Lothar Gall, Berlin 1972, pp. 182-186, Benjamin Constant criticized the rigorism of Kant's moral philosophy and its alleged acceptance of the death of innocent human lives in favor of the absolute prohibition of lies (although Kant never wrote the like) and wanted to introduce "mediating principles" to make the strict "primary principles" of morality better applicable. In response to this, Kant argued

Thus, the relationship between politics and morality from the point of view of Kant's critical works and the concept of political subjectivity is so far discussed that the investigation can proceed to the related problem of politics and religion, which here, as mentioned in the introduction to this chapter, is treated as the relationship between *reflection* and *faith*. For if the consciousness philosophical approach is to be followed, then the functional methods of social theory, which no longer have any reference to the individual subject, must be systematically avoided. However, this does not mean that functionalism is not instructive, which is why we should now take a look at its achievements, so that it becomes clear what articulates the specificity of a consciousness-philosophical and judgment-analytical approach.

The first and equally famous and notorious functionalist design in modern religious theory was presented by Thomas Hobbes in his *Leviathan*, in the third part of which, *Of Christian Common-Wealth*, he developed a religious doctrine supporting his doctrine of state. One of the central statements about which such an analogy should be made is: "The Gospel was, that Christ was King."[703] Since religion raises a vital and for public order extraordinarily relevant question of truth, the disposal of this truth must be placed in the hands of the sovereign who constitutes the soul of the "artificial God", the Leviathan, in favor of inner and outer peace. That is why Hobbes tries in his writing to give the sovereign immediate guidance

---

strictly against such a bending of the first principles in the short treatise *Über ein vermeintliches Recht aus Menschenliebe zu lügen* [On a Supposed Right to Lie from Philanthropy], Werke VIII, pp. 637-643, and only conceded the application and administration of the decreed law to what he understood by politics and its mediating principles. He concluded: "The law must never be adapted to politics, but politics must always be adapted to the law." (ibid., p. 642) It is clear that there is no way of realizing political subjectivity in this, for the exclusion of the entire *finding* of justice from the political process actually restricts Kant's explicit concept of the political to the "exercising administration of justice," as Vollrath quoted him further above. However, since all those involved in this dispute, i.e. neither Constant, Kant, Sassenbach nor Vollrath, clearly named the *subject of the political* and distinguished it from the moral or legal subject, the outcome of this conflict can be judged as undecided for lack of clarity in the concerns of the individual parties. The concept of political subjectivity has hopefully enabled a better articulation of the question in this chapter and given reason enough to schedule a new session in this important dispute.

[703] Hobbes, Thomas, *Leviathan or the Matter, Forme, & Power of a Common-Wealth Ecclesiasticall and Civill*, [1651] edited by C. B. Macpherson, London 1968, III/32, p. 413.

on how the Bible should be interpreted so that it works functionally for the maintenance of peace and the continuity of rule.[704] There must therefore be a state definition and supervision of the religious cult to be practiced in public. Hobbes, who was probably not an areligious person,[705] completely abstracted in social theory from the belief-relevant sensitivities and judgments of individuals, which he only wanted to bring into a functioning public order. Chapter B.1.7.3 already mentioned in another context how much Carl Schmitt blamed this methodically consistent and unobjectionable concession of an internal reservation of faith for the epidemic spread of liberalism and the decline of Leviathan.[706]

In his writings, the Grand Master of the sociology of religion, Max Weber, has primarily researched the relative functionality of the various religions for the accumulation of capital and the formation of a professsional administration. With completely different objectives, closely related to Hobbes and Weber's approach, Niklas Luhmann has described the function of religion for society, which in systems theory does not consist of subjects but only of communication, as one of several communication systems differentiated since the 17th century. Like these other subsystems of society, the religious system has the task of *reducing complexity* and meaning in specific respects, whereby Luhmann explicitly and leitmotivically poses the question of whether religion as religious communication is still possible at all.[707] For it could be that other, functionally equivalent

---

[704] One of the hermeneutical problems is then that the state-bearing interpretation of the New Testament must be *radically anti-trinitarian*, because political theology can only unfold its highest ambition and its greatest literary power under unrestricted monotheistic conditions; cf. the study by Erik Petersen, *Der Monotheismus als politisches Problem. Ein Beitrag zur politischen Theologie im Imperium Romanum* [Monotheism as a Political problem. A Contribution to Political Theology in the Imperium Romanum], Leipzig 1935, in which the author elaborates that all political theology since Hobbes has been anti-trinitarian.

[705] Although at the end of his life he was suspiciously unpassionate about his death and said that he would "crawl out of the world through a narrow hole"; cf. the literary portrait of the philosopher by John Aubrey, the biographer of prominent thinkers of his time and secretary of Francis Bacon, in: Aubrey, *Brief Lives*, London 1949.

[706] Schmitt, Carl, *Der Leviathan in der Staatslehre des Thomas Hobbes. Sinn und Fehlschlag eines Symbols* [The Leviathan in the Theory of Thomas Hobbes. Meaning and Failure of a Symbol], Tübingen 1938.

[707] Luhmann, Niklas, *Funktion der Religion* [The Function of Religion, 1977], 2nd ed.,

institutions of society that can take over or have long since taken over bundled services in religious communication – which in the case of psychotherapy as a form of deaconry and the vulgate of the exact sciences as a form of immanent theology would have to be considered. But if the function of religion itself is treated as a problem, then inevitably, also in functionalist analysis, a constitutive reference to 'psychic systems' – that is: individualized subjects – comes about. For the problem of religion in modern societies, at least in some churches and denominations, is above all the inadequate 'micro-motivation' of private participants.[708] Nevertheless, the causes of religious communication – threats to existence, evil in the world and death – naturally remain in principle. They are simply no longer so intensively communicated via ecclesiastically institutionalized denominations but obtain corresponding services from an industry that is well established in the market of religious products, namely esotericism.

This change in individual religious practice is described as modern *secularization* by an epochal term and as *privatization* by a pseudo-legal term aimed at the withdrawal of the individual itself and is usually deplored at the same time. In this context, de-solidarization, loss of the religiously founded and morally necessary community or lack of respect for the order of creation are associated, e.g. as an ecological risk or as a dwindling respect for religiously demanded morals (e.g. heterosexuality, prohibition of contraception and abortion). It may be that the collective faith under common and obedient observance of cults was in many respects more functional than the privatization of religious practice in some industrialized countries, which can now be clearly observed not only sociologically. At the same time, however, it seems that only the historical development in the course of the formation and release of the individual (cf. chapter A.1) has uncovered the actual origin of religiosity in the subject, which is necessarily as 'private' as moral judgment before one's own conscience. This is not a new idea at all, but one of the thoughts through which the religious critic Kant in 1794 drew upon himself the threat of the "highest disgrace" of the pious Minister of Culture von Wöllner and the King himself.

"It sounds questionable, but it is by no means reprehensible to say: that

---

Frankfurt 1990, p. 8; cf. the interesting answers to Luhmann's theses in Welker, Michael (ed.), *Theologie und funktionale Systemtheorie. Luhmanns Religionssoziologie in theologischer Diskussion* [Theology and Functional Systems Theory. Luhmann's Sociology of Religion in Theological Discussion], Frankfurt 1985.

[708] Luhmann, *Funktion der Religion*, loc. cit., p. 262.

every man *makes* himself a god, yes, according to moral concepts... *had to make* one himself to worship the one who made him. For in whatever way also a being as god wants to appear to him as such (if that is possible), he must first of all hold this idea together with his ideal in order to judge whether he is authorized to consider it as a deity and to worship it. By mere revelation, without first laying this concept in its purity, as a testing stone, as the basis, there can therefore be no religion and all worship of God would be *idolatry*."[709]

This immediacy of the reflecting believer to God determines individualism in religious terms. Here, functional and philosophical considerations of consciousness are surprisingly intertwined, for Luhmann writes definetively: "We can understand secularization as the socio-structural relevance of privatizing religious decision-making."[710] It is thus also stated that secularization is not necessarily connected with the increase of irreligiousness in subjective perception, but rather only refers to the processing of this outflow of religiousness into the "private" by the denominational-ecclesiastical organizations, which see themselves as the actual institutions of religious "public". It would therefore be premature to conclude directly from the privatization of faith that cults are being liberalized and that immanence is gaining in importance in religious judgment. The places of religious communication (sects, transcendental meditation, yoga, esoteric circles for re-birthing or soul migration, etc.) that many individuals visit in a compensatory manner often demand a *much stricter ritual practice* and encourage the most amazing ideas of intensely experienceable transcendence, such as the Davidians in the USA, the Aum sect in Japan or the Solar Templers in Switzerland. This is not to say that non-denominational practices of faith necessarily lead to dangerous dogmas and criminal devotion, because the examples are far too numerous, not only in European history, to overlook the aberrations of the atrocities tolerated or even demanded by denominations. Rather, this rigour and willingness to deny oneself only shows what dictatorial claim the religious judgment in the subject can exercise over its secular existence. Because one thing is hard to deny: The Hamas fighters on their way into martyrdom, the Japanese kamikaze pilots carried by the divine wind to the enemy and the Sufis living under the strictest rules of fasting and prayer are thoroughly *religious*. The outwardly observable power of their faith corresponds to

---

[709] Kant, Immanuel, *Die Religion innerhalb der Grenzen der reinen Vernunft* [Religion within the Limits of Pure Reason], Werke VIII, addition of B, B 257 [839-840].

[710] Luhmann, *Funktion der Religion*, loc. cit., p. 232.

the severity of a moral demand which must always underlie their religious feeling, to which they submit their conscience and even their life. If their action does not come for such a moral reason, Kant also believes, then their religion is *idolatry*, which draws its mythical power *not from a moral consciousness, but from fear*. The diminished form of this is the 'religious mania', which still stands on the ground of moral consciousness, but overestimates cult and dogma and is thus prepared to threaten the freedom of faith and opinion of others, as Kant knows from experience:

> "To consider this statuary faith (which is at best limited to one people and cannot contain the general world religion) as essential in the service of God in general, and to make it the supreme condition of the divine pleasure in man, this is a *religious mania* whose observance is an after-service, i.e. such a supposed worship of God, whereby the true service demanded by himself is just counteracted."[711]

The relationship between religion and politics is usually addressed as the relationship between church and state or church and society, the latter variant being cultivated in Germany especially since the founding of the Federal Republic. According to Oskar Nell-Breunig, political Catholicism and Christian social doctrine were very much in favor of the Second Vatican Council (1962-65), because the reforms mainly related to the rights and needs of the religious individual (abolition of the Latin liturgy, position of the laity in the Church). A new type of religious reflection emerged, namely the 'theology of the world', in which the Catholic Church tried to adapt to the democratic order of the world after the war and from which progressive South American priests derived 'theology of liberation." In the lines of the Catholic theologian Johann Baptist Metz, who wanted to redefine political theology, one finds the religious enthusiasm of that time in political matters, but also the trace of the conditions to be overcome:

> "Here the positive task of political theology becomes apparent: It seeks to redefine the relationship between religion and society, between church and social public, between eschatological faith and social practice – not pre-critically, with the intention of a new identification of both realities, but retro-critically, in the sense of a 'second reflection'."[712]

The identification of religious and political reality is the main characteristic

---

[711] Kant, *Die Religion innerhalb der Grenzen der reinen Vernunft* [Religion within the Limits of Pure Reason], loc. cit., B 256 [839].

[712] Metz, Johannes Baptist, *Zur Theologie der Welt* [On the Theology of the World], Munich 1968, p. 99.

of most of the connections between the two areas, whereby historically it was primarily the reality of faith that wanted to impose its truth on political reality.[713] Metz vehemently distances himself from any "reactionary neo-politization of faith", but wants to let the sphere of faith participate in the achievements of liberal democracies and political modernity, of which the *public sphere* is the most important for him:

> "Church criticism of society will only be credible and efficient in the long run if it is increasingly supported by a *critical public within this church itself*. For who, if not this critical public sphere, should ensure that the church as an institution does not depict in itself what it is criticizing in others? Of course, the description of such a critical public in the Church still has little material today... "[714]

The differentiation between the political and religious spheres in the structure of the individual judgment has so far not been attempted by anyone in German-language religious studies literature.[715] Yet in a country of the

---

[713] Cf. the chapters on Augustinian *Eschatology*, *The Bolshevik Church* and *Hitler* in Dolf Sternbergers excellent *Drei Wurzeln der Politik* [Three Roots of Politics], Frankfurt 1984, pp. 307-361 and 412-439; cf. of course Karl Löwith's *Weltgeschichte und Heilsgeschehen. Die theologischen Voraussetzungen der Geschichtsphilosophie* [World History and Salvation. The Theological Prerequisites of Philosophy of History], [1953] Stuttgart 1985.

[714] Metz, *Zur Theologie der Welt* [On the Theology of the World], loc. cit., p. 113.

[715] The anthology *Gottesrede – Glaubenspraxis. Perspektiven theologischer Handlungstheorie* [Speech of God - Practice of Faith. Perspectives of a Theological Theory of Action], ed. by Edmund Arens., Darmstadt 1994, makes clear how new the question of the communicative performance of the religious subject still is. However, the essays consistently concentrate on the Christian-communicative, intersubjective pragmatics of discourse, i.e. they are limited to the claims to validity of linguistic utterances. A real subject-related potential in action theory lies in the writings of René Girard, who marked the violent origin of all mythical religions in his main work, *Das Heilige und die Gewalt* [Violence and the Sacred], Frankfurt 1992. Against this background he interpreted in *Das Ende der Gewalt* [Of Things hidden Since the Foundation of the World], Freiburg i. B. 1980, and in *Ausstoßung und Verfolgung. Eine historische Theorie des Sündenbocks* [The Scapegoat], Frankfurt 1992, the meaning of Judeo-Christian revelation as an elucidation of the human fatal attraction to violence. The theory of conflictual mimetism underlying this interpretation is centered on the subject's consciousness, its self-delusion and production of culture and myth based on the human sacrifice. Cf. Grünenberg, Reginald, *Gründungsgewalt und Politik. René Girards Kulturtheorie im Spiegel der Politikwissenschaft* [Founding Violence and Politics. René Girard's Theory of Culture as Reflected in Political Science]

Islamic world, where the struggle of different radical-theocratic to secular beliefs currently constitutes an essential part of the social and political crisis, a subject-related differentiation of the various achievements has been developed. Indeed, even secular scholars still living in Islamic countries are generally so convinced of the reality of Mohammed's revelation of Allah that they can only distinguish between religion and politics along the lines of the history of Islam. But one of the leading philosophers of the Islamic-Arab world, Mohammed Abed Al-Jabri, who taught until 2013 in Rabat/Morocco, subjected his own culture to a critique of its "epistemological foundations" in a Kantian manner, while his approach remains explicitly intra-cultural. Most Arab intellectuals, he said, criticize Islamic culture from a point of view of European educated exteriority, whereby they lose sight of the peculiarity of the subjective, religious-practical experience and thus of the role of tradition (turâth), which is constitutive for the understanding of religion. His own ambitious work in three volumes, the third volume of which is dedicated to the theme of *La Raison politique arabe* [The Political Arab Reason] develops – one could say – a subversive model of individual reflection from this subjective experience of the connection between Islam and politics.[716] For him, the key situation is the subjective experience of reading in the Holy Texts. Al-Jabri tries to show that the political deficit in Arab culture is connected with the fact that in the traditionally taught ways the sacred texts are read (i.e. fundamentalist, liberal or Marxist), the *separation of read object and reading subject is not carried out*. For fourteen centuries, the Arabic language has not changed and has become identical with the sense of authenticity in Arab culture, giving the language itself a sacred character.

> "Why do we insist so much on the separation of subject and object in our proposed reading of tradition? Because the contemporary Arab reader is limited by his tradition and burdened by his present; which means first of all that tradition absorbs him, takes away his independence and freedom. Since his birth, the tradition of language and

---

in: academia.edu, Berlin 2010.

[716] The original title of Al-Jabri's *Critique of Arab Reason* is: Naqd al-'aql al-'arabî, I- Takwîn al-'aql al-'arabî, Beiruth-Casablanca 1982; II-Binyat al-'aql al-'arabî: dirâsa tahlîliyya naqdiyya li- nuzum al ma'rifa fî al-thaqâfa al-'arabiyya, Beiruth-Casablanca 1986; III. Al-'Aql al-siyâsi al-'arabi: muhaddidâtuh wa tajalliyyâtuh, Beiruth-Casablanca 1989. The introduction of Al-Jabri to his own work, *Introduction à la Critique de la raison arabe*, Paris 1994, Casablanca 1995, translated from Arabic and introduced by Ahmed Mahfoud and Marc Geoffroy, is therefore helpful.

thought in the form of a specific vocabulary and concepts has not ceased to be hammered into his head. As fables, legends and imaginary ideas, as a certain kind of relationship to things and as a way of thinking. As knowledge and truths. He receives all this without the slightest effort, without a trace of critical spirit... Under these conditions, the practice of thinking is more of a memory game; when the Arab reader bends over his texts, his reading of these texts is *reminiscent*, but by no means *exploratory* and *thoughtful*."[717]

Here Al-Jabri carefully tries to *dissuade* Arab scholars and intellectuals from a hermeneutic maxim that Dilthey and Gadamer – always with reference to Schleiermacher's misunderstood concept of 'divination' – wanted to *restore* in our latitudes.[718] Or, with reference to the European Enlightenment, Al-Jabri undertakes a *critique of tradition and prejudice on a non-universal basis*, not based on the knowledge of objective laws of nature and reason, but on reflection on the *individual and its historical and cultural positionality*.[719] Of course, this results in a pathos of enlightenment that does

---

[717] Al-Jabri, Introduction, loc. cit., p. 51.

[718] See Schleiermacher, Friedrich, *Hermeneutik und Kritik*, Frankfurt 1990, ed. by Manfred Frank, introduction by the editor: "Some of the students and commentators of Schleiermacher (e. g. Boeckh and Dilthey) regarded the divination as a kind of congenial reenactment of the interpreter's speech. Others – such as Gadamer – have discussed and suspected the divination theorem in the context of the time-dependence between interpreter and text, conjuring up in its name the possibility of 'flying over' the location-dependence of the interpreter and imagining oneself empathetic of a foreign soul." (ibid., p. 46) An example from Hans-Georg Gadamer's main work shows that he and Al-Jabri could reach out on the threshold of tradition and modernity, *coming from opposite directions*: "The authority of persons has […] its last reason not in an act of submission and the *abdication of reason*, but in an act of *recognition* and *knowledge* – the realization that the other is superior to one in judgment and insight and that therefore his judgment takes precedence, i.e. over one's own judgment. It has nothing to do with blind 'carcass obedience'. Yes, authority has absolutely nothing to do with obedience, but with *knowledge*." (Gadamer, *Wahrheit und Methode. Grundzüge einer philosophischen Hermeneutik, Gesammelte Werke* [Truth and Method. Collected Works], vol. I, 5, Tübingen 1986, p. 263) The same applies to texts and traditions. This hermeneutic attitude would suit the traditionalist Coran scholars very well. But they don't need to know Gadamer, because they follow this method anyway – and for such a long time that it preceds Gadamer's birth by more than a millennium.

[719] Thus, he represented a position similar in cultural philosophy to Mohammed Arkoun, emeritus for Islamic intellectual history at the Sorbonne, philosopher

not achieve the radicalism and tabula rasa mentality of European thought in the 17th and 18th centuries, but is possibly *politically* appropriate in a culture in which the dominant principles of order will depend on religious legitimation for an unforeseeable future.[720] The European Enlightenment, on the other hand, had the advantage of encountering a Christianity weakened by church schism and princely absolutism, the relativization of which had thus already been initiated in the form of the secularization that had begun.

Al-Jabri is treated in such detail here because, in a non-Christian cultural area on a completely different basis, in a situation that we knew so similarly in 18th century Europe, he opens up the political in a philosophizing way. The decisive difference is probably that for him the theocratic claim of his religion was the biggest problem, whereas in Europe it was absolutist feudal rule. Al-Jabri works culturally and philosophically on the level of the great formations of intellectual history. His isolation of the 'unconscious realities' of the cultural production of thought, however, does not correspond, as one might assume, to Foucault's impressive discourse-analytical attempt to divide Western history since the Renaissance into various *epistemes*, these "systems of non-formal knowledge" that have always structured the thinking of individuals in advance and were inaccessible to reflection.[721] In contrast to Foucault, Al-Jabri obviously

---

in the tradition of Ibn Rushd (Averroes) and most prominent representative of a rational understanding of Islam. In an interview he described how Islam could preserve its historical peculiarity even within the horizon of European universalism: "It would be important to go beyond the criticism that has so far been realized by the critical thinking of the West. This has always referred only to its own model, without ever including other models in its critical models. What's new about the current situation is that it's about anthropological integration of the other models." ("We need visionaries", in: die tageszeitung, 6.2.1996, p. 14); cf. also Arkoun, Mohammed, *Westliche Vernunft contra islamische Vernunft* [Western Reason against Islamic Reason], in: Lüders, Michael, Der Islam im Aufbruch, 2nd ed., Munich 1993.

[720] Much more radical than Al-Jabri's philosophical work, for example, was the book by the liberal scholar Alî Abd al-Râziq of Al-Azhar University in Cairo, published in 1925 under the title *Islam and the Foundations of Political Rule* (reissued in French translation under the title *L'Islam et les fondements du pouvoir*, Casblanca 1995). In it, the author claimed that there was simply no clear justification for political rule in the Quran or in the Sunnah and that the concept of the Caliphate had no equivalent in the Revelation. Al-Râziq was then excluded from the teaching staff by the palace's intervention.

[721] Cf. Foucault, Michel, *Les mots et les choses* [The Order of Things. An Archeology

believed in a subjective ability *to make the epistemic change consciously and reflectingly*, whereas for the systems theorist Foucault, this change must also be *pre-structured by the totality of the discourse*. But if one wants to stick to this vocabulary, then one could formulate it in such a way that Al-Jabri wants to prepare the *transition in the rules of discourse from the episteme of faith to the episteme of opinion*, because in essence it is about **the simple demand to be *able to have* and to be *allowed to have* an opinion regarding tradition and faith**. This development of an individual competence of *opinion-based knowledge* in connection with the legal guarantee of being allowed to make use of it *publicly*[722], these were the most important features of the historical change presented in Part A in the new experience of the self and others which makes up modernity. But also in a systematic way, the concept of political subjectivity is close to Al-Jabri's philosophical critique of culture. His hermeneutic method, which he develops from the critique of "acte[s] mental[s]" [mental acts], he calls a "lecture disjonctive-rejonctive" [a disconnecting-recombining lecture].[723] This separation and reconnection of the reading subject in relation to the text is nothing other than **the opening of the syntactic field between individuality and order through reflection in political judgment** (which was thoroughly discussed here; cf. chapter B.1.7.2.1). The subject should be able to separate from the text in order to recognize the object character of the traditional religious order and itself as an individual. At this moment, reflection on alternatives to order, or the compatibility between the order symbolically embodied in the text (e.g. of criminal law, the interest economy or the caliphate – according to the traditional reading) and the individual perspective on the same.[724] Al-Jabri describes the recombination as the "intuit-

---

of the Human Sciences], Paris 1966.

[722] See also Goitein, Shelomo Dev, *Individualism and Conformity in Classical Islam*, in: Banani, Amin and Vryonis, Speros (ed.), *Individualism and Conformity in Classical Islam*, Wiesbaden 1977, pp. 3-18.

[723] Al-Jabri, loc. cit., p. 47; the disconnecting-recombining method could be considered a similar sounding interpretation of Hobbes' resolutive-compositive epistemology, but the heuristic processes in both cases are easy to distinguish: "Hobbes found it in the method used by Galileo – the 'resolutive-compositive' method. The resolutive part was the way to reach the required simple basic propositions; the compositive was the way to build the complex ones from those." Macpherson, Crawford Brough, Editor's Introduction, in: Hobbes, Thomas, *Leviathan or the Matter, Forme, & Power of a Common-Wealth Ecclesiasticall and Civill* [1651], London 1968, pp. 25-26.

[724] In Al-Jabri, this 'putting into perspective' is the expression that comes closest to

tion exploratrice" [exploring intuition], which can encompass ("embrasser") the reading and the read self ("moi-lu et moi-lisant"). In the language of the concept of political subjectivity it would mean that *the individual that has individualized itself through reflection must at the same time reflect itself as a part of the subjective order*, that is, place its peculiarity reflectingly in the horizon of a general public, where it appears once again, but as one among many non-identically schematized others. Al-Jabri's distinction between *moi-lu* (the read 'I') and *moi-lisant* (the reading 'I') is a vivid representation of this process of reflection previously examined here in abstract, which was described, among other things, as the integration of a comparison of judgments (publicity) between the poles of individuality and order.[725] Above all, he intensely describes this *confluence of horizons of individual and order*, for reflection is not only intended to release the individual, but as part of the social order **to enable it to have a genuinely political orientation therein**.[726]

To return to the question of religion, a final example of the similarity of Al-Jabri's critique of political reason in Arabo-Islamic culture and the philosophy of political subjectivity is given. The function of *political creation of time* developed here in chapter B.1.7.2.3 by the type of reflection of the mathematically sublime is also discussed by Al-Jabri on the basis of the excellently contrasting examples of *depoliticizing concepts of time in the fundamentalist reading of tradition*.[727] These observations can be condensed into a general rule: The prescribed fixation of subjective time, whether as an eschatological escape out of the world or, as here, as an overwhelming and all-enlightening presence of the usually gloriously presented past in

---

the concept of reflection that he avoids. In my opinion, the metaphor of perspective judgment is an attempt to depict the judgment-logical process of reflection, which can already be observed in Leibniz' monadology (cf. chapter A.1.2), but also in Friedrich Kaulbach's work; cf. Kaulbach, *Philosophie der Perspektivismus*, vol. I, *Wahrheit und Perspektive bei Kant, Hegel und Nietzsche*, Tübingen 1990.

[725] See chapter B.1.7.3 Al-Jabri, by the way, insists that this "exploratory intuition" should not be confused with intuition in the sense of Bergson, personalism or phenomenology; see Al-Jabri, *Introduction*, loc. cit., p. 56.

[726] Al-Jabri thus expressly fights against the *transcendentalization of politics by religion*, whereby politics is presented as timeless and without alternative on the basis of text exegesis; cf. Al-Jabri, Mohammed Abed, *Extrémisme et attitude rationaliste dans la pensée arabo-islamique* [Extremism and Rational Attitude in Arabo-Islamic Thinking], in: Cordellier, Serge (ed.), *L'islamisme*, Paris 1994.

[727] Al-Jabri, *Introduction*, loc. cit., p. 33.

the less pleasing present, is the *symbolic or even authoritarian suppression of free disposal over the subjective time structure of past, present and future*. There is a freedom in relation to the subjective use of time based on the heautonomous constitution of reflecting judgment. Those who cannot reflect do not have this freedom, which is an important dimension in political judgment. But the same applies in reverse: **whoever is denied this freedom is deceived of his reflectivity.**

Politics as subjective orderly thinking is not necessarily limited by the imagined lifetime and can have a reference to the life of the individual soul in an otherworldly order after physical death.[728] This idea does not necessarily have to take place within the framework of a confessional faith, but it can, as we know, certainly be motivated by a mystical or philosophical faith, which often has a private religious character.[729] But as in moral judgment before one's own conscience there is in any case a moment of radical privacy in faith judgment, to which Kant has already pointed out further above. This is mainly due to the fact that morality and faith have the same origin in judgment analysis; only that morality as an insight into the binding nature and legality of the compulsory concept *systematically precedes and must form the basis of faith* – even if, of course, from a historical point of view, it seems the other way round. In principle, it has so far at least been ensured that religion and politics are by no means mutually exclusive in principle, just as little as morality and politics. However, in order for these dimensions to be interconnected in the subject, the development and admission of reflection is necessary in both cases. It is known that moral and religious judgment can be radically a-

---

[728] On the relationship between human time and world time as an imposition and deadline, cf. Metz, Johann Baptist, *Gotteskrise. Ein Portrait des zeitgenössischen Christentums* [Crisis of God. A Portrait of Contemporary Christianity], in: Süddeutsche Zeitung, 24/25 July 1993. These ideas of the resurrection after death are articulated very differently in the revealed religions. In Judaism, the resurrection has long been a highly controversial topic, for it is documented in only one place in the Hebrew Bible, namely in the book of Daniel 12:3 (cf. Küng, Hans, *Das Judentum*, Munich 1991, p. 163). In the Quran, on the other hand, there are relevant passages in almost half of all 114 Suras.

[729] Mysticism is the experience of encounter and unity with the divine in this world. Peter Slotderdijk has noted that an anthropology of the mystical should explain not only the naturalness but also the rarity of mystical states; see Sloterdijk, *Der mystische Imperativ. Bemerkungen zum Formwandel des Religiösen in der Neuzeit* [The Mystical Imperative. Remarks on the Change of Form of Religion in Modern Times], in: Sloterdijk (ed.), *Mystische Zeugnisse aller Zeiten und Völker*, Munich 1993, a new edition of Martin Buber's *Ecstatic Confessions*, Jena 1909, p. 36.

political or even anti-political. Morality and faith can, however, open the political judgment in a completely legitimate way to *over-empirical worlds*, to a world of *'intelligent beings'* in the moral 'second nature', as Kant puts it, and to a world of *holy beings*, the *highest ends* and the *resurrected souls*. The imaginary orders of the transcendent worlds then usually initiate a retroactive effect and the formation of expectations for this-sided notions of order. **A political theory that cannot grasp this sphere of political transcendence for lack of a powerful philosophical foundation, or even specifically denies it, is forced into a series of reductionisms** that pose all questions of faith and moral action under the terms of a social-functional need, benefit or a communicative follow-up operation and thus underestimates the judgments of the political subjects. The religious origin of genuine political achievements is unmistakable, even if the historical development up to then was often extremely conflictual. The mediation of the most important Christian principles, for example in state founding acts such as constitutions that give rise to enforceable rights, shows that political subjectivity as a human ability must not only defend itself against hegemonic claims of institutionally consoledated religious practices or theories. **There is no doubt that all forms of liberal democracy and the rule of law owe their existence to a valuable religious tradition, of which it is no longer clear, however, whether it would have the strength to do the same again or what would have to replace it.** The trace of individual reflection on morality and faith, which can also be interpreted as the trace of the emerging political subjectivity in history, is indelible everywhere. Now it can also be read.

B.1.9 Excursus I: *Hypostases of Identity* – The Second Tradition of Philosophy of Consciousness

The location of the foundation of political subjectivity, which has so far been exposed in the deeper layers of Kant's *Critique of the Power of Judgment*, must now be determined within the framework of a philosophical topography relative to the known theorems of subjectivity. With the 'reconstruction' of the *CPJ*, a claim to its own philosophy of subjectivity is articulated, which determines the origin of political quality. The following discussion therefore serves as orientation and clarification, for it must not be overlooked that the philosophy of political subjectivity does not reinvent anything, but only follows a continuance, an inheritance, in which its context was still unarticulated and waited for its discovery – this is the thesis. A schematic representation of the traditions of the so-called philosophy of consciousness and its critique points to the existence of a previously unnoticed moment in the genealogy of subjectivity. **There is a philosophy of the individual based on the criticism of judgment, which has not yet been developed.** Anti- or post-metaphysicists have always too quickly added the empirical subject to psychology, sociology or linguistics. The following overview is initially oriented towards the two currently most important social theories and attempts to differentiate the various versions of the concept of self as the epitome of subjectivity by means of the spelling. Ernst Tugendhat's proposal to change from 'I' (as the nominated pronoun of the first person singular [in German fittingly spelled out as the lower case vowel]) to 'I' (as a non-nominalized pronoun appearing in the sentence as a grammatical subject) gave me the idea.[730] The following diagram is thus an attempt to draw an *egological pedigree of modern subjectivity theories*, so that the model of **political subjectivity, as developed here, can be assigned its own, previously unoccupied place.**

---

[730] Cf. Tugendhat, Ernst, *Selbstbewusstsein und Selbstbestimmung. Sprachanalytische Interpretationenen* [Self-consciousness and Self-determination. Analytic Interpretations], 5th ed., Frankfurt 1993, [1979]; here in particular the 4th lecture *Descent from the I to the 'I'* (ibid., pp. 68-90).

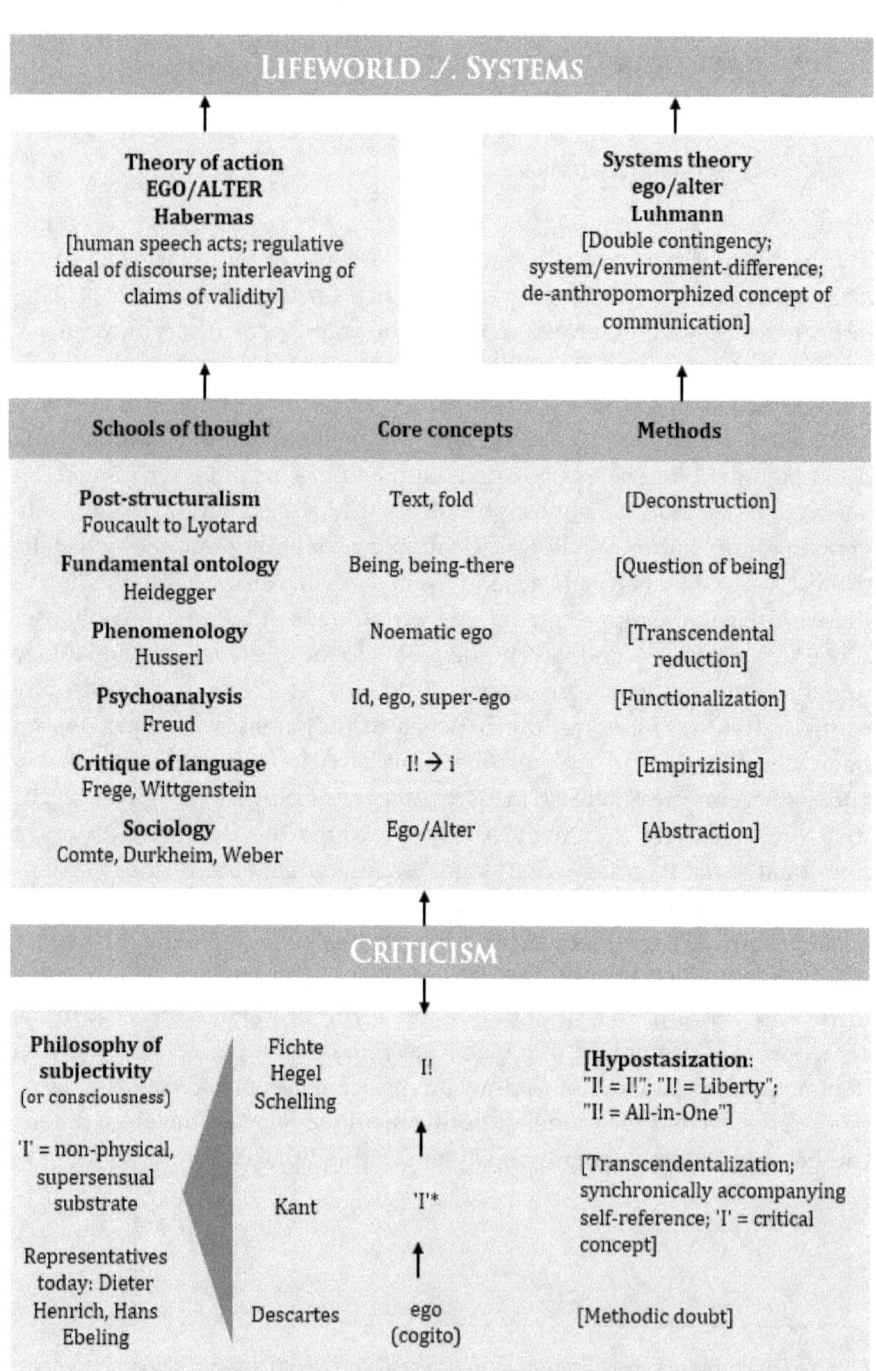

Chart IV: The egological pedigree of modernity
[*see the continuation from this point on in chart V]

As already mentioned, many philosophers and social theorists call our epoch an age of 'post-metaphysical' theory. In an astonishing agreement of the parties disputing on all other points, the so-called philosophy of consciousness is assumed as a first, but thoroughly failed experiment of the observation of consciousness under the condition of self-reference. The starting point of the critique lies clearly in Kant's *Critique of Pure Reason*, more precisely: in the chapter on the transcendental deduction of categories. The presentation of the formal 'I' concept made there, which must accompany all thoughts so that they can be attributed to reason, is regarded as the most difficult passage in modern philosophy. Kant's contemporaries and immediate philosophical successors already believed they had to base their transcendental philosophy on another elementary philosophy. They criticized the lack of insight into the structure of consciousness, whose central concept of an 'I' holds all mental achievements together. Nobody had the idea that Kant's concept of 'I'-consciousness as the so-called "synthetic unity of transcendental apperception", the highest point at which everything must be hung, was meant as sparingly as it appeared in the text. If the 'I' only really has to accompany all thoughts, then it is nothing more than an accompanying self-reference, so that the thinking mind can organize itself as a system, i.e. its operations are self-calculating and differ from other systems depending on the application to the form of sensuality or will. The 'I' concept would then be a technical term, only the "form of understanding,"[731] which has nothing to do with the abyss of a human concept of self. It would be the not further decomposable basic element for the self-referential systems, to which Kant gave the names "pure theoretical" and "pure practical reason." Instead, under the quills of Kant's first critics, suddenly such great and questionable dimensions of spirit and freedom appeared inside this purely technical concept of 'I', *freed from its critical quotation marks*, which needed a philosophical intuition to be opened up, but whose crypto-religious nature was evident even then. Finally, a whole series of alleged moral demands and political-historical provisions were discovered in the veiled nature of Kant's alleged concept of self.

From the very beginning, subject theory had the task of explaining the connection between the phenomena consciousness, knowledge of nature, morality and faith. Applied to social reality, for a time it benefited from a normative idea of society and the forces holding it together. This made the task quite easy at first. But already in the course of the 19th century, the

---

[731] *CPuRe*, B 169 [266].

problems accumulated to the extent that empiricism revealed a completely unexpectedly complex image of society that could no longer be held together by moral concepts as a framework. As a result, the entire tradition of consciousness theory was at issue. The era of the great experiments in consciousness philosophy from Descartes to Husserl, and after them in the the theory of intersubjectivity, is considered over for Luhmann, here representing many other authors:

> "Since a double horizon [alter and ego as special horizons and aggregates of meaningful reference] is also constitutive in this respect for the independence of a dimension of meaning, **social matters cannot be traced back to the achievements of consciousness of a monadic subject. All attempts at a theory of the subjective constitution of 'intersubjectivity' have failed.**"[732]

Older sociology, however, was not yet qualified to cross this border to philosophy, for it was itself much too dependent on the notion of 'subject' and 'reflection', which was now perceived as inadequate. Luhmann's systems theory is known to be one of the reactions to this state diagnosed as a 'crisis of theory.'[733] Historically, he describes the process as follows:

---

[732] Luhmann, Niklas, *Soziale Systeme. Grundriß einer allgemeinen Theorie* [Social Systems. Ground Plan for a General Theory], Frankfurt 1984, p. 120 [highlight by me]. In the following the excursion will mainly deal with Luhmann's objecttions inspired by systems theory, for he has frequently and relatively extensively commented on this speculative core of subject philosophy. Habermas' rejection of this tradition, which goes back to Kant's reflections, is more oriented towards the supposedly missing transition from categorical imperative or from practical reason to communication in the lifeworld, whereby of course he also indirectly refers to a deficit of the formal concept of the subject. However, where Habermas is directly concerned with subjectivity, Kant's text appears only in the blind mirror of Hegel's criticism (cf. Habermas, Jürgen, *Nachmetaphysisches Denken. Philosophische Essays* [Post-Metaphysical Thinking. Philosophical Essays], Frankfurt 1988, pp. 18-34; or Habermas, *Der philosophische Diskurs der Moderne. Zwölf Vorlesungen* [The Philosophical Discourse of Modernity. Twelve Lectures], Frankfurt 1985, pp. 26-33). Luhmann, in my opinion, on the other hand, recognized and described the problem more clearly when he attested to the philosophy of consciousness a **superficial and unquailfied concept of reflection** (see Habermas, Jürgen u. Luhmann, Niklas, *Theorie der Gesellschaft oder Sozialtechnologie* [Theory of Society or Social Technology], Frankfurt 1971, p. 27). It is precisely this shortcoming that I am trying to remedy with this study on the basis of the Kantian texts.

[733] Luhmann, *Soziale Systeme*, loc. cit., p. 7. Another reaction is the whole tradition of the linguistic turn from Frege to Davidson.

"One can see the reflecting conceptuality of German idealism and Romanticism as a first experiment with a difference-oriented observation and historically recognize in it the semantics of a transitional period. Nevertheless, and precisely for this reason, the otherness of the series of terms *distinction-description-form-observation-description* must be emphasized. We do not tie in with a concept of reflection that starts from consciousness and therefore cannot get rid of the problem of intentionality, of self-objectification, of always only secondary division into self as subject and self as object and the [impossible; RG] synthesis connected to it. Theoretically at least, philosophy of consciousness has not succeeded, although such intentions to understand difference as the first and last thing become apparent."[734]

---

[734] Luhmann, Niklas, *Weltkunst* [World Art], in: Luhmann & Bunsen, Frederick D. & Baecker, Dirk, *Unbeobachtbare Welt. Über Kunst und Architektur* [Unobservable World. On Art and Architecture], Bielefeld 1990, pp. 7-45, here pp. 12 – with an important reference to Dieter Henrich's treatise *Fichtes ursprüngliche Einsicht* [Fichte's Original Insight], Frankfurt 1967. In the Zeitschrift für Soziologie (ZfS), several attempts have taken place to separate sociology written in systems theory from the philosophy of consciousness or to locate it in supposedly dangerous proximity to it; see Kneer, Georg u. Nassehi, Armin, *Verstehen des Verstehens. Eine systemtheoretische Revision der Hermeneutik* [Understanding of Understanding. A Systems Theoretical Revision of Hermeneutics], in: ZfS 5/1991, p. 341-356; Wagner, Gerhard u. Zipprian, Heinz, *Identität oder Differenz? Bemerkungen zu einer Aporie in Niklas Luhmanns Theorie selbstreferentieller Systeme* [Identity or Difference? Remarks on an Aporia in Niklas Luhmann's Theory of Self-Referential Systems], in: ZfS 6/1992, pp. 394-405; Luhmann, N., *Bemerkungen zu "Selbstreferenz" und zu "Differenzierungen" aus Anlaß von Beiträgen im Heft 6, 1992, der Zeitschrift für Soziologie* [Remarks on "Self-Reference" and on "Differentiation" on the Occasion of Articles in Issue 6, 1992, of the Zeitschrift für Soziologie], in: ZfS 2/1993, pp. 141-146; Nassehi, A., *Das Identische "ist" das Nicht-Identische. Bemerkungen zu einer theoretischen Diskussion um Identität und Differenz* [The Identical "is" the Non-Identical. Notes on a Theoretical Discussion about Identity and Difference], in: ZfS 6/1993, p. 477-481; Bohnen, Alfred, *Die Systemtheorie und das Dogma von der Irreduzibilität des Sozialen* [Systems Theory and the Dogma of the Irreducibility of the Social], in: ZfS 4/1994, p. 292-305; Wagner, G., *Am Ende der systemtheoretischen Soziologie. Niklas Luhmann und die Dialektik* [At the Endpoint of Systems-Theoretical Sociology. Niklas Luhmann and Dialectics], in: ZfS 4/1994, p. 275-291; Luhmann, N., *Gesellschaft als Differenz. Zu den Beiträgen von Gerhard Wagner und von Alfred Bohnen in der Zeitschrift für Soziologie 4/1994* [Society as Difference. On the Contributions of Gerhard Wagner and Alfred Bohnen in the Zeitschrift für Soziologie 4/1994], in: ZfS 6/1994, p. 477-481.

Consequently, in systems theory the key terms 'reflection', 'action' and 'meaning' were separated from the subject and converted to *system references*, because the subject – according to the accusation – became conceptually, as an active carrier of consciousness, even after the greatest efforts neither conclusive in its rationality nor in its irrationality. These problems of consciousness-oriented theories of action at the individual level intensified as soon as the analysis of collective processes in groups and societies was required. The insistence on the subject's self-decoupling as an ineluctable circle, also observed by Luhmann, is typical of the post-idealist critique of Kant's system. Is this criticism justified? If we look at the problems of Kant's philosophy: Is the accusation that Kant assumes identity confirmed? Is it true that he simply postulated identity without being able to reflect it to its root, where there would undoubtedly be another difference? There is not much evidence that Kant could have assumed identity, but the 'I' of transcendental apperception and the doctrine of the "fact of reason" were clues that were appointed as evidence. Post-Kantian criticism has adhered to this indictment and the charge has given rise to a trial that has now lasted for over two centuries.[735]

Since the success of systems theory, the social science theories of action, which are still based on consciousness, have been under increased pressure to explain. They are forced to specify their subject reference, because often their relation to consciousness is not determined enough, imprecise or even only intuitive and implicit. However, the subject theory, which could explain individual and collective action based on consciousness, has not been further developed philosophically, but has practically stagnated

---

[735] We cannot delve into this huge complex of philosophy of subjectivity and this central problem of the interpretation of Kant's critical philosophy here. At least it may be noticed that the excellent Kant scholar Beatrice Longuenesse has just recently voiced her doubts about the traditional interpretations of Kant's transcendental apperception and the function of the 'I' therein. In her book *I, Me, Mine: Back to Kant, and Back Again*, Oxford 2017, she advocates for a double use of the 'I' in Kant, whereby the 'I' of transcendental apperception is strictly non-psychological and purely technical. In *Laws of Singularity*, 2017, I explained a similar setup, including a hypothesis about how the psychic 'i' of individuality came historically into being, how it was and still is a prerequisite to get access to the epistemic 'I' of transcendental apperception – and how and why the psychic-individual 'i' needs to be stripped-off of all its empirical, psychic-individual qualities to enter the holy of the holies of pure theoretical Reason and to adopt temporarily the role/function of the empstemic 'I'.

since Kant's critique of the subject of knowledge, because **the subsequent egological efforts primarily aimed at delimiting or dissolveing the concept of the ego.** When it comes to the philosophical dimension of classical-idealistic subjectivity today, the focus of attention is usually on the works of Dieter Henrich, the most important representative of subject theory – possibly because he is the last scholar to make conclusive or at least criticism-worthy considerations.[736] In particular, the influence of his opusculum on Fichte was enormous.[737] It showed that Fichte struggled throughout his life to break through the logical circle which he thought he had seen as the condition of consciousness in Kant's definition of the 'I'. The alleged circle consists in the fact that Kant's self-consciousness is only to be gained through reflection, but that this reflection in turn already imputes the acquaintance of an ego with itself, without naming it. For many years, Fichte tested different metaphors in order to avoid the logical trap of this circularity. The "I as a set"; or: the "eye that sees itself"; or: "the power that an eye is inserted to" – these are only some of his attempts to find a formulation for what is now called self-reference. An important distinction has been (re-)discovered: There is *pure* and *concurrent*, i.e. *accompanying self-reference*. Of these two forms of possible self-reference, Luhmann has described the accompanying one as the only promising theoretical instrument.[738] At this point in his main work to date he also refers to the *possible discussion between transcendental theory and systems theory*, which should have exactly this **theorem of the accompanying self-reference as its starting point**. Since Fichte, in contrast to Kant, no longer distinguished between accompanying and pure self-reference and instead

---

[736] There are other, albeit philosophically less influential German authors, such as Henrich's former student Manfred Frank, who has written very useful introductions and historical overviews, which he regularly enriches with his own theses inspired by the Anglo-American philosophy of mind; see, for example, Manfred Frank's study *Selbstbewusstsein und Selbsterkenntnis. Essays zur analytischen Philosophie der Subjektivität* [Self-Consciousness and Self-Knowledge. Essays in Analytical Philosophy of Subjectivity], Stuttgart 1991. Finally, there is Hans Ebeling, whose writings on subjectivity as a death struggle clearly show auto-therapeutic features but contribute nothing to the matter; cf. Ebeling, *Neue Subjektivität. Die Selbstbehauptung der Vernunft* [New Subjectivity. The Self-Assertion of Reason], Würzburg 1990. An exhaustive and most compelling overview on Henrich's work and the whole strand of philosophy of subjectivity can be found in Dieter Freundlieb's excellent study *Dieter Henrich and Contemporary Philosophy: The Return to Subjectivity*, Hants and Burlington 2003.

[737] Henrich, Dieter, *Fichtes ursprüngliche Einsicht*, op. cit.

[738] Luhmann, *Soziale Systeme*, loc. cit., p. 604 ff.

struggled with the metaphors of the mentioned pure self-reference, he could neither develop a system of knowledge nor somehow underpin the Kantian system. Henrich, on the other hand, supports Fichte's infertile idea wherever he can. Not for a moment does he defend the Kantian text against Fichte's thesis. On the contrary. It is appropriate to give a small sample of the subtle interventions in the original Kantian text with which the key question of subjectivity was turned in favor of the Kant critics at this decisive point. Henrich writes:

> "He [Kant] made the ego the 'highest point' <u>of</u> transcendental philosophy, to which all logic and, according to it, the doctrine of recognizing objects must first be attached."[739]

The highlighting of the genitive is intended to focus attention on the essentials of Kant's own formulation, to which Henrich refers and which is often quoted:

> "And thus the synthetic unity of apperception is the highest point to which one must affix all use of the understanding, even the whole of logic <u>and, after it, transcendental philosophy</u>; indeed this faculty is the understanding itself."[740]

While Henrich makes the **ego the highest point of transcendental philosophy itself**, even at Kant it hangs two levels lower, namely below logic. Henrich knew what he wrote, for with the "doctrine of the recognition of objects" he only correctly paraphrased the term "transcendental philosophy." What will happen to the sentence if the term is used again in place of Henrich's paraphrase? **Transcendental philosophy then hangs at its highest point, the ego; underneath also hangs the whole logic, and then, surprisingly, transcendental philosophy comes again. It somehow hangs under the science that should be attached to it.**

Why this bending of the original text? **It is in the service of concentrating all attention on the unity of the I concept as identity, on this mystical event that awaits its interpretation and can only be understood with the right faith or a special philosophical attitude.** In this I-technique the whole performance of understanding and reason shall be presented at one point in such a condensed way that something essential appears again, which Kant tried to settle outside philosophy and beyond the limits of possible knowledge, namely in *faith*. For Henrich, too, who sees himself as

---

[739] Henrich, *Fichtes ursprüngliche Einsicht*, loc. cit., p. 10 [highlighted by me].

[740] *CPuRe*, B 134, fn. [247] [highlighted by me].

a descendant of idealism, everything points to the same *crypto-religious entanglement*, to the **search for a philosophically unassailable religion at the heart of philosophy**. For at the latest since Hegel we have known that only philosophy resembles theology in its secularizing power. Henrich's monumental work on Hölderlin even confirms and reinforces the impression that he is concerned with regaining a reason in the I that is unconditional, but above all direct to being.[741] The piety of the author has dressed up as a philosophical project.

This misunderstanding, which is admittedly beautiful in an unconventional way, has contaminated the entire commentary literature on Kant.[742] Henrich in his fixation on the 'I!'as identity actually wanted to hang the whole transcendental philosophy directly on it. He again endowed this already not entirely new goal of interpretation with the highest scientific authority – and many have followed his instructions. Elsewhere, in a hardly less influential work, he wrote:

"This theory [Kant's theory of cognition] further claims that the necessity inherent in such concepts and principles [which are not derived from experience itself] can be *justified* by the constitution of that self-consciousness which Kant calls the 'transcendental unity of apperception.'"[743]

---

[741] Henrich, Dieter, *Der Grund des Bewusstseins. Untersuchungen zu Hölderlins Denken (1794-1795)* [The Ground of Consciousness. Studies on Hölderlin's Thinking (1794-1795)], Stuttgart 1992.

[742] One can measure the astonishing gravitational force of Henrich's misinterpretation by how much it keeps even outstanding authors trapped in its orbit. Konrad Cramer, for example, wrote a precise and profound essay on the "I think" in the *CPuRe*. But at the moment when it promises to become really exciting on the occasion of the question of the self of the respective consciousness, this is held back as if by an invisible hand. Almost three decades after Henrich's study on Fichte, its authority is completely unbroken, and Cramer can only send a cautious signal in a footnote that he intends to challenge it one day: "I can only assert here that the 'circle' of self-consciousness [*CPuRe* B 404] described by critics has nothing to do with the circle of the so-called 'theory of reflection' of self-consciousness as a theory explaining this fact. I hope to be able to prove this claim in other places." (Cramer, Konrad, *Über Kants Satz: "Das: Ich denke, muss alle meine Vorstellungen begleiten können* [About Kant's Sentence: "That: I Think, Must be Able to Accompany all my Representations], in: Cramer et al. (ed.), *Theorie der Subjektivität, Festschrift zum 60. Geburtstag von Dieter Henrich*, Frankfurt 1990, p.167-202, here p. 201, fn.)

[743] Henrich, Dieter, *Identität und Objektivität. Eine Untersuchung über Kants transzen-*

This is a serious assertion – for which there is nowhere proof in Kant – because it is simply wrong. The Marburg philosopher Reinhard Brandt was able to convincingly show that this path must finally be regarded as closed for permanent failure.[744] He pointed out that there is no justification at all in the Kantian text for generations of philosophy professors digging into the concept of 'I' of transcendental apperception and making a living of it. Henrich, like many before him, brought his intention or even his philosophical helplessness to Kant's work and stood up against the text – and he did that many times. The equation of empirical and transcendental subjectivity as identity has led to an impermissible reification of the formal 'I' concept of transcendental apperception.[745] Such a process has been described in theology with the concept of *hypostasis*, whose forgotten theoretical potential has not yet been recovered.[746]

---

dentale Deduktion [Identity and Objectivity. A Study on Kant's Transcendental Deduction], Heidelberg 1976, p. 16 [highlight by me].

[744] Cf. Brandt, Reinhard, *Die Urteilstafel. Die Kritik der reinen Vernunft A 67-76; B 92-201*, Kant-Forschungen, vol. 4, Hamburg 1991.

[745] In the B-version of the much too little-noticed chapter on the paralogisms in the *CPuRe*, Kant unmistakably writes:"... but this identity of the subject, of which I can become conscious in every representation, does not concern the intuition of it, through which it is given as object, and thus cannot signify the identity of the person either [....] But I do not thereby know at all whether this consciousness of myself would even be possible without things outside me through which representations are given to me, and thus whether I could exist merely as a thinking being (without being a human being) [...]*The logical exposition of thinking in general is falsely held to be a metaphysical determination of the object.*" In the following sentence, Kant even claims that **such a hypostasis of identity, if it could prove its legitimacy, would be the only objection that could overturn the entire Critique of Pure Reason**: "It would be a great, or indeed the only stumbling block to our entire critique, if it were possible to prove *a priori* that all thinking beings are in themselves simple substances, thus (as a consequence of the same ground of proof) that personality is inseparable from them, and that they are conscious of their existence as detached from all matter." (*CPuRe* B 408-410 [446-7]). Henrich probably noticed this distinction of *subject* and *person* in the chapter on paralogisms. Significantly, however, *he quotes the text in the A version, which suits his interpretation but was obviously outdated in Kant's eyes*. He also downplays the importance of this problem by pointing out that Kant offered two different solutions to this problem, "both of which are equally unsatisfactory." (Henrich, *Identität und Objektivität*, loc. cit., p. 55, fn.)

[746] It forms the contrast to Kant's concept of *hypotyposis*, which has already been discussed here (cf. chapter B.1.7.2.2), in that it describes the *illegitimate, uncritical objectification of a symbolic hypotyposis*, i.e. a superposition of what is actually

It was a convenient solution for a number of prominent post-metaphysicists to lean on Henrich's opusculum on Fichte in order to disqualify the philosophy of subjectivity as fixated on identity.[747] This was an interesting and worthwhile strategy in terms of a minimal-effort approach. It covered their backs against annoying questions from Kant's subject theory and left them free hand for their own research. That is undoubtedly perfectly legitimate. However, the history of subject theory has thus become a memorial to a supposedly aporetic approach. Henrich has led the sympathizers as well as the declared opponents of the philosophy of consciousness on the wrong track. Not that he would really be to blame because he just followed his own agenda. Those who relied on him could have taken the trouble to study the sources themselves more thoroughly.[748]

---

symbolic by a schematic hypotyposis. Kant did not deal with the logical relationship between hypostasis and hypotyposis at any point specifically. However, not only the common use of the word indicates this meaning of hypostasis, but at least one place also proves Kant's corresponding use of the term. In the Transcendental Dialectic of the *CPuRe*, he writes the following about *perverted reason* (perversa ratio): "Instead of this, one reverses the matter and begins by grounding things hypostatically on the actuality of a principled of purposive unity; because it is entirely inscrutable, **the concept of such a highest intelligence is determined anthropomorphically, and then one imposes ends on nature forcibly and dictatorially,** instead of seeking for them reasonably on the path of physical investigation,..." (*CPuRe* B 720 [617] [highlight by me]). This describes the hypostasis of a regulatory principle, namely the idea of a systematic unity of nature, which of course can only be formed critically, i.e. legitimately in relation to the respective use of reason, by the teleologically reflecting power of judgment.

[747] See Tugendhat, Ernst, *Selbstbewusstsein und Selbstbestimmung*, Frankfurt 1979, p. 69; Habermas, Jürgen, *Theorie des kommunikativen Handelns*, Frankfurt 1981, vol. 1, p. 526-529; Luhmann, Niklas, *Weltkunst,* op. cit, pp. 7-45, here p. 12; and even Manfred Frank attunes himself to this choir, in *Selbstbewusstsein und Selbsterkenntnis*, loc. cit., p. 166. The passages cited here are only exemplary; all the authors mentioned referred to Henrich's early text on Fichte several times in this manner.

[748] A particularly clear example of this attitude, which benefits from Henrich's work without any certainty of its own, can be found in Jürgen Habermas: "Henrich makes no attempt to defend the paradigm of philosophy of consciousness that came to power with Kant against a criticism that has been repeatedly voiced since Nietzsche. He insists on the intuitive experience of self-consciousness as well as on a 'discursive-free presence of final reasons'. *This can hardly satisfy in the face of a dilemma that Henrich himself has worked out with all desirable clarity as Fichte's original insight:* the spontaneity of the suddenly

Despite this philosophical-historically mediated partiality, Luhmann welcomed the expected return of consciousness and subject theoretical themes and ambitions in several places, especially in the chapter *Interpenetration* of his main work.[749] However, he immediately concentrated on an assumed autonomy of the consciousness presented as a unit in its "potential transcending all social experiences" and on the autopoietic self-occupation of this consciousness – with bibliographic reference to Dieter Henrich's investigation of "interpretations of life" and their forms of meaning 'happiness' and 'need'.[750] This was hastily and too early broken off. Convergences are much more far-reaching. Above all, however, Luhmann gets involved with Henrich's motives, who wants to establish consciousness as pure self-reference and identity. Henrich's meditative and truly profound thoughts in their sometimes-top-class literary form are of course impressive. But the main thing is that Luhmann can be pleased about such a modest philosophy of consciousness, which no longer manages to bridge the gap to social and political empiricism. The misleading concept of the unity of consciousness has encouraged this philosophical autism and led to the isolation of subject philosophy. Kant, on the other hand, has identified several important differences in consciousness that

---

familiar subjectivity must evade the self-relationship of a subject that inevitably becomes an object. (Habermas, *Nachmetaphysisches Denken. Philosophische Aufsätze* [Post-Metaphysical Thinking. Philosophical Essays], Frankfurt 1988, 2nd edition, p. 275 [highlighted by me]) Here perhaps a scholarly side note to 1.) Nietzsche as a Kant-critic, whom Habermas would like to present as a suitable witness and 2) on the thoroughness of philosophical reading then as now: "**The numerous treatises that address Nietzsche's relationship to Kant's philosophy do not seem to be interested in such philological quisquilia as punctual accountability, in which edition Nietzsche might have got to know the work of the Königsberger.** The Nietzsche interpreters love the conversation of the great spirits without worrying about the materiality of such inevitably text-dependent inter-auctorial communication processes, and philology has not yet finished exploring Nietzsche's library and readings – at least in Kant's case it apparently didn't find any trace of him yet in Nietzsche's library." (Zelle, Carsten, *Die doppelte Ästhetik der Moderne. Revisionen des Schönen von Boileau bis Nietzsche* [The Double Aesthetics of Modernism. Revisions of Beauty from Boileau to Nietzsche], Stuttgart 1995, p. 311) In other words, there is a good chance that Nietzsche had no idea what he was talking, i.e. writing about when it came to Kant. He had his knowledge on Kantian philosophy probably exclusively from (bad) secondary literature.

[749] Luhmann, *Soziale Systeme*, loc. cit., p. 299.

[750] Henrich, Dieter, *Fluchtlinien. Philosophische Essays* [Vanishing Lines. Philosophical Essays], Frankfurt 1982.

result in a completely different picture. The distinction between understanding, reason and judgment must be regarded as a distinction between different systems of thought. All three use the medium of consciousness and are dependent on each other. It is difficult to overlook, especially in the Kantian text, that consciousness consists of several systems. It cannot be described as a single system, but even less as the product and outflow of a uniform 'I'-concept.

If one now describes the text structure of Kant's critical works with system-theoretical terminology on an experimental basis, the result is a surprisingly coherent and extremely memorable picture. According to this, pure theoretical reason and (pure) practical reason, presented in the two books *CPuRe* and *CPraRe*, are two operationally closed systems and 'environments' for each other in the medium of consciousness. The *Critique of the Power of Judgment* no longer belongs to the 'system' of transcendental philosophy, which actually consists only of natural and moral philosophy,[751] but it contains the reason for the possible transition from concepts of nature to concepts of freedom, namely in the human capacity to produce pleasure and displeasure by reflecting on subjective states.[752]

Luhmann has already made an interesting assumption about the origin of psychological systems in terms of difference theory: "In general one can perhaps regard the pleasure/displeasure scheme as the basic rule for the

---

[751] *CPJ*, First Introduction, p. 57 and B X [58].

[752] Reiner Wiehl came very close to this interpretation; cf. Wiehl, *Die Komplementarität von Selbstsein und Bewusstsein* [The Complimentarity of Self-Being and Self-Consciousness], in: Cramer, Konrad et al. (ed.), *Theorie der Subjektivität, Festschrift zum 60. Geburtstag von Dieter Henrich*, Frankfurt 1990, p. 44-75. He notes the problem of complementary togetherness (complementarity) of *identity of the subject and individuality of the finite person* and sees it solved by Kant in the *CPJ* for the purpose of the transcendental philosophical system. Instead of discussing this highly interesting solution, which he has just found, Wiehl passes it by and believes he has to search immediately for what *ontological remains* have not been taken into account by the Kantian argumentation. With Husserl and Whitehead, Wiehl wants to deepen the question phenomenologically or "onto-cosmologically" and explore the "space left in the undetermined between perception and judgment of perception as a space of 'prepredicative' experience." (ibid., p. 74) The limits of the *sayable* in Kantian philosophy remain unexplored, because the *unsayable* in its concealment (*Ver*borgenheit) promises ontological security (*Ge*borgenheit) and invites us to fly over the limits of judgment with intuition.

construction of psychic systems..."[753] He also admits that the anthropology of the 18th century rightly turned to this difference. The oscillating difference pleasure/ displeasure is not only the compass for getting to know the world, but also the impulse generator for the entire critical system of Kant. No previously known 'anthropology' has made so much use of the difference between pleasure and displeasure to develop an entire cultural theory, including science and philosophy, as this keystone of Kant's transcendental philosophy: the *Critique of the Power of Judgment*. It is not a direct anthropology, but formally it contains everything an anthropology would have to report on. It has hardly been noticed so far that the *CPJ* must describe the entire developmental mechanism that enables finite beings to at some point fix something like transcendental philosophy in writing or to construct an internal combustion engine.[754] Kant's so-called 'aesthetics' and 'teleology' contains all the terms that are necessary to make the representability (symbol, language, schema) of critical philosophy circular, i.e. self-referential. The *CPJ* therefore contains important cognitive-theoretical concepts and models that determine the evolutionary access of the empirical-historical subject to the transcendental subject, as the individual analyses of the forms of judgment have shown. Kant's third *Critique* contains the theoretical elements that justify the conceivability of relative and absolute quantities, orders, proportions, preformations, harmonies and symmetries.

Kant was concerned not to give a "plaster cast of a living person"[755] in the system of transcendental philosophy – i.e. exclusively in the first two *Critiques*. The entire revision of the B-version of the *Critique of Pure Reason* was devoted to the effort to erase all evidence from the first part of the critical enterprise that it could already be a transcendental anthropology. **With inexhaustible perseverance, however, the commentators have pursued the *re-anthropologization* of the *CPuRe* - in the 20th century above all Heidegger.**[756] Luhmann's frequent polemic against the humanist

---

[753] Luhmann, Niklas, Individuum, Individualität, Individualismus, in: Luhmann, Gesellschaftsstruktur und Semantik, Studien zur Wissenssoziologie der modernen Gesellschaft, vol. 3, p. 149-258, here p. 237.

[754] Except for Volker Gerhardt and Friedrich Kaulbach in *Kant*, Darmstadt 1979, series *Erträge der Forschung*, p. 127, which also point out that an investigation of this important aspect of the *CPJ* is still missing.

[755] *CPuRe*, B 864 [693].

[756] Cf. Heidegger, Martin, *Kant und das Problem der Metaphysik*, 4th ed., Frankfurt 1973; and in response the review by Ernst Cassirer, "*Kant und das Problem der*

philosophers, they must finally state in which or whose brain reason should really sit, misses its goal. The reference 'brain' as a real substrate and material condition sine qua non for reason as a system and for knowledge is far too restrictive. This only articulates the long practiced self-restriction of a theorist who wants to leave systems-theoretical constructivism under the control of dogmatic empiricism. The empirical subject appears only in the third *Critique* as a *psychological system*, namely as its specifically human condition, which can be attributed to the capacity of the feeling of pleasure and displeasure.[757] This is the astonishing course of Kant's work: It begins in the *Critique of Pure Reason* with the systematic representation of the subject of the knowledge of nature; from there, in the *Critique of Practical Reason*, it carefully opens up the possibility of thinking of a subject of morality through freedom, and only at the end does it reach the individual human being as an individual living together in society in the *Critique of the Power of Judgment*. Through nature (understanding) and freedom (reason) two transcendentally explorable legislations already work in one subject;[758] but now a third one is added, which makes the transition from one legislation to another possible. **Only a psychic system with a special disposition for reflection has the possibility to set off on the path to the knowledge of reason and understanding**. In this respect, understanding, reason and judgmental, psychic subject are the **results of inter-systemic co-evolution**. In this sense, the first sentence of the *CPuRe* is to be understood:

> "There is no doubt whatever that all our cognition begins with experience; [...] As far as time is concerned, then, no cognition in us precedes experience, and with experience every cognition begins."[759]

Also, only in a systemic understanding of the various achievements of consciousness does it make sense that Kant deduces the categories of mind not as a "system of preformation" but as a "system of epigenesis,"[760] which

---

Metaphysik". Bemerkungen zu Martin Heideggers Kant-Interpretation ["Kant and the Problem of Metaphysics." Remarks on Martin Heidegger's Interpretation of Kant], in: *Kantstudien*, vol. XXXVI, 1-2/1931, p. 1-26.

[757] *CPJ*, B XXIII [65].

[758] *CPJ*, B XVIII [62].

[759] *CPuRe*, B 1 [136].

[760] CPuRe, B 167 [265]. Cf. Ingensiep, H.-W., *Die biologischen Analogien und die epistemischen Alternativen in Kant's Kritik der reinen Vernunft B § 27* [The Biological Analogies and Epistemic Alternatives in Kant's Critique of Pure Reason B §27] in: *Kant-Studien* 85/1994, pp. 381-393.

becomes decisive for all three *Critiques*. The empirical subject, which has reflecting, i.e. pre-scientific, non-mechanical and non-moral power of judgment, contains the impulse generator of the entire consciousness and its systemically composed achievements, namely the oscillating difference of desire/unpleasure. This difference can only be connected on the pleasure side, i.e. the difference can only be re-entered on the pleasure side.[761] Reinhard Brandt indirectly confirmed this systems-theoretical description by showing that in the *CPJ* no judgment of the 'un-beauty' and ugliness would be possible.[762] Even the sublime of an "ocean set into a rage", which one observes from a secure point of view, is nevertheless the object of a 'negative pleasure' as an imaginary threat. Finally, the form of judgment that combines pleasure as an individual-subjective state with other states and subjects is the reflecting power of judgment or simply: *sensus communis*, common sense. This formally understood common sense as judgment is the consciousness-side of social interaction and thus its counterpart. This pure public spirit has no moral dimension in itself. It is only the potential of consciousness that must be added to communication in order for the interpenetration of both media consciousness and sociality as systems to become possible. Exactly this fact has been presented above on the level of the analysis of judgments with the difference between meta- and object-language in the understanding of the term *publicity*.

If you think about it further, it follows that the *psychological system falls into the environment of both forms of reason*. Finally, the uniform concept of consciousness disintegrates into exactly **three operationally closed systems: understanding and reason, both only accessible through the third,**

---

[761] 'Re-entry' is a key operative term from George Spencer Brown's fascinating book *Laws of Form*, London 1969, which develops an algebraic calculus of form in which Luhmann and other systems theorists and constructivists now see the most successful formal expression for 'self-reference.' Re-entry means that a difference as a whole reappears on one of its two distinct sides without there being a logical contradiction. The difference between right and wrong can, for example, be further processed in the right and thus enables an operationally closed functional system of justice, which allows further re-entries of connecting operations.

[762] See Brandt, Reinhard, *Die Schönheit der Kristalle. Zum Gegenstand und zur Logik des ästhetischen Urteils bei Kant* [The Beauty of Crystals. On the Subject and Logic of Kant's AestheticJudgment], in: Brandt & Stark, Werner (ed.), *Autographen, Dokumente und Berichte. Zu Amtsgeschäften und Werk Immanuel Kants* [Autographs, Documents and Reports. On Official Business and Work of Immanuel Kant], Kant-Forschungen, vol. 5, Hamburg 1994, pp. 32-35.

a **judicious psyche**. Furthermore, there are at least *two separate ego functions*. Kant means this when he writes:"... and the ego of the human being is indeed twofold in form (the way of conception), but not in matter (the content)."[763] This is a completely different constellation from the inclusion of a dialectical movement within a single 'I' term, namely that of transcendental apperception, attempted by post-Kantian subjectivity theory. This is nothing but a necessarily accompanying self-reference of all thought activity, which constitutes another *focus imaginarius* about which we know nothing more than that we need it for thinking. The name of this self-reference, 'I', is only the uniform principle of deduction of categories. One recognizes its completely metatheoretical character with regard to every possible knowledge by the fact that it cannot yet be given the predicate of finiteness in any way. Only the categories of mind that can be determined with his help outline the totality of possible knowledge and finiteness.

The fact of empirical consciousness must therefore *not be directly bound to the notion of transcendental identity*, for it is in a sense only 'borrowed'. Identity in this sense is lent to the psychic system at the moment of the use of understanding or reason. This means: empirical consciousness and transcendental identity of the subject coincide only *as long as* theoretical or moral thinking (based on concepts of nature or freedom) is practiced. Putting Kant's concept of identity into one with the fact of psychological consciousness is an impermissible reification, a *hypostasis*. Kant writes at the decisive point in transcendental deduction:

> "For the empirical consciousness that accompanies different representtations is by itself dispersed and without relation to the identity of the subject."[764]

That mischievous smile at a "transcendental-theoretical foundation of individuality" was therefore premature.[765] The Kantian transcendental philosophy obviously has no difficulties with self-reference.[766] Accordingly,

---

[763] Kant, Immanuel, *Anthropologie*, Werke XII, p. 417 [BA 15].

[764] *CPuRe*, B 134 [247].

[765] Luhmann, *Soziale Systeme*, loc. cit., p. 347.

[766] An interest of systems-theoretical authors in Kant has therefore already made itself felt; cf. Disselbeck, Klaus, *Die Ausdifferenzierung der Kunst als Problem der Ästhetik*, in: Berg, Henk u. Prangel, Matthias (ed.), *Kommunikation und Differenz. Ansätze in der Literatur- und Kunstwissenschaft*, Opladen 1993, 137-158. Disselbeck is claiming that Kant's form of aesthetics would be the last chance of thinking about returning beauty from nature and the world to man. Therefore,

Luhmann's following remark on transcendental-theoretical authorship does not fit Kant:

> "According to his own theory, the transcendental theorist must then postulate himself as a free and thus unrecognizable individual, that is, as a theorist who cannot be seen in the cards."[767]

Nothing would be more inaccurate regarding the *Critique of the Power of Judgment*. Willi Goetschel has shown how much Kant has exposed and committed himself to his authorship as an individual by also making his literary practice part of his philosophy.[768] At the same time, as we have seen (cf. chapter B.1.5), Kant has probably recognized the dubious ontological status of the concept of individuality in the works of Leibniz and Wolff and has therefore used the 'individual' exclusively as a biological complement to the specie, thus always in an empirical sense. The form of man as a single being, if one may say so, lies entirely in his *dividuality*. Nothing else means the distinction between transcendental and empirical subject, whereby, as shown above, the empirical subject of consciousness is developed from the difference pleasure/displeasure and the transcendental subject is split into the subject of understanding and the subject of reason. The problems of consciousness as being identical to itself in the 'I' concept, only emerged with Fichte or were read into Kant's philosophy out of incomprehension. The 'I' was thus, as in the tradition of ancient metaphysics, *quasi-substantialized and hypostasized*. Luhmann has promised to come to the aid of this theory of consciousness with systems theory:

> "Whether and how to get out of known difficulties of a philosophy of self-referential consciousness (such as Fichte's breed) must be left to a later examination."[769]

The time for this test has actually come and systems theory can now move on to its work. After all, so far it has only worked its way through the historical shadow of Kant's subject theory in idealism. The present study on political subjectivity now provides the systems theory with instruments

---

the *CPJ* contains the "theory of reflection for the differentiated art system" (ibid., p. 152). This meets in some respects the cultural anthropological interpretation of Kant's philosophy, which is developed here in chapter B.2.3.

[767] Luhmann, *Soziale Systeme*, loc. cit., p. 347, fn.

[768] Cf. Goetschel, Willi, *Constituting Critique. Kant's Writing as Critical Praxis*, Durham & London 1994.

[769] Luhmann, *Soziale Systeme*, loc. cit., p. 355.

and hints.

The foundations in the reflecting power of judgment that could carry a philosophy of political subjectivity that had come to light here so far were buried under the collapsed ruins of these frozen, undercomplex concepts of the subject. Some authors had an idea of the possibility of a different philosophy of consciousness; some even found their way in. But the enormous weight of the entire Kantian system and the commentary literature seemed to block this entrance. Cassirer and Vollrath obviously did not want to recover the entire treasure, but they only needed selected individual pieces which they finally skillfully smuggled out to complete their own philosophical buildings. In contrast, Alfred Baeumler and Luc Ferry were certainly the ones who pushed ahead with the systematic excavation. In the context of his program of "non-metaphysical humanism," Luc Ferry and his colleague Alain Renaut have defined the whole field by analyzing the connection between the critique of taste and politics in the 18th century and by defusing some influential metaphysics-critical arguments against any subject philosophy (as alienation, reification, etc.).[770] However, there is still no thorough investigation of the *CPJ* by the two authors, although they consider it necessary and have held out the prospect of one several times. In his classic of aesthetic history, Alfred Baeumler also announced that in a second volume he would expand the work into a *logic of individuality*, from which he was prevented by all kinds of adverse circumstances. Ultimately, he also thought he had to realize that such a philosophical definition of the individual cannot exist. Here is just a quote to recall how clearly Baeumler still had the problem in mind in his earlier study, which Hannah Arendt would hardly have formulated differently.

"But only in the aesthetic sphere is man recognized as a human being, and that is why living individuality could only become an object of thought in the epoch of taste. As a *subject of religion*, man is bound to an objective reality and evades any conceptual knowledge. As a *subject of science*, he is no longer a living, concrete human being, but only a theoretical being. As a natural creature, it is subject to the general laws

---

[770] Cf. Ferry, Luc, *Homo aestheticus. L'invention du goût à l'âge démocratique*, [The Human Being as an Aesthete. The Invention of Taste in the Age of Democracy], Paris 1990; Ferry, *Le nouvel ordre écologique. L'arbre, l'animal et l'homme*, Paris 1992; cf. also Ferry & Renaut, Alain, *La pensée 68th. Essai sur l'antihumanisme contemporain*, Paris 1988; finally, Alain Renauts excellent book *L'ère de l'individu. Contribution à l'histoire de la subjectivité*, Paris 1989.

of the body; anthropology is therefore not a fundamentally new science. Only ethics seems to take man into account in his entire concretion – *but ethics in particular is always in danger of placing an individuality-extinguishing norm in the foreground* and losing the idea of the concrete man above that of an unconditional law or a social subject."[771]

The concept of political subjectivity has hopefully taken this tradition of another philosophy of consciousness a step further, because here the *CPJ* has been thoroughly worked through for the first time and, without having to exert greater pressure on the text, a quite solid basic concept of political reality arose. Essential here was the step from subject to individual, which also means that individuality is a much more fragile asset directly exposed to the storm of history and cultural change, which alone cannot do much in objective terms, i.e. with regard to mathematical knowledge of nature and principles of morality. **Individuality has proven to be a polycentric, evolutionary and systemically organized entity of very different subjects**. As political subjectivity, it is always dependent on higher faculties of understanding and reason in order to arrive at the solid form of subjectivity as practical and theoretical knowledge. Political subjectivity is a complex asset, because many conditions have to coincide for its realization. By comparison, its achievements are modest – even if the world today would have no idea of such concepts as 'citizens', 'democracy', 'participation', 'parliamentarism', etc. without this special ability to judge. Finally to this digression, this **buried second tradition of philosophy of consciousness**, as it could be called, and the history of the previous search for it is presented in chart V, in which it forms a side arm that was still suppressed in chart IV.[772] With reference to the philosophically recon-

---

[771] Baeumler, Alfred, *Das Irrationalitätsproblem in der Ästhetik und Logik des 18. Jahrhunderts bis zur Kritik der Urteilskraft*, 1923, Neudruck Darmstadt 1975, p.3; cf. on the history of the non-written sequel the epilogue from 1967. However, Baeumler does not let his readers know whether his Nazi commitment in Alfred Rosenberg's office also belonged to the "adverse circumstances."

[772] Apart from Cassirer, Arendt, Vollrath, Ferry and Renaut, Friedrich Kaulbach also seems to have had an inkling of the fact that a second philosophy of subjectivity could be consistently developed from the reflecting power of judgment; cf. Kaulbach, Friedrich, *Ästhetische Welterkenntnis bei Kant* [Aesthetic Knowledge of the World in Kant], Würzburg 1984, chapter *Asthetische Version der Identität von Ich- und Weltgefühl* [Aesthetic Version of the Identity of Self- and World-Feeling], S. 57-60. Overall, Kaulbach's later developed *philosophy of perspectivism*, which had been announced long before, seems to me to be – if one may say so – a Leibnizian-monadological reading of the reflecting power of

structible formation of pronouns, it is proposed here to list all six pronouns customary in the German language as products of reflection, because it has perhaps become clear in the previous investigation that there *is no exclusivity of the self in the politically-reflecting formation of judgment.* The consequence of this is that the ego must always be taken into account in the various possible forms of alterity and that its performance as an individual lies precisely in being able to go through this reflection in relation to all (or pragmatically: as many) non-egos as possible and to think along with it.

---

judgment in the *CPJ*, which is intended to make individuality explainable; see Kaulbach, *Philosophie des Perspektivismus*, Band I, *Wahrheit und Perspektive bei Kant, Hegel und Nietzsche* [Philosophy of Perspectivism, vol. I, Truth and Perspective in Kant, Hegel and Nietzsche], Tübingen 1990, but it is not included here in Scheme V, because this approach, if I have interpreted it correctly, is not explicit enough with regard to the problem of individuality. In the memorial to Kaulbach's honor there is in any case no contribution that specifically addresses a perspective-philosophical version of individuality, although here, too, the idea is somehow in the air; cf. Gerhardt, Volker & Herold, Norbert (ed.), *Perspektiven des Perspektivismus. Gedenkschrift zum Tode Friedrich Kaulbachs,* Würzburg 1992.

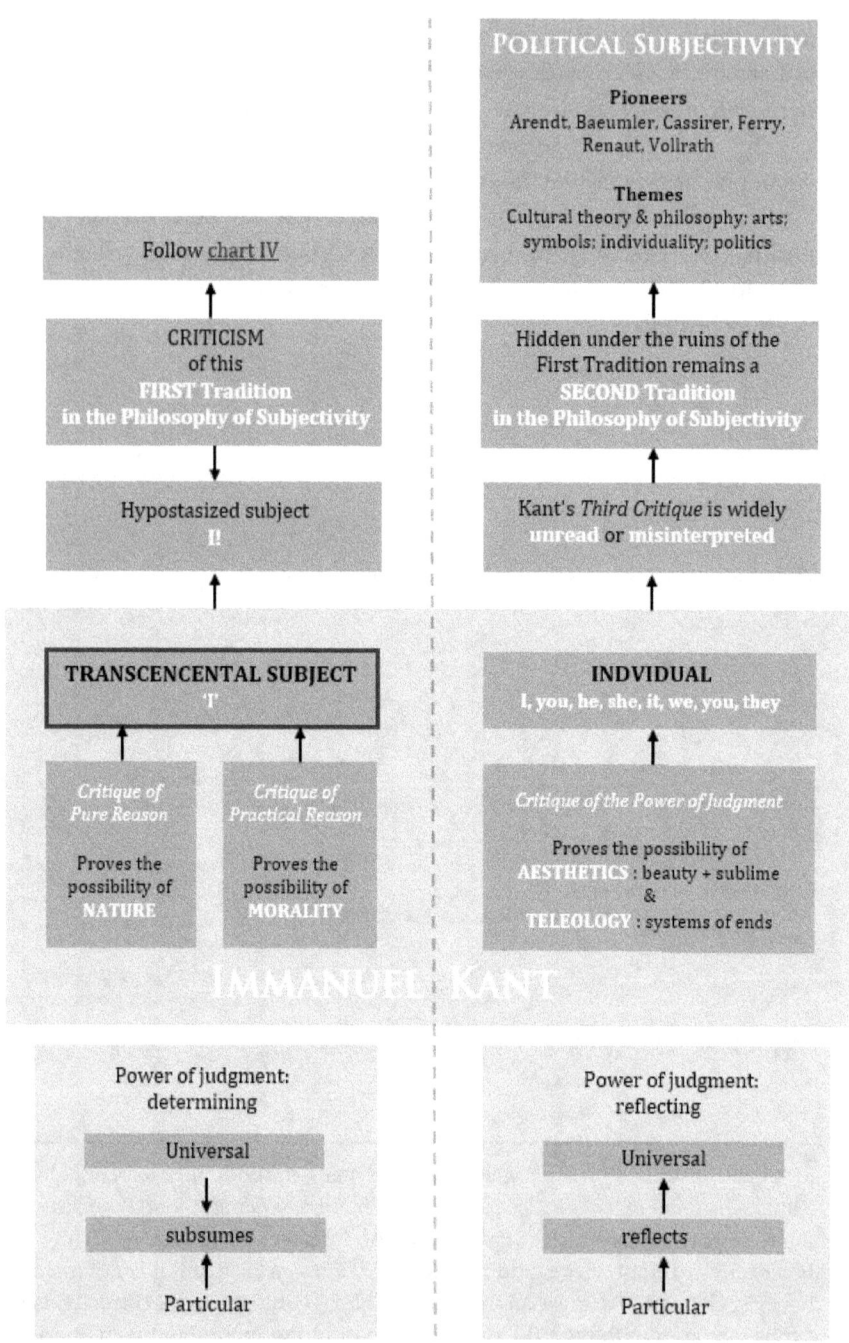

Chart V: The *Second Tradition* of the philosophy of subjectivity [this is the continuation of the egological pedigree in chart IV]

B.2 Political Quality: Subject-Philosophical Reconstruction of Political Phenomena

As a rule, philosophical investigations end as soon as they consider their theses to have been proven within the scope of the task at the conceptual level. The result is then only tested on itself and the negative test criterion is that the individual speculations, derivations and conclusions must not contradict each other. A great deal of trust is placed in that the empiricists of the disciplines mentioned will already endeavor to find a suitable reality for the new construct. In this way, one's own failure is given a good chance for reasons unrelated to the theory. A greater concession in the sense of interdisciplinary cooperation, on the other hand, could protect philosophical theses from misunderstandings as well as from undeserved disregard. In the present case, such a plausibility check of the philosophical concept of political subjectivity should exist in its application to social-scientific and real-political material. It is possible that some of the previous philosophical discussions will only become accessible and understandable with the help of this experiment.

Although the range of phenomena of the political is unmanageable in its breadth, its depth can be explored relatively well. First of all, it would have been obvious to choose a political phenomenon that is directly accessible to the common sense of politics, such as the strange form of communication of people in parliaments, the faces of politicians on television, the mysterious rationality of elections[773], the charming intrusiveness of political architecture or finally the essential difference between subjects and citizens. The questions could then be discussed as to whether the shape of parliament corresponds to the form and unity of political judgment[774] or why no individual can symbolically embody a parliament,

---

[773] Cf. with reference to political subjectivity the instructive treatises by Georges Lavau, *Is the Voter an Individualist?* and by Alessandro Pizzorno, *On Rationality and Democratic Choice*, both in: Birnbaum, Pierre & Leca, Jean (ed.), *Individualism. Theories and Methods*, Oxford 1990, pp. 269-294 and pp. 295-331.

[774] Ernst Vollrath has already dealt with this question in *Handlungshermeneutik als Alternative zur systemtheoretischen Interpretation politischer Institutionen* [Hermeneutics of Action as an Alternative to Systems-Theoretical Interpretations of Political Institutions], in: Gerhardt, Volker (ed.), *Der Begriff der Politik. Bedingungen und Gründe für politisches Handeln* [The Concept of Politics. Conditions and Reasons for Political Action], Stuttgart 1990, pp. 204-212, referring to the

which can very well succeed with a government, for example. Because the form of parliament is an ingenious invention and a corrective to the symbolic hypostasis that characterizes non-reflecting forms of rule in pre-democratic societies? Such considerations could be interesting, but they would be too speculative, because the discussion of the examples and the plausibility of political subjectivity would need to rely on too little scientific literature that could not provide sufficient support. It is therefore necessary to search in a narrowly defined section, the dimensions of which are given by the terms that initially put us on the historical trail of political subjectivity.

---

universal form of the reflecting judgment, but not to the unity of political judgment dedicated here as a *reflection on public order*.

B.2.1 Charisma

If an object is sought at the intersection of politics and aesthetics to test the previous theses, after an initial examination of the possibilities one inevitably encounters the phenomenon of charisma. A second look at this topical method reveals that another element of the historical triad would be taken into account with this sociological concept, namely the public sphere. The considerable amount of scientific literature on charisma makes it a first-class experimental object.

B.2.1.1 Max Weber's Objective Charisma

Since Max Weber's monumental work *Wirtschaft und Gesellschaft* [Economy and Society], the term 'charismatic rule' has made an impressive career. The communist and soon also the National Socialist dictatorship, which was already in the making during Weber's lifetime, were exemplary embodiments of a crossover of rational-bureaucratic and charismatic rule. The three ideal types – rational, traditional and charismatic rule – proved to be excellent means of interpretation for 20th century politics. However, a special magic came from the concept of charisma, because liberal democracies still need charismatic elements of power today. Charisma offered itself as a selection criterion for statesmanlike aptitude and corresponding teachings from the skillful (instead of only 'good') state leader as master of the symbolic language. In the concept of charism, politics shows itself from a very pragmatic side, which does not have to worry about moral values and can make success the exclusive goal. So, it is no coincidence that social science research has since concentrated with astonishing one-sidedness on a single figure of the concept: the charismatic leader.[775] In Weber's text, on the other hand, the term charisma is used to describe a much broader theoretical structure that is extraordinarily demanding and whose potential has not been exhausted by commentary

---

[775] Cf. in summary and exemplarily until the end of the 1970s Arnold Zingerle's study *Max Webers historische Soziologie* [Max Weber's Historical Sociology], Darmstadt 1981, p. 130ff; until the beginning of the 1990s cf. also Gebhardt, Winfried, *Grundlinien einer Entwicklung des Charismakonzeptes* [Sketch of the Evolution of the Concept of Charisma], in Gebhardt & Zingerle, Arnold u. Ebertz, Michael (ed.), *Charisma: Theorie, Religion, Politik*, series *Materiale Soziologie* TB3, Berlin and N. Y. 1993, p. 1-12, here p. 2.

and research literature.

Therefore, it makes sense to go to Weber's text first. The first quote in *Wirtschaft und Gesellschaft* is also one that has invited people to simplify the concept of charisma:

> "There are three pure types of legitimate rule. Their legitimacy can be primarily: 1. [rational] ... 2... or finally 3. *charismatic* character: charismatic rule rests on the extraordinary devotion to holiness or the heroic power or the model of a person and the order revealed or created by him."[776]

Here it is impossible to overlook the charisma of a leader. In the first and at the same time definitory paragraph of the detailed description of charismatic rule, it is even more exclusively tailored to human beings:

> "*Charisma* means a quality of personality that is regarded as extraordinary (originally, both in prophets as well as in therapeutic and legal ways as in hunting guides as in war heroes: as magical), that is assumed to be gifted with supernatural or superhuman or at least extraordinary powers or qualities or is regarded as sent by God or as exemplary and therefore as a *leader*. How the quality in question would be assessed 'objectively' from any ethical, aesthetic or other point of view is of course completely indifferent conceptually: it depends solely on how it is actually evaluated by the charismatically dominated, the *'followers.'*"[777]

These *charismatically dominated subjects* give validity to the charisma through recognition: "But this is (with genuine charisma) not the *reason* for legitimacy, but rather it is *duty* of the ones called upon [by the charismatic leader; R.G.] by vocation and probation to recognize this quality." Now follows the first sentence, which will be particularly important for the rest: "This *recognition* is psychologically a faithful, very personal devotion born of enthusiasm or misery and hope."[778] Furthermore, the pure charisma is "specifically unfamiliar to the economy" because it is not receptive to the charm of bureaucratic resource management and time planning; but above all, it represents "the great revolutionary power in traditionally bound

---

[776] Weber, Max, *Wirtschaft und Gesellschaft. Grundriß der verstehenden Soziologie* [Economy and Society. An Outline for Interpretive Sociology], 5. rev. ed., Tübingen 1985, p. 124; emphasis by the author – also in all further quotations.

[777] Ibid., p. 140.

[778] Ibid.

epochs". Charisma can be a transformation from within, which, "born of need and enthusiasm, means a change of central attitudes and actions with a complete reorientation of all attitudes towards all individual forms of life and towards the *world* at large."[779] This is now a formulation that no longer relates exclusively to the rule of charismatic persons. In the following Weber then describes the "everydayization of charisma", which becomes unavoidable in particular due to the technical question of succession and its organization. As a result, economic interests and measures to secure the social position of the immediate followers participating in the rule will take a further step in everyday life. In this developmental scheme, however, the charisma does not disappear, but rather it is transformed and searches for or is controlled by *new objects*. The temporal stabilization of power beyond the life span of the charismatic primordial leader was regulated quite efficiently by the *heredity* of the charisma. The entire European aristocracy has legitimized itself through the original deeds of its first title-holders. The hereditary charism thus drew more attention to the dynasties of clans, sects or families formed by descent, rather than requiring the individual aristocratic person to embody and repeat the founding act. Finally, a clear distinction can be observed in European divine grace between the personal charisma of the monarch and the much more important official charisma.[780]

So, it is clear that charisma is not a moment of socialization limited to rulers. What Weber has already begun up to this point, he continues in the part of the book that deals with the sociology of religion: the development of a much more general concept of charisma, which expands into an anthropological theory of action.[781] The charismatic objects are no longer only persons, but also things[782], presented objects and finally ideas. Friedrich Tenbruck made the breakthrough to such an anthropological theory of

---

[779] Ibid., p. 142.

[780] In this context the already discussed *two-body doctrine* of the Middle Ages is to be seen, whereby the holiness of the office was made legally independent of the minor or spiritual insane monarch; cf. Kantorowicz, Ernst, *Die zwei Körper des Königs. Eine Studie zur politischen Theologie des Mittelalters*, München 1990 [The King's Two Bodies. A Study in Medieval Political Theology, Princeton 1957].

[781] Weber, *Wirtschaft und Gesellschaft*, loc. cit., pp. 245-381.

[782] Talismans, fetishes, magic objects of witch cults and anti-cults, radiant or protective crystals in esotericism, and finally objects with which 'prestige' is simply connected – which means that people can also be prestige objects of other people.

charisma, which is still entirely based on Weber's text.[783] A general approach that, going beyond Weber's works, distinguishes the structurally necessary stages of change of charisma, from the regionally and culturally differentiated, historical-concrete effect of charisma to the modern charisma of reason, is found in Wolfgang Schluchter.[784]

Since the political propaganda in World War II, charisma has also become relevant in media theory, because electronic communication media are known to have an extremely charismatic effect, dissolve the physicality of charismatic persons in order to synthetically resurrect them and for the first time connect masses of people all over the world to form followers.[785]

Finally, Wolfgang Lipp's first 'generative theory' of charisma is to be mentioned, for in recent research it is regarded as a further breakthrough.[786] Up to now, the existence of charisma has simply been noted historically and accepted as such. Lipp was the first to ask: "How does charisma come about? What forces, what basic conditions support the process?"[787] His thesis is that there is an interrelation of *stigma* and charisma. Stigmatized subjects can reverse the process in which they are destined to become victims and enjoy the charisma through "self-stigmatization". To support this model Lipp refers to the ethnological observations of the rites de passage or to the alternation of 'structure' and 'antistructure', which denotes moments of abrupt symmetrical reversal of order in ethnological societies.[788] For him it is essential that the impulse for action

---

[783] Cf. Tenbruck, Friedrich, *Das Werk Max Webers*, in: Kölner Zeitschrift für Soziologie und Sozialpsychologie 27/1975, pp. 663-702; Tenbruck, *Anthropologie des Handelns*, in: Lenk, Hans (ed.), *Handlungstheorien - interdisziplinär*, vol. 2, Munich 1978, pp. 89-138.

[784] Schluchter, Wolfgang, *Die Entwicklung des okzidentalen Rationalismus. Eine Analyse von Max Webers Gesellschaftsgeschichte* [The Development of Occidental Rationalism. An Analysis of Max Weber's Social History], Tübingen 1979.

[785] References in Gebhardt, *Grundlinien*, loc. cit., p. 12, note 14.

[786] Lipp, Wolfgang, *Schuld und Gnade. Soziale Konstruktion, Kulturdynamik, Handlungsdrama* [Charisma – Guilt and Mercy. Social Construction, Cultural Dynamics, Drama of Action], in: Gebhardt et al. (eds.), *Charisma*, loc. cit., pp. 15-32.

[787] Ibid., p. 16.

[788] The theory cannot be discussed and commented on in detail here. However, in my opinion, already in this sketch a serious theoretical misapprehension of action is discernible. The imputation that the passage from stigma to charisma is a conscious act of the stigmatized/charismatic subject is extremely romantic. The sacrificial rites can only be reconstructed with an excess of naivety or

emanates from the still stigmatized charismatic, who can reverse the pattern of order *from persecution to worship through self-persecution.*

All previously mentioned models of charisma[789] can now be combined with regard to the structuring of their subject area. Without exception in research it was assumed that there is a phenomenon in charisma which essentially starts from a *person*, the *vicarious representation of a person* or from an *impersonal thing* (thing, imagined object, idea). The emanation of charisma, which works from a carrier medium, forms the field of the charismatically dominated or influenced and materializes a *charismatic order*. This operating mode should be described here as the description of *objective charisma.*[790] The vectors of this force, whatever its nature, go clearly and exclusively *from the charismatic carrier medium to the recipients*, who are puzzlingly socialized by this force. Is there another way to build this field in a coherent way that takes full account of the empirical evidence to date?

---

cynicism according to the pattern of the victim's autonomous action. Lipp knows the works of René Girard and refers to them with approval, but obviously has not read them: Girard develops a reconstruction of the sacralization of victims that is exactly opposite to Lipp's theory and is based on the *collective subconscious of the sacrificial community* and the charismatic victim as an averting of the dangerous, because structurally conflictual, "mimetic desire". The charismatic phase is only a postponement of sacrifice in order to make it effective, for the sacrifice must paradoxically be both the object of persecution and sanctification. This paradox is stretched in time by a series of 1.) worship, 2.) persecution and murder, 3.) sanctification in the hereafter. Thus, the victim functions as a construction of transcendence. Cf. Grünenberg, Reginald, *Gründungsgewalt und Politik. René Girards Kulturtheorie im Spiegel der Politikwissenschaft* [Founding Violence and Politics. René Girard's Theory of Culture as Reflected in Political Science] in: academia.edu, Berlin 2010.

[789] The following description also applies to all models that cannot be discussed in detail here.

[790] That this scheme is the undisputed structure of all theoretical works on charisma has not yet been noticed – not even in Arnold Zingerle's summarizing treatise; cf. Zingerle, *Theoretische Probleme und Perspektiven der Charisma-Forschung. Ein kritischer Rückblick*, [Theoretical Problems and Perspectives of Charisma Research. A Critical Review], in: Gebhardt et al. (ed.), *Charisma*, loc. cit., pp. 249-266.

B.2.1.2 The Qualitative Turnaround: The Subjective-Political Charisma

The constitution of the charismatic leader and charismatic objects, as well as the contexts that promote or hinder the charisma of these objects, have already been the subject of numerous studies. It is therefore striking that *so little attention has been paid to the recipients of the charismatic message*. Andreas Dörner, who analyzed the political myth as a charismatic staging, therefore rightly observes:

> "The impact research developed to date is far from advanced enough to allow statements to be made about what certain audiences actually think at reception, how they perceive a situation, how they react cognitively or emotionally."[791]

Perhaps the scattered references in Weber's text to the individual reception of charisma will help in this situation. The passage on Weber's theory of the psychological validity and effect of charisma already quoted above reports of a "very personal devotion" that is born of need or hope. In the definitional article Weber formulates the conditions for recognition of the charism as an "evaluation" on the part of the charismatically dominated subject, whose freedom of choice he immediately limits and describes the valuation itself as *duty*, which the charismatically gifted person calls (without pronouncing it) to follow. Elsewhere, Weber emphasizes that in the genuine charisma, no dissenting election, no majority rule and minority formation can be permissible within the succession regulation: "Only one can be the right one; so the dissenting voters commit an outrage."[792] Finally, there is a general provision of the mode of validity or effect that extends to all three ideal types of rule, namely the *subjective "belief in legitimacy"*. Interestingly, Weber formulates the juxtaposition with the other, objective side of legitimacy as follows: "It is therefore *expedient* to distinguish the types of rule according to their typical claim to legitimacy" – as if he saw the reverse thematization, namely from the side of faith and evaluation, already as the possible, albeit more difficult alternative.[793] This

---

[791] Dörner, Andreas, *Politischer Mythos und symbolische Politik. Sinnstiftung durch symbolische Formen am Beispiel des Hermannsmythos* [Political Myth and Symbolic Politics. Creating Meaning Through Symbolic Forms Using the Example of the Hermann Myth], Opladen 1995, p. 14.

[792] Weber, *Wirtschaft und Gesellschaft*, loc. cit., p. 665.

[793] Ibid., p. 122.

recalls Kant's methodical decision to present the beauty of nature in an exemplary and pure way to make the structure of the judgment of beauty better discernible. This observation should encourage us to take this difficult path again with Weber.

First of all, the simple fact that charisma is an *aesthetic phenomenon* deserves attention. It undoubtedly has a psychic and psychologically analyzable dimension, but we are not so much interested in the libidinal or mimetic driving forces of the psychosomatic body, which charismatically connect it with the medium. For it is only through the aesthetic dimension that one reaches the subject to which this investigation is devoted, namely the particular form of judgment in the subject, which makes it politically addressable. The receptivity of the subjects in the process described as objective charisma should be called, whenever judgments are part of the process, *subjective charisma*. This gives the description of the phenomenon a constructivist twist, for it now looks as if it is the charismatically dominated subjects who aggregate their judgments to form the *charismatic field around the alleged carrier medium*. That is exactly what is intended. Now it can be discussed in which way the modes of reflecting judgment in the individual bring about this construction.

The basic syntactic tension in the political judgment exists between the elementary concepts of individuality and order.[794] They divide the entire field of possible judgments, provided that they are political, under the direction of reflecting judgment.[795] The charisma does not necessarily separate these two syntactic elementary concepts, as Weber has clearly shown, but rather the 'genuine charisma' as the sacral force of communization has exactly the opposite consequence. As in Islamic orthodox Quran reading, which the Moroccan philosopher Al-Jabri criticized here (cf. chapter B.1.8), the sacral-charismatic character of objects does not permit any distancing between reflecting subject and reflected object, so that the distinction between individuality and order does not come about in the political judgment, or no political judgment at all can be found in the subject. This does not mean, however, that there is no reflection at all, for the aesthetic and teleological aspects are completely indispensable in the charismatic experience. How could a sacred being be worshipped, the power of a charismatic person feared, or the meaning of a ritual sensed if

---

[794] On the provisional use of 'syntactic' and 'semantic', see chapter B.1.7.2.1.

[795] To justify this small limitation, it was necessary to deduce its claim by presenting the particular unity of political judgment, namely as a *reflection on public order*; cf. chapter B.1.7.1.

the reflecting power of judgment did not come to the aid of its various types of reflection? The notions of beauty, sublime and end had to fulfil their respective tasks right into the primordial beginnings of human history; therefore, however, they did not always take on the complex form of a political reflection judgment.

On this occasion it becomes clear that the charisma covers a larger area of phenomena than the concept of political subjectivity. All forms of ritual publicity can be categorized under it, whereas the genuinely political character is denied here precisely in this form of social communication. Political subjectivity therefore describes events that belong to a narrower concept of charisma. This special limitation is found in what Weber called the *everydayization of charisma*, that is, the dissolution of its sacred binding power. However, everydayisation is not only supported by social rationalization processes and opportunities to increase complexity, such as bureaucratization. The reconstruction from a political-subjective point of view makes other moments visible. This process can be described as a *spreading (in the sense of widening) of the genuine charisma* through politically qualified reflection, as well as the historically situated emergence of a new power of judgment.

There is obviously a *reciprocal relationship* between the developmental histories of charisma and political subjectivity. **While charisma has apparently lost its intensity and significance in the everyday life of progressive modernity, political subjectivity took its place in modern history to the opposite extent.** It is, as is assumed here, one and the same reflecting activity that has only individualized itself in order to gain autonomy in relation to collective social processes. It then does not only behave in such a way that orders and effective forces, which promise superhuman threats or chances of redemption, <u>can</u> be more and more difficultly constructed by political subjects. Rather, in addition to this objective-sociological conditionality of disenchantment, a reflection on the individual <u>will</u>, or rather <u>a need for reflection</u>, manifests itself, which the historian Nipperdey has described as the need for a special form of *conviviality* that spread in 18th century Europe.[796] But this sociability in turn led to the multiplication of charismatic objects, because the clasp of the sacred had broken open and one began to argue publicly and to form

---

[796] Cf. Nipperdey, Thomas, *Die anthropologische Dimension der Geschichtswissenschaft* [The Anthropological Dimension of History, in: Nipperdey, *Gesellschaft, Kultur, Theorie. Gesammelte Aufsätze zur neueren Geschichte* [Society, Culture, Theory. Collected Essays on Modern History], Göttingen 1976, pp. 33-58; cf. chapter A.3.

dissenting opinions about the virtue of the rulers, the Christianity of the princes of the church and the glory of God – without letting the sociability immediately lead to violence. Since then, the spectrum of possible subjective orders has been growing steadily: nature has been domesticated in agriculture and its yields have been mechanically and chemically optimized so that the cyclical famines, that threatened all of humanity until far into the 19th century, cease and generalized prosperity develops; medical care is beginning to protect and prolong life; and finally, in the course of the claims for freedom of speech, faith and political decisions are being privatized, with the result that the forces most directly affecting the imagination of mankind have already been broken by reflection in the past history. The world experienced the disappearance of the sublime because nature and God were forced to retreat.

The increasing number of competing charismas led to the individual charisma becoming smaller. The increasingly detailed background knowledge about their private lives and their biographies has a levelling effect on political figures in public life in the industrial nations in terms of subjective perception and reflecting assessment, but certainly meets a need of the political subjects.[797] **It therefore becomes much more difficult for politicians to create an aura of mystery, political genius, extraordinary competence or simply fortune.**[798] The formation of a solid charismatic field around a person or even around an idea takes longer and is subject to much more difficult trials than under sacral or hereditary conditions. Charisma is more than ever linked to real proof in this respect. This is also connected with the fact that journalistic researching media[799] mainly report on political mistakes and failures. After all, as charismatic as the media

---

[797] But this is precisely what Richard Sennett sees as the deplorable "tyranny of intimacy" when he reports that American presidents (Polish and many others now also) sit down with working families to prove their closeness to the people; cf. Sennett, *The Fall of Public Man*, 1974.

[798] There is the anecdote of Napoleon's Foreign Minister Talleyrand, who wanted to hire a talented young man in diplomatic service. The latter thanked for this favor with the moving words that this was the best day of his life, because he had never had fortune before. To which Talleyrand replied horrified: "Excuse me? You haven't had any fortune yet? Then I can't have you here. You are dismissed!"

[799] This refers to the opposite of media reporting which, due to a lack of own research, can only make statements about the information made available to it by the respective political PR departments. After all, about 80 % of the policy-related reports in Germany are prefabricated in these departments.

may be, they can also hinder or destroy it; after all, they still say: "Only bad news are good news." This has not been true to the same extent for business leaders, since they have limited accountability, their individual decisions and actions are more difficult to observe, their private lives are better protected, and their economic successes have a stronger connotation of objectivity in political judgment. But overall it has become more difficult to embody a certain 'greatness' in a person of public life who represents an imagined order. Worship or hatred for the charismatic leaders has historically dwindled with the power of the imaginary worlds associated with them, leaving just *sympathy* or *antipathy*. Again, however, this only shows how preconditioned and less trivial such simple dispositions can be. In this process there is no cultural decline, but undoubtedly an increase in individual judgment and communication skills. It may be difficult to be a superman today under these conditions. **What is worrying, however, is how many people still believe they need supermen to worship and control themselves, and with what intensity they therefore seek objectively charismatic relationships that are untroubled by reflection.** There are only a few areas of public life left that offer such an opportunity of super-humanity for a limited period of time, namely those who are most probate to celebrity worship: movies, sports and music.[800]

There is an interesting analogy between subjective charisma and reflection, which is further proof of the conditional identity of charisma and reflection. Indeed, genuine charisma is "specifically irrational in the sense of alienation from the rules."[801] In its structure it resembles reflecting judgment in general and aesthetic judgment in particular. Here too, an objective characteristic of the charisma finds an equivalent in the subjective judgment of the individual. These analogical connections are now to be discussed against the background of the conceptuality of political subjectivity previously developed in the study.

The subjective charisma thus opens up a field of reflection between the poles of individuality and imagined, subjective order in the course of everyday life. In this syntactic unity of political judgment as a reflection on public order, the types of reflection on beauty and sublimity then find their

---

[800] Although the reflecting power of judgment also has an effect in these areas, it is usually no longer based on a politically qualifiable concept of order. Instead, it creates mostly cinematic, sporty or musically sublimated ritual public spheres, accompanied by aesthetic individuality in the reflection on the beauty or sublime of the respective symbolically hypotyped or hypostasized phenomena.

[801] Weber, *Wirtschaft und Gesellschaft*, loc. cit., p. 141.

respective places *by inscribing the states of the judging subject as semantic values in the judgment of reflection*. As shown in chapter B.1.7.2.2.2-4, the subjective-political elementary concepts of morality, justice, time, body and power are made possible and produced as ideas. It is a logical consequence that in subjective charisma the symbolic-hypotypical moment must be clearly to be found, i.e. it is always a *sensualization of a representation*, be it an idea, a term, or, as it is constitutive for political judgment: a subjective order. This abstract discussion can be illustrated without difficulty by the example of the American president, to whose office and charismatic significance most of the charismatic research literature is devoted.[802] The president is no longer a representative of God on earth and no longer has any sacred attributes but is an American citizen. The (television) audience watching him recognizes him as an ordinary, albeit privileged person and has usually gained the necessary minimal distance of reflection to him as a charismatic object. Thus, in their charismatic relationship with their president, the participants of this audience have the freedom to see themselves as individuals connected to him in a certain respect. If this president manages to induce the formation of a charismatic field around his person and his office by the political subjects, then he has succeeded, because he has been **chosen by the individuals as the object of the sensualization of their subjective concept of order**. His face, his speeches, his attitude, his program and what other individuals already say about him: all this is collected in political judgment in order *to judge the appropriateness of this person as a sensualization for one's own ideas of order*. Of course, it also depends on how large the number of individuals reflecting on it in a charismatic relationship is, because the charisma is formed, among other things, through the semantic reflection value of subjective power, i.e. **the respective own concept of order is based on a presidentiable appearance with a corresponding will through which it can also be reflected with the corresponding power and can be trusted to realize the subjective order of the judging individual**. The already formed judgment of other individuals often has a *catalytic effect* on one's own judgment. This is understandable, because if the judgment-forming individual cannot observe any effect of the presidential phenomenon and its power reflected as will in his own neighbors and friends, for example, he includes this deficit in the hypotyposis that accompanies his own judgment. This does not damage the syntactic relationship between individuality and subjective

---

[802] The Pope ranks immediately after the American President; see Gebhardt, *Grundlinien*, loc. cit., p. 3.

order, but the semantic value of reflected power (by means of the dynamically sublime) overwhelms the candidate's *offer of embodiment*, because he is ultimately considered too weak to realize the imagined order. Incidentally, this can be very different in nature – for example, predominantly of a moral, religious, economic or social nature – as long as it is stretched only through reflection. In subjective charisma, the relative power of order develops above all a strong feeling of dynamic sublimity. The person, the object or the idea becomes the *representation* of my reflecting idea of an order that is not determined in any particular degree, but always *subjectively*-determined.

In this way, charisma has a so far undiscovered and undefined quality that does not make the subject appear to be dependent on the charismatic forces and imprisoned by them in the attitude of devotion and the faith born of need. This could no longer convince anyone, because the usual political judgment and decision making is generally rather undramatic. Today in particular, subjective charisma is an emotion that can be experienced on a daily basis through a person, an object or a 'theme', which is also based on a subjective performance of judgment – which, although not as absolute moral autonomy, can nevertheless be appreciated as the *autonomy of the reflecting power of judgment in the individual*. Common sense in political matters that can be felt and experienced in this way has its own dignity, which must not always be crushed by the majesty of moral law (cf. chapter B.1.8).

With these considerations, an empirical-cognitive and impact research, which Dörner has announced above as a desideratum, is of course not yet anticipated, but they serve such only as a theoretical offer. As a rule, however, all cognitive-theoretical approaches are written so far under abstraction from the references to consciousness or reflection. Here a subject-philosophical alternative would be formulated, which is waiting for its empirical testing.

B.2.2 Excursus II: Ethnological and Cultural-Anthropological Dimensions of Political Subjectivity

The historical location of the political, here understood as the temporal determination of the emergence of political subjectivity, was made in Part A of the study, in the European 18th century with special consideration of Germany. This was an attempt to solve the task in an exemplary and ideal-typical manner. The assertion that the special capacity for political judgment develops in people at certain times and in certain places and not in others, however, requires a broader confirmation than only in the more recent history of Christian Europe. Finally, both temporally and spatially, the dimensional limits of the narrower initial hypothesis are to be broken in order, where not to prove it, to at least defend the claim to the universal validity of the concept of political subjectivity. The question "What is political?", which has been dealt with and answered in great detail here, is followed by the no less interesting temporalized questions "When and where is or was something political?" and "What will be political?" In this way, the perspective of a new, genuinely political cultural theory can be added to the horizon in the short term. This can no longer be explained here[803], but at least the ethnological and cultural-anthropological foundations should be discussed.

If the emergence of political subjectivity is linked to cultural history, it would have to be possible to find dispositions in the *Critique of the Power of Judgment*, for it was from this that all elements for the political judgment could ultimately be drawn. Although several authors claimed or mention-

---

[803] About as thoroughly as Jürgen Habermas, who developed his own social theorem of evolution on the basis of the concept of communicative action, to which he assigned an appropriate space in his *Theorie des kommunikativen Handelns* [Theory of Communicative Action], vol. 2, Frankfurt 1981, in the chapters *Rationale Struktur der Versprachlichung des Sakralen* [Rational Structure of the Linguisticization of the Sacred] (ibid., p. 118-170) and *Entkoppelung von System und Lebenswelt* [Decoupling of System and Lifeworld] (ibid., p. 229-290). Niklas Luhmann's systems theory also rests on a broad base of [fascinating!] studies on the evolution of social systems in Europe since the 17th century; cf. Luhmann, *Gesellschaftsstruktur und Semantik. Studien zur Wissenssoziologie der modernen Gesellschaft* [Social Structure and Semantics. Studies on the Sociology of Knowledge in Modern Society], 3 vol., Frankfurt 1993.

ed that the *CPJ* contained a theory of culture[804], nobody has bothered to isolate this theory from the systematic requirements of the critique of knowledge and to present it specifically.[805] Some cultural-philosophical attempts even referred more to the first two *Critiques*. Arnold Gehlen, for example, sought reinsurance in Kant's text for his own anthropology, but none of these came from the *CPJ*.[806] There is a certain consequence to this, for the cultural theory of Johann Gottfried Herders,[807] which is much more important for Gehlen, appeared before Kant's third Critique and could not yet have been influenced by it.[808] More astonishing, however, is the fact that Ernst Cassierer's cultural theory in his work *Philosophie der symbollischen Formen* [Philosophy of Symbolic Forms], which was intended to establish a "critique of culture", cannot be traced back to Kant's third *Critique*, or that all of Cassirer's borrowings from the *CPJ* have largely remained uncommented.[809] In the final instance, Hegel's influence, espe-

---

[804] So also Jacques Derrida in *Die Wahrheit in der Malerei* [The Truth in Painting], loc. cit., p. 132.

[805] Friedrich Kaulbach, for example, sees an *Ästhetische Welterkenntnis bei Kant* [Aesthetik Knowledge of the World in Kant], Würzburg 1984, but in what this empirically manifests itself, he can only show this in the field of art. Nowhere else does he find a bridge to cultural, social and political reality in the system of Kantian terms.

[806] Cf. Gehlen, Arnold, *Der Mensch. Seine Natur und seine Stellung in der Welt* [Man. His Nature and his Position in the World], 1940, 9. revised. [and ideologically streamlined; R.G.] ed. Wiesbaden 1972, passim.

[807] Herder, Gottfried Johann, *Ideen zur Philosophie der Geschichte der Menschheit* [Ideas on the Philosophy of the History of Humanity], 4 vols., Riga and Leipzig 1784-1791.

[808] It is obvious that Gehlen only wanted to obtain a certain philosophical authority for his anthropology with the quotes from Kant, for no work was criticized as sharply by Kant as the philosophy of history of his pupil Herder, who tried to give shape to the theory of man as if there had not yet been a critique of the subject of reason by a certain Kant. Abstaining from all metaphysical questions – in the Kantian sense: from the philosophical problems of subjectivity – makes Herder's work the precursor of today's reductionism and functionalism in the social sciences. Gehlen has contributed to this tradition and the line can be extended to the works of Niklas Luhmann. To call Kant of all people as witnesses to the defense of this method is a label fraud; cf. Kant, Immanuel, , *Rezension zu Gottfried Herders "Ideen zur Philosophie der Geschichte der Menschheit"* [Review of Gottfried Herder's "Ideas on the Philosophy of the History of Humanity"], in: Kant, Werke XII, pp. 781-806.

[809] This has already been mentioned above; cf. Philonenko, Alexis, *Cassirer. Lecteur*

cially his *Phenomenology of the Spirit*, seems to have been decisive for Cassirer's enterprise, for it offered itself to short-circuit such an elegant model of the evolution of the mind on its way to itself with the collection of cultural-historical forms of its various sensualizations, from myth to the theory of relativity. **Thus, this topic is still completely unresolved, and so much so that the studies in chapters B.1.3 to B.1.7.3 are probably the closest to the text and the most material-rich discussions of the *CPJ* in cultural theory to date.**

In the introduction to this work, reference was made to the "anthropological side entrance", which Ottfried Höffe encouraged. Here is a small confession: Despite all the enthusiastic reference to this invitation, I did not mention that the present study is about something completely different, if not the exact opposite of what Höffe had in mind. For the political anthropology to which **the concept of political subjectivity refers must be *descriptive*, i.e. oriented towards historical and ethnological reality**. In this it is supported and informed by George Balandier's older works, which have received far too little attention. His *Political Anthropology* is completely foreign to the normative-philosophical approach of German political science.[810] He has examined the ethnological literature on the problem of the political and combined it with his own empirical-ethnological findings gained during his expeditions and research in Africa to form an *ethnographically based theory of the political*. The aim of this teaching

---

et interprète de Kant [Cassirer. Reader and Interpreter of Kant], in: Seidengart, Jean (ed.), *Ernst Cassirer. De Marbourg à New York. L'itinéraire philosophique, Actes du colloque de Nanterre, 12-14 octobre 1988*, p. 43-54. In his *Philosophie der symbolischen Formen* [Philosophy of Symbolic Forms], Darmstadt 1954, there are exactly three references to the *CPJ*, but twenty-one to the *CPuRe*. In the third volume of the work, there is a longer discussion of Kant's criticism, in which Cassirer complains that it is only about world-*recognizing*, pure science whose horizon must transcend the philosophy of symbolic forms as a world-*understanding* discipline – and the *CPJ* is not mentioned with a word (ibid., vol. 3, p. 7-16). Cassirer's later remark that the *CPJ* is primarily an extension of the question of knowledge by the dimension of biological life is also irritating; cf. Cassirer, Ernst, *Zur Logik des Symbolbegriffs*, in: Cassirer, *Wesen und Wirkung des Symbolbegriffs*, [1938] Darmstadt 1994, special edition, p. 201-230, here p. 228.

[810] Cf. Balandier, George, *Politische Anthropologie*, Munich 1976. The difference is already evident in the composition of the texts on political anthropology in Höffe's volume *Der Mensch - ein politisches Tier? Essays zur politischen Anthropologie* [Man – A Political Anima? Essays on political anthropology], Stuttgart 1992; all contributions are only comments on classical texts of political theory from Aristotle to Foucault and have nothing to do with empirical anthropology.

should be to overcome the prejudice that *primitive peoples have no history* and many of them, especially those without observable forms of state, would *not know any kind of politics*.[811] Especially the structuralist school has denied primitive societies any historico-political dimension. On behalf of this view, Louis Dumont blamed the ideological individualism of modernity and its researchers for what he considered to be an aberrant attribution of political quality among primitive peoples.[812] Dumont's diatribes against individualism have been mentioned here several times; in summary, his later works were only a symptom of the underdevelopment of empirically founded theorems of individuality or individualization.[813] In recent research, Dumont's assessment of modern societies is judged as so thwarted by his sympathy for holistic-hierarchical societies that it no longer even mentions him. It was probably a kind of overconfidence when Dumont said that after his interesting and instructive book about India's *Homo hierarchicus*,[814] he already knew its counterpart, the *Homo individualis*, well enough to be able to condemn and exhort him.

Remarkable for our purposes is Balandier's extraordinarily pronounced methodical awareness of the problem. For a true "world history of political thought"[815] to be written, he believes, the question of the definition of the political must be asked anew. Balandier makes a detailed comparison of the various offers formulated in the works of earlier political anthropologists.[816] While some anthropologists speak of the political, where kinship ends, certain characteristics of space (territory, inner/outer difference) or action (reference to power instead of authority) are given, for others only the function of the political in the form of achievements for society as a

---

[811] See also Balandier, George, *Anthropo-Logiques*, 2nd revised and extended edition, Paris 1985, pp. 5-27, 203-248.

[812] Dumont, Louis, *Préface*, in: Evans-Pritchard, E.E., *Les Nuer*, Paris 1969.

[813] Cf. Dumont, Louis, *Essais sur l'individualisme. Une perspective anthropologique sur l'idéologie moderne*, Paris 1983; cf. also here chapter A.1.

[814] Cf. Dumont, Louis, *Homo hierachicus*, Paris 1967.

[815] Balandier, *Politische Anthropologie*, loc. cit., p. 20.

[816] Cf. Easton, David, Political Anthropology, in: Biennial Review of Anthropology, 1959, p. 226 et seq.; Eisenstadt, S. N., Primitive Political Systems, in: American Anthropologist 61/1959; Radcliffe-Brown, A. R., Structure and Function in Primitive Society, London 1952; Schapera, I., Government and Politics in Tribal Societies, London 1956; Sutton, F. X., Representation and Nature of Political Systems, in: Comparative Studies in Society and History, 2/1959.

whole counts (cooperation, integrity, decision making, security).[817] Balandier states provisionally:

> "The political can neither be reduced to a 'code' (such as language or myth) nor to a 'network of relationships' (such as kinship or exchange); **it remains a comprehensive system that has not yet received satisfactory formal treatment.**"[818]

Balandier saw his own work as preparation for a new discipline, not as its final form. Overall, however, thanks to his conscientiousness, his conclusion is so cautious and necessarily skeptical that it hardly seems possible to contradict Dumont's thesis that there is nothing political in primitive cultures. The empirically proceeding and politically interested ethnology, with which we wanted to inform ourselves, obviously does **not yet have an effective criterion for differentiating between the political and the non-political**. Political anthropology could therefore be released from an embarrassment if it used the concept of political subjectivity. However, even then Balandier's high expectations remained unfulfilled, for "history" certainly cannot be "rehabilitated" in this way. The view of the ability to the political can only be gained by means of a thorough *disillusionment of all historical – and thus always crypto-metaphysical – hopes*. Balandier's concluding formula is characterized by this very assumption of an alleged subjugation of political subjectivity under a historical subjectivity of whatever kind in which of individuality is no longer a trace.[819]

---

[817] Balandier, *Politische Anthropologie*, a.a.O., S. 37-48.

[818] Ibid., p. 62 [highlight by me].

[819] Cf. Wilhelm Dilthey's profound studies on this problem of individuality and historical reason, *Der Aufbau der geschichtlichen Welt in den Geisteswissenschaften. Gesammelte Schriften VII*, Leipzig 1927 and by Stephan Otto, *Rekonstruktion der Geschichte. Zur Kritik der historischen Vernunft* [Reconstruction of History. On the Critique of Historical Reason], 2 vol., Munich 1982 and 1992. Dilthey wrote: "Throughout the entire concept of the spiritual world such fundamental experience of community passes through, in which consciousness of the unified self and that of similarity with others, the same nature of man and individuality are connected with one another" (Loc. cit., p. 141). As so often, the normative levelling of the real challenge of individuality can also be observed here. These studies make clear what Hannah Arendt already suspected, namely that for logical and methodological reasons individuality can be conceptually extraordinarily difficult to grasp. The efforts Dilthey and Otto have put into their respective experiments is impressive. Therefore, Balandier's implicit anti-individualism is not a program, but rather the symptom of a methodical problem.

> "All human societies produce politics, all are – for the same reasons – exposed to the stream of history."[820]

But it would be another disappointment to accept, for it looks as if the concept of political subjectivity should partially support Dumont's assertion: political phenomena existed only in a few cultures and not in all historical epochs either. Ancient historian Christian Meier, whose entire work is the search for answers to two questions, would also agree:

> "How did the Greeks, unlike all other cultures before and beside them, develop democracies? And what was the political of the Greeks, which made it excellent as a determined/determining life-element of their society?"[821]

Elsewhere he also called this approach an attempt in "political ethnology."[822] This approach presupposes an awareness for the peculiarity, for the historical positionality and the improbability of the political. So, it seems that the Greeks differed exactly by the political from ethnological societies or cultures, which suggests that the political in the latter was (and still is) probably not at all or only very little pronounced.

In the course of the investigation it became clear that a very demanding ability of individuality must be realized in order for something like a political judgment and thus political subjectivity to come into being. Since political ethnology has unfortunately not been continued in a form as sophisticated and problem-aware as Balandier's, the concept of individuality can for the time being be used as an indicator of the potential feasibility of political subjectivity in archaic and ethnological cultures. The elementary concept of individuality is now anything but simple. Newer ethnology has had to realize through intercultural comparison that there are not only very different concepts of individuality, but that some cultures know nothing of the sort. It has been shown that individuality has so far been above all a metaphysical concept of monotheistic-Christian Europe. The attribution of all actions of a being to a thought center in its body, i.e. under the concept of unity of action, can be found in almost no archaic culture.[823] Steven Lukes, the author of the philosophical studies on

---

[820] Balandier, *Politische Anthropologie*, loc. cit., p. 204.

[821] Meier, Christian, *Die Entstehung des Politischen bei den Griechen* [The Origin of the Political in the Greeks], Frankfurt 1980, p. 12.

[822] Meier, Christian, *Politik und Anmut* [Politics and Grace], Berlin 1985, p. 23.

[823] Cf. the well-documented essays in the anthology of the Laboratoire d'Ethno-

individuality[824], which have become decisive in the Anglo-American language area, has also pointed out that the question of individuality is fundamentally ethnocentric in color – but therefore by no means useless.[825] The main problem of this cultural anthropological research on individuality is therefore the uncertainty as to whether the European scheme of individuality is suitable at all for intercultural comparison. Most work in this field precedes its otherwise thorough ethnological and philological investigations with such a meagre framework of individuality theory that this concern for incommensurability seems justified. However, the problem is not 'European individuality' per se, but the inadequate level of its philosophically and sociologically reflected representation.[826] Sociologist Marcel Mauss, for example, has summarized the empirically observable changes in social behavior towards a European individuality conceived as perfection in a judgment that appears evolutionary theory. Yet, it is not a real theory, but only a teleologically inspired sequence of characteristic changes. The essential is missing, namely a theorem that explains the transitions and the performances or functions condensed therein:

"From a simple masquerade to the mask, from a 'role' (personnage) to a 'person' (personne), to a name, to an individual; from the latter to a being possessing metaphysical and moral value; from a moral con-

---

logie et de Sociologie Comparative, *Singularités. Les voies d'émergence individuelle* [Singularities. The Paths to to the Emergence of the Individual], Paris 1989; this is also the conclusion of the results in another anthology which has already been translated into English; see Birnbaum, Pierre u. Leca, Jean (ed.), *Sur l'individualisme. Théories et méthodes*, Paris 1986 [Individualism. Theories and Methods, Oxford 1990].

[824] See Lukes, Steven, *Individualism*, Oxford 1973.

[825] Lukes, Steven, *The Use of Ethnocentricity*, in: Lukes, *Moral Conflict and Politics*, Oxford 1991, p. 71-80. Lukes note ironically "...that an ethnocentric question – 'Under what conditions did the individual emerge?' – can yield a rich variety of compelling and rigorous indigenous answers" (ibid., p. 80). This essay also precedes the commemorative publication for Eric de Dampierre, *Singularités*, loc. cit.

[826] This also applies to the standard work by Stephen Lukes, *Individualism*, op.cit., which tells no more than a brief and rhapsodic history of literature about individuality. The motto of this book and at the same time of his essay *The Use of Ethnocentricity*, loc. cit., is a completely remote passage from Joseph de Maistres *Extrait d'une conversation*, which took place in 1820 and was only published in 1884. Lukes really believes that individuality was only perceived as a problem and thoroughly reflected upon in the 19th century – a very uninformed thesis, as shown here in chapter A.1.

sciousness to a sacred being; from the latter to a fundamental form of thought and action – the course is accomplished."[827]

This "fundamental form of thought and action" is nowhere explicitly elaborated and describes only a very vaguely assumed metaphysical claim of European individualism. As is the rule with other authors, it is not even clarified whether individuality is a social system or structural achievement, an artifact of communication, a moral discourse a priori or, for instance, the productive achievement of a differentiating consciousness at the level of psychic systems. Against the background of Chinese cultural history, Irene Bloom has gone the opposite way and has proposed that the figure of imaginary and perhaps also lived individuality can be resurrected from the early Confucian and Taoist texts themselves, instead of using European individualism as a template.[828] The amazing thing is that the image of early Chinese-aristocratic individualism quickly becomes much more concrete and detailed than the European template set aside. But if one renounces a conceptual basis of individuality as a heuristic guideline and as a topical minimal criterion, then of course the individual can arise even from the most ritualistic thinking in which only the pronoun 'I' has to play any role.[829] But what for the Moroccan philosopher Al-Jabri, for

---

[827] Mauss, Marcel, *Une catégorie de l'esprit humain: La notion de Personne, celle de 'moi'*, first published in: The Journal of the Royal Anthropological Institute 68/1938, reprinted in: Mauss, The Category of the Person. Anthropology, Philosophy, History, edited by M. Carrithers, S. Collins and S. Lukes, Cambridge 1985.

[828] Bloom, Irene, On the Matter of Mind. The Metaphysical Basis of the Expanded Self, in: Munro, David (ed.), Individualism and Holism. Studies in Confucian an Taoist Values, Michigan 1985, pp. 293-330.

[829] This way also myths and stories are often read, for example about the hunter's isolation or the solitude of kings and heroes. One could assume that the classic model for such readings is the interpretation of the Ulysses figure in the transition from the Iliad to the Odyssey, i.e. from the mythical and cruel hero to the cunning, sometimes desperate individual who reckons with his human weaknesses. However, this Greek story is much younger in terms of cultural history than the above-mentioned old legends. The myth and its historical context are over-civilized by the underpinning of such simple schemes of individuality. This process belongs to the hypostases of identity discussed in chapter B.1.8, the *Excursus I*, which cause the 'I' of the epistemic subject to coincide with the reflecting consciousness of the individual. In the case of the Confucian and Taoist values discussed in Munro's anthology, *Individualism and Holism*, loc. cit., it is characteristic that only the moral subject is connected to the person as an individual. In the following passage, the editor approvingly

example, as we have seen above (cf. chapter B.1.8), is the decisive condition for civil society impulses and for a political and cultural 'take-off' of Islam imprisoned in its tradition, namely individuality, is of course only talked away with such defensive-relativist or normative strategies of social theory and cultural anthropology. What is unsatisfactory about this is that these floating images of individuality are again structurally identical to the European philosophy of individuality – but only in the form of their Vulgate, which has long been traded under the title *atomism*.[830] I am therefore not aware of any historical research that has investigated the phenomenon of individuality more carefully and at the same time more convincingly than Christian Meier's *Die Entstehung des Politischen bei den Griechen* [The Origin of the Political in the Greeks]. By contrasting the "ability-consciousness" of individual citizens, characteristic of the antique polis of the 5th century B.C., with the "modern progressive thinking", he does not even find himself in the embarrassment of having to use the concept of the individual. He describes the historical situation in which an Attic small town, which has grown into a world power since the Persian Wars, has to find ways and means to cope with and withstand this enormous change. The decisive role was played by the theatre, in which the citizens of Athens experienced themselves and from the perspective of others (*The Persians* by Aeschylus) as well as their own ability to dispose of orders (*Eumenides*, third part of the *Orestie* of Aeschylus):

"It was no longer a question of whether public (monarchic or aristocratic) order should be or not, and no longer of who holds the rule and how it should be structured in detail. No, now one was wondering what fundamentally different constitutions one wanted to have. Whether the nobility or the demos should rule was the problem;

---

quotes Arthur Danto's contribution, *Philosophical Individualism in Chinese and Western Thought*, in the same volume: "Arthur Danto writes of Immanuel Kant that 'the rational being is perceived as a legislator, but then each legislator, or rational being, enacts only those principles each other legislator would enact upon suitable ratiocination, so that in the end everyone must think alike.' With suitable modification, this conclusion would be affirmed by most Confucians as well." (ibid., p. 15) It is not further insisted here that such a definition of individualism as "in the end everyone must think alike" would do to the here developed theorem of individuality hypostasizing violence.

[830] Cf. Taylor, Charles, *Atomism*, in: Taylor, *Philosophical Papers*, vol. II, Cambridge 1985, pp. 187-210. In this respect, feminist research has not brought any progress either; see Fox-Genovese, Elisabeth, *Feminism without Illusions. A Critique of Individualism*, North Carolina 1991.

whether the governed should be decisively involved in the government... order became completely the object of politics. This is the central realization of the *Eumenides*."[831]

Meier's study has the inestimable advantage of implicitly dealing with the question of individuality and explicitly linking it to the possibility of the political as an individual availability of order ("ability-consciousness") – just as it is necessary for the philosophy of political subjectivity to make it plausible. From here the question of the *minimal cultural conditions for the emergence of political subjectivity* can now be asked.

Part A of the study was based on the extraordinarily complex context of European and in particular German culture in the 18th century, because there was an inviting simultaneous interpretation of individuality, individualistic aesthetics and new practice of publicity. At the same time, it was acknowledged that the same foundations of political subjectivity can also be formed very condensed in historical events and deeds (e.g. the American Revolution), instead of in scholarly treatises and decades of cautious, authoritarian discussions. What is obviously decisive is that a consciousness forms in people that enables them to distinguish themselves from the given order and to imagine this order itself as subjectively available. The basic requirement therefore seems to be that *something, no matter what and in what way, provokes the construction of a field of tension for reflection in the judging subject*, in that the structure of individuality and public order becomes imaginable as distanced and yet coherent. As a rule, one could extrapolate without great danger, the first issue is that the sacrality or dogmatism of transcendental concepts of order, insofar as these are dictatorially determining, is softened or broken up until the practice of faith is hierarchically downgraded to a limited (e.g. private) area of social life or even functionally differentiated into its own, specialized communication system. The ancient Polis had good conditions to offer in this respect, because there was a great tolerance towards the multitude of Near Eastern religions. The trial against Socrates seems to contradict this, but in fact it is only the inglorious exception, because the prosecution would have been formally inadmissible – which Socrates knew very well yet did everything to be sentenced to death.[832]

---

[831] Meier, *Die Entstehung des Politischen*, loc. cit., p. 150; cf. Also Meier, *Die politische Kunst der griechischen Tragödie* [The Political Art of Greek Tragedy], Munich 1988.

[832] The fascinating book by American journalist Isidor F. Stone, *The Trial of Socrates*, 1988, shows a rather cold-blooded and arrogant Socrates, who, seconded by

On the other hand, it follows that these necessary foundations for political subjectivity tend not to be found in archaic forms of human life. The strong congruence of self-image, institutional and transcendental order in segmental societies, such as pre-state tribal societies, makes the construction and stabilization of subjective scope for reflection between individuality and order unlikely.[833] Individuality is an achievement of judgment that can develop in the co-evolution of consciousness and tendentially functionally differentiating social systems. Incidentally, these considerations make it vividly clear that political subjectivity cannot only not be categorized under Habermas' (originally Husserl's) concept of the *lifeworld*, but is complementary to it:

> "The design of a collectively shared homogeneous world is certainly an idealization; but due to their familial, social and mythical structures of consciousness, archaic societies more or less approach this ideal type."[834]

To return to the initial thesis of the digression: If the derivation of political subjectivity from the power of reflecting judgment is well-founded, then

---

other worshippers of Sparta such as his student Plato, leaves no stone unturned in damaging Athenian democracy. The only documented place, by the way, where a law against blasphemy was ever considered in the Polis, is ironically, and yet with subtle subversive consequence, the 10th book of Plato's *Nomoi*.

[833] For example, if Andreas Dörner writes of the "myth as a medium of reflection", then it is the Hermann myth after its destruction that coincides with the defeat of National Socialism. **The strong, unconditional archaic myth is certainly not a medium of reflection, but the opposite: a relief from (or a protection against) reflection.** Dörner, on the other hand, is looking for a kind of political standard mythology that could also function in modern, secularized democracies as an aesthetic-emotional principle of socialization; cf. Dörner. *Politischer Mythos und symbolische Politik. Sinnstiftung durch symbolische Formen am Beispiel des Hermannsmythos* [Political Myth and Symbolic Politics. Creation of Meaning Through Symbolic Forms Using the Example of the Hermann Myth], Opladen 1995.

[834] Habermas, Jürgen, *Theorie des kommunikativen Handelns*, loc. cit., vol. 2, p. 234. This statement does not match the public discussion of the term 'lifeworld', but it does agree with the author's more recent portrayals of it: "The private core areas of the world, which are characterized by intimacy, i.e. protection from publicity, structure encounters between relatives, friends, acquaintances etc. and interlock, at the level of these simple interactions, the life stories of the relatives. The public sphere is complementary to this private sphere from which the public is recruited as the bearer of the publicity." (Habermas, *Faktizität und Geltung* [Truth and Justifikation], Frankfurt 1992, p. 429)

the entire history of political culture must be *formally* inscribed in the *CPJ*. The *content* of the work has already been reviewed in chapter B.1.6 with regard to its political themes and examples. In addition, some illustrations and examples were found in the course of the study which directly followed the Kantian argumentation by testing it against cultural and political-historical facts of modern times up to the present. However, when it comes to a universal formula for determining the emergence of political subjectivity, the concrete examples in the *CPJ* can only be read as traces that must first be connected with one another so that something like the *form* of a general rule can be interpreted from them. With the guidelines of these examples in hand, the excursion therefore leads once again through the labyrinth of Kant's text, where a formal connection between aesthetics, culture, politics and history is sought.

The assessment of beauty maintains an important relationship with nature in more ways than one. Not only that the best examples of beauty can be found in the "outdoors", which are suitable for a critique of aesthetic taste, in which the judgments must always be as pure as possible. Rather, someone's "immediately and certainly intellectual interest in beauty"[835] is at all times the "characteristic of a good soul" and, if this interest is habitual, indicates "at least a mood favorable to moral feeling."[836] In the preceding paragraph Kant deals with the interest in beauty from an empirical point of view and links the philosophical constitution of beauty with flawless ethnological observations, which are of the greatest interest here. In this respect, beauty is an "original" ability to communicate emotions, ...

> ".... and thus, at first to be sure only charms, e.g., colors for painting oneself (roucou among the Caribs and cinnabar among the Iroquois), or flowers, mussel shells, beautifully colored birds' feathers, but with time also beautiful forms (as on canoes, clothes, etc.) that do not in themselves provide any gratification, i.e., satisfaction of enjoyment, become important in society and combined with great interest, until finally civilization that has reached the highest point makes of this almost the chief work of refined inclination, and sensations have value only to the extent that they may be universally communicated;..."[837]

The empirical, indirect interest in beauty is thus determined by an "inclination towards society" (ibid.). Thus, there is an – albeit "only very

---

[835] *CPJ*, B 167 [179].
[836] *CPJ*, B 166 [178].
[837] *CPJ*, B 164-5 [177].

ambiguous [–] transition from the pleasant to the good."[838] Once this transition is entered, however, nature loses its *constitutive* function for the judgment of taste, as soon as it has begun to point out man's moral feeling, and becomes an *optional* but still particularly suitable *example* among many for the assessment of beauty in its purity. This historical distancing of nature in beauty, which in itself is very considerate, is described much more radically in the feeling of the sublime. This reflecting capacity is not suitable for anything else but to form the first resistance against "raw nature" and finally to overcome it. It is, through the imagination as a tool of reason and its ideas, "a power to assert our independence in the face of the influences of nature."[839] Included in this are the gods, who are thought in the feeling of the dynamic and sublime as the will of this threatening nature. Only the sublime forms the necessary resistance to overcome the *fear* of these gods and the enormous monuments of their destructive power in nature, the "upheaval of oceans", "monuments of ancient, powerful devastations", "eruptions both fiery and watery" and "fossils."[840] In the feeling of the sublime, humanity remains 'un-humiliated', as Kant writes, in the person, although it is exposed to the superior power of the gods and nature. At another point Kant periodizes the history of reason by describing *fear* and *anxiety* as the oldest origin of the diversity of gods and demons, which was broken with the *awareness of moral principles* – and here it should be inserted: by means of the feeling of the sublime and beautiful – which, after a long period of polytheism, finally also produced the concept of a unified God.[841] But the historically "earliest germination of human reason" lies unambiguously in the moral feeling that has become apparent before all teleological observation of nature: "As soon as human beings began to reflect on right and wrong, at a time when they still indifferently overlooked the purposiveness of nature,..." it could no longer be the same whether someone lies or tells the truth, whether someone behaves violently or peacefully. "It is as if they heard an inner voice that things must come out differently."[842] These early people, about whom Kant speculates here, still had the greatest difficulties to think together the unmanageable diversity of nature with the inner moral law without resorting to a supreme cause of the world:

---

[838] *CPJ*, B 165 [177].
[839] *CPJ*, B 118 [152].
[840] *CPJ*, B 385 [295-6].
[841] *CPJ*, B 418 [312].
[842] *CPJ*, B 438 [316].

"Now they could have hatched up a lot of nonsense about the inner constitution of that world-cause, but that moral relation in the government of the world always remained the same, universally comprehensible for the most uncultivated reason as soon as it considers itself as practical even though speculative reason is far from being able to stay in step with it."[843]

This means that **practical reason has always been faster, more thorough and simpler than speculative reason**. This points to a *primacy of practical reason* that has also been demonstrated in cultural history. Kant thus claims nothing less than that the *fact of reason* occurs first in the reflection on right and wrong. When teleological research of nature then began, the ideas created by pure practical reason found "incidental confirmation from natural ends."[844] So the history of reason is written from its dialectics. That's where it was trapped most of the time. It could not penetrate appearances, was limited to its primary, practical and reflecting operations and could not use the theoretical understanding. Only since recent science, especially mathematical-experimental physics since Galileo and Newton, succeeded in bringing nature itself before Kant's famous *Court of Reason*, only in this new epoch of the history of pure reason could the fundamental *formal* coexistence of the knowledge of nature and morality be proven[845] – in two books written by a certain Immanuel Kant, in the *Critique of Pure Reason* and in the *Critique of Practical Reason*!

On the one hand, this far-reaching discussion serves to demonstrate Kant's willingness to historically situate the individual faculties of thought, namely understanding, reason and aesthetic as well as teleological judgment.[846] By the way, he has kept a promise here that he had made in

---

[843] *CPJ*, B 439 [323].

[844] *CPJ*, B 415 [311].

[845] This formal unity of law of nature and morality exists only in the *form of the law*, which is used by practical reason just as by the theoretical understanding – with two essential differences, namely 1.) the spontaneity of the will to be bound by law (instead of the receptivity of pure sensuality) and 2.) the causality of freedom (instead of causality of nature): "If the maxim of the action is not so constituted as to stand the test against the *form of a natural law* in general, then it is morally impossible [...]. Hence using the nature of the world of sense as the type of an intelligible nature is also permitted, so long as I do not transfer to the latter any intuitions and what depends on them but refer to it merely the *form of lawfulness* as such." (*CPraRe*, A 124 [92])

[846] Of course, this has not only been the subject of the *CPJ* but appears in almost all

the last chapter of the *CPuRe* on the *History of Pure Reason*: "This title stands only here to designate a place that is left open in the system and must be filled in the future."[847] Another motive of this digression, however, refers directly to the above agreed search for a rule for the emergence of political subjectivity in the historical traces of the *CPJ*. To this end, the chronology of the individual faculties must be re-examined.

The origin of all judgment lies in the – however darkly thought – ideas of *reason*, especially freedom, which points to a moral ability that can be felt. Only this reason as practical faculty calls the reflecting power of judgment on the plan to form a common reason for the transition to nature assessment. According to Kant, the feeling of the *sublime* is entitled to the rank of the oldest child of practical reason, because only this feeling makes it possible to form from the 'negative pleasure' of the terror of nature a positive idea of an 'un-humiliated' counter-power embodied in man. Beauty in nature can only be experienced after this self-perception of the subject as a *citizen of a second nature*, for only in this distanced peace can the lack of interest and contemplation necessary for beauty be realized, whereby the harmony of moral and spatiotemporal nature and laws can become the object of admiration.[848] *Teleology* has already been effective in all this, because from the beginning it has been about ends and their connections up to the highest end of the world.[849] But it enjoys its greatest

---

texts of the critical phase, such as in *Metaphysical Foundations of Natural Science* or in *Anthropology in Pragmatic Perspective*.

[847] *CPuRe* B 880 [702].

[848] Cf. *CPJ* B 111-2 [149]; also here chapter B.1.7.2.2 on the symbolic hypotyposis of morality in natural beauty.

[849] "Teleology considers nature as a kingdom of ends, morality a possible kingdom of ends as a kingdom of nature." (Kant, Immanuel *Grundlegung zur Metaphysik der Sitten* [Groundwork of the Metaphysics of Morals], Werke VII, BA 81 [70]) This could now be followed by a further discussion of one of the greatest problems of the interpretation of Kant's philosophy, namely the nature of the 'fact of reason'. The primacy of practical reason is obviously also historically situated, namely as an *original ability to judge reasonably at all*. Through the spontaneity of will, practical reason has an extraordinary advantage over the theoretically judging understanding in that it is not dependent on the receptive forms of intuition to construct a nature according to laws in space and time but can nevertheless strive for the categories of mind. The special nature of which practical reason is capable, namely the intelligibly, i.e. moral nature, it can build up and make arise without any help and completely on its own – as a realm of ends, i.e. as a system of future causes that have their effects against the chronology in the past. From a cultural-historical point of view, this only refers

reputation in the time in which many legal systems already existed, the existence of God according to his revelations should also be proved from the very *concept* of such a perfect being and empirical research into nature had assumed systematic traits by means of a teleological heuristics.[850]

The narrowing down of purposiveness of nature and a moral realm of ends under a single world creator was still on the path of sensualistic or idealistic analogies[851], but it cannot be overlooked to what extent nature was increasingly distanced and made a *mirror of the subject*.[852] The next step, namely the discovery of the understanding as a principle of the lawfulness of nature a priori, was experienced by Kant as a Copernican turn and a "revolution of the way of thinking," which was only comparable with Aristotle's foundation of logic and the "happy idea of a single man,"

---

to the gap between the first legal concepts and systems of world history and the age when it was recognized that mathematics can be applied to nature. Here, too, Dieter Henrich has acted as an 'obfuscater' of the Kantian text, for he has reinterpreted his own lack of understanding of the concept of ends as another ambiguity of the *CPJ*: "Although Kant argued that these usages point to the notion of a final end, he could hardly overlook the need for an account of the source from which this notion is generated. It can, to be sure, emerge only within the moral context. But in precisely what way? Kant doesn't address this question in the Critique of Judgment." ("*The Moral Image of the World*, in: Henrich, *Aesthetic Judgment and the Moral Image of the World*, Stanford 1992, p. 27)

[850] Especially since the founding of empirical sciences by Aristotle, which for Kant belongs to an epoch before the decisive new revolutions of exact science and world-exploring (in contrast to Aristotle's logic, which itself represents one of these revolutions!); Kant's laconic remark: "To be sure, we no longer detect any noticeable pleasure in the comprehensibility of nature and the unity of its division into genera and species, by means of which alone empirical concepts are possible through which we cognize it in its particular laws; but it must certainly have been there in its time, and only because the most common experience would not be possible without it has it gradually become mixed up with mere cognition and is no longer specially noticed." (*CPJ* B XL [p. 74])

[851] Cf. *CPuRe* B 881 [702].

[852] Richard Rorty's voluminous farewell letter to academic philosophy is very stimulating and instructive in this respect. But one clearly notices where the metaphor of the mirror is no longer useful as an instrument for exposing metaphysical dreams and self-deceptions: with Kant. Rorty also succeeds in completely overlooking what great philosophical and scientific achievements have been made possible by this way of distancing oneself from nature. The problem is certainly not that he does not know these achievements; cf. Rorty, *Philosophy and the Mirror of Nature*, 1979.

namely (allegedly) Thales, of whom Diogenes Laertios reported that a light had risen in him in the construction of an equilateral triangle. This man was the first to realize that all mathematical (and geometric) propositions are synthetic and a priori, thus apodictic. What Thales had achieved for mathematics and the great natural scientists Galilei, Bacon and Newton for experimental physics, Kant wanted to achieve for philosophy in order to inaugurate a new epoch of science and philosophy, namely "the end of infinite errors."[853] From this moment on, the subject of reason had not only come into the full possession of its own understanding for the first time, but the relationship to nature had completely changed: for the first time the natural scientists had understood that reason...

> "... it must take the lead with principles for its judgments according to constant laws and *compel nature to answer its questions*, rather than letting nature guide its movements by keeping reason, as it were, in leading-strings."[854]

In contrast, Galileo's famous sentences "God created everything by number, weight and measure" or "The Book of Nature is written in the language of mathematics"[855] were almost cautious and pedagogical; but for him the aim was the same: "rifare i cervelli degli uomini", to make over the brains of humans. One could now think that the up-and-coming movement of the subject of reason in world history – from its birth from the mighty *womb of nature* into the reflecting position of a *mirror* and finally into the superior position of *judge* – would already be completed. If that was true, then the Western history of thought really would not be much more than a metaphysics of the subject, which inevitably makes everything, including itself, into a 'framework' [*Gestell*], as Heidegger insistently called the essence of technology.[856] For it is undisputed that this subject is jointly responsible for the devastation of the planet and for its still threatening nuclear or ecological destruction.

Overall, however, this summary underestimates the Kant's critical philosophy, the abilities of rational beings and these beings themselves as individuals explored in it – and not only because there have been earth-

---

[853] Kant's motto taken from Bacon's *Instauratio magna, CPuRe,* B II [91].

[854] *CPuRe,* B XIV [109].

[855] Galilei, Galileo, *Saggiatore IV,* 52 and VI, 232.

[856] Heidegger, Martin, *Die Frage nach der Technik* [The Question of Technology], in: Heidegger, *Vorlesungen und Essays* [Lectures and Essays], Pfullingen 1954, 4th ed. 1978.

shattering events that could give cause for hope in the meantime. **My thesis is that the emancipation of the subject from nature is not finished with the discovery of the nature-constituting understanding, for at the same time a** *separation of a completely different kind from nature* **has taken place, namely in the form of the emergence of political subjectivity.** The political triad described in Part A coincides approximately with the scientific revolutions and there is no doubt that these scientific insights into nature and its principles had repercussions on the social and cultural conditions of political subjectivity. However, it would be a mistake to see the discovery of the various natural mechanisms (from the chemical elements and their reactions to the mechanics of the celestial bodies, e.g. the formation of spiral galaxies, which Kant was the first to recognize) as the real reason for the emergence of political judgment in individuals. The separation from nature, which enables political judgment in reflection, is not necessarily of the kind that Kant characterized in his second preface to the *CPuRe* as the authority of the judicial subject over the nature to be heard (which in all cases is violated in the process[857]). This would only be the consequence of the separation of the epistemic subject of pure reason from nature until it itself determines what and how nature has to be. The peculiarity of the European Enlightenment is rather that pure, speculative reason and political judgment take their respective places in history at the same time. We have seen that the emergence of an 'ability-consciousness' among the Greeks was determined by a historical constellation that had nothing to do with a scientific revolution, yet undoubtedly ushered in a cultural epoch of political subjectivity. In the Athenian polis, the chronology of Kant's history of reason can even be clearly reversed in relation to the emergence of political subjectivity: *at first the Greeks discovered the political, and only then logic, science and knowledge of nature.* Even Socrates would probably have been inconceivable anywhere in the world except in this extraordinary political community, for which he went to war, as was his duty, but otherwise showed no sympathy. In one single respect Plato was certainly a committed fighter for the political, albeit in a metaphysical-dogmatic version: he wanted to purify all ideas about the public order of the community from the last traces of the nature-religious myth, to emancipate it from sensually-teleologically understood nature and to lead it to ideality. Essential for our purposes here is the observation that the overcoming of nature in the understanding of political subjectivity is not

---

[857] This already happens when nature is forced to fulfil people's ideas of end in the form of houses, ships and clocks; cf. *CPuRe* B 654 [580-581].

identical with the achievement of that uniform transcendental subjectivity that can actually "uncoveringly" [Heidegger's "entbergend"] turn everything into the ontological 'framework' [which is equated by Heidegger to the 'maximum forgetfulness of being']. For the subject of the political is always an individual that has perceived itself in an aesthetic-teleological, i.e. in a reflecting way and has recognized the order of external nature as something separate from itself. Kant was, long before he could classify the achievements of the great scientists as a Copernican turn, seized by this other, actually not at all silent revolution, for it had finally induced him to discover a reflecting judgment in himself, whereby the *citizen* Immanuel Kant could resurrect from the *subject* or even *serf* in his person.[858] Only as such could he even think that as an individual he had the ability and even a certain cause to put up for discussion in public some sort of alternative concepts of order regarding the coexistence of all people in one state or all over the world. Obviously, he had an idea that the existing social, economic and legal order was only one of many possible; above all, however, he still believed to have in mind exactly which order in his opinion should be (bourgeois-republican[859]). He had long since shared this faculty, namely that of the *subjective genesis of order*, but it took an thorough and complicated reading of the *Criticism of the Power of Judgment* to find the form and the composition of judgment required for this achievement. This reading was presented here in chapter B.1.4, and it turned out that the teleological judgment provides all functions for the subjective (later also called syntactical) tension between self-perception and public order. We have also just seen here that this faculty cannot by far be assumed to be activated and realized in all people, at any time in history and at any place on the planet. The formal rule for the historically contingent emergence of political subjectivity can therefore now be determined: **The teleological structure of subject and natural order in the reflecting judgment must be broken up in such a way that the subject becomes aware of the optionality of this order in dependence on its own reflected states (opinions), whereby it simultaneously individuates itself.** The natural order pre-

---

[858] Willi Goetschel describes this convincingly on the level of literary activity in *Constituting Critique. Kant's Writing as Critical Praxis*, Durham and London 1994. This is an unusual interpretation because, among other things, it elaborates the political character of the *Critique ofPure Reason* very vividly – with a clear reference to Kant's efforts to constitute himself as a literary-political subject, and thus as an individual.

[859] Nowhere is this more clearly stated than in *Zum Ewigen Frieden* [On Eternal Peace], loc. cit., Werke XI, pp. 193-251.

viously thought to be stable and objective can be shaken by various events and made accessible to the construction of the syntactic field of tension between individuality and subjective order, for example through *natural disasters, wars* (Greek polis)[860], *colonization, crises of faith* and *new insights into nature* (European Enlightenment). Nature, which previously corresponded to the idea of an objective order, thus changed sides to a certain extent and is suddenly available to political judgment as a transcendental principle of nature in an individualized consciousness (cf. chapter B.1.4). The 'old nature', the *natura naturans*, therefore naturally continues to exist, but its reflecting value has migrated into the subject and has made it an individual.[861] Dieter Claessens, a sociologist who has long concerned him-

---

[860] One recalls Ludwig Tieck's invocation of the Greeks in the storm of the French Revolutionary Wars; here cited in chapter A 1.6. Cf. also Meier, Christian, *Die Rolle des Krieges im klassischen Athen* [The Role of War in Classic Athens], in: Historische Zeitschrift 251/1990, pp.555-605.

[861] This observation in Kant's work of an unavoidable cultural-historical *retreat of nature as a representation and idea of the predominant objectivity into reflection* has to my knowledge not yet been specifically worked out by anyone. Nothing like this can be found in the relevant literature; cf. for example Böhme, Gernot, *Geschichte der Natur* [History of Nature], in: Böhme, *Philosophieren mit Kant. Zur Rekonstruktion der Kantischen Erkenntnis- und Wissenschaftstheorie* [Philosophizing with Kant. On the Reconstruction of Kant's Theory of Cognition and Science], Frankfurt 1986, p. 34-41; Lepenies, Wolf, *Das Ende der Naturgeschichte* [The End of Natural History], Munich 1976; Wolters, Gereon, *Immanuel Kant*, in: Böhme, Gernot (ed.), *Klassiker der Naturphilosophie. Von den Vorsokratikern bis zu Kopenhagener Schule* [Classics of Natural Philosophy. From the Pre-Socratic to the Copenhagen School], Munich 1989, pp. 203-219. In his scholarly and exciting book, which also deals with Kant, Lepenies discusses his topic only from the side of the history and sociology of positive natural and historical sciences but does not seek the philosophical foundation that he could also have found in Kant. The Böhme brothers' great enterprise of developing an aesthetic of nature that makes nature itself appear, i.e. of securing a share in the action of its own revelation, is purposefully repulsing itself from the subject philosophy. Above all, they try to overcome the natural aesthetics of the *CPJ* in the form of its reconstruction through the very precise book by Martin Seel, *Eine Ästhetik der Natur* [An Aesthetics of Nature] Frankfurt 1991. They rightly reproach Seel for presenting a temporally static, synchronic model of natural aesthetics and thus ignoring the essential questions of emergence, natural and cultural evolution. But they are mistaken in implying this lack of diachrony and evolutionary awareness of the *CPJ* itself, as has been shown here. Paradoxically, in order to escape the consequences of their rejection of subject-philosophical references, their well-meant, "listening" natural aesthetics is transformed into a *radical anthropomorphic nature or ontotheology* underhand. It illogically ascribes nature

self with 'hominization', writes about it:

"The unemotional treatment of worldly things for transformation into tools and the use of tools to create nature, only to get rid of the old imposing nature, the discovery that the creation becomes independent (one talks to it while carving, curses it, makes friends with it, mourns its loss), the discovery that it is something confronting, this central capacity for experience that came about with the relief of the old nature through these tools, all this is indifferent alienation: the prize for the chance to humanity."[862]

At one single point in the *CPJ* one could think that Kant had sensed the possibility of such a modified and the disposability of nature (subjectively) radicalizing reading of the *CPJ*, which points to its own political faculty. There, in the penultimate paragraph of the *Critique of Aesthetic Judgment*, he prophesies the end of the direct relationship with nature and warns that its patterns are at least remembered by the intelligent analogy, the moral ideas and the moral feeling:

"With difficulty will a later age dispense with that model, because it will always be further from nature, and ultimately, without having enduring examples of it, will hardly be in a position to form a concept of the happy union of the lawful constraint of the highest culture with the force and correctness of a free nature, feeling its own worth, in one and the same people."[863]

---

the "silence" of an offended and maltreated being, so that *it cannot be claimed that nature is in fact the subject of its actions* and has probably initiated its own retreat with the help of man as one of its beings in a planned manner and appointed him as heir by speaking through him. The whole effort of the Boehme brothers bears the imprint of an ontological basic conviction of man as "shepherd of being", as Heideggger developed it in the *Letter on Humanism*: Man as an agent, a thrown one, who may see his dignity in the preservation of the truth of being; a passage of being, which wants to become visible to itself; cf. Böhme, Hartmut, *Aussichten einer ästhetischen Theorie der Natur* [Outlook to an Aesthetic Theory of Nature], in: Haberl, Horst Gerhard et. Al. (ed.), *Entdecken/Verdecken. Eine Nomadologie der Neunziger*, Graz 1991, pp. 15-34; cf. also Seel's critical comment on the enterprise of the Böhme brothers in Seel, *Ästhetik der Natur*, loc. Cit., S. 128-132.

[862] Claessens, Dieter, *Nova Natura. Anthropologische Grundlagen modernen Denkens* [Nova Natura. Anthropological Foundations of Modern Thought], Düsseldorf 1970, p. 19.

[863] *CPJ*, B 263 [230].

The patterns that we have received from the sensually experienceable nature were formed, for example, by the feeling of beauty and sublimity. Where is the sublime of this kind today? Where can we still experience nature as a real power or as a greatness that makes us feel a negative desire, when we go to the summit of the four-thousand-meter peak with the underground 'Metro-Alpin' (in Saas-Fee, Switzerland) on our ski holiday and relax in the evening in front of the TV at *K2 – The Last Adventure*? The occasional observation of everyday culture (science fiction, children's toys, computer games, American cinema) provides interesting information. The feeling of the sublime seeks space and the distant future (*Star Trek* including all future generations: *Next Generation*; *Deep Space Nine*; *Voyager*), the deep sea (*Seaquest DSV*, soon to be *The Swarm*, based on the novel of the same name by Frank Schätzing) and the archaic past in the present (*Highländer* or *Jurassic Park*) as well as the frequent presence of organic monsters (from *King Kong* to *Godzilla* to *Alien(s)*) in each of these dimensions.[864] It is precisely such areas and experiences of life that we can only imagine and from which, for the time being, no disappointments or even the enlightenment of our fantasies of greatness, power and violence threaten to have a retroactive effect. The sensually experienceable nature on Earth is so far deprived and exhausted that it becomes more and more the most urgent political program to save it. Nature has become an object of everyday politics and even elected representatives sit in our parliaments to represent its interests (which for some of them are not necessarily those of the people). A monstrous thought in the truest sense of the word against the background of the overcome, formerly objective ideas of natural order, which was at the same time also the social order! Meanwhile, nature is only an interest dependent on legal and political representation, which has

---

[864] Mechanical beings are not included here because they are not natural phenomena. But it is precisely in James Camron's *Terminator II* that one can study where the future of the sublime lies: in the *power of machines*. This fabulously successful film, which was watched by millions of spectators all over the planet, presents the last step of forgetting nature with the liquid metal robot of the T 2000 series, because this machine was designed by machines themselves. The reflecting judgment is obviously very receptive to this idea: in the face of the violence of mega-machines, all the power of nature is nothing. These include the synthetic natures generated by computers, such as cyberspace, whose reality is not yet particularly exciting because today's computers only support a few truly interactive applications due to their lack of capacity. But it is probably only a matter of a few years before these technical hurdles are overcome. The feature film has already reached this stage, namely with *Matrix* [this was my take on this subject in 1996 and then again in 2006]

to rank among the many other particular interests in everyday democratic pluralism. Today, individuals must *come to the aid of nature* in a political way, i.e. convincingly declare the remains of nature as a part of their desired public order worth preserving before the assembly of all (represented) individual concepts of order. One could also describe the political sense of ecology with regard to this cultural anthropological evolution as an *active memory and recognition of a nature discarded, forgotten and left outside by reflection*. The political capacity of the individuals can therefore be a corrective to the 'framework'[865], even if this political action of the individuals can never bring nature back into the intimate relationship that we still maintained with it in the age of myth and cults. Similarly, with reference to reflecting judgment and animal welfare, it has been expressed by Luc Ferry in an inspired essay in which he attacks the dogmatic-hypostatic and antipolitical claims of 'deep ecology', ecofeminism and radical utilitarianism (Peter Singer et al.):

> "Between the 'let-be', the Heideggerian serenity and the imperious 'civilizing' action of the Cartesians, we need a synthetic concept. Is the limited respect that we owe to animals, far from being inscribed in nature, far from being obeyed by civilization, in this sense a matter of *politeness* and *civility*?"[866]

These thoughts, that one could make friends with nature or make it a contractual part of the order of civil society (e.g. as a constitutional determination as state objectives), cannot be grasped at all, unlike under the leadership of the new faculty of political subjectivity. As long as the fabric of the grossly mistreated nature does not rip, as long as its forgotten violence does not suddenly resurface – for example as the collapse of the climate system predicted by climate researchers for a long time – individu-

---

[865] Instead of art, as the late Heidegger imagined the encounter with the ambivalent nature of technology. The early Heidegger saw this hope of a planetary containment of technology in National Socialism.

[866] Ferry, Luc, *Le nouvel ordre écologique. L'arbre, l'animal et l'homme* [The New Ecological Order. The Tree, the Animal and Man], Paris 1992, p. 128. The most important concern of Ferry in this essay can also be found in Martin Seel's subject-theoretical natural aesthetics: "The recognition of nature as a subject is the false recognition of nature." (Seel, *Ästhetik der Natur*, loc. cit., p. 366). An example of the opposite position: Holland-Cunz, Barbara, *Soziales Subjekt Natur. Natur und Geschlechterverhältnis in emanzipatorischen politischen Theorien* [Social Subject Nature. Nature and Gender Relations in Emancipatory Political Theories], Frankfurt 1994.

als have just as long to use their judgment in favor of a civilized handling of nature. Sceptics like Niklas Luhmann believe that this "ecological communication" can only take place very slowly in order not to completely deregulate society in its multitude of functional systems – which implicitly also denotes the contingency of an ecological dictatorship.[867] But the real miracle is, however, as much time as it takes for nature to behave in such a way that it can even become a part of the society of individuals.

---

[867] Luhmann sees a small chance of successfully introducing ecological communication in the educational system and in the New Social Movements. This gives the other functional systems time to organise adaptation; cf. Luhmann, Niklas, *Ökologische Kommunikation. Kann die moderne Gesellschaft sich auf ökologische Gefährdungen einstellen?* [Ecological Communication. Can Modern Society Adapt to Ecological Hazards?], Opladen 1988.

B.3 Connecting Points for the Philosophy of Political Subjectivity

As already mentioned, new philosophical approaches are generally recommended purely as such and without reference to their possible applications, unless cursory. In order to counteract the fact that such a multitude of theoretical and empirical-social-scientific consequences, which apparently emerge from the investigation of political subjectivity, are not taken into consideration because of the complexity of their philosophical origin, some offers for the continuation and completion of the approach are made in the following. The chapter on charisma (B.2.1.1-2) was to some extent an anticipation of these offers, in which the main features of the operationalization of the philosophical concept were demonstrated using a suitable subject as an example.

B.3.1 Systems and Discourse Theory

In the foreword it was mentioned that the present study of the foundations of political subjectivity should not be burdened with the demands and limitations by Luhmann's systems theory and Habermas' theory of discourse.[868] Nevertheless, a reasonable demand was to compare this analysis of basic political concepts, which was trained in Kant's idealism, with the previously common epistemologies of the social sciences, which already happened here in *Excursusus II* in order not to make the transcendental-philosophical approach come under suspicion of normative and ontological reciprocity. It is also certain that the concept of political subjectivity cannot make a decisive contribution to the theoretical buildings of systems and discourse theory as such. This explains why these two great and enormously fruitful social theories could not at any point become the subject of a thorough criticism, for from the standpoint of political subjectivity there are no objections to the reconstruction of the concept of communication from a functionalist or linguistic-pragmatic perspective. Therefore, no direct application is recommended in this first section, but it

---

[868] This did not mean that the findings of the two theories would not be taken into account. On the contrary: Only the discourse-centered and systems-theoretical concepts of society and communication have made an appropriate narrowing of the theorem of political subjectivity possible.

should only be pointed out that the philosophy of political subjectivity developed here seems to be a **suitable complement to systems and discourse theory** – which, conversely, of course, also means that *they* are a systematic completion of the philosophy of political subjectivity with regard to the *overall possible perspectives in which reality can be conceptually grasped*. In the concepts of political subjectivity, therefore, what falls out of the sociological as well as the normative-linguistic perspective on communication can be addressed and yet fills the intuition of everyday understanding: **the obstinate self-experience as an individual and political being.**

In Habermas' theory of discourse, the communication event only begins in the material of intersubjectively divided language, whereby this does not become theoretically relevant in its entire spectrum of meaning, but only according to the claims of validity conveyed in it. This building material is used to construct a conceptual successor for what used to be called 'practical reason'. However, one judges the success of this great enterprise, it is at least clear that this kind of intersubjective discourse theory tries to reconstruct the possibility of moral communication after the so-called linguistic turn, but only, among other things, lectures on the political phenomena. Genuine lifeworldly understanding under the linguistically immanent ideal of domination-free communication should provide the basic material for much more than just political action. It is intended to keep in reserve the entire rationality through which any form of social system formation (e.g. law) becomes possible. Thus, the political is not only in no way specifically determined by communication theory and instead conventionally assumed, but the normative content, whose linguistic pragmatic possibility and reality is to be proven, is accommodated only in the political, among other things. An overlapping of discourse theory and political subjectivity therefore only exists in the area where – in the words of the present concept – normative contents are communicated politically, or, as stated in chapter B.1.8, where *the determining judgment rides on the back of the reflecting judgment into the public sphere*. Otherwise, the framework of the theory of communicative action is much larger than the political philosophy of reflectively judging consciousness presented here, for it still claims to be a general theory of social integration and system formation – from which the philosophy of political subjectivity is far removed.[869]

---

[869] On the traits of Habermas' theory described here see in particular *Faktizität und Geltung* [Truth and Justification], Frankfurt 1992.

The rejection of any kind of philosophy of subject or consciousness is absolute and categorical at Habermas. Surprisingly, a series of transitions between consciousness (reflection) and communication (functional social systems) can be found in systems theory, which Luhmann has left open, but without working them out and making them solid. That would be the task of philosophy, as he has rightly pointed out several times. The hypostases of identity philosophy discussed in *Excursus I* (chapter B.1.9) and Luhmann's rather cautious-pragmatic objections against it, which nowhere really slammed the door, suggest that from the point of view of this theory there may be possibilities of mediation between social systems and consciousness; although it is always clear that the border nevertheless remains clearly drawn between the spheres. In his work, Luhmann deals in great detail with both the concept of individuality[870] and the concept of the public.[871] Both are constitutive for the philosophy of political subjectivity. It has already been pointed out that the exclusion of subjects (by which Luhmann means psychological systems) from the theory of society provides a pragmatic answer to a tradition of aporias of sociological theory formation that goes back more than one hundred years. Luhmann and many others regard it as an exhausted and unsuccessful approach to start the analysis of society from the consciousness of an epistemic, moral or psychological subject. Nevertheless, the systems-theoretical reconstruction of individualism as the 'semantics' of modern society is close to the heart of all sociological functionalism, for it puts systems theory to the test. A

---

[870] Luhmann, Niklas, *Soziale Systeme*, loc. cit., the chapters *Interpenetration* (ibid., p. 286-345) and *Die Individualität psychischer Systeme* [The Individuality of Psychic Systems] (ibid., p. 346-376); cf. Luhmann, *Individuum, Individualität, Individualismus*, in: Luhmann, *Gesellschaftsstruktur und Semantik*, loc. cit., vol. 3, p. 149-258.

[871] Luhmann, Niklas, *Öffentliche Meinung* [Public Opinion], in: Luhmann, *Politische Planung* [Political Planning], Opladen 1971, pp. 9-34; Luhmann, *Gesellschaftliche Komplexität und öffentliche Meinung* [Social Complexity and Public Opinion], in: Luhmann, *Soziologische Aufklärung 5. Konstruktivistische Perspektiven*, Opladen 1990, pp. 170-182; Luhmann, *Veränderungen im System gesellschaftlicher Kommunikation und die Massenmedien* [Changes in the System of Social Communication and the Mass Media], in: Luhmann, *Soziologische Aufklärung 3*, Opladen 1981; Luhmann, *Die Beobachtung der Beobachter im politischen System: Zur Theorie der öffentlichen Meinung* [The Observer of the Observer in the Political System. On the Theory of Public Opinion], in: Willke, Jürgen (ed.), *Öffentliche Meinung. Theorien, Methoden, Befunde. Beiträge zu Ehren von Elisabeth Noelle-Neumann*, Opladen 1992, pp. 77-86; ders., *Die Wirklichkeit der Massenmedien*, Opladen 1996; Luhmann, *Öffentliche Meinung* [Public Opinion], in: Luhmann, *Die Politik der Gesellschaft* [The Politics of Society], Frankfurt 2000, pp. 274-318.

theory of communication that could not process this phenomenon, be it as an artifact, as systems theory does it, or as a condition of this communication, would simply be useless. Political subjectivity means a reversal of the question of systems theory and is therefore on the side of individuality as a condition of political communication.[872] Of course, this does not mean that the whole systems theory is 'turned upside down' or 'on its feet' in a pretentious manner. There must be no doubt that functional-structural systems theory according to Niklas Luhmann also has a much more extensive and more general theoretical format that is richer in consequences than everything presented here under the name political subjectivity. It is the most complex and at the same time most explanatory universal communication theory there is, and it will undoubtedly play an important role in the social sciences and thus also in political science in the future. For good reason, because for the first time a theorist has laid out and expanded his methodological foundation so deeply that the concepts in which the laws and phenomena of social communication are reconstructed systematically build on and refer to one another. It is only a matter of time before this very complex theory, which is dependent on extremely intensive learning work, is generally mastered and assumed by an entire generation of social scientists.[873] Such a 'soft' social science discipline as political science, in which there have been no reliable terminological conventions to date, let alone common methodological approaches or even a thoroughly related theory of reflection on the subject or the discipline, will have nothing to oppose the pressure of such a *nomothetically* proceeding social theory except its helpless reference to 'pluralism of methods', 'interdisciplinarity' etc. Political scientists had no other choice than to work *ideographically* in a bad sense because of the framework of conditions that have existed since the discipline was invented (this is no different in Germany than in the

---

[872] I see the most interesting opening to subject-philosophical questions such as this one in Luhmann's model of the 'interpenetration' of systems, with which the co-evolution of consciousness and communication can be reconstructed; cf. Luhmann, *Soziale Systeme*, loc. cit., pp. 286-345: cf. also here *Excursus I*, chapter B.1.9. That consciousness is also organized as a self-referential autopoetic system was not disputed here at any point, but rather confirmed and emphasized.

[873] The appropriate didactic resources for this are now being made available. In addition to the increasingly better and more comprehensible introductions to Luhmann's work, there is now also a handbook on conceptual navigation in the cosmos of systems theory; see Baraldi, Claudio u. Corsi, Giancarlo u. Esposito, Elena, *GLU. Glossar zu Niklas Luhmanns Theorie sozialer Systeme* [GLU. Glossary on Niklas Luhmann's Theory of Social Systems], Frankfurt 1996.

USA), namely insofar as their science could generally only be the *learned appearance of their respective individual political opinions*.

The basic lines of a philosophy of political subjectivity presented here are intended to remedy precisely this shortcoming. It is a theory of reflection for the subject that can finally answer the intrusive and irrefutable question of "What is political?" in a satisfactory manner and at the same time reassures political science as an epistemologically autonomous enterprise. This is now protected from the takeover bids negotiated at theory exchanges by the various social theories, which not only cooperate in often welcome ways in the interests of political science, but also always form real competition in the system of sciences in epistemic and social terms.[874] **The result of the investigation on political subjectivity can rightly be regarded as the political science complement to sociological systems theory.** Here, the topoi and concepts are intercepted which until now had to be feared that systems theory would undermine and kidnap them with its functionalist method[875], and provide them with their own, philosophically founded legitimation. I am so confident that I dare to claim: **The foundation of the political in the subject is now exposed and there is no longer any possibility of contesting the responsibility of political science for this piece of world (reflection and reality) with good prospects.**

B.3.2 Political Psychology and Cognition

In the introduction it was already pointed out that there is indeed a *similarity between political subjectivity and political individual psychology* – with the essential difference that political subjectivity only examines *judgments* and *reconstructs the generation of their forms*. Overall, political psychology as a sub-discipline of political science is mainly located in the

---

[874] The first two decades of political science in Germany are just an example. In a long series of conferences of specialists, principals and ministry officials, all social sciences and the humanities called for the *dissolution of political science*, which was regarded as an imposition of the victorious powers for 're-education' at universities.

[875] Robert Spaemann formulated this most clearly in his laudation for the Hegel Prize winner in 1989; see Spaemann, *Niklas Luhmanns Herausforderung der Philosophie* [Niklas Luhmann's Challenge of Philosophy], in: Luhmann, Niklas, *Paradigm Lost: Über die ethische Reflexion der Moral* [Paradigm Lost. On the Ethical Reflection of Morals], Frankfurt 1990, p. 62.

U.S. However, skepticism about the viability of 'personality studies' and 'social cognition' to date, which in Germany is partly based on ideology-critical reasons, is also repeatedly voiced in the U.S. because of the methodological weaknesses.[876] The basic assumption of an individual or collective unconscious in the sense of psychoanalysis, the simple aggregation of empirical observations with the following extrapolating derivation of rule, the focus on 'political leaders', the neglect of the systemic conditionality of political action and the overestimation of its scope – these unfavorable circumstances are the reasons for the reluctance towards the psychological approach. Why go to all this trouble if such research can at best report what every interested observer with common sense perceives anyway or predicts with greater subjective certainty of judgment?

However, there are now efforts to compile the theoretical instruments for a more complex and cognitive approach. Gerhard Vowe, who sees the solution of psychological problems in a theory of political cognition, writes:

"I will try to show that it is analytically fruitful to systematically link the political with the cognitive, i.e. with thinking, knowledge, perception, judging, ordering, drawing conclusions and learning – or to replace the one by the other. This approach focuses on the cognitive structuring of political action by the actors, on the structure of their knowledge base and thought processes, which are updated in political action. This implies that systemic structures, e.g. roles and organizations, are seen as emergent contexts for action; [...] *that the guiding orientations of the interacting actors are not to be reduced to motives, interests and norms*, but cognitions form a constitutive component of the orientations for action."[877]

To this end, Vowe outlines the use of first concepts such as "cognitive schemes", "abstraction" and "association heuristics", "script" and "planning". Although these concepts – and with them the entire approach – are implicitly tailored to the actions of political decision-makers, i.e. more to

---

[876] Cf. Greenstein, Fred I., Can Personality and Politics be Studied Systematically? in: Political Psychology 1/1992, p. 105-128; cf. also Immelmann, Aubrey, The Assessment of Political Personality: A Psychodiagnostically Relevant Conceptualization and Methodology, in: Political Psychology 4/1993, p. 725-741.

[877] Vowe, Gehard, *Politische Kognition. Umrisse eines kognitionsorientierten Ansatzes für die Analyse politischen Handelns* [Political Cognition. Outlines of a Cognitive Approach for the Analysis of Political Action], in: Politische Vierteljahresschrift, special edition 25, 1994, pp. 423-447, here p. 424 [highlight by me].

the various (in the Kantian sense mechanical) prudence teachings and 'state art,' nothing prohibits a generalization of these concepts to make them accessible for reflecting judgment, such as 'heuristics,' which are inconceivable without a basis in reflection and which cannot hide their origin. A cognitive theory of political action meets the objectives of the concept of political subjectivity above all in judgment analysis, but the difference between the two approaches is also immediately apparent, which lies prima facie in the philosophically founded reinsurance of all concepts of political subjectivity through a general system of all cognitive abilities, which one justifiably still calls reason. Nevertheless, the doctrine of judgment, which constitutes the core of the philosophy of political subjectivity, proves to be extremely adaptable to recent developments in political psychology and cognition.

B.3.3 Political Communication and Media Theory

Communication under the conditions of modern information technology is also part of the topic of cognition. More specifically, it is about the qualified political aspect of the human-machine complex formed in the technically supported communication event. Although the electronic medium is a kind of *additional organ of perception for human subjects*, it conditions the ability of the same subjects to judge in retrospect. This was no different with the old communication media. Up to now, however, the printing press, telegraph, radio and television have been trivial in terms of communication theory, because the flow of information[878] ran single-track from the news source to the destination. The importance of information, its semantics and pragmatics, was ignored in this model and still is today, because the determination of the semantics of information appeared to be irrelevant for the technical development of the medium. With the new dimension of interactivity made possible by sophisticated network informatics and more powerful hardware (processor and digital cable capacities), the artificial data dream, called cyberspace and virtual reality, has already caught up with the political system of some industrialized countries. The essential, namely qualitative progress lies in the fact that virtually every person can become an 'information receiver/destination' and also a 'sender/source'. The "Electronic Town Hall" has been circulating as an idea in the USA since the 1970s. In the meantime, the networked

---

[878] In the sense of Claude Elwood Shannon's classic of information theory, *The Mathematic Theory of Information* (1948), as the quantity of bit transmission units.

town hall, with the possibility of organizing direct access to files for citizens, surveys or referendums in this way, is no longer a dream of the future. Conservative presidential candidate Ross Perot even went into the election campaign in 1991 with this topic and with far-reaching promises of more direct democracy supported by information technology. On the Internet, we can find this largest and currently exponentially growing worldwide data network; several European cities have meanwhile each founded a 'municipal' cyberspace. The hopes placed in this kind of public sphere and the uncontrollable freedom in cyberspace are extraordinarily high.[879] The emerging momentum of the Internet is so fascinating that experts now believe that the Internet itself will soon become the center of all IT activities. The development of program languages such as Java or Jini seem to be right, because this makes the network so powerful that it can feed all the software used via a telephone line into the simplest computer. The network becomes increasingly independent of the individual user hardware.

But how the path to the information society will look politically depends not only on the capacity of computers and data networks or the marketing opportunities of new technologies, but above all on *the way political subjects can cultivate, articulate and realize their ability in this new medium*. However, the little that has been said about political subjects in political science so far will not get us very far when it comes to designing a well-founded theory of democracy for the information age, which the new medium can adequately grasp with regard to its political potentials. The concept of political subjectivity developed here already meets the structure of the question in that the political judgment is distinguishable according to its semantic and syntactic contents. The concept of politically qualifiable reflection, as a procedural concept of the public sphere (in consciousness and in social communication) and generative distancing between the individual and the subjective order, is suitable for reconstructing the political conditions of judgment in artificial data spaces due to its formal character. The question becomes interesting above all at the level of semantic values, i.e. the way in which individual states are obtained for judgment. The progressive derealization and simulation of one's own body in the data space and the possibility of almost boundless proportioning in the representation of size, power and time certainly leaves its mark on the constitution of the reflected self as an individual. Especially in these

---

[879] Cf. Buchstein, Hubertus, *Virtuelle Demokratie* [Virtual Democracy], in: Neue Gesellschaft – Frankfurter Hefte 2/1996, pp. 165-169.

communication worlds emerging on the horizon, the concept of political subjectivity could prove itself, because it not only assures the individual a 'status', but also a certain philosophical dignity. Because of the cybernetic-systemic constitution of these new media dimensions, **there is hardly any area that would have less need for subject reference of its own accord and which thus clings so much to radical constructivism and functionalism.**

B.3.4 Women's Studies and Gender Anthropology

It took a while, but in the meantime the so-called Second Women's Movement[880] has also been institutionalized scientifically. Not only that women are (and should be) positively discriminated in the appointments to university chairs, but above all a new discipline has emerged from the movement, women's studies or feminist science. It has made it its first and to this day a priority task to work out the implicit gender-specific patterns in the sciences, which describe themselves (almost folkloristically) as 'value-free' – also in political science.[881] The tenor - pardon: the soprano of feminist criticism sounds as follows: "The central concepts of political science (state, public, politics, power, institutions, interests, decisions,

---

[880] The First Women's Movement arose in the second half of the 19th century in connection with the founding of socially charitable, denominational associations (Allgemeiner Deutscher Frauenverein ADF 1865) and formed a radical wing around 1900. The Second Women's Movement was formed in 1968/69 in Germany in the milieu of politically active students in reaction to the male-aligned organization of the Socialist German Student Union (SDS). But a real broad impact could only develop in the course of the §218-campaigns [abortion] and demonstrations; cf. Schenk, Herrad *Die feministische Herausforderung. 150 Jahre Frauenbewegung in Deutschland* [The Feminist Challenge. 150 Years of the Women's Movement in Germany], 5th edition, Munich 1990.

[881] It should not be overlooked that political science is by no means the home of women's studies. On the contrary. In very few universities in Germany, political science departments offer events on women's studies or gender studies (in an extended sense now accepted by leading feminist scholars). Up to now, this discipline has found shelter mainly in literary studies, psychology and sociology. This is rightly seen as a symptom of structural, political and scientific conservatism in German political science. What is always disappointing about this discipline is its incomprehensible lack of curiosity and pleasure in new problems. For this reason, political science does not have any kind of opinion leadership in any political or social-theoretical topic, nor does it even have a competence advantage that is justifiably attributed to it.

conflicts, participation, etc.) reflect a male-centered and male-dominated world."[882] In the quoted volume, the authors jointly state that political science has not achieved much in defining its political object. The concept of the public sphere, or the difference between 'public' and 'private', which is constitutive for political science, has also reconstructed the area of phenomena experienced by women as politically sub-complex, to which feminist critique has in the meantime reacted by 'gendering' the public sphere.[883] In feminist research it has become clearer than anywhere else that the difference between public and private cannot be the basis for politics, but is itself one of many political contents. The concept of political subjectivity offers itself here in order to address gender in general, but above all female individuality as a special positionality in the reflected order structure of public and private sphere. Since political judgment is essentially based on individual, reflected self-perception in the horizon of subjective and objective orders, the physical or rather symbolic aspect[884] of femininity can be taken into account in the foundation of all political reality, namely in reflecting judgment. The same could of course apply to men, but even more so to a political gender anthropology that incorporates gender and physicality in the political and political science contexts in general.

B.3.5 Political Education

The concept of political subjectivity takes into account the empirically well documented fact that in the civil self-image, perceived by many people in the western hemisphere as original and natural, and in democratic

---

[882] Kreisky, Eva, *Gegen geschlechterhalbierte Wahrheiten. Feministische Kritik an der Politikwissenschaft im deutschsprachigen Raum* [Against Gender Halved Truths. Feminist Criticism of Political Science in German-Speaking Countries], in: Kreisky & Sauer, Birgit, *Feministische Standpunkte in der Politikwissenschaft. Eine Einführung*, Frankfurt 1995, p. 32.

[883] Lang, Sabine, *Öffentlichkeit und Geschlechterverhältnis. Überlegungen zu einer Politologie der öffentlichen Sphäre* [Publicity and Gender Relation. Reflections on a Political Science of the Public Sphere], in: ibid. pp. 83-121; cf. also List, Elisabeth, *Homo politicus – femina privata. Thesen zur Kritik der politischen Anthropologie* [Homo Politicus – Femina Privata. Theses on the Critique of Political Anthropology], in: List, *Die Präsenz des Anderen. Theorie und Geschlechterpolitik* [The Presence of the Other. Theory and Gender Policy], Frankfurt 1993, pp. 155-173.

[884] In the sense that the body is the symbol of the individual; cf. chapter B.1.7.2.3.

judgment a high cognitive performance and evolutionary improbability is condensed. This becomes particularly clear when a democracy feels the shortcomings of these abilities among its citizens. Political subjectivity, which one could also call *cognitive political competence*, is obviously a rapidly degradable and destructible resource in modern political societies. One of the hopes that this resource will continue to exist, and regenerate, lies in the educational system. Political education should be an institutional guarantee for general access to an individualizing education that promotes critical thinking and generates political ability. The content of political education as a school subject in Germany after 1945 often gave rise to fierce political debates. Even if the pedagogical pathos was cultivated by the individual as the center of teaching and the ideal of autonomy, the factual dimension almost always prevailed in political education. This means nothing else than that curricular teaching to this day is generally about questionable knowledge, namely the structure of the state, institutional theory, the foundations of constitutional law and the legal system, economic and social order. Although one cannot exactly speak of a 'strengthening democratic consensus' in Germany, the subject has regressed in terms of both content and quantity since the early 1980s in favor of science teaching.[885] One of the main problems is the lack of motivation on the part of the pupils, who thus react when politics (also under the title of social studies) is taught little, discontinuously and by teachers from outside the subject. Due to the lack of historical models and traditions, the situation in Germany is difficult enough anyway, because there is no event in German history in which a democratic consciousness could sustainably focus and symbolize itself in a reminiscent manner. Instead of the fact that the German Reunification would have formed such a moment, the unforgotten bad experiences (now especially of parents) with the old 'civic doctrine' are added in the new federal states. The neglect of the subject of politics on the part of the ministries and schools is noticed by the pupils in any case and is considered not without reason as a general disregard of the political itself.

Here is a content-related starting point for the concept of political subjectivity: the appreciation of the political. The introduction spoke of political subjectivity as a kind of *exoticism of the present*, which consists in showing what surprising complexity the judgment-related consciousness

---

[885] Cf. Gagel, Walter, *Geschichte der politischen Bildung in der Bundesrepublik Deutschland 1945-1989* [History of Political Education in Germany, 1945-1989], 2nd ed. Opladen 1995.

must provide for something like an ordinary political judgment to come about. This wealth of historical or cultural-anthropological and judgment-logical prerequisites for the reflected experience of a political everyday-life and for the awareness of a political opinion forms a suitable background for making the **most common features of a democratic culture appear astonishing and downright adventurous.** This is an interesting, productive opportunity for alienation. For what seems so devalued through everyday-use, the political, can be reappropriated in a new form through this representation as a complex, almost miraculous ability. Not only in school lessons, but also in university seminars and in adult education, pupils and students are not only confronted with the legal, economic and administrative problems of a large, anonymous political system, which they have to acquire through learning work. Rather, they can also learn something about one of their most astonishing abilities, namely the ability to form a political judgment.

Recap

Political Subjectivity –
A Cultural Achievement Under Siege

The answer to the question of how people can politically become subjects of their history spanned a wide range. First, three apparitions were outlined in a historical field considered to be the origin of political modernity. The investigation of the phenomena of *individuality, aesthetics* and *publicity* in the 18th century, the interrelation of which has hardly been taken into account so far, had as a result clear indication of a new, generalizing self-understanding of people, which was accompanied by an accentuated, individual need for expression (A.1-3). At the same time, it became apparent that the realization of this need required a certain ability, which had to be just as new. On the basis of this finding, it seemed permissible to see in the simultaneity of events the ideal type of a historically situated *emergence of political subjectivity* – even if it was not yet clear what this subjectivity consists of in detail. Now that all thinking that produces action and knowledge must be a kind of judgment, the quality of this capacity was to be sought in a particular *form of judgment*. Following an intuition of Hannah Arendt, the key to the problem of a specifically political capacity for thought was sought in the reflecting judgment that Kant had discovered and analyzed in the *Critique of the Power of Judgment* (B.1.1-2).

At this time of the investigation, however, it was not yet possible to foresee how the judgment-related concept of the political could be read into a philosophical work that deals only with aesthetics and teleology. The previous attempts, in which reflecting judgment was translated as a very shadowy *common sense* or an equally indefinite *capacity for common sense*, were characterized by a highly selective perception of Kant's work. The task was therefore to show that Kant's philosophical system had left a place unoccupied in which a capacity for judgment could be established that could be specifically qualified as political. Only when the methodological shell of the third *Critique* was broken up did perspectives of subjectivity appear that could be commensurate with the cultural-historical emergence of politics. The developed *counter-method*, with which Kant's work was to be *rebuilt* for the purposes of a philosophy of the political, consisted in the *controlled back-mixing* of the types of judgment he had analyzed and kept pure (B.1.3). This also made the transcendental principle of judgment by means of its concept of nature interesting as a function in the political judgment (B.1.4). The real guideline for the back-mixing of the pure concepts of beauty, sublime and ends was finally the determination of the unity of political judgment as a *reflection on public order* (B.1.7.1). Thus, it soon became clear that the aesthetic and teleological functions in the political judgment are analogous to the relationship between pure intuition and understanding in the theoretical use of reason. The overall function of the aesthetic concepts of reflection of the beautiful and sublime lies in the identification of individual states. These *semantic assignments*, as they were called, had to be combined with the teleological concepts of individuality and order, which in turn constitute the *syntactic* part of judgment (B.1.7.2). The concept of order, which the social sciences and political philosophy had so far only conventionally presupposed, not only experienced a philosophical deepening long overdue, but above all a surprising *subjective turn*, whereby it qualified itself as the actual elementary concept of political subjectivity. The conjugation of the possibilities of linking then resulted in the complete number of *semantic elementary concepts* for the political judgment. This is the preliminary result of the philosophical investigation of political subjectivity in the CPJ: *One* uniform action (reflection) as a structural principle (public sphere) of political judgment and *two* syntactic elementary concepts (individuality and order), which can be put into relation according to *four* semantic elementary concepts (morals/justice, time, body, might).

A large number of examples were used to illustrate how the concepts of reflection of the beautiful and the sublime unexpectedly systematically fill political judgments with familiar contents if they are only placed under the condition of being linked to certain notions of ends, namely individuality and order (B.1.7.2 - B.1.7.3). However, the plausibility checks of the developed model should not stop there. The important question was how moral and political subjectivity relate to each other (B.1.8). After all, the important significance of the religious moment in the political judgment could not be overlooked. Within this complex of problems, minimal conditions of the compatibility of morality and faith with the structural characteristics of political judgments were found – among other things with the help of the reflections of the Moroccan philosopher Al-Jabri, which themselves stem from a theory of political subjectivity as cultural criticism. It turned out, among other things, that an individual is a *polycentric entity of qualitatively different subjects*, each of whom is responsible for specific performances of judgment.

In Excursus I, *Hypostases of Identity* (B.1.9), an attempt was then made to localize political subjectivity as a special variant of the philosophy of subjectivity that had previously hardly been perceived. The resulting topography of the theoretical landscape is perhaps one of the welcome by-products of this investigation. So far, there are hardly any scientific maps with which one can reliably orient oneself on the wild continent between sociology, political science and philosophy. These disciplines, including their various epistemological approaches and traditions, were put into a comprehensible relationship by means of a historical genealogy of subjectivity theorems, in order to show that the disqualifying speech of the 'monologism of the subject' was based on an insufficient reading and understanding of key texts. The prevailing social-theoretical conception of the primacy of socialization through communication was confronted with a new dimension containing the individual contribution to political sociality. The concept of political subjectivity was thus attested its own origin and finally assigned a certain place between social philosophy and theory of society.

The sociological connectivity of the concept was finally tested on the phenomenon of *charisma*. The previous empirical findings of charisma research could be interpreted in a new and rather unusual way. For the first time it was possible to ask the question of what capacity in the subject makes it accessible for the various forms of charisma and in what way political judgment is involved in this process. The process, which Max Weber called the 'everydayization' of charisma, proved to be a historical sublimation of the charismatic structure, which only released political subjectivity, or which was only made possible by political subjectivity. The choice between these two aspects of the same event depends on whether one takes the *objective* or the *subjective charisma* as a reference. I think that the application of political subjectivity has thus already achieved a first result that can be helpful for the theoretical framing of a genuinely *political aesthetic of charism*.

Since Part A of the study contained the ideal-typical construction of an original situation of the political in Europe in the 18th century, a general theorem on the historical emergence of the political was developed in Excursus II (B.2.2), so that the methodological procedure of the first part is theoretically reassured. This was based on the previous findings of political ethnology and cultural anthropology. Once again, the concept of order redefined here proved to be extraordinarily helpful and progressive, because the theorem of political emergence gained from it not only determines the conditions of the historical realization of political subjectivity and the resulting new relationship between political societies and nature. Rather, this theorem also makes it clear that Europe's political modernity, which believes itself to be founded primarily on the achievements of the natural sciences and the rationality associated with them, as well as the bourgeois revolutions, is not the only possible form of the emergence of the political.

This closes the circle in which the answer to the question of the cause of the political is contained. **What came to light is a weak, derived, in its structure rather filigree and culturally-historically rare ability in human subjects. It can easily be undermined, hindered or completely extinguished by other abilities, such as moral, religious or mechanical judgments, as well as by needs, libidinal ties and psychosomatic dependencies.** It is anything but a robust, anthropological institution given to individuals by birth. At the same time, however, the insights gained here can reverse the direction of view. This evolutionary improbability of political subjectivity also indicates what an astonishing cultural achievement it represents. Its conceptual model, which could be developed from Kant's *Critique of the Power of Judgment* and a series of important recourses to his philosophical system, is intended to help cultivate people's political faculty and preserve its achievements rather than to atrophy it.

Glossary

The most important terms of Kant's philosophy are listed here, as far as they are important for the understanding of his critical works and for the investigation of political subjectivity. I have added nothing to these terms and used them exactly as I found them in Kant's opus. To describe them, however, I have partly chosen my own formulations, which cannot be found in Kant, but which better characterize my use of his terms.

Analytics is the decomposition and isolation of judgments into elementary concepts. Kant also calls it the "logic of truth."

Appearance is the indefinite object of an *empirical intuition* if it is only *perceived*. It is also the epitome of the things that we can *recognize* with the understanding in connection with pure intuition. Then it is not about physical objects as objects of sensual perception, but about the *laws that constitute them*.

Concepts are either constructed, then they are *mathematical*, or they are confirmed by a critique of the subject and founding knowledge (conceptus ratiocinatus), then they are *philosophical*.

Deduction is the procedure in which the justification of the validity claims of (in theoretical or practical philosophy) concepts or (in the critique of taste and teleology) maxims (because the reflective judgment is not capable of concepts and laws) is examined.

Dialectics is the 'logic of' – with Kant: necessary – 'illusion'. Theoretical and practical reason, but also reflective judgment, always become dialectical when they direct their judgments towards the totality of things. Reason then comes into conflict with itself.

Freedom is the name for the principle of causality of an intelligible nature (i.e. problematically thinkable in analogy to the objective nature, but not recognizable like the latter). This causality is not an eternally upward and downward chain of cause and effect, but assumes the *spontaneity of original causes*, which are not themselves conditioned by previous effects, as is the case in sensual nature. Freedom as a concept is the condition of the possibility of morality.

Hypostasis is an inadmissible, illegitimate reification of concepts and ideas with regard to the critical use of reason. This over-attribution of materiality occurs because of an *uncritical hypotyposis*, i.e. concepts or ideas that cannot be schematically hypotyped are based on intuitions a priori (i.e. presumptuously recognized like a law of nature) or even directly thought intuitively (like a god who *thinks* the thing as such instead or recognizing it, which one cannot have at all). The concept, which would actually only be suitable for reflection, is thereby hypostasized and given a semblance of objectivity.

Hypotyposis is any kind of representation, i.e. the sensualization of concepts. It is either *schematic* when concepts of understanding are connected with the forms of contemplation (space and time; a priori); or *symbolic* when concepts of reason, to which no intuition a priori can be appropriate, are analogously underpinned by an intuition a posteriori.

Intuition is the way in which imagination refers to objects. If it is done through sensual perception, the intuition is *empirical*; if it is only done through the *forms of sensuality*, the perception is *pure*. The only known forms of sensuality are space and time. When drawing a triangle on paper or calculating the trajectory of a projectile, the object is constructed in pure intuition.

Knowledge is objective when understanding and intuition have produced the object by themselves, i.e. have constructed it according to the functions of understanding. This very narrow concept of knowledge, which is determined by the causal-mechanical and experimentally controlled construction of nature, must be taken into account when Kant states, for example, that the judgment of beauty is not a judgment of knowledge.

Metaphysically, a connection can be called if the *conditions of its possibility*, which belong to the transcendental investigation of the same connection, has already been clarified and the synthetic propositions are collected a priori as first-degree possibilities (e.g. the categorical imperative or the law of causality) and their consequences examined. The law of causality enables (1st stage, the *possibility of knowledge*, i.e. metaphysically) knowledge about the lever; the law itself is enabled (2nd stage, the *condition of possibility*, i.e. transcendental) through the categories of mind and the forms of intuition.

Methodology is the name of the sections in the three *Critiques* devoted to the applications or transition from pure conceptual analysis to the applied sciences. This piece is missing in aesthetics because there is *no science of beauty*.

Nature is the epitome of things, as long as they are subject to general laws. The sensual, i.e. physical or phenomenal nature is the existence of things under *given* empirical laws (heteronomy). The extrasensory, i.e. moral, intelligible or noumenal nature encompasses things that exist under the *self-given* laws of reason (autonomy). Man as a 'citizen of both worlds' belongs to both natures.

Order is in *objective* meaning limited variability. In *subjective* meaning, i.e. as an achievement of the judging subject, order is an *imagined connection of ends*. It is either *aggregative*, i.e. it is formed from a finite number of hypothetically assumed individual purposes without a recognizable overall purpose. Then the judgment was formed under the idea of (material-objective) relative purposiveness. Or this purposiveness is presented *internally*, i.e. the single purposes form a system or an organ, which contains the total purpose of the appearance as a necessary for each other of the whole and its parts. In this case, appearance would be both cause and effect of itself and thus order would be *organic*.

Perception is the connection of an apparition through its sensation with consciousness.

Reason is the system of concepts that the understanding produces when it aims at totality and transcends the limits of sensuality. The critical use of these transcendent concepts, namely *world*, *God* and *freedom*, is the main task of the critical system. They do not generate knowledge, but they do pose irrefutable tasks that are at the same time a priori unsolvable.

Reflecting power of judgment is the ability to think a logical transition from the particular (own state, observation) to the universal in a judgment, whereby the universal (rule, law) is unknown and is sought. For methodological reasons – in order to arrive at as 'pure' a type of judgment as possible – the reflecting power of judgment is almost exclusively applied to (empirical, raw, free) nature in the *CPJ*. Its output is differentiated into the reflection of the *beautiful*, the *mathematically* and the *dynamically sublime*, and finally the *relative* and the *internal* purposiveness (aggregates and organisms).

Reflection is the process of finding out the conditions in order to arrive at concepts. In reflection, the faculty of judging looks at itself in order to arrive at concepts or to present them in a sensual way.

Sensation is the reception of a sensory stimulus that affects the subjective feeling of pleasure and displeasure. The sensation is not itself bound to consciousness.

Thing in itself is an object as an *intuitive* mind could look at it, i.e. it would create it *thinkingly*. The human mind is *discursive*, it requires intuition in connection with understanding and can only *constructively* create objects. The thing itself designates the perspective of a divine mind on the world. Accordingly, it always denotes the way in which we cannot *recognize* an object but can *think* it problematically. Reason itself is a thing in itself and also man, insofar as he is a being of reason, which stands under the law of the causality of freedom, but not of nature.

Thinking is always: judging! Thinking is exclusively the direct (pure natural science and practical philosophy) or indirect (aesthetics, teleology) activity of the mind. 'Indirect' means that the principles of the mind are 'dark', 'confused' and not specifically recognized. Intuition does not think.

Transcendental refers to a context in which the *condition of the possibility of something* is thematized. It is a *double conditioning*, which is actually a *two-stage inquiry into the possibilities of possibility*. The *condition* of the *possibility* (e.g. metaphysics of morals, which contains the law of morality) of morality (virtue as the practical realization of moral law) is the concept of freedom. The condition is always a second-degree possibility. The conditions of the possibility of causal-mechanical knowledge of nature are the categories. Typically transcendental is the question: "How is nature (as a knowledge-founding concept of the natural whole, deduced by the critique of the subject, as a conceptus rationcinatus) possible"?

Understanding is nothing other than the arid framework of the twelve categories of the table of judgments under the titles quantity, quality, relation, and modality. They contain all the functions in judgments that thinking requires if it aims at knowledge. It is the 'capacity of concepts', of 'thinking' and of 'judgments.' These few concepts and their derivations in the *CPuRe* have undoubtedly been the center of Kant's philosophy and at the same time the biggest problem of its interpretation to date.

Words are *names for concepts* or designations of sensual or super-sensual objects.

Bibliography

For a better understanding and orientation, tentative English translations of the titles are given in square brackets [].

1. Monographs

Adam, Armin, *Rekonstruktion des Politischen. Carl Schmitt und die Krise der Staatlichkeit 1912-1933* [Reconstruction of the Political. Carl Schmitt and the Crisis of Statehood 1912-1933], Weinheim 1992.

Al-Jabri, Mohammed Abed, Naqd al-'aql al-'arabî, I-Takwîn al-'aql al-'arabî [Critique of Arab Reason I] Beiruth-Casablanca 1982.

- : Binyat al-'aql al-'arabî: dirâsa tahlîliyya naqdiyya li- nuzum al ma'rifa fî al-thaqâfa al-'arabiyya, [Critique of Arab Reason II], Beiruth-Casablanca 1986.

- : Al-'Aql al-siyâsi al-'arabi: muhaddidâtuh wa tajalliyyâtuh [Arab Political Reason III], Beiruth-Casablanca 1989.

- : *Introduction à la Critique de la raison arabe* [Introduction to the Critique of Arab Reason], Paris 1994, Casablanca 1995.

Al-Râziq, Alî Abd, *L'Islam et les fondements du pouvoir* [Islam and the Foundations of Power] Casblanca 1995.

Althusius, Johannes, Politica methodice digesta atque exemplis sacris et profanis illustrata, [1603] 3rd ed. Herborn 1614, reprint Aalen 1961.

Anderson, Benedict, *Die Entstehung der Nation* [The Origin of the Nation], Frankfurt 1988.

Anter, Andreas, *Die Macht der Ordnung. Aspekte einer Grundkategorie des Politischen* [The Power of Order. Aspects of a Basic Category of Politics], Tübingen 2004

Arendt, Hannah, *Eichmann in Jerusalem*, N.Y. 1968.

- : *Über die Revolution* [On Revolution], Munich 1974.

- : *Die verborgene Tradition. Acht Essays* [The Hidden Tradition. Eight Essays], Frankfurt 1976.

- : *Vom Leben des Geistes*, vol. I: *Das Denken*, vol. II: *Das Wollen*, Munich 1979.

- : *Vita activa oder vom tätigen Leben* [Vita activa], Munich 1983.

- : *Das Urteilen. Texte zu Kants politischer Philosophie* [Judging. Texts on Kant's Political Philosophy], ed. and with an essay by Roland Beiner, Munich 1985.

- : *Was ist Politik? Fragmente aus dem Nachla* [What is Politics? Fragments from the Estate], edited by Ursula Ludz, Munich 1993.

Aristotle, *Metaphysik. Schriften zur Ersten Philosophie* [Metaphysics. Writings on First Philosophy], ed. by Franz F. Schwarz, Stuttgart 1970.

- : *Politik. Schriften zur Staatstheorie* [Politics: Writings on the Theory of State], transl. and ed. by Franz F. Schwarz, Stuttgart 1989.

Aubrey, John, *Brief Lives*, London 1949.

Baeumler, Alfred, *Das Irrationalitätsproblem in der Ästhetik und Logik des 18. Jahrhunderts bis zur Kritik der Urteilskraft* [The Problem of Irrationality in Aesthetics and Logics in the 18th Century up to the *Critique of the Power of Judgment*], 1923, reprint Darmstadt 1975.

Balandier, George, *Politische Anthropologie* [Political Anthropology], Munich 1976.

- : *Anthropo-Logiques*, Paris 1985.

Bardy, Gustave, *Menschen werden Christen. Das Drama der Bekehrung in den ersten Jahrhunderten* [People Become Christians. The Drama of Conversion in the First Centuries, Freiburg 1988 [French orig. *La Conversion au Christianisme durant les premiers siècles*, Paris 1949]

Bartuschat, Wolfgang, *Zum systematischen Ort von Kants Kritik der Urteilskraft* [On the Systematic Site of Kant's Critique of Judgment], Frankfurt 1972.

Bateson, Gregory, *Ökologie des Geistes. Anthropologische, psychologische, biologische und epistemologische Perspektiven* [Ecology of Mind. Anthropological, Psychological, Biological and Epistemological Perspectives], Frankfurt 1981.

- : *Geist und Natur. Eine notwendige Einheit* [Spirit and Nature. A Necessary Unity], Frankfurt 1987.

Batteux, Charles, *Einschränkung der schönen Künste auf einen einzigen Grundsatz* [Limitation of the Fine Arts to a Single Principle], 1746], transl. by J. A. Schlegel, Hildesheim 1976.

Bauer, Wilhelm, *Die öffentliche Meinung* [Public Opinion], Tübingen 1914.

- : *Die öffentliche Meinung in der Weltgeschichte* [Public Opinion in World History], Potsdam 1930.

Baumgarten, Alexander Gottlieb, *Metaphysica*, Halle 1739, photomechanical reprint Hildesheim 1969.

- : *Texte zur Grundlegung der Ästhetik* [Texts on the Foundation of Aesthetics], ed. by Hans Rudolf Schweizer, Hamburg 1983.

Beck, Ulrich, *Risikogesellschaft. Auf dem Weg in eine andere Moderne* [Risk Society. Towards Another Modernity], Frankfurt 1986

- : *Die Erfindung des Politischen. Zu einer Theorie reflexiver Modernisierung* [The Invention of the Political. Towards a Theory of Reflexive Modernization], Frankfurt 1993.

Beck, Ulrich and Beck-Gernsheim, Elisabeth, *Riskante Freiheiten – Zur Individualisierung der Lebensformen in der Moderne* [Risky Liberties – On Individualization of Life Forms in Modernity], Frankfurt 1993.

Beiner, Ronald, *Political Judgement*, London 1983.

Benjamin, Walter, *Das Kunstwerk im Zeitalter seiner technischen Reproduzierbarkeit*, Frankfurt 1977.

Berger, Peter and Luckmann, Thomas, *Die gesellschaftliche Konstruktion der Wirklichkeit. Eine Theorie der Wissenssoziologie* [The Social Construction of Reality. A Theory of Sociology of Knowledge; N.Y. 1966], Frankfurt 1995.

Bergson, Henri, *Zeit und Freiheit. Eine Abhandlung über die unmittelbaren Bewusstseinstatsachen* [French orig. *Essai sur les données immédiates de la conscience*, 1889] [Time and Freedom. A Treatise on the Immediate Facts of Consciousness], Jena 1911.

Blumenberg, Hans, *Die Legitimität der Neuzeit* [The Legitimacy of Modern Times], Frankfurt 1966.

Böhme, Gernot, *Philosophieren mit Kant. Zur Rekonstruktion der Kantischen Erkenntnis- und Wissenschaftstheorie* [Philosophizing with Kant. On the Reconstruction of Kant's Theory of Knowledge and Science], Frankfurt 1986.

Boileau-Despréaux, Nicolas, *Epîtres*, in: *Oeuvres II*, ed. by S. Menant, Paris 1969.

- : *Art poétique*, ed. by August Buck, Munich 1970.

Bohrer, Karl Heinz, *Das absolute Präsens. Die Semantik ästhetischer Zeit* [The Absolute Presence. The Semantics of Aesthetic Time], Frankfurt 1994.

Bornscheuer, Lothar, *Topik. Zur Struktur der gesellschaftlichen Einbildungskraft* [Topics. On the Structure of Social Imagination], Frankfurt 1976.

Brandt, Reinhard, , *D'Artagnan und die Urteilstafel. Über ein Ordnungsprinzip der europäischen Kulturgeschichte (1,2,3/4)* [D'Artagnan and the Table of Judgments. On a Principle of Order in European Cultural History (1,2,3/4)], Stuttgart 1991.

- : *Die Urteilstafel. Kritik der reinen Vernunft A 67-76; B 92-201* [The Table of Judgements. Critique of Pure Reason A 67-76; B 92-201], Kant-Forschungen Volume 4, Hamburg 1991.

Brentano, Lujo, *A History of the Economic Development of England*, vol, 2: *The Time of Mercantilism*, New York1968.

Brückner, Jutta, *Staatswissenschaften, Kameralismus und Naturrecht. Ein Beitrag zur Geschichte der Politischen Wissenschaft im Deutschland des späten 17. und frühen 18. Jahrhunderts* [Political Sciences, Cameralism and Natural Law. A Contribution to the History of Political Science in Germany in the Late 17th and early 18th Centuries], Munich 1977.

Brunkhorst, Hauke, *Staatswissenschaften, Kameralismus und Naturrecht. Ein Beitrag zur Geschichte der Politischen Wissenschaft im Deutschland des späten 17. und frühen 18. Jahrhunderts* [Democracy and Difference. From the Classical to the Modern Concept of the Political], Frankfurt 1994.

Bullinger, Martin, *Öffentliches Recht und Privatrecht. Studien über Sinn und Funktion der Unterscheidung* [Public Law and Private Law. Studies on the Meaning and Function of this Difference], Stuttgart 1968.

Cassirer, Ernst, *Kants Leben und Lehre* [Kant's Life and Teaching], Berlin 1918.

- : *Philosophie der symbolischen Formen* [Philosophy of Symbolic Forms], 3 vol., 1923, Darmstadt 1994.

- : *Die Philosophie der Aufklärung* [The Philosophy of the Enlightenment], Tübingen 1932.

- : *An Essay on Man. An Introduction to a Philosophy of Human Culture*, New Haven 1944, German translation Stuttgart 1960.

Cassirer, Heinrich W., *A Commentary on Kant's Critique of Judgement*, London 1930, reprint 1970.

Cicero, Marcus Tullius, *De re publica (Vom Gemeinwesen)*, Stuttgart 1979.

Claessens, Dieter, *Nova Natura. Anthropologische Grundlagen modernen Denkens* [Nova Natura. Anthropological Foundations of Modern Thought], Düsseldorf 1970.

Clausewitz, Carl von, *Verstreute kleine Schriften* [Scattered Small Writings], edited by Werner Hahlweg, Osnabrück 1979.

Derrida, Jacques, *Gesetzeskraft. Der "mystische Grund der Autorität"* [The Power of Law. The "Mystical Ground of Authority"], Frankfurt 1991.

- : *Die Wahrheit in der Malerei* [The Truth in Painting], Vienna 1992.

Diehle, Albrecht, *Die Griechen und die Fremden* [The Greeks and the Foreigners], Munich 1994.

Dilthey, Wilhelm, *Der Aufbau der geschichtlichen Welt in den Geisteswissenschaften. Gesammelte Schriften VII* [The Structure of the Historical World in the Humanities. Collected Writings VII], Leipzig 1927.

Dörner, Andreas, *Politischer Mythos und symbolische Politik. Sinnstiftung durch symbolische Formen am Beispiel des Hermannsmythos* [Political Myth and Symbolic Politics. The Creation of Meaning Through Symbolic Forms Using the Example of the Hermann Myth], Opladen 1995.

Dumont, Louis, *Gesellschaft in Indien. Die Soziologie des Kastenwesens* [Society in India. The Sociology of the Caste System], Vienna 1976 (*Homo hierachicus*, Paris 1967).

- : *Essais sur l'individualisme. Une perspective anthropologique sur l'idéologie moderne*, Paris 1983.

- : *Homo aequalis. Genèse et épanouissement de l'idéologie économique*, Paris 1985.

Düsing, Karl, *Die Teleologie in Kants Weltbegriff* [The Teleology in Kant's World Concept], Bonn 1968.

Dux, Günter, *Die Zeit in der Geschichte. Ihre Entwicklungslogik vom Mythos zur Weltzeit. Mit kulturvergleichenden Untersuchungen in Brasilien (J.Mensing), Indien (G. Dux / K. Kälble / J. Meßmer) und Deutschland (B. Kiesel)* [Time in History. Its Logic of Development from Myth to World Time. With Comparative Cultural Studies in Brazil (J. Mensing), India (G. Dux / K. Kälble / J. Meßmer) and Germany (B. Kiesel)], Frankfurt 1989.

Eagleton, Terry, *Ästhetik. Die Geschichte ihrer Ideologie* [Aesthetics. The History of its Ideology, 1990], Stuttgart 1994.

Ebeling, Hans, *Neue Subjektivität. Die Selbstbehauptung der Vernunft* [New

Subjectivity. The Self-Assertion of Reason], Würzburg 1990.

Eco, Umberto, *Einführung in die Semiotik* [Introduction to Semiotics], Munich 1985.

Eder, Klaus, *Geschichte als Lernprozeß? Zur Pathogenese politischer Moderne in Deutschland* [History as a Learning Process? On the Pathogenesis of Political Modernity in Germany], Frankfurt 1985.

Eichberger, Tassilo, *Die Architektur der Vernunft* [The Architecture of Reason], Freiburg 1999.

Elias, Norbert, *Über den Prozeß der Zivilisation* [On the Process of Civilization], 2 vol., 14th ed., Frankfurt 1987.

- : *Die Gesellschaft der Individuen* [The Society of Individuals], Frankfurt 1987.

Eppler, Erhard, *Kavaleriepferde beim Hornsignal. Die Krise der Politik im Spiegel der Sprache* [Cavalry Horses at the Bugle Call. The Crisis of Politics in the Mirror of Language], Frankfurt 1992.

Erasmus of Rotterdam, Desiderius, *Süß scheint der Krieg den Unerfahrenen* [War is Sweet for those who haven't Experienced it], transl. and ed. by Brigitte Hannemann, Munich 1987.

Laboratoire d'Ethnologie et de Sociologie Comparative, *Singularités. Les voies d'émergence individuelle*, anniversary publication for Eric de Dampierre, Paris 1989.

Farge, Arlette, *Lauffeuer in Paris. Die Stimme des Volkes im 18. Jahrhundert* [Wildfire in Paris. The Voice of the People in the 18th Century], Stuttgart 1993.

Ferry, Luc, *Philosophie politique I. Le droit: la nouvelle querelle des anciens et des modernes*, Paris 1983.

- : *Philosophie politique II. Le système des philosophies de l'histoire*, Paris 1984.

- : *Homo aestheticus. L'invention du goût à l'âge démocratique*, Paris 1990 [*Der Mensch als Ästhet. Die Erfindung des Geschmacks im Zeitalter der Demokratie*, Stuttgart 1992].

- *Le nouvel ordre écologique. L'arbre, l'animal et l'homme*, Paris 1992.

Ferry, Luc and Renaut, Alain, *Philosophie politique III. Des droits de l'homme à l'idée républicaine*, Paris 1985.

- : *La pensée 68. Essai sur l'antihumanisme contemporain*, Paris 1988.

Finkielkraut, Alain, *Verlust der Menschlichkeit. Versuch über das 20. Jahrhundert* [Loss of Humanity. Essay on the 20th Century], Stuttgart 1999.

Foster, Georg, *Über die öffentliche Meinung* [On Public Opinion], Akademie-Ausgabe vol. 8, Berlin 1974.

Foucault, Michel, *Die Ordnung der Dinge* [The Order of Things. An Archaeology of the Human Sciences], Frankfurt 1991 [*Les mots et les choses*, Paris 1966].

Fox-Genovese, Elisabeth, *Feminism without Illusions. A Critique of Individualism*, North Carolina 1991.

Fraenkel, Ernst, *Deutschland und die westlichen Demokratien* [Germany and the Western Democracies], ed. by Alexander v. Brünneck, Frankfurt 1991.

- : *Öffentliche Meinung und internationale Politik* [Public Opinion and International Politics], Tübingen 1962.

- : *Selbstbewusstsein und Selbsterkenntnis. Essays zur analytischen Philosophie der Subjektivität* [Self-Confidence and Self-Knowledge. Essays on the Analytical Philosophy of Subjectivity], Stuttgart 1991.

Freud, Sigmund, *Abriß der Psychoanalyse*, Frankfurt 1985.

Fricke, Christel, *Kants Theorie des reinen Geschmacksurteils* [Kant's Theory of Pure Judgment of Taste], Berlin 1990.

Friedell, Egon, *Kulturgeschichte der Neuzeit* [Cultural History of Modern Times], 3 vol. [1927-32], Frankfurt 1984.

Friedmann, Friedrich G., *Hannah Arendt. Eine deutsche Jüdin im Zeitalter des Totalitarismus* [Hannah Arendt. A German Jewess in the Age of Totalitarianism], Munich 1985.

Gadamer, Hans-Georg, *Wahrheit und Methode. Grundzüge einer philosophischen Hermeneutik* [Truth and Method. Fundamentals of Philosophical Hermeneutics], Gesammelte Werke vol. I, 5th ext. ed., Tübingen 1986.

Gagel, Walter, *Geschichte der politischen Bildung in der Bundesrepublik Deutschland 1945-1989* [History of Political Education in the Federal Republic of Germany 1945-1989], 2nd ed., Opladen 1995.

Garcia, Jorge E., *Introduction to the Problem of Individuation in the Early Middle Ages* [Introduction to the Problem of Individuation in the Early Middle Ages], Munich 1984.

Gehlen, Arnold, *Der Mensch. Seine Natur und seine Stellung in der Welt* [Man.

His Nature and His Position in the World, 1940], 9th rev. ed., Wiesbaden 1972.

Gerhards, Jürgen & Neidhardt, Friedhelm, *Strukturen und Funktionen moderner Öffentlichkeit. Fragestellungen und Ansätze* [Structures and Functions of the Modern Public Sphere. Questions and Approaches], working paper of the department "Public Spheres and Social Movement" of the WZB, Berlin 1990, FS III 90-101.

Gerhardt, Volker, *Immanuel Kants Entwurf "Zum Ewigen Frieden". Eine Theorie der Politik*, [Immanuel Kant's Draft "On Eternal Peace". A Theory of Politics], Darmstadt 1995.

Gerhardt, Volker & Kaulbach, Friedrich, *Das Prinzip der Handlung in der Philosophie Kants* [The Principle of Action in Kant's Philosophy], Berlin & New York 1978.

- : *Kant*, Darmstadt 1979.

Girard, René, *Das Ende der Gewalt* [The End of Violence], Freiburg i. B. 1980 [*Des choses cachées depuis la fondation du monde*, Paris 1978].

- : *Das Heilige und die Gewalt* [Violence and the Sacred], Frankfurt 1992 [*La violence et le sacré*, Paris 1972].

- : *Ausstoßung und Verfolgung. Eine historische Theorie des Sündenbocks* [The Scapegoat], Frankfurt 1992 [Le bouc émissaire, Paris 1982].

- : *Shakespeare. Les feux de l'envie* [Shakespeare. A Theater of Envie], Paris 1990.

Goetschel, Willi, *Constituting Critique. Kant's Writing as Critical Praxis*, Durham and London 1994.

Guggenberger, Bernd, *Die politische Aktualität des Ästhetischen* [The Political Topicality of Aesthetics], Eggingen 1992.

Grünenberg, Reginald, *Your Are Many – The Polycentric Subject*, expected in 2019.

Habermas, Jürgen, *Strukturwandel der Öffentlichkeit. Untersuchungen zu einer Kategorie der bürgerlichen Gesellschaft* [Structural Change of the Public Sphere. Studies on a Category of Bourgeois Society], Darmstadt, Neuwied 1962, 2nd ed., Frankfurt 1991, with a foreword to the new edition.

- : *Theorie des kommunikativen Handelns* [Theory of Communicative Action], 2 vol., Frankfurt 1981.

- : *Der philosophische Diskurs der Moderne. Zwölf Vorlesungen* [The

Philosophical Discourse of Modernity. Twelve Lectures], Frankfurt 1985.

- : *Nachmetaphysisches Denken. Philosophische Aufsätze* [Post-Metaphysical Thinking. Philosophical Essays], 2nd ed., Frankfurt 1988.

- : *Faktizität und Geltung* [Truth and Verification], Frankfurt 1992.

Hartmann, Nicolai, *Neue Wege der Ontologie* [1943], 4th ed., Stuttgart 1964.

Hegel, Georg Wilhelm Friedrich, *Philosophie der Geschichte* [Philosophy of History], 1830-31, Frankfurt 1970.

- : *Phänomenologie des Geistes* [Phenomenology of the Spirit], Frankfurt 1972.

Heidegger, Martin, [Kant and the Problem of Metaphysics], [1929] Frankfurt 1973, 4th and ext. ed.

- : *Nietzsche*, vol. I, Pfullingen 1961.

Heinsohn, Gunnar, *Warum Auschwitz? Hitlers Plan und die Ratlosigkeit der Nachwelt* [Why Auschwitz? Hitler's Plan and the Perplexity of Posterity], Reinbek b. Hamburg 1995.

Henrich, Dieter, *Fichtes ursprüngliche Einsicht* [Fichte's Original Insight], Frankfurt 1967.

- : *Identität und Objektivität. Eine Untersuchung über Kants transzendentale Deduktion* [Identity and Objectivity. A study on Kant's Transcendental Deduction], Heidelberg 1976.

- : *Fluchtlinien. Philosophische Essays* [Vanishing Lines. Philosophical Essays], Frankfurt 1982.

- : *Der Grund des Bewusstseins. Untersuchungen zu Hölderlins Denken (1794-1795)* [The Ground of Consciousness. Studies on Hölderlin's Thinking (1794-1795)], Stuttgart 1992.

- : *Aesthetic Judgement and the Moral Image of the World*, Stanford 1992.

Hensmann, Volker, *Staat und Absolutismus im Denken der Physiokraten* [State and Absolutism in Physiocratic Thought], Frankfurt 1975.

Herder, Gottfried Johann, *Metakritik zur Kritik der reinen Vernunft* [Meta-Critique to the *Critique of Pure Reason*], Berlin 1955.

Hobbes, Thomas, *Leviathan or the Matter, Forme, & Power of a Common-Wealth Ecclesiasticall and Civill*, [1651] ed. by C. B. Macpherson, London 1968.

Höffe, Otfried, *Ethik und Politik. Grundmodelle und -probleme der praktischen*

Philosophie [Ethics and Politics. Basic Models and Problems of Practical Philosophy], Frankfurt 1979.

- : *Immanuel Kant*, Munich 1983.

Hoffman, Arndt, *Zufall und Kontingenz in der Geschichtstheorie. Mit zwei Studien zur Theorie und Praxis der Sozialgeschichte* [Chance and Contingency in Historical Theory. With Two Studies on the Theory and Practice of Social History], Frankfurt 2005.

Holland-Cunz, Barbara, *Soziales Subjekt Natur. Natur und Geschlechterverhältnis in emanzipatorischen politischen Theorien* [Social Subject Nature. Nature and Gender Relations in Emancipatory Political Theories], F. a M. 1994.

Hölscher, Lucian, , *Öffentlichkeit und Geheimnis. Eine begriffsgeschichtliche Untersuchung zur Entstehung der Öffentlichkeit in der frühen Neuzeit* [Public Sphere and Mystery. A Conceptual-Historical Investigation of the Emergence of the Public Sphere in the Early Modern Period], Stuttgart 1976.

Hölscher, Lucian, *Geschichte der protestantischen Frömmigkeit in Deutschland* [History of Protestant Piety in Germany], Munich 2005

Hösle, Vittorio, *Hegels System. Der Idealismus und das Problem der Intersubjektivität* [Hegel's System. Idealism and the Problem of Intersubjectivity], 2 vol., Hamburg 1987.

Honneth, Axel, *Kampf um Anerkennung. Zur moralischen Grammatik sozialer Konflikte* [Fight for Recognition. On the Moral Grammar of Social Conflicts], Frankfurt 1992.

Huizinga, Johan, *Herbst des Mittelalters. Studien über Lebens- und Geistesformen des 14. und 15. Jahrhunderts in Frankreich und in den Niederlanden* [Autumn of the Middle Ages. Studies on Life Forms and Mentalities of the 14th and 15th centuries in France and in the Netherlands], Stuttgart 1975.

Hume, David, *Of the Standards of Taste and other Essays*, ed. by John W. Lenz, Indianapolis 1975.

- : *Eine Untersuchung über den menschlichen Verstand* [A Study of the Human Mind], ed. by Herbert Herring, Stuttgart 1986.

Husserl, Edmund, *Zur Phänomenologie des inneren Zeitbewusstseins (1893-1917)* [On the Phenomenology of the Inner Consciousness of Time (1893-1917)], ed. by R. Boehm, The Hague 1966, Husserliana vol. X.

Jauß, Hans Robert, *Literaturgeschichte als Provokation* [Literary History as Provocation], Frankfurt 1970

- : *Studien zum Epochenwandel der ästhetischen Moderne* [Studies on the Epochal Change of Aesthetic Modernism], Frankfurt 1989.

Jochmann, Carl Gustav, *Über die Sprache* [On Language], Riga 1828, reprinted 1968.

Kant, Immanuel, *Werkausgabe I-XII* [Edition of Completed Works I-XII], 12 vol., ed. by Wilhelm Weischedel, 7th edition, Frankfurt 1988.

- : *Critique of Pure Reason*, transl. by Paul Guyer & Allen Wood, Cambridge 1998.

- : *Critique of Practical Reson*, transl. by Werner S. Pluhar, Indianapolis 2002.

- : *Critique of the Power of Judgment*, transl. by Paul Guyer, Cambridge 2000.

Kantorowicz, Ernst, *The King's Two Bodies. A Study in Medieval Political Theology*, Princeton 1957.

Kaulbach, Friedrich, *Einführung in die Philosophie des Handelns* [Introduction to the Philosophy of Action], Darmstadt 1982.

- : *Ästhetische Welterkenntnis bei Kant* [Aesthetic Knowledge of the World in Kant], Würzburg 1984.

- : *Philosophie des Perspektivismus. Band I, Wahrheit und Perspektive bei Kant, Hegel und Nietzsche* [Philosophy of Perspectivism, vol. I, Truth and Perspective in Kant, Hegel and Nietzsche], Tübingen 1990.

Kersting, Christa, *Die Genese der Pädagogik im 18. Jahrhundert. Campes "Allgemeine Revision" im Kontext der neuzeitlichen Wissenschaft* [The Genesis of Education in the 18th Century. Campes "General Revision" in the Context of Modern Science], Weinheim 1992.

Kersting, Wolfgang, *Die politische Philosophie des Gesellschaftsvertrags* [The Political Philosophy of the Social Contract], Darmstadt 1994.

Keynes, John Maynard, *General Theory of Employment, Interest and Money*, in: Keynes, *Collected Writings Vol. VII*, [1936] Cambridge 1973.

Koch, Anton, *Subjektivität in Raum und Zeit* [Subjectivity in Space and Time], Frankfurt 1990.

Kohler, Georg, *Geschmackmacksurteil und ästhetische Erfahrung. Beiträge zur Interpretation von Kant's "Kritik der ästhetischen Urteilskraft"* [Judgment of Taste and Aesthetic Experience. Contributions to the Interpretation of

Kant's Critique of Aesthetic Judgment], Kantstudien Ergänzungshefte, vol. 111, Berlin, N. Y. 1980.

Koselleck, Reinhart, *Vergangene Zukunft. Zur Semantik geschichtlicher Zeiten* [Past Future. On the Semantics of Historical Times], 3rd ed., Frankfurt 1984.

- : *Kritik und Krise* [Critique and Crisis], Frankfurt 1973.

Küng, Hans, *Das Judentum* [Judaism], Munich 1991.

Küppers, Bernd-Olaf, *Der Ursprung biologischer Information. Zur Naturphilosophie der Lebensentstehung* [The Origin of Biological Information. On the Natural Philosophy of the Origin of Life], Munich 1986.

Kues, Nikolaus von, *Über den Beryll* [On the Beryl], 1458, Hamburg 1987.

Kulenkampff, Jens, *Kants Logik des ästhetischen Urteils* [Kant's Logic of Aesthetic Judgment], Frankfurt 1978.

Lahrem, Stephan & Weißenbach, Olaf, *Grenzen des Politischen. Philosophische Grundlagen für ein neues politisches Denken* [Limits of the Political. Philosophical Foundations for a New Political Thinking], Stuttgart 2000

Langer, Claudia, *Reform nach Prinzipien* [Reform According to Principles], Stuttgart 1986.

Lefort, Claude , *Essais sur le politique*, Paris 1985.

- : *L'invention démocratique. Les limites de la domination totalitaire*, Paris 1981.

Leibniz, Gottfried Wilhelm, *Monadologie* [Monadology], Stuttgart 1990.

Leidhold, Wolfgang, *Politische Philosophie* [Political Philosophy], Würzburg 2003.

Lepenies, Wolf, *Das Ende der Naturgeschichte* [The End of Natural History], Munich 1976.

Lévi-Strauss, Claude, *Traurige Tropen* [Triste Tropiques], Frankfurt 1989.

- : *Das wilde Denken* [The Savage Mind], Frankfurt 1989.

- : *Strukturale Anthropologie* [Structural Anthropology], 2 vol., Frankfurt 1975.

Liedtke, Max, *Der Begriff der reflektierenden Urteilskraft in Kants Kritik der reinen Vernunft* [The Concept of Reflecting Judgment in Kant's Critique of Pure Reason], Hamburg 1964.

Longuenesse, Beatrice, *I, Me, Mine: Back to Kant, and Back Again*, Oxford

2017.

Lottes, Günther, *Politische Aufklärung und plebejisches Publikum. Zur Theorie und Praxis des englischen Radikalismus im späten 18. Jahrhundert* [Political Enlightenment and Plebeian Audience. On the Theory and Practice of English Radicalism in the Late 18th Century], Munich 1979.

Luhmann, Niklas, *Grundrechte als Institution. Ein Beitrag zur politischen Soziologie* [Fundamental Rights as an Institution. A Contribution to Political Sociology], Berlin 1965.

- : *Politische Planung* [Political Planning], Opladen 1971.

- : *Vertrauen. Ein Mechanismus der Reduktion sozialer Komplexität* [Confidence. A Mechanism of Reduction of Social Complexity], 2nd and ext. ed., Stuttgart 1973.

- : *Macht* [Power], Stuttgart 1975.

- : *Funktion der Religion* [The Function of Religion], 1977, 2nd ed., Frankfurt 1990.

- : *Liebe als Passion. Zur Codierung von Intimität* [Love as Passion. On the Coding of Intimacy], Frankfurt 1982.

- : *Soziale Systeme. Grundriß einer allgemeinen Theorie* [Social Systems. Outline of a General Theory], Frankfurt 1984.

- : *Ökologische Kommunikation. Kann die moderne Gesellschaft sich auf ökologische Gefährdungen einstellen?* [Ecological Communication. Can Modern Society Adapt to Ecological Threats?], Opladen 1988.

- : *Paradigm Lost: Über die ethische Reflexion der Moral* [Paradigm Lost: On the Ethical Reflection of Morality], Frankfurt 1990.

- : : *Gesellschaftsstruktur und Semantik, Studien zur Wissenssoziologie der modernen Gesellschaft* [Social Structure and Semantics. Studies on the Sociology of Knowledge of Modern Society], 3 vol., Frankfurt 1993.

- : *Die Realität der Massenmedien* [The Reality of the Mass Media], Opladen 1996.

- : *Die Politik der Gesellschaft* [The Politics of Society], Frankfurt 2000.

Lukes, Steven, *Individualism*, Oxford 1973.

Lyotard, Francois, *Der Widerstreit* [The Clash], Munich 1987.

- : *Leçons sur l'Analytique du sublime. Kant, Critique de la faculté de juger*, §§ 23-29, Paris 1991.

Lypp, Bernhard, *Ästhetischer Absolutismus und politische Vernunft* [Aesthetic Absolutism and Political Reason], Frankfurt 1972.

Macpherson, Crawford Brough, *Die politische Theorie des Besitzindividualismus* [The Political Theory of Ownership Individualism, Oxford 1962], Frankfurt 1990.

Mandeville, Bernard, *The Fable of the Bees: or, Private Vices, Public Benefits*, ed. by Kaye, F. B., Oxford 1924.

Man, Michael, *The Source of Social Power. A History of Power from the Beginning to AD 1790*, 1986.

Mause, Ingeborg, *Zur Aufklärung der Demokratietheorie. Rechts- und Demokratietheoretische Überlegungen im Anschluß an Kant* [On the Enlightenment of Democratic Theory. Considerations in Legal and Democratic Theory Following Kant], Frankfurt 1992.

Mc Farlane, Alan, *The Origins of English Individualism*, Oxford 1979.

Meier, Christian, *Die Entstehung des Politischen bei den Griechen* [The Origin of the Political in the Greeks], Frankfurt 1980.

- : *Die Ohnmacht des allmächtigen Dictators Caesar. Drei biographische Skizzen* [The Powerlessness of the Almighty Dictator Caesar. Three Biographical Sketches], Frankfurt 1980.

- : *Politik und Anmut* [Politics and Grace], Berlin 1985.

- : *Die politische Kunst der griechischen Tragödie* [The Political Art of Greek Tragedy], Munich 1988.

Merleau-Ponty, Maurice, *Phänomenologie der Wahrnehmung* [Phenomenology of Perception], Berlin 1966.

Metz, Johann Baptist, *Zur Theologie der Welt* [On the Theology of the World], Munich 1968.

Möller, Horst, *Vernunft und Kritik. Deutsche Aufklärung im 17. und 18. Jahrhundert* [Reason and Critique. German Enlightenment in the 17th and 18th Centuries], Frankfurt 1986.

Morris, Colin, *The Discovery of the Individual 1050-1200*, London 1972.

Kluge, Alexander & Negt, Oskar, *Öffentlichkeit und Erfahrung. Zur Organisationsanalyse von bürgerlicher und proletarischer Öffentlichkeit* [Publicity and Experience. On the Organizational Analysis of the Bourgeois and Proletarian Public], Frankfurt 1972.

Niethammer, Immanuel, , *Der Streit des Philantropismus und Humanismus in der Theorie des Erziehungsunterrichts unserer Zeit* [The Controversy of Philantropism and Humanism in the Theory of Education in our Time], Jena 1808, reprint Weinheim 1968.

Oncken, August, *Adam Smith und Immanuel Kant. Der Einklang und das Wechselverhältnis ihrer Lehren über Sitte, Staat und Wirtschaft* [Adam Smith and Immanuel Kant. The Harmony and Interrelation of Their Teachings on Customs, State and Economy], Leipzig 1877.

Orozco, Teresa, *Platonische Gewalt. Gadamers politische Hermeneutik der NS-Zeit* [Platonic Violence. Gadamer's Political Hermeneutics of the NS Era], Hamburg 1995.

Ortega y Gasset, José, *Über das römische Imperium* [About the Roman Empire], Stuttgart 1942.

Otto, Stephan, *Rekonstruktion der Geschichte. Zur Kritik der historischen Vernunft* [Reconstruction of History. On the Critique of Historical Reason], 2 vol., Munich 1982 and 1992.

Paine, Thomas, *Common Sense*, Stuttgart 1982.

Paul, Jean, *Vorschule der Ästhetik* [Preschool of Aesthetics], 1804, critical ed. 1/11, Leipzig 1935.

Peter, Joachim, *Das transzendentale Prinzip der Urteilskraft. Eine Untersuchung zur Funktion und Struktur der reflektierenden Urteilskraft bei Kant* [The Transcendental Principle of Judgment. An Investigation into the Function and Structure of Reflective Judgment in Kant], Kantstudien Ergänzungshefte, vol. 126, Berlin, N. Y. 1992.

Petersen, Erik, *Der Monotheismus als politisches Problem. Ein Beitrag zur politischen Theologie im Imperium Romanum* [Monotheism as a Political Problem. A Contribution to Political Theology in the Roman Empire], Leipzig 1935.

Philonenko, Alexis, *La théorie kantienne de l'histoire*, Paris 1986.

Pfetsch, Frank R., *Dimensionen des Politischen* [Dimensions of the Political], 3 vol., Darmstadt 1995; vol. I: *Erkenntnis und Politik. Philosophische Dimensionen des Politischen* [Knowledge and Politics. Philosophical Dimensions of the Political].

Piaget, Jean, *Le développement de la notion de temps chez l'enfant*, Paris 1973.

Popper, Karl Raymund, *The Open Society and its Enemies*, 2 vol., [1945] London 1984.

Prignitz, Christoph, *Vaterlandsliebe und Freiheit. Deutscher Patriotismus von 1750-1850* [Patriotism and Freedom. German Patriotism from 1750-1850], Wiesbaden 1981.

Radcliffe-Brown, A. R., *Structure and Function in Primitive Society*, London 1952.

Rawls, John, *Eine Theorie der Gerechtigkeit* [A Theory of Justice], Frankfurt 1972.

- : *Die Idee des politischen Liberalismus. Aufsätze 1978-89* [The Idea of Political Liberalism. Essays 1978-89], ed. by Wilfried Hinsch, Frankfurt 1992.

Reble, Albert, Geschichte der Pädagogik [History of Pedagogics], Stuttgart 1980.

Renaut, Alain, *L'ère de l'individu. Contribution à l'histoire de la subjectivité*, Paris 1989.

Ritter, Joachim, *Metaphysik und Politik. Studien zu Aristoteles und Hegel* [Metaphysics and Politics. Studies on Aristotle and Hegel], Frankfurt 1969.

Rodis-Lewis, Geneviève, *Descartes*, Paris 1979.

Rorty, Richard, Philosophy and the Mirror of Nature, 1979.

- : *Kontingenz, Ironie und Solidarität* [Contingency, Irony and Solidarity], Frankfurt 1991.

Rousseau, Jean-Jacques, *Emile oder Über die Erziehung* [Emile or On Education], [1762] Stuttgart 1993.

Sarcinelli, Ulrich, *Demokratische Streitkultur* [Democratic Culture of Controversy], Opladen 1990.

Sartori, Giovanni, *Demokratietheorie* [Theory of Democracy], Darmstadt 1992.

Sassenbach, Ulrich, *Der Begriff des Politischen bei Immanuel Kant* [The Concept of the Political in Immanuel Kant], Würzburg 1992.

Schaeffer, Jean-Marie, *L'art de l'âge moderne. L'esthétique et la philosophie de l'art du XVIIIe siècle à nos jours*, Paris 1992.

Shama, Simon, *Citizen. A Chronicle of the French Revolution*, N.Y. 1989.

Schapera, I., *Government and Politics in Tribal Societies*, London 1956.

Schenk, Herrad, *Die feministische Herausforderung. 150 Jahre Frauenbewegung in Deutschland* [The Feminist Challenge. 150 Years of Women's Movement in Germany], 5th ed., Munich 1990.

Schefczyk, Michael, *Moral ohne Nutzen. Eine Apologie des Kantischen Formalismus* [Morals Without Benefits. An Apology of Kantian Formalism], Sankt Augustin 1995.

Schleiermacher, Friedrich, *Hermeneutik und Kritik* [Hermeneutics and Criticism], ed. by Manfred Frank, Frankfurt 1990.

Schmitt, Carl, *Politische Theologie, Vier Kapitel zur Lehre von der Souveränität* [Political Theology, Four Chapters on the Teaching of Sovereignty], [1922] 3rd ed., Berlin 1979.

- : *Der Begriff des Politischen. Text von 1932 mit einem Vorwort und 3 Corrolarien* [The Concept of the Political. Text from 1932 with a foreword and 3 corollaries], Berlin 1963.

- : *Der Leviathan in der Staatslehre des Thomas Hobbes. Sinn und Fehlschlag eines Symbols* [The Leviathan in Thomas Hobbes' Theory of State. Sense and Failure of a Symbol], Tübingen 1938.

- : *Über die drei Arten des rechtswissenschaftlichen Denkens* [On the Three Types of Jurisprudential Thinking], Hamburg 1934.

- *Hamlet oder Hekuba. Der Einbruch der Zeit in das Spiel* [Hamlet or Hekuba. The Intrusion of Time into the Play], Düsseldorf 1956, unchanged reprint, Stuttgart 1985.

Schmitt, Eberhard, *Repräsentation und Revolution. Eine Untersuchung zur Genesis der kontinentalen Theorie und Praxis parlamentarischer Repräsentation aus der Herrschaftspraxis des Ancien Régime in Frankreich (1760-1789)* [Representation and Revolution. A Study on the Genesis of Continental Theory and Practice of Parliamentary Representation from the Practice of the Ancien Régime in France (1760-1789)], Munich 1969.

Schössler, Dietmar, *Carl von Clausewitz*, Reinbek 1991.

Schulze, Winfried, *Deutsche Geschichte im 16. Jahrhundert 1500-1618* [German History in the 16th Century 1500-1618], Munich 1987.

Schumpeter, Joseph A., *History of Economic Analysis*, [1954], London 1982.

Schwan, Alexander, *Politische Philosophie im Denken Heideggers* [Political Philosophy in Heidegger's Thinking], 1965, 2nd ed., Opladen 1989.

Schweizer, Hans Rudolf, *Ästhetik als Philosophie der sinnlichen Erkenntnis. Eine Interpretation der ‚Aesthetica' A. G. Baumgartens mit teilweiser Wiedergabe des lateinischen Textes und deutscher Übersetzung* [Aesthetics as Philosophy of Sensual Knowledge. An interpretation of the 'Aesthetica' of A. G. Baumgarten with partial reproduction of the Latin text and German translation], Stuttgart 1973.

Seitter, Walter, *Menschenfassungen. Studien zur Erkenntnispolitikwissenschaft* [Versions of the Human. Studies in Political Epistemology], Munich 1985.

Seel, Martin, *Eine Ästhetik der Natur* [An Aesthetic of Nature], Frankfurt 1991.

Sen, Amartya, *Poverty and Famines*, Oxford 1981.

Sennett, Richard, *Verfall und Ende des öffentlichen Lebens. Die Tyrannei der Intimität* [The Fall of Public Man], Frankfurt 1986.

- : *Flesh and Stone*, N.Y. and London 1994.

Shaftesbury, Third Earl of, *An Old Spelling. Critical Edition of Shaftesbury's 'Letter Concerning Enthusiasm' and 'Sensus communis: An Essay on the Freedom of Wit an Humor'*, ed. by Richard B. Wolf, N.Y. 1988.

- : *Standard Edition. Sämtliche Werke, ausgewählte Briefe und nachgelassene Schriften* [Standard Edition. All Works, Selected Letters and Posthumous Writings], vol. I.3, *Ästhetik*, ed. by Wolfram Benda et al., Stuttgart 1992.

Simmel, Georg, *Grundfragen der Soziologie. Individuum und Gesellschaft* [Basic Questions of Sociology. Individual and Society], Berlin 1917.

Smith, Adam, *An Inquiry into the Nature and Causes of the Wealth of Nations*, Harmondsworth/Middlesex (Penguin) 1970.

- : *Theorie der ethischen Gefühle* [Theory of Moral Sentiment], 2 vol., Hamburg 1977.

Spencer Brown, George, *Laws of Form*, London 1969.

Stamm, Karl-Heinz, *Alternative Öffentlichkeit. Die Erfahrungsproduktion neuer sozialer Bewegungen* [Alternative Public Sphere. The Production of Experience of New Social Movements], Frankfurt 1988.

Stankiewicz, William J., *Politics and Religion in Seventeenth-Century France. A Study of Political Ideas from the Monarchomachs to Bayle, as Reflected in the Toleration Controversy*, Berkley/Los Angeles 1960.

Steinberger, Peter J., *The Concept of Political Judgement*, Chicago and London 1993.

Sternberger, Dolf, *Drei Wurzeln der Politik* [Three Roots of Politics], Frankfurt 1984.

Stone, Isidor F., *The Trial of Socrates*, 1988.

Strawson, Peter Frederick, *Einzelding und logisches Subjekt. Ein Beitrag zur deskriptiven Metaphysik* [*Individuals*, London 1964], Stuttgart 1972.

Tarnowski, Wolfgang, *Gladiatoren* [Gladiators], Nuremberg 1987.

Tarski, Alfred, *Logic, Semantics, Metamathematics*, Oxford 1956.

Teichert, Dieter, *Immanuel Kant: "Kritik der Urteilskraft* [Immanuel Kant: "Critique of Judgment"], Paderborn 1992.

Toennis, Ferdinand, *Kritik der öffentlichen Meinung* [Critique of Public Opinion], Berlin 1922.

Trapp, Christian Ernst, *Versuch einer Pädagogik* [Tentative Pedagogics], Berlin 1780, repr. by Theodor Fritzsch, Leipzig 1913.

Tugendhat, Ernst, *Selbstbewusstsein und Selbstbestimmung. Sprachanalytische Interpretationen* [Self-confidence and Self-determination. Analytical Interpretations], 5th ed., Frankfurt 1993.

Valjavec, Fritz, *Die Entstehung der politischen Strömungen in Deutschland 1770-1815* [The Origins of Political Currents in Germany 1770-1815], Munich 1951.

Virilio, Paul, *Die Eroberung des Körpers. Vom Übermenschen zum überreizten Menschen* [The Conquest of the Body. From the Superhuman to the Over-Excited Human Being], Munich 1994.

Vollrath, Ernst, *Grundlegung einer philosophischen Theorie des Politischen* [Foundation of a Philosophical Theory of the Political], Würzburg 1987.

- : *Was ist das Politische? Eine Theorie der Politik und ihrer Wahrnehmung* [What is the Political? A Theory of Politics and its Perception], Würzburg 2003.

Voltaire, *Le siècle de Louis XIV*, 2 vol., Paris 1929.

Weber, Max, *Die Protestantische Ethik und der Geist des Kapitalismus* [Protestant Ethics and the Spirit of Capitalism], in: Weber, *Gesammelte Aufsätze zur Religionssoziologie* [Collected Essays on the Sociology of Religion], vol. I, Tübingen, 6th ed. 1972.

- : *Wirtschaft und Gesellschaft. Grundriß der verstehenden Soziologie* [Economy and Society. Ground Plan of an Understanding Sociology], 5th rev. ed., Tübingen 1985.

Wehler, Hans-Ulrich, *Deutsche Gesellschaftsgeschichte* [German Social

History], vol. 1: *Vom Feudalismus des Alten Reiches bis zur Defensiven Modernisierung der Reformära: 1700-1815* [From the Feudalism of the Old Reich to the Defensive Modernization of the Reform Era 1700-1815] Munich 1987.

Wohlfeil, Rainer, *Einführung in die Geschichte der deutschen Reformation* [Introduction to the History of the German Reformation], Munich 1982.

Zaller, John R., *The Nature and Origin of Mass Opinion*, Cambridge 1992.

2. Anthologies

Arens, Edmund (ed.), *Gottesrede – Glaubenspraxis. Perspektiven theologischer Handlungstheorie* [Speech of God – Practice of Faith. Perspectives of a Theological Theorie of Action], Darmstadt 1994.

Aretin, K.O. Frh. v. (ed.), *Der aufgeklärte Absolutismus* [The Enlightened Absolutism], Cologne 1974.

Ariès, Philippe (ed.), *L'enfant et la vie familiale sous l'Ancien Régime*, Paris 1960.

Ariès, Philippe and Duby, Georges (ed.), *Histoire de la vie privée*, vol. 2, *De l'Europe féodale à la Renaissance*, Paris 1985.

- : *Histoire de la vie privée*, vol. 3, *De la Renaissance au Lumières*, Paris 1986.

Baraldi, Claudio and Corsi, Giancarlo and Esposito, Elena, *GLU. Glossar zu Niklas Luhmanns Theorie sozialer Systeme* [GLU. Glossary on Niklas Luhmann's Theory of Social Systems], Frankfurt 1996.

Birnbaum, Pierre and Leca, Jean (ed.), *Sur l'individualisme. Théories et méthodes*, Paris 1986.

Brumlik, Michael and Brunkhorst, Hauke (ed.), *Gemeinschaft und Gerechtigkeit* [Community and Justice], Frankfurt 1993.

Bürger, Christa & Bürger, Peter (ed.), *Aufklärung und literarische Öffentlichkeit* [Enlightenment and Literary Publicity], Frankfurt 1980.

Cavalieri, Paola & Singer, Peter (ed.), *The Great Ape Project*, London 1993

Cramer, Konrad et al. (ed.), *Theorie der Subjektivität* [Theory of Subjectivity], Festschrift for the 60. anniversary of Dieter Henrich, Frankfurt 1990.

Forum for Philosophy Bad Homburg (ed.), *Ästhetische Reflexion und kommunikative Vernunft* [Aesthetic Reflection and Communicative Reason],

Bad Homburg 1993.

Frank, Manfred (ed.), *Selbstbewusstseinstheorien von Fichte bis Sartre* [Theories of Self-Consciousness from Fichte to Sartre], Frankfurt 1991.

Frank, Martin & Haverkamp, Anselm (ed.), *Individualität* [Individuality], in: *Poetik und Hermeneutik XIII*, Munich 1988.

Funke, Gerhard (ed.), *Akten des 7. Internationalen Kant-Kongresses, Mainz, 28. März-01. April 1990* [Files of the 7th International Kant Congress, Mainz, 28 March - 01 April, 1990], 3 vol., Bonn and Berlin 1991.

Gebhardt, Winfried & Zingerle, Arnold & Ebertz, Michael (ed.), *Charisma: Theorie, Religion, Politik* [Charisma: Theory, Religion, Politics], series *Materiale Soziologie* TB3, Berlin & N. Y. 1993.

Gerhardt, Volker (ed.), *Der Begriff der Politik. Bedingungen und Gründe für politisches Handeln* [The Concept of Politics. Conditions and Reasons for Political Action], Stuttgart 1990.

Gerhardt, Volker & Herold, Norbert (ed.), *Perspektiven des Perspektivismus. Gedenkschrift zum Tode Friedrich Kaulbachs* [Perspectives of Perspectivism. Commemorative publication on the death of Friedrich Kaulbach], Würzburg 1992.

Göhler, Gerhard (ed.), *Grundfragen der Theorie politischer Institutionen. Forschungsstand - Probleme - Perspektiven* [Basic Questions of the Theory of Political Institutions. State of Research – Problems – Perspectives], Opladen 1987.

- : *Politische Institutionen im gesellschaftlichen Umbruch. Ideengeschichtliche Beiträge zur Theorie politischer Institutionen* [Political Institutions in Social Upheaval. Historical Contributions to the Theory of Political Institutions], Opladen 1990.

Hard Nibbig, Christiaan L. (ed.), *Was heißt darstellen?* [What Does it Mean to Represent?], Frankfurt 1994.

Höffe, Otfried (ed.), *Der Mensch - ein politisches Tier? Essays zur politischen Anthropologie* [Man – A Political Animal? Essays in Political Anthropology], Stuttgart 1992.

Kluxen, Kurt (ed.), [Parliamentarism,] Cologne 1967.

Kreisky, Eva & Sauer, Birgit (ed.), *Feministische Standpunkte in der Politikwissenschaft. Eine Einführung* [Feminist Positions in Political Science. An Introduction], Frankfurt 1995.

Kulenkampff, Jens (ed.), *Materialien zu Kants "Kritik der Urteilskraft"* [Materials on Kant's "Critique of Judgment"], Frankfurt 1974.

Löffler, Martin (ed.), *Die öffentliche Meinung. Publizistik als Medium und Faktor der öffentlichen Meinung* [Public Opinion. Publishing as a Medium and Factor of Public Opinion], ed. Deutsche Studiengesellschaft für Publizistik, Munich 1962.

Mahrenholz, Ernst Gottfried et al., *Bericht zur Lage des Fernsehens (für den Präsidenten der Bundesrepublik Richard von Weizsäcker)* [Report on the State of Television (for the President of the Federal Republic Richard von Weizsäcker)], ed. by Bundespräsidialamt, February 1994.

Martin, Gottfried (ed.), *Allgemeiner Kantindex zu Kants gesammelten Schriften* [General Index to Kant's Collected Works], 2 vol., Berlin 1967.

Merten, Klaus & Schmidt, Siegfried (ed.), *Die Wirklichkeit der Medien. Eine Einführung in die Kommmunikationswissenschaft* [The Reality of the Media. An Introduction to Communication Science], Opladen 1994.

Pries, Christine (ed.), *Das Erhabene. Zwischen Grenzerfahrung und Größenwahn* [The Sublime. Between Border Experience and Delusions of Grandeur], Weinheim 1989.

Quaritsch, Helmut (ed.), *Complexio oppositorum. Über Carl Schmitt* [Complexio oppositorum. About Carl Schmitt], Berlin 1988.

Rossi, Pietro (ed.), *Theorie der modernen Geschichtsschreibung* [Theory of Modern Historiography], Frankfurt 1987.

Schmitt, Charles B. and Skinner, Quentin (ed.), *The Cambridge History of Renaissance Philosophy*, Cambridge 1988.

Vowinckel, Gerhard (ed.), *Clausewitz-Kolloquium - Theorie des Krieges als Sozialwissenschaft* [Clausewitz Colloquium – Theory of War as Social Science], Berlin 1993.

Welker, Michael (ed.), *Theologie und funktionale Systemtheorie. Luhmanns Religionssoziologie in theologischer Diskussion* [Theology and Functional Systems Theory. Luhmann's Sociology of Religion in Theological Discussion], Frankfurt 1985.

3. Articles

Al-Jabri, Mohammed Abed, *Extrémisme et attitude rationaliste dans la pensée arabo-islamique*, in: Cordellier, Serge (ed.), *L'islamisme*, Paris 1994.

Arkoun, Mohammed, *Westliche Vernunft contra islamische Vernunft* [Western Reason versus Islamic Reason], in: Lüders, Michael, *Der Islam im Aufbruch*, 2nd ed., Munich 1993.

Beiner, Roland, *Hannah Arendt über das Urteilen* [Hannah Arendt on Judgment], in: Arendt, Hannah, *Das Urteilen. Texte zu Kants politischer Philosophie*, ed, by Roland Beiner, Munich 1985, pp. 115-197.

Bermbach, Udo, *Widerstandsrecht, Souveränität, Kirche und Staat: Frankreich und Spanien im 16. Jahrhundert* [Law of Resistance, Sovereignty, Church and State: France and Spain in the 16th Century], in: *Pipers Handbuch der politischen Ideen*, ed. by Irving Fetscher and Herfried Münkler, Munich 1985, Volume III, pp. 101-160.

Bittner, Rüdiger, *Maximen* [Maxims], in: *Akten des 4. Internationalen Kant-Kongresses Mainz 6.-10.1974* [Files of the 4th International Kant Congress Mainz 6.-10.1974], Part II, section 2, pp. 485-498.

Blasche, Siegfried, *Zur kommunikationsphilosophischen Rekonstruktion der Zwecklichkeit in Kant's Kritik der Urteilskraft*, in: Forum für Philosophie Bad Homburg (ed.), *Ästhetische Reflexion und kommunikative Vernunft*, Bad Homburg 1993, pp. 11-40.

Bloom, Irene, *On the Matter of Mind. The Metaphysical Basis of the Expanded Self*, in: Munro, Donald (ed.), *Individualism and Holism. Studies in Confucian an Taoist Values*, Michigan 1985, pp. 293-330.

Böhme, Hartmut, *Aussichten einer ästhetischen Theorie der Natur* [Outlooks of an Aesthetic Theory of Nature], in: Haberl, Horst Gerhard et al. (ed.), *Entdecken/Verdecken. Eine Nomadologie der Neunziger*, Graz 1991, pp. 15-34.

Brandt, Reinhard, *Die Schönheit der Kristalle. Zum Gegenstand und zur Logik des ästhetischen Urteils bei Kant*, [The Beauty of Crystals. On the Object and Logic of Aesthetic Judgment in Kant], in: Brandt & Stark, Werner (ed.), *Autographen, Dokumente, und Berichte. Zu Amtsgeschäften und Werk Immanuel Kants*, in: *Kant-Forschungen*, vol. 5, Hamburg 1994, pp. 19-57.

- : *Anthropologie bei Kant (und Hegel)* [Anthropology in Kant (and Hegel)], in: *Psychologie und Anthropologie oder Philosophie des Geistes. Beiträge zu einer Hegeltagung in Marburg*, ed. by F. Hespe and B. Tuschling, Stuttgart 1991.

- : *Die politische Institution bei Kant* [The Political Institution in Kant], in: Göhler, Gerhard et al. (ed.), *Politische Institutionen im gesellschaftlichen Umbruch. Ideengeschichtliche Beiträge zur Theorie politischer Institutionen*, Opladen 1990, pp. 335-357.

- : *Kant als Metaphysiker* [Kant as Metaphysicist], in: Gerhardt, Volker (ed.), *Der Begriff der Politik. Bedingungen und Gründe für politisches Handeln*, Stuttgart 1990, pp. 57-93.

Brunkhorst, Hauke, *Kommunale Macht und Öffentliche Freiheit. Zur Theorie des Politischen im Anschluß an Hannah Arendt* [Communal Power and Public Freedom. On the Theory of the Political Following Hannah Arendt], in: *Kurswechsel*, 4/1991, S. 70-80.

Buchstein, Hubertus, *Virtuelle Demokratie* [Virtual Democracy], in: *Neue Gesellschaft / Frankfurter Hefte* 2/1996, S. 165-169.

Bubner, Rüdiger, *Wie wichtig ist Subjektivität? Über einige Selbstverständlichkeiten und mögliche Mißverständnisse der Gegenwart* [How Important is Subjectivity? On Some Self-Evident Facts and Possible Misunderstandings of the Present], in: *Merkur* 3/1995, S. 229-239.

Burnier, DeLysa, *Constructing Political Reality: Language, Symbols, and Meaning in Politics. A Review Essay*, in: *Political Research Quaterly* 1/1994, S. 239-253.

Cassirer, Ernst, "*Kant und das Problem der Metaphysik". Bemerkungen zu Martin Heideggers Kant-Interpretation* ["Kant and the Problem of Metaphysics." Remarks on Martin Heidegger's Interpretation of Kant], in: *Kantstudien*, vol. XXXVI, 1-2/1931, pp. 1-26.

- : *Kant und die moderne Biologie* [Kant and Modern Biology], in: Cassirer, *Geist und Leben. Schriften zu den Lebensordnungen von Natur und Kunst, Geschichte und Sprache*, ed. by Ernst Wolfgang Orth, Leipzig 1993, pp. 61-93.

- : *Zur Logik des Symbolbegriffs* [On the Logic of the Concept of Symbol], in: Cassirer, *Wesen und Wirkung des Symbolbegriffs*, [1938] Darmstadt 1994, spec. ed., pp. 201-230.

Cazeneuve, Jean, *La connaissance d'autrui dans les sociétés archaïques*, in: *Cahiers internationaux de sociologie XXV*, July-December 1958, pp. 75-99.

Combe, Pierre J. de la, *Rationalization of the Law and Tragic Invention. The Eumenides and the Heroic Individual*, in: *International Journal of Philosophy* 2/1993, pp. 244-253.

Cramer, Konrad, *Über Kants Satz: "Das: Ich denke, muss alle meine*

Vorstellungen begleiten können [On Kant's Sentence: "This: I think, must be able to accompany all my ideas"], in: Cramer et al. (ed.), *Theorie der Subjektivität, Festschrift zum 60. Geburtstag von Dieter Henrich*, Frankfurt 1990, p.167-202.

Danto, Arthur C., *Philosophical Individualism in Chinese and Western Thought*, in: Munro, Donald (ed.), *Individualism and Holism. Studies in Confucian and Taoist Values*, Michigan 1985, pp. 385-90.

De Bondt, Werner & Thaler, Richard, *Does the Stock Market Overreact?*, in: *Journal of Finance*, vol. 40, issue 3, *Papers and Proceedings of the Forty-Third Annual Meeting American Finance Association, Dallas/Texas, 28-30 December 1984* (July 1985), pp. 793-805.

Derrida, Jacques, *"Il faut bien manger" ou le calcul du sujet*, interview with Jean-Luc Nancy, in: *Confrontation*, No. 20, Paris 1989.

Detel, Wolfgang, *Griechen und Barbaren. Zu den Anfängen des abendländischen Rassismus* [Greeks and Barbarians. On the Beginnings of Occidental Racism], in: *Zeitschrift für Philosophie* 6/1995, S. 1019-1043.

Dietrich, Rainer, *Carl von Clausewitz als Psychologe - Die "moralischen Größen" im Lichte der Persönlichkeitspsychologie* [Carl von Clausewitz as Psychologist – The "Moral Factors" in the Light of Personality Psychology], in: Vowinckel, Gerhard (ed.), *Clausewitz-Kolloquium - Theorie des Krieges als Sozialwissenschaft*, Berlin 1993, pp. 111-136.

Disselbeck, Klaus, *Die Ausdifferenzierung der Kunst als Problem der Ästhetik* [The Differentiation of Art as a Problem of Aesthetics], in: Berg, Henk de and Prangel, Matthias (ed.), *Kommunikation und Differenz. Ansätze in der Literatur- und Kunstwissenschaft*, Opladen 1993, 137-158.

Dumouchel, Daniel, *La découverte de la faculté de juger réfléchissante. Le rôle heuristique de la "Critique du goût" dans la formation de la Critique de la faculté de juger*, in: *Kant-Studien*, Vol. 85, 1994, pp. 419-442.

Easton, David, *Political Anthropology*, in: *Biennal Review of Anthropology*, 1959, p. 226ff.

Eisenstadt, S. N., *Primitive Political Systems*, in: *American Anthropologist* 61/1959, p. 156-174.

Engelsing, Rolf, *Die Perioden der Lesegeschichte in der Neuzeit. Das statistische Ausmaß und die soziokulturelle Bedeutung der Lektüre* [The Periods of Reading History in Modern Times. The Statistical Extent and Socio-Cultural Significance of Reading], in: *Archiv für Geschichte des Buchwesens* 10/1970, pp. 877-896.

Frank, Manfred, *Fragmente einer Geschichte der Selbstbewusstseins-Theorien von Kant bis Sartre*, [Fragments of a History of Theories of Self-Consciousness from Kant to Sartre], in: Frank, (ed.), *Selbstbewusstseinstheorien von Fichte bis Sartre*, Frankfurt 1991, 415-599.

- : *Wider den apriorischen Intersubjektivismus. Gegenvorschläge aus Sartrescher Inspiration* [Against A Priori Intersubjectivism. Counterproposals from Sartric Inspiration], in: Brumlik, Michael & Brunkhorst, Hauke (ed.), *Gemeinschaft und Gerechtigkeit*, Frankfurt 1993, pp. 273-289.

Gasché, Rudolph, *Überlegungen zum Begriff der Hypotypose bei Kant* [Reflections on the Concept of Hypotyposis in Kant], in: Hard Nibbig, Christiaan L.(ed.), *Was bedeutet darstellen?*, Frankfurt 1994, pp. 152-174.

Gerhards, Jürgen, *Dimensionen und Strategien öffentlicher Diskurse* [Dimensions and Strategies of Public Discourses], in: *Journal für Sozialforschung*, 32/1992, pp. 307-318.

- : *Europäische Öffentlichkeit durch Massenmedien?* [A European Public Sphere Through Mass Media?], in: Schäfers, Bernhard (ed.), *Lebensverhältnisse und soziale Konflikte im neuen Europa. 26. Deutscher Soziologentag 1992*, Frankfurt 1993, pp. 558-567.

- : *Politische Veranstaltungen in der Bundesrepublik. Nachfrager und wahrgenommenes Angebot einer 'kleinen' Form von Öffentlichkeit* [Political Events in the Federal Republic of Germany. Demanders and Accepted Offer of a 'Small' Form of Publicity], in: *Kölner Zeitschrift für Sozialpsychologie*, 44/1992, p. 766-779.

- : *Westeuropäische Integration und die Schwierigkeiten der Entstehung einer europäischen Öffentlichkeit* [Western European Integration and the Difficulties of the Emergence of a European Public Sphere], in: *Zeitschrift für Soziologie*, 2/1993, p. 96-110.

Gerhards, Jürgen & Neidhardt, Friedhelm, *Strukturen und Funktionen moderner Öffentlichkeit –Fragestellungen und Ansätze* [Structures and Functions of a Modern Public Sphere – Questions and Approaches], in: Wolfgang R. Langenbucher, Wolfgang R. (ed.), *Politische Kommunikation – Grundlagen, Strukturen*, Vienna 1993, pp. 52-88.

Gerhards, Jürgen, Neidhardt, Friedhelm et al., *Öffentlichkeit und öffentliche Meinungsbildung im Ländervergleich USA-BRD* [Public Sphere and Public Opinion Formation in Comparison of Countries USA-Germany, in: Meulemann, Heiner & Elting-Camus, Agnes (ed.), *26. Deutscher*

Soziologentag Düsseldorf 1992, vol. II, Opladen 1993, pp. 188-191.

Gerhardt, Volker, *Politische Subjekte* [Political Subjects], in: Nagl-Docekal, H. & Vetter, H. (ed.) *Death of the Subject?* Vienna and Munich 1987, pp. 201-229.

- : *Vernunft aus Geschichte. Ernst Cassirers systematischer Beitrag zu einer Philosophie der Politik* [Reason from History. Ernst Cassirer's Systematic Contribution to a Philosophy of Politics], in: Braun, H.-J. & Holzhey, H. E & Orth, E.-W. (ed.), *Über Ernst Cassirer's Philosophie der symbolischen Formen*, Frankfurt 1988, pp. 220-248.

- : *Politik und Metaphysik. Rahmenbedingungen einer Begriffsbestimmung der Politik* [Politics and Metaphysics. Framework of a Definition of Politics], in: Gerhard (ed.), *Der Begriff der Politik. Bedingungen und Gründe für politisches Handeln*, Stuttgart 1990, pp. 1-19.

- : *Politisches Handeln* [Political Action], in: Gerhard (ed.), *Der Begriff der Politik. Bedingungen und Gründe für politisches Handeln*, Stuttgart 1990, pp. 291-309.

Goitein, Shelomo Dev, *Individualism and Conformity in Classical Islam*, in: Banani, Amin & Vryonis, Speros (ed.), *Individualism and Conformity in Classical Islam*, Wiesbaden 1977, pp. 3-18.

Greenstein, Fred I., *Can Personality and Politics be Studied Systematically?* in: *Political Psychology* 1/1992, p. 105-128.

Grünenberg, Reginald, *Gründungsgewalt und Politik. René Girards Kulturtheorie im Spiegel der Politikwissenschaft*, in: academia.edu, Berlin 2010.

- : *Laws of Singularity*, in: academia.edu, Berlin 2017.

- : *What is a Democrat? An Attempt to define the Democratic Personality*, in: *Fikrunn wa Fann*, Goethe-Institut, June 2012.

Habermas, Jürgen, *Volkssouveränität als Verfahren. Ein normativer Begriff der Öffentlichkeit?* [Popular Sovereignty as a Procedure. A Normative Concept of the Public Sphere?], in: Forum für Philosophie (ed.), *Die Ideen von 1789 in der deutschen Rezeption*, Frankfurt 1989, pp. 7-36.

Höffe, Otfried, *Wiederbelebung im Seiteneinstieg* [Revival in the Side Entrance], in: Höffe (ed.), *Der Mensch – ein politisches Tier? Essays on Political Anthropology*, Stuttgart 1992, pp. 5-13.

Hölscher, Lucian, *Öffentlichkeit* [Public Sphere], in: : *Geschichtliche Grundbegriffe. Historisches Lexikon zur politisch-sozialen Sprache in Deutschland*, ed. by Brunner, Otto & Conze, Werner & Koselleck, Reinhart,

Stuttgart 1978.

Holldack, Heinz, *Der Physiokratismus und die absolute Monarchie* [Physiocrat Doctrin and Absolute Monarchy] in: Aretin, K. O. Freiherr von (ed.), *Der aufgeklärte Absolutismus*, Cologne 1974, pp. 137-162.

Ibanez-Noé, Javier, *Urteilskraft und Darstellung* [Power of Judgment and Representation], in: Funke, Gerhard (ed.), *Akten des 7. Internationalen Kant-Kongresses, Mainz, 28. März-01. April 1990*, 2 vol., Bonn and Berlin 1991.

Immelmann, Aubrey, *The Assessment of Political Personality: A Psychodiagnostically Relevant Conceptualization and Methodology*, in: *Political Psychology* 4/1993, S. 725-741.

Ingensiep, H.-W., *Die biologischen Analogien und die erkenntnistheoretischen Alternativen in Kants Kritik der reinen Vernunft B § 27* [The Biological Analogies and the Epistemological Alternatives in Kant's Critique of Pure Reason B § 27], in: *Kant-Studien* 85/1994, S. 381-393.

Jäger, Hans Wolf, *Öffentlichkeit im 18. Jahrhundert* [Public in the 18th Century], in: *Das achtzehnte Jahrhundert* 1/1992, p. 10-11.

Jauß, Hans Robert, *Ursprung und Bedeutung der Fortschrittsidee in der Querelle des Anciens et des Modernes* [Origin and Meaning of the Idea of Progress in the 'Dispute between the Ancients and Moderns'], in: Kuhn, H. & Wiedemann, F. (ed.), *Die Philosophie und die Frage nach dem Fortschritt*, Munich 1964, pp. 51-80.

- : *Ästhetische Normen und geschichtliche Reflexion in der Querelle des Anciens et des Modernes* [Aesthetic Norms and Historical Reflection in the 'Dispute between the Ancients and Moderns'] in: Perrault, Charles, *Parallèle des Anciens et des Modernes en ce qui regarde les Arts et les Sciences*, Munich 1964, pp. 8-64.

- : *Negativität und Identifikation. Versuch zu einer Theorie der ästhetischen Erfahrung* [Negativity and Identification. Attempt at a Theory of Aesthetic Experience], in: *Poetik und Hermeneutik* VI, 1975, pp. 263-339.

Jay, Martin, *Im Reich des Blicks: Foucault und die Diffamierung des Sehens im Französischen Denken des zwanzigsten Jahrhunderts* [In the Empire of Gaze. Foucault and the Diffamation of View in French Thinking in the 20th Century], in: Couzens Hoy, David (ed.), *Foucault: A Critical Reader*, Oxford 1988.

- : *Negativität und Identifikation. Versuch zu einer Theorie der ästhetischen Erfahrung* [The Orders of Seeing in Modern Times], in: *Tumult. Zeitschrift für Verkehrswissenschaft,* 1990 ed.: *The Visible,* pp. 40-55.

- : *Hannah Arendt und die 'Ideologie des Ästhetischen' oder: Die Ästhetisierung des Politischen* [Hannah Arendt and the 'Ideology of Aesthetics' or: The Aesthetization of the Political], in: Kemper, P. (ed.), *Die Zukunft des Politischen,* Frankfurt 1993, p. 123ff.

Jensen, Stefan, *Im Kerngehäuse* [Within the Core], in: Rusch, Gerhard et al. (ed.), *DELFIN 1993. Konstruktivismus und Sozialtheorie,* Frankfurt 1994, pp. 47-108.

Jochmann, Carl Gustav, *Über die Öffentlichkeit* [On the Public Sphere], in: *Prometheus. Für Licht und Recht. Zeitschrift in zwanglosen Heften, hrsg. v. Heinrich Zschokke und seinen Freunden,* part three, 1833, pp. 149-178; reprint in: Haufe, Eberhard *Carl Gustav Jochmann. Die unzeitige Wahrheit. Aphorismen. Glossen,* Leipzig 1979, pp. 205-243.

Kahl, Sinikka, *Mit der Kürbisflasche gegen das Böse* [With the Pumpkin Bottle Against Evil, in: *die tageszeitung,* 29.9.1995, pp. 15-16.

Kaiser, Joseph H., *Konkretes Ordnungsdenken* [Concrete Order Thinking], in: Quaritsch, Helmut (ed.), *Complexio oppositorum. Über Carl Schmitt,* Berlin 1988, with discussion, pp. 319-340.

Kavolis, Vytaulas, *Logic of Selfhood and Modes of Order: Civilisational Strutures for Individual Identities,* in: Robertson, Roland & Holzner, Burkart (ed.), *Identity and Authority,* Oxford 1980, pp. 40-60.

Konersmann, Ralf, *Person. Ein bedeutungsgeschichtliches Panorama* [Person. A panorama of the History of its Meaning], in: *Internationale Zeitschrift für Philosophie* 2/1993, pp. 199-227.

Kunisch, Johannes, *Absolutismus und Öffentlichkeit* [Absolutism and Public Sphere] in: *Der Staat,* 2/1995, p. 183-198.

Lavau, Georges, *Is the Voter an Individualist?* in: Birnbaum, Pierre & Leca, Jean (ed.), *Individualism. Theories and Methods,* Oxford 1990, pp. 269-294.

Legros, Robert, *La critique hégélienne de l'individualisme,* in: *International Journal of Philosophy* 2/1993, pp. 254-265.

Liedtke, Max, *Der Begriff der Reflexion bei Kant* [The Concept of Reflection in Kant], in: *Archiv für Geschichte der Philosophie,* 48/1966, p. 207-216.

Lipp, Wolfgang, *Charisma – Schuld und Gnade. Soziale Konstruktion, Kulturdynamik, Handlungsdrama* [Charisma – Guilt and Grace. Social Construction, Cultural Dynamics, Drama of Actin], in: Gebhardt, Winfried et al. (ed.), *Charisma - Schuld und Gnade. Soziale Konstruktion, Kulturdynamik,*

Handlungsdrama, series 'Materiale Soziologie' TB3, Berlin & N. Y. 1993, p. 16-32.

List, Elisabeth, *Wissenskörper: Von der Theorie des Subjekts zur Politik symbolischer Repräsentationen,* in: List, *Die Präsenz des Anderen. Theorie und Geschlechterpolitik,* Frankfurt 1993, pp. 111-122.

Luhmann, Niklas, *Öffentliche Meinung* [Public Opinion], in: Luhmann, *Politische Planung,* Opladen 1971, pp. 9-34.

- : *Einführende Bemerkungen zu einer Theorie symbolisch generalisierter Kommunikationsmedien* [Introductory Remarks to a Theory of Symbolically Generalized Communication Media], in: Luhmann, *Soziologische Aufklärung 2,* Opladen 1975, pp. 170-192.

- : *Weltzeit und Systemgeschichte. Über Beziehungen zwischen Zeithorizonten und sozialen Strukturen gesellschaftlicher Systeme* [World Time and System History. On Relations Between Time Horizons and Social Structures of Social Systems], in: Oelmüller, Willi (ed.), *Wozu noch Geschichte?,* Munich 1977, pp. 203-252.

- : *Veränderungen im System gesellschaftlicher Kommunikation und die Massenmedien* [Changes in the System of Social Communication and the Mass Media], in: Luhmann, *Soziologische Aufklärung 3,* Opladen 1981.

- : *Gesellschaftliche Komplexität und öffentliche Meinung* [Social Complexity and Public Opinion], in: Luhmann, Sociological Enlightenment 5. Constructivist Perspectives, Opladen 1990, pp. 170-182.

- : *Weltkunst* [World Art]in: Luhmann & Bunsen, Frederick D. & Baecker, Dirk, *Unbeobachtbare Welt. Über Kunst und Architektur,* Bielefeld 1990, pp. 7-45.

- : *Die Beobachtung der Beobachter im politischen System: Zur Theorie der öffentlichen Meinung* [The Obervation of Observers in Political Systems. On the Theory of Public Opinion], in: Willke, Jürgen (ed *Öffentliche Meinung. Theorien, Methoden, Befunde. Beiträge zu Ehren von Elisabeth Noelle-Neumann,* Opladen1992, pp. 77-86.

- : *Theoriesubstitution in der Erziehungswissenschaft. Von der Philantropie zum Neuhumanismus* [Theory Substitution in Educational Science. From Philanthropy to New Humanism], in: Luhmann, Social Structure and Semantics. Studies on the Sociology of Knowledge of Modern Society, Volume 2, Frankfurt 1993, pp. 105-194.

- : *Individuum, Individualität, Individualismus* [Individual, Individuality,

Individualism], in: Luhmann, *Gesellschaftsstruktur und Semantik, Studien zur Wissenssoziologie der modernen Gesellschaft*, vol. 3, Frankfurt 1993, pp. 149-258.

- *Öffentliche Meinung* [Public Opinion], in: Luhmann, *Die Politik der Gesellschaft*, Frankfurt S. 119-143.

Lukes, Steven, *The Use of Ethnocentricity*, in: Lukes, *Moral Conflict and Politics*, Oxford 1991, pp. 71-80.

Macpherson, Crawford Brough, *Editor's Introduction*, in: Hobbes, Thomas, *Leviathan or the Matter, Forme, & Power of a Common-Wealth Ecclesiasticall and Civill*, [1651] London 1968, pp. 9-63.

Makreel, Rudolf, *Reconciling Dogmatic and Reflective Interpretations of History*, contribution to the 8th International Congress on Kant – Kant and the Problem of Peace, 1.-5. March, 1995, Memphis/Tennessee, USA, 1996.

Mandt, Hella, *Antipolitik*, in: *Zeitschrift für Politik* 4/1987, p. 383-395.

Maus, Ingeborg, *Zur Theorie der Institutionalisierung bei Kant* [On the Theorie of Institution Building in Kant], in: Göhler, Gerhard et al. (ed.), *Politische Institutionen im gesellschaftlichen Umbruch. Ideengeschichtliche Beiträge zur Theorie politischer Institutionen*, Opladen 1990, pp. 358-385.

Mauss, Marcel, *Une catégorie de l'esprit humain: La notion de Personne, celle de 'moi'*, first published in: *The Journal of the Royal Anthropological Institute* 68/1938, reprint in Maus, *The Category of the Person. Anthropology, Philosophy, History*, ed. by M. Carrithers, S. Collins and S. Lukes, Cambridge 1985.

Meier, Christian, *Zu Carl Schmitts Begriffsbildung – Das Politische und der Nomos* [On Building of Concepts in Carl Schmitt – The Political and the Nomos], in: Quaritsch, Helmut (ed.), *Complexio oppositorum. Über Carl Schmitt*, Berlin 1988, pp. 537-556.

Mesnard, Pierre, *Le commerce épistolaire comme expression sociale de l'individualisme humaniste*, in: *Individu et société dans la Renaissance, Colloque internationale 1965*, Brussels 1967, pp. 13-31.

Metz, Johann Baptist, *Gotteskrise. Ein Portrait des zeitgenössischen Christentums* [God Crisis. A Portrait of Contemporary Christianity], in: Süddeutsche Zeitung, 24/25 July 1993.

Müller, Max, *Person und Funktion* [Person and Function], in: *Philosophisches Jahrbuch* 69/2, 1962, pp. 371-404.

- : *Philosophische Grundlagen der Politik* [Philosophical Foundations of

Politics], in: *Existenz und Ordnung. Festschrift für Erik Wolf zum 60. Geburtstag*, Frankfurt 1962, pp. 282-308.

Münkler, Herfried, *Die Moral der Politik. Politik, Politikwissenschaft und die sozio-moralische Dimension politischer Ordnung* [The Morality of Politics. Politics, Political Science and the Socio-Moral Dimension of Political Order], in: Leggewie, Claus (ed.), *Wozu Politikwissenschaft? Über das neue in der Politik*, Darmstadt 1994, pp. 228-242.

Neidhardt, Friedhelm, *Öffentlichkeit* [Publicity], in: Enderle, Georges & Homann, Karl et al. (ed.), *Lexikon der Wirtschaftsethik*, Freiburg i. B. 1993, pp. 775-780.

Nipperdey, Thomas, *Die anthropologische Dimension der Geschichtswissenschaft* [The Anthropological Dimension of Historical Science], in: Nipperdey, *Gesellschaft, Kultur, Theorie. Gesammelte Aufsätze zur neueren Geschichte*, Göttingen 1976, pp. 33-58.

- : *Verein als soziale Struktur im späten 18. und frühen 19. Jahrhundert* [Association as Social Structure in the late 18th and early 19th Century] in: Nipperdey, *Gesellschaft, Kultur, Theorie. Gesammelte Aufsätze zur neueren Geschichte*, Göttingen 1976, pp. 174-205.

Nitschke, Peter, *Zwischen Innovation und Tradition: der politische Aristotelismus in der deutschen politischen Philosophie der Prämoderne* [Between Innovation and Tradition: Political Aristotelism in German Pre-Modern Political Philosophy], in: *Zeitschrift für Politik* 1/1995, S. 27-40.

Philonenko, Alexis, *Cassirer. Lecteur et interprète de Kant*, in: Seidengart, Jean (ed.), *Ernst Cassirer. De Marbourg à New York. L'itinéraire philosophique, Actes du colloque de Nanterre, 12-14 October 1988*, pp. 43-54.

- : *Kant. Critique de la faculté de juger – "Streiten und Disputieren": l'antinomie du goût*, in: Philonenko, *Le transcendental et la pensée moderne. Etudes d'histoire de la philosophie*, Paris 1990, pp. 212-235.

Pizzorno, Alessandro, *On Rationality and Democratic Choice*, in: Birnbaum, Pierre & Leca, Jean (ed.), *Individualism. Theories and Methods*, Oxford 1990, pp. 295-331.

Post, Jerrold M. & Robins, Robert S., *Political Paranoia. The Psychopolitics of Hate*, Yale 1995

Rudolph, Enno, *De servo individuo. Kants Weg von der Person zur Persönlichkeit* [De servo individuo. Kant's Path from Person to Personality], in: *Internationale Zeitschrift für Philosophie* 2/1993, pp. 228-243.

Schwan, Alexander, *Philosophie der Gegenwart vor dem Problem des Pluralismus* [Contemporary Philosophy and the Problem of Pluralism], in: Simon, Josef (ed.), *Freiheit. Theoretische und praktische Aspekte des Problems*, Freiburg and Munich 1977, pp. 171-203.

Sloterdijk, Peter, *Der mystische Imperativ. Bemerkungen zum Formwandel des Religiösen in der Neuzeit* [The Mystical Imperative. Remarks on the Change of Form of the Religious in Modern Times], in: Sloterdijk (ed.), *Mystische Zeugnisse aller Zeiten und Völker*, Munich 1993 [New Edition of Martin Buber's *Ecstatic Confessions*, Jena 1909], pp. 9-42.

Sternberger, Dolf, *Begriff des Politischen. Heidelberger Antrittsvorlesung* [Concept of the Political. Inaugural Lecture], in: Sternberger, *Die Politik und der Friede*, Frankfurt 1986, pp. 69-88.

Stützel-Prüsener, Marlies, *Die deutschen Lesegesellschaften im Zeitalter der Aufklärung* [German Reading Societies During Enlightenment], in: Dann, Otto (ed.), *Lesegesellschaften und bürgerliche Emanzipation. Ein europäischer Vergleich*, Munich 1981, pp. 71-86.

Sumic-Riha, Jelica, *Über die Inexistenz von Kants politischer Philosophie* [On the Inexistence of Kant's Political Philosophy], in: Mladen Dolar et al., *Kant und das Unbewusste*, Vienna 19944.

Sutton, Frederick X., *Representation and Nature of Political Systems*, in: *Comparative Studies in Society and History*, 2/1959, pp. 19-32.

Taylor, Charles, *Atomism*, in: Taylor, *Philosophical Papers*, vol. II, Cambridge 1985, pp. 187-210.

Tenbruck, Friedrich, *Anthropologie des Handelns* [Anthropology of Acting], in: Lenk, Hans (ed.), *Handlungstheorien – interdisziplinär*, Volume 2, Munich 1978, pp. 89-138.

- : *Das Werk Max Webers* [The Work of Max Weber], in: *Kölner Zeitschrift für Soziologie und Sozialpsychologie* 27/1975, pp. 663-702.

Theunissen, Michael, *Die verdrängte Intersubjektivität in Hegels Philosophie des Rechts* [The Repressed Intersubjectivity in Hegel's Philosophy of Law, in: Henrich, Dieter & Horstmann, R.-P. (ed.), *Hegels Philosophie des Rechts. Die Theorie der Rechtsformen und ihre Logik*, Stuttgart 1982, pp. 317-381.

Topitsch, Ernst, , *Über die Möglichkeit besonderer Verfahren in den Sozialwissenschaften* [On the Possibility of Special Procedures in the Social Sciences], in: Topitsch (ed.), *Logik der Sozialwissenschaften*, Cologne 1965, p. 254.

Tversky, Amos & Kahemann Daniel, *Judgement under Uncertainty: Heuristics and Biases*, in: *Science*, New Series, vol. 185, issue 4157 (September 27, 1974), pp. 1124-1131.

Voegelin, Eric, *What is Nature?* in: Voegelin, *Anamnesis*, London 1978, pp. 71-88.

Vollrath, Ernst, *Hannah Arendt über Meinung und Urteilskraft* [Hannah Arendt on Opinion and the Power of Judgment], in: Reif, Adelbert (ed.), *Hannah Arendt. Materialien zu ihrem Wer*, Munich 1979, pp. 85-107.

- : *Hannah Arendt und die Methode des politischen Denkens* [Hannah Arendt and the Method of Political Thinking], in: Reif, Adelbert (ed.), *Hannah Arendt. Materialien zu ihrem Werk*, Munich 1979, pp. 79-84.

- : *'Neue Wege der Klugheit.' Zum methodischen Prinzip der Theorie des Handelns bei Clausewitz* ['New Ways of Wisdom'. On the Methodical Principle of the Theory of Action in Clausewitz], in: *Zeitschrift für Politik*, 1984/1, p. 53 ff.

- : *Politische Philosophie - Gibt es das überhaupt (noch)?* [Politische Philosophie – Does this (Still) Exist?] in: *Zeitschrift für Politik* 3/1987, S. 221-232.

- : *Die Kultur des Politischen. Konzepte politischer Wahrnehmung in Deutschland* [The Culture of the Political. Concepts of Political Perception in Germany], in: Gerhardt, Volker (ed.), *Der Begriff der Politik. Bedingungen und Gründe für politisches Handeln*, Stuttgart 1990, pp. 268-290.

- : *Handlungshermeneutik als Alternative zur systemtheoretischen Interpretation politischer Institutionen* [Hermeneutics of Action as an Alternative to Systems-Theoretical Interpretations of Political Institutions], in: Gerhardt, Volker (ed.), *Der Begriff der Politik. Bedingungen und Gründe für politisches Handeln*, Stuttgart 1990, pp. 204-212.

- : *Sittliche oder politische Urteilskraft?* [Ethical or Political Power of Judgment], in: *Politische Vierteljahresschrift* 4/1991, S. 654-661.

- : *Die Philosophie des Politischen in Deutschland. Kritische Bemerkungen* [The Philosophy of the Political in Germany. Critical Remarks], in: *Information Philosophie*, March 1992, pp. 35-40

- : *Carl von Clausewitz: Eine mit dem Handeln befreundete Theorie* [Carl von Clausewitz: A Theory Befriended with Action], in: Vowinckel, Gerhard (ed.), *Clausewitz-Kolloquium - Theorie des Krieges als Sozialwissenschaft*, Berlin 1993, pp. 63-78.

Vowe, Gehard, *Politische Kognition. Umrisse eines kognitionsorientierten*

Ansatzes für die Analyse politischen Handelns [Political Cognition. Outlines of a Cognitive Approach to the Analysis of Political Action], in: *Politische Vierteljahresschrift*, special edition 25, 1994, pp. 423-447.

Wagner, Gerhard and Zipprian, Heinz, *Identität oder Differenz. Bemerkungen zu einer Aporie Niklas Luhmanns Theorie selbstreferentieller System* [Identity or Difference. Remarks on an Aporia in Niklas Luhmann's Theory of Self-Referential Systems], in: *Zeitschrift für Soziologie* 6/1992, S. 394-405.

Welke, Martin, *Gemeinsame Lektüre und frühe Formen von Gruppenbildung im 17. und 18. Jahrhundert. Zeitungslesen in Deutschland* [Joint Reading and Early Forms of Group Formation in the 17th and 18th Centuries. Newspaper Reading in Germany], in: Dann, Otto (ed.), *Vereinswesen und bürgerliche Gesellschaft in Deutschland*, Munich 1984, pp. 29-53.

Wenzel, Uwe-Justus, *Fundamentaltheorie des Politischen oder politische Theorie des Fundamentalen* [Fundamental Theory of the Political or Political Theory of the Fundamental], in: *Archiv für Rechts- und Sozialphilosophie*, 4/1988, p. 531-441.

- : *Moral im Abstand. Die "Operation der Reflexion" im moralischen Grenzfall* [Morality at a Distance. The "Operation of Reflection" in Moral Borderline Cases], in: Funke, Gerhard (ed.), .), *Akten des 7. Internationalen Kant-Kongresses, Mainz, 28. März-01. April 1990*, 2 vol., Bonn and Berlin 1991, pp. 439-53.

Wiehl, Reiner, *Die Komplementarität von Selbstsein und Bewusstsein* [The Complementarity of Self-Being and Consciousness] in: Cramer, Konrad et al. (ed.), *Theory of Subjectivity*, Festschrift on the occasion of the 60. Birthday of Dieter Henrich, Frankfurt 1990, pp. 44-75.

Wittmann, Reinhard, *Der lesende Landmann. Zur Rezeption der aufklärerischen Bemühungen durch die bäuerliche Bevölkerung im 18. Jahrhundert* [The Reading Peasant. On the Reception of the Efforts of Enlightenment on the Agrarian Population in the Late 18th Century], in: Berindei, D. & a. (ed.), *Der Bauer Mittel- und Osteuropas im sozioökonomischen Wandel des 18. und 19. Jahrhunderts*, Cologne 1973, p. 142-189.

Wolters, Gereon, *Immanuel Kant*, in: Böhme, Gernot (ed.), *Klassiker der Naturphilosophie. Von den Vorsokratikern bis zu Kopenhagener Schule*, Munich 1989, pp. 203-219.

Cell, Carsten, *Öffentlichkeit im 18. Jahrhundert. Tagung der Deutschen Gesellschaft für die Erforschung des 18. Jahrhunderts, 18-20. November 1992 in Meersburg/Bodensee* [The Public in the 18th Century. Conference of the

German Society for the Study of the 18th Century, 18-20 November 1992 in Meersburg/Bodensee], conference report, in: *Das achtzehnte Jahrhundert* 1/1993, S. 12-13.

Zingerle, Arnold, *Theoretische Probleme und Perspektiven der Charisma-Forschung. Ein kritischer Rückblick* [Theoretical Problems and Perspectives of Charisma Research. A Critical Retrospective], in: Gebhardt, Winfried & a. (ed.), *Charisma: Theorie, Religion, Politik,* series 'Materiale Soziologie' TB3, Berlin & N. Y. 1993, pp. 249-266.

Index of Persons

Adam, Armin 53, 60, 64, 65, 66, 67, 246, 302, 419, 433, 436, 476
Al-Jabri , Mohammed Abed 332, 333, 334, 335, 336, 337, 369, 382, 412, 419, 441, 485
Al-Râziq, Alî Abd 334, 419
Althusius, Johannes 68, 69, 419
Anderson, Benedict 280, 419
Anter, Andreas 212, 245, 419
Arendt, Hannah 7, 10, 17, 24, 25, 26, 27, 28, 30, 80, 81, 145, 146, 151, 152, 153, 154, 156, 176, 186, 196, 239, 251, 275, 276, 289, 290, 291, 313, 315, 325, 358, 359, 379, 411, 419, 425, 441, 442, 447, 452, 476
Arens, Edmund 331, 438
Aretin, Karl-Otto Freiherr von 60, 438, 446
Ariès, Philippe 40, 41, 42, 438
Aristoteles 78, 434
Arkoun, Mohammed 334, 441
Aubrey, John 327, 404, 420, 446
Baeumler, Alfred 86, 92, 103, 107, 109, 357, 358, 420
Balandier, George 377, 378, 379, 380, 420, 484
Baraldi, Claudio 402, 438
Bardy, Gustave 310, 420
Bartuschat, Wolfgang 193, 420
Bateson, Gregory 194, 420
Batteux, Charles 91, 420
Bauer, Wilhelm 129, 136, 421, 454
Baumgarten, Alexander 14, 95, 104, 105, 106, 107, 108, 109, 111, 161, 199, 421, 436
Beck , Ulrich 34, 297, 421
Beck-Gernsheim, Elisabeth 421
Beiner, Ronald 151, 152, 420, 421, 441
Benjamin, Walter 250, 251, 312, 326, 421
Berger, Peter 249, 421
Bergson, Henri 265, 336, 421
Bermbach, Udo 121, 441
Birnbaum, Pierre 40, 361, 381, 438, 448, 451
Bittner, Rüdiger 318, 441
Blasche Siegfried 260, 317, 441
Bloom, Harold 382, 441
Blumenberg, Hans 39, 128, 421

Böhme, Gernot 394, 421, 441, 454
Bohrer, Karl Heinz 86, 267, 422
Boileau-Despréaux, Nicolas 85, 88, 90, 91, 92, 95, 98, 100, 103, 263, 350, 421
Bornscheuer, Lothar 422
Brandt, Reinhard 133, 168, 190, 292, 296, 348, 354, 422, 441
Brentano, Lujo 63, 422
Brückner, Jutta 62, 422
Brumlik, Michael 111, 439, 444
Brunkhorst, Hauke 24, 111, 152, 422, 439, 442, 444
Bubner, Rüdiger 442
Buchstein, Hubertus 406, 442
Bullinger, Martin 123, 422
Bürger, Christa 439
Bürger, Peter 439
Burnier, DeLysa 253, 442
Canetti, Elias 276
Cassirer, Ernst 26, 44, 45, 86, 96, 98, 100, 101, 106, 148, 156, 190, 214, 256, 353, 357, 359, 376, 377, 422, 442, 445, 450
Cavalieri, Paola 197, 439
Cazeneuve, Jean 199, 283, 443
Cicero, Marcus Tullius 75, 97, 112, 191, 248, 423
Claessens, Dieter 394, 395, 423
Clausewitz, Carl von 77, 80, 81, 82, 83, 155, 229, 423, 435, 440, 443, 452, 453, 476, 480
Combe, Pierre J. de la 443
Corsi, Giancarlo 402, 438
Cramer, Konrad 347, 351, 439, 443, 453
Danto, Artuhr C. 46, 85, 195, 383, 443
De Bondt, Werner 67, 443
Derrida, Jacques 150, 163, 169, 170, 187, 197, 255, 376, 423, 443
Detel, Wolfgang 202, 443
Diehle, Albrecht 202, 423
Dietrich, Rainer 77, 443
Dilthey, Wilhelm 199, 333, 379, 423
Disselbeck, Klaus 356, 443
Dörner, Andreas 26, 252, 368, 374, 385, 423
Dumont, Louis 40, 49, 66, 69, 158, 195, 378, 379, 380, 423, 483
Dumouchel, Daniel 165, 443
Düsing, Karl 423
Dux 265, 266, 269, 423
Eagleton, Terry 84, 151, 424

Easton, David 378, 444
Ebeling, Hans 345, 424
Ebertz, Michael 363, 439
Eco, Umberto 255, 271, 424
Eder, Klaus 118, 424
Eichberger, Tassilo 424
Eisenstadt, S. N. 378, 444
Elias, Norbert 41, 42, 43, 53, 276, 424
Engelsing, Rolf 132, 444
Eppler, Erhard 135, 424
Erasmus von Rotterdam, Desiderius 41, 230, 424
Esposito, Elena 402, 438
Farge, Arlette 424
Ferry, Luc 29, 30, 84, 85, 93, 95, 96, 104, 106, 111, 128, 149, 151, 156, 157, 158, 197, 201, 204, 239, 283, 357, 359, 397, 398, 424, 425, 476
Finkielkraut, Alain 17, 425
Foster, Georg 126, 127, 425
Foucault, Michel 14, 76, 158, 200, 272, 285, 335, 377, 425, 447
Fox-Genovese, Elisabeth 383, 425
Fraenkel, Ernst 130, 425
Frank, Manfred 285, 439, 444
Freud, Sigmund 34, 203, 276, 425, 482
Fricke, Christel 425
Friedell, Egon 228, 425
Friedmann, Friedrich 152, 425
Funke, Gerhard 256, 318, 439, 446, 453
Gadamer, Hans-Georg 85, 109, 111, 112, 113, 333, 425, 433
Gagel, Walter 409, 425
Garcia, Jorge 426
Gasché, Rudolph 256, 444
Gebhardt , Winfried 363, 366, 367, 373, 439, 448, 454
Gehlen, Arnold 376, 426
Gerhards, Jürgen 426, 444, 445
Gerhardt, Volker 289, 313, 359, 361, 426, 439, 442, 445, 452, 453
Girard, René 202, 208, 268, 274, 293, 332, 367, 426
Goetschel, Willi 165, 294, 356, 393, 426
Göhler, Gerhardt 133, 292, 439, 442, 449
Goitein, Shelomo Dev 335, 445
Greenstein, Fred I. 404, 445
Grünenberg, Reginald 1, 10, 142, 148, 202, 208, 274, 293, 332, 367, 426, 445, 488, 489

Guggenberger, Bernd 251, 426
Guyer, Paul 8, 9, 87, 147, 227, 429
Habermas, Jürgen 10, 21, 24, 29, 31, 34, 111, 116, 117, 118, 122, 123, 124, 126, 155, 205, 216, 261, 298, 300, 301, 303, 309, 342, 349, 350, 375, 385, 399, 400, 401, 426, 446, 483
Hartmann, Nicolai 94, 427
Haverkamp, Anselm 40, 439
Hegel, Georg Willhelm Friedrich 11, 26, 30, 71, 72, 75, 77, 78, 114, 125, 126, 147, 148, 150, 151, 152, 236, 270, 336, 342, 347, 359, 377, 403, 427, 428, 429, 434, 442, 452, 480
Heidegger, Martin 14, 50, 84, 147, 148, 149, 156, 157, 247, 257, 271, 308, 353, 392, 393, 397, 427, 436, 442, 473
Heinsohn, Gunnar 197, 427
Henrich, Dieter 10, 11, 22, 31, 152, 181, 255, 309, 343, 345, 346, 347, 348, 349, 350, 351, 390, 427, 439, 443, 452, 454
Hensmann, Volker 60, 427
Herder, Gottfried Johann 265, 376, 427
Herold, Norbert 359, 439
Hobbes, Thomas 23, 70, 122, 156, 186, 225, 228, 274, 300, 310, 326, 327, 328, 335, 428, 435, 449
Höffe, Otfried 18, 152, 158, 161, 312, 318, 377, 428, 440, 446
Hoffman, Arndt 19, 428
Holland-Cunz, Barbara 398, 428
Holldack, Heinz 60, 446
Hölscher, Lucian 117, 118, 123, 124, 126, 127, 128, 310, 428, 446
Honneth, Axel 428
Hösle, Vittorio 152, 428
Huizinga, Johan 40, 278, 293, 428
Hume, David 71, 96, 97, 98, 100, 101, 105, 170, 428, 480
Husserl, Edmund 6, 271, 342, 352, 385, 429
Ibanez-Noé, Javier 256, 446
Immelmann, Aubrey 404, 446
Ingensiep, H.-W. 354, 446
Jäger, Hans Wolf 446
Jauß, Hans Robert 40, 90, 109, 429, 446
Jay, Martin 200, 447
Jean Paul 104
Jensen, Stefan 288, 447
Jochmann, Carl Gustav 131, 132, 133, 134, 135, 429, 447
Kahemann, Daniel 452
Kahl, Sinikka 200, 447

Kaiser, Joseph H. 246, 447
Kant, Immanuel 3, 5, 7, 8, 10, 11, 14, 15, 18, 20, 21, 26, 28, 29, 30, 32, 33, 34, 36, 37, 45, 52, 57, 58, 59, 66, 72, 73, 74, 78, 79, 80, 81, 83, 84, 85, 86, 99, 100, 101, 104, 105, 106, 107, 108, 109, 111, 113, 114, 123, 133, 134, 138, 139, 145, 146, 147, 148, 149, 150, 151, 152, 153, 154, 155, 156, 157, 158, 160, 161, 162, 163, 164, 165, 166, 167, 168, 169, 170, 172, 174, 175, 176, 177, 178, 179, 180, 181, 182, 183, 184, 185, 186, 187, 188, 189, 192, 193, 197, 201, 203, 206, 207, 208, 213, 214, 215, 216, 219, 220, 221, 222, 223, 225, 226, 227, 228, 229, 230, 231, 232, 233, 234, 235, 236, 238, 240, 241, 243, 244, 251, 252, 253, 254, 255, 256, 257, 258, 259, 260, 263, 264, 265, 266, 271, 275, 276, 277, 285, 289, 291, 292, 293, 294, 296, 298, 299, 300, 302, 304, 307, 308, 312, 313, 314, 315, 316, 317, 318, 319, 320, 321, 322, 323, 324, 325, 326, 329, 330, 336, 338, 339, 341, 342, 344, 345, 346, 347, 348, 349, 350, 351, 352, 353, 354, 355, 356, 357, 359, 369, 376, 377, 383, 386, 387, 388, 389, 390, 391, 392, 393, 394, 396, 399, 411, 414, 415, 416, 418, 420, 421, 422, 423, 425, 426, 427, 428, 429, 430, 431, 432, 433, 434, 437, 439, 440, 441, 442, 443, 444, 446, 448, 449, 450, 451, 453, 454, 476, 480
Kantorowicz, Ernst 273, 365, 429
Kaulbach, Friedrich 167, 190, 216, 313, 336, 352, 359, 376, 426, 429, 439
Kavolis, Vytaulas 447
Kersting, Christa 429
Kersting, Wolfgang 69, 429
Keynes, John Maynard 61, 429, 482
Kluge, Alexander 433
Kluxen, Kurt 130, 440
Koch, Anton 430
Kohler, Georg 182, 189, 430
Konersmann, Ralf 447
Koselleck, Reinhart 117, 122, 269, 270, 430, 446
Kreisky, Eva 408, 440
Kues, Nicolas of 430
Kulenkampff, Jens 181, 430, 440
Küng, Hans 337, 430
Kunisch, Johannes 124, 447
Küppers, Bernd-Olaf 214, 430
Lahrem, Stephan 430
Lavau, Georges 361, 448
Leca, Jean 40, 361, 381, 438, 448, 451
Lefort, Claude 274, 430
Legros, Robert 79, 448

Leibniz, Gottfried Willhelm 14, 39, 47, 49, 50, 51, 52, 99, 100, 104, 106, 107, 109, 201, 220, 294, 336, 356, 430, 476, 480
Leidhold, Wolfgang 257, 430
Lepenies, Wolf 394, 430
Lévi-Strauss, Claude 17, 201, 227, 283, 430
Liedtke, Max 166, 431, 448
Lipp, Wolfgang 366, 367, 448
List, Elisabeth 286, 408, 448
Löffler, Martin 115, 116, 122, 440
Longuenesse, Beatrice 344, 431
Lottes, Günther 431
Luckmann, Thomas 249, 421
Luhmann, Niklas 10, 11, 15, 16, 18, 31, 33, 34, 46, 57, 58, 65, 119, 155, 171, 205, 216, 233, 245, 261, 270, 277, 296, 303, 307, 328, 329, 342, 343, 344, 345, 346, 349, 350, 352, 353, 354, 356, 357, 375, 376, 398, 399, 401, 402, 403, 431, 438, 441, 448, 449, 453, 475, 476, 481, 482
Lukes, Steven 381, 382, 432, 449
Lyotard, François 86, 111, 149, 150, 152, 432
Lypp, Bernhard 432
Macpherson, Crawford 70, 72, 327, 336, 428, 432, 449
Mahrenholz, Ernst Gottfried 305, 440
Makreel, Rudolf 230, 449
Mandeville, Bernard de 62, 63, 64, 66, 432
Mandt, Hella 306, 449
Martin, Gottfried 256, 440
Maus, Ingeborg 157, 449
Mauss, Marcel 381, 382, 449
Mc Farlane, Alain 432
Meier, Christian 82, 107, 140, 248, 249, 250, 380, 383, 384, 394, 432, 449, 484
Merleau-Ponty, Maurice 272, 432
Merten, Klaus 440
Mesnard, Pierre 43, 450
Metz, Johann Baptist 331, 337, 432, 450
Möller, Horst 125, 126, 132, 135, 136, 138, 139, 432
Morris, Colin 433
Müller, Max 284, 450
Münkler, Herfried 19, 20, 121, 306, 441, 450
Negt, Oskar 433
Neidhardt, Friedhelm 426, 445, 450
Niethammer, Immanuel 433
Nipperdey, Thomas 36, 130, 139, 370, 450

Nitschke, Peter 124, 245, 450
Oncken, August 66, 433
Orozco, Teresa 112, 433
Ortega y Gasset, José 112, 433
Otto, Stephan 43, 433
Paine, Thomas 110, 111, 212, 433
Peter, Joachim 433
Petersen, Erik 327, 433
Pfetsch, Frank 237, 434
Philonenko, Alexis 190, 230, 256, 299, 300, 377, 433, 450, 451
Piaget, Jean 34, 265, 434, 482
Pizzorno, Alessandro 361, 451
Popper; Karl 49, 295, 434
Post, Jerrold 224, 451
Pries, Christine 86, 149, 440
Prignitz, Christoph 141, 434
Quaritsch, Helmut 246, 248, 440, 447, 450
Radcliffe-Brown, A. R. 378, 434
Rawls, John 72, 124, 152, 434
Reble, Albert 53, 56, 57, 434
Renaut, Alain 30, 49, 50, 51, 156, 357, 359, 425, 434
Ritter, Joachim 78, 434
Robins, Robert S. 224, 451
Rodis-Lewis, Geneviève 48, 434
Rorty, Richard 196, 391, 434
Rossi, Pietroy 269, 440
Rousseau, Jean-Jacques 54, 55, 56, 57, 59, 69, 70, 72, 73, 127, 232, 434, 480
Rudolph, Enno 451
Sarcinelli, Ulrich 434
Sartori, Giovanni 68, 70, 434
Sassenbach, Ulrich 153, 186, 225, 312, 313, 314, 315, 326, 434
Sauer, Birgit 408, 440
Schaeffer, Jean-Marie 84, 435
Schama, Simon 127
Schapera, I. 378, 435
Schefczyk, Michael 308, 435
Schenk, Herrad 407, 435
Schleiermacher, Friedrich 333, 435
Schmidt, Siegfried 440
Schmitt, Carl 40, 45, 46, 121, 122, 186, 234, 245, 246, 247, 248, 249, 250, 268, 300, 310, 327, 419, 435, 440, 447, 449, 479

Schössler, Dietmar 83, 435
Schulze, Winfried 121, 436
Schumpeter, Joseph A. 61, 64, 436, 482
Schwan, Alexander 284, 309, 436, 451
Schweizer, Hans Rudolf 108, 436
Seel, Martin 266, 395, 398, 436
Seitter, Walter 278, 436
Sen, Amartya 228, 436
Sennett, Richard 271, 371, 436
Shaftesbury, Third Earl of 14, 98, 99, 100, 113, 216, 436, 476
Simmel, Georg 436
Singer, Peter 196, 197, 397, 439
Skinner, Quentin 23, 40, 45, 46, 440
Sloterdijk, Peter 337, 451
Smith, Adam 14, 60, 64, 65, 66, 67, 302, 433, 436, 476, 480, 482
Spencer Brown, George 354, 436
Stamm, Karl-Heinz 436
Stankiewicz, William J. 121, 437
Steinberger, Peter J. 30, 110, 155, 176, 244, 313, 437
Sternberger , Dolf 152, 280, 291, 437, 451
Stone, Isidor F. 271, 385, 436, 437
Strawson, Peter Frederick 40, 201, 204, 310, 437
Stützel-Prüsener, Marlies 139, 451
Sumic-Riha, Jelica 315, 451
Sutton, Frederick X. 378, 451
Tarnowski, Wolfgang 288, 437
Tarski, Alfred 296, 437
Taylor, Charles 383, 451, 489
Teichert, Dieter 160, 437
Tenbruck, Friedrich 365, 366, 451
Thaler, Richard 67, 443
Theunissen, Michael 152, 267, 452
Toennis, Ferdinand 117, 437
Topitsch, Ernst 215, 452
Trapp, Christian Ernst 56, 437
Tugendhat, Ernst 207, 339, 349, 437
Tversky, Amos 67, 452
Valjavec, Fritz 138, 140, 437
Virilio, Paul 288, 437
Voegelin, Eric 191, 212, 452

Vollrath, Vollrath 28, 30, 80, 81, 151, 152, 153, 154, 155, 157, 176, 186, 239, 248, 249, 297, 308, 312, 313, 326, 357, 359, 361, 437, 452
Voltaire 56, 93, 438
Vowe, Gerhard 404, 405, 453
Vowinckel, Gerhard 77, 81, 440, 443, 453
Wagner, Gerhard 119, 343, 453
Weber, Max 3, 32, 37, 40, 63, 180, 211, 233, 272, 279, 327, 363, 364, 365, 366, 368, 369, 370, 372, 413, 438, 452, 482
Wehler, Ulrich 19, 62, 118, 131, 132, 136, 137, 141, 438
Weißenbach, Olaf 430
Welke, Martin 134, 140, 453
Welker, Michael 328, 441
Wenzel, Uwe-Justus 153, 318, 453
Wiehl, Reiner 351, 453
Wittmann, Reinhard 132, 136, 454
Wohlfeil, Rainer 121, 438
Wolters, Gereon 394, 454
Zaller, John R. 438
Zelle, Carsten 85, 87, 91, 115, 263, 350
Zingerle, Arnold 363, 367, 439, 454
Zipprian, Heinz 119, 343, 453

Picture Credits and Graphics

Picture Credits

Cover: *The Tennis Court Oath* by Jacques-Louis David (1748-1825), 1791.

Fig.1: Mario Laserna and Albert Einstein, original photo ©Mario Laserna.

Fig.2: Niklas Luhmann (1927-1998) ©Archiv Landeszeitung Lüneburg.

Fig.3: Hannah Arendt (1906-1975) ©Hannah Arendt Bluecher Literary Trust.

Fig.4: Luc Ferry ©Edition Grasset, Irmeli Jung.

Fig.5: Gottfried Wilhelm von Leibniz (1646-1713), oil painting by Bernhard Christoph Francke, ca. 1700.

Fig.6: Adam Smith (1723-1790), engraving after a medallion by James Tassie, ca. 1787.

Fig.7: Carl von Clausewitz (1780-1831), portrait by Wilhelm Wach, ca. 1830.

Fig.8: Anthony Ashley-Cooper, Third Earl of Shaftesbury (1671-1712), Archive for Art and History Berlin.

Fig.9: Immanuel Kant (1724-1804), Anonymus.

Portrait of the author: ©Jernimus van Pelt, www.jeronimusvanpelt.nl

Graphics

Chart 0: Overview of political subjectivity within the individual

Table 1: Faculties of the mind

Chart I: Thematic structure of the Critique of the Power of Judgment

Chart II: The path of judgment

Chart III: The human individual – a polycentric subject

Chart IV: The egological pedigree of modernity

Chart V: The Second Tradition of philosophy of subjectivity

Bonus

It is extremely difficult to define exactly what qualifies a person as 'democratic'. Political science cannot answer this simple question because the 'science' part in it is not up to the standard of other social sciences and humanities. Under the meta-theoretical dominance of 'structures', 'systems' and 'discourses', political science has completely lost out of sight the reference 'subject'. In order to develop a democratic personality, people first need the cognitive capacity to imagine political alternatives. Then they need the freedom and the intention to use it. The following essay appeared in June 2012 in German, English, French, Arab and Farsi in the intercultural magazine *Fikrun wa Fann*, published by the German Goethe Institute. The English translation was made by Aingeal Flanagan.

What Is a Democrat? An Attempt to Define the Democratic Personality

When Educated Guesses Fail

The question that forms the title of this essay sounds very simple indeed, and one might think that there is a short and concise answer to it. But all attempts to come up with an answer promptly fail. Try it yourself! Explain in a few short sentences what a democrat is. Answers such as 'a person who lives in a democracy' or 'the kind of people who make up a democracy' are invalid because some democracies can cope with a large number of non-democrats and there are democrats in countries that are anything but democratic. Moreover, such answers are just an attempt to use the known to explain the unknown instead of explaining the unknown on the basis of what it is. A correct definition would also have to provide criteria that allow us to differentiate between democrats and non-democrats.

See? Not as easy as it looks, is it? Okay, let's give it another try. Go onto the internet and enter the term 'democrat' or even 'what is a democrat?' in German in the search engine. Aha: so they're members of some political parties who call themselves 'democrats'. Okay. That's not the answer either. Fine, let's give it one more go. Perhaps it's only us Germans who don't know what a democrat is. Try asking the question in English. After all, the English-speaking world is much larger and has always been one step ahead of the game in terms of democracy. But here too the results are disappointing.

This is all the more astonishing when we consider that here in the 'West' we not only hold democracy in very high regard, we also want to export it worldwide, and in so doing bring joy into other peoples' lives. Logically, this is understandable and is in line with the experience that a democracy needs a certain – as yet undefined – number of democrats to survive, but we still don't even know what a democrat is. Nevertheless, we want to democratize Iraq, Afghanistan, and – while we're at it – China too, not to mention the Arab nations that have just liberated themselves from their despots in such a spectacular and unexpected manner. We feel what it is like to be a democrat and we have an idea of what it means, but we can't put it into words. I will now have to disappoint you by saying that we will not be able to solve this definition problem here either, because the extent and consequences of it are much more far-reaching than this simple little question leads us to believe.

Individual – Political Subject – Democrat

If we go up a level and look at the more general term 'political subject', the category to which the term 'democrat' belongs, we experience the same problem. Here too we could ask, 'What is a political subject?' Here too we don't have an answer at hand, and the internet is no help either. The whole thing just becomes more confusing, because according to Marxist theory the political subject is the working class; from Lenin onwards, however, it is the Communist Party. For the Nazi jurist Carl Schmitt, on the other hand, the political subject was the dictator, who had the power to impose the state of emergency. This doesn't help us at all. If we move up to the next higher level of abstraction, we come to the *individual*. Using our intuition, we can assume that people are individuals and that, as such, they *can* at least be political subjects too, and as such they *can* also be democrats. However, if we then apprehensively ask, 'What is an individual?', we are overwhelmed by a mountain of different philosophical, sociological, and psychological answers, none of which are of any help to us in this matter.

We will not be able to satisfactorily fill and complete the syllogistic chain *individual-political subject-democrat* with definitions here because we would only be explaining one mystery with another. There are, however, a few tantalizing hints as to why these terms were either *not* focused on and defined or why they were *no longer* focused on and defined. Furthermore, I have developed my own approach to the middle term, the 'political subject', which I would like to discuss here. Perhaps, by the end of this article, we will manage to have at least a rough outline of what a democrat is.

Individualism emerged in the eighteenth century in an era of upheaval characterized by the civil revolutions in England, America, and France. It was the result of two things: firstly, the *actions* of enraged citizens, who were fighting for greater justice, self-determination, and participation in political power, and secondly, *treatises* in which the greatest minds of the day tried to show what this historically significant individuality means in detail. A variety of schemata for the individual were developed in a variety of disciplines, above all the individual as a complex 'subject' with astonishing horizons in *philosophy* (Descartes, Leibniz, Kant); then the individual as the object of education in *pedagogy* (Locke, Rousseau, Pestalozzi); as a player on the markets in *economics* (Smith); as a legally responsible entity in the *contracts of government and social contracts* (Locke, Hume, Rousseau); and finally, as a soldier who fights on the basis of his own convictions in *war*(Clausewitz). This development reached its pinnacle sometime around the year 1800 with the critical philosophy of Immanuel Kant, in which most of the above-mentioned ideas were brought together to create a compact philosophy of civil republicanism and individualism.

However, this also marked the end of the *Golden Age of the Individual*. Above all in Germany, which had not managed to have its own civil revolution, the speculative idealism of Fichte, Schelling, and Hegel – who wanted to 'outdo' and 'overcome' Kant – displaced concrete civil and philosophical individualism as a philosophical theme. Instead, either the foundation for a truth that would encompass both religion and science was sought in the abstract 'I' concept of the transcendental subject, or the world spirit was evoked, a world-spirit in which all people were supposed to find peace, by means of dialectic 'sublation', beyond their disturbing individuality and in an all-overarching state. These attempts (including the Communist attempt) all failed, which has meant that since the middle of the nineteenth century, the philosophy of the subject – and with it the theme of individuality – has been increasingly discredited.

Epistemological Anti-Individualism

We are still noticing the after-effects of this to this day, insofar as a metatheoretical dogma is predominant in all cultural sciences, social sciences, and humanities, without exception. This dogma declares that one can no longer assume the model of the thinking subject – and certainly not the concrete individual – as the carrier of actions. Today, there is no serious theory of action that still traces social, political, economic, scientific, or artistic action back to subjects or individuals and deals with their inner horizons. Instead, theories are developed exclusively on the basis of 'systems' and 'structures' (history, economics, psychology, political science, sociology), 'contexts' and 'discourses' (literature, art, philosophy).

From this perspective, the question 'What is a democrat?' must sound like the reactionary attempt to revive a dead tradition, namely early *bourgeois* individualism and its 'naive' theory of action, which was based on the assumption of subjects of sound mind and bodily individuals. That being said, in modern – and in above all democratic – societies, the exploration of individuality should indeed be an important theme, because by making it so these societies would be focusing on their own, fundamental preconditions.

Astonishingly, it was the most radical but also the most brilliant and most sensitive system theoretician who highlighted this problem. 'The modern concept of the individual belongs, therefore, in a society that could thus consider itself called upon to reach some clarity about itself,' was how Niklas Luhmann began his assessment of the inadequate theoretical performance in this field in 1992. After all, 'after years of de-focusing, it seems as if a re-focusing on the individual is beginning. However, the classics in this discipline [sociology] are hardly any help: with the *split paradigm* of personal/social identity or with superficial borrowings from transcendental philosophy they contented themselves with the word *subject*, and never bored down deeper towards individuality.'

Once one is aware of this meta-theoretical anti-individualism, one also understands the indignation of the academic world when the historian Daniel Goldhagen published his book *Hitler's Willing Executioners* in 1996. In this book, the author refused to continue writing 'structure history' or 'social history' because structures and the social do not denounce and murder human beings. Instead, in accordance with the Anglo-American tradition of 'thick description' (Clifford Geertz), he examined the motives of the individual perpetrators. The impoverishment of the theory of action in sociology, which in this way he attacked in an exemplary manner, is the first reason why we cannot provide an answer to the questions 'what is a democrat?' and 'what is a political subject?', because we don't even know what their logical and historical predecessor, the individual, is.

The second and third reasons for this inability are both particularly prevalent in Germany. First of all, there is in this country a completely unbroken tradition of deriving the political from the state and never from the individual *as a* political subject. In good Aristotelian manner, the human is seen as a state-related animal (*zoon politikon*). The being is always deduced from the state order that is to be represented, the state order that the being has to support and to tolerate. The inner complexity of this being is completely ignored. Another German peculiarity is to judge the political subject solely using the standards of morality, or even to construct it altogether. Political philosophy in this country applies exclusively *normative* values to the political subject, *i.e.* it is not in the least bit interested in what it *is*, but solely in what it *should be*. This is immediately followed by noble calls for an orientation towards the common good and (completely misunderstood) solidarity. It is impossible to teach German thinkers that the normative – *i.e.* the morally structured *discourse* – can only ever produce an 'I must' and a 'we must', whereas in the case of the individual as a political subject, the cheeky 'I want – and others should!' rears its head. This *political moralism* is a thread that runs through the publications of most academically educated authors and the political comments pages and features sections of newspapers. Just think for a moment of the recently discovered 'ego-democrats' and 'enraged citizens' that the German press so likes to bang on about. The resulting *positive* concept of the democrat can only be that of an obdurate follower or a political saint. So it really is no wonder that we cannot actually define what a democrat is. After all, we know neither what an individual is, nor what constitutes a political subject. This is evidence of the inadequacy of political science, which has to this day not even come close to coming up with its own basic concepts. This applies equally to the concept of the political and to the concept of the political subject. Economics (Smith, Malthus, Ricardo, Schumpeter, Keynes *etc.*), sociology (Durkheim, Weber, Parsons, Luhmann), and psychology (Freud, Adler, Jung, Piaget, Erikson *etc.*) have all come up with sound concept structures that could be developed. This was not the case with political science, neither in Germany, nor elsewhere. *Because they know neither what they do, nor what they are talking about.*

The Ability to Think Political Order

Let us now turn to the constructive part, to see whether we can come up with something useful that does justice to the democrats, who are obviously out there and do exist. In my own academic work entitled *Political Subjectivity. The Philosophical Foundation of Democratic Individualism* (2006), I tried to pick up where the aforementioned Golden Age of Individualism left off and to further develop its findings. In short: *political subjectivity is the ability to reflect on public order*. This is what a human being must have in order to develop thoughts and judgments that could be qualified as *political*. The main philosophical task is to show what the terms 'reflection', 'public sphere' and 'order' mean in this definition. When coming up with this definition, I did not take any existing political orders as a starting point but examined instead the intellectual power that allows human beings to *create* these orders in the first place so that they can then *participate* in these orders as individuals, political subjects, and ultimately as 'citizens' (as opposed to subjects). This is why the concepts 'public sphere' and 'order' are not just about the things that each of us finds ready-made in the world, but about how we, as thinking and judging beings, can allow these concepts to develop in us so that we can reflect on them. The 'public sphere' aspect in the aforementioned formula does not, therefore, refer solely to the empirical, civil public sphere such as the one outlined in Jürgen Habermas' *Structural Transformation of the Public Sphere* (1962), with all its media, conversations, reading groups, parliaments, newspapers, and televisions, (to which we today could of course add the internet, Twitter etc.), but also to a structural principle of our thought, namely when we discuss our interests, wishes, and ideals in a *thought* public sphere in which we can also confront ourselves with *imagined* opposing opinions.

Accordingly, the 'order' mentioned in the formula is not only the existing, given order, but the *order that we conceive in our minds* and, above all, *desire* (of the economy, political rule, customs, religion etc.). Only then can we compare it with the real order that exists outside ourselves and bring our approval or rejection into a real, empirical public sphere, e.g. in the form of conversations, political activities, the publication of books and newspapers, television appearances and – in democracies – participation in elections. So, a political subject is characterized by its ability to imagine that something could *be different to what it currently is*. In other words, a political subject has cognitive access to the concept of the *option*. In those cases, where there is no such cognitive access, a *political* thought will never develop in a human being! For Europeans, who are so used to democracy, this might seem exaggerated. If so, it is only because they have forgotten how small the world-historical window through which they were themselves given access to this faculty of thought actually is. A theory of the political subject that is as universal as this should, therefore, be verifiable using ethnological observations and anthropological considerations. And indeed, it can.

Political Science and Ethnology

Louis Dumont's studies of *Homo hierarchicus* (1966) are famous. He found the best example of this *homo hierarchicus* in India's caste society. In this society, there is – or was (the situation has changed in the meantime) – no trace of political capacity for reflection and no notion that the given order could be a different one. Even more informative are the works of the French sociologist, ethnologist, and anthropologist Georges Balandier, which receive too little attention. His very descriptive *Political Anthropology* (1972) is completely and utterly different to the normative, philosophical approach adopted by German political science. Balandier examined ethnological literature on the problem of the political and sought to combine it with his own empirical ethnological findings from his African research to create an ethnologically supported theory of the political. The objective of this theory was to do away with the prejudice that primitive peoples had no history and that many of them, especially those without any discernible forms of state, had no knowledge of any form of politics. The structuralist school in particular disputed that primitive societies had any historical-political dimension. Balandier's marked methodological awareness of the problem is noteworthy. As far as he was concerned, in order to ensure that a true 'world history of political thought' could one day be written, it was essential to re-pose the question as to the definition of the political. Balandier undertook a detailed comparison of the various definitions formulated in the works of earlier political anthropologists. While some anthropologists spoke of the political as being where family relationships end or where specific characteristics of space (territory, difference between the internal and the external) or action (reference to power instead of to authority) prevailed, others only considered the function of the political in the form of services to society as a whole (cooperation, integrity, decision-making, security). Balandier concludes: 'The political can be reduced neither to a "code" (such as language or myth), nor to a "network of relationships" (such as relatives or exchanges); it remains a comprehensive system that has not to date been formally addressed in a satisfactory manner.' For our purposes, what is decisive is that he sought to find evidence of the political or a form of political subjectivity in ethnological societies – and did not succeed in doing so. So there are forms of culture where a thought that can be qualified as *political* never arises and never can arise, because everything is rite, magic, and timeless order.

Christian Meier, a scholar of ancient history, did the reverse. His entire *oeuvre* is determined by the search for answers to two questions: 'How is it that the Greeks, and not any of the other cultures that existed before them or at the same time as them, developed democracies? And what constituted the political aspect of the Greeks, what characterized this political aspect as the specific/specifying life element in their society?' Elsewhere, he described this approach as an attempt at 'political ethnology'. This approach stipulates an awareness of the special, of the historical emergence, and the unlikelihood of the political. It seemed to Meier that it was this very aspect, *i.e.* the political, that set the Greeks apart from other peoples and cultures, by which he assumed that the political in other cultures was probably either non-existent or not very pronounced at all. No one formulated the above-mentioned cognitive concept of the *option* as a prerequisite for the genuine political thought of the individual better and more comprehensibly than Meier. The most important result of his research is the 'capability awareness' that developed in individual Greeks after this small Mediterranean state succeeded in defeating the huge Persian Empire with its million-strong army, contrary to all expectations.

I would also like to mention the Moroccan philosopher Mohammed Abed al-Jabri, another important authority on a historical-anthropological basic structure for political subjectivity, who investigated this question in the context of a religion-based culture. In his monumental four-volume work, *Critique of Arab Reason* (1984-2001), which examines the current deficits and delays in the Arab world on the basis of its own cultural sources, he describes a key, concrete situation with which most Arab children are familiar and have been for centuries: children reading and learning by heart the holy scriptures together in Koranic schools. Al-Jabri vividly demonstrates how the separation of the object that is read and the subject who is reading is not completed in the case of this kind of reading, which involves the internalization of the text. This condition is also facilitated by the fact that many Arabs who can read are only familiar with the Koran. This moved Al-Jabri to pose the following question: *who is reading whom here?* The official Arabic language (in contrast to the spoken Arabic dialects) has not changed in over one and a half millennia and has, during this time, been the guarantee of authenticity in Arab culture. Moreover, through the revelation and the canonization of the Koran, it has also taken on a sacred character. In this cultural force field, the style of Koran lessons has led to a fatal reversal: *now, the holy scriptures are reading the people.* This, according to al-Jabri, has resulted in an underdevelopment of the capacity for reflection and the inhibition of the individualization of the reading subject. With this he is turning against a concept of tradition that is restricted to the repetition of history. He calls his hermeneutic method a 'disjunctive and simultaneously re-junctive reading' ('lecture disjonctive-rejonctive'). The subject should be able to separate itself from the text in order to identify the object character of the traditionally religious order and himself as an individual. It is only at this moment that reflection about alternatives to the prevailing order becomes possible. This means reflecting on the compatibility between the order that is symbolically embodied in the texts on the one hand (for example the order of criminal law, of the Islamic economy, or of the caliphate) and the individual *perspective* on this order on the other. Al-Jabri describes the 'rejunction' ('rejonction') as the 'explorative intuition' ('intuition exploratrice') that can encompass the 'reading and the read I' ('moi-lu et moi-lisant'). In particular, he describes the connection of the horizons of the individual and the order vividly because the reflection is not supposed just to release the individual but to make *genuine political orientation* possible for him as part of the social order.

A First Attempt of a Definition

Based on these ethnological and anthropological observations, we can now say with some certainty that the political subject is a human individual who is capable of reflecting on patterns of public order. But what is a democrat? What special kind of political subject is the democrat and what are the properties that distinguish the democrat from the non-democrat? There follows a first attempt at answering this question:

The democrat is someone who wants to see the *thought* public sphere, which he is capable of imagining, realized in the *real* public sphere so that he can – in conversations, media, parties, and parliaments – contribute his own idea of order without sanctions or fear of death. The motive for the democrat to get involved in this real public sphere is the fundamental opportunity that he can, through his actions, also make his political will part of the process of rule and legislation by joining a party, publishing in the media, setting up a new party, taking part in demonstrations and elections etc. The democrat schematizes the real individuals who are his opponents in the real public sphere because they hold different opinions, not as *existential enemies*, but as *political opponents*. This also means that his ideas of public order are always characterized by a toleration of the opposition, because he himself could find himself in the opposition at any time. The democrat also abstains from hypostasizing his ideas of order as timeless ontological truths and instead recognizes them as personal, subjective interests that he would like to see implemented by the government in the structure that comprises government and opposition and therefore become generally applicable.

This is only a first sketch, an outline that makes it clear that we still have to discover and conduct more research on the democrat. Together with the considerations mentioned earlier, it also shows why there can be no simple answer to the question 'what is a democrat?', because no one is born a democrat. It is this very complexity that shows us how astonishingly beautiful and fragile this product of our spiritual and cultural evolution is, and also how many preconditions it entails.

About the Author

Reginald 'Reggie' Grünenberg (*1963) is a German philosopher, political scientist, writer-producer and novelist. He studied political science, history, and philosophy in Paris (Sciences Po), Munich (LMU), and Berlin (HU) up to the doctorate. He also studied later on at Bocconi School of Management in Milan, SOAS in London and Waseda University in Tokyo. As a grant holder of the EU Commission, he became a certified expert on Japan in 2008. Reggie's homepage is www.reggies.world.

Published Papers

Gründungsgewalt und Politik. René Girards Kulturtheorie im Spiegel der Politikwissenschaft, in: academia.edu, Berlin 2010.

Laws of Singularity, in: academia.edu, Berlin 2017.

What is a Democrat? An Attempt to Define the Democratic Personality, in: Fikrunn wa Fann, Goethe-Institut, June 2012.

Upcoming Book

Your Are Many – The Polycentric Subject, expected in 2019; preview on academia.edu.

Novel

Nippon trilogy *The Discovery of the East Pole*, published in English in 2018 (Chinese in 2019).

Imprint

Political Subjectivity –

The Philosophical Foundation of Democratic Individualism

Printed version

Language: American English

Author: Reginald Grünenberg

Translated by: Bayard Taylor & DeepL.com

Cover design: Mondart

Publisher: Perlen Verlag, Berlin

ISBN 978-3-942662-33-8

© Perlen Verlag 2018

www.ingramcontent.com/pod-product-compliance
Lightning Source LLC
Chambersburg PA
CBHW071056230426
43666CB00009B/1728